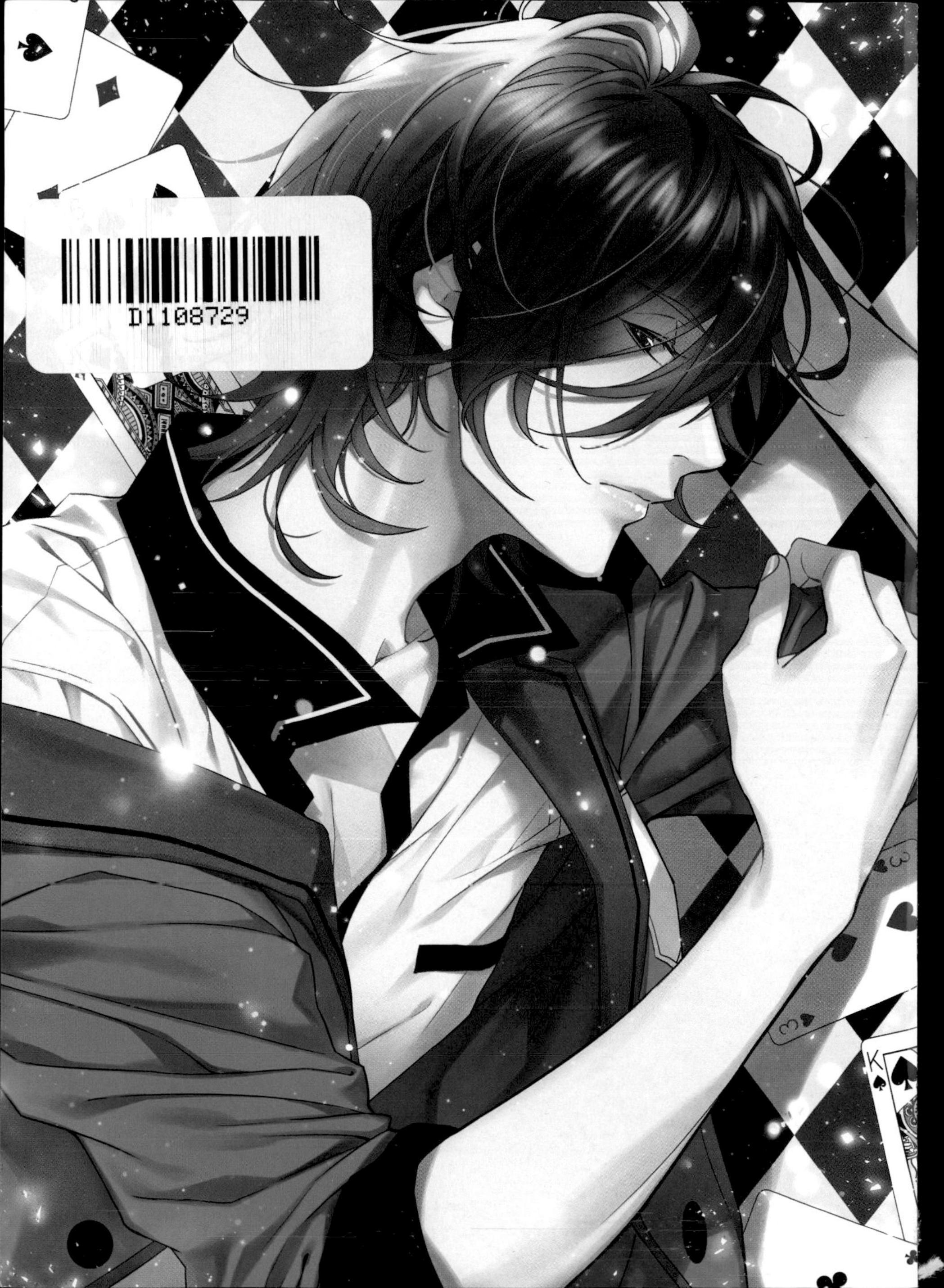

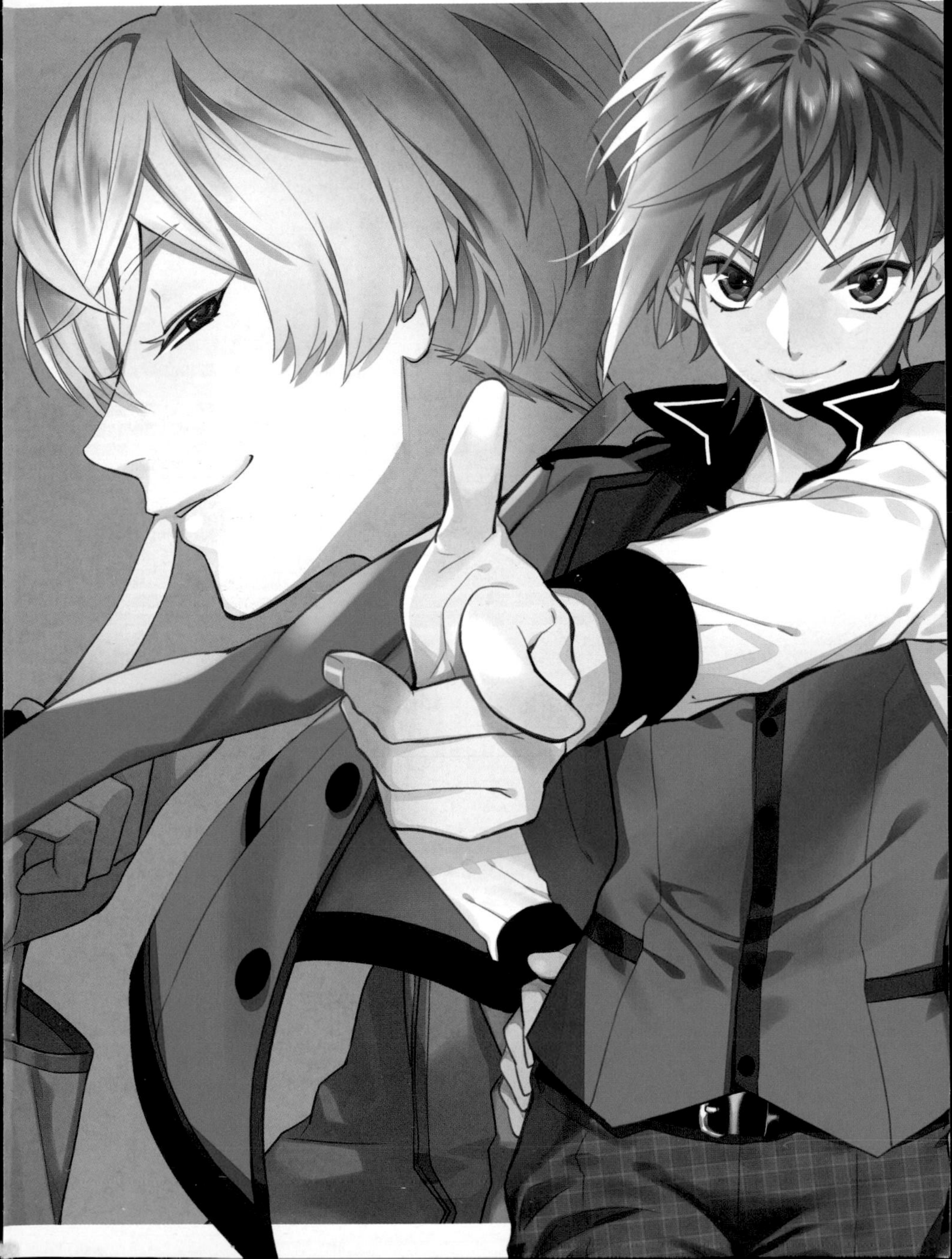

PRETTY BOY DETECTIVE CLUB

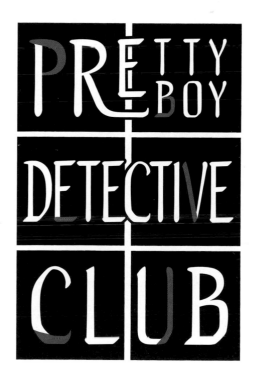

Original Story:
NISIOISIN
Manga:
Suzuka Oda
Original Character Design:
Kinako

PRETTY BOY DETECTIVE CLUB

2

CONTENTS

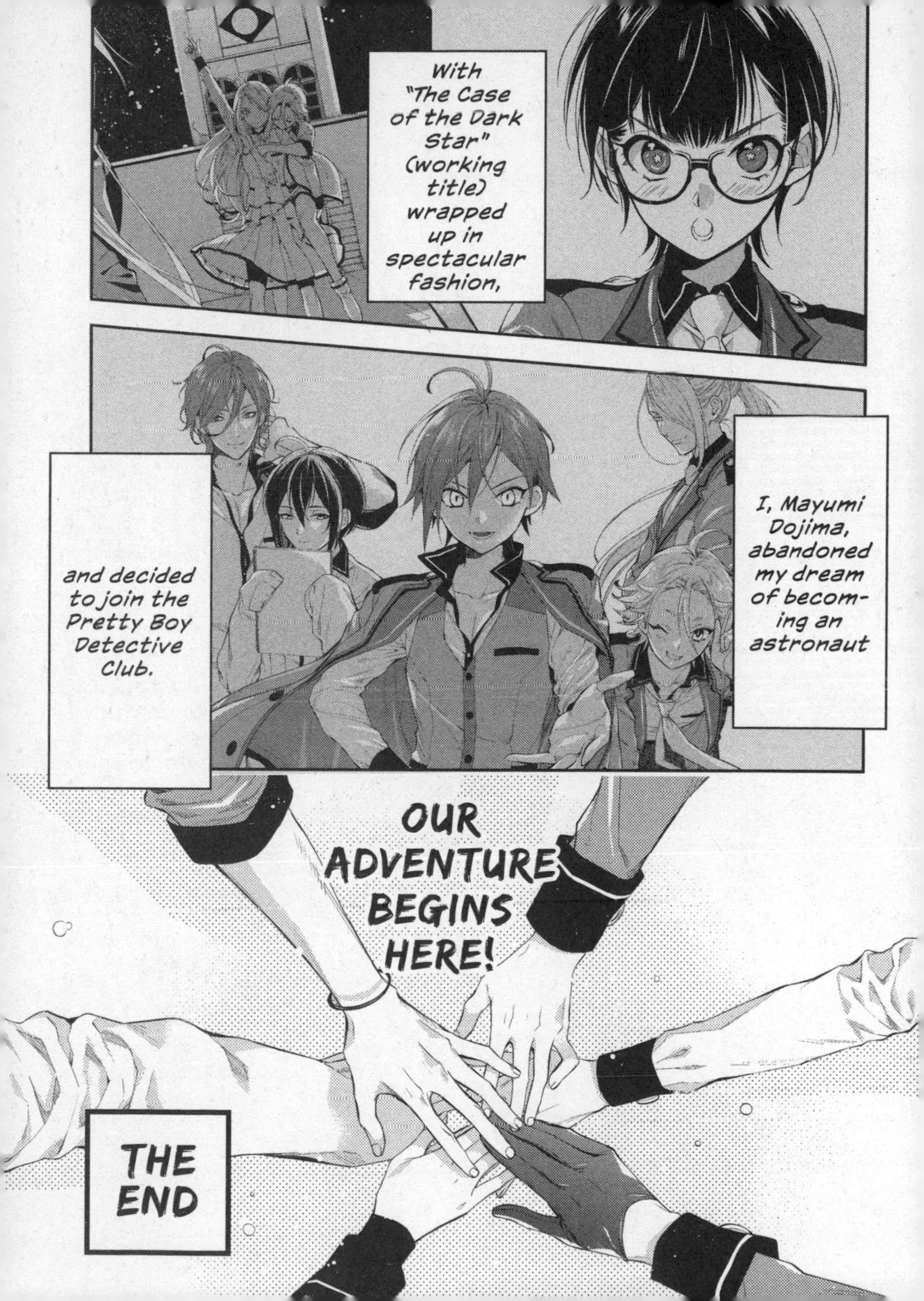
With "The Case of the Dark Star" (working title) wrapped up in spectacular fashion,
I, Mayumi Dojima, abandoned my dream of becoming an astronaut
and decided to join the Pretty Boy Detective Club.
OUR ADVENTURE BEGINS HERE!
THE END

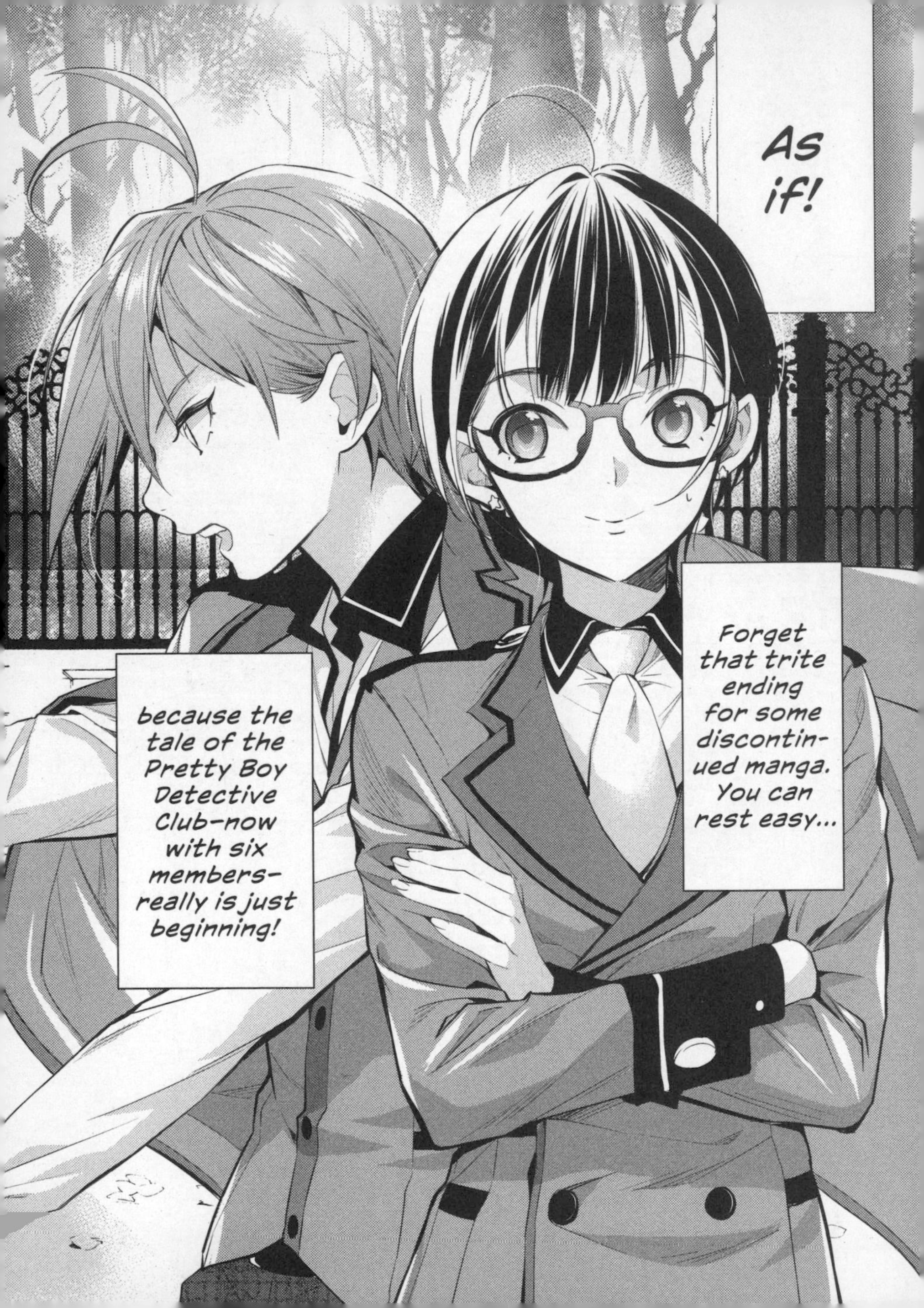
As if!
Forget that trite ending for some discontin-ued manga. You can rest easy...
because the tale of the Pretty Boy Detective Club—now with six members—really is just beginning!

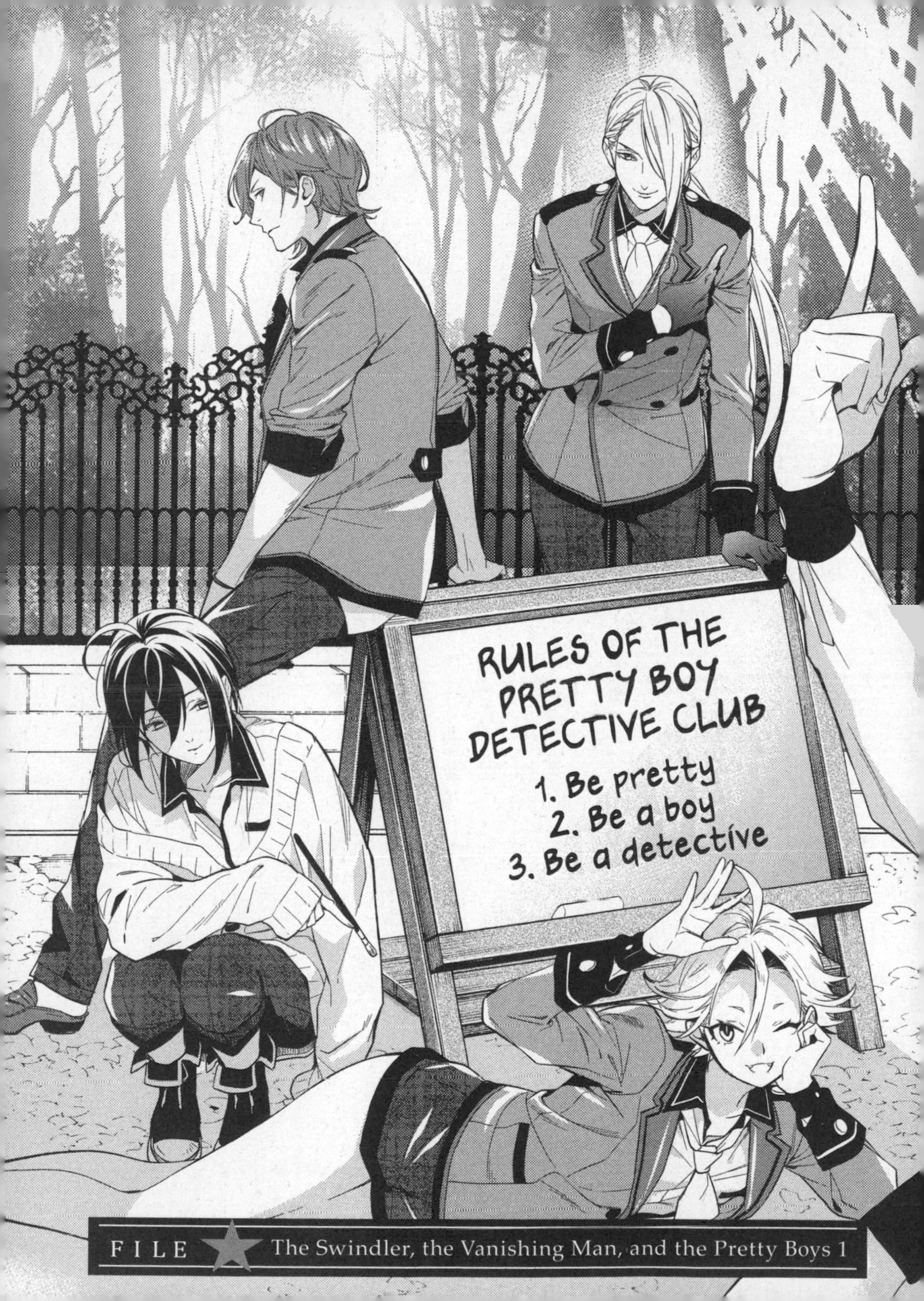
RULES OF THE PRETTY BOY DETECTIVE CLUB
1. Be pretty
2. Be a boy
3. Be a detective

FILE ★ The Swindler, the Vanishing Man, and the Pretty Boys 1

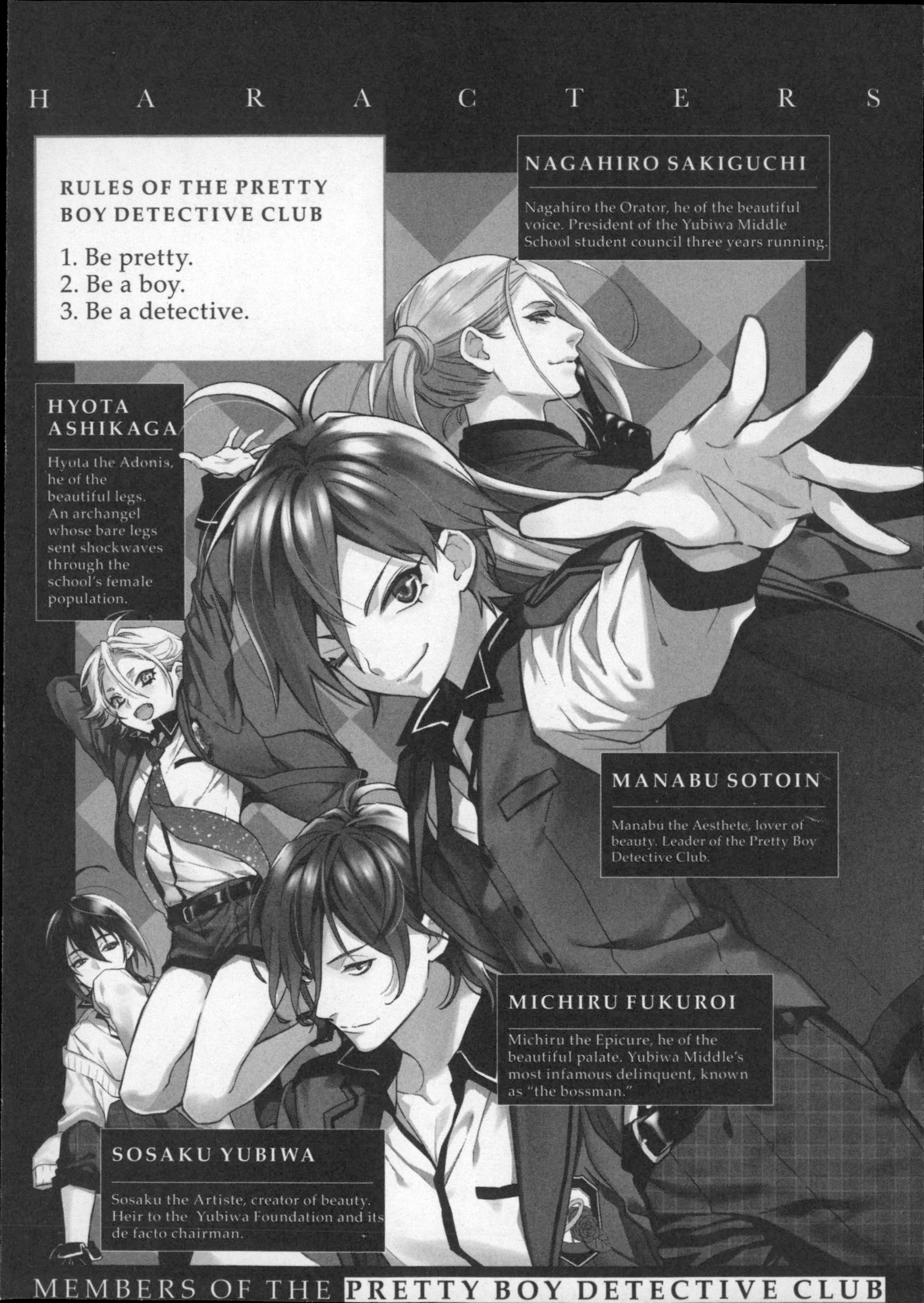
HARACTERS
RULES OF THE PRETTY BOY DETECTIVE CLUB
1. Be pretty.
2. Be a boy.
3. Be a detective.
NAGAHIRO SAKIGUCHI
Nagahiro the Orator, he of the beautiful voice. President of the Yubiwa Middle School student council three years running.
HYOTA ASHIKAGA
Hyota the Adonis, he of the beautiful legs. An archangel whose bare legs sent shockwaves through the school's female population.
MANABU SOTOIN
Manabu the Aesthete, lover of beauty. Leader of the Pretty Boy Detective Club.
MICHIRU FUKUROI
Michiru the Epicure, he of the beautiful palate. Yubiwa Middle's most infamous delinquent, known as "the bossman."
SOSAKU YUBIWA
Sosaku the Artiste, creator of beauty. Heir to the Yubiwa Foundation and its de facto chairman.
MEMBERS OF THE PRETTY BOY DETECTIVE CLUB

S T O R Y & C

PRETTY BOY DETECTIVE CLUB

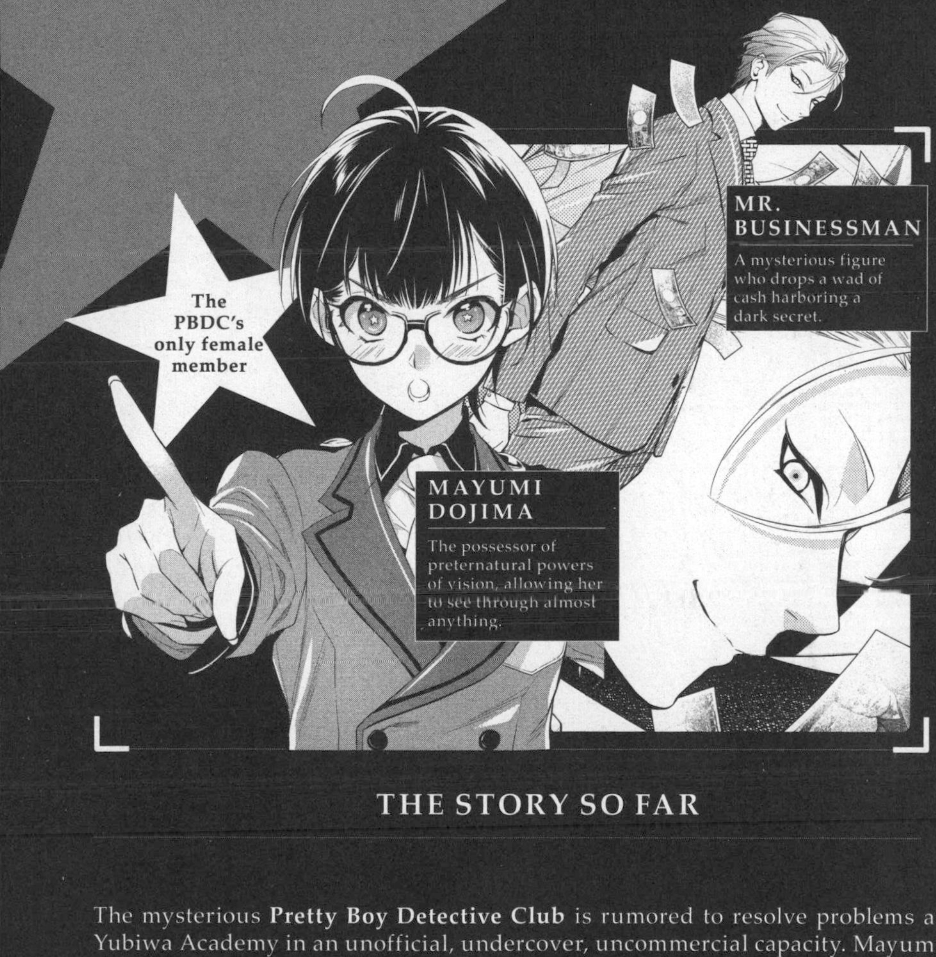
MR. BUSINESSMAN
A mysterious figure who drops a wad of cash harboring a dark secret.
The PBDC's only female member
MAYUMI DOJIMA
The possessor of preternatural powers of vision, allowing her to see through almost anything.

THE STORY SO FAR

The mysterious **Pretty Boy Detective Club** is rumored to resolve problems at Yubiwa Academy in an unofficial, undercover, uncommercial capacity. Mayumi Dojima, a second-year student at the school, commissions the club to help her find a star she saw just once, ten years ago. Their investigation reveals that her "star" was actually the flash of a military satellite being shot down by a nuclear missile in a top-secret operation! Mayumi is kidnapped by a professional delivery service called the Twenties, but Nagahiro the Orator uses his brains and chameleon-like voice to fool the leader of the Twenties and resolve the matter without incident. Mayumi joins the Pretty Boy Detective Club as Mayumi the Seer—and her first test as a member of the club is waiting just around the corner!

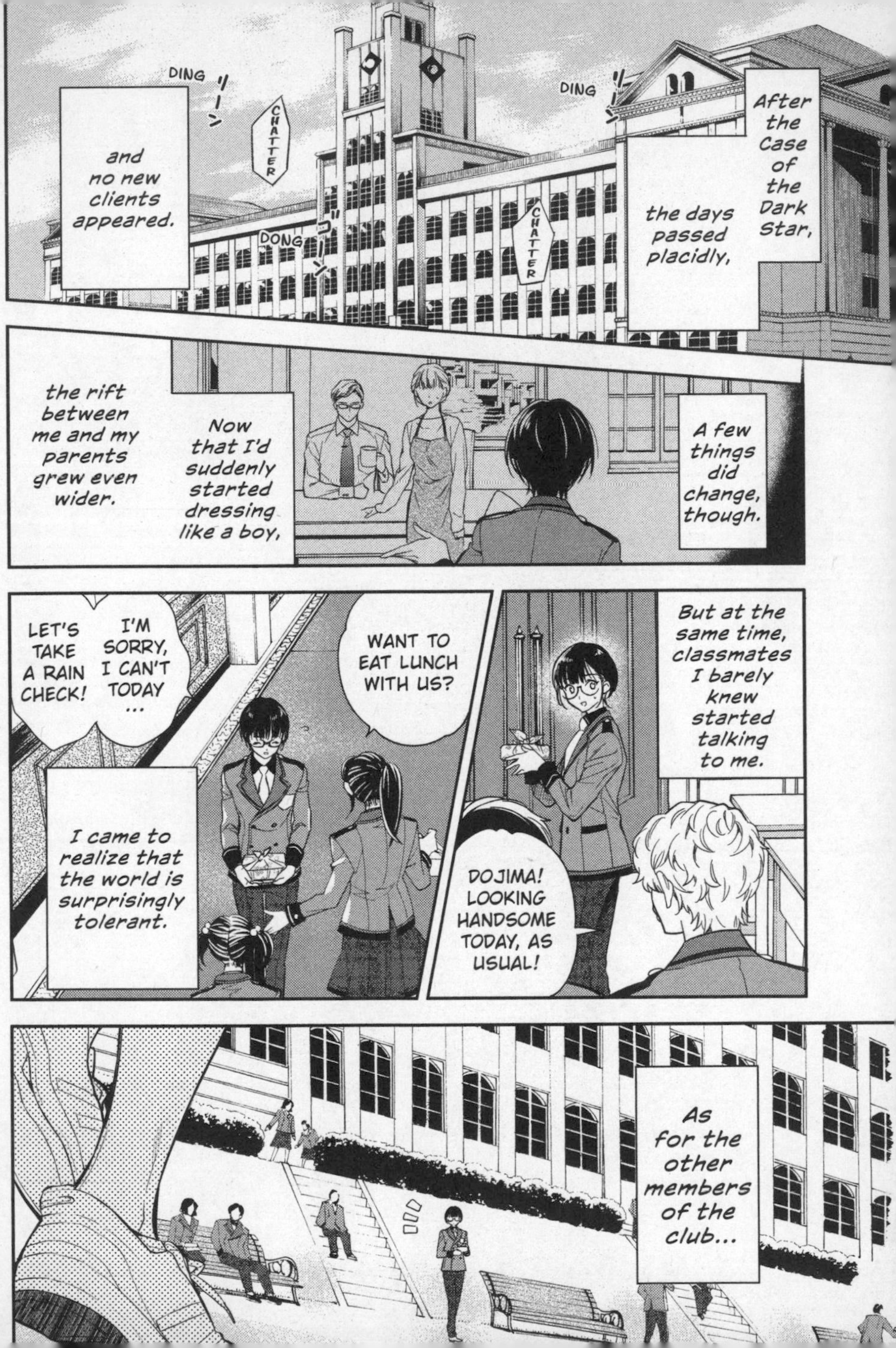
After the Case of the Dark Star,
DING
the days passed placidly,
CHATTER
DING
CHATTER
DONG
and no new clients appeared.
A few things did change, though.
Now that I'd suddenly started dressing like a boy,
the rift between me and my parents grew even wider.
But at the same time, classmates I barely knew started talking to me.
DOJIMA! LOOKING HANDSOME TODAY, AS USUAL!
WANT TO EAT LUNCH WITH US?
I'M SORRY, I CAN'T TODAY...
LET'S TAKE A RAIN CHECK!
I came to realize that the world is surprisingly tolerant.
As for the other members of the club...

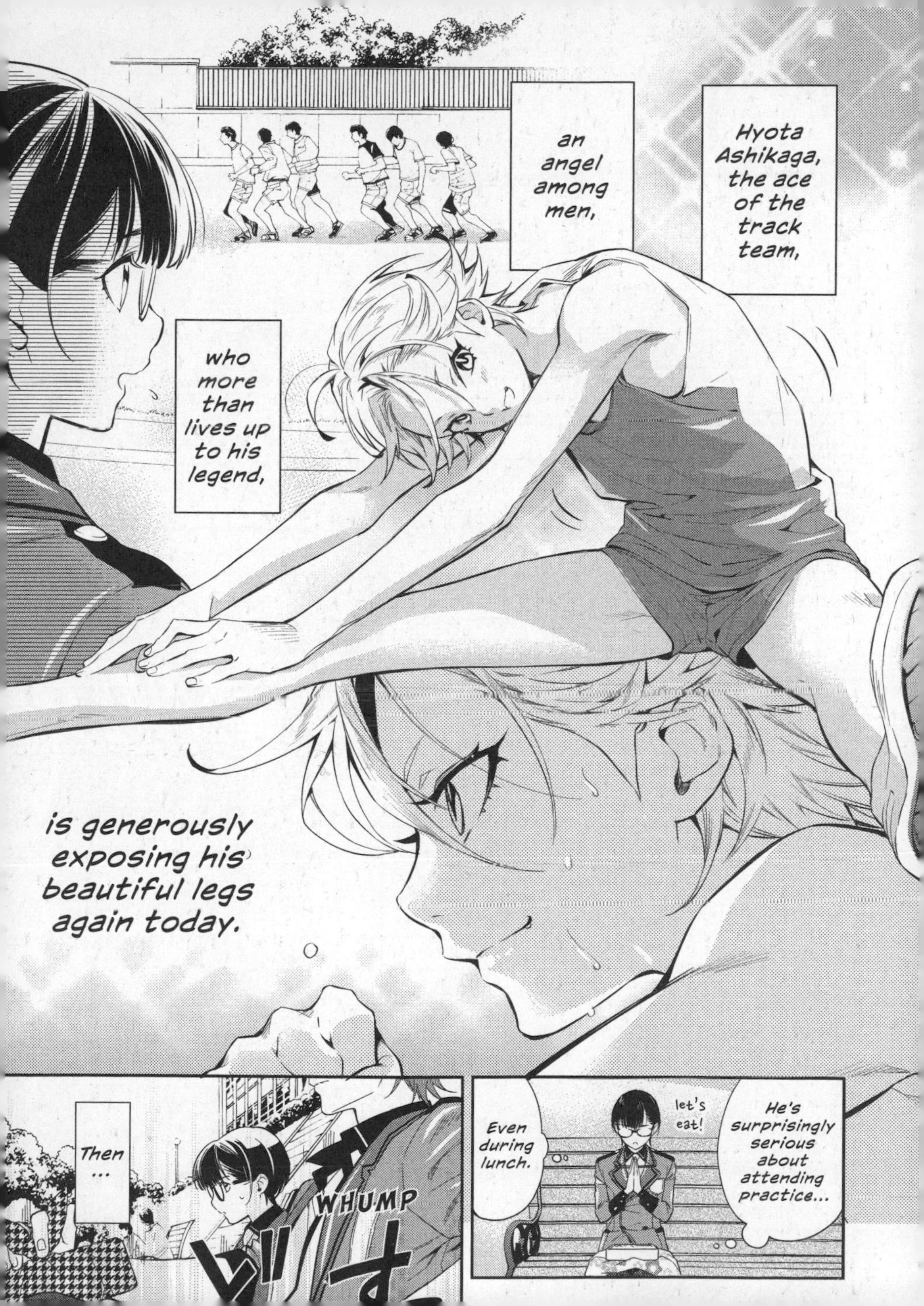
Hyota Ashikaga, the ace of the track team,
an angel among men,
who more than lives up to his legend,
is generously exposing his beautiful legs again today.
He's surprisingly serious about attending practice...
let's eat!
Even during lunch.
Then ...
WHUMP

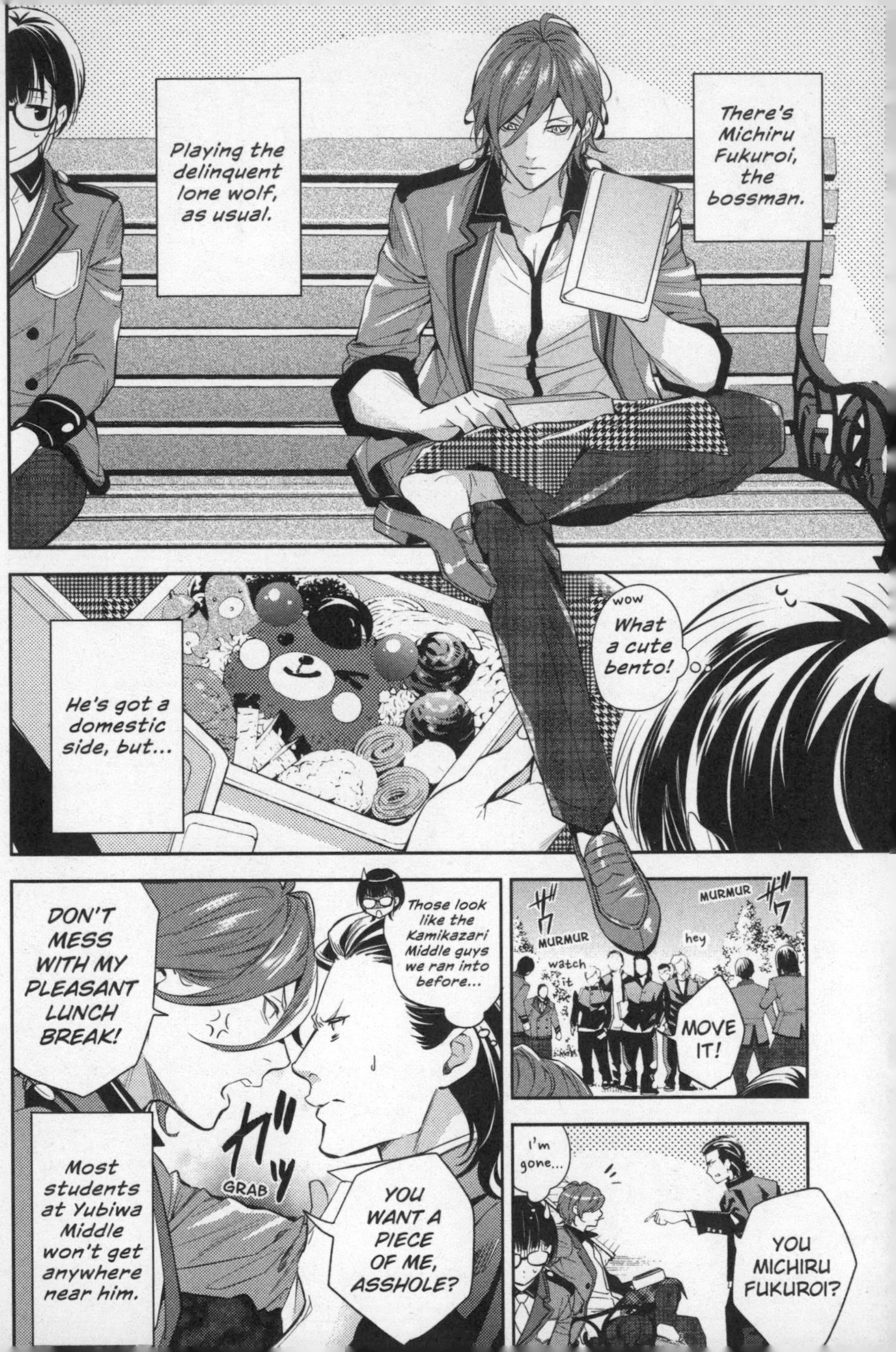
There's Michiru Fukuroi, the bossman.
Playing the delinquent lone wolf, as usual.
wow
What a cute bento!
He's got a domestic side, but...
MURMUR
hey
MOVE IT!
MURMUR
watch it
YOU MICHIRU FUKUROI?
I'm gone...
Those look like the Kamikazari Middle guys we ran into before...
DON'T MESS WITH MY PLEASANT LUNCH BREAK!
YOU WANT A PIECE OF ME, ASSHOLE?
GRAB
Most students at Yubiwa Middle won't get anywhere near him.

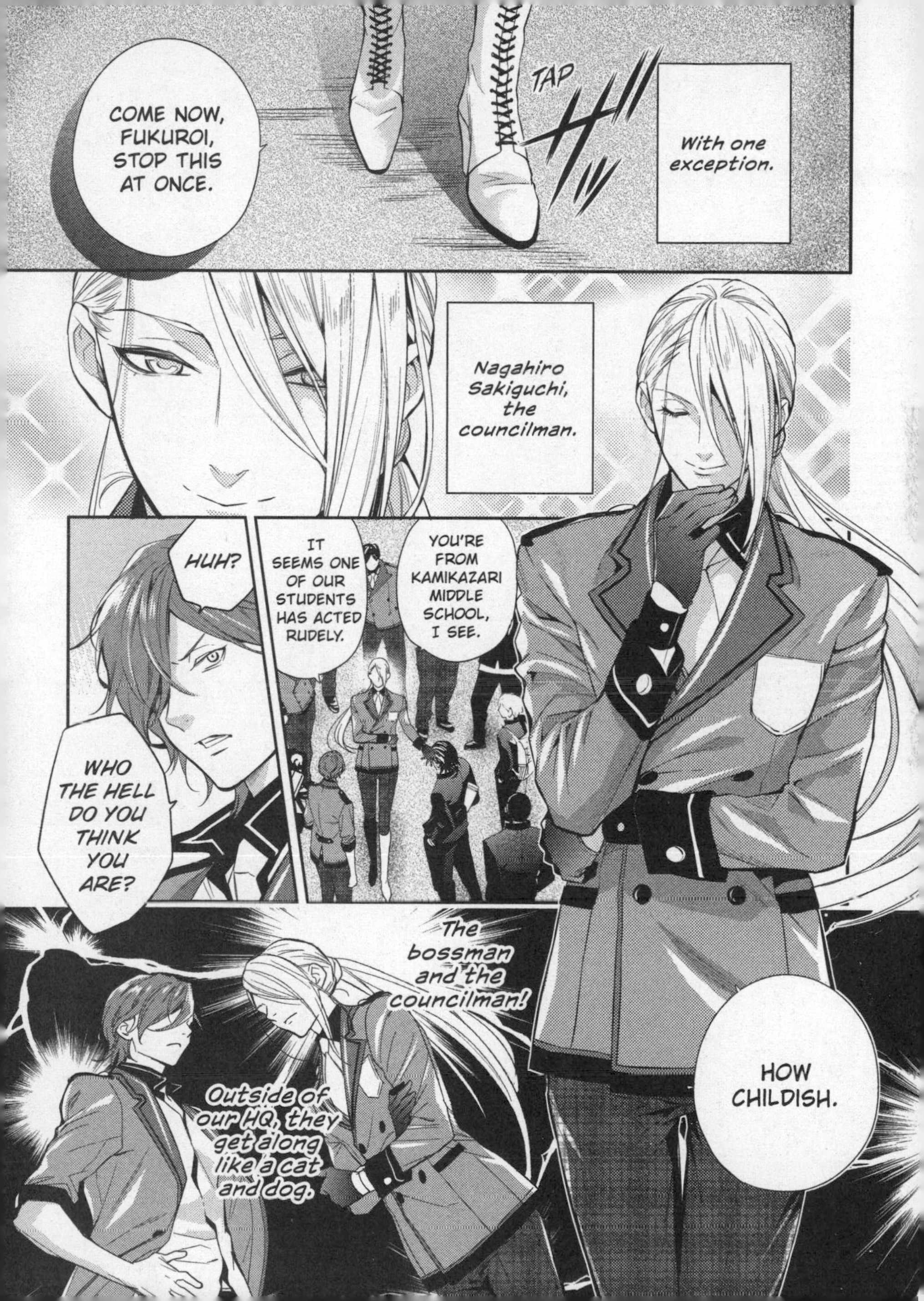
With one exception.
TAP
COME NOW, FUKUROI, STOP THIS AT ONCE.
Nagahiro Sakiguchi, the councilman.
YOU'RE FROM KAMIKAZARI MIDDLE SCHOOL, I SEE.
IT SEEMS ONE OF OUR STUDENTS HAS ACTED RUDELY.
HUH?
WHO THE HELL DO YOU THINK YOU ARE?
HOW CHILDISH.
The bossman and the councilman!
Outside of our HQ, they get along like a cat and dog.

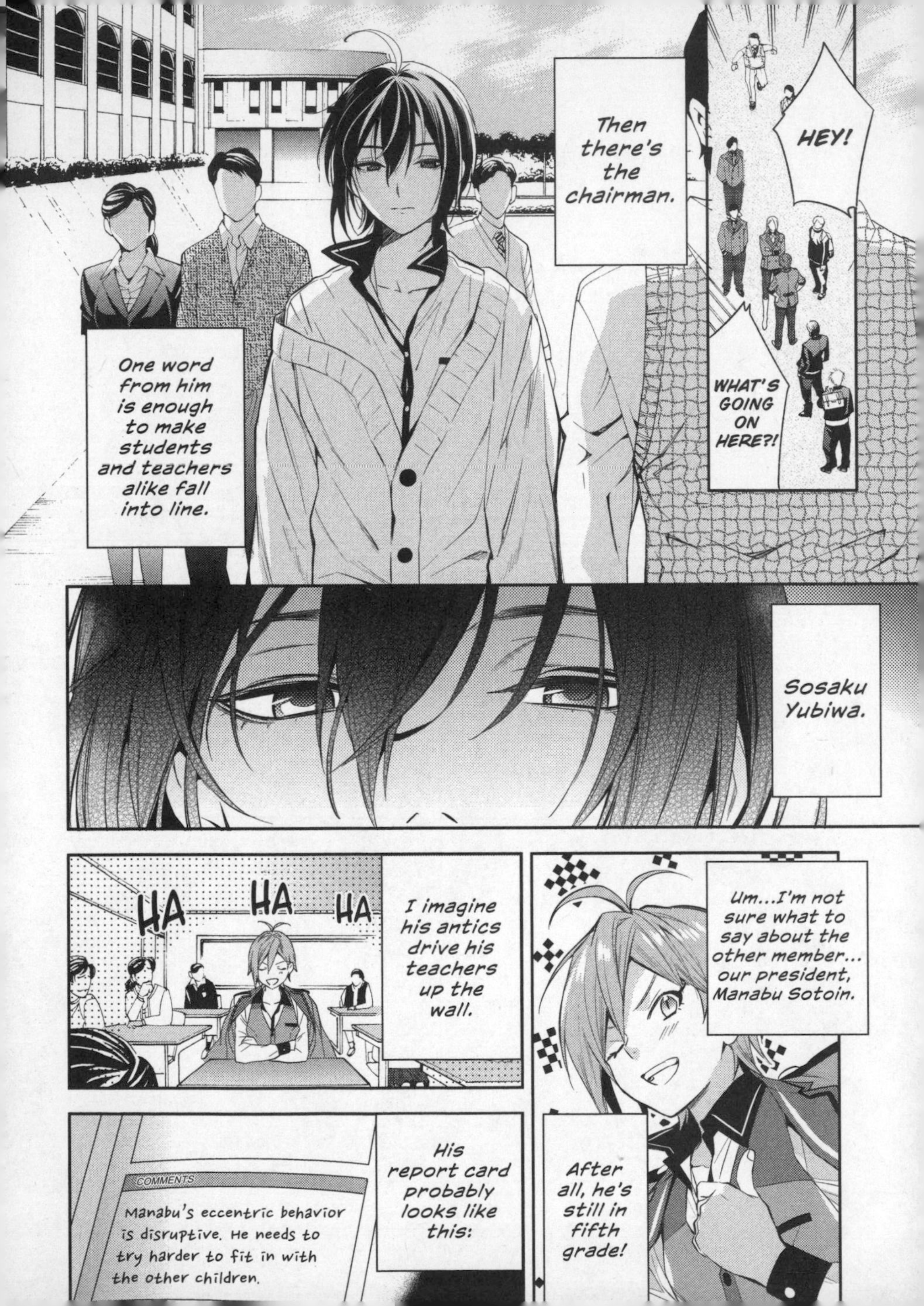
HEY!
WHAT'S GOING ON HERE?!
Then there's the chairman.
One word from him is enough to make students and teachers alike fall into line.
Sosaku Yubiwa.
Um...I'm not sure what to say about the other member... our president, Manabu Sotoin.
After all, he's still in fifth grade!
I imagine his antics drive his teachers up the wall.
HA HA HA
His report card probably looks like this:
COMMENTS
Manabu's eccentric behavior is disruptive. He needs to try harder to fit in with the other children.

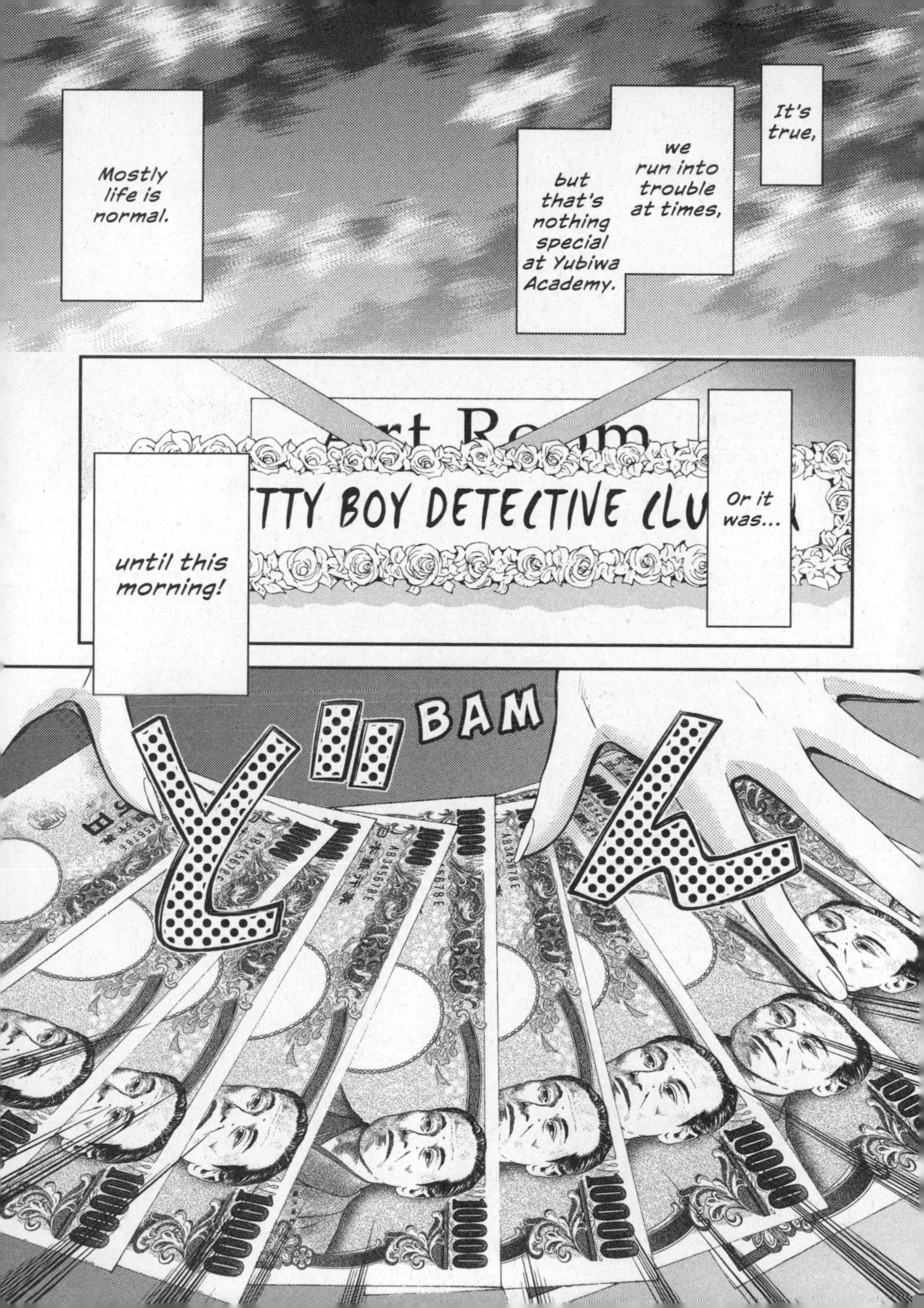
It's true,
we run into trouble at times,
but that's nothing special at Yubiwa Academy.
Mostly life is normal.
Or it was...
until this morning!
BAM

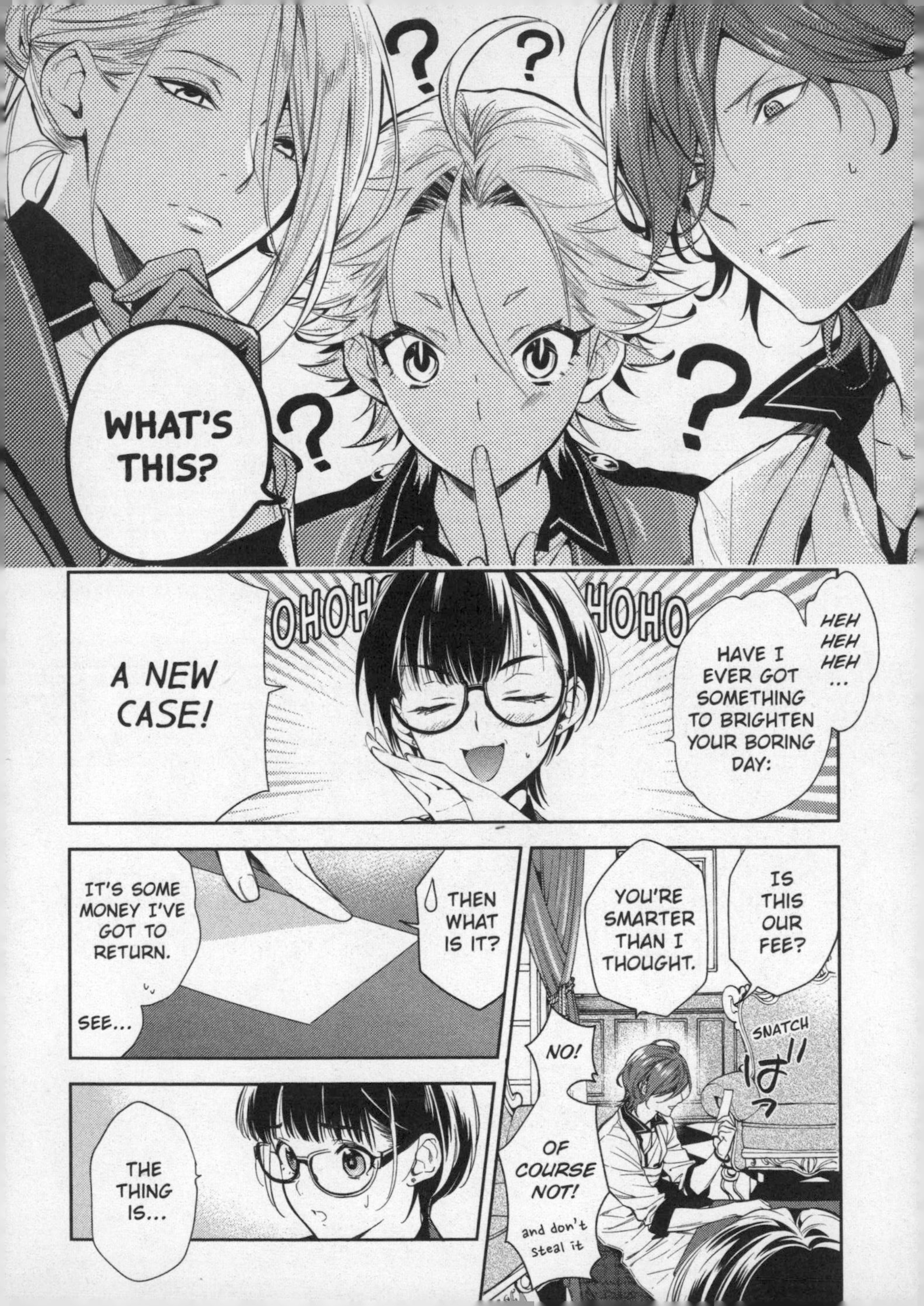
WHAT'S THIS?
HEH HEH HEH ...
HAVE I EVER GOT SOMETHING TO BRIGHTEN YOUR BORING DAY:
OHOHO HOHO
A NEW CASE!
IS THIS OUR FEE?
YOU'RE SMARTER THAN I THOUGHT.
SNATCH
NO!
OF COURSE NOT!
and don't steal it
THEN WHAT IS IT?
IT'S SOME MONEY I'VE GOT TO RETURN.
SEE...
THE THING IS...

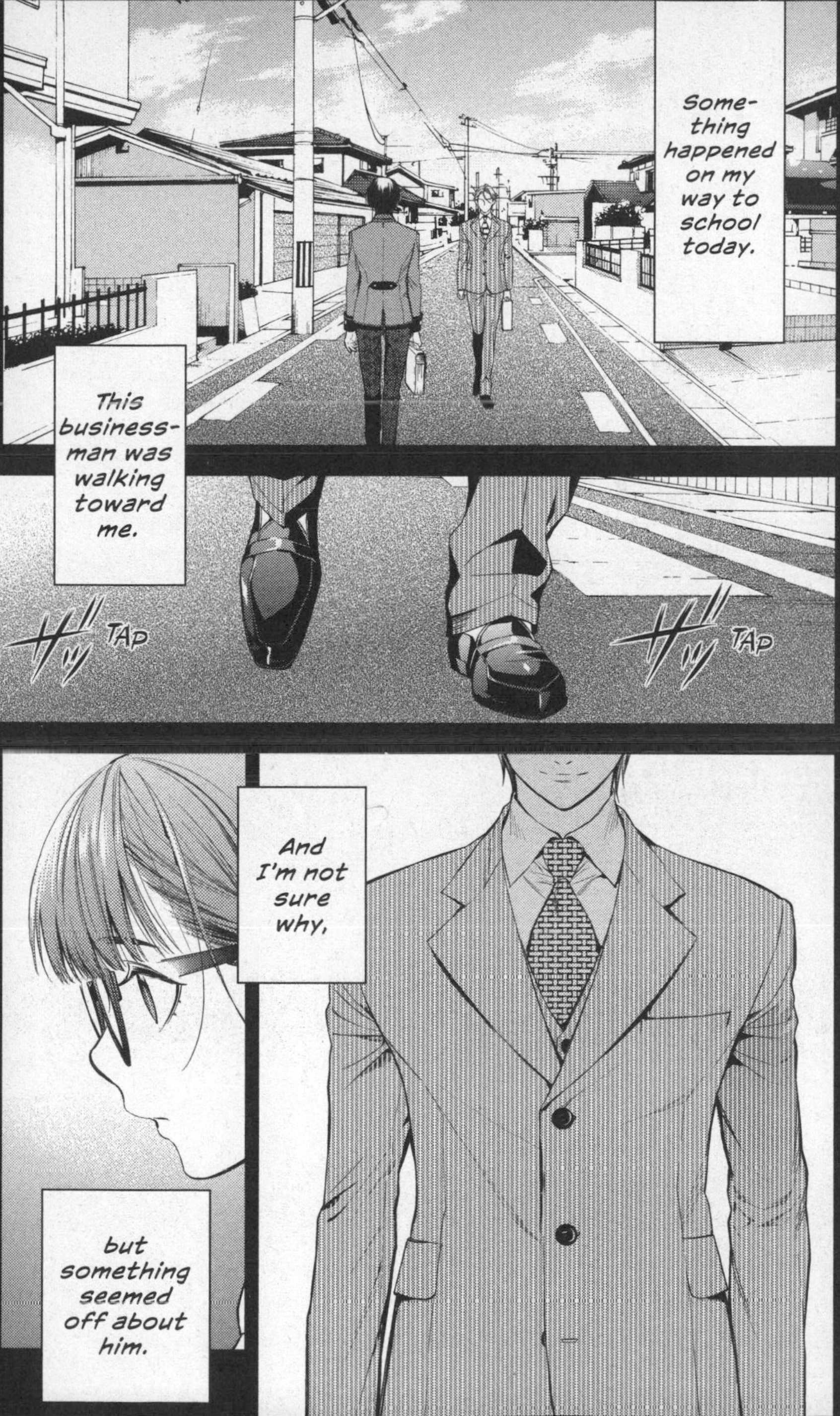

Something happened on my way to school today.
This businessman was walking toward me.
TAP
TAP
And I'm not sure why,
but something seemed off about him.

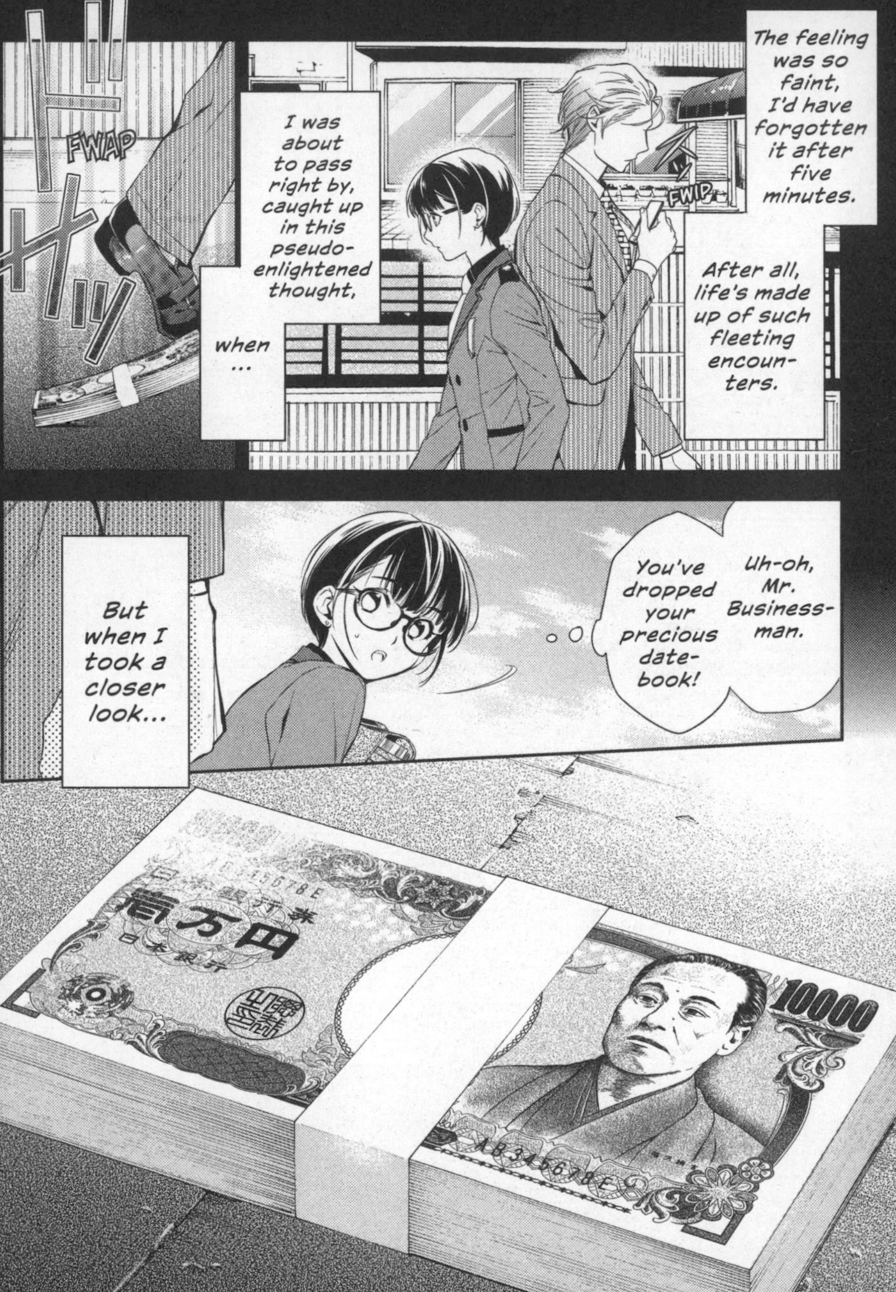
The feeling was so faint, I'd have forgotten it after five minutes.
After all, life's made up of such fleeting encounters.
FWIP
I was about to pass right by, caught up in this pseudo-enlightened thought,
when ...
FWAP
Uh-oh, Mr. Businessman.
You've dropped your precious datebook!
But when I took a closer look...
日本銀行券
壱万円
日本銀行
10000

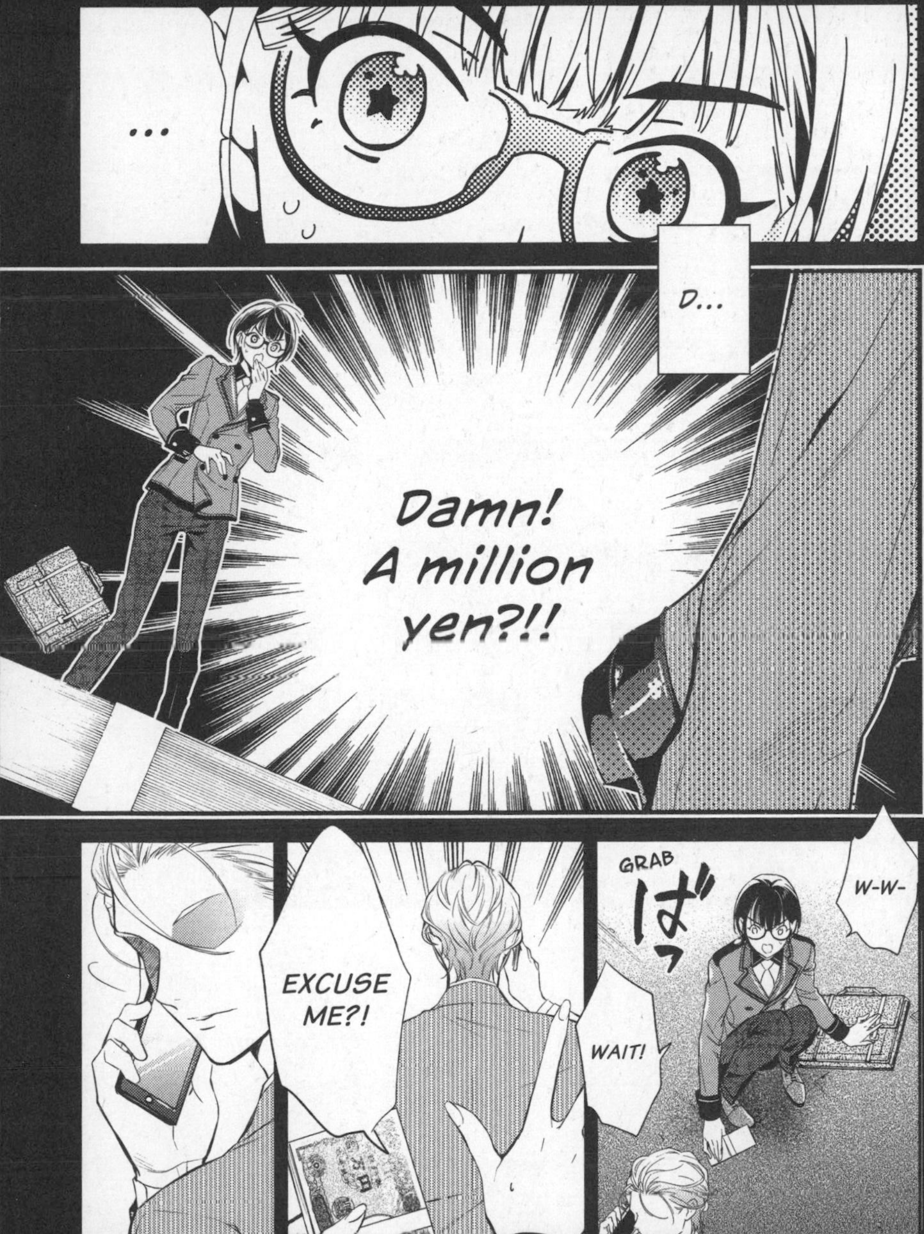
...
D...
Damn! A million yen?!!
W-W-
GRAB
ばっ
WAIT!
EXCUSE ME?!

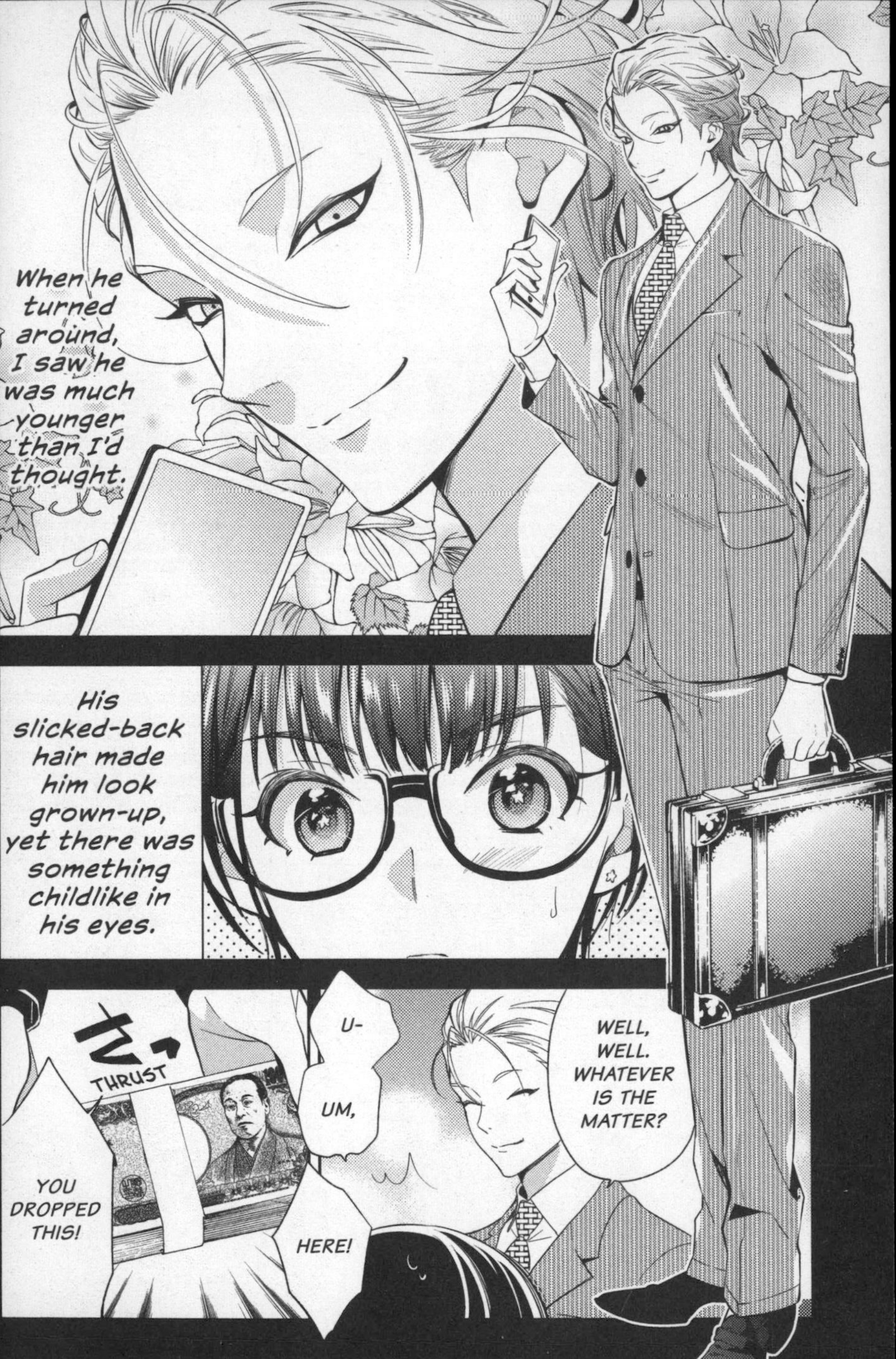
When he turned around, I saw he was much younger than I'd thought.
His slicked-back hair made him look grown-up, yet there was something childlike in his eyes.
WELL, WELL. WHATEVER IS THE MATTER?
U-
UM,
HERE!
THRUST
YOU DROPPED THIS!

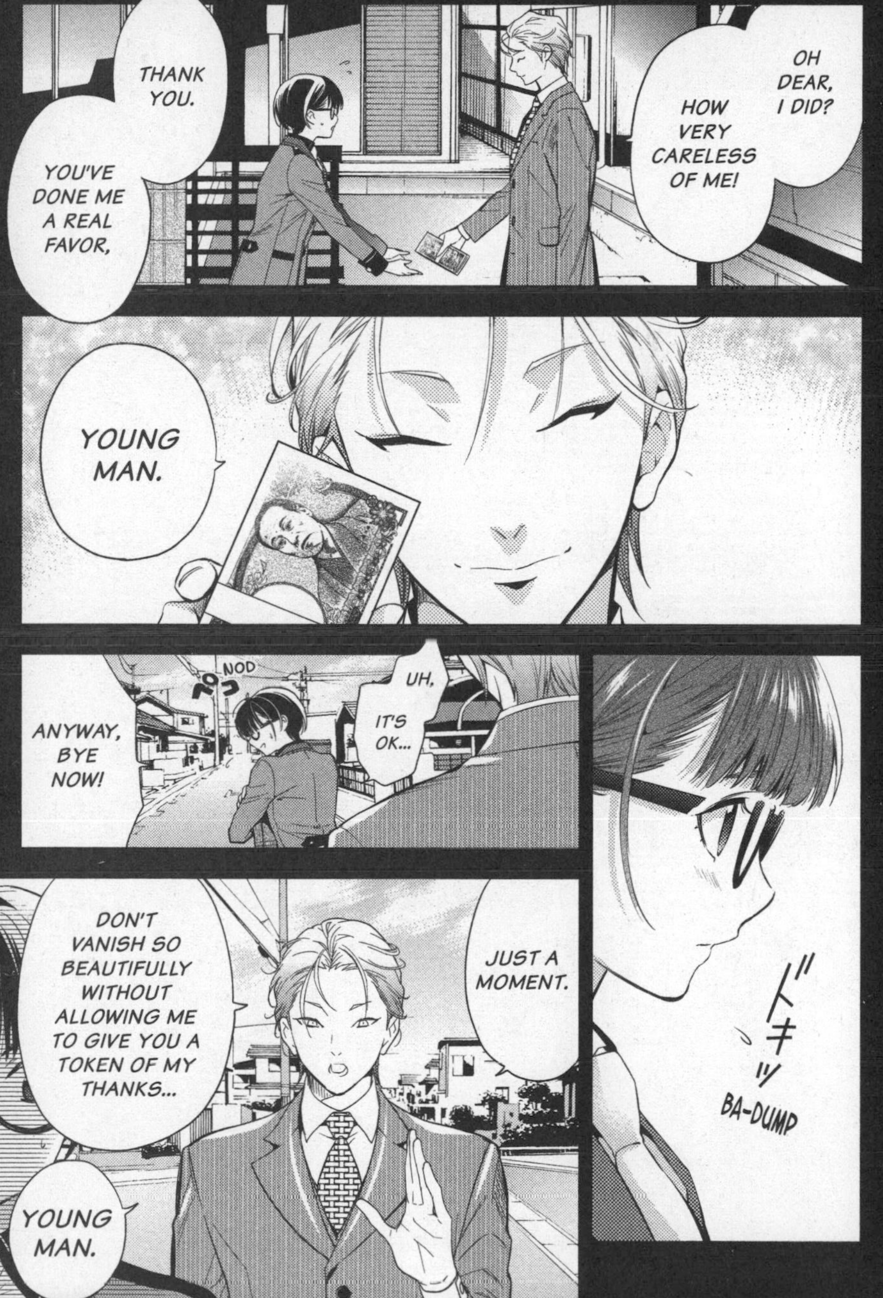
OH DEAR, I DID?
HOW VERY CARELESS OF ME!
THANK YOU.
YOU'VE DONE ME A REAL FAVOR,
YOUNG MAN.
ドキッ
BA-DUMP
UH, IT'S OK...
NOD
ANYWAY, BYE NOW!
JUST A MOMENT.
DON'T VANISH SO BEAUTIFULLY WITHOUT ALLOWING ME TO GIVE YOU A TOKEN OF MY THANKS...
YOUNG MAN.

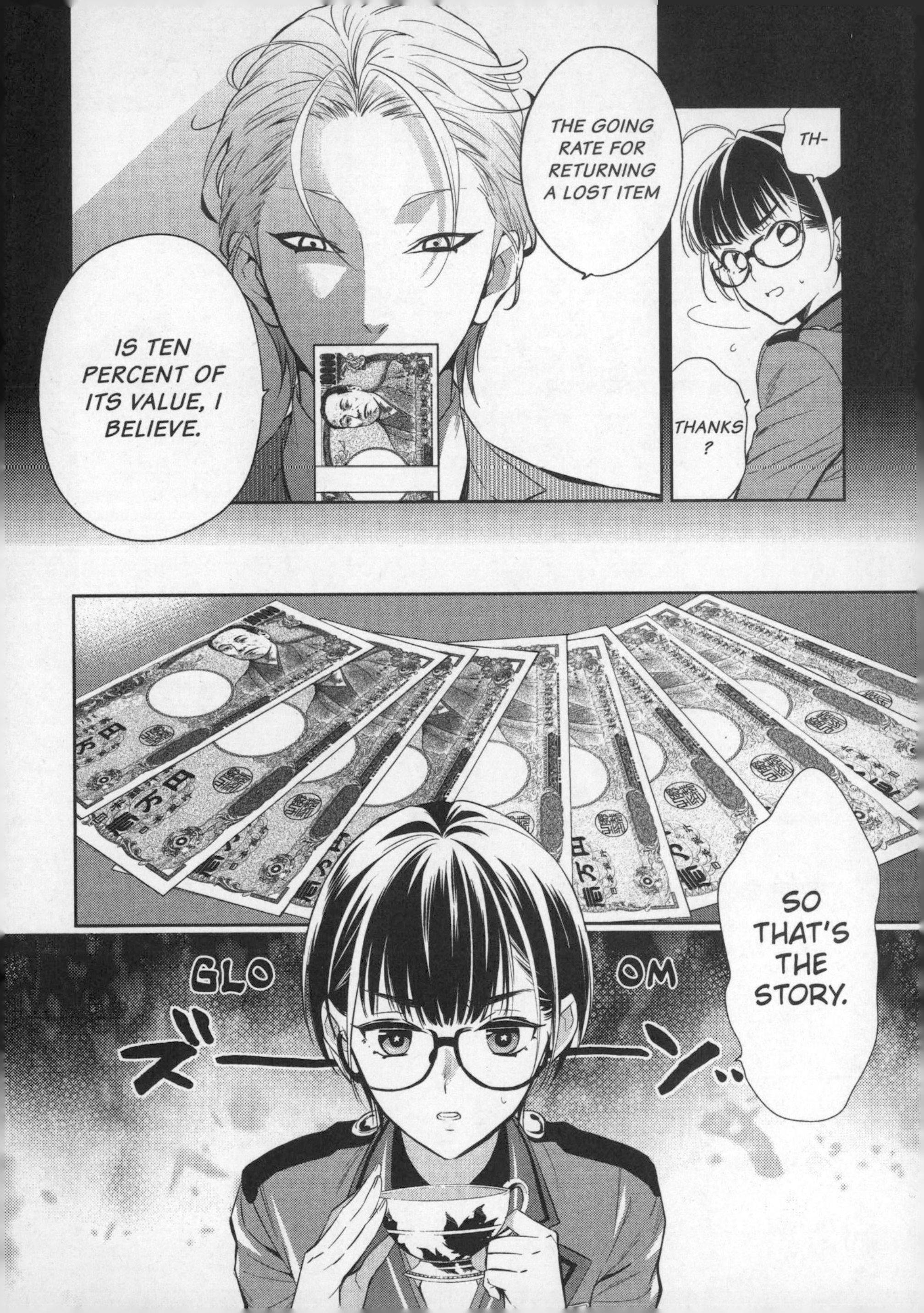
TH-
THANKS ?
THE GOING RATE FOR RETURNING A LOST ITEM
IS TEN PERCENT OF ITS VALUE, I BELIEVE.
SO THAT'S THE STORY.
GLO OM
ズーン

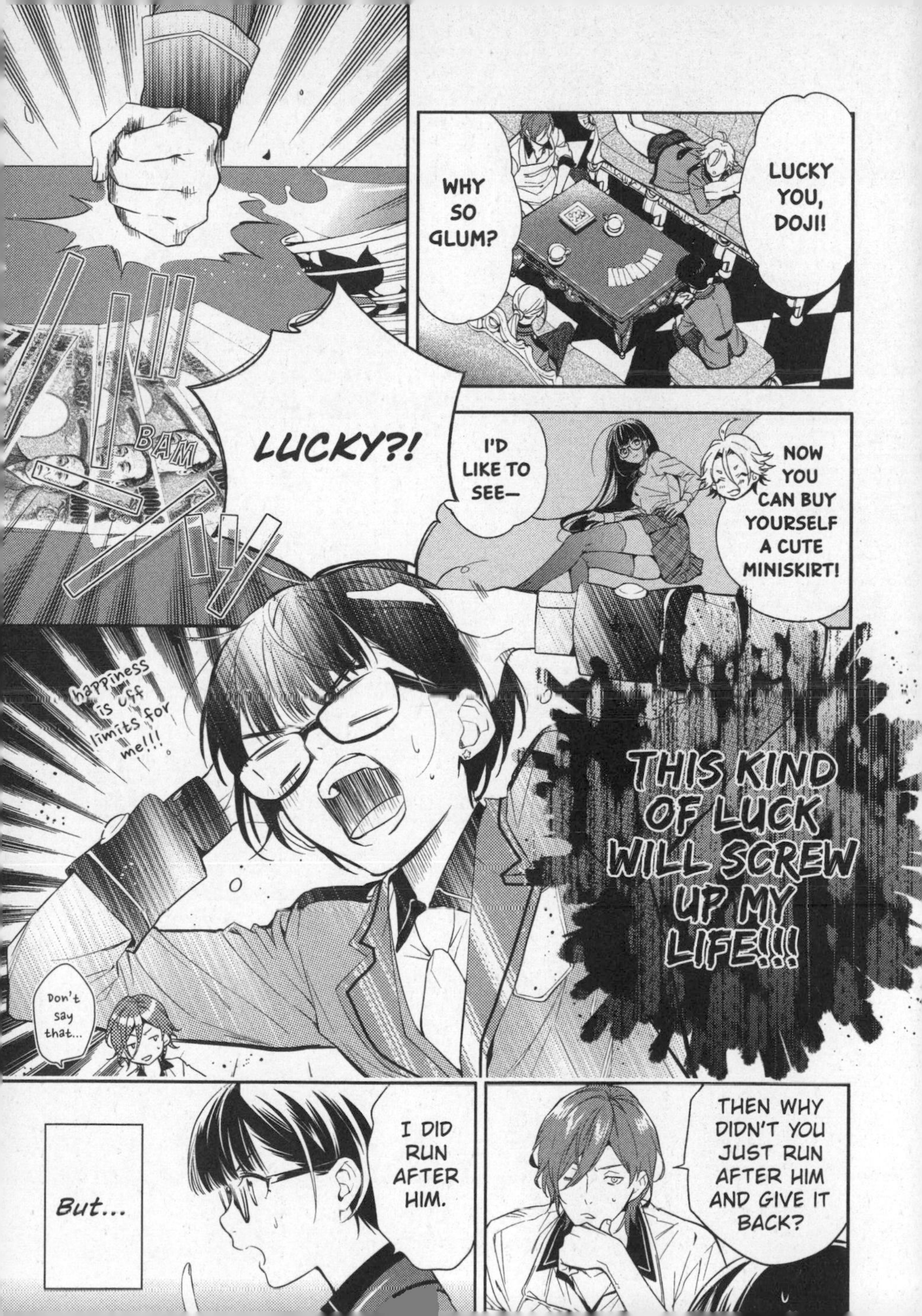
LUCKY YOU, DOJI!
WHY SO GLUM?
NOW YOU CAN BUY YOURSELF A CUTE MINISKIRT!
I'D LIKE TO SEE—
LUCKY?!
BAM
THIS KIND OF LUCK WILL SCREW UP MY LIFE!!!
happiness is off limits for me!!!
Don't say that...
THEN WHY DIDN'T YOU JUST RUN AFTER HIM AND GIVE IT BACK?
I DID RUN AFTER HIM.
But...

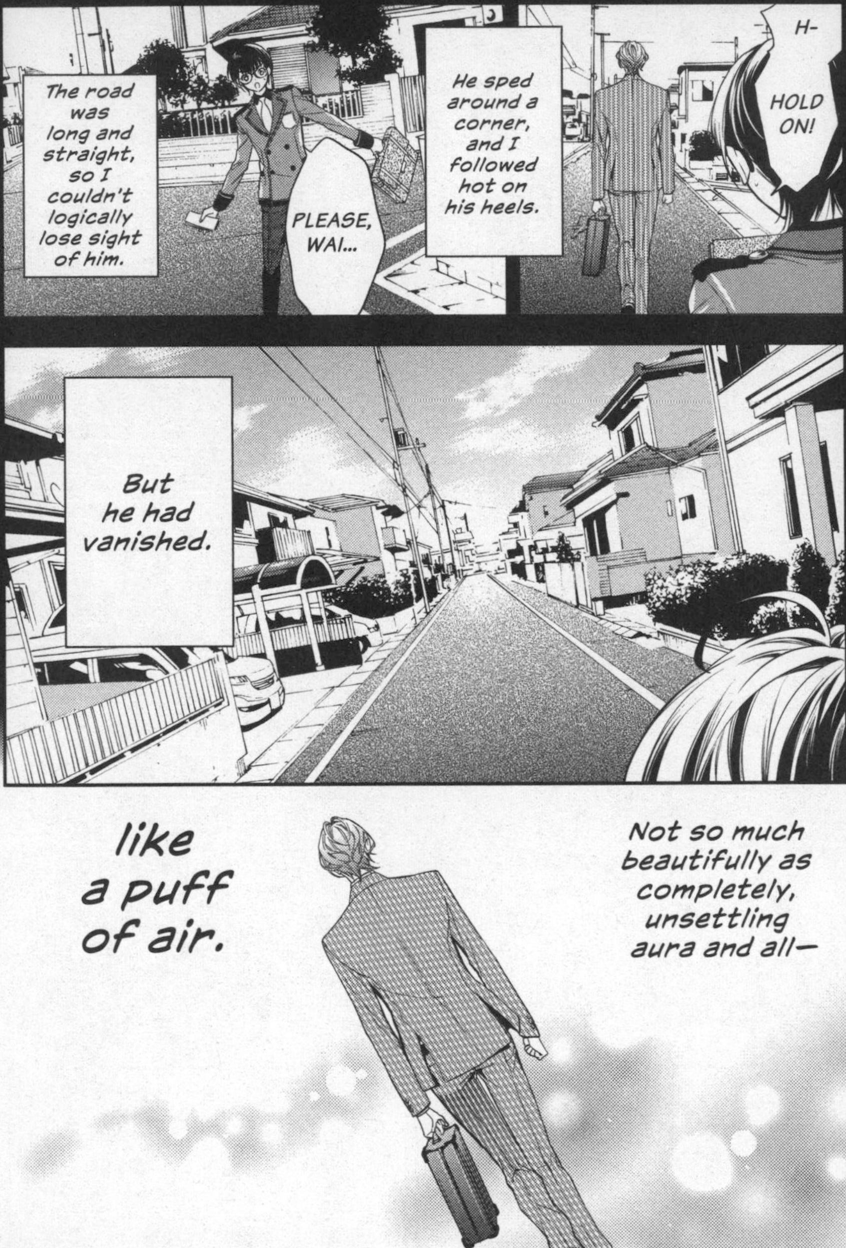

H-
HOLD ON!
He sped around a corner, and I followed hot on his heels.
PLEASE, WAI...
The road was long and straight, so I couldn't logically lose sight of him.
But he had vanished.
Not so much beautifully as completely, unsettling aura and all—
like a puff of air.

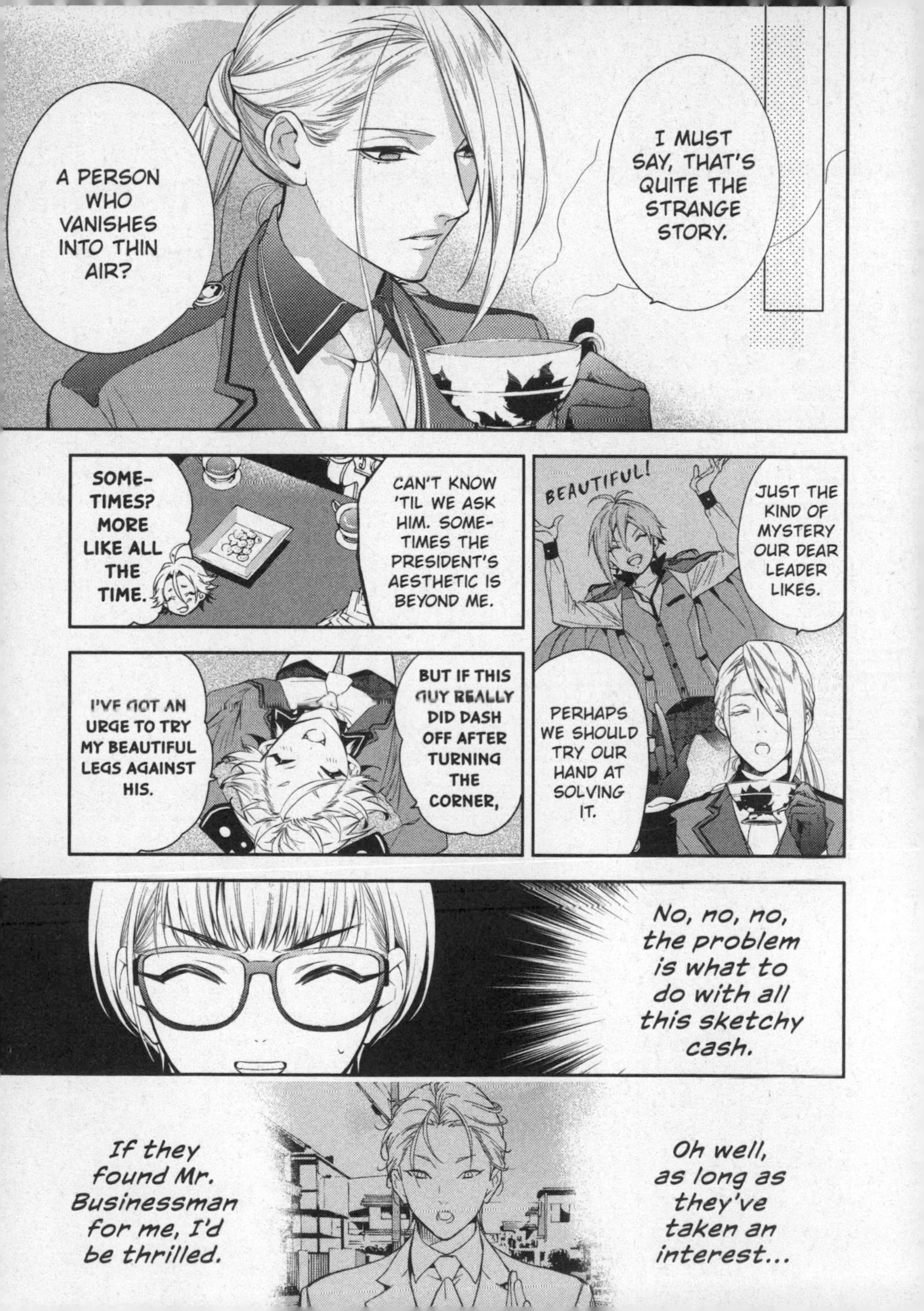
I MUST SAY, THAT'S QUITE THE STRANGE STORY.
A PERSON WHO VANISHES INTO THIN AIR?
BEAUTIFUL!
JUST THE KIND OF MYSTERY OUR DEAR LEADER LIKES.
PERHAPS WE SHOULD TRY OUR HAND AT SOLVING IT.
CAN'T KNOW 'TIL WE ASK HIM. SOME-TIMES THE PRESIDENT'S AESTHETIC IS BEYOND ME.
SOME-TIMES? MORE LIKE ALL THE TIME.
BUT IF THIS GUY REALLY DID DASH OFF AFTER TURNING THE CORNER,
I'VE GOT AN URGE TO TRY MY BEAUTIFUL LEGS AGAINST HIS.
No, no, no, the problem is what to do with all this sketchy cash.
Oh well, as long as they've taken an interest...
If they found Mr. Businessman for me, I'd be thrilled.

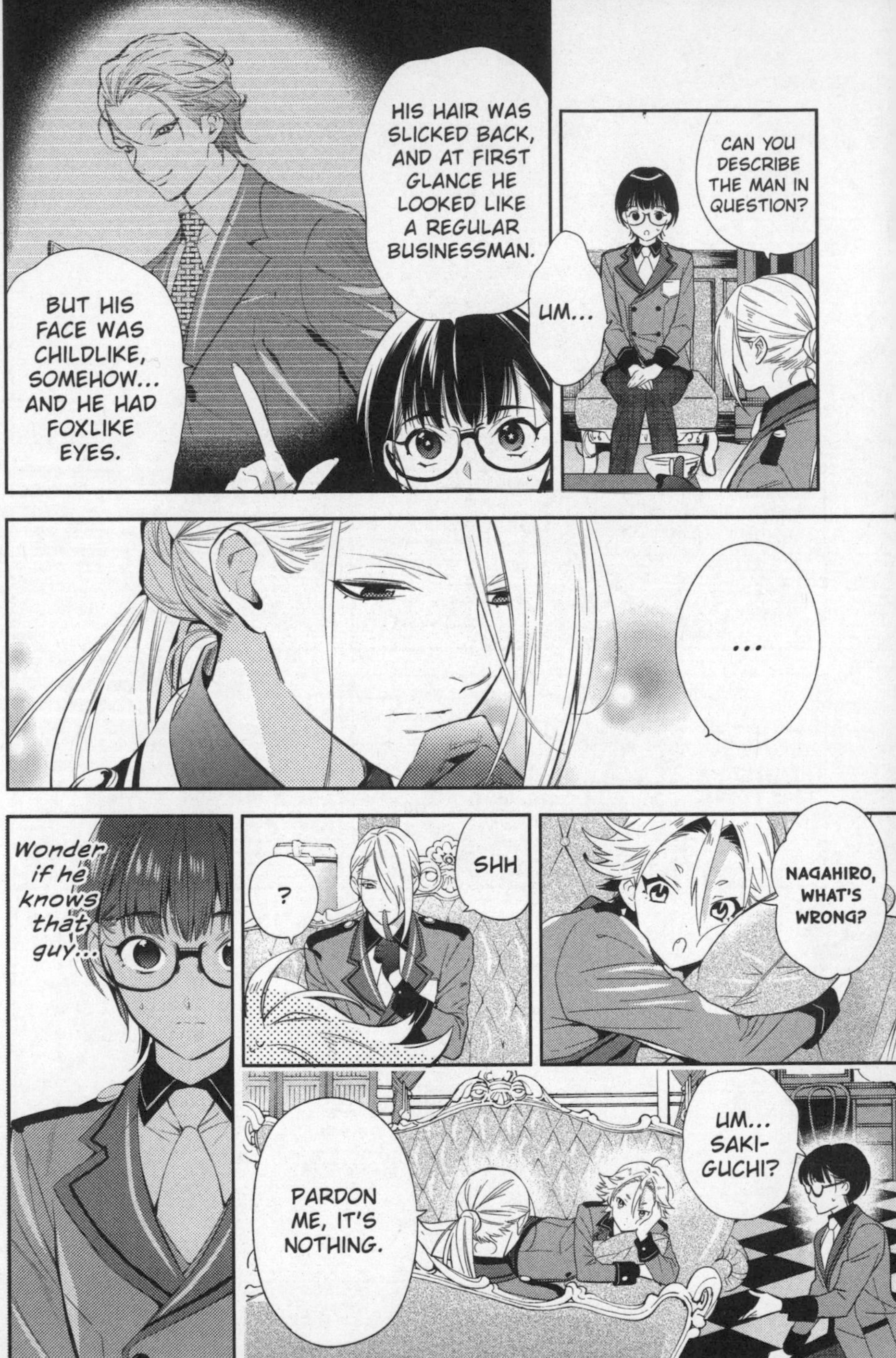
CAN YOU DESCRIBE THE MAN IN QUESTION?
UM...
HIS HAIR WAS SLICKED BACK, AND AT FIRST GLANCE HE LOOKED LIKE A REGULAR BUSINESSMAN.
BUT HIS FACE WAS CHILDLIKE, SOMEHOW... AND HE HAD FOXLIKE EYES.
...
NAGAHIRO, WHAT'S WRONG?
SHH
?
UM... SAKI-GUCHI?
PARDON ME, IT'S NOTHING.
Wonder if he knows that guy...

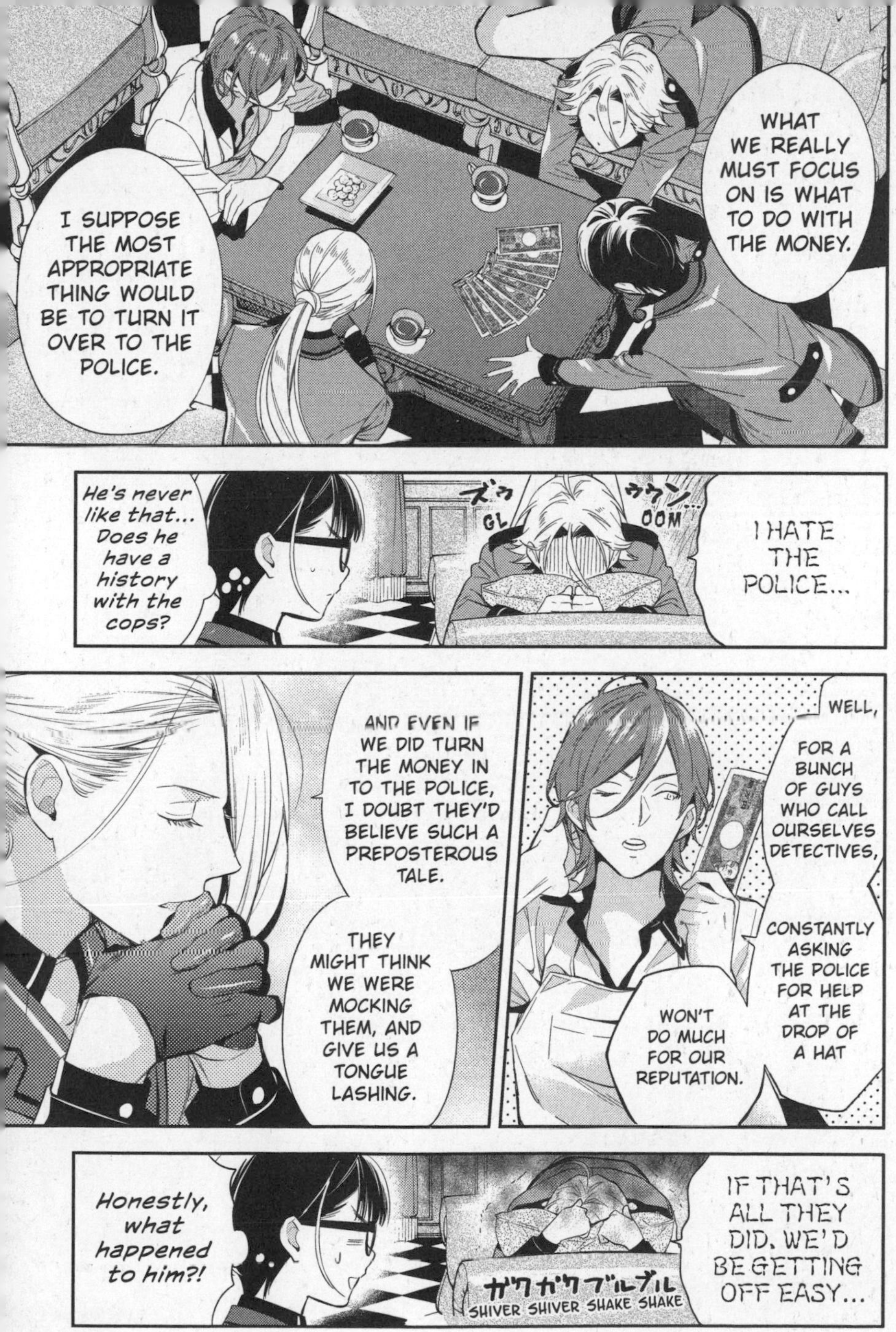
WHAT WE REALLY MUST FOCUS ON IS WHAT TO DO WITH THE MONEY.
I SUPPOSE THE MOST APPROPRIATE THING WOULD BE TO TURN IT OVER TO THE POLICE.
I HATE THE POLICE...
OOM
GL
He's never like that... Does he have a history with the cops?
WELL,
FOR A BUNCH OF GUYS WHO CALL OURSELVES DETECTIVES,
CONSTANTLY ASKING THE POLICE FOR HELP AT THE DROP OF A HAT
WON'T DO MUCH FOR OUR REPUTATION.
AND EVEN IF WE DID TURN THE MONEY IN TO THE POLICE, I DOUBT THEY'D BELIEVE SUCH A PREPOSTEROUS TALE.
THEY MIGHT THINK WE WERE MOCKING THEM, AND GIVE US A TONGUE LASHING.
IF THAT'S ALL THEY DID, WE'D BE GETTING OFF EASY...
ガクガクブルブル
SHIVER SHIVER SHAKE SHAKE
Honestly, what happened to him?!

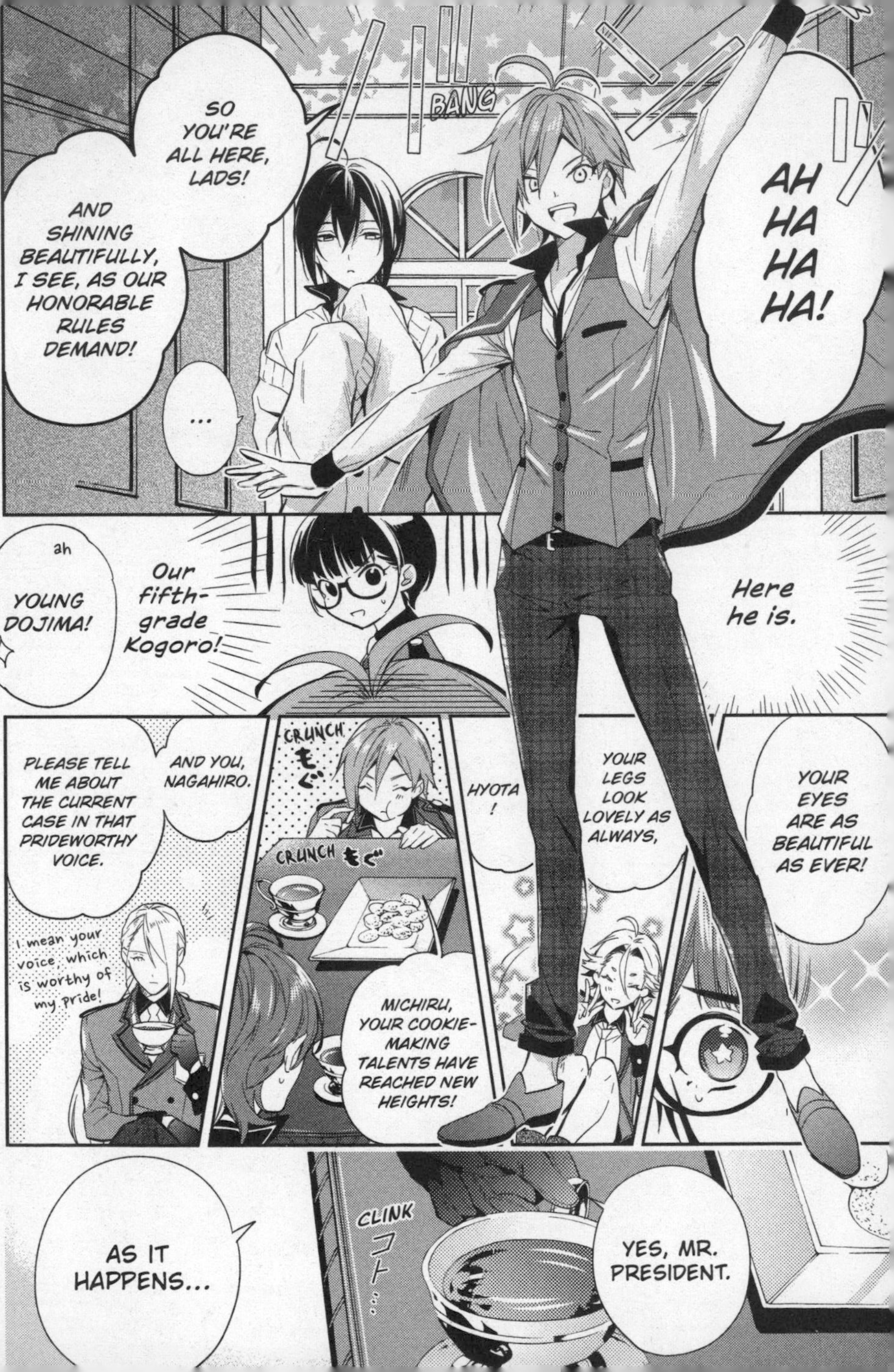
BANG
AH HA HA HA!
SO YOU'RE ALL HERE, LADS!
AND SHINING BEAUTIFULLY, I SEE, AS OUR HONORABLE RULES DEMAND!
...
Here he is.
Our fifth-grade Kogoro!
ah
YOUNG DOJIMA!
YOUR EYES ARE AS BEAUTIFUL AS EVER!
YOUR LEGS LOOK LOVELY AS ALWAYS,
HYOTA!
CRUNCH もぐ
CRUNCH もぐ
MICHIRU, YOUR COOKIE-MAKING TALENTS HAVE REACHED NEW HEIGHTS!
AND YOU, NAGAHIRO.
PLEASE TELL ME ABOUT THE CURRENT CASE IN THAT PRIDEWORTHY VOICE.
I mean your voice, which is worthy of my pride!
YES, MR. PRESIDENT.
CLINK コト…
AS IT HAPPENS...

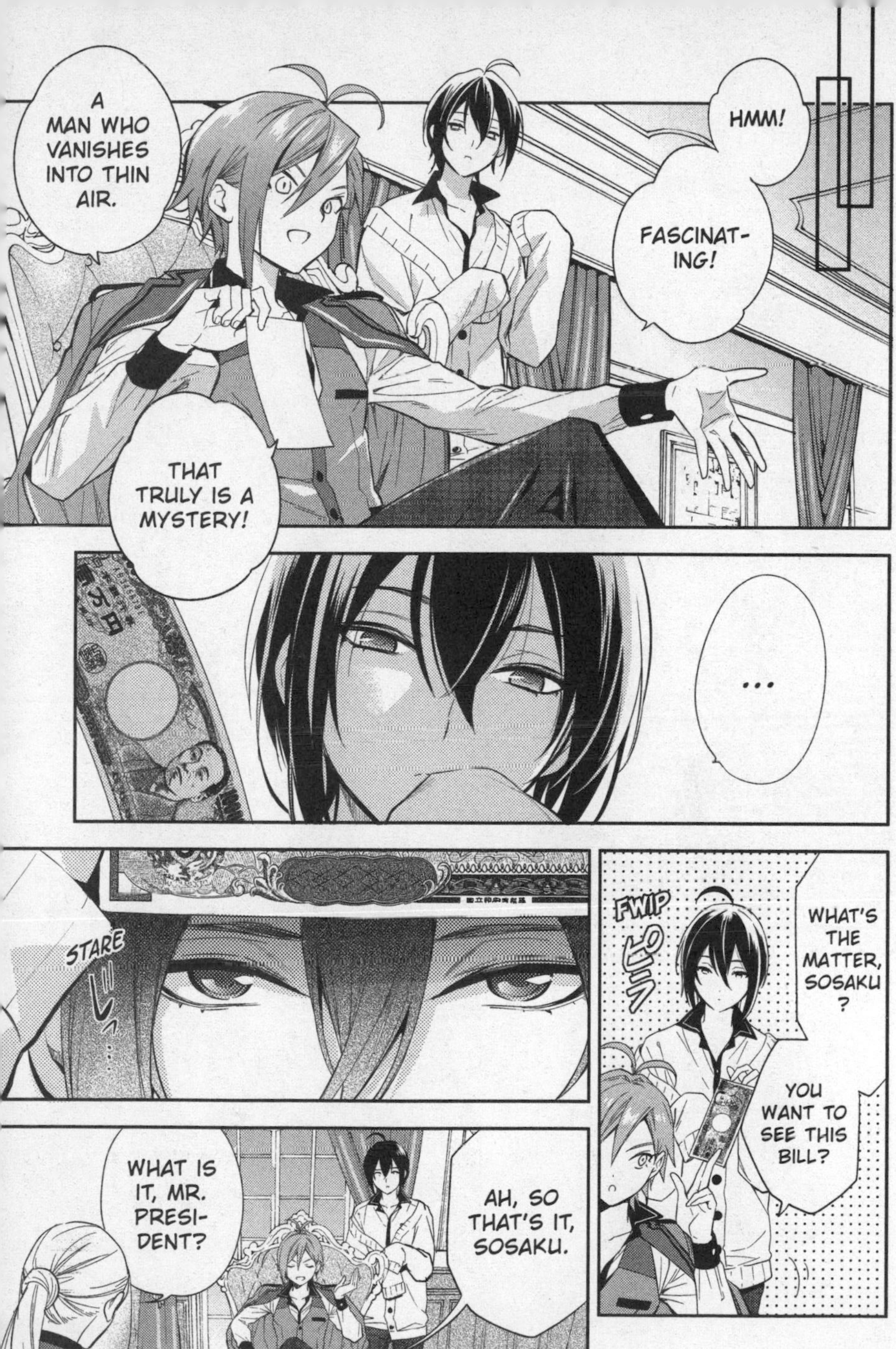
HMM!
FASCINATING!
A MAN WHO VANISHES INTO THIN AIR.
THAT TRULY IS A MYSTERY!
...
FWIP
WHAT'S THE MATTER, SOSAKU?
YOU WANT TO SEE THIS BILL?
STARE
AH, SO THAT'S IT, SOSAKU.
WHAT IS IT, MR. PRESIDENT?

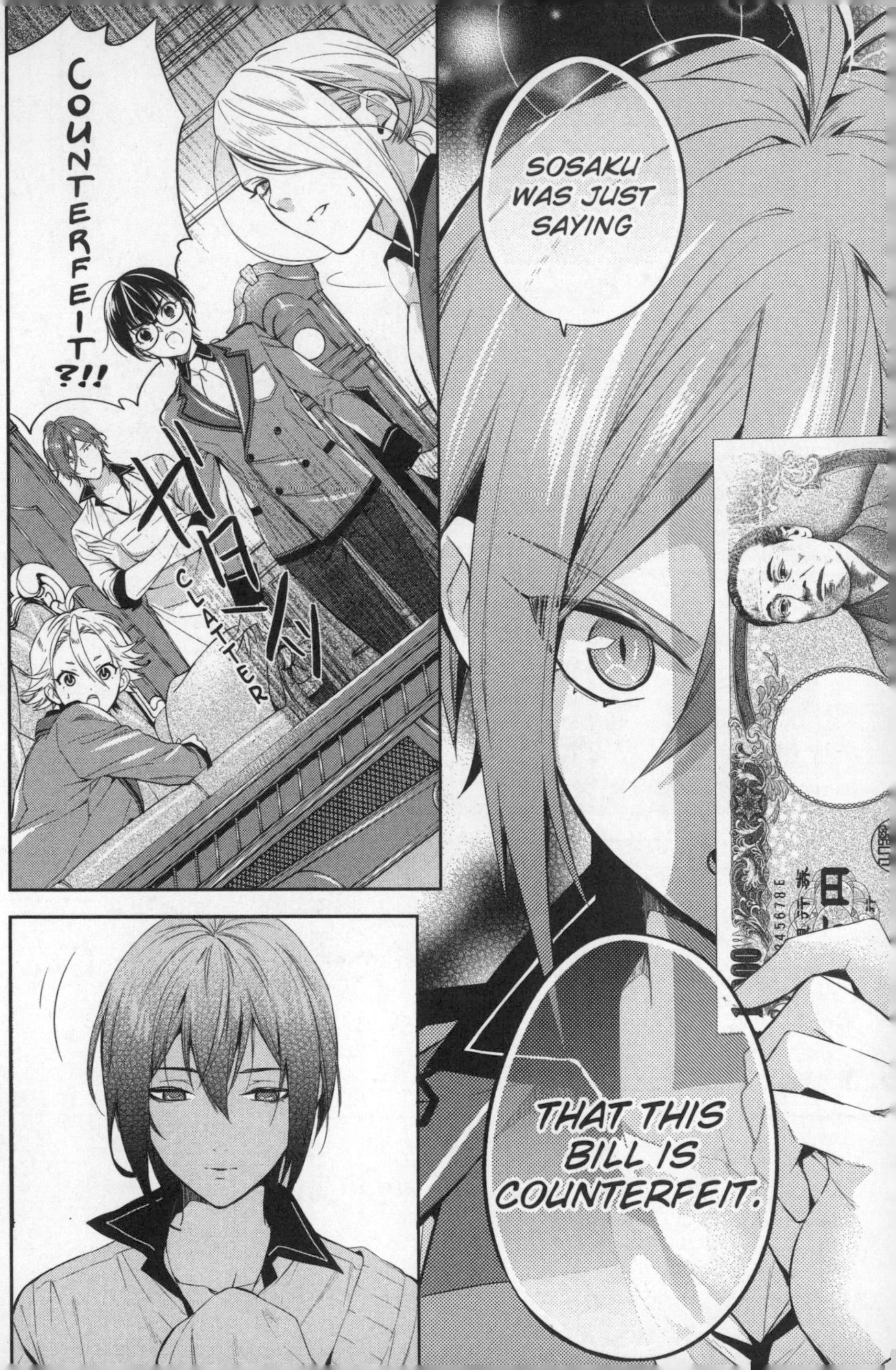
SOSAKU WAS JUST SAYING
THAT THIS BILL IS COUNTERFEIT.
COUNTERFEIT?!!
CLATTER

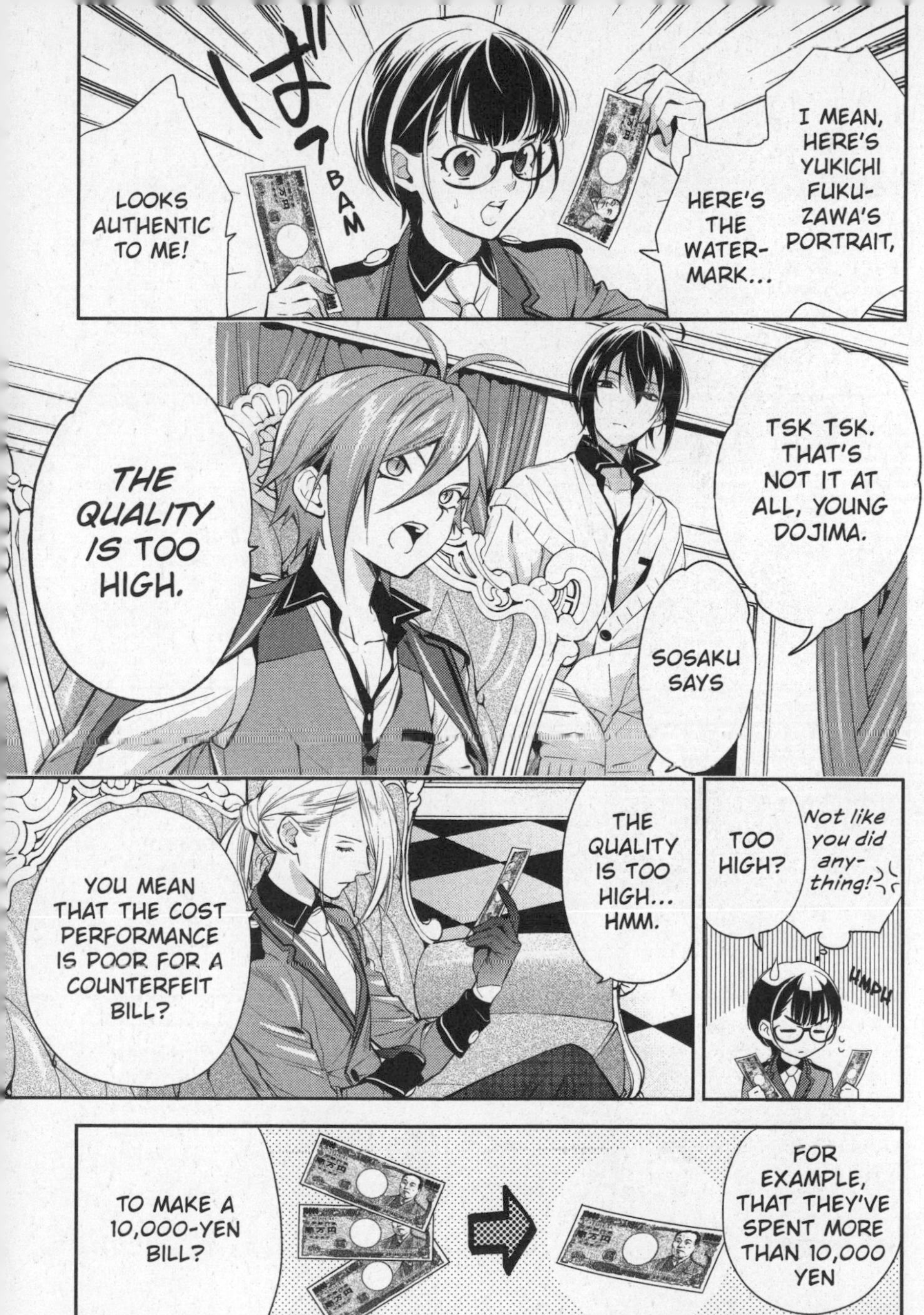
I MEAN, HERE'S YUKICHI FUKU-ZAWA'S PORTRAIT,
HERE'S THE WATER-MARK...
BAM
LOOKS AUTHENTIC TO ME!
TSK TSK. THAT'S NOT IT AT ALL, YOUNG DOJIMA.
SOSAKU SAYS
THE QUALITY IS TOO HIGH.
Not like you did any-thing!
TOO HIGH?
HMPH
THE QUALITY IS TOO HIGH... HMM.
YOU MEAN THAT THE COST PERFORMANCE IS POOR FOR A COUNTERFEIT BILL?
FOR EXAMPLE, THAT THEY'VE SPENT MORE THAN 10,000 YEN
TO MAKE A 10,000-YEN BILL?

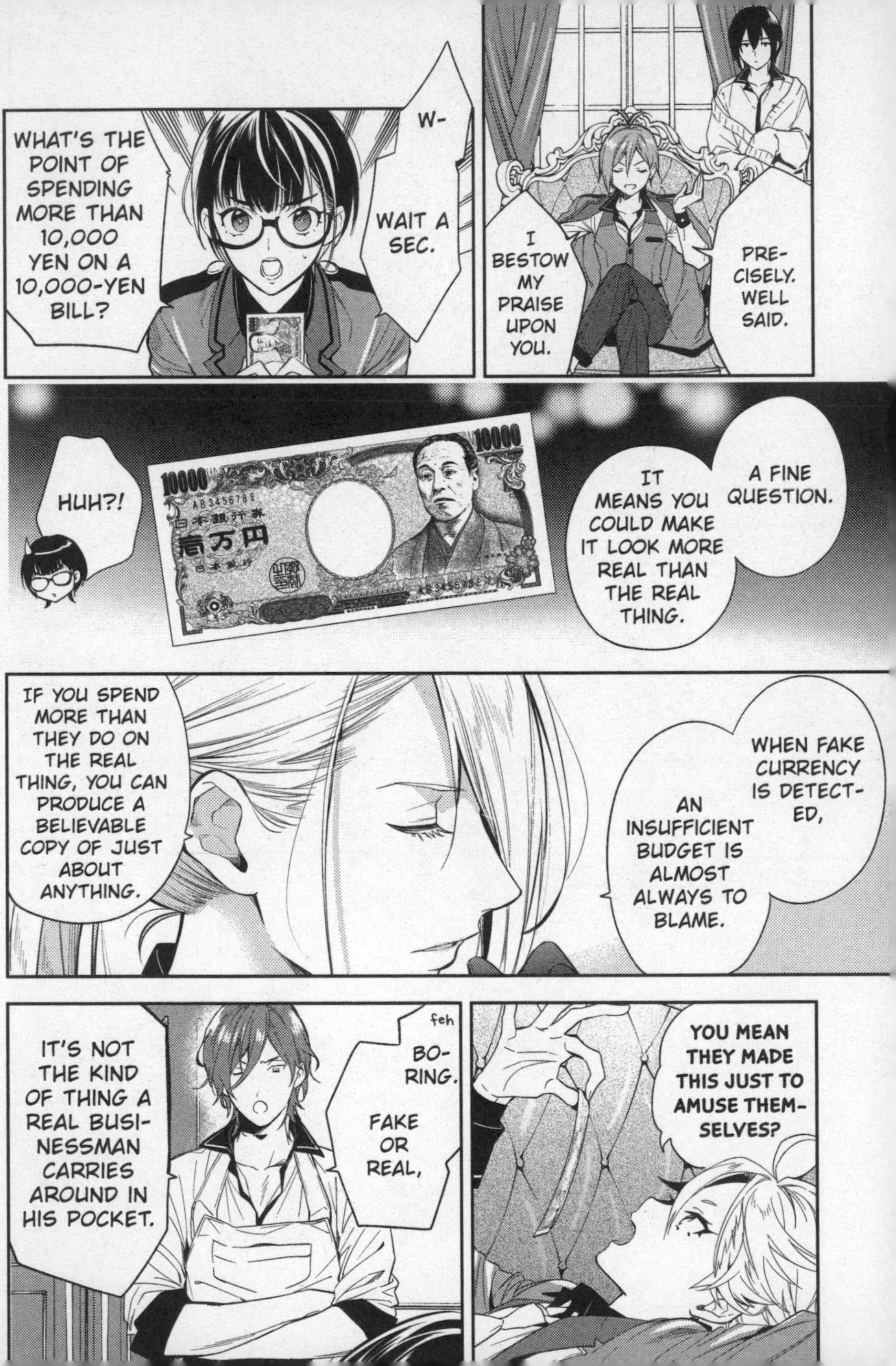
PRE-CISELY. WELL SAID.
I BESTOW MY PRAISE UPON YOU.
W-
WAIT A SEC.
WHAT'S THE POINT OF SPENDING MORE THAN 10,000 YEN ON A 10,000-YEN BILL?
A FINE QUESTION.
IT MEANS YOU COULD MAKE IT LOOK MORE REAL THAN THE REAL THING.
HUH?!
WHEN FAKE CURRENCY IS DETECT-ED,
AN INSUFFICIENT BUDGET IS ALMOST ALWAYS TO BLAME.
IF YOU SPEND MORE THAN THEY DO ON THE REAL THING, YOU CAN PRODUCE A BELIEVABLE COPY OF JUST ABOUT ANYTHING.
YOU MEAN THEY MADE THIS JUST TO AMUSE THEM-SELVES?
feh
BO-RING.
FAKE OR REAL,
IT'S NOT THE KIND OF THING A REAL BUSI-NESSMAN CARRIES AROUND IN HIS POCKET.

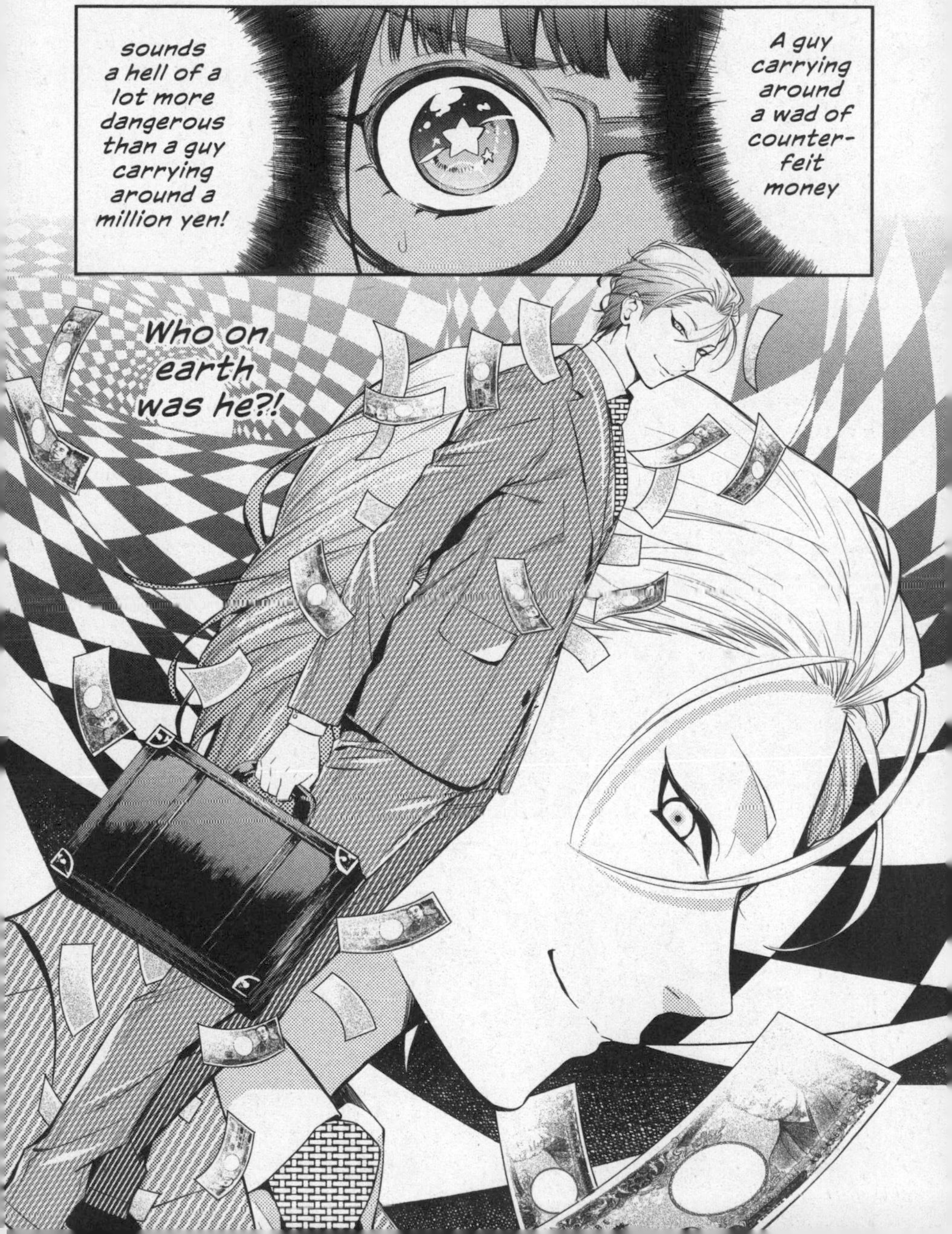
A guy carrying around a wad of counter-feit money
sounds a hell of a lot more dangerous than a guy carrying around a million yen!
Who on earth was he?!

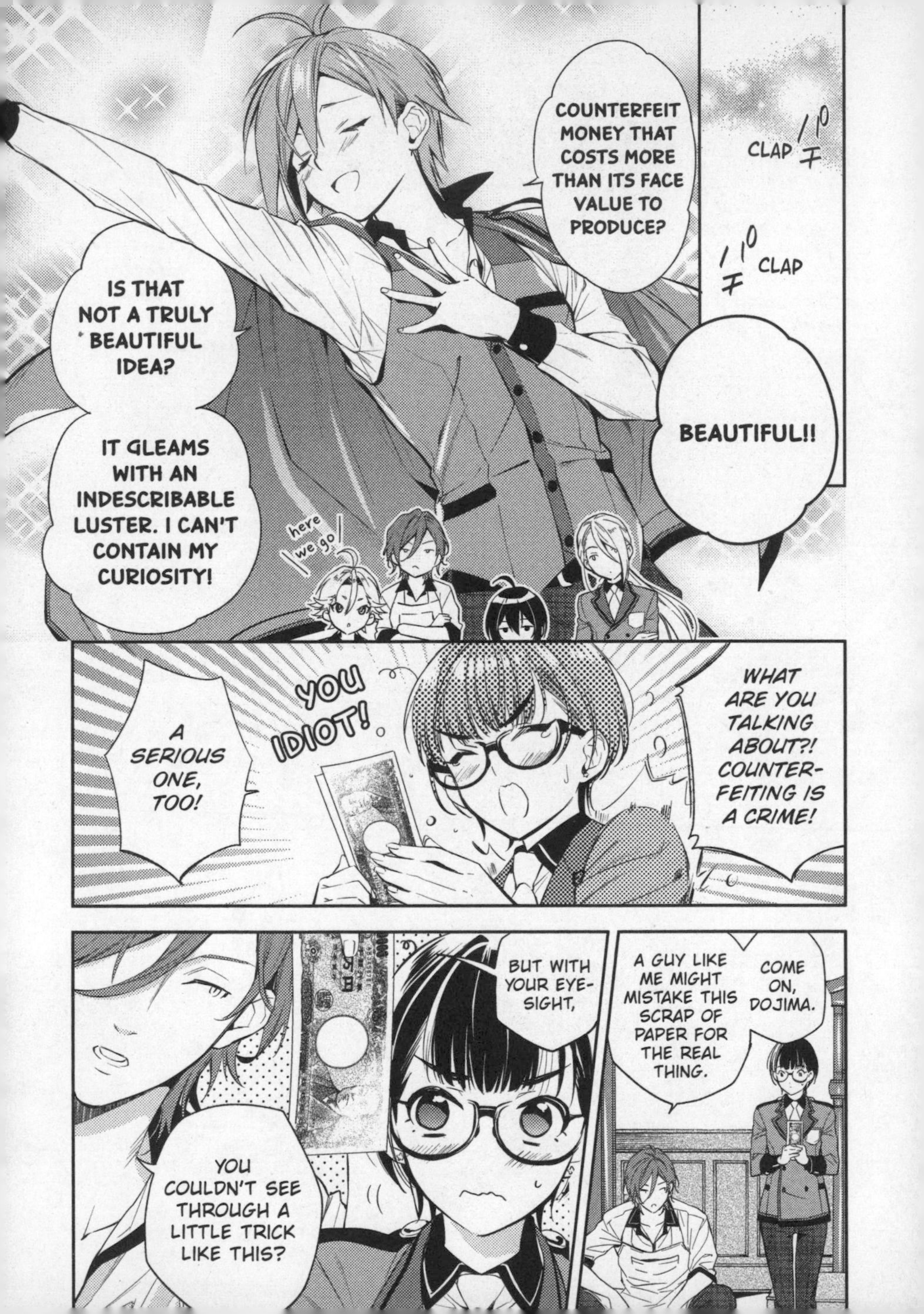
COUNTERFEIT MONEY THAT COSTS MORE THAN ITS FACE VALUE TO PRODUCE?
CLAP
CLAP
BEAUTIFUL!!
IS THAT NOT A TRULY BEAUTIFUL IDEA?
IT GLEAMS WITH AN INDESCRIBABLE LUSTER. I CAN'T CONTAIN MY CURIOSITY!
here we go
WHAT ARE YOU TALKING ABOUT?! COUNTER-FEITING IS A CRIME!
YOU IDIOT!
A SERIOUS ONE, TOO!
COME ON, DOJIMA.
A GUY LIKE ME MIGHT MISTAKE THIS SCRAP OF PAPER FOR THE REAL THING.
BUT WITH YOUR EYE-SIGHT,
YOU COULDN'T SEE THROUGH A LITTLE TRICK LIKE THIS?

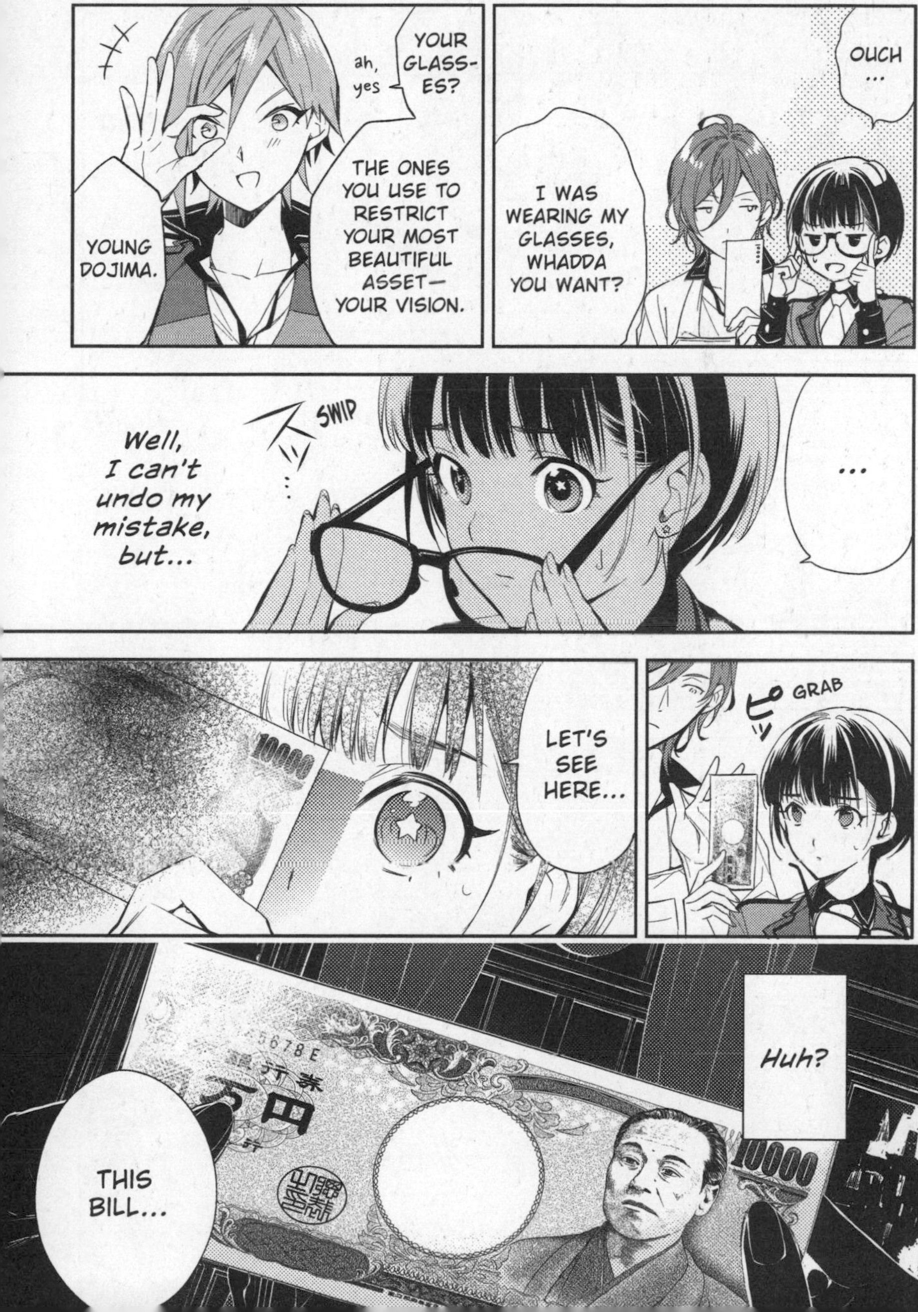
OUCH ...
I WAS WEARING MY GLASSES, WHADDA YOU WANT?
YOUR GLASS-ES?
ah, yes
THE ONES YOU USE TO RESTRICT YOUR MOST BEAUTIFUL ASSET—YOUR VISION.
YOUNG DOJIMA.
...
SWIP
Well, I can't undo my mistake, but...
GRAB
LET'S SEE HERE...
Huh?
THIS BILL...

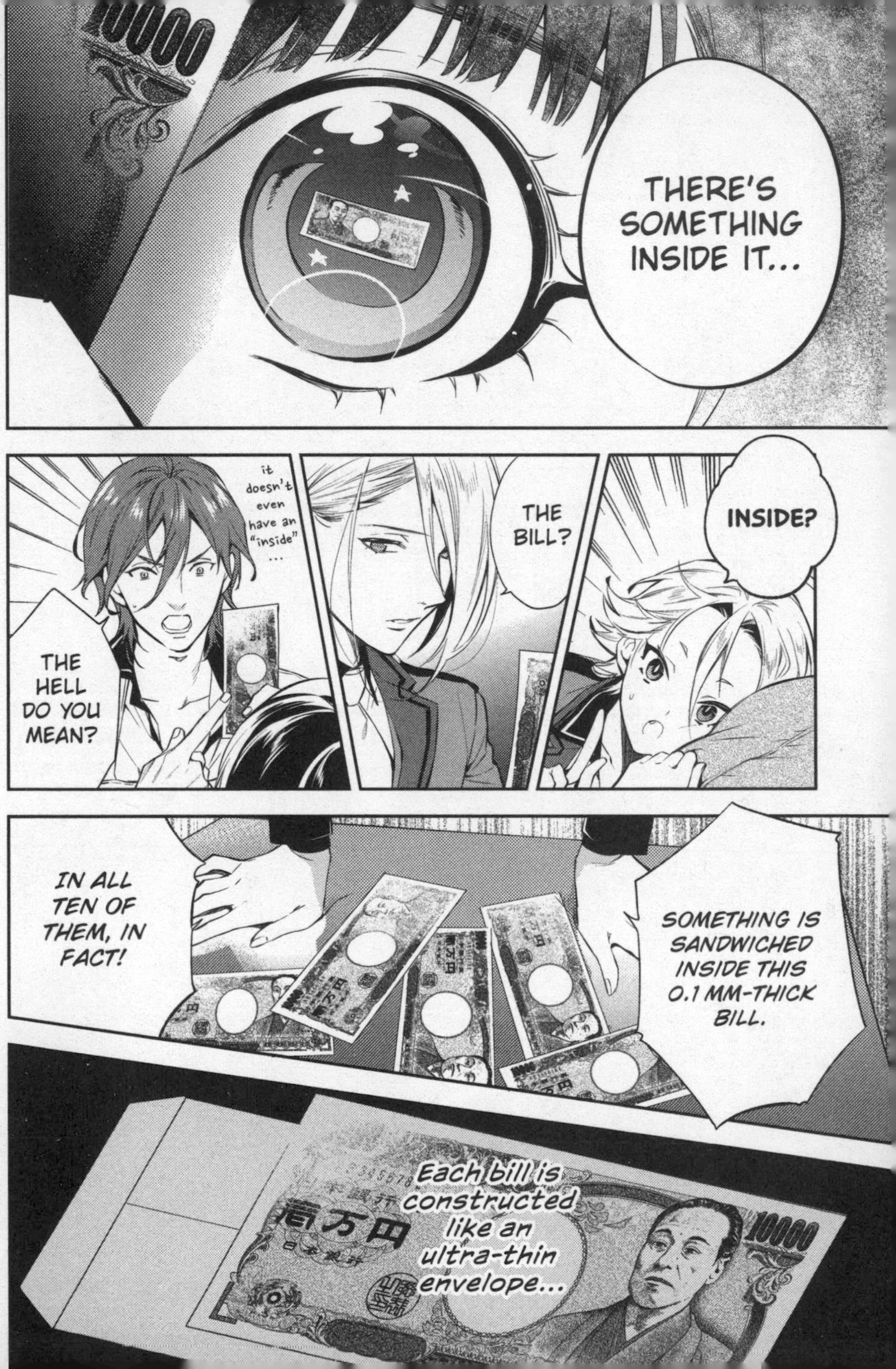
THERE'S SOMETHING INSIDE IT...
INSIDE?
THE BILL?
it doesn't even have an "inside"...
THE HELL DO YOU MEAN?
SOMETHING IS SANDWICHED INSIDE THIS 0.1 MM-THICK BILL.
IN ALL TEN OF THEM, IN FACT!
Each bill is constructed like an ultra-thin envelope...

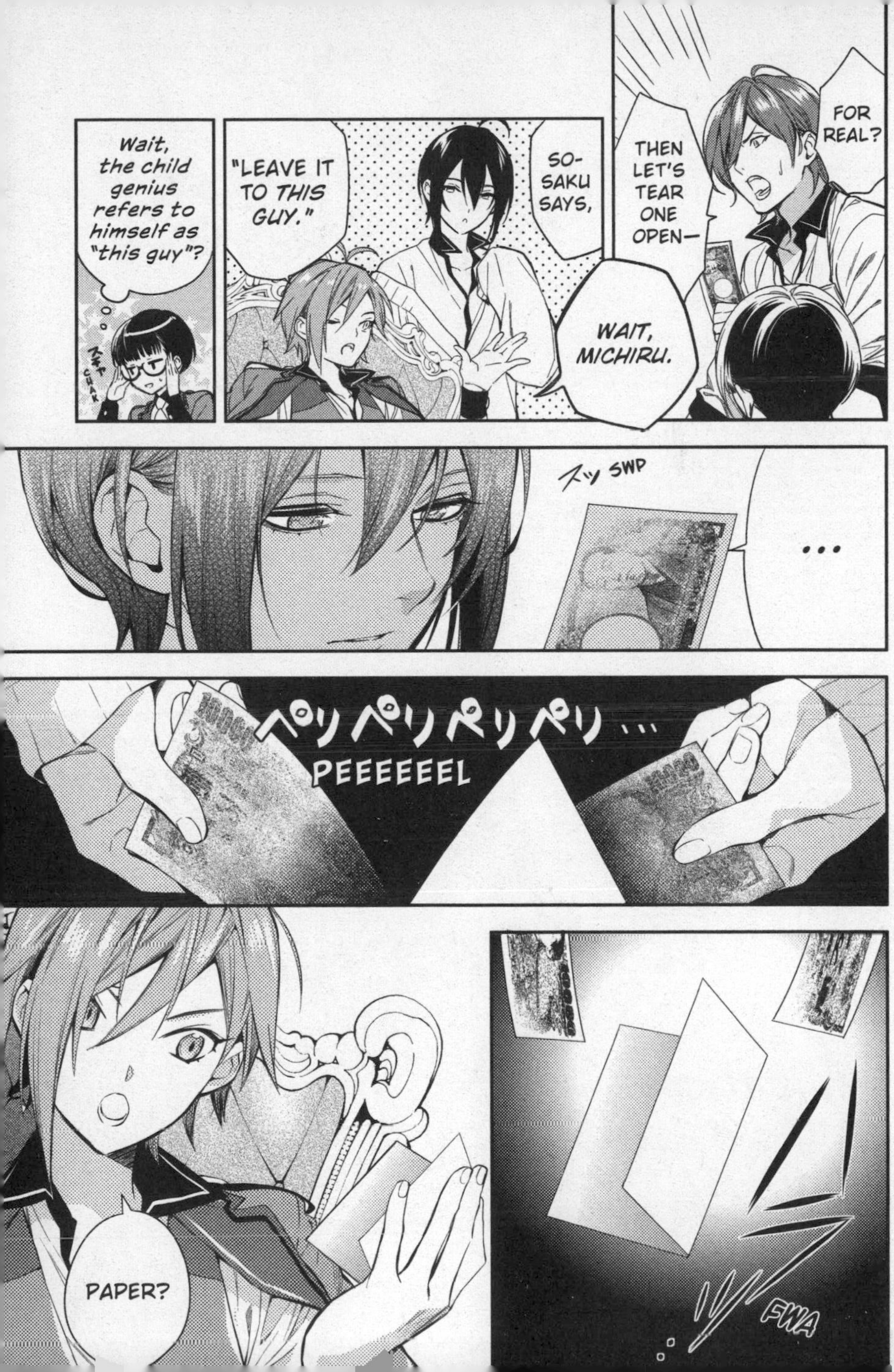
FOR REAL?
THEN LET'S TEAR ONE OPEN—
WAIT, MICHIRU.
SO-SAKU SAYS,
"LEAVE IT TO THIS GUY."
Wait, the child genius refers to himself as "this guy"?
スチャ CHAK
...
ズッ SWP
ペリペリペリペリ…
PEEEEEEL
FWA
PAPER?

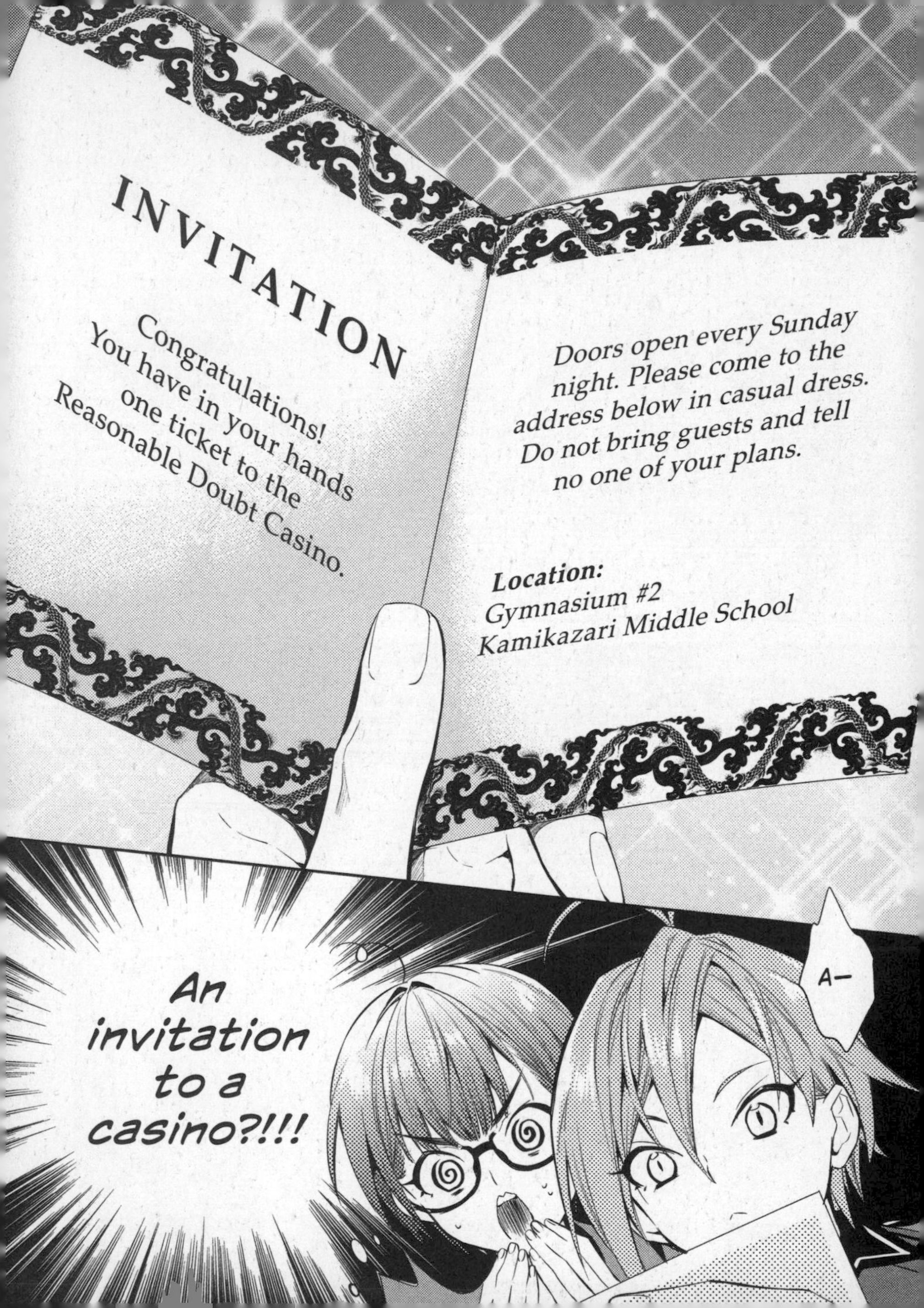
INVITATION
Congratulations!
You have in your hands one ticket to the Reasonable Doubt Casino.
Doors open every Sunday night. Please come to the address below in casual dress. Do not bring guests and tell no one of your plans.
Location:
Gymnasium #2
Kamikazari Middle School
A—
An invitation to a casino?!!!

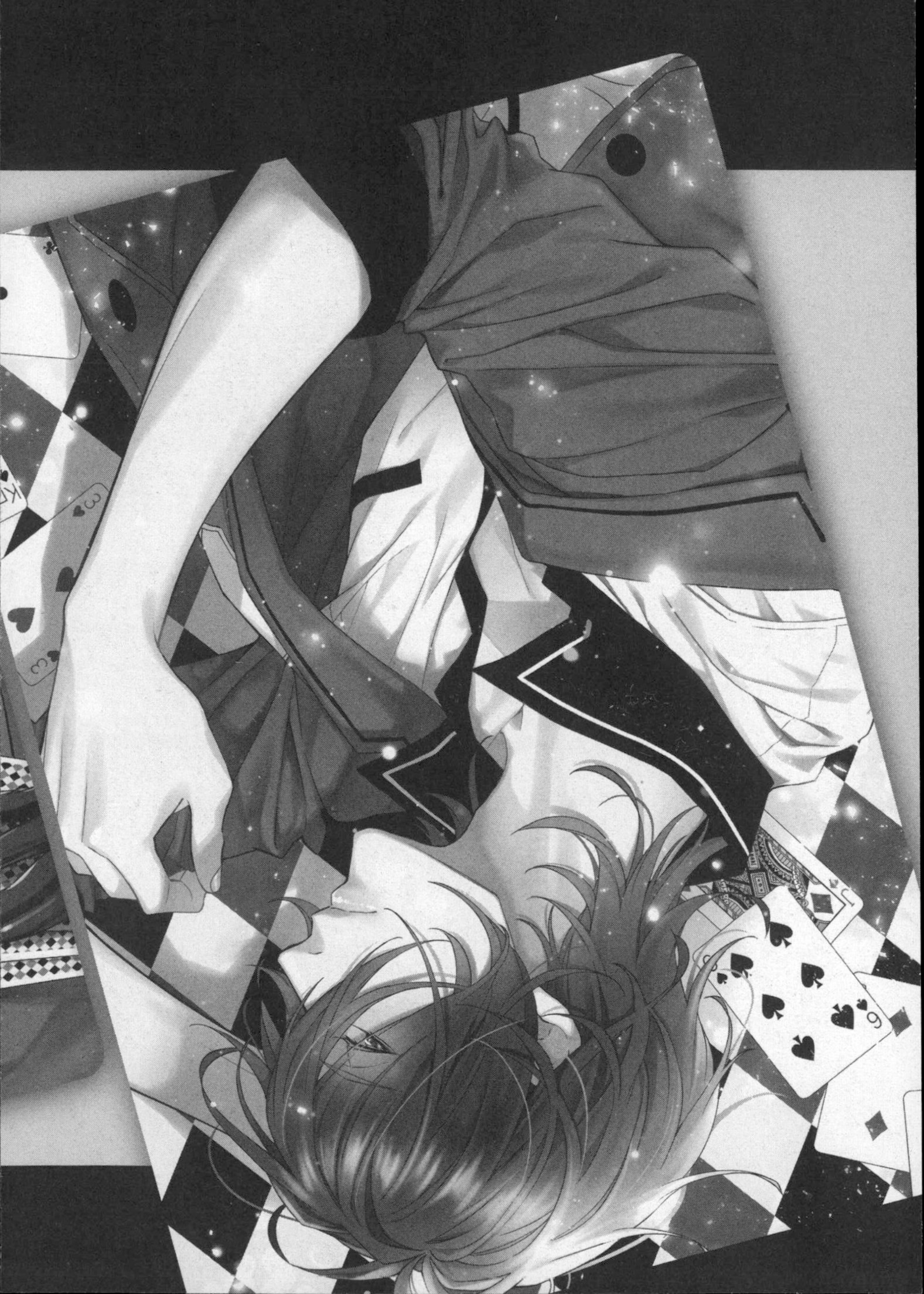

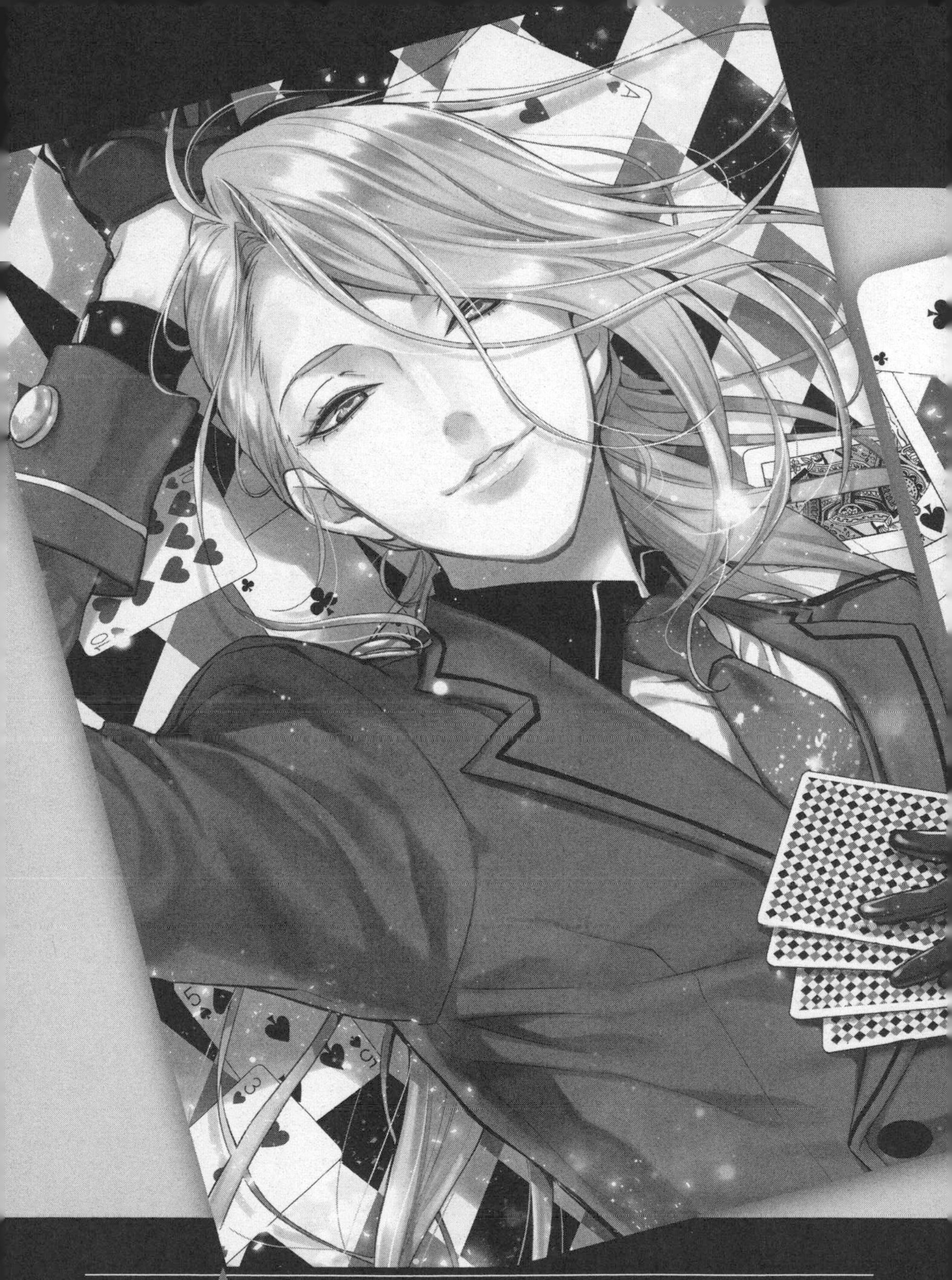

FILE ★ The Swindler, the Vanishing Man, and the Pretty Boys 2

PRETTY BOY

DETECTIVE CLUB!!

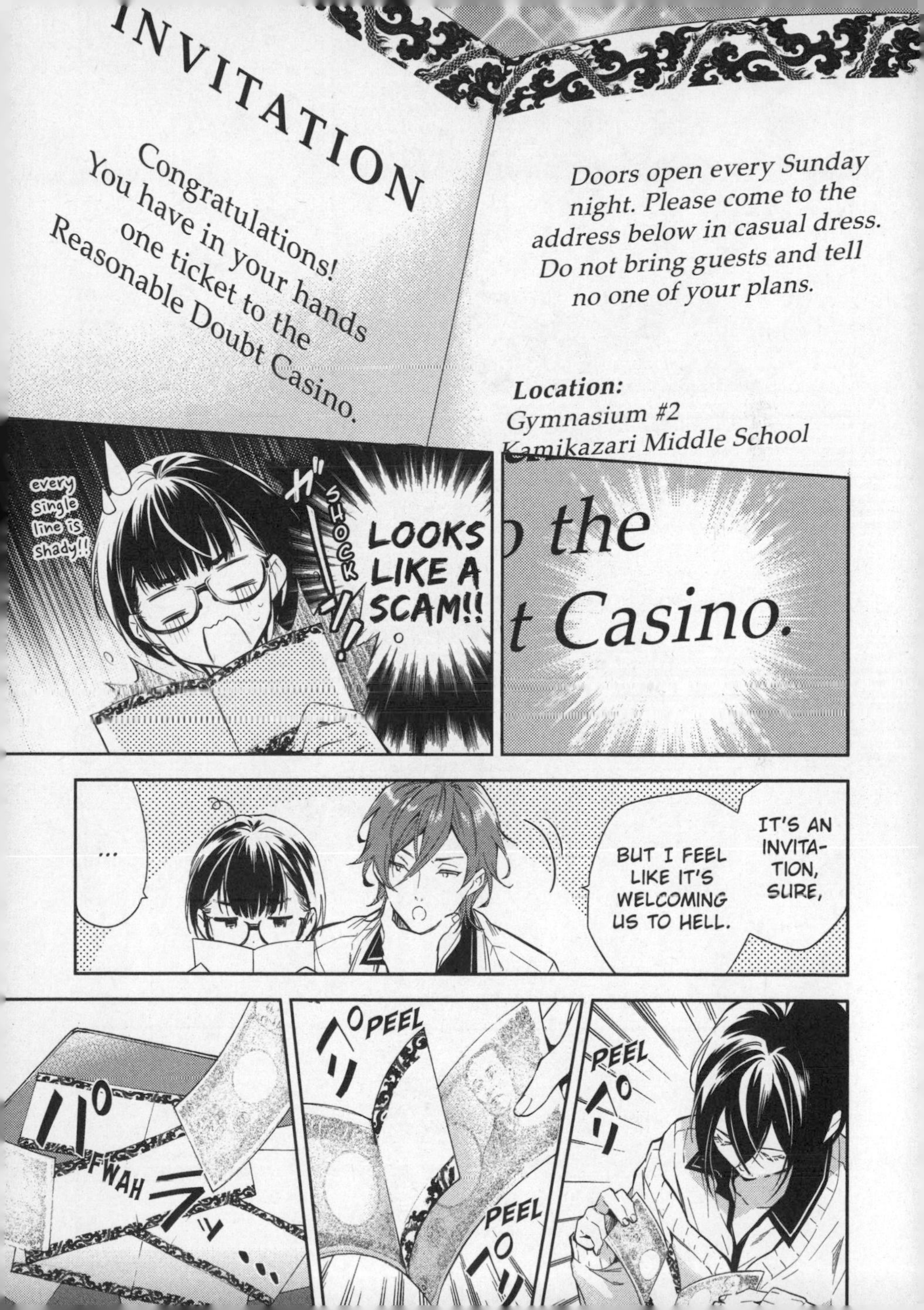
INVITATION
Congratulations! You have in your hands one ticket to the Reasonable Doubt Casino.
Doors open every Sunday night. Please come to the address below in casual dress. Do not bring guests and tell no one of your plans.
Location:
Gymnasium #2
Kamikazari Middle School
o the
t Casino.
SHOCK
LOOKS LIKE A SCAM!!
every single line is shady!!
IT'S AN INVITATION, SURE,
BUT I FEEL LIKE IT'S WELCOMING US TO HELL.
...
PEEL
PEEL
PEEL
FWAH
...

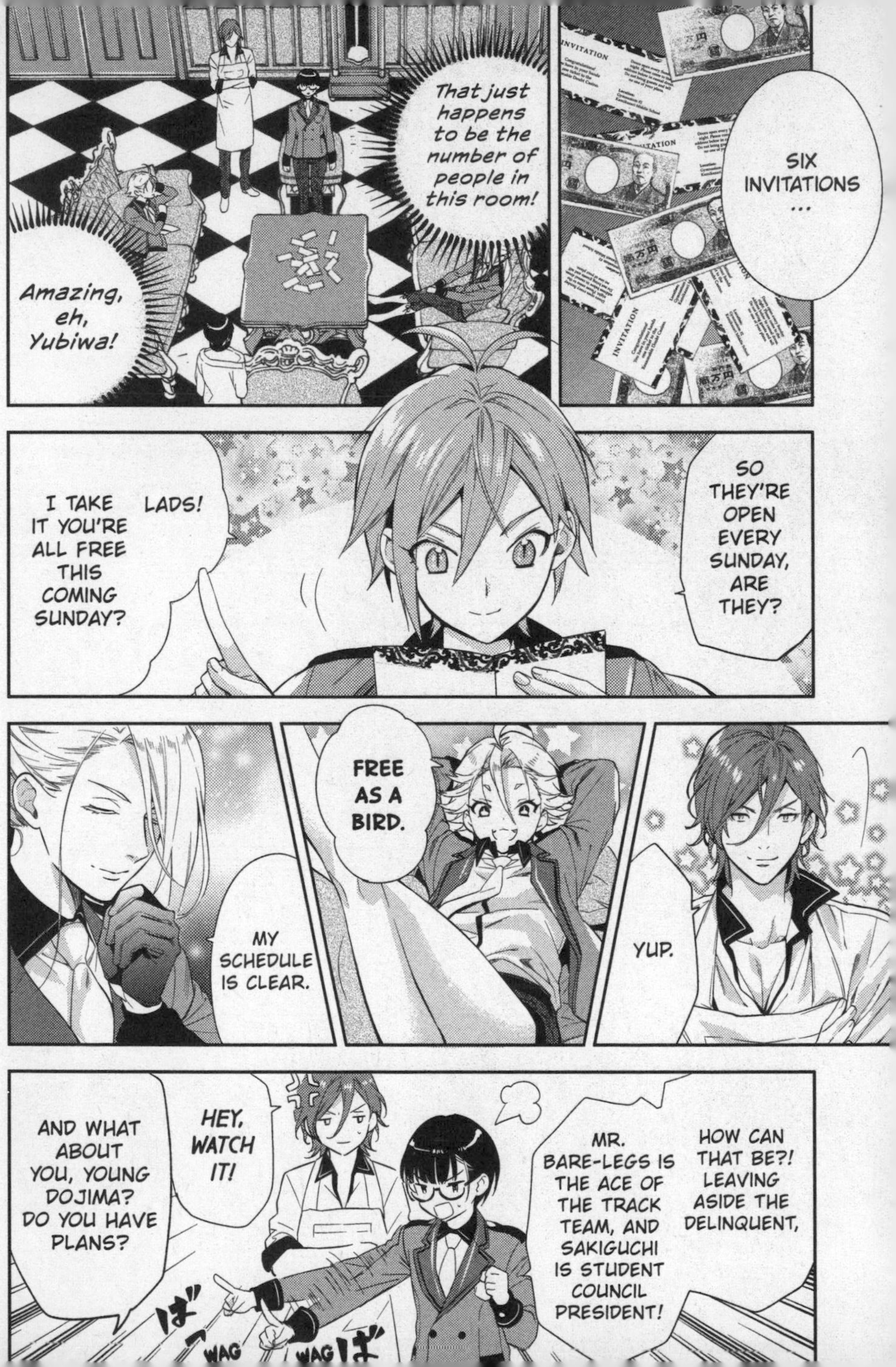

SIX INVITATIONS ...
That just happens to be the number of people in this room!
Amazing, eh, Yubiwa!
SO THEY'RE OPEN EVERY SUNDAY, ARE THEY?
LADS!
I TAKE IT YOU'RE ALL FREE THIS COMING SUNDAY?
YUP.
FREE AS A BIRD.
MY SCHEDULE IS CLEAR.
HOW CAN THAT BE?! LEAVING ASIDE THE DELINQUENT,
MR. BARE-LEGS IS THE ACE OF THE TRACK TEAM, AND SAKIGUCHI IS STUDENT COUNCIL PRESIDENT!
HEY, WATCH IT!
AND WHAT ABOUT YOU, YOUNG DOJIMA? DO YOU HAVE PLANS?
ば WAG
ば WAG

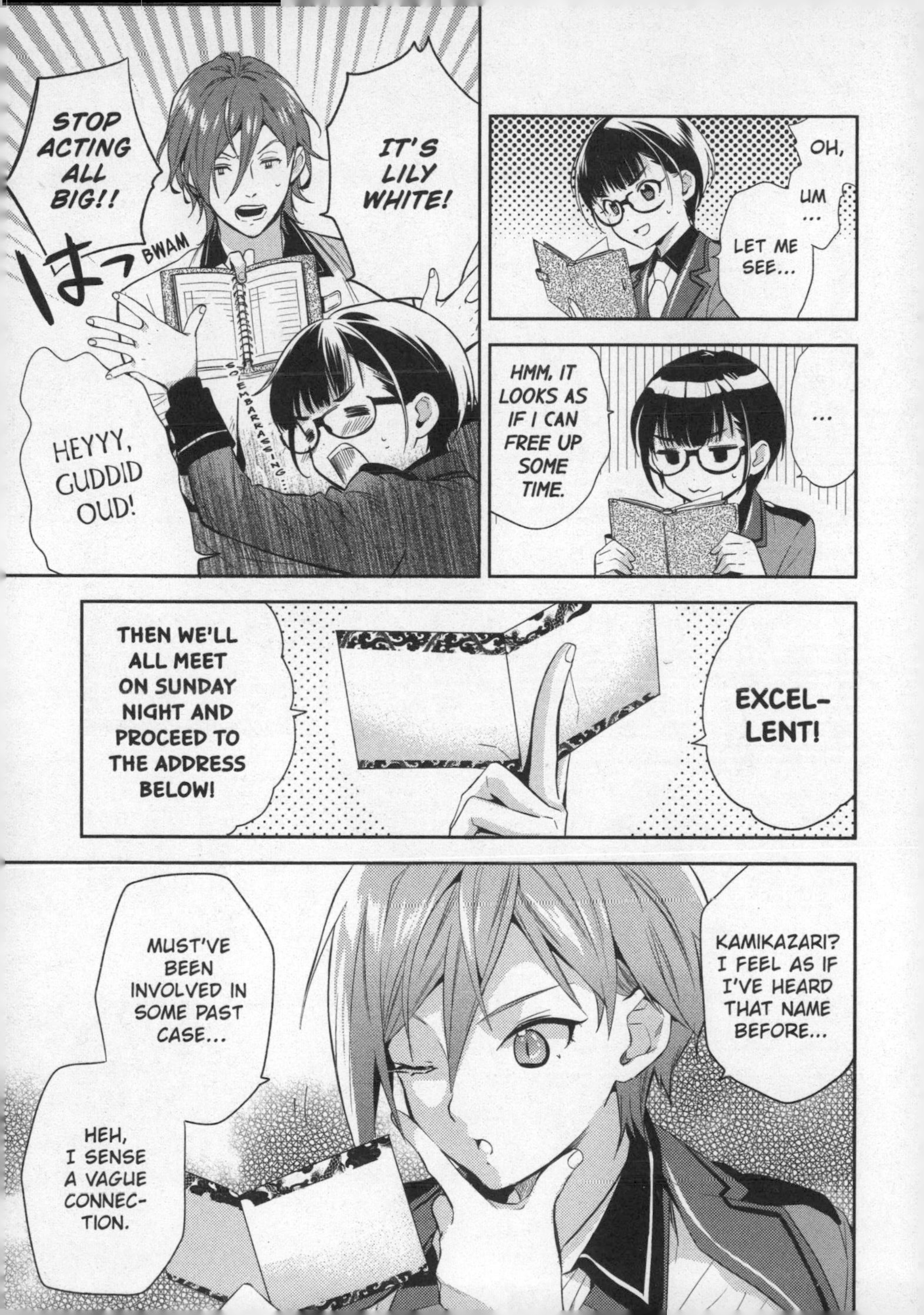
OH,
UM ...
LET ME SEE...
...
HMM. IT LOOKS AS IF I CAN FREE UP SOME TIME.
IT'S LILY WHITE!
STOP ACTING ALL BIG!!
はっ
BWAM
SO EMBARRASSING...
HEYYY, GUDDID OUD!
EXCEL-LENT!
THEN WE'LL ALL MEET ON SUNDAY NIGHT AND PROCEED TO THE ADDRESS BELOW!
KAMIKAZARI? I FEEL AS IF I'VE HEARD THAT NAME BEFORE...
MUST'VE BEEN INVOLVED IN SOME PAST CASE...
HEH, I SENSE A VAGUE CONNECTION.

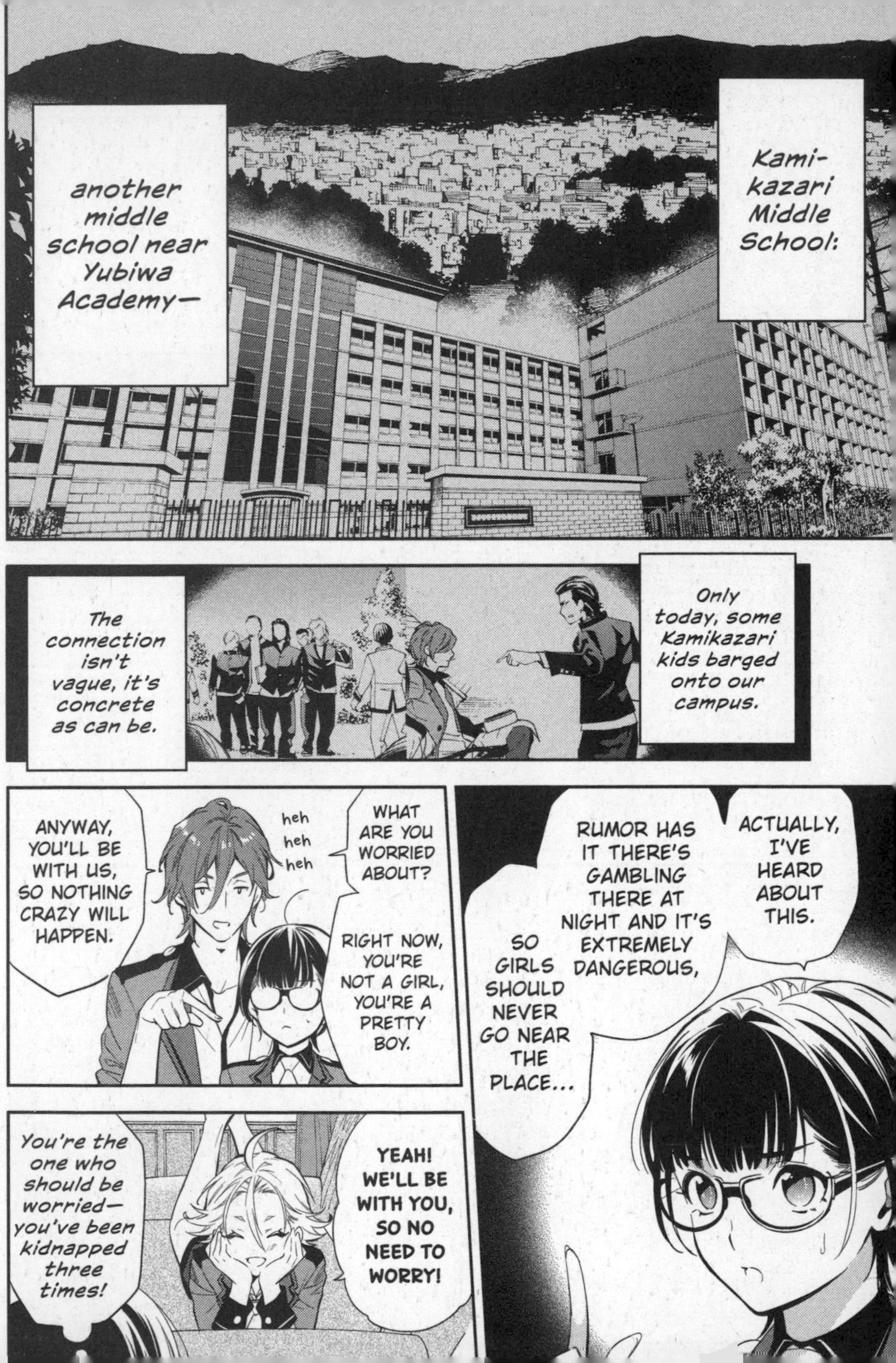
Kami-kazari Middle School:
another middle school near Yubiwa Academy—
Only today, some Kamikazari kids barged onto our campus.
The connection isn't vague, it's concrete as can be.
ACTUALLY, I'VE HEARD ABOUT THIS.
RUMOR HAS IT THERE'S GAMBLING THERE AT NIGHT AND IT'S EXTREMELY DANGEROUS,
SO GIRLS SHOULD NEVER GO NEAR THE PLACE...
WHAT ARE YOU WORRIED ABOUT?
heh heh heh
RIGHT NOW, YOU'RE NOT A GIRL, YOU'RE A PRETTY BOY.
ANYWAY, YOU'LL BE WITH US, SO NOTHING CRAZY WILL HAPPEN.
YEAH! WE'LL BE WITH YOU, SO NO NEED TO WORRY!
You're the one who should be worried—you've been kidnapped three times!

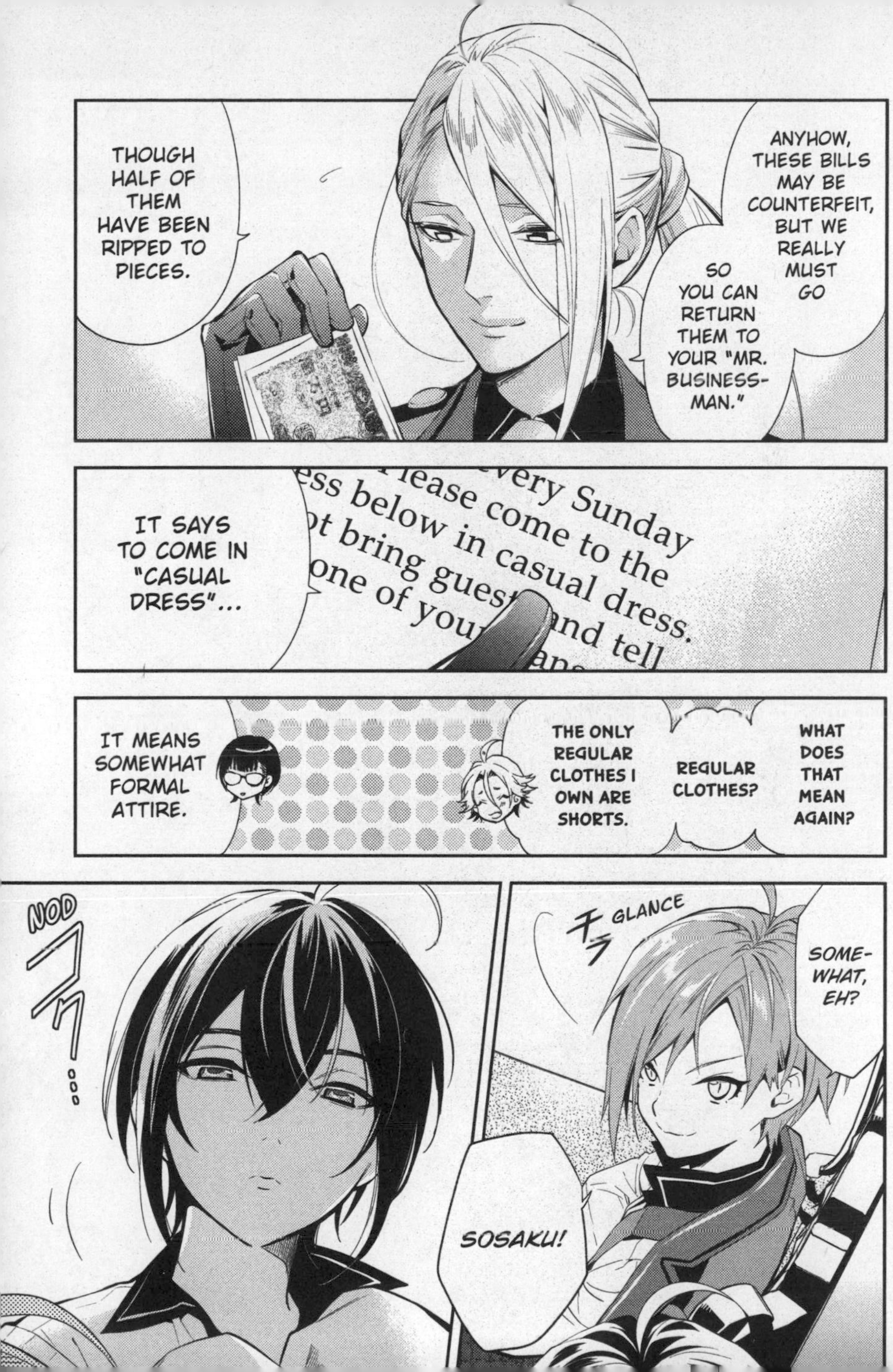
ANYHOW, THESE BILLS MAY BE COUNTERFEIT, BUT WE REALLY MUST GO
SO YOU CAN RETURN THEM TO YOUR "MR. BUSINESS-MAN."
THOUGH HALF OF THEM HAVE BEEN RIPPED TO PIECES.
very Sunday
lease come to the
ess below in casual dress.
ot bring guest and tell
one of you
IT SAYS TO COME IN "CASUAL DRESS"...
WHAT DOES THAT MEAN AGAIN?
REGULAR CLOTHES?
THE ONLY REGULAR CLOTHES I OWN ARE SHORTS.
IT MEANS SOMEWHAT FORMAL ATTIRE.
GLANCE
SOME-WHAT, EH?
SOSAKU!
NOD

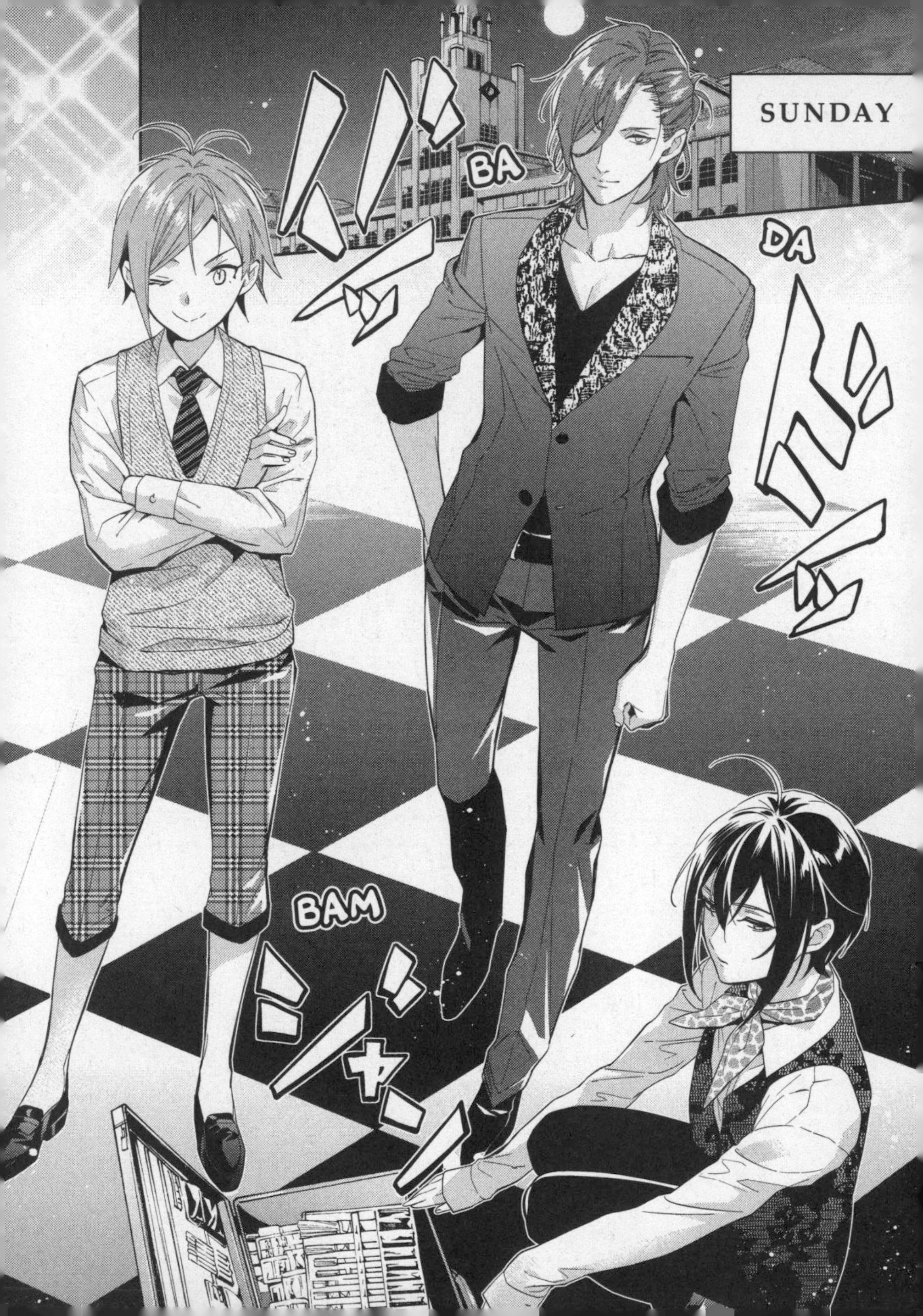
SUNDAY
BA
DA
BAM

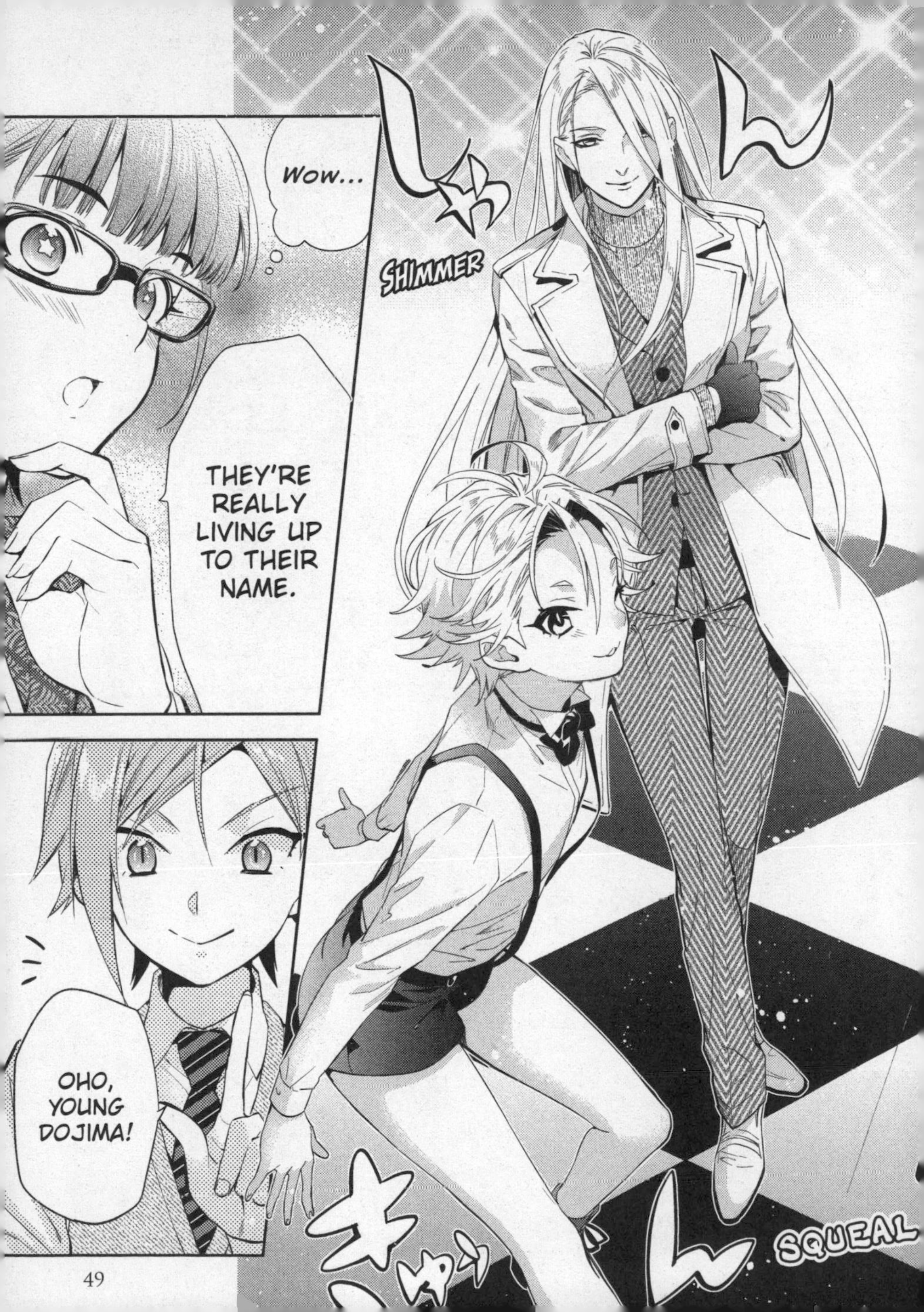
SHIMMER
SQUEAL
WOW...
THEY'RE REALLY LIVING UP TO THEIR NAME.
OHO, YOUNG DOJIMA!

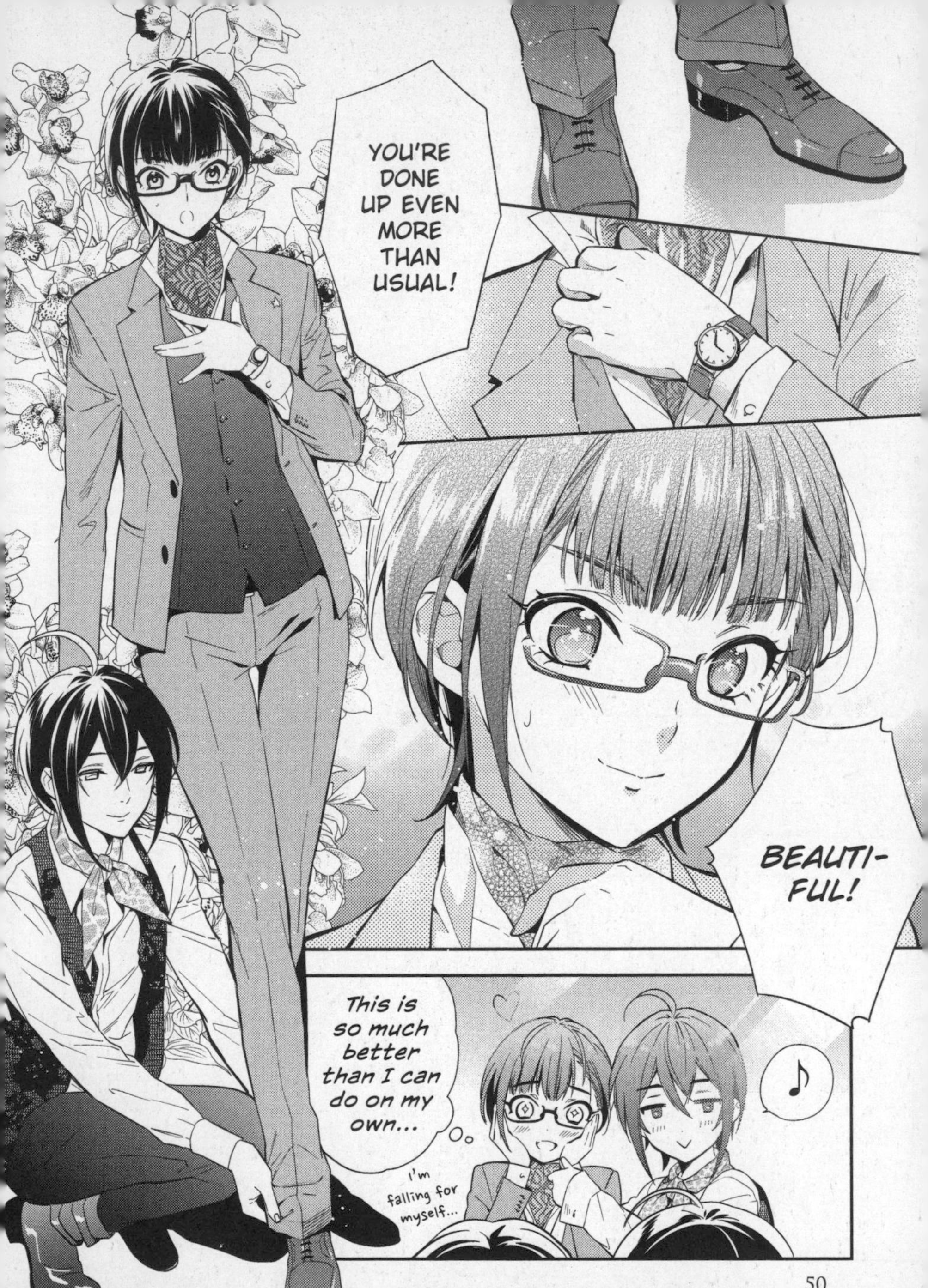
YOU'RE DONE UP EVEN MORE THAN USUAL!
BEAUTI-FUL!
♪
This is so much better than I can do on my own...
I'm falling for myself...

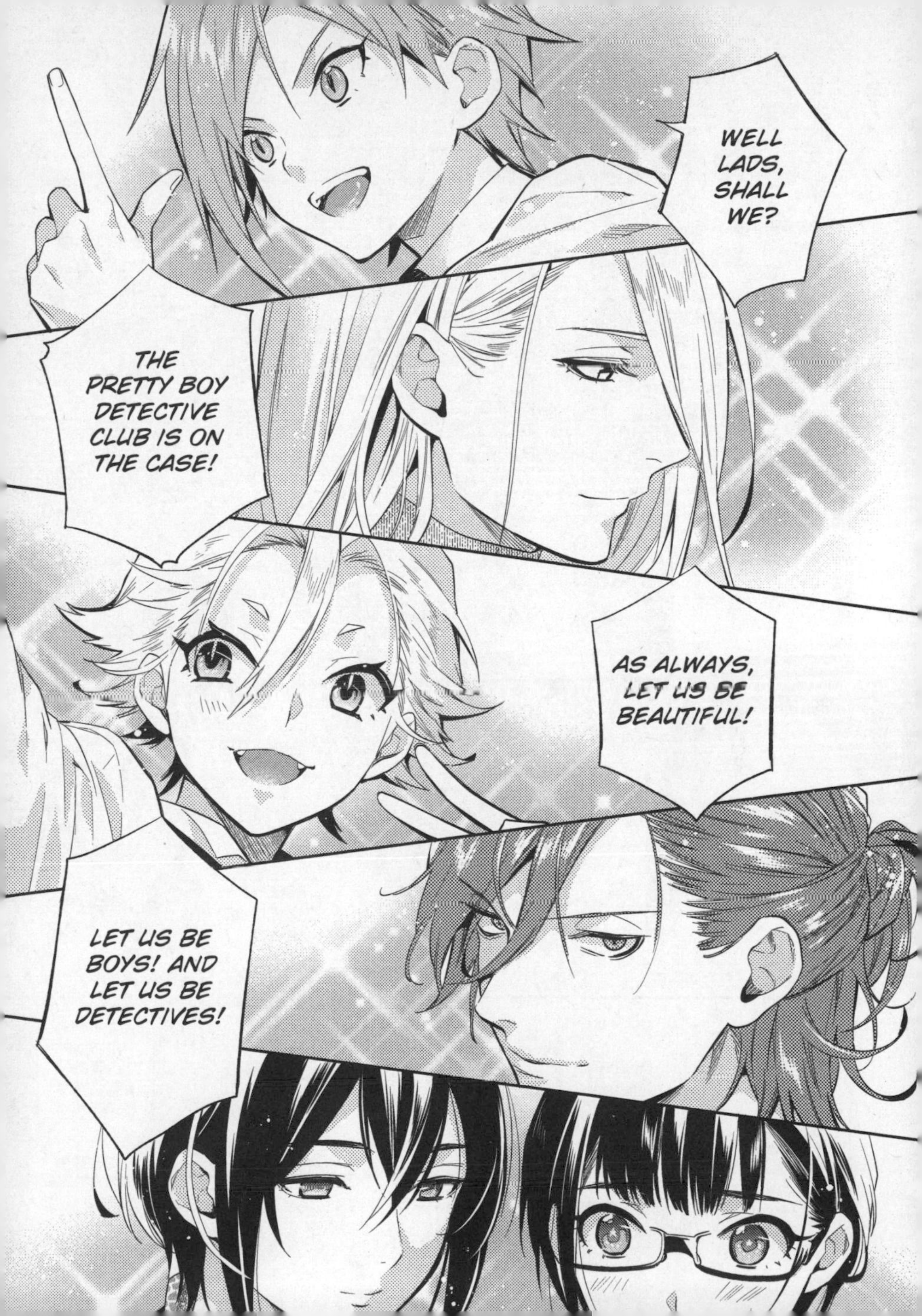
WELL LADS, SHALL WE?
THE PRETTY BOY DETECTIVE CLUB IS ON THE CASE!
AS ALWAYS, LET US BE BEAUTIFUL!
LET US BE BOYS! AND LET US BE DETECTIVES!

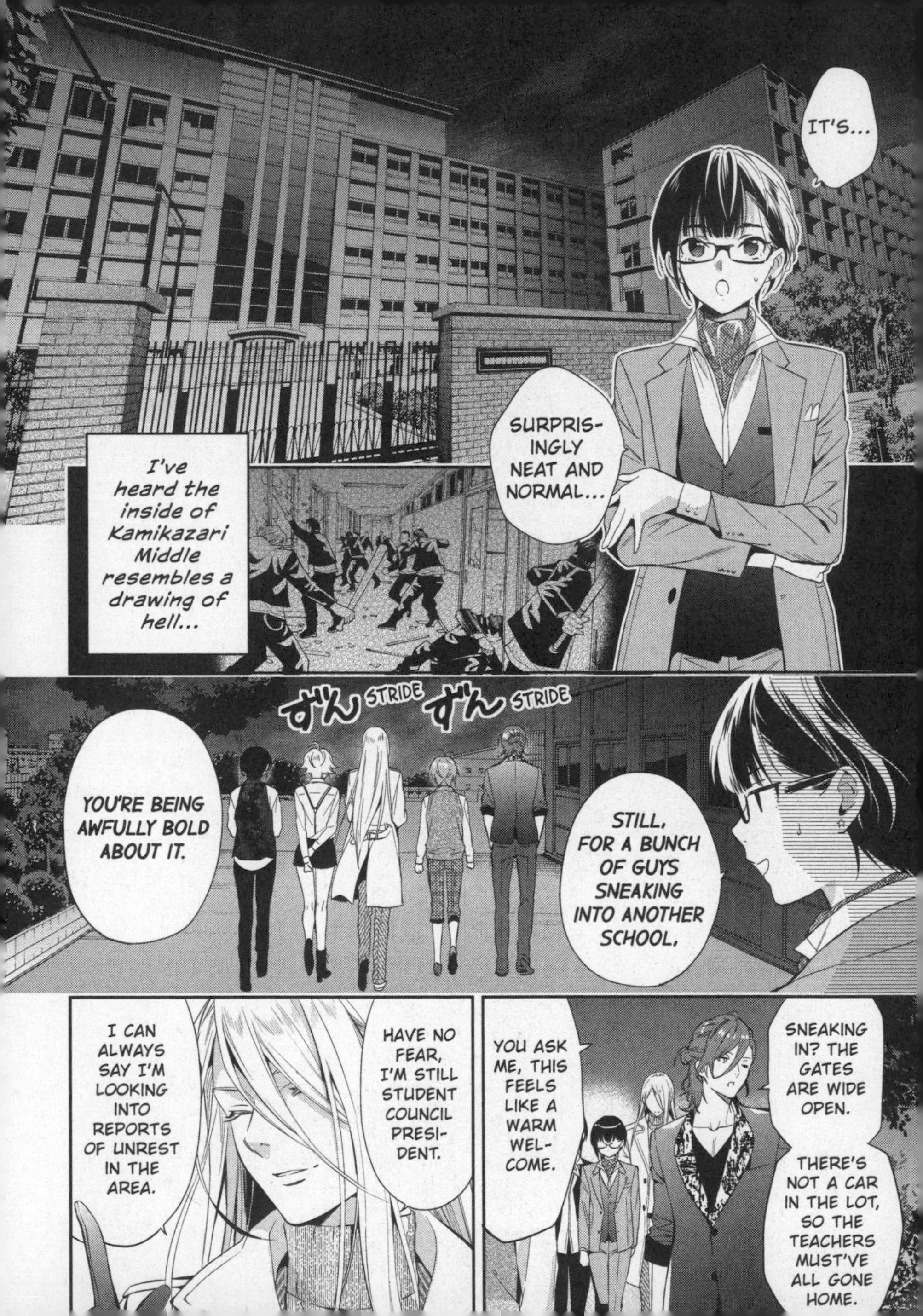
IT'S...
SURPRIS-INGLY NEAT AND NORMAL...
I've heard the inside of Kamikazari Middle resembles a drawing of hell...
ずん STRIDE ずん STRIDE
STILL, FOR A BUNCH OF GUYS SNEAKING INTO ANOTHER SCHOOL,
YOU'RE BEING AWFULLY BOLD ABOUT IT.
SNEAKING IN? THE GATES ARE WIDE OPEN.
THERE'S NOT A CAR IN THE LOT, SO THE TEACHERS MUST'VE ALL GONE HOME.
YOU ASK ME, THIS FEELS LIKE A WARM WEL-COME.
HAVE NO FEAR, I'M STILL STUDENT COUNCIL PRESI-DENT.
I CAN ALWAYS SAY I'M LOOKING INTO REPORTS OF UNREST IN THE AREA.

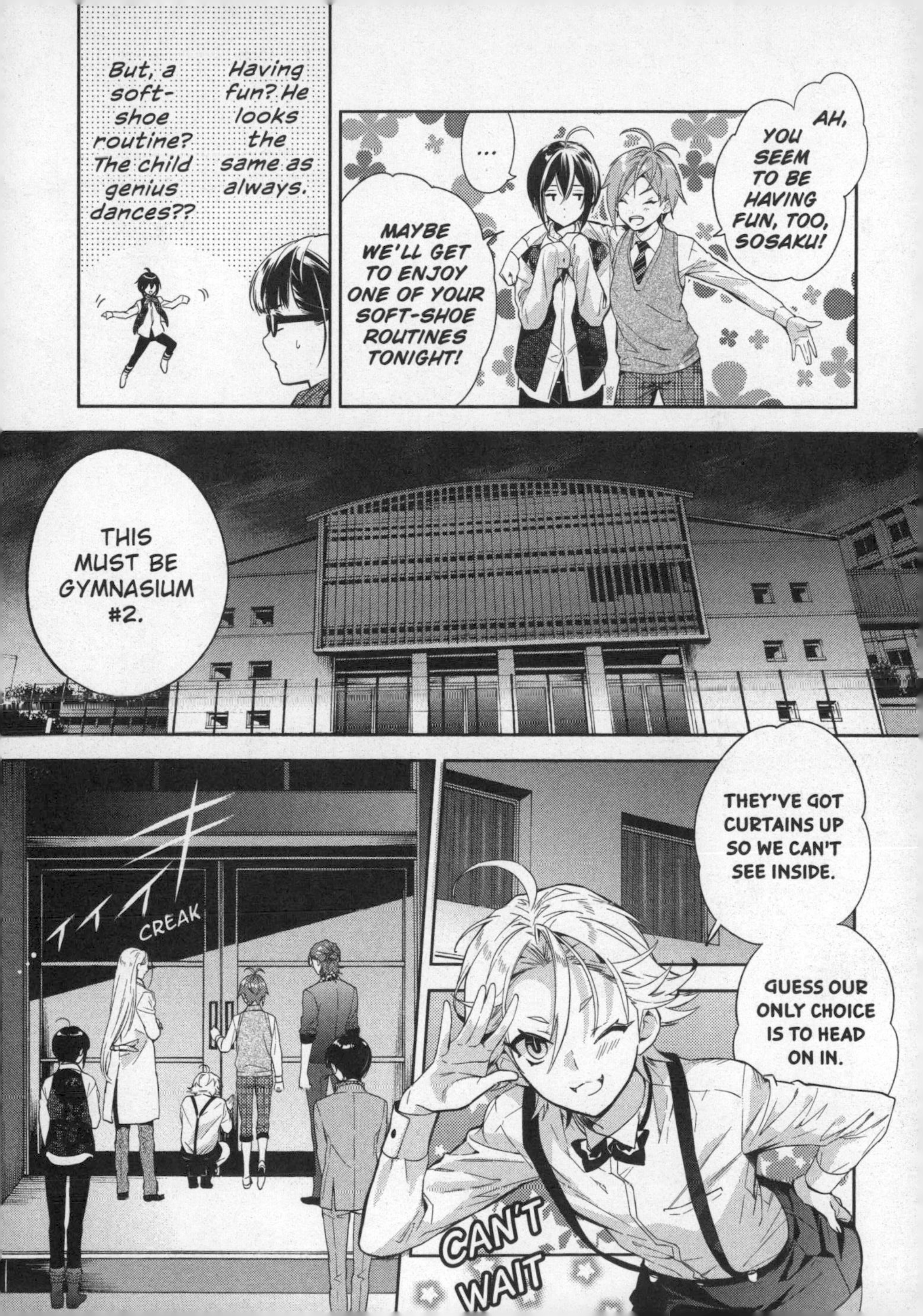
AH, YOU SEEM TO BE HAVING FUN, TOO, SOSAKU!
...
MAYBE WE'LL GET TO ENJOY ONE OF YOUR SOFT-SHOE ROUTINES TONIGHT!
Having fun? He looks the same as always.
But, a soft-shoe routine? The child genius dances??
THIS MUST BE GYMNASIUM #2.
THEY'VE GOT CURTAINS UP SO WE CAN'T SEE INSIDE.
GUESS OUR ONLY CHOICE IS TO HEAD ON IN.
CAN'T WAIT
CREAK

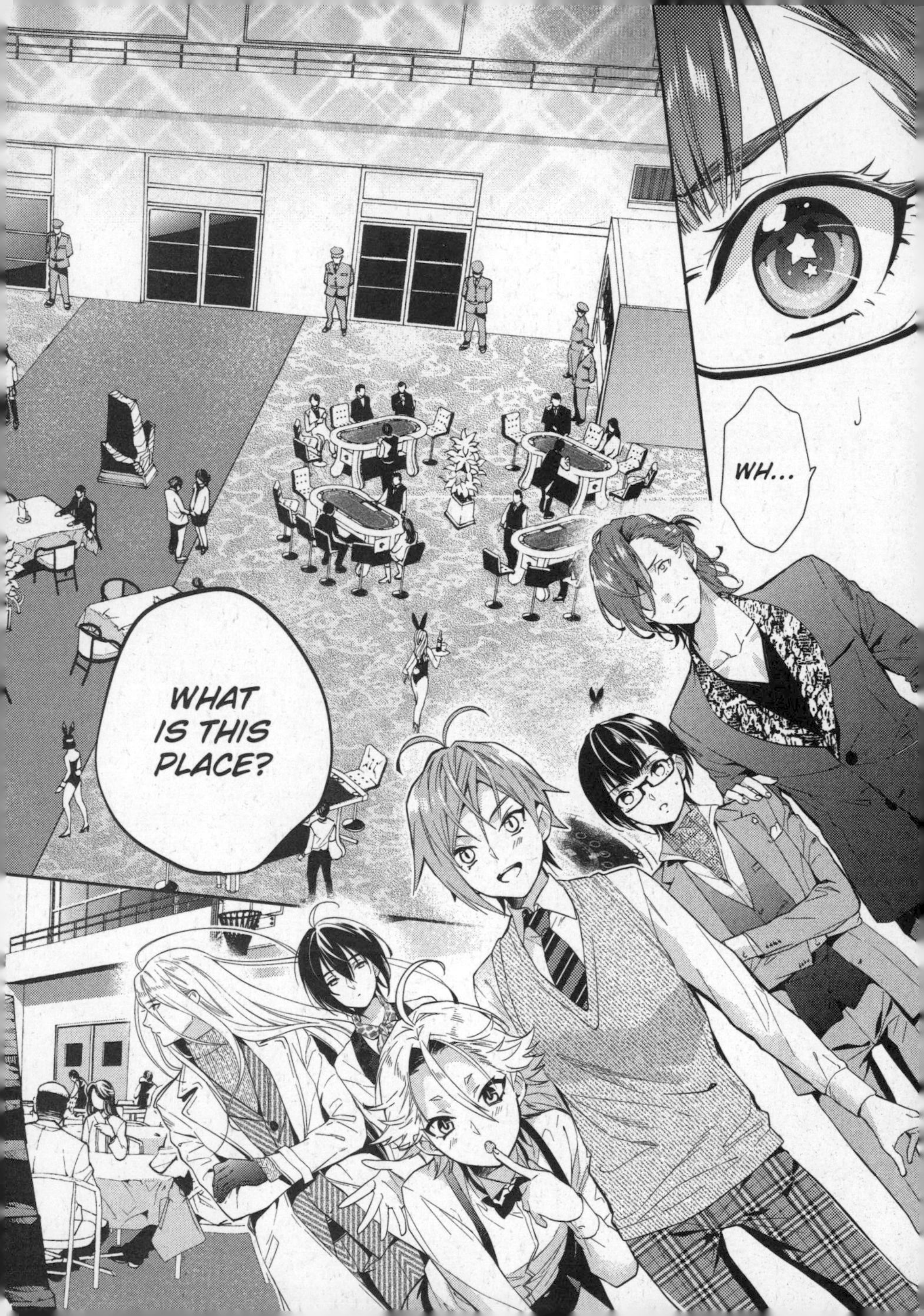
WH...
WHAT IS THIS PLACE?

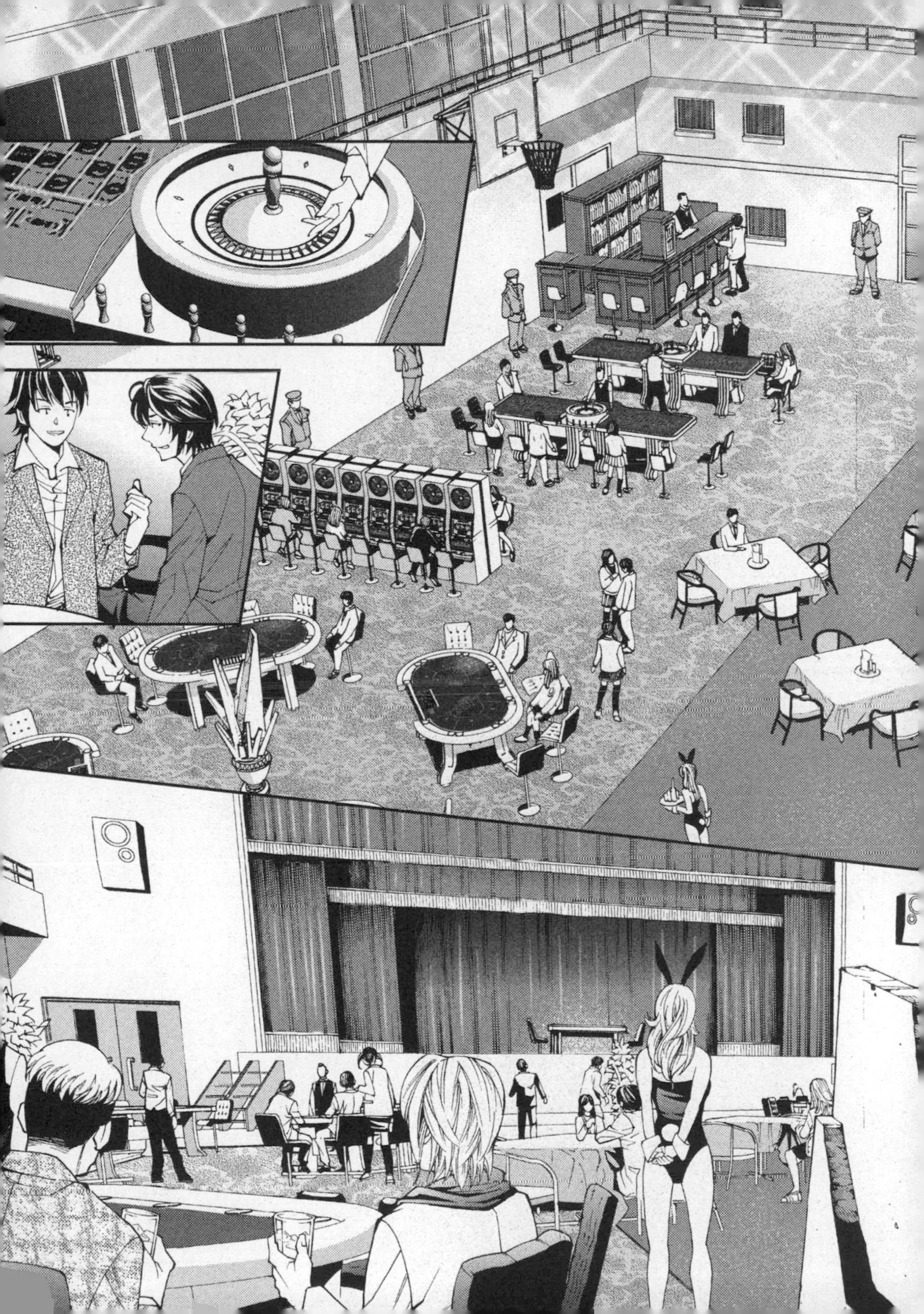

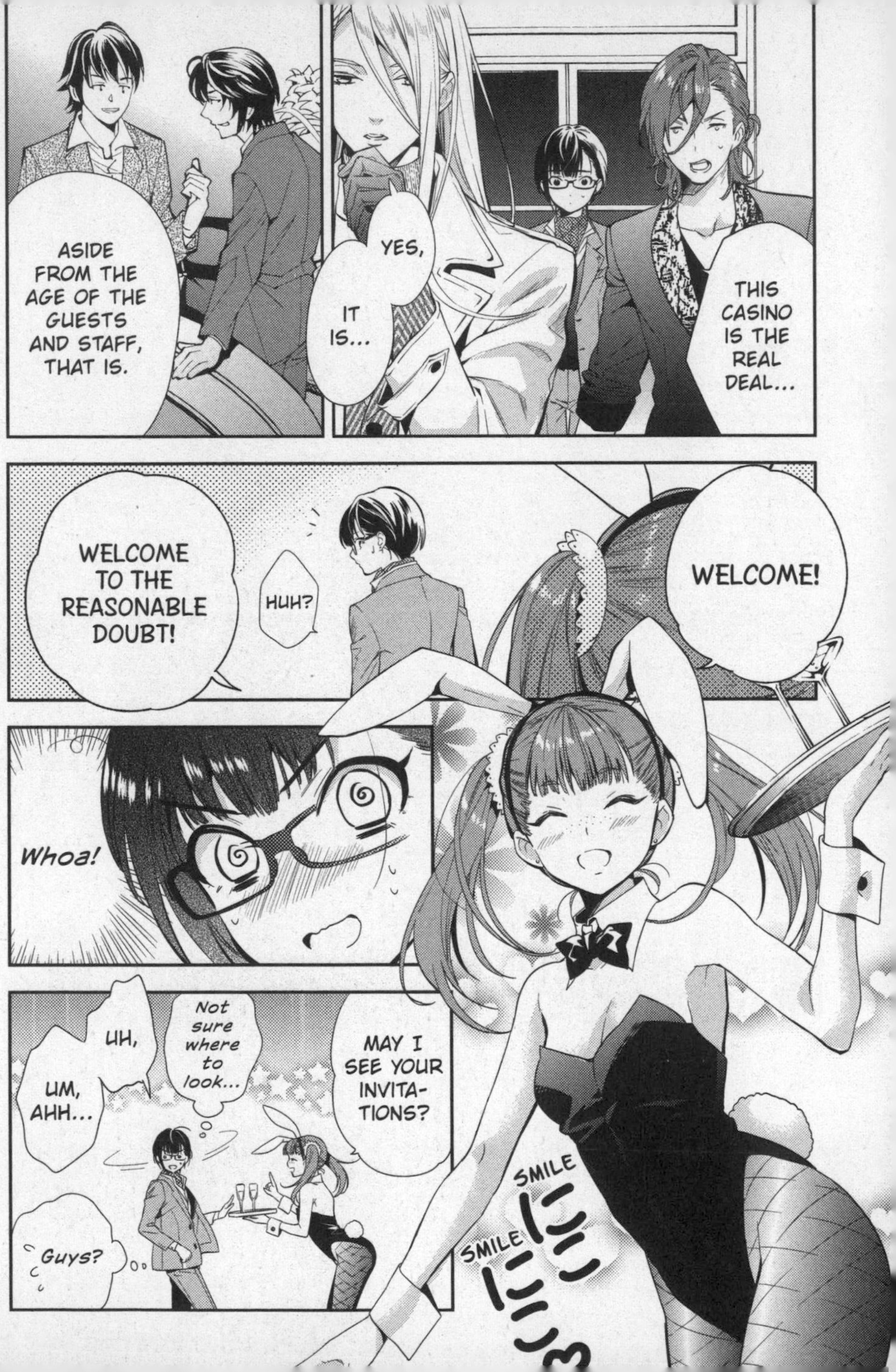
THIS CASINO IS THE REAL DEAL...
YES, IT IS...
ASIDE FROM THE AGE OF THE GUESTS AND STAFF, THAT IS.
WELCOME!
HUH?
WELCOME TO THE REASONABLE DOUBT!
SMILE
SMILE
Whoa!
MAY I SEE YOUR INVITATIONS?
Not sure where to look...
UH,
UM, AHH...
Guys?

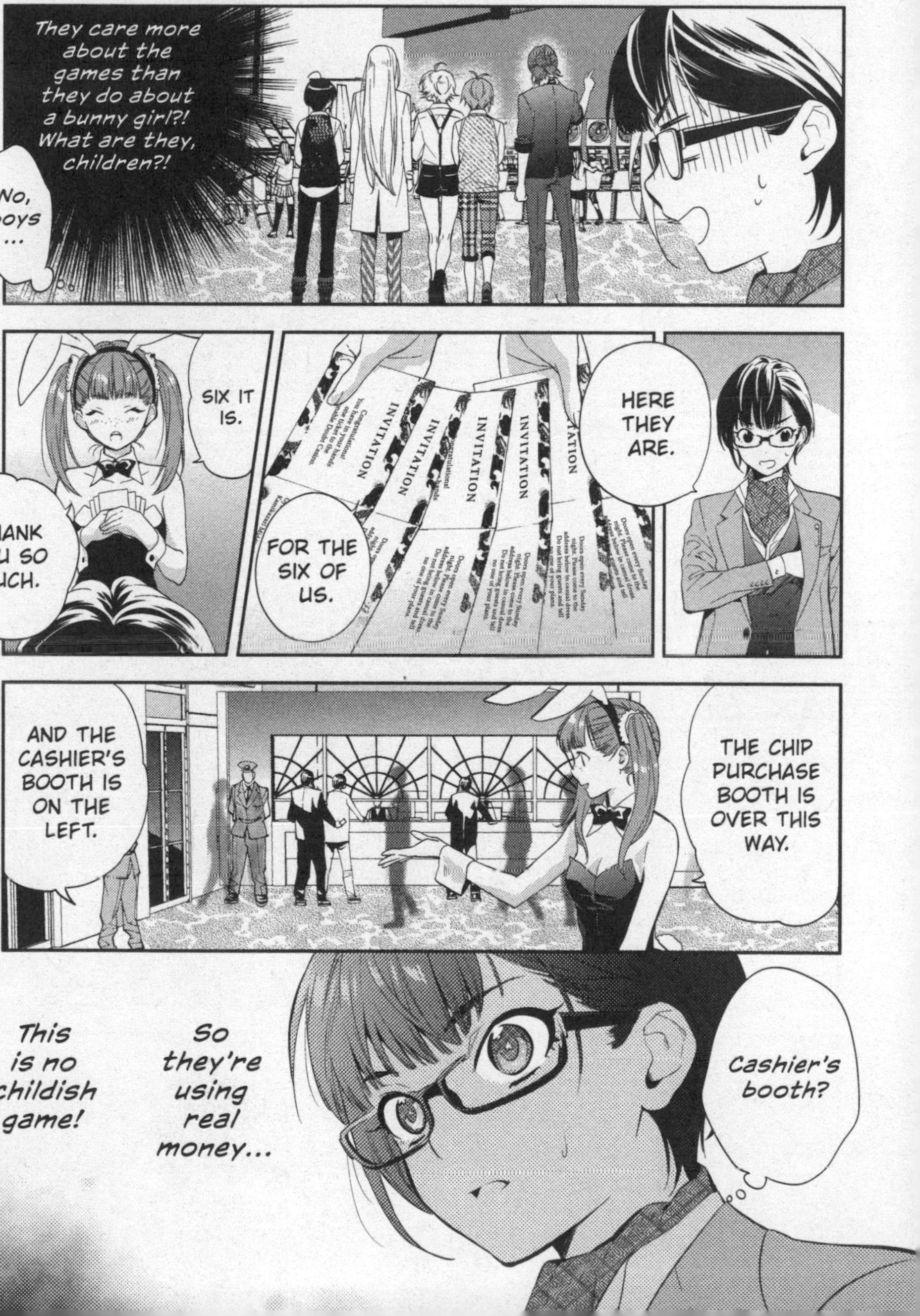
They care more about the games than they do about a bunny girl?! What are they, children?!
No, boys ...
HERE THEY ARE.
INVITATION
INVITATION
INVITATION
INVITATION
FOR THE SIX OF US.
SIX IT IS.
THANK YOU SO MUCH.
THE CHIP PURCHASE BOOTH IS OVER THIS WAY.
AND THE CASHIER'S BOOTH IS ON THE LEFT.
Cashier's booth?
So they're using real money...
This is no childish game!

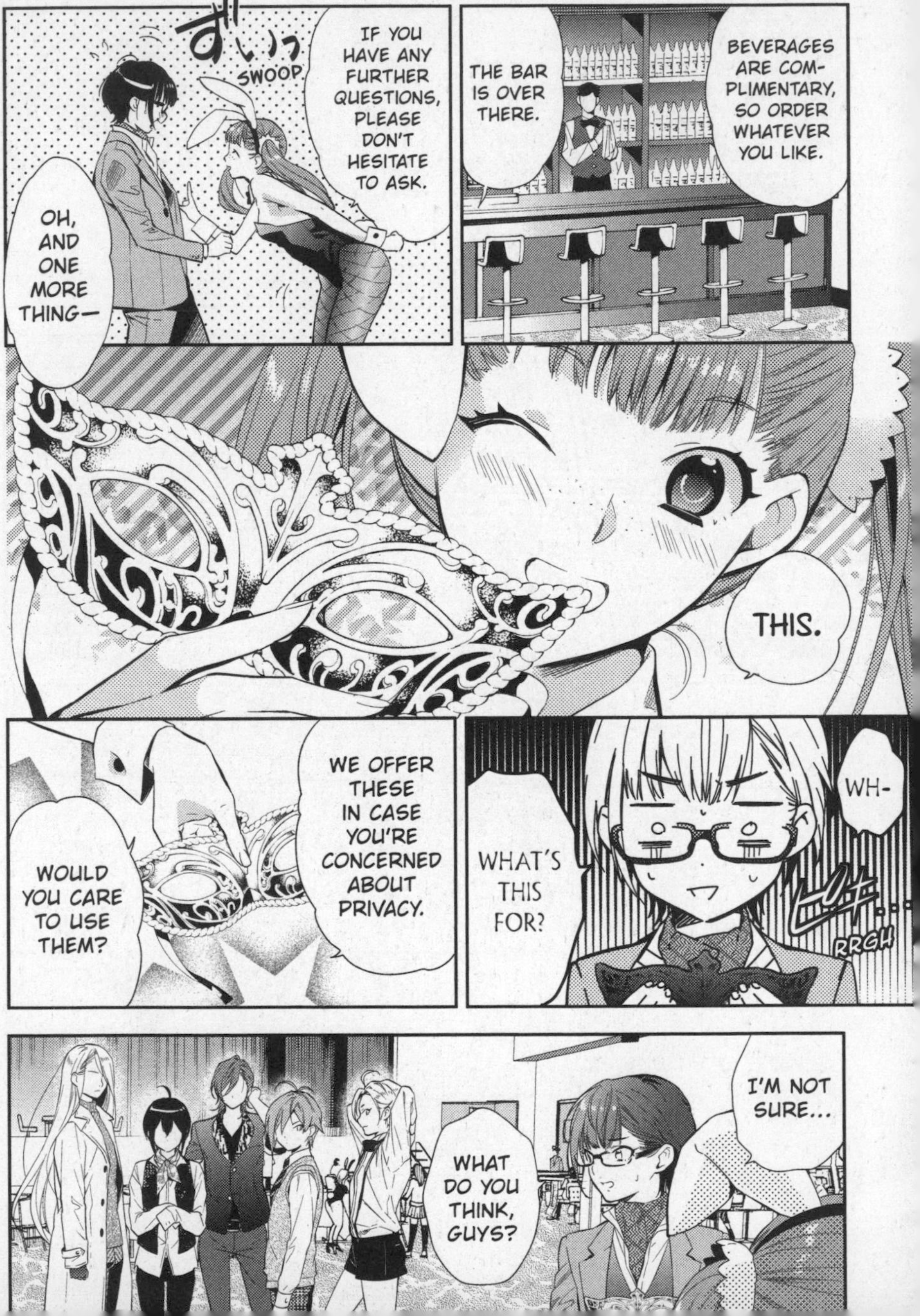
BEVERAGES ARE COMPLIMENTARY, SO ORDER WHATEVER YOU LIKE.
THE BAR IS OVER THERE.
IF YOU HAVE ANY FURTHER QUESTIONS, PLEASE DON'T HESITATE TO ASK.
SWOOP
OH, AND ONE MORE THING—
THIS.
WH-
WHAT'S THIS FOR?
RRGH
WE OFFER THESE IN CASE YOU'RE CONCERNED ABOUT PRIVACY.
WOULD YOU CARE TO USE THEM?
I'M NOT SURE...
WHAT DO YOU THINK, GUYS?

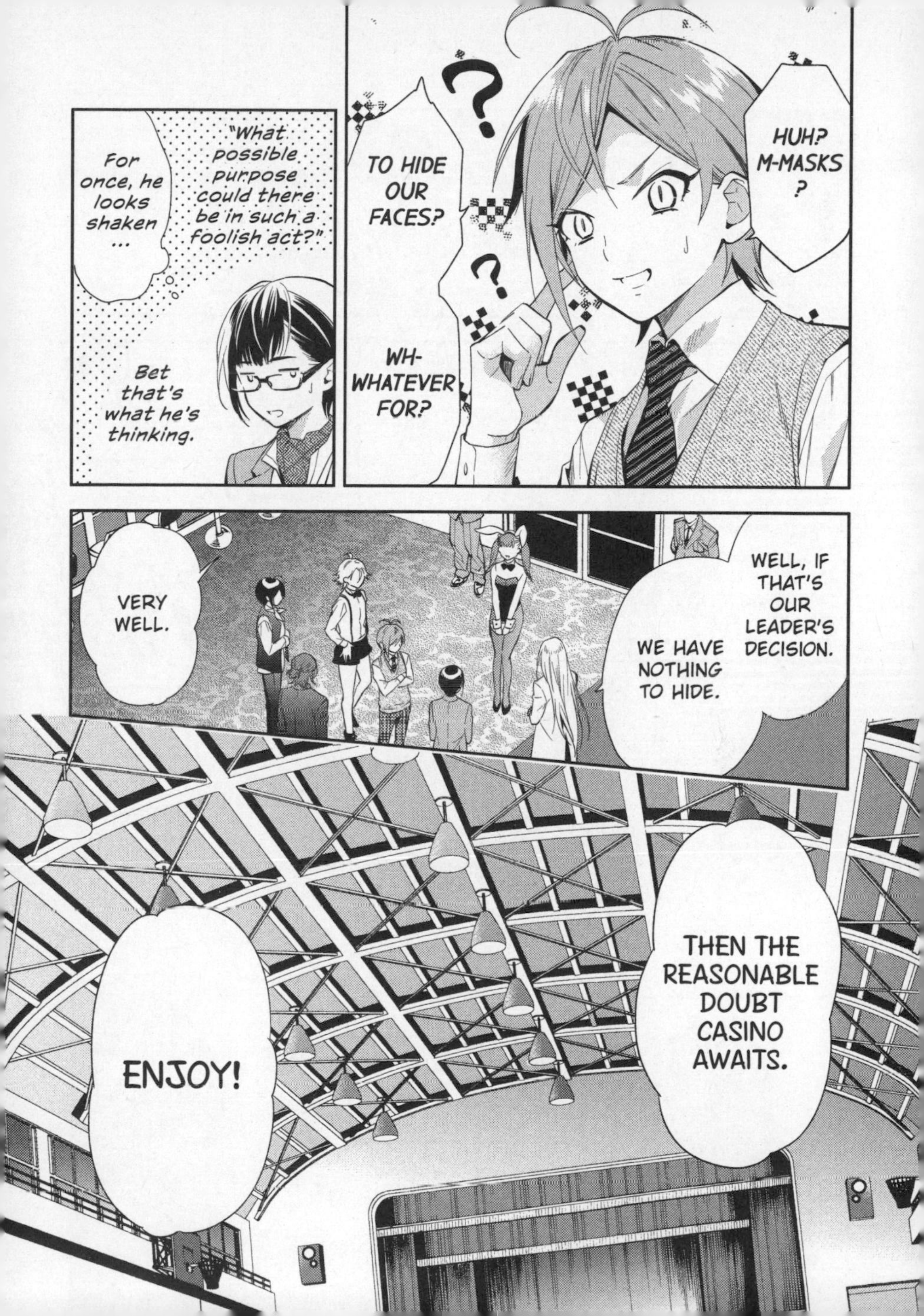
HUH? M-MASKS?
TO HIDE OUR FACES?
WH-WHATEVER FOR?
"What possible purpose could there be in such a foolish act?"
For once, he looks shaken...
Bet that's what he's thinking.
WELL, IF THAT'S OUR LEADER'S DECISION.
WE HAVE NOTHING TO HIDE.
VERY WELL.
THEN THE REASONABLE DOUBT CASINO AWAITS.
ENJOY!

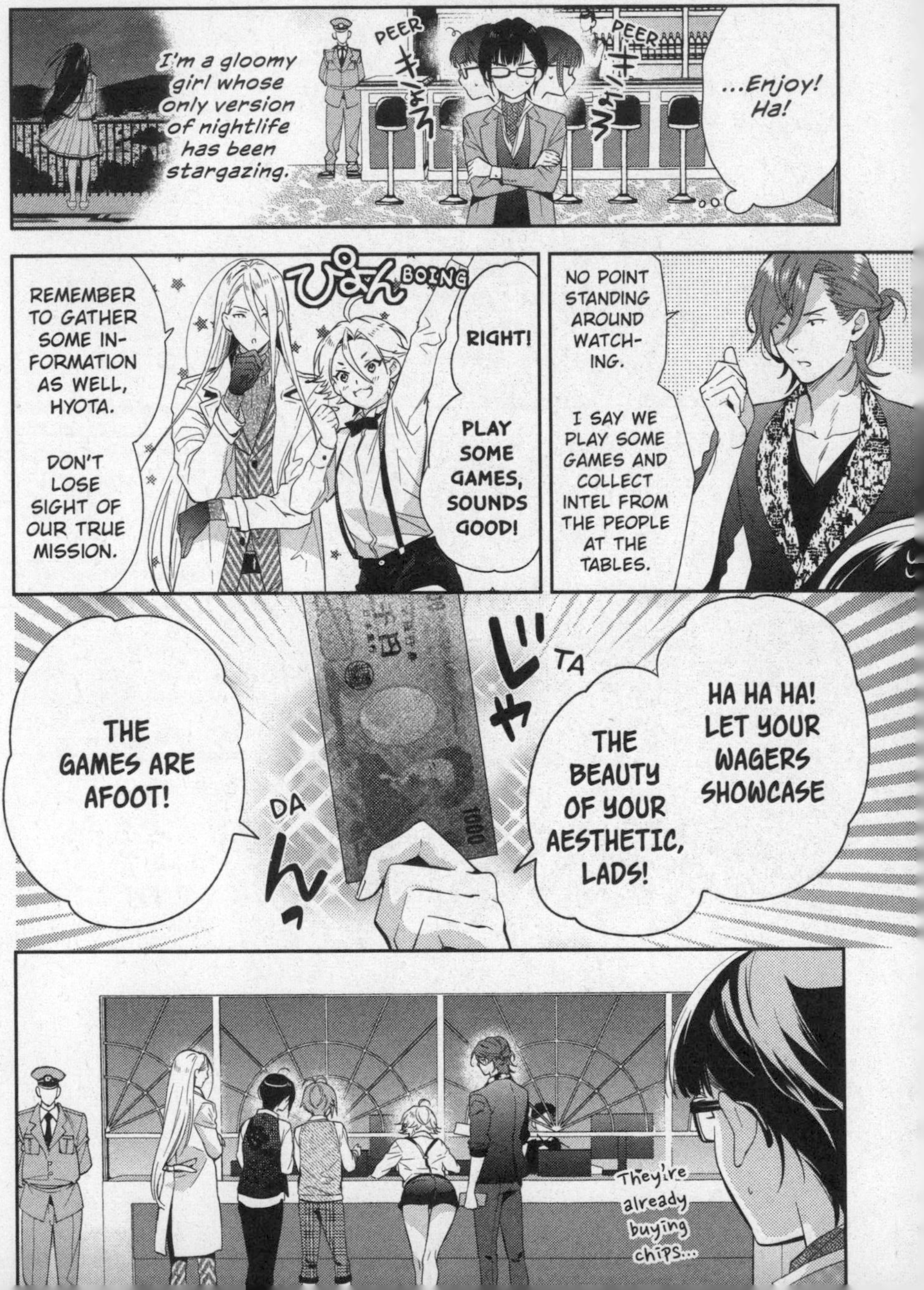
...Enjoy! Ha!
PEER
PEER
I'm a gloomy girl whose only version of nightlife has been stargazing.
NO POINT STANDING AROUND WATCHING.
I SAY WE PLAY SOME GAMES AND COLLECT INTEL FROM THE PEOPLE AT THE TABLES.
RIGHT!
PLAY SOME GAMES, SOUNDS GOOD!
ぴょん BOING
REMEMBER TO GATHER SOME INFORMATION AS WELL, HYOTA.
DON'T LOSE SIGHT OF OUR TRUE MISSION.
HA HA HA! LET YOUR WAGERS SHOWCASE
THE BEAUTY OF YOUR AESTHETIC, LADS!
TA
DA
THE GAMES ARE AFOOT!
They're already buying chips...

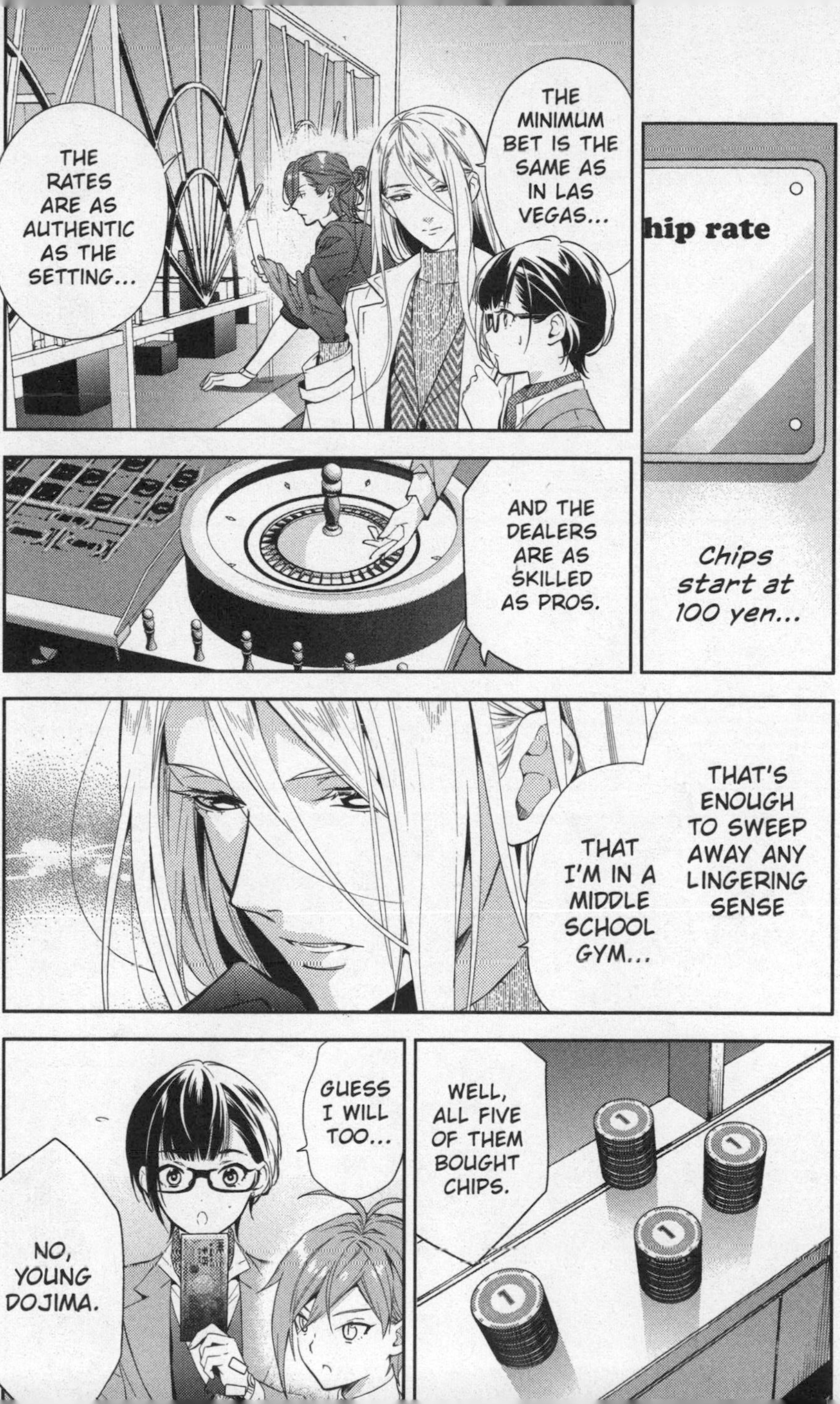
hip rate
Chips start at 100 yen...
THE MINIMUM BET IS THE SAME AS IN LAS VEGAS...
THE RATES ARE AS AUTHENTIC AS THE SETTING...
AND THE DEALERS ARE AS SKILLED AS PROS.
THAT'S ENOUGH TO SWEEP AWAY ANY LINGERING SENSE
THAT I'M IN A MIDDLE SCHOOL GYM...
WELL, ALL FIVE OF THEM BOUGHT CHIPS.
GUESS I WILL TOO...
NO, YOUNG DOJIMA.

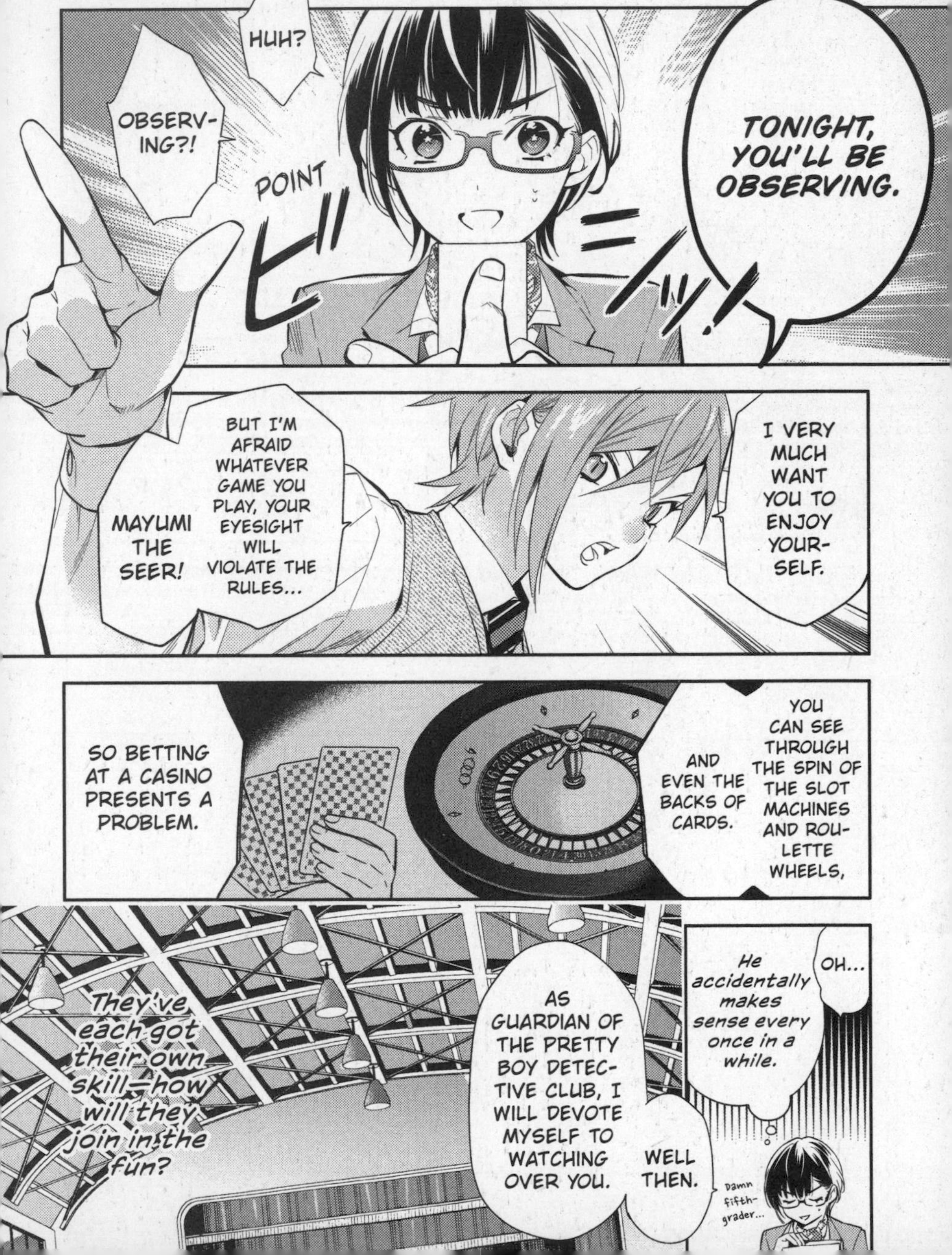
TONIGHT, YOU'LL BE OBSERVING.
ビシッ!
HUH?
OBSERVING?!
POINT
I VERY MUCH WANT YOU TO ENJOY YOURSELF.
BUT I'M AFRAID WHATEVER GAME YOU PLAY, YOUR EYESIGHT WILL VIOLATE THE RULES...
MAYUMI THE SEER!
YOU CAN SEE THROUGH THE SPIN OF THE SLOT MACHINES AND ROULETTE WHEELS,
AND EVEN THE BACKS OF CARDS.
SO BETTING AT A CASINO PRESENTS A PROBLEM.
OH...
He accidentally makes sense every once in a while.
Damn fifth-grader...
WELL THEN.
AS GUARDIAN OF THE PRETTY BOY DETECTIVE CLUB, I WILL DEVOTE MYSELF TO WATCHING OVER YOU.
They've each got their own skill—how will they join in the fun?

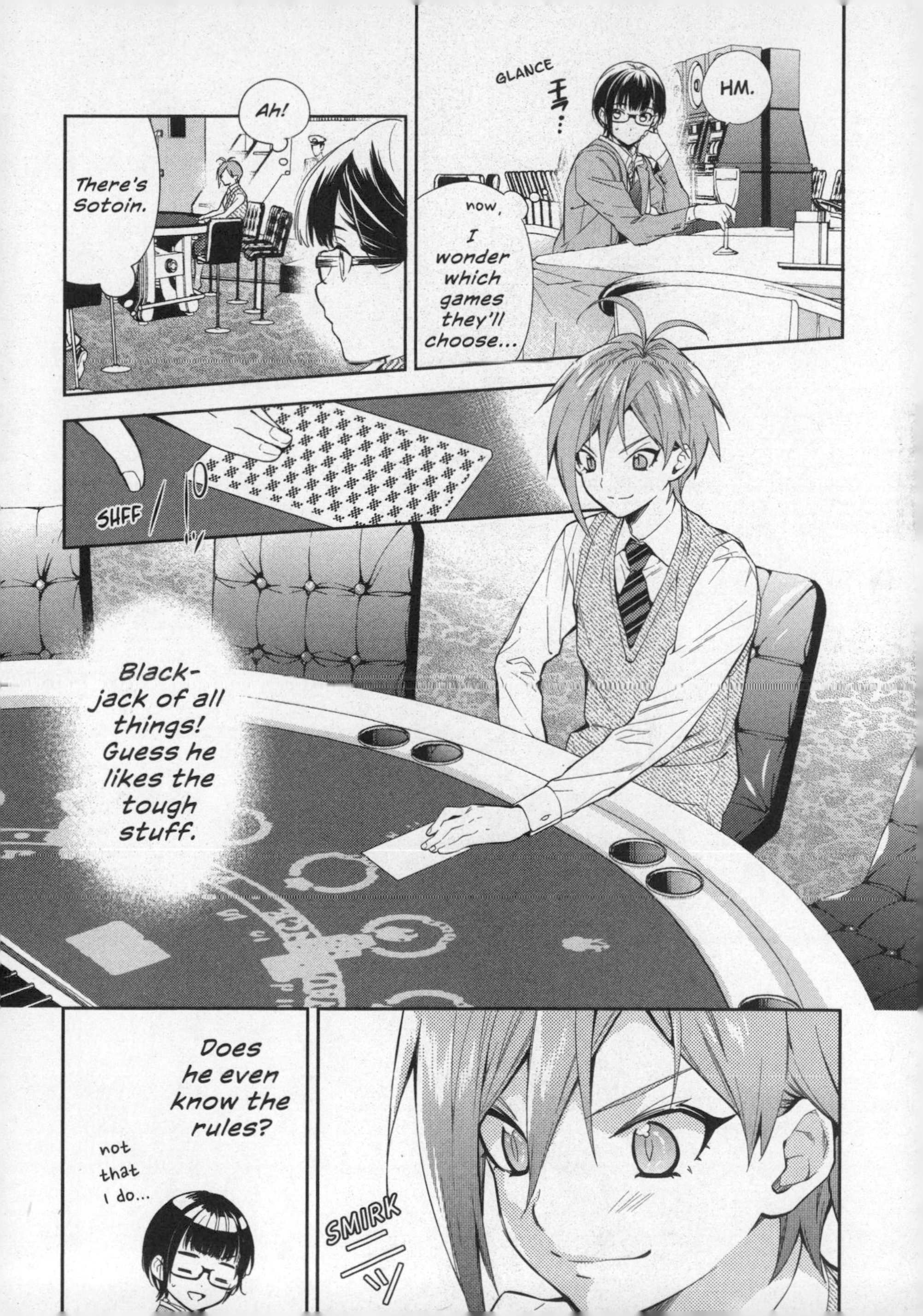
HM.
GLANCE
now, I wonder which games they'll choose...
Ah!
There's Sotoin.
SHFF
Black-jack of all things! Guess he likes the tough stuff.
SMIRK
Does he even know the rules?
not that I do...

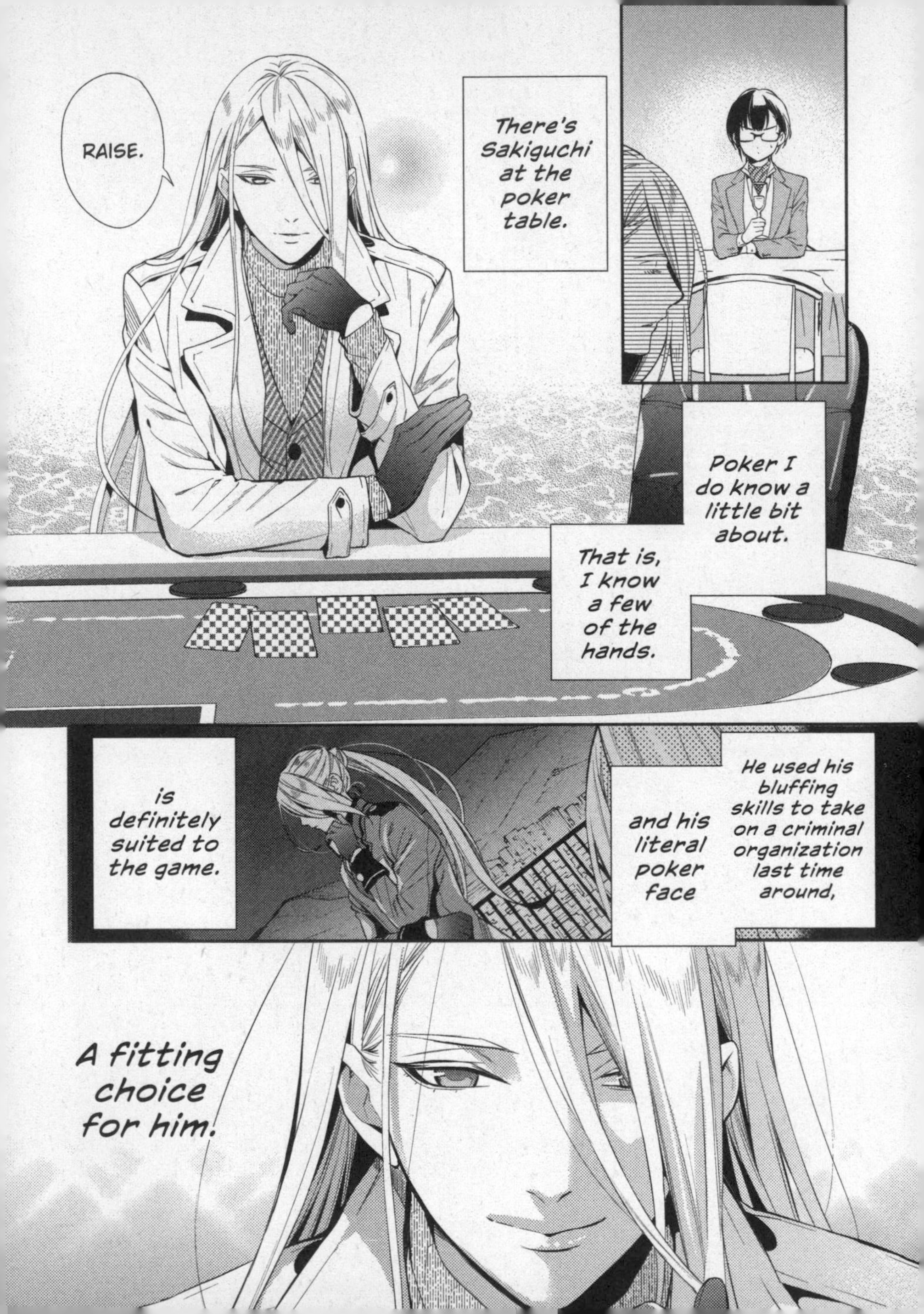
There's Sakiguchi at the poker table.
RAISE.
Poker I do know a little bit about.
That is, I know a few of the hands.
He used his bluffing skills to take on a criminal organization last time around,
and his literal poker face
is definitely suited to the game.
A fitting choice for him.

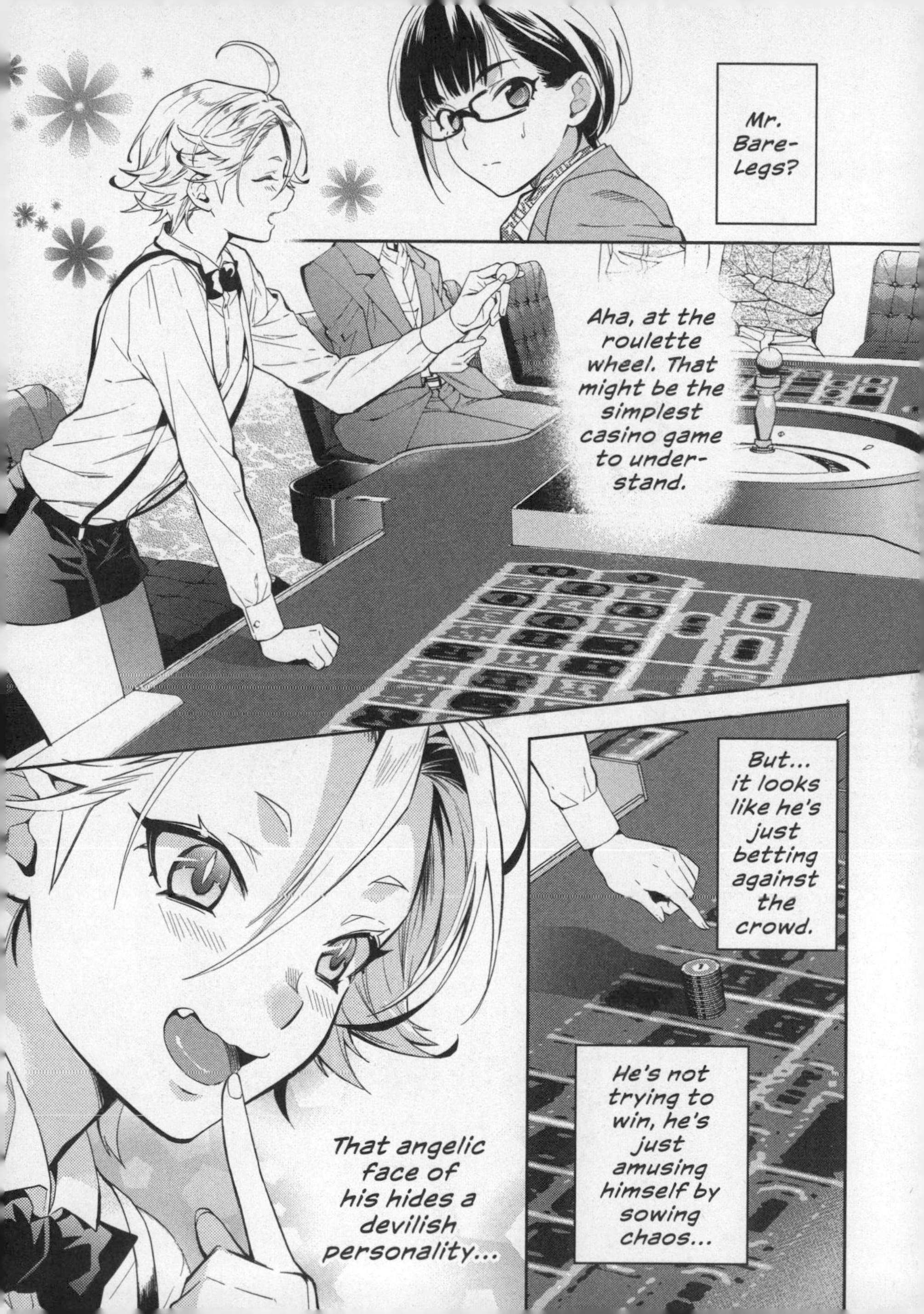
Mr. Bare-Legs?
Aha, at the roulette wheel. That might be the simplest casino game to understand.
But... it looks like he's just betting against the crowd.
He's not trying to win, he's just amusing himself by sowing chaos...
That angelic face of his hides a devilish personality...

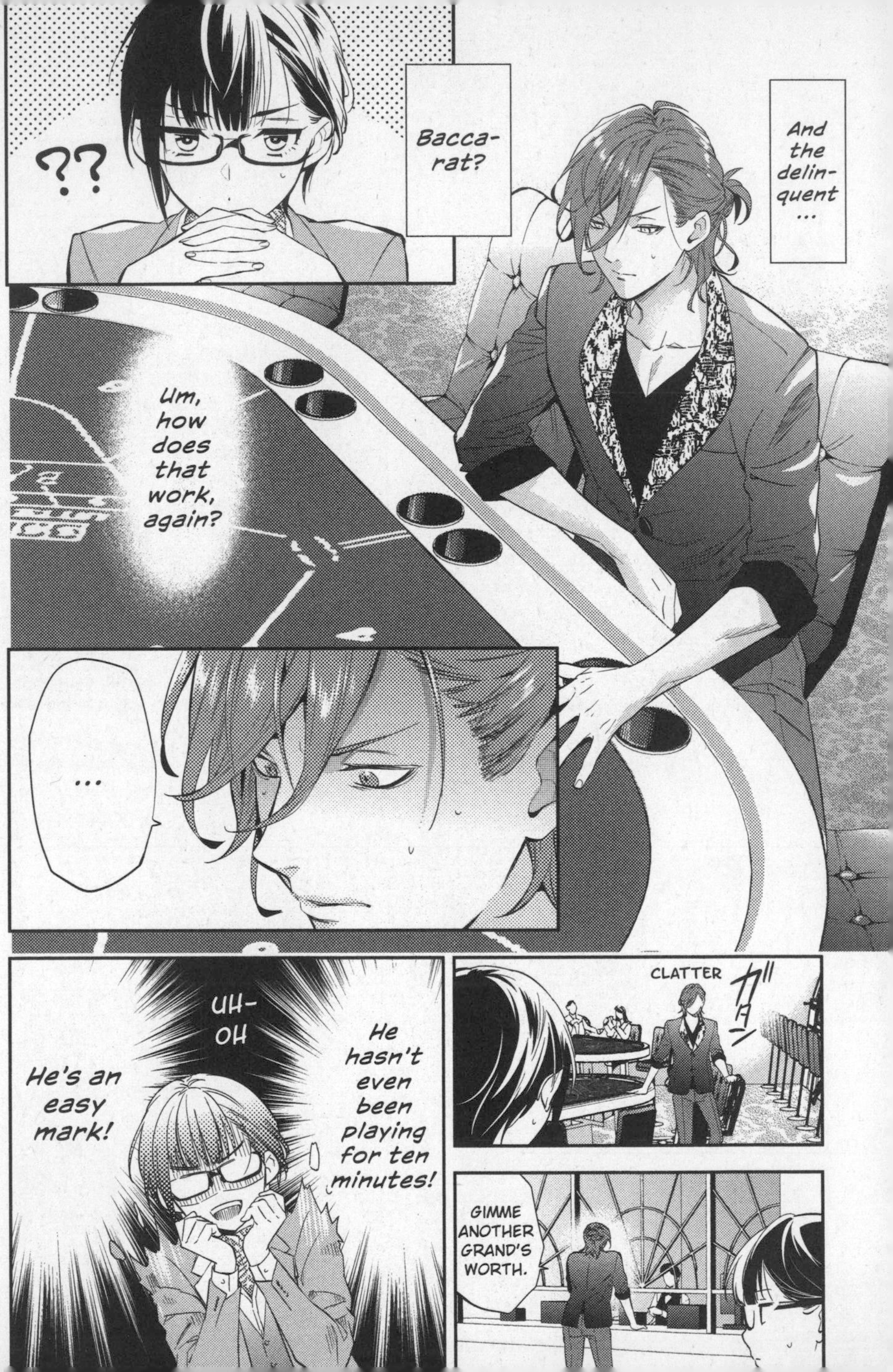
And the delinquent...
Baccarat?
??
Um, how does that work, again?
...
CLATTER
ガタン
GIMME ANOTHER GRAND'S WORTH.
UH-OH
He hasn't even been playing for ten minutes!
He's an easy mark!

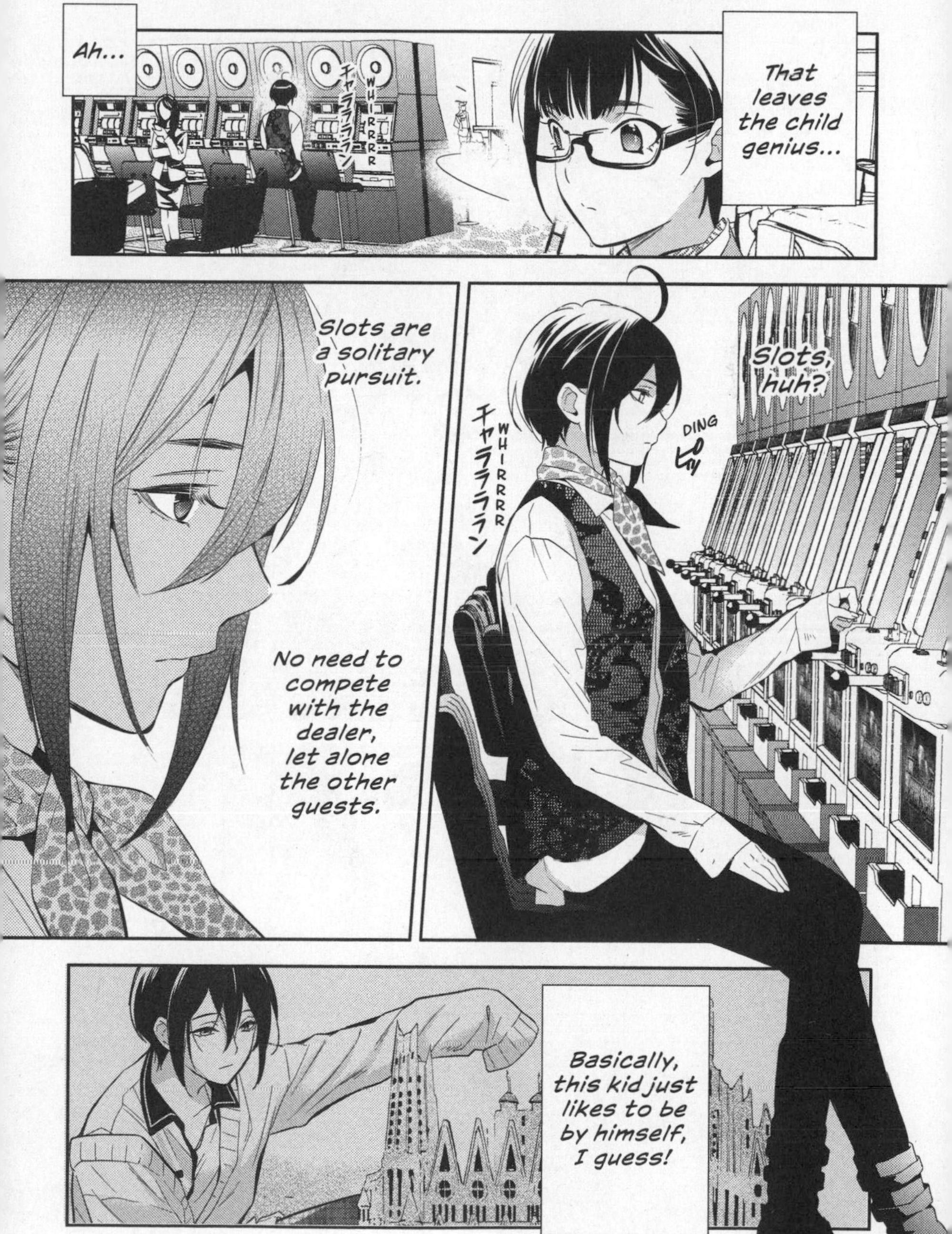
That leaves the child genius...
Ah...
WHIRRR
チャラララン
Slots, huh?
DING
ピッ
WHIRRR
チャラララン
Slots are a solitary pursuit.
No need to compete with the dealer, let alone the other guests.
Basically, this kid just likes to be by himself, I guess!

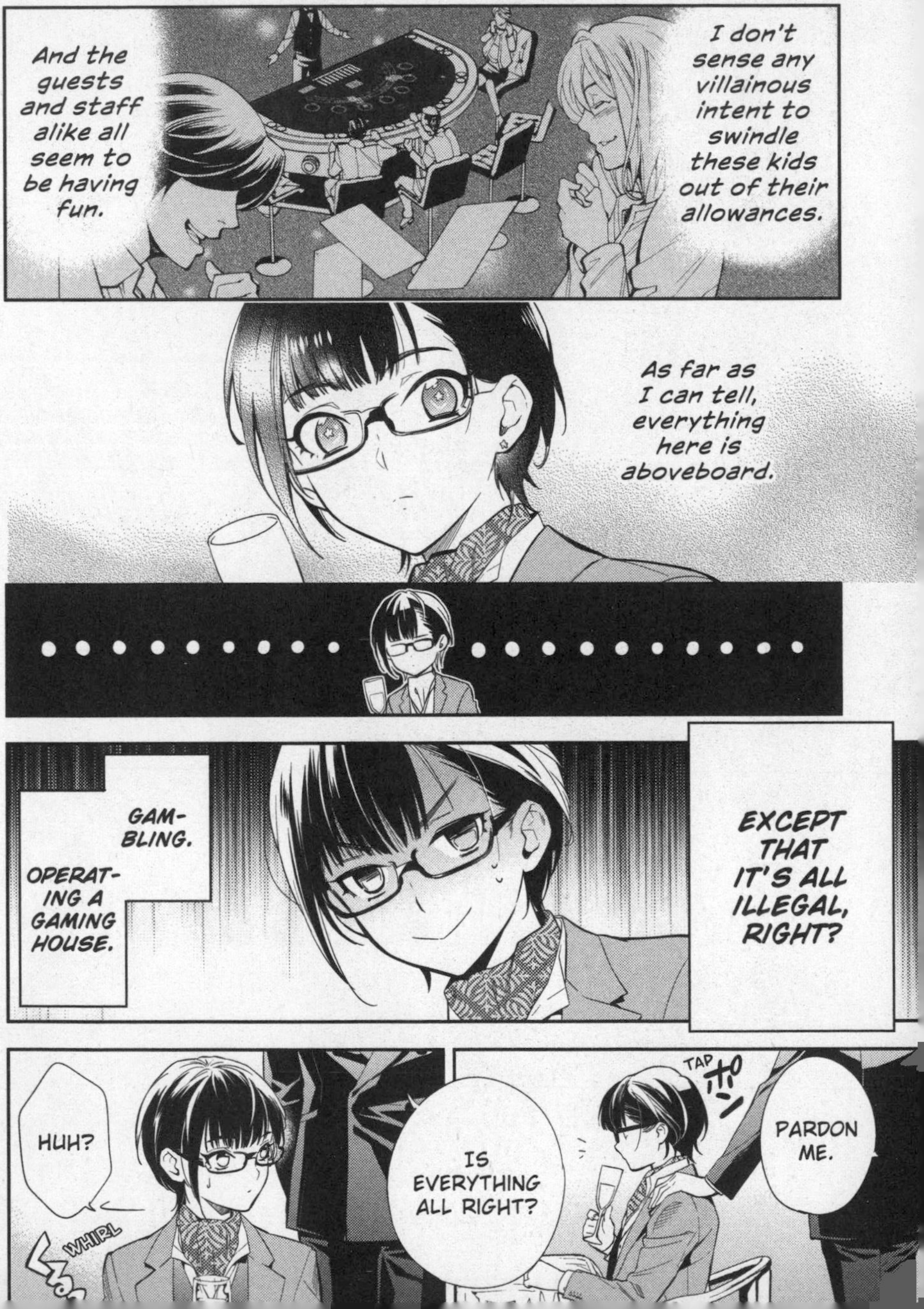
I don't sense any villainous intent to swindle these kids out of their allowances.
And the guests and staff alike all seem to be having fun.
As far as I can tell, everything here is aboveboard.
• • • • • • • • • • • • • • • • • • • •
EXCEPT THAT IT'S ALL ILLEGAL, RIGHT?
GAM-BLING.
OPERAT-ING A GAMING HOUSE.
TAP
PARDON ME.
IS EVERYTHING ALL RIGHT?
HUH?
WHIRL

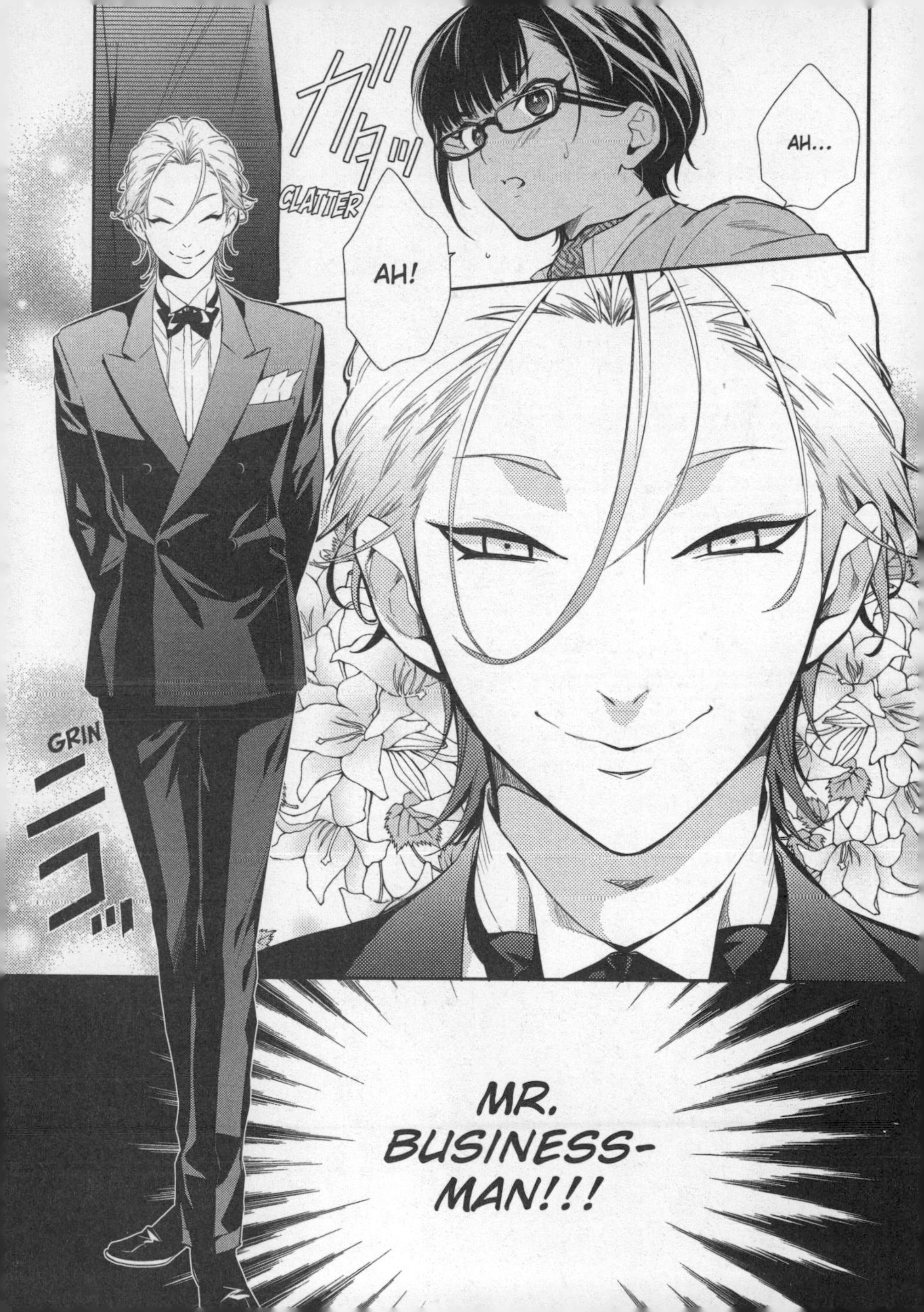
AH...
CLATTER
AH!
GRIN
MR. BUSINESS-MAN!!!

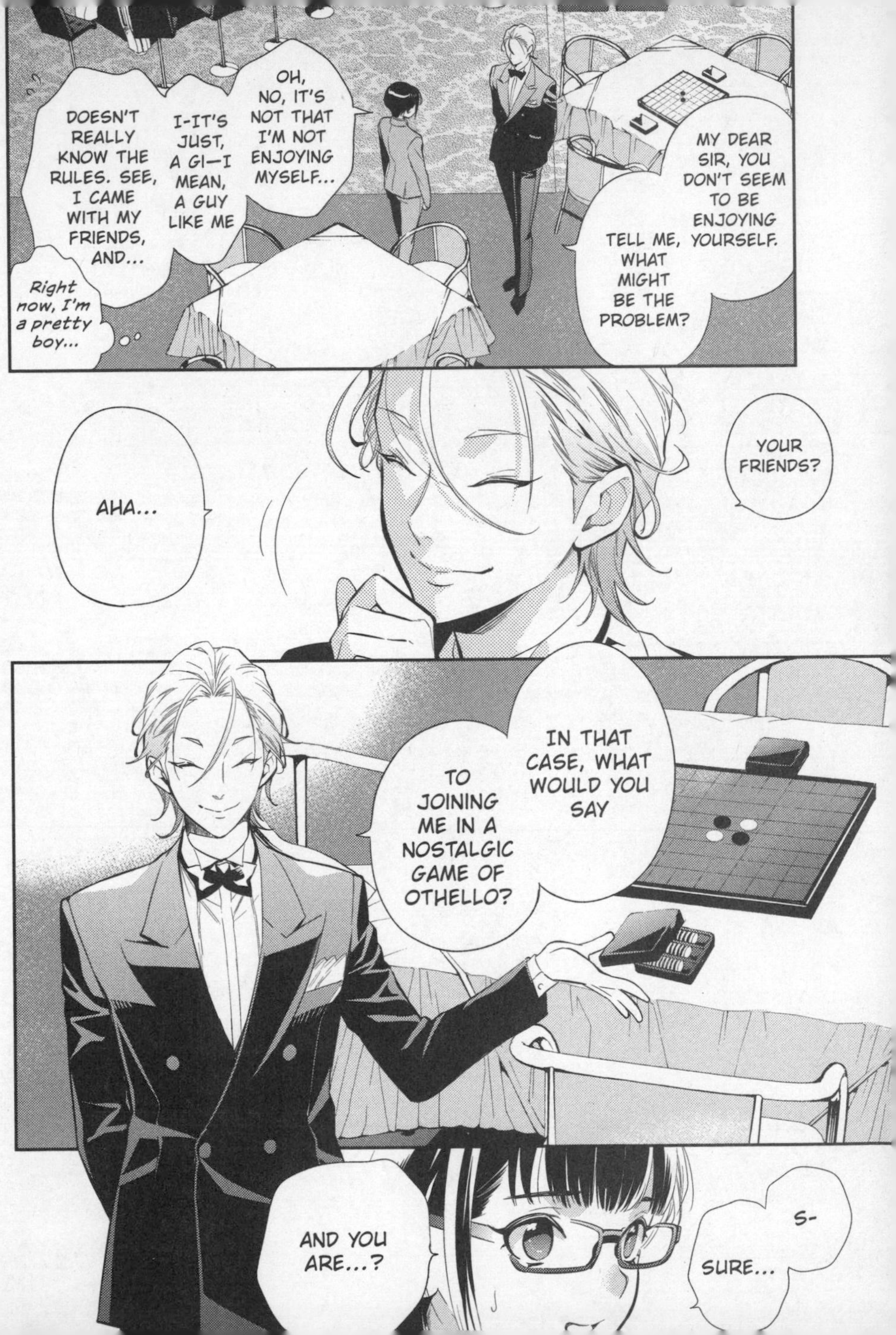
MY DEAR SIR, YOU DON'T SEEM TO BE ENJOYING YOURSELF.
TELL ME, WHAT MIGHT BE THE PROBLEM?
OH, NO, IT'S NOT THAT I'M NOT ENJOYING MYSELF...
I-IT'S JUST, A GI—I MEAN, A GUY LIKE ME
DOESN'T REALLY KNOW THE RULES. SEE, I CAME WITH MY FRIENDS, AND...
Right now, I'm a pretty boy...
YOUR FRIENDS?
AHA...
IN THAT CASE, WHAT WOULD YOU SAY
TO JOINING ME IN A NOSTALGIC GAME OF OTHELLO?
S-
SURE...
AND YOU ARE...?

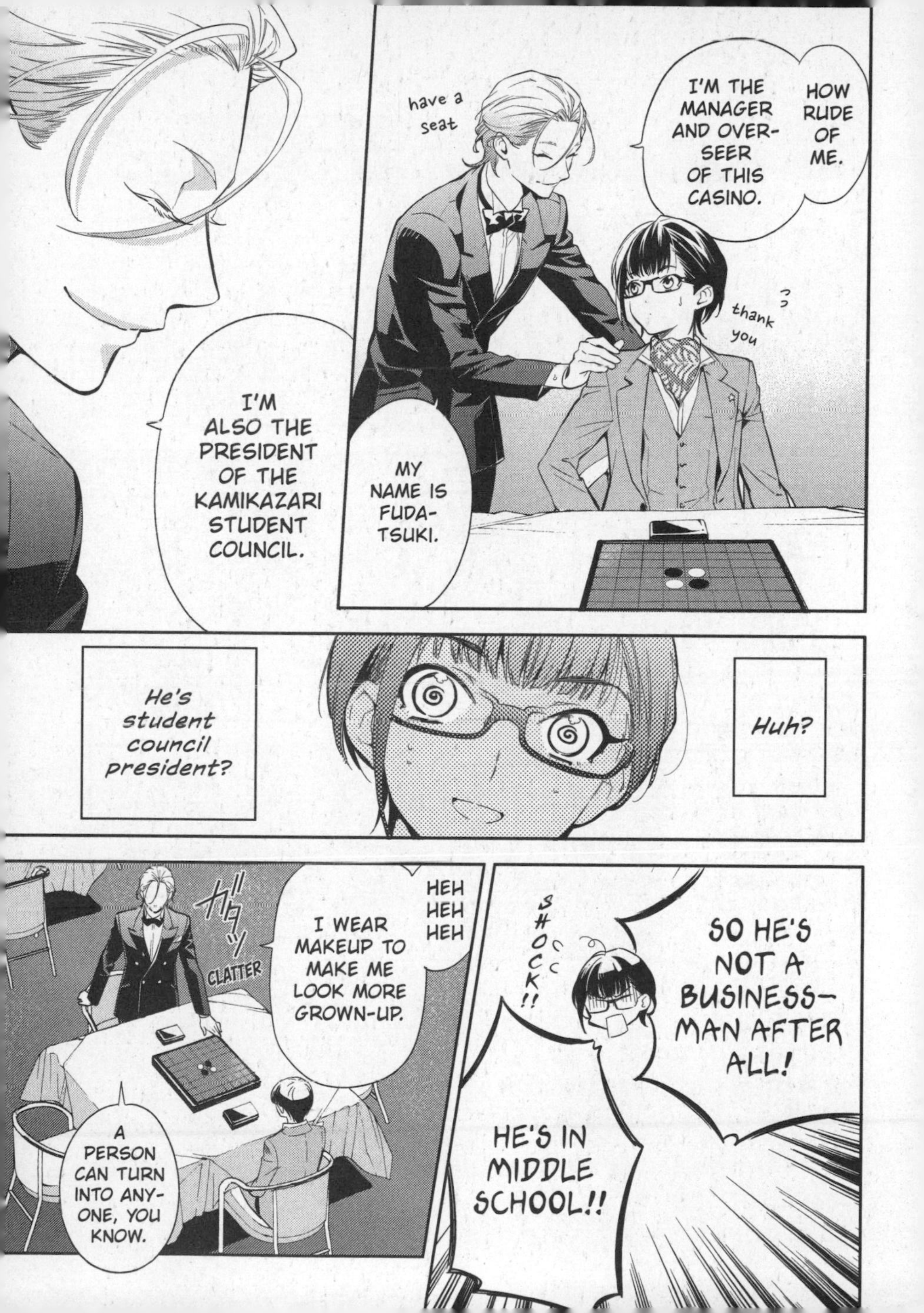
HOW RUDE OF ME.
I'M THE MANAGER AND OVERSEER OF THIS CASINO.
have a seat
thank you
MY NAME IS FUDATSUKI.
I'M ALSO THE PRESIDENT OF THE KAMIKAZARI STUDENT COUNCIL.
Huh?
He's student council president?
SO HE'S NOT A BUSINESSMAN AFTER ALL!
SHOCK!!
HE'S IN MIDDLE SCHOOL!!
HEH HEH HEH
I WEAR MAKEUP TO MAKE ME LOOK MORE GROWN-UP.
CLATTER
A PERSON CAN TURN INTO ANYONE, YOU KNOW.

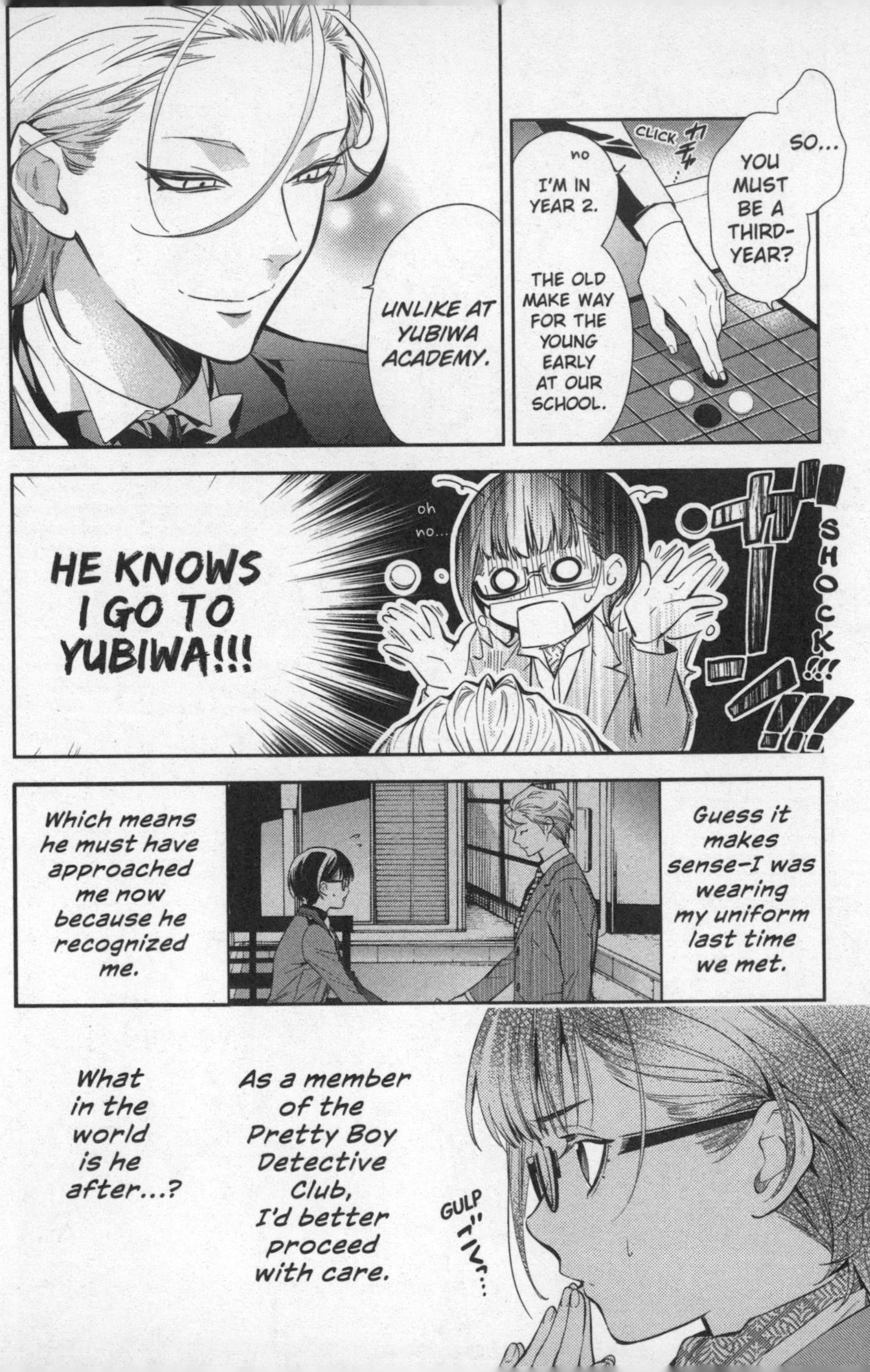
CLICK
SO... YOU MUST BE A THIRD-YEAR?
no
I'M IN YEAR 2.
THE OLD MAKE WAY FOR THE YOUNG EARLY AT OUR SCHOOL.
UNLIKE AT YUBIWA ACADEMY.
SHOCK!!!
oh no...
HE KNOWS I GO TO YUBIWA!!!
Guess it makes sense—I was wearing my uniform last time we met.
Which means he must have approached me now because he recognized me.
GULP
As a member of the Pretty Boy Detective Club, I'd better proceed with care.
What in the world is he after...?

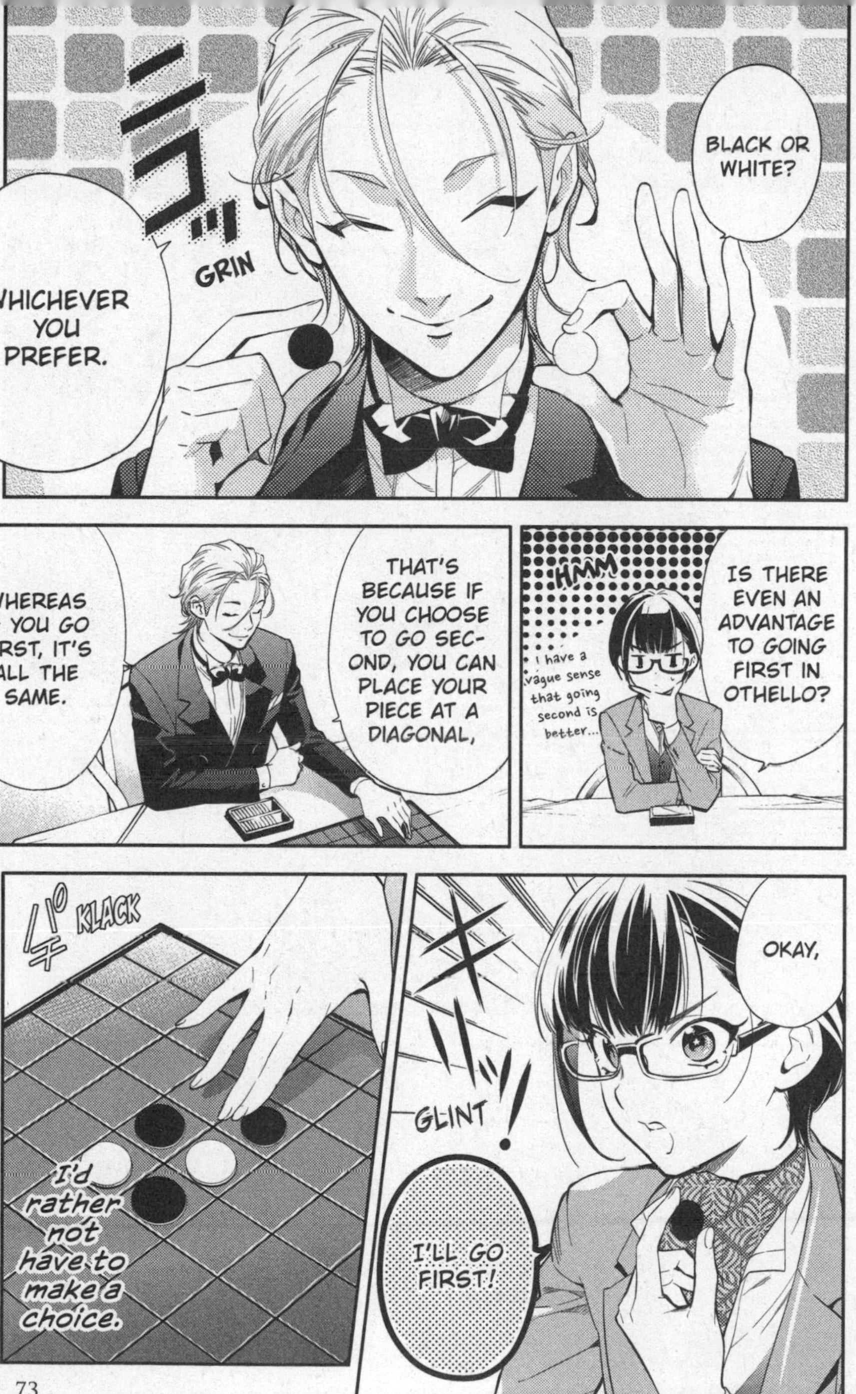
BLACK OR WHITE?
GRIN
WHICHEVER YOU PREFER.
HMM
IS THERE EVEN AN ADVANTAGE TO GOING FIRST IN OTHELLO?
I have a vague sense that going second is better...
THAT'S BECAUSE IF YOU CHOOSE TO GO SEC-OND, YOU CAN PLACE YOUR PIECE AT A DIAGONAL,
WHEREAS IF YOU GO FIRST, IT'S ALL THE SAME.
OKAY,
GLINT
I'LL GO FIRST!
KLACK
I'd rather not have to make a choice.

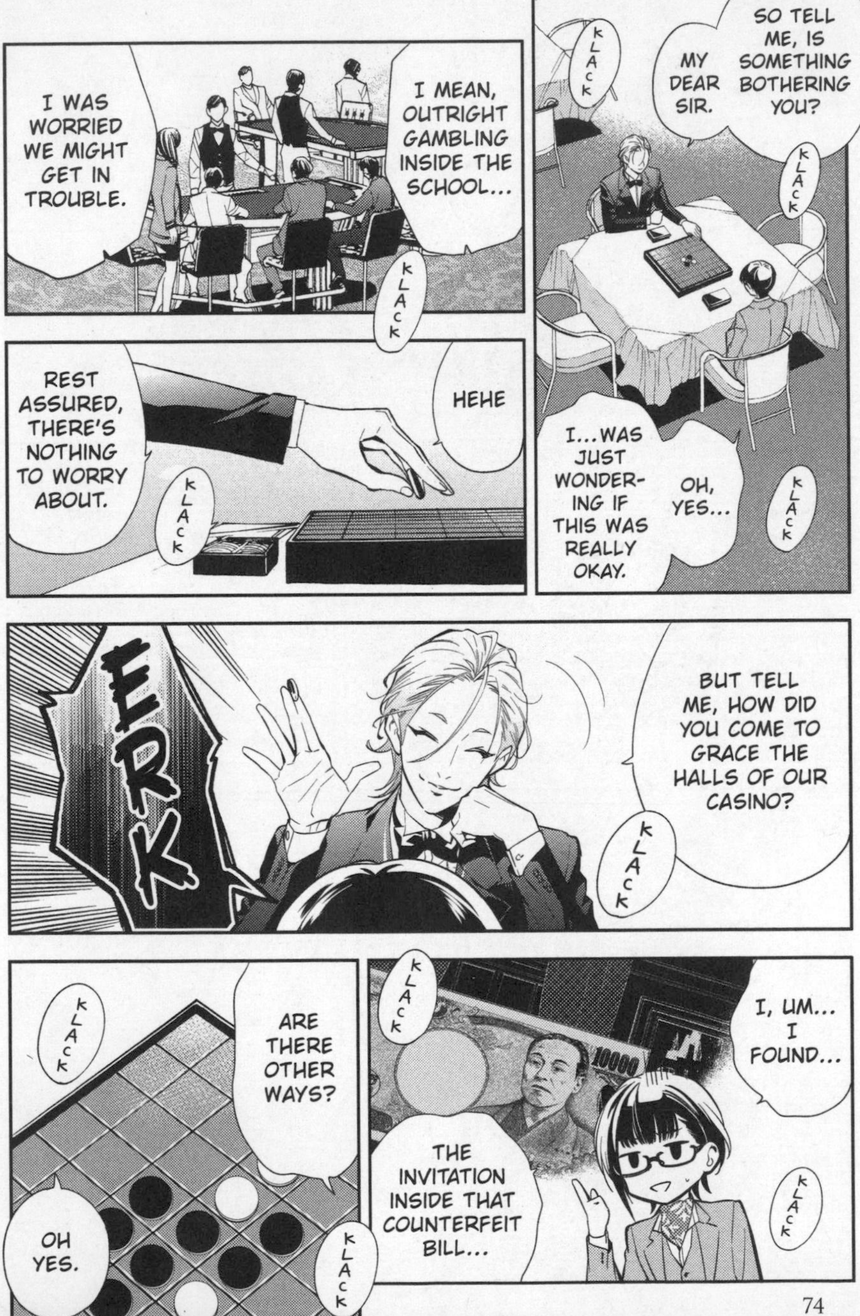
SO TELL ME, IS SOMETHING BOTHERING YOU?
MY DEAR SIR.
KLACK
KLACK
KLACK
OH, YES...
I...WAS JUST WONDERING IF THIS WAS REALLY OKAY.
KLACK
I MEAN, OUTRIGHT GAMBLING INSIDE THE SCHOOL...
I WAS WORRIED WE MIGHT GET IN TROUBLE.
HEHE
REST ASSURED, THERE'S NOTHING TO WORRY ABOUT.
KLACK
BUT TELL ME, HOW DID YOU COME TO GRACE THE HALLS OF OUR CASINO?
KLACK
ERRK
KLACK
I, UM... I FOUND...
KLACK
THE INVITATION INSIDE THAT COUNTERFEIT BILL...
ARE THERE OTHER WAYS?
KLACK
KLACK
OH YES.

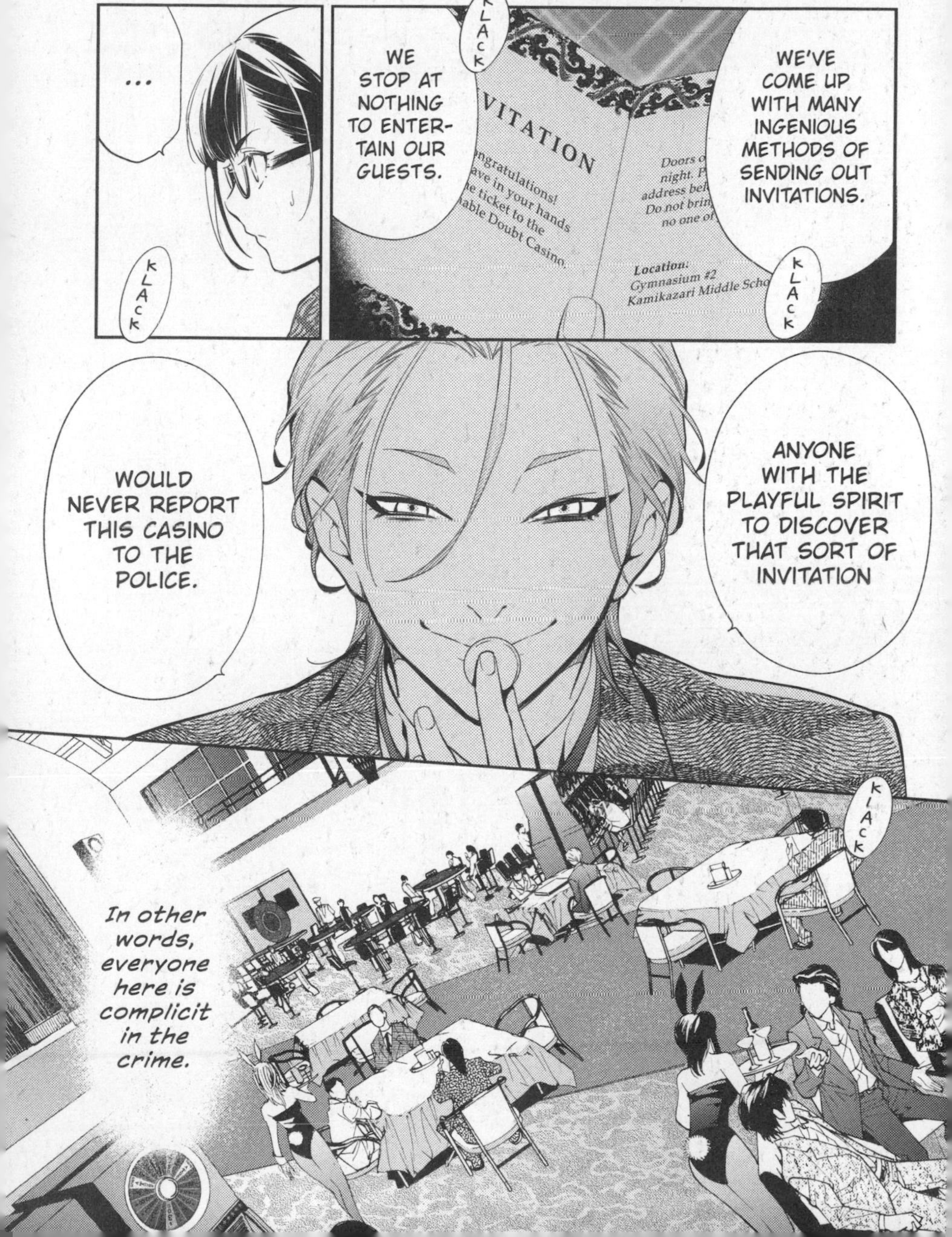
WE'VE COME UP WITH MANY INGENIOUS METHODS OF SENDING OUT INVITATIONS.
KLACK
Location:
Gymnasium #2
WE STOP AT NOTHING TO ENTER-TAIN OUR GUESTS.
KLACK
...
KLACK
ANYONE WITH THE PLAYFUL SPIRIT TO DISCOVER THAT SORT OF INVITATION
WOULD NEVER REPORT THIS CASINO TO THE POLICE.
KLACK
In other words, everyone here is complicit in the crime.

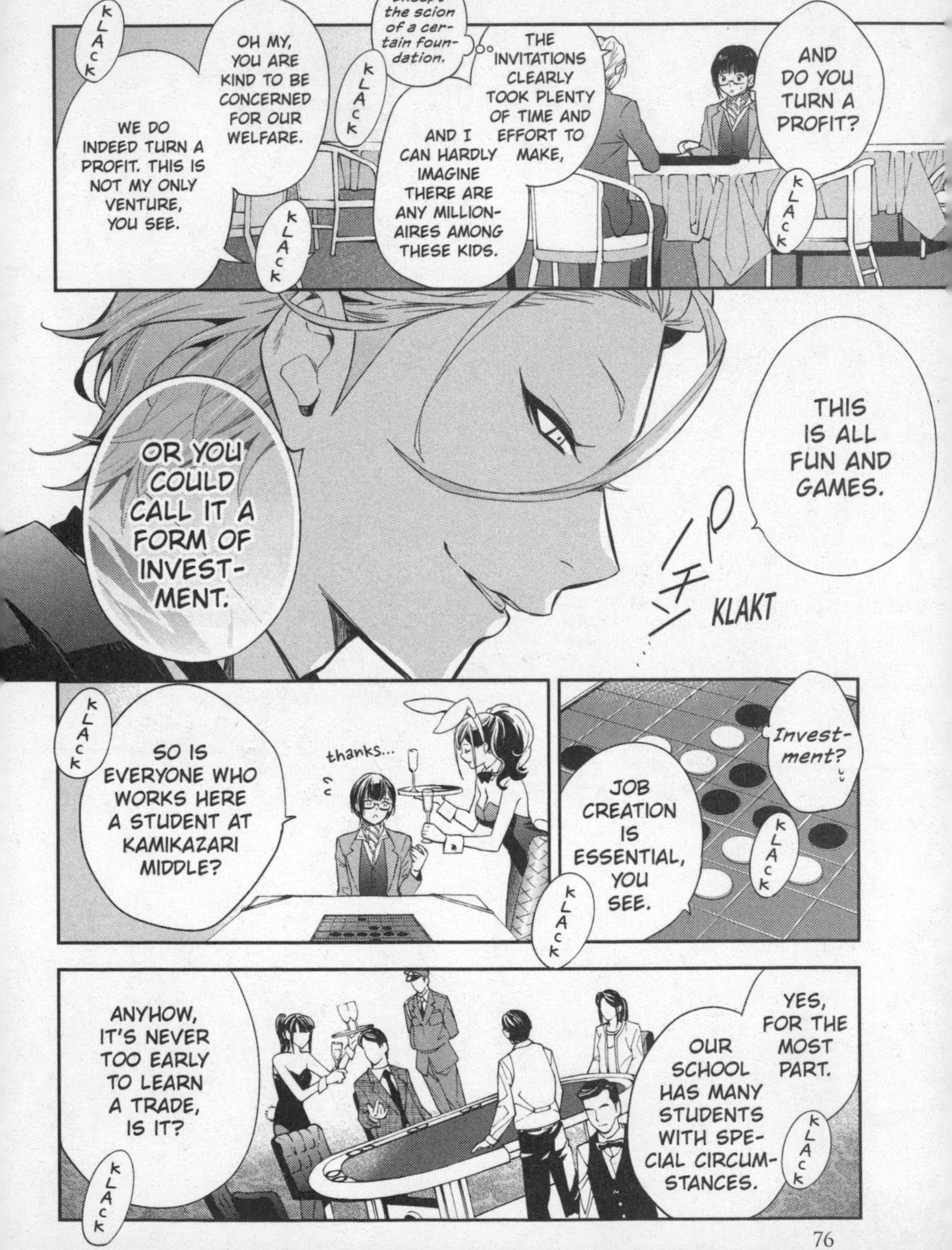
AND DO YOU TURN A PROFIT?
KLACK
THE INVITATIONS CLEARLY TOOK PLENTY OF TIME AND EFFORT TO MAKE,
AND I CAN HARDLY IMAGINE THERE ARE ANY MILLION-AIRES AMONG THESE KIDS.
Except the scion of a cer-tain foun-dation.
KLACK
OH MY, YOU ARE KIND TO BE CONCERNED FOR OUR WELFARE.
WE DO INDEED TURN A PROFIT. THIS IS NOT MY ONLY VENTURE, YOU SEE.
KLACK
KLACK
THIS IS ALL FUN AND GAMES.
KLAKT
OR YOU COULD CALL IT A FORM OF INVEST-MENT.
Invest-ment?
KLACK
JOB CREATION IS ESSENTIAL, YOU SEE.
KLACK
KLACK
SO IS EVERYONE WHO WORKS HERE A STUDENT AT KAMIKAZARI MIDDLE?
thanks...
YES, FOR THE MOST PART.
OUR SCHOOL HAS MANY STUDENTS WITH SPE-CIAL CIRCUM-STANCES.
KLACK
ANYHOW, IT'S NEVER TOO EARLY TO LEARN A TRADE, IS IT?
KLACK

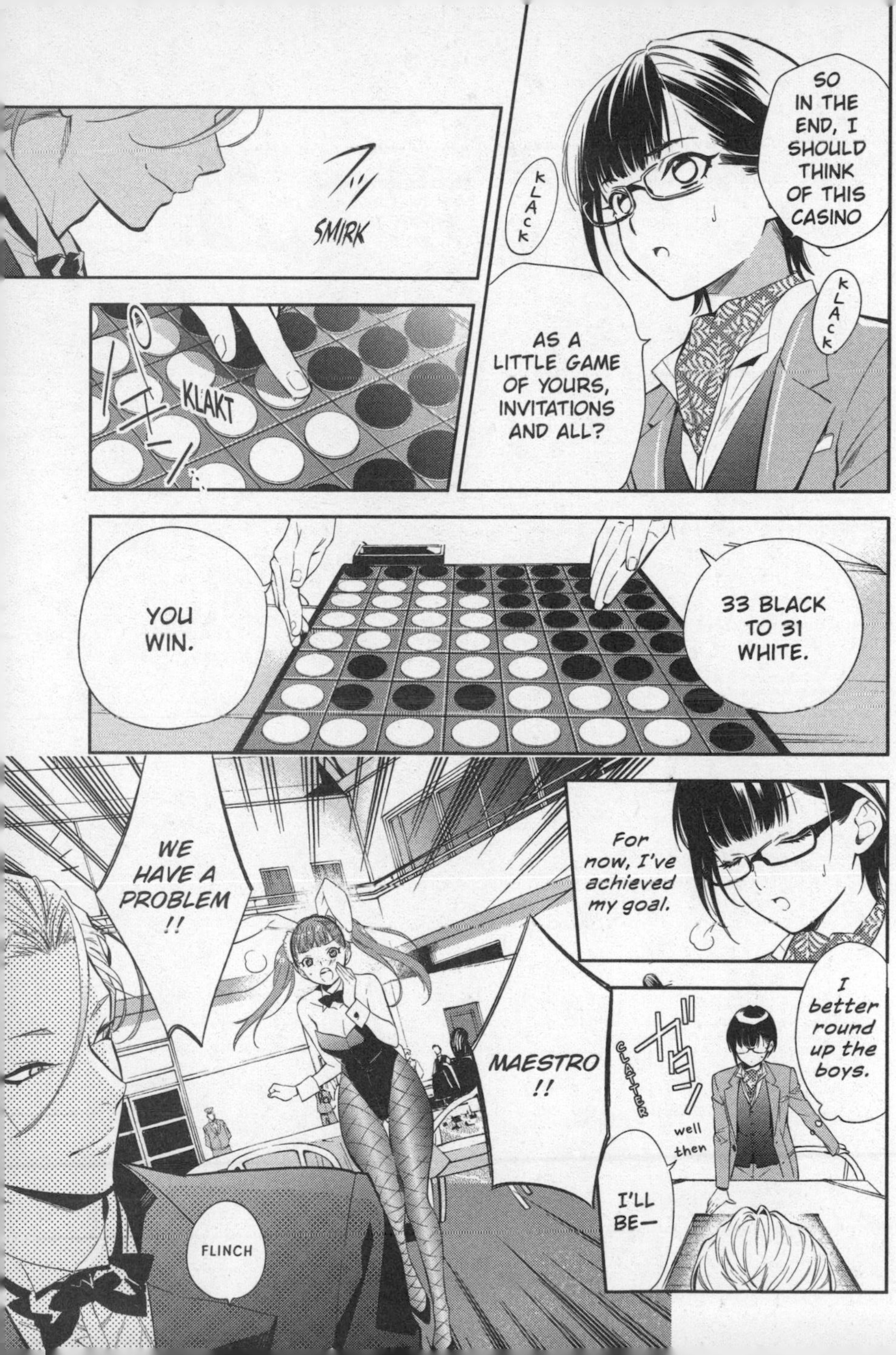
SO IN THE END, I SHOULD THINK OF THIS CASINO
KLACK
KLACK
AS A LITTLE GAME OF YOURS, INVITATIONS AND ALL?
SMIRK
KLAKT
33 BLACK TO 31 WHITE.
YOU WIN.
For now, I've achieved my goal.
I better round up the boys.
CLATTER
well then
I'LL BE—
WE HAVE A PROBLEM!!
MAESTRO!!
FLINCH

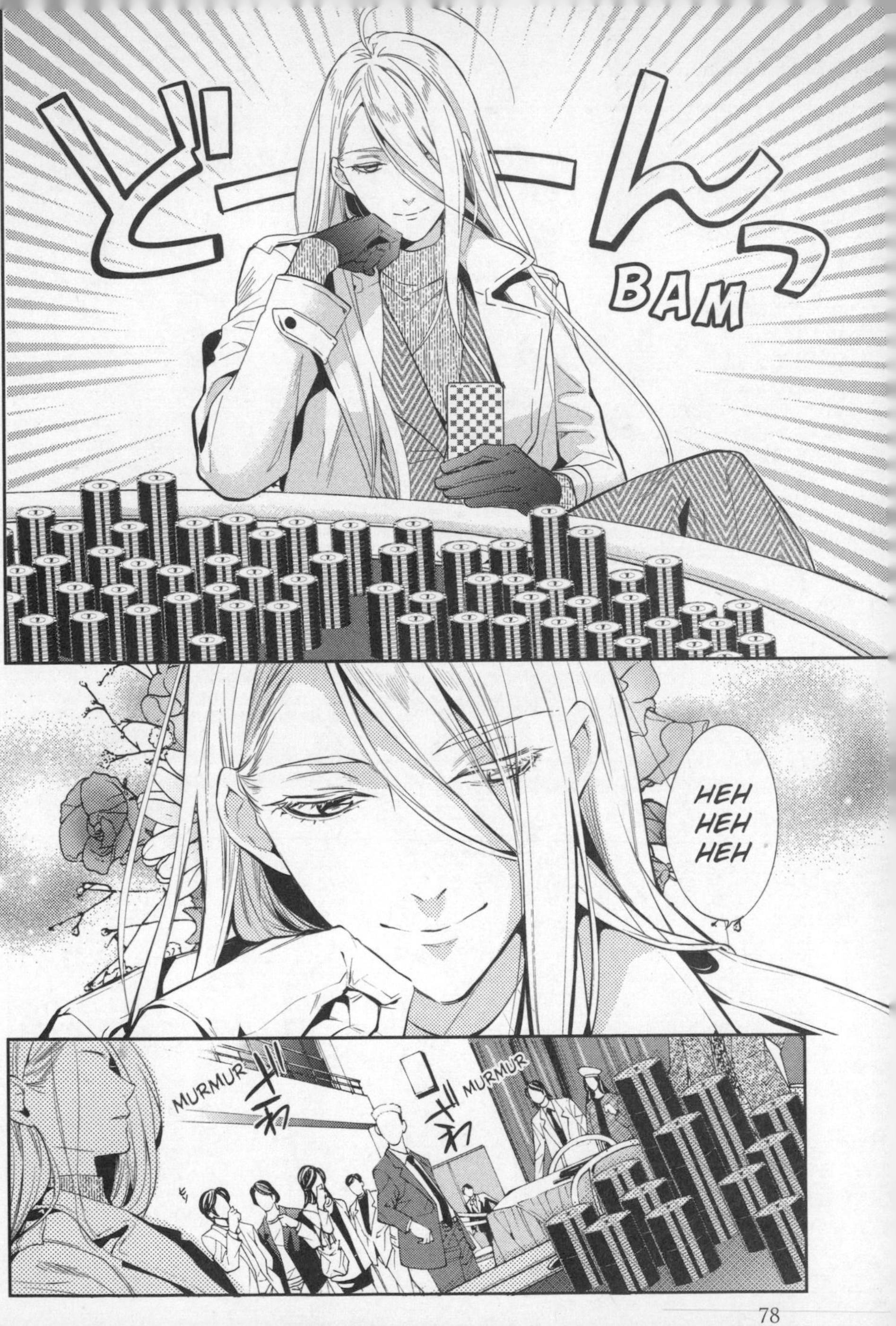
どーんっ
BAM
HEH HEH HEH
ザワ
MURMUR
ザワ
MURMUR

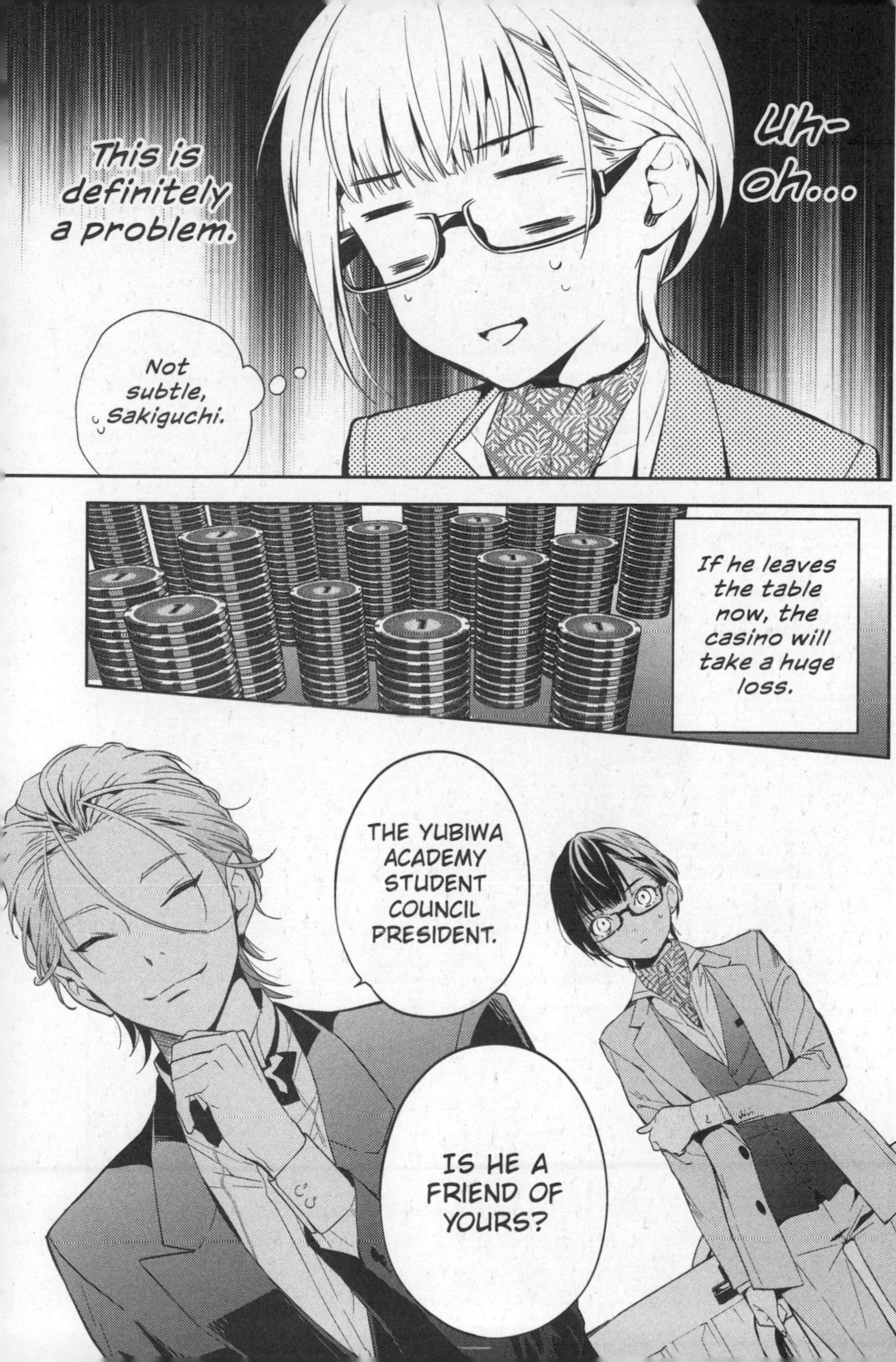
Uh-oh...
This is definitely a problem.
Not subtle, Sakiguchi.
If he leaves the table now, the casino will take a huge loss.
THE YUBIWA ACADEMY STUDENT COUNCIL PRESIDENT.
IS HE A FRIEND OF YOURS?

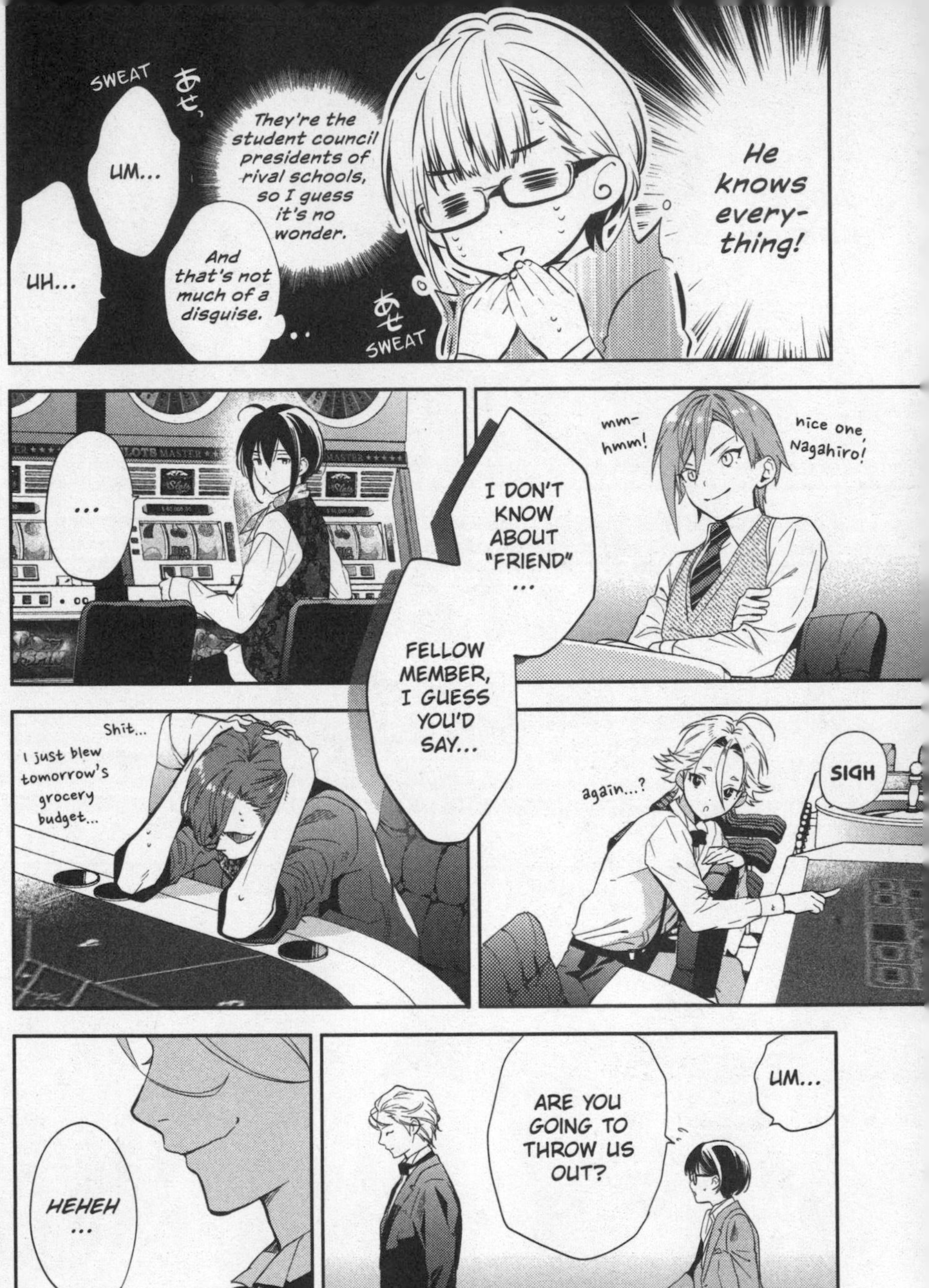
He knows everything!
あせ
SWEAT
They're the student council presidents of rival schools, so I guess it's no wonder.
And that's not much of a disguise.
..
あせ,
SWEAT
UM...
UH...
nice one, Nagahiro!
mm-hmm!
I DON'T KNOW ABOUT "FRIEND"...
FELLOW MEMBER, I GUESS YOU'D SAY...
...
SIGH
again...?
Shit...
I just blew tomorrow's grocery budget...
UM...
ARE YOU GOING TO THROW US OUT?
HEHEH...

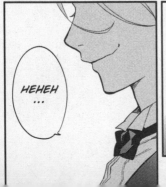

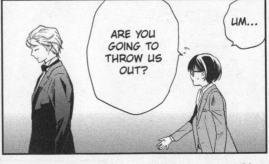

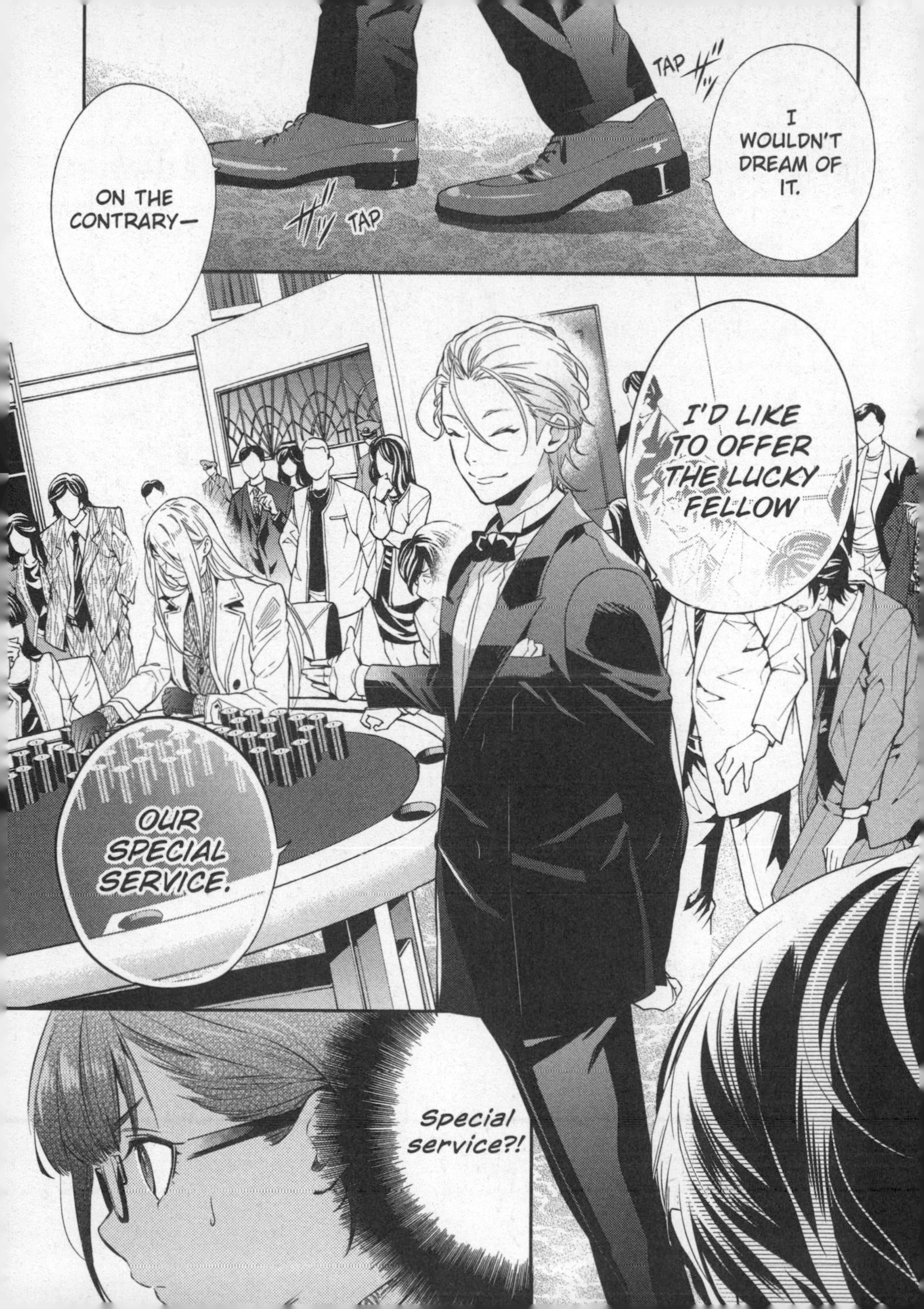
TAP
I WOULDN'T DREAM OF IT.
TAP
ON THE CONTRARY—
I'D LIKE TO OFFER THE LUCKY FELLOW
OUR SPECIAL SERVICE.
Special service?!

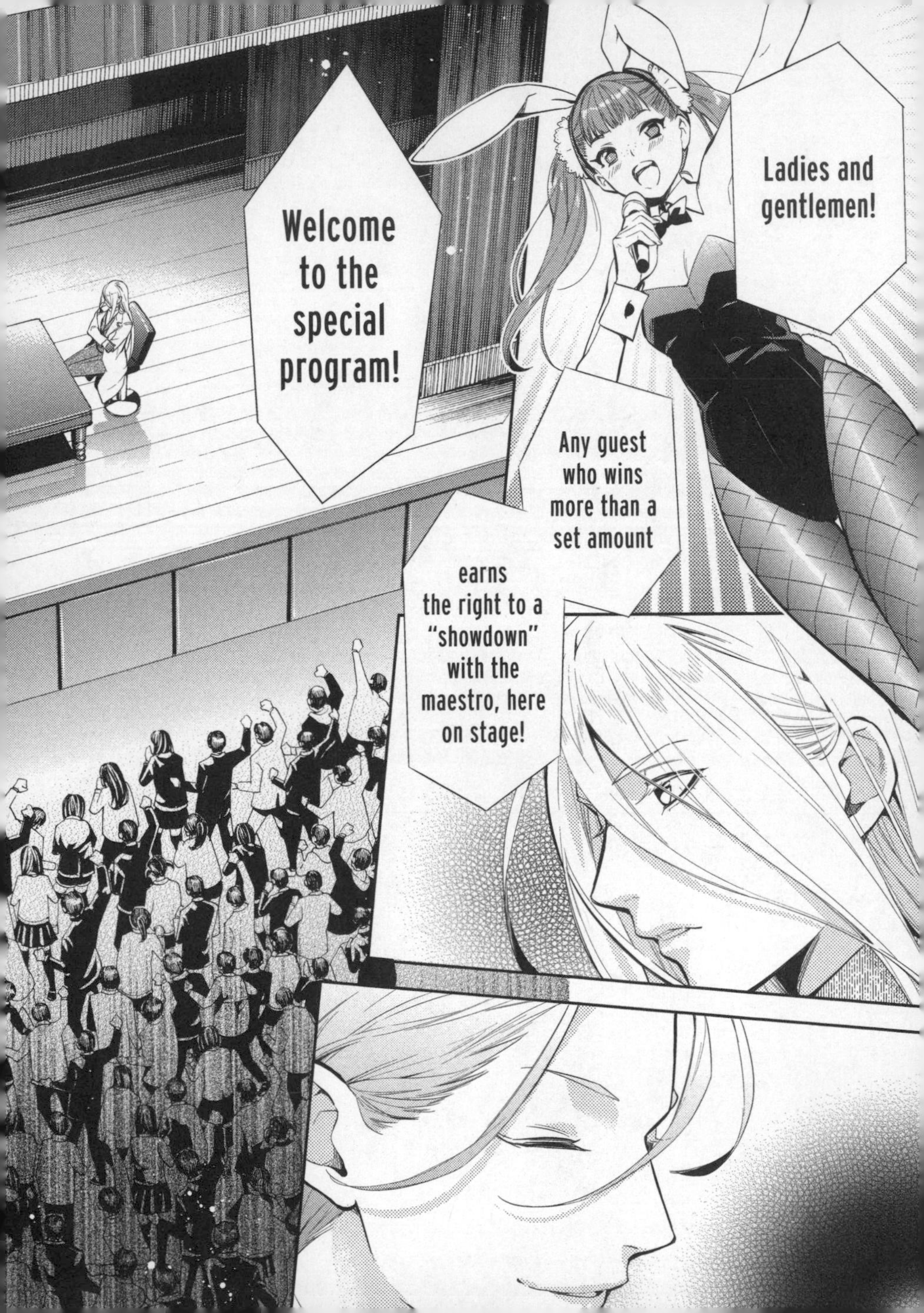
Ladies and gentlemen!
Welcome to the special program!
Any guest who wins more than a set amount
earns the right to a "showdown" with the maestro, here on stage!

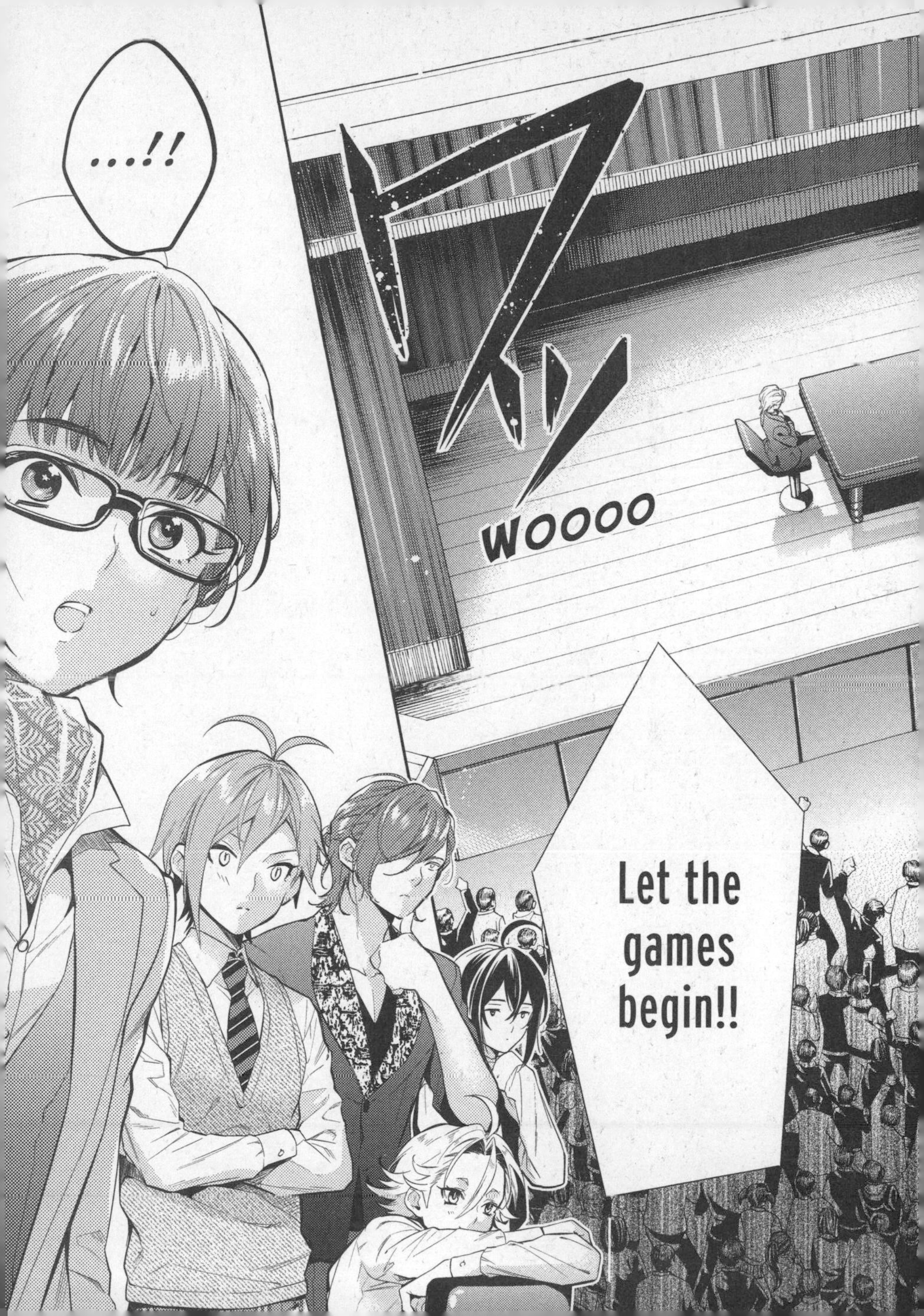
WOOOO
Let the games begin!!
...!!

PRETTY BOY

DETECTIVE CLUB!!

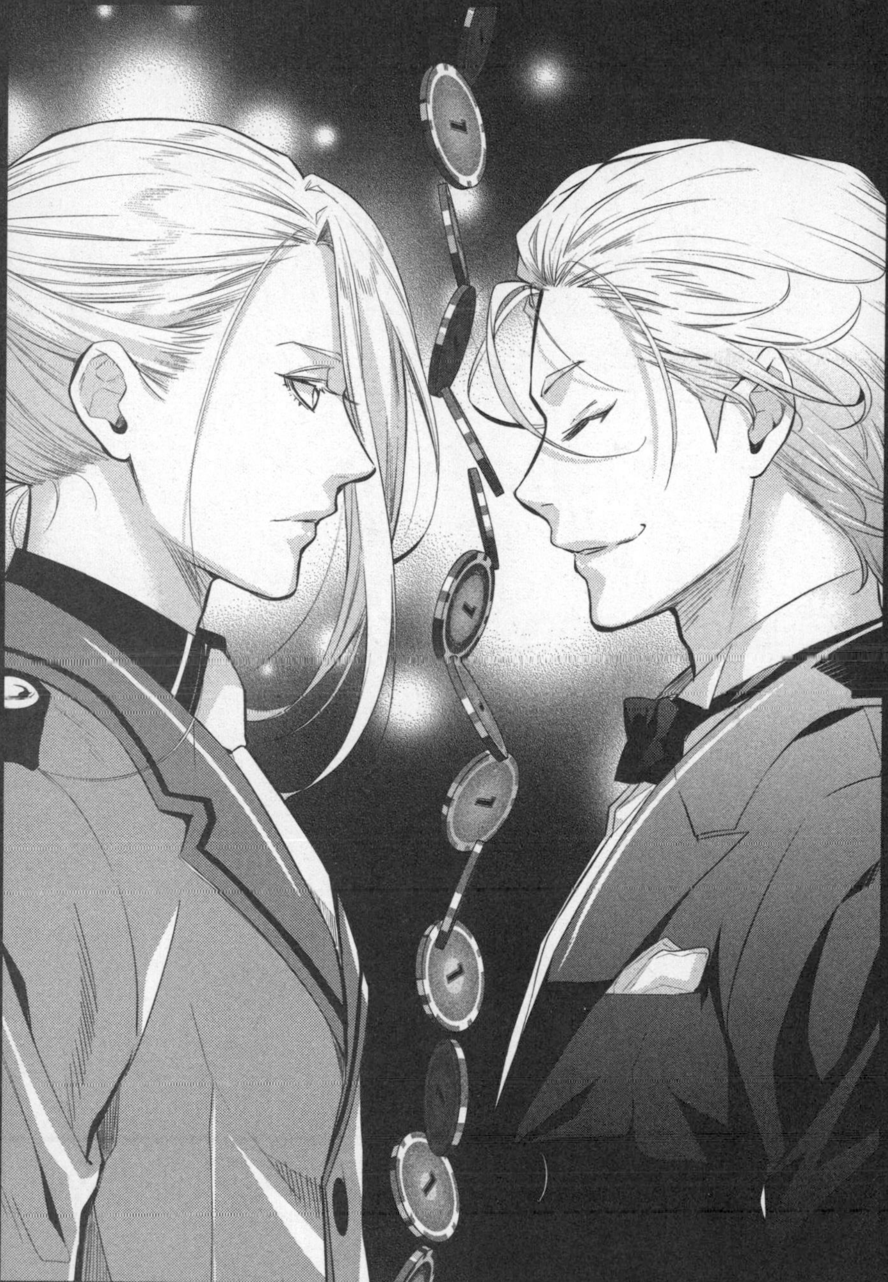

FILE ★ The Swindler, the Vanishing Man, and the Pretty Boys 3

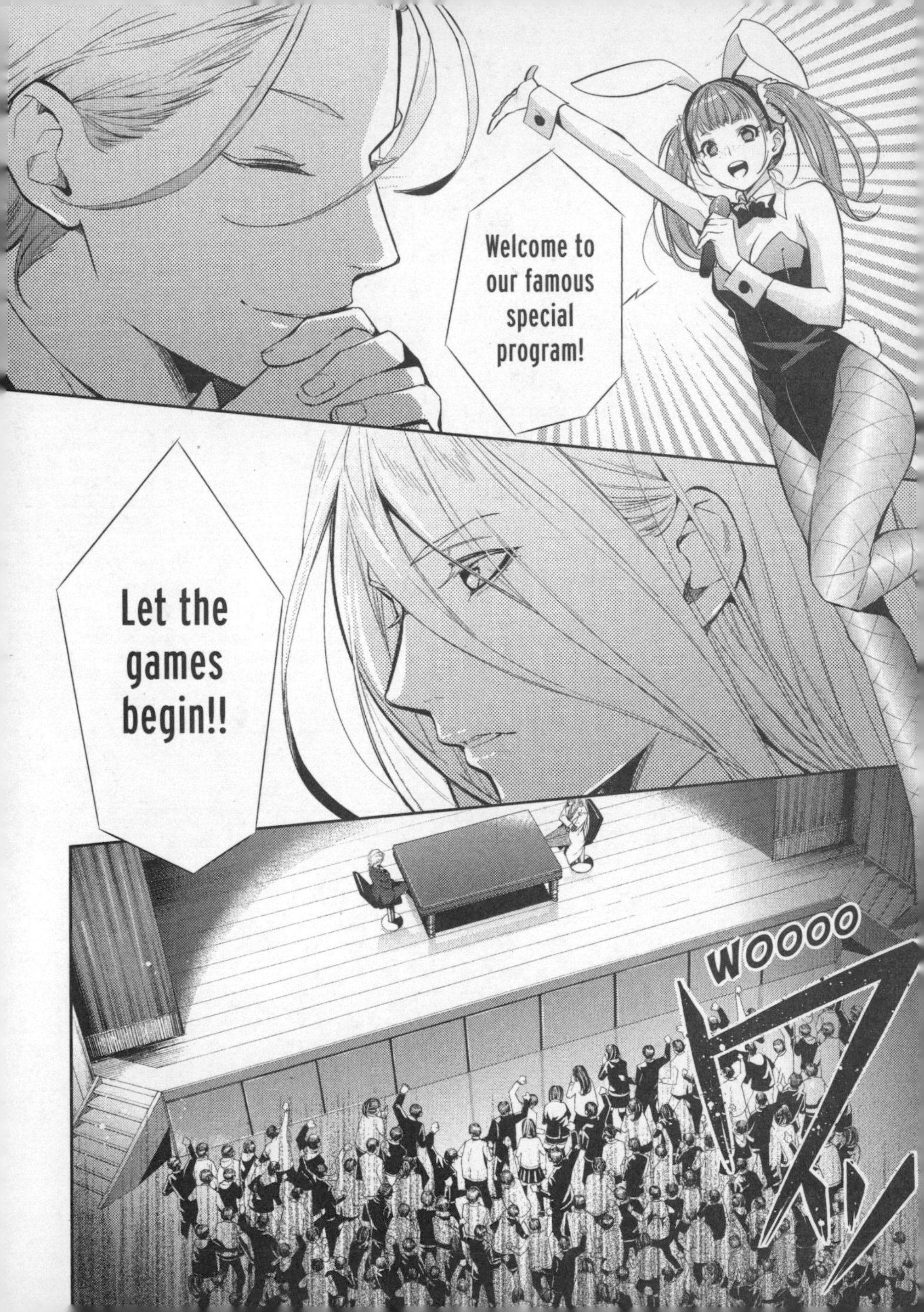
Welcome to our famous special program!
Let the games begin!!
WOOOO

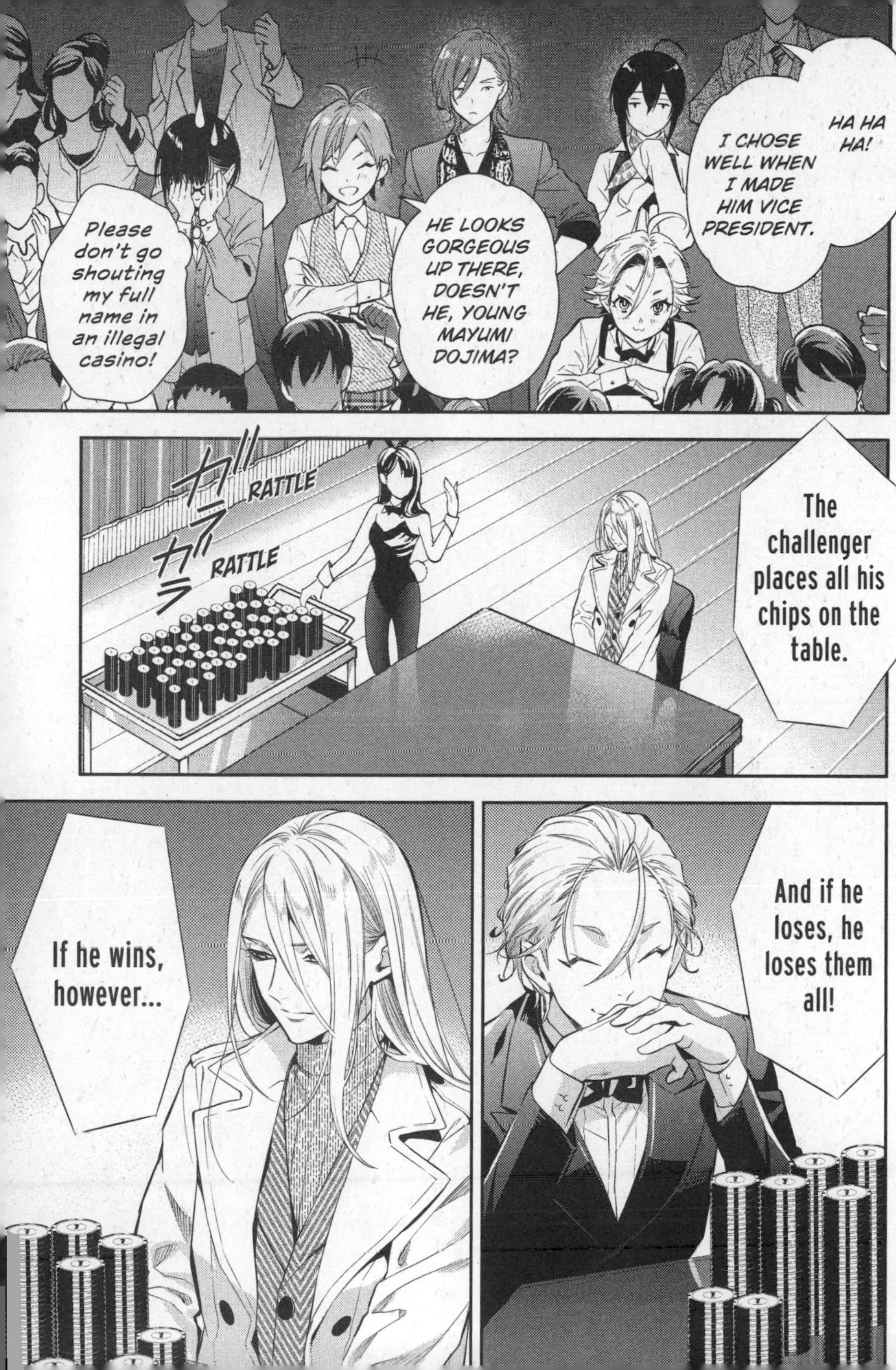
HA HA HA!
I CHOSE WELL WHEN I MADE HIM VICE PRESIDENT.
HE LOOKS GORGEOUS UP THERE, DOESN'T HE, YOUNG MAYUMI DOJIMA?
Please don't go shouting my full name in an illegal casino!
The challenger places all his chips on the table.
RATTLE
RATTLE
And if he loses, he loses them all!
If he wins, however...

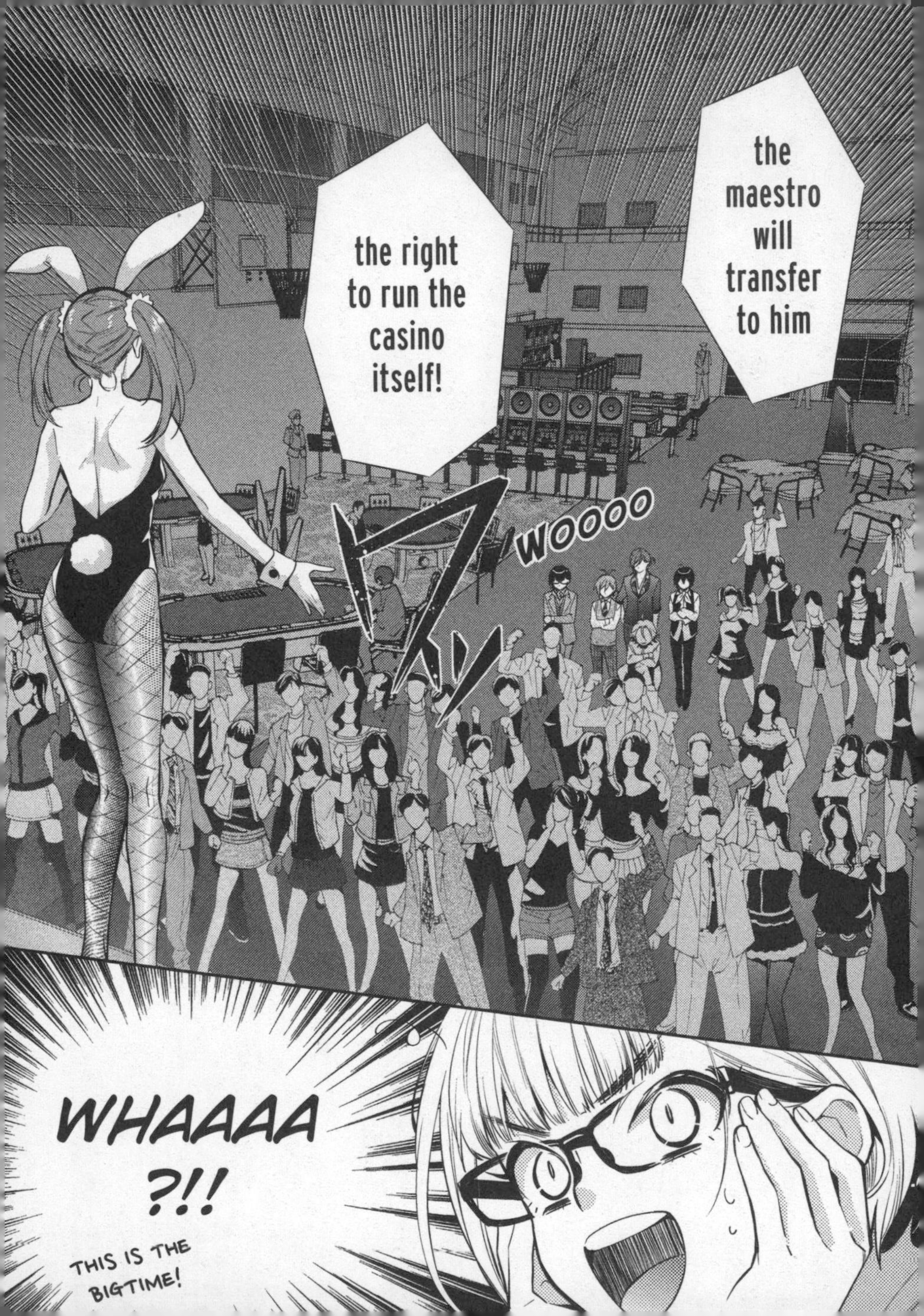
the maestro will transfer to him
the right to run the casino itself!
ワッ
WOOOO
WHAAAA ?!!
THIS IS THE BIGTIME!

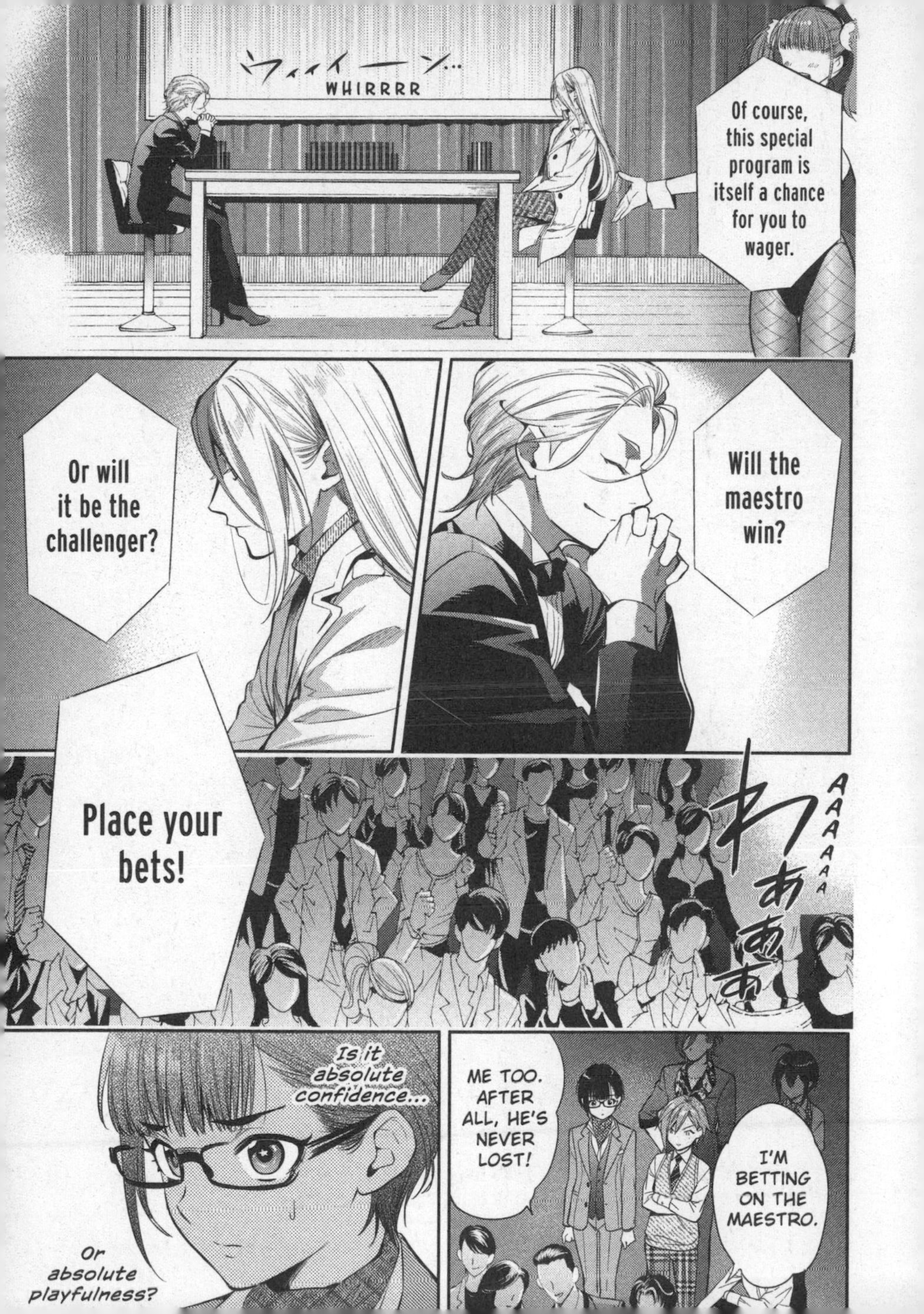
ウィィィーーン…
WHIRRRR
Of course, this special program is itself a chance for you to wager.
Will the maestro win?
Or will it be the challenger?
Place your bets!
わあああ
AAAAAA
I'M BETTING ON THE MAESTRO.
ME TOO. AFTER ALL, HE'S NEVER LOST!
Is it absolute confidence...
Or absolute playfulness?

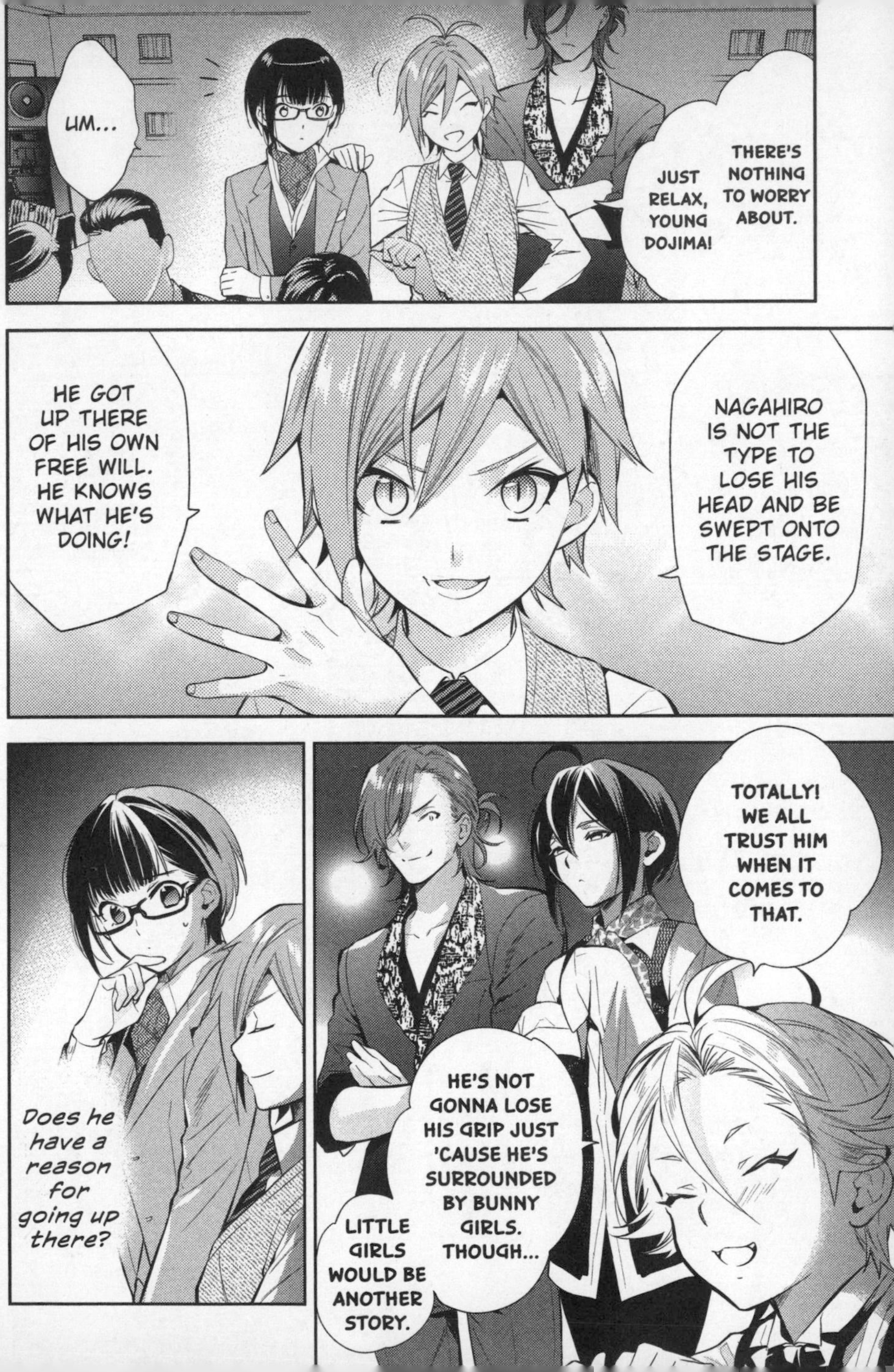
THERE'S NOTHING TO WORRY ABOUT.
JUST RELAX, YOUNG DOJIMA!
UM...
NAGAHIRO IS NOT THE TYPE TO LOSE HIS HEAD AND BE SWEPT ONTO THE STAGE.
HE GOT UP THERE OF HIS OWN FREE WILL. HE KNOWS WHAT HE'S DOING!
TOTALLY! WE ALL TRUST HIM WHEN IT COMES TO THAT.
HE'S NOT GONNA LOSE HIS GRIP JUST 'CAUSE HE'S SURROUNDED BY BUNNY GIRLS. THOUGH...
LITTLE GIRLS WOULD BE ANOTHER STORY.
Does he have a reason for going up there?

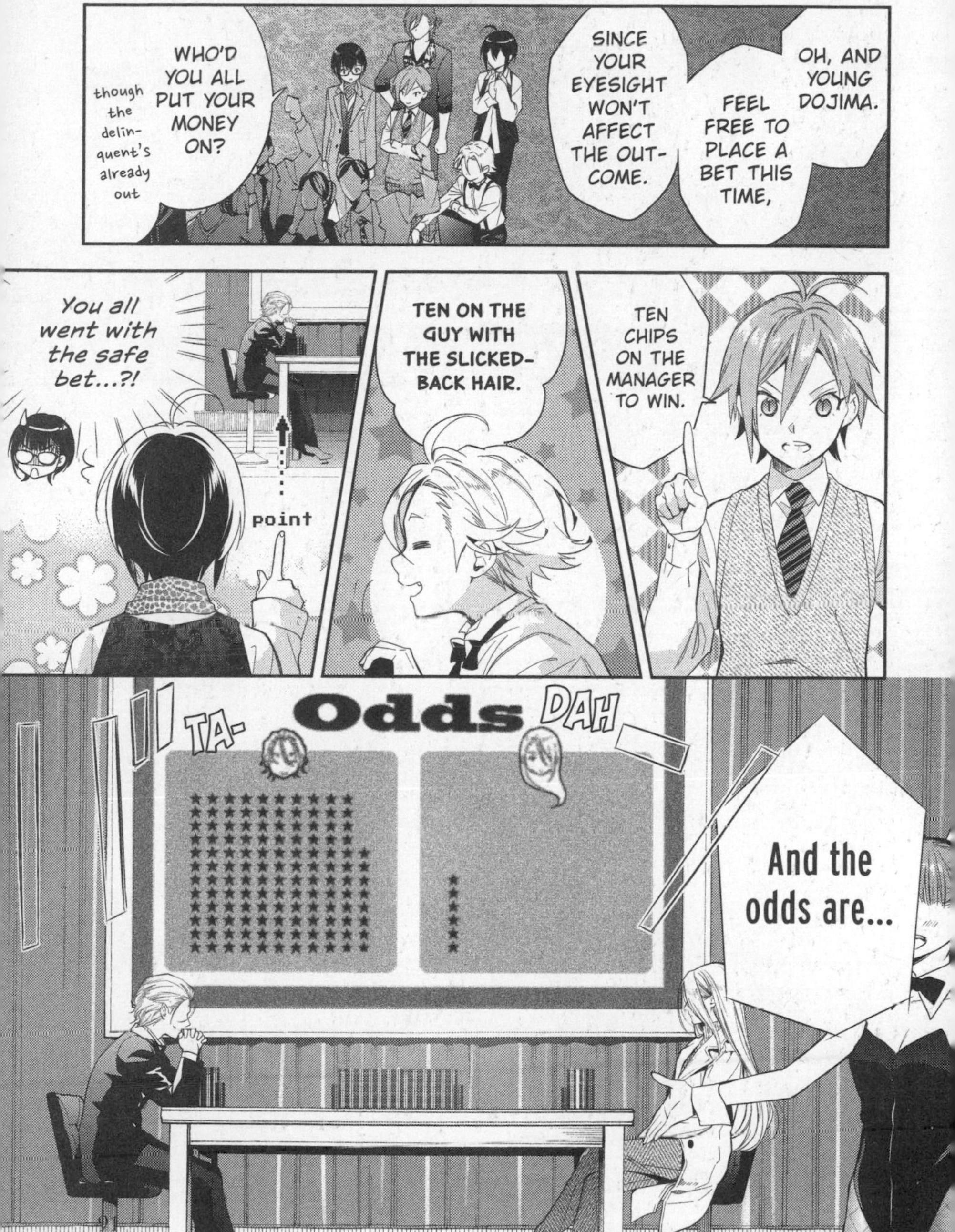
OH, AND YOUNG DOJIMA.
FEEL FREE TO PLACE A BET THIS TIME,
SINCE YOUR EYESIGHT WON'T AFFECT THE OUT-COME.
WHO'D YOU ALL PUT YOUR MONEY ON?
though the delin-quent's already out
TEN CHIPS ON THE MANAGER TO WIN.
TEN ON THE GUY WITH THE SLICKED-BACK HAIR.
You all went with the safe bet...?!
point
TA-
DAH
Odds
And the odds are...

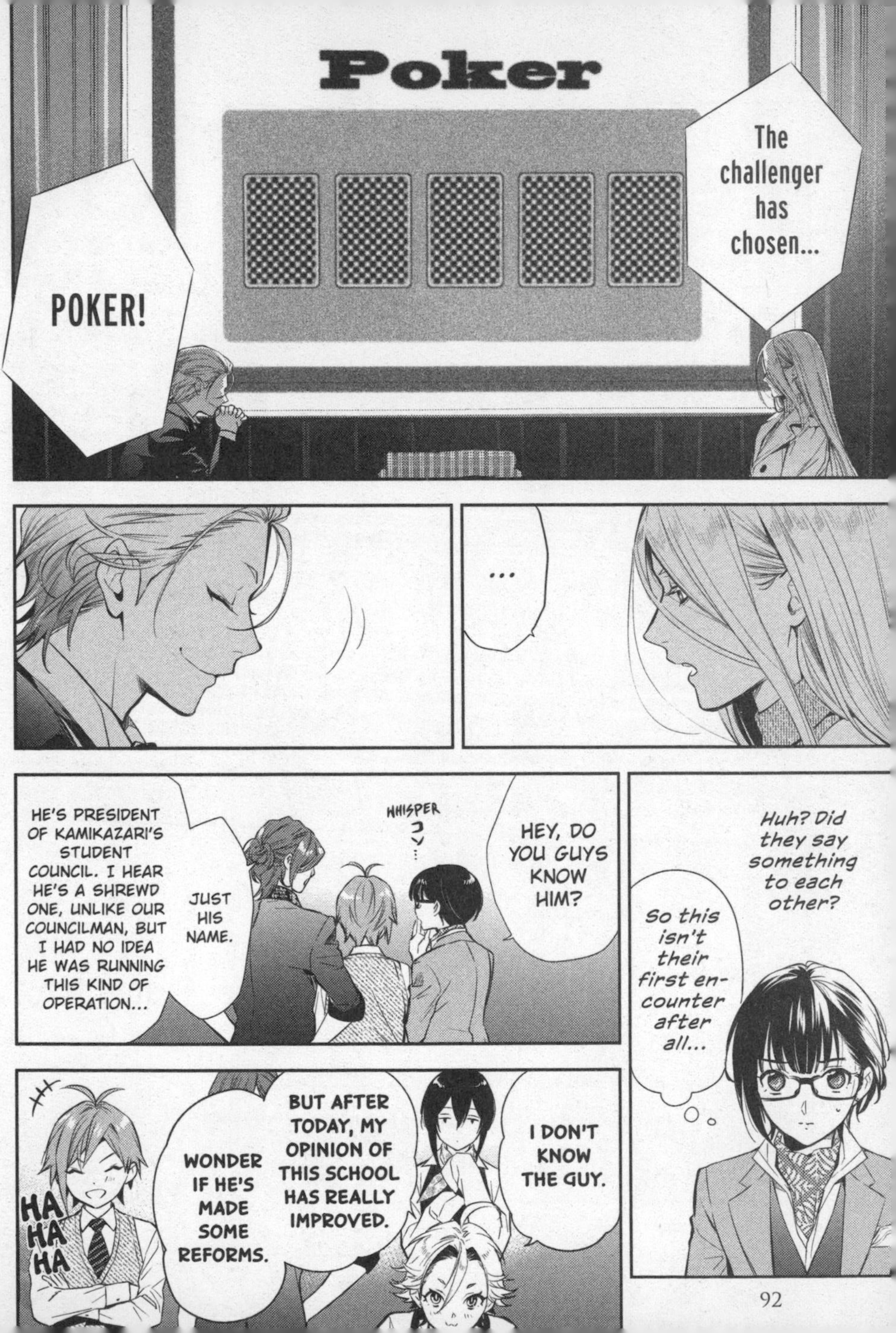
Poker
The challenger has chosen...
POKER!
...
Huh? Did they say something to each other?
So this isn't their first encounter after all...
HEY, DO YOU GUYS KNOW HIM?
WHISPER
コソ…
JUST HIS NAME.
HE'S PRESIDENT OF KAMIKAZARI'S STUDENT COUNCIL. I HEAR HE'S A SHREWD ONE, UNLIKE OUR COUNCILMAN, BUT I HAD NO IDEA HE WAS RUNNING THIS KIND OF OPERATION...
I DON'T KNOW THE GUY.
BUT AFTER TODAY, MY OPINION OF THIS SCHOOL HAS REALLY IMPROVED.
WONDER IF HE'S MADE SOME REFORMS.
HA HA HA

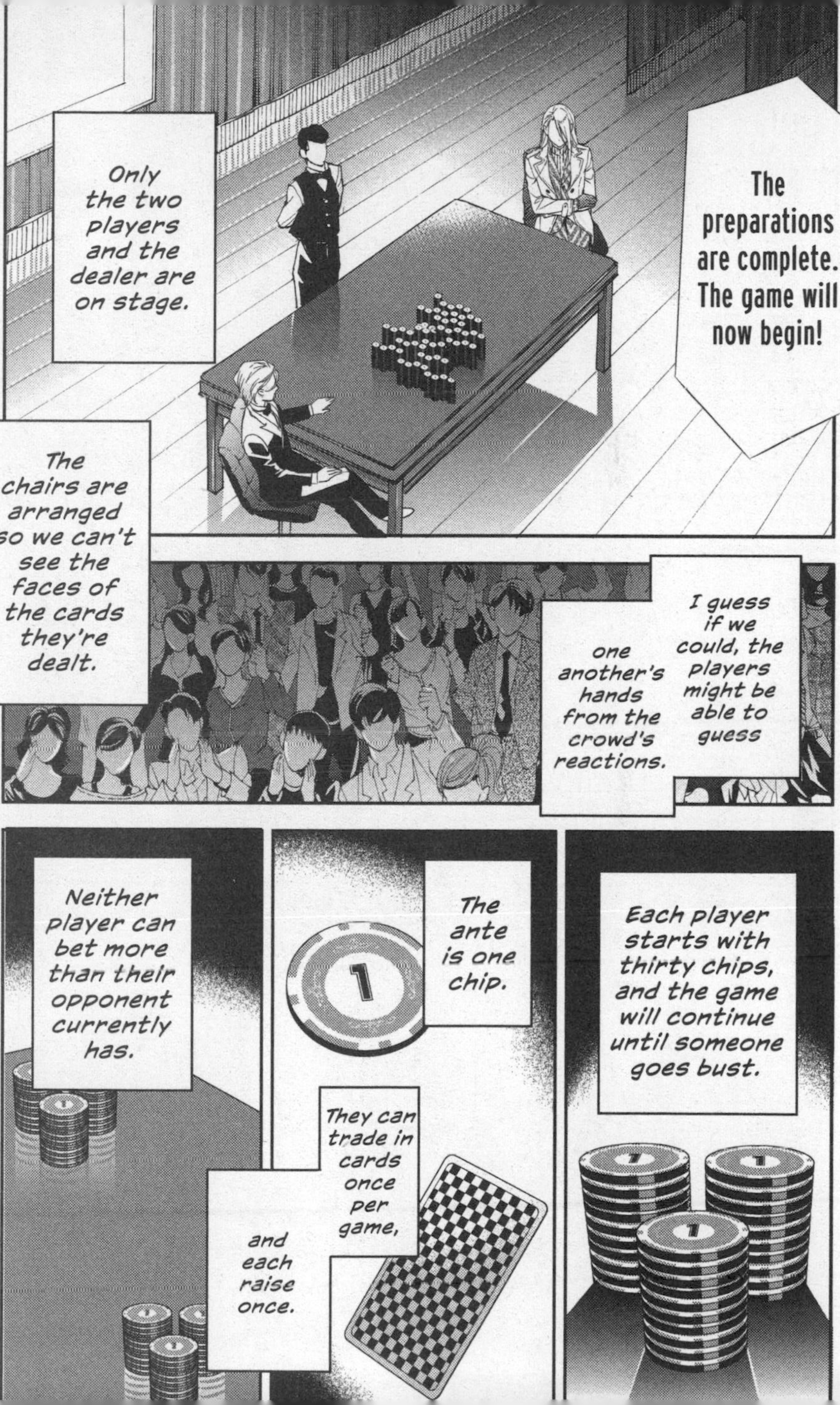
The preparations are complete. The game will now begin!
Only the two players and the dealer are on stage.
The chairs are arranged so we can't see the faces of the cards they're dealt.
I guess if we could, the players might be able to guess
one another's hands from the crowd's reactions.
Each player starts with thirty chips, and the game will continue until someone goes bust.
The ante is one chip.
They can trade in cards once per game,
and each raise once.
Neither player can bet more than their opponent currently has.

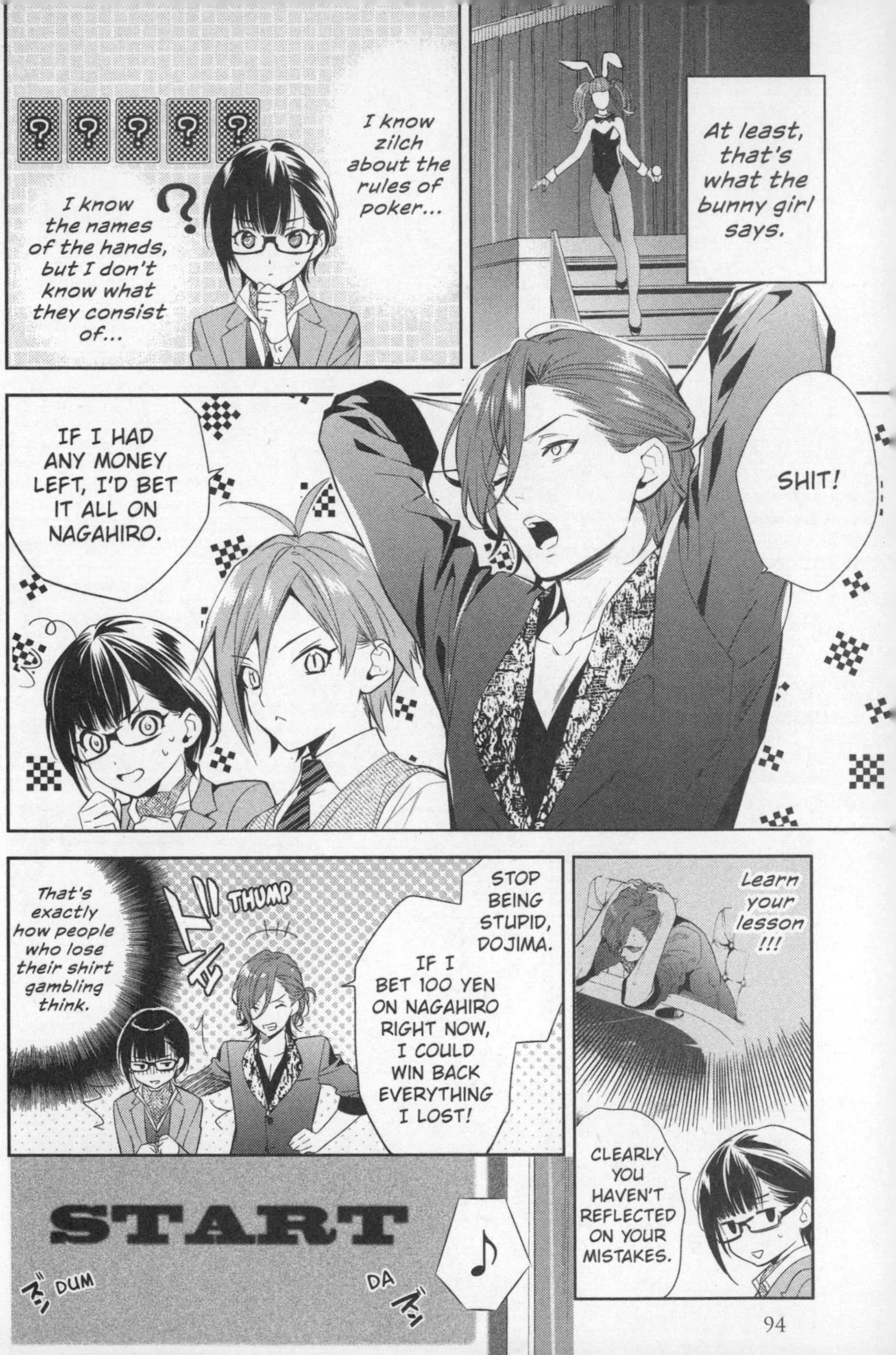
At least, that's what the bunny girl says.
I know zilch about the rules of poker...
I know the names of the hands, but I don't know what they consist of...
SHIT!
IF I HAD ANY MONEY LEFT, I'D BET IT ALL ON NAGAHIRO.
Learn your lesson !!!
STOP BEING STUPID, DOJIMA.
IF I BET 100 YEN ON NAGAHIRO RIGHT NOW, I COULD WIN BACK EVERYTHING I LOST!
THUMP
That's exactly how people who lose their shirt gambling think.
CLEARLY YOU HAVEN'T REFLECTED ON YOUR MISTAKES.
♪
DA
START
DUM

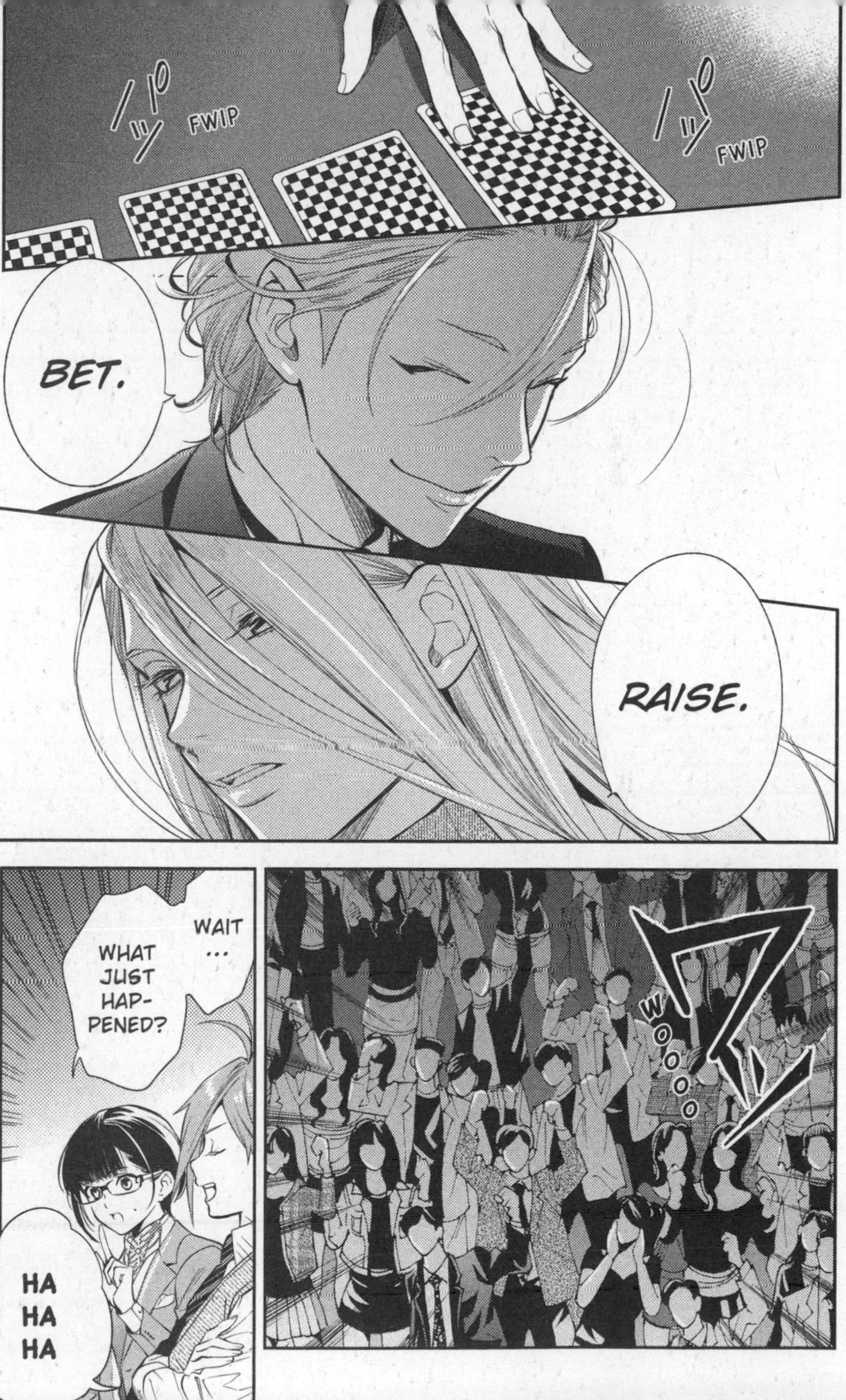
FWIP
FWIP
BET.
RAISE.
WOOOOO
WAIT ... WHAT JUST HAP-PENED?
HA HA HA

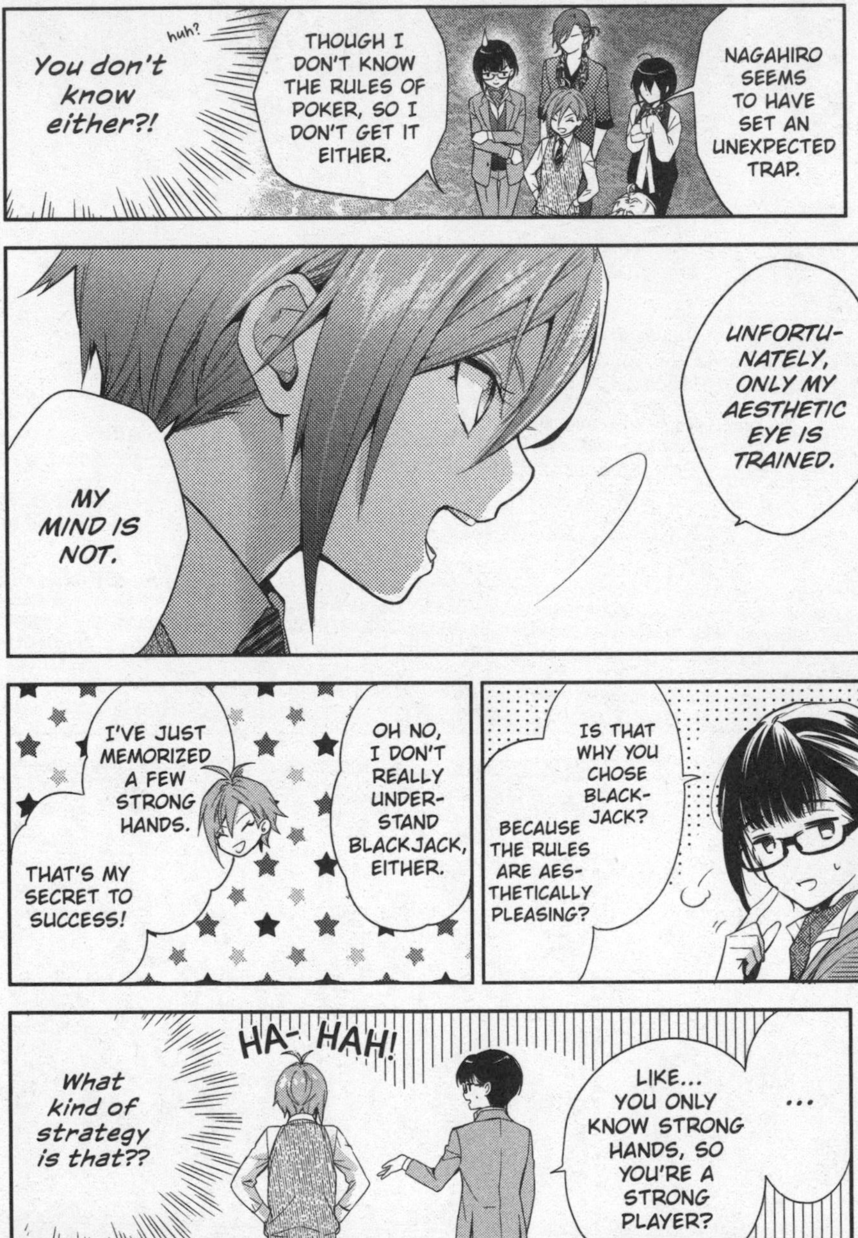
NAGAHIRO SEEMS TO HAVE SET AN UNEXPECTED TRAP.
THOUGH I DON'T KNOW THE RULES OF POKER, SO I DON'T GET IT EITHER.
huh?
You don't know either?!
UNFORTUNATELY, ONLY MY AESTHETIC EYE IS TRAINED.
MY MIND IS NOT.
IS THAT WHY YOU CHOSE BLACKJACK?
BECAUSE THE RULES ARE AESTHETICALLY PLEASING?
OH NO, I DON'T REALLY UNDERSTAND BLACKJACK, EITHER.
I'VE JUST MEMORIZED A FEW STRONG HANDS.
THAT'S MY SECRET TO SUCCESS!
...
LIKE... YOU ONLY KNOW STRONG HANDS, SO YOU'RE A STRONG PLAYER?
HA-HAH!
What kind of strategy is that??

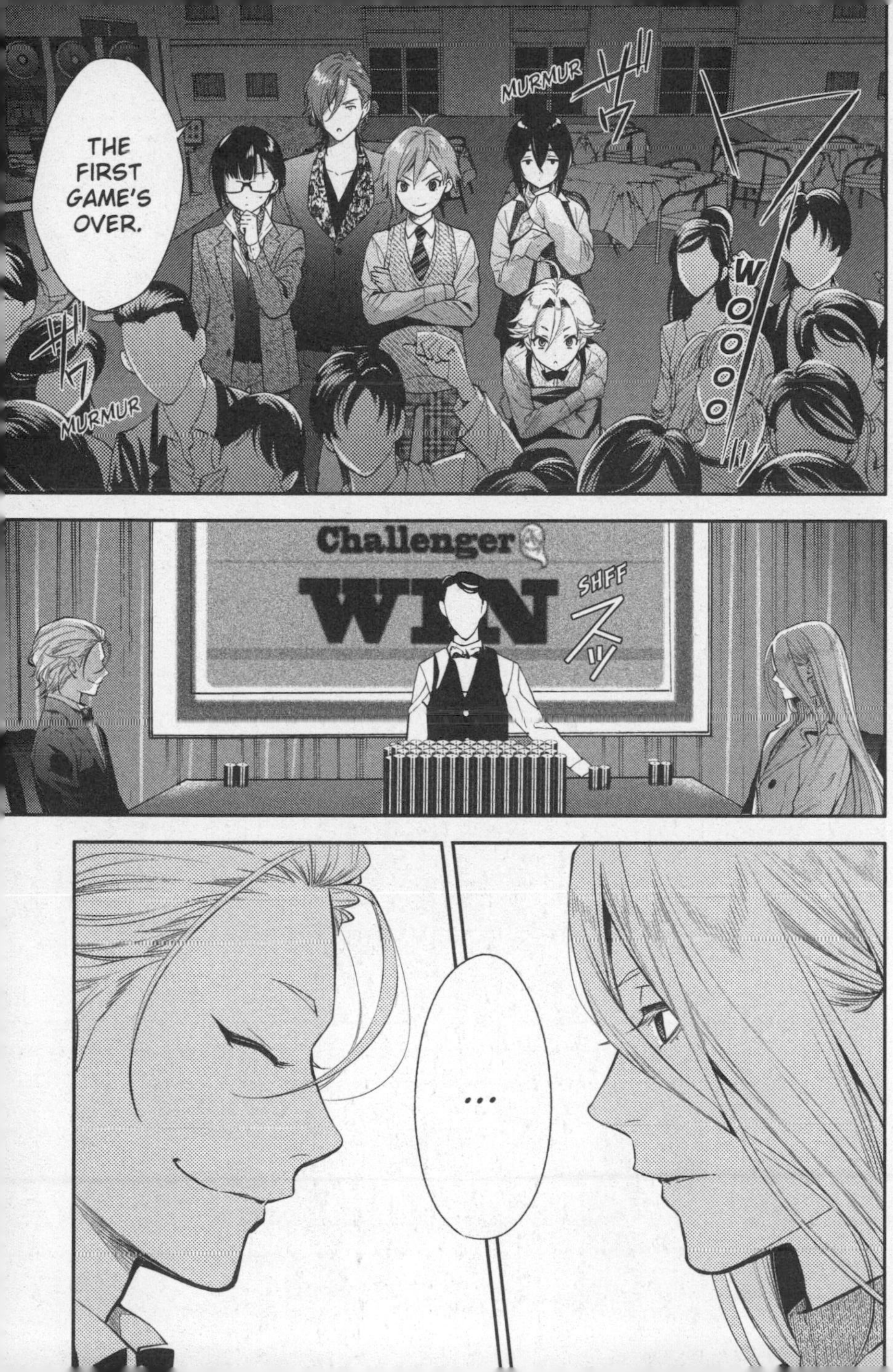
WOOOOOO
MURMUR
MURMUR
THE FIRST GAME'S OVER.
Challenger
WIN
SHFF
...

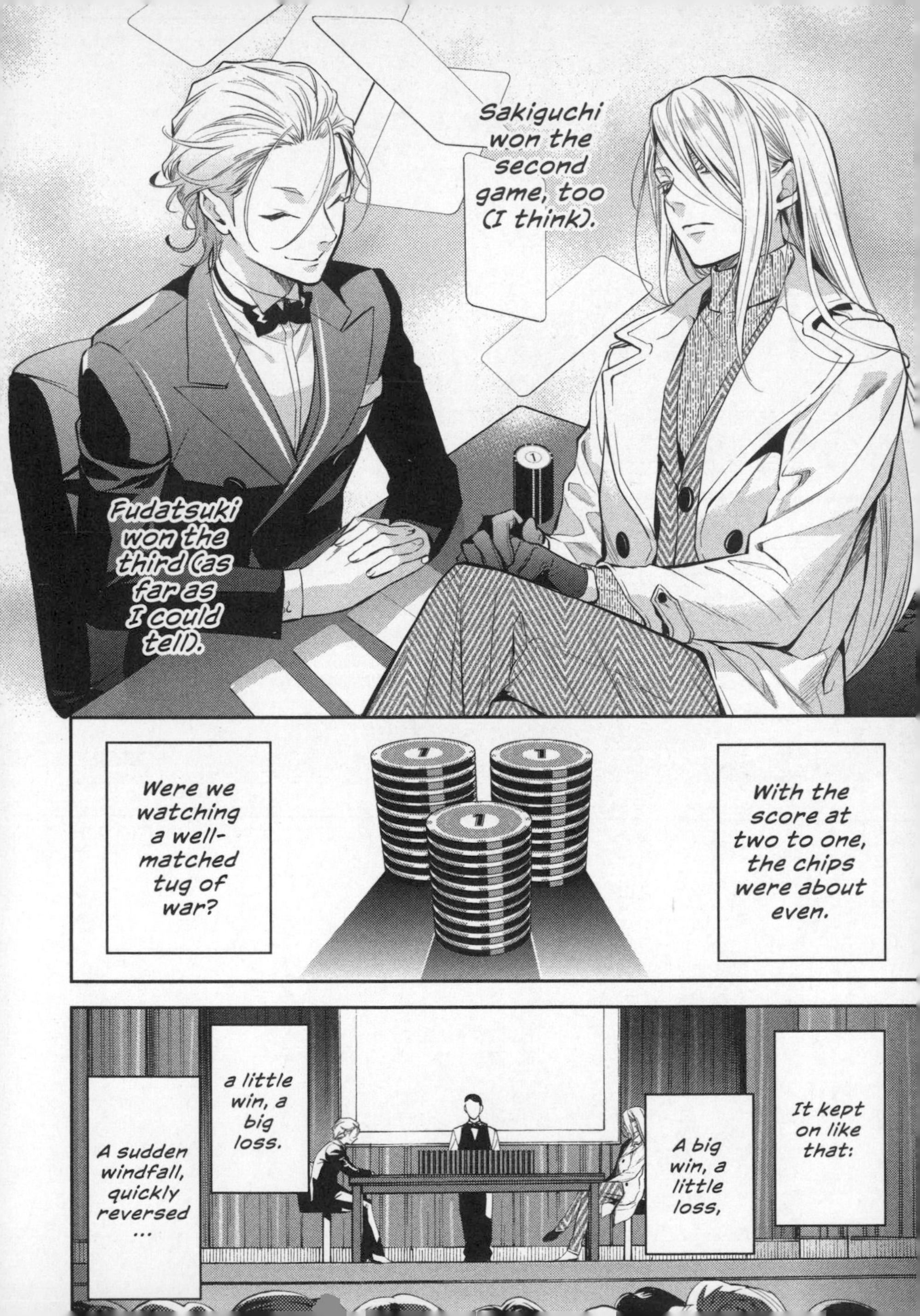
Sakiguchi won the second game, too (I think).
Fudatsuki won the third (as far as I could tell).
With the score at two to one, the chips were about even.
Were we watching a well-matched tug of war?
It kept on like that:
A big win, a little loss,
a little win, a big loss.
A sudden windfall, quickly reversed ...

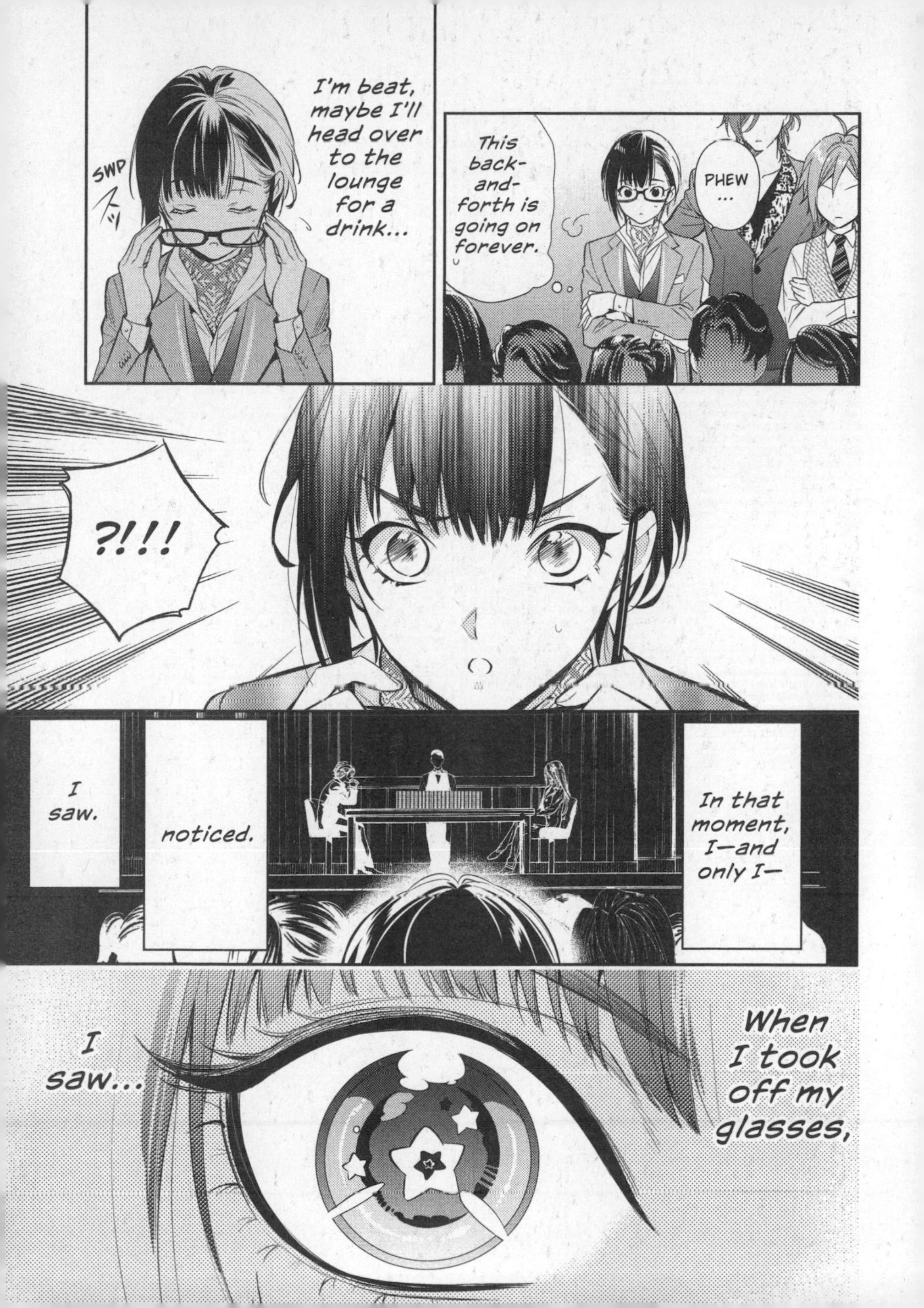
PHEW...
This back-and-forth is going on forever.
I'm beat, maybe I'll head over to the lounge for a drink...
SWP
?!!!
In that moment, I—and only I—
noticed.
I saw.
When I took off my glasses,
I saw...

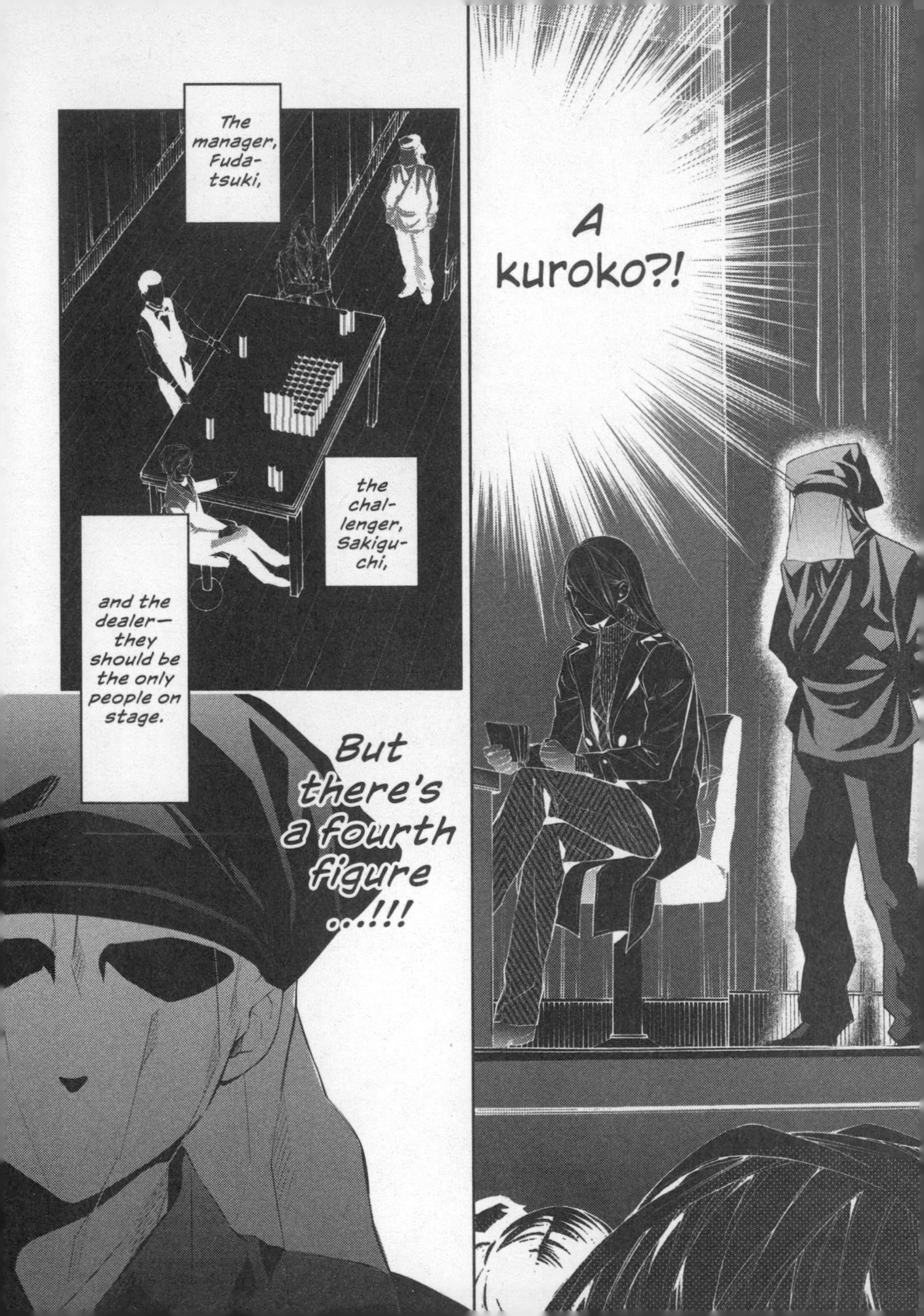

A kuroko?!
The manager, Fuda-tsuki,
the chal-lenger, Sakigu-chi,
and the dealer—they should be the only people on stage.
But there's a fourth figure ...!!!

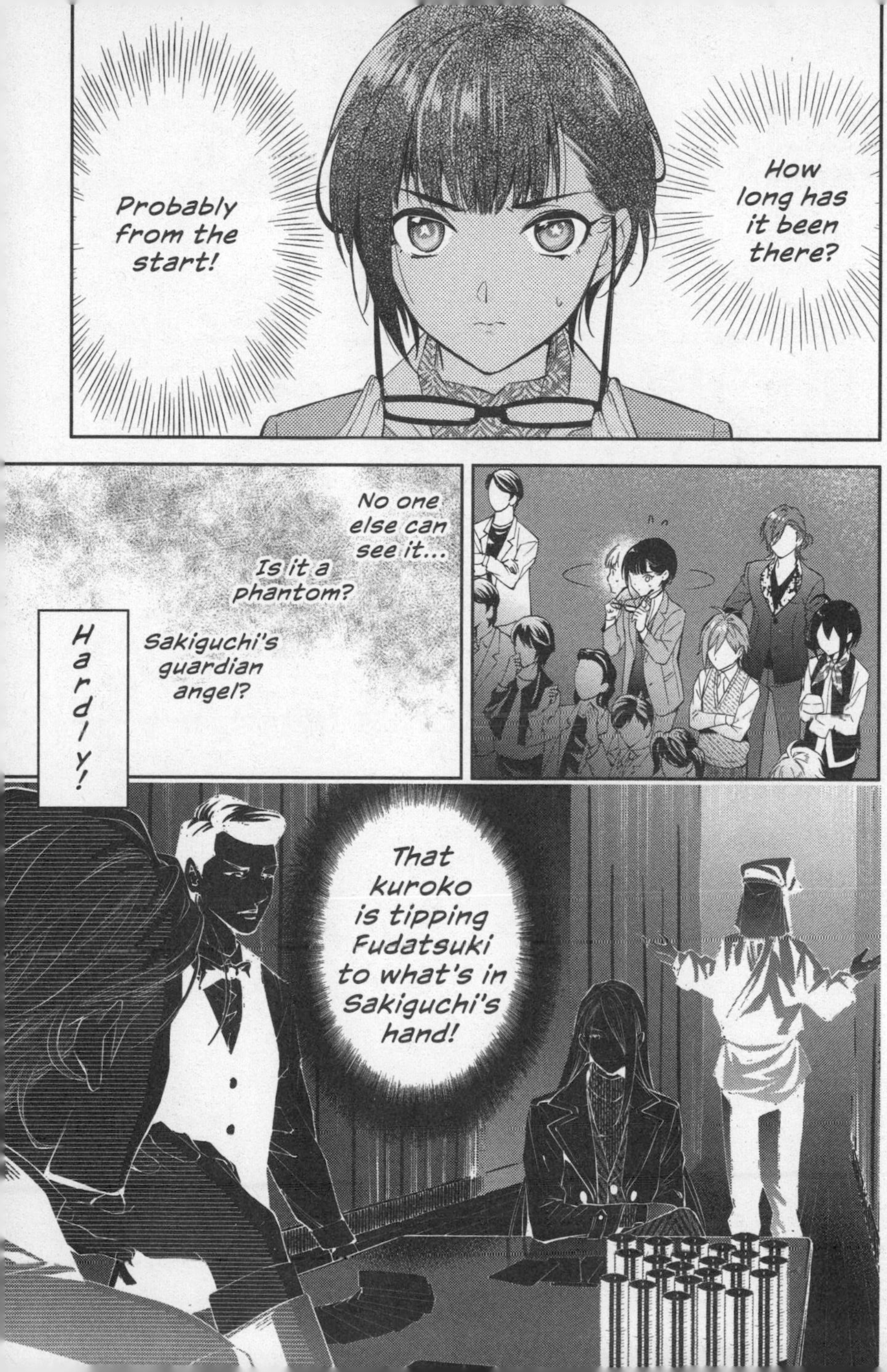
How long has it been there?
Probably from the start!
No one else can see it...
Is it a phantom?
Sakiguchi's guardian angel?
Hardly!
That kuroko is tipping Fudatsuki to what's in Sakiguchi's hand!

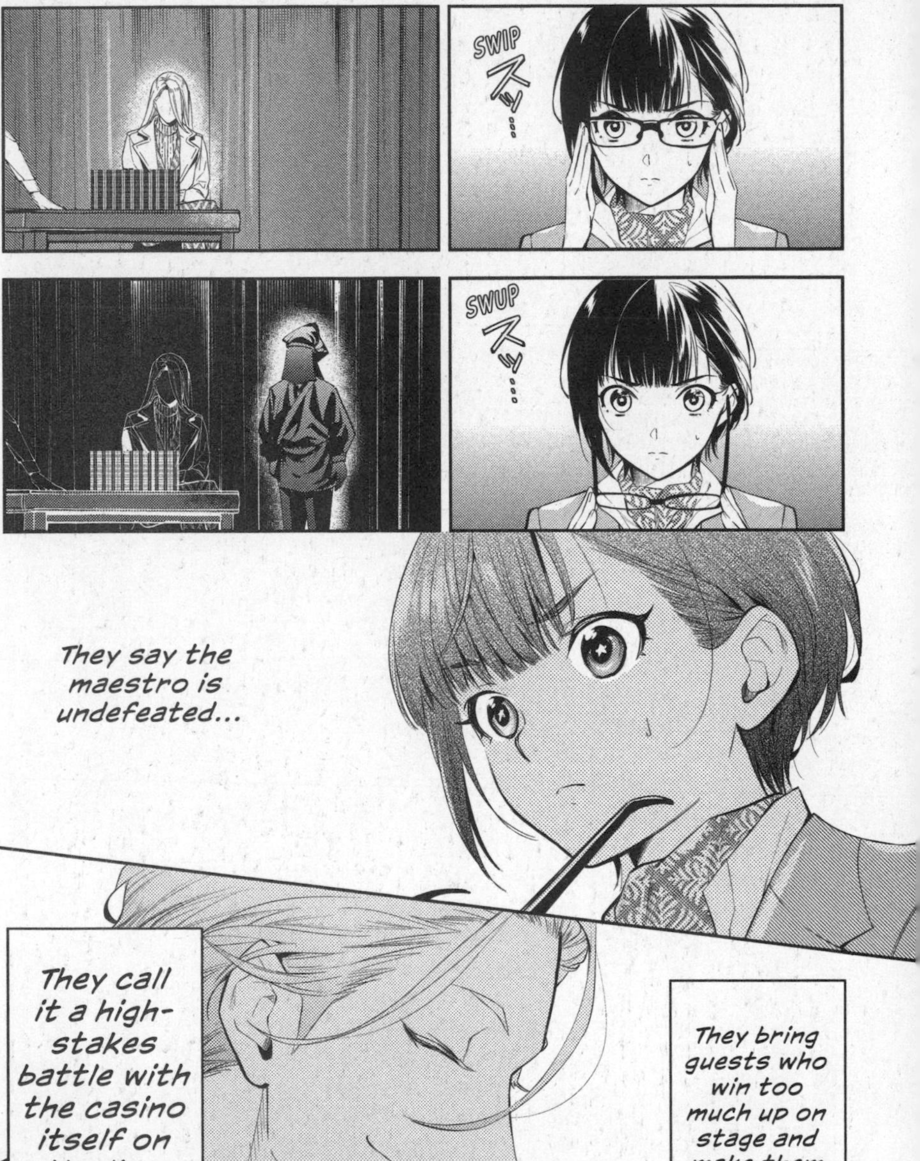
SWIP
スッ…
SWUP
スッ…
They say the maestro is undefeated...
They bring guests who win too much up on stage and make them bet every-thing.
They call it a high-stakes battle with the casino itself on the line, but...

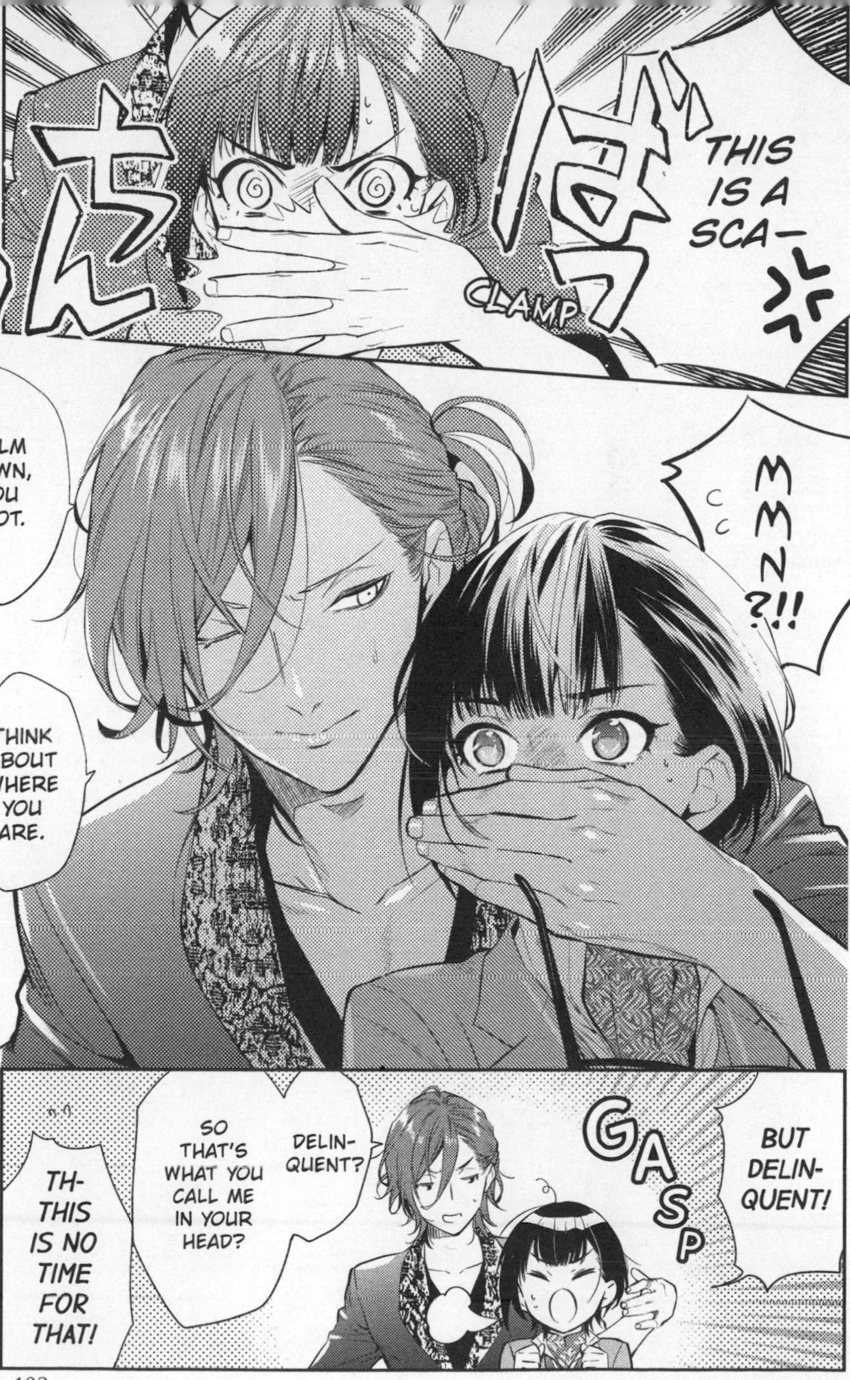
THIS IS A SCA—
CLAMP
MMN?!!
CALM DOWN, YOU IDIOT.
THINK ABOUT WHERE YOU ARE.
BUT DELIN-QUENT!
GASP
DELIN-QUENT?
SO THAT'S WHAT YOU CALL ME IN YOUR HEAD?
TH-THIS IS NO TIME FOR THAT!

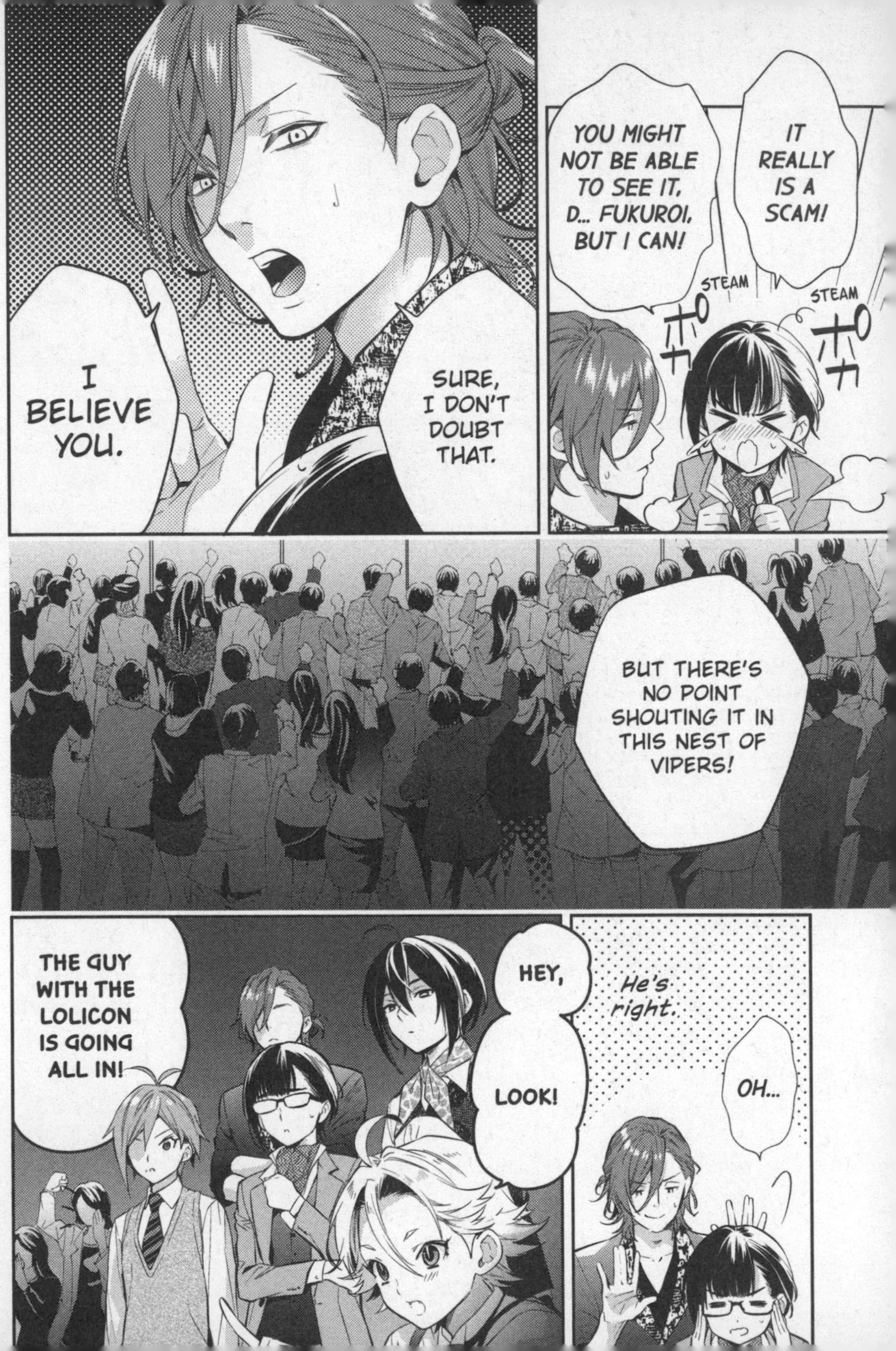
IT REALLY IS A SCAM!
YOU MIGHT NOT BE ABLE TO SEE IT, D... FUKUROI, BUT I CAN!
STEAM
STEAM
SURE, I DON'T DOUBT THAT.
I BELIEVE YOU.
BUT THERE'S NO POINT SHOUTING IT IN THIS NEST OF VIPERS!
He's right.
OH...
HEY,
LOOK!
THE GUY WITH THE LOLICON IS GOING ALL IN!

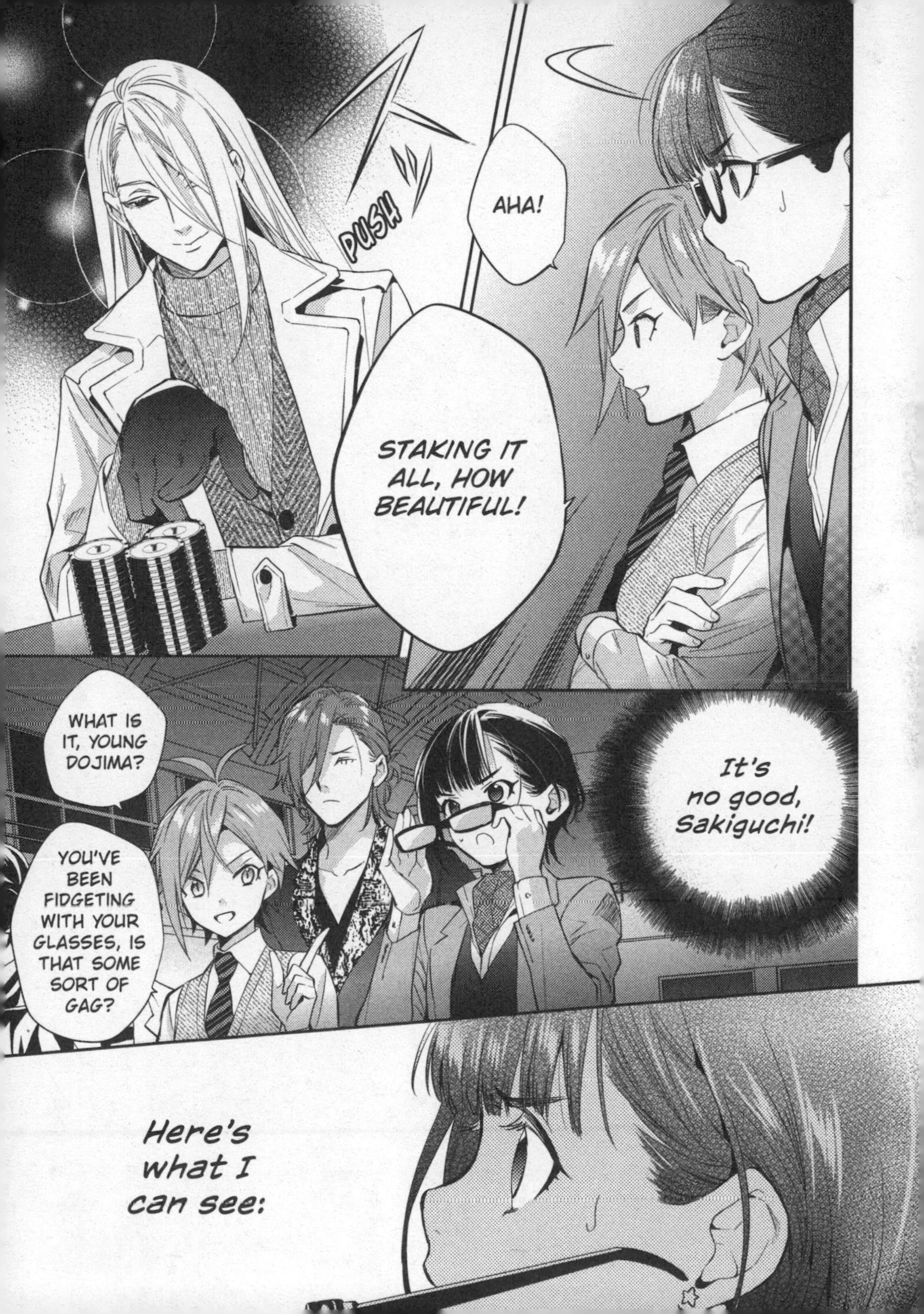
AHA!
STAKING IT ALL, HOW BEAUTIFUL!
PUSH
It's no good, Sakiguchi!
WHAT IS IT, YOUNG DOJIMA?
YOU'VE BEEN FIDGETING WITH YOUR GLASSES, IS THAT SOME SORT OF GAG?
Here's what I can see:

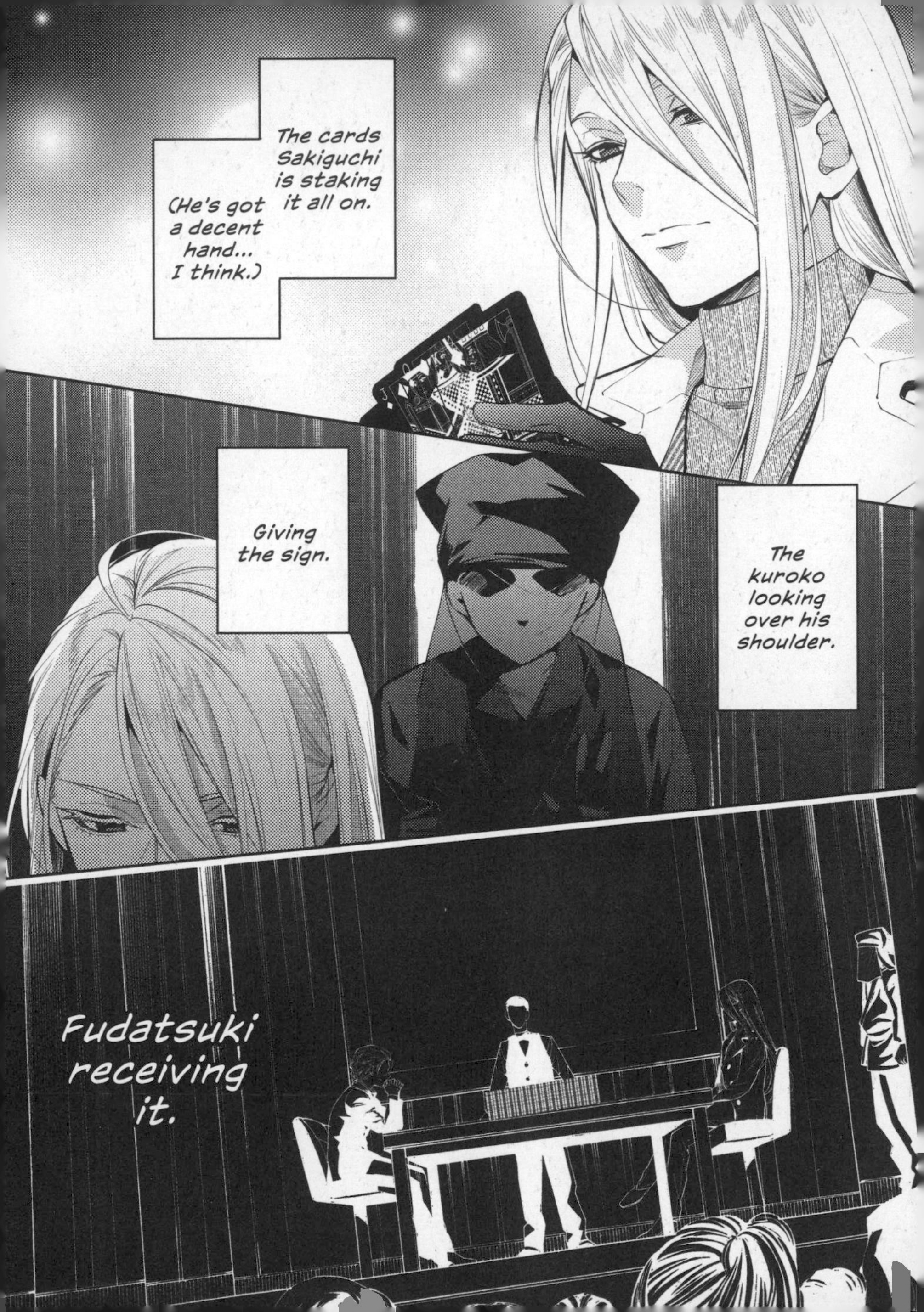
The cards Sakiguchi is staking it all on.
(He's got a decent hand... I think.)
The kuroko looking over his shoulder.
Giving the sign.
Fudatsuki receiving it.

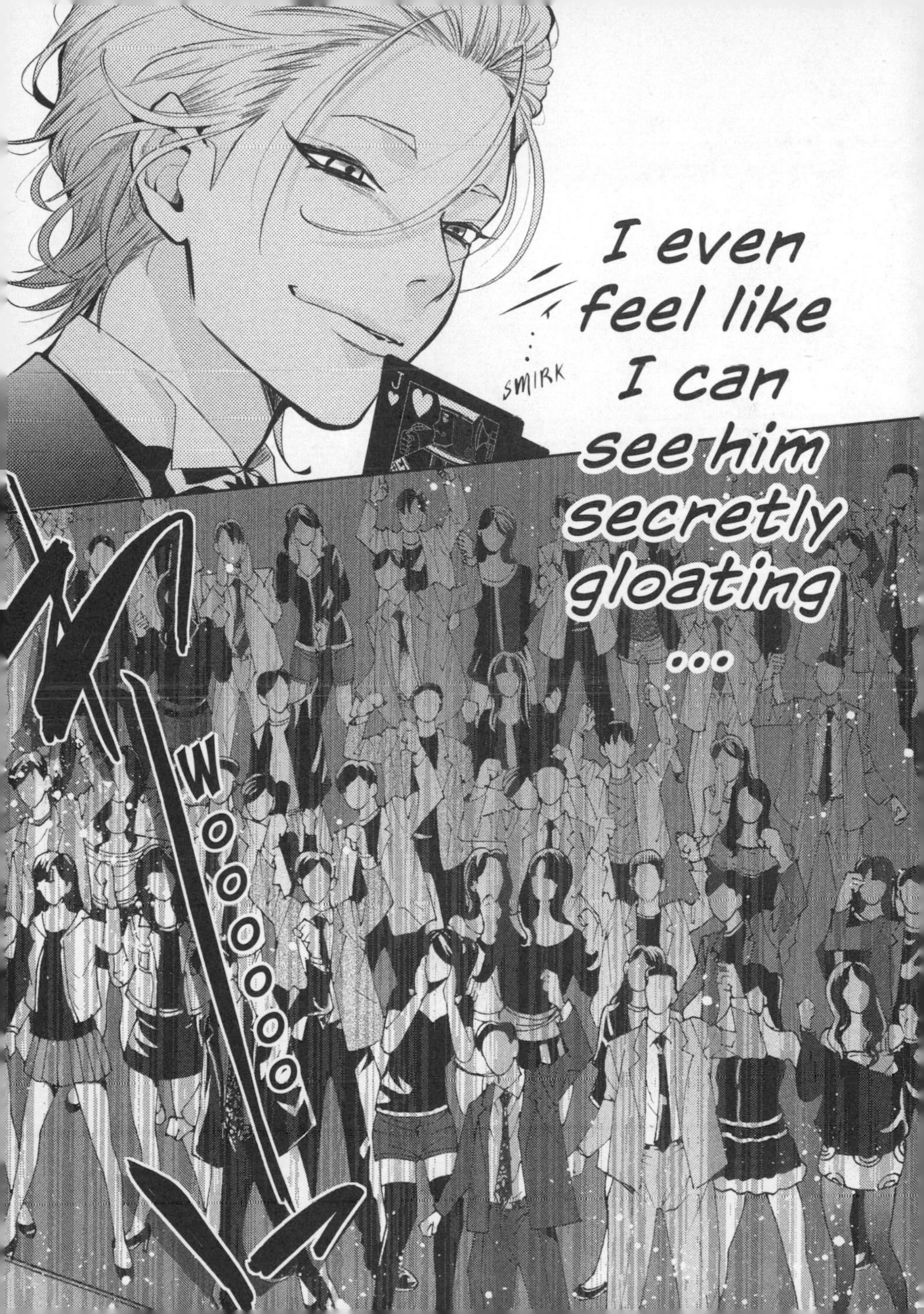
I even feel like I can see him secretly gloating...
SMIRK
WOOOOOOO

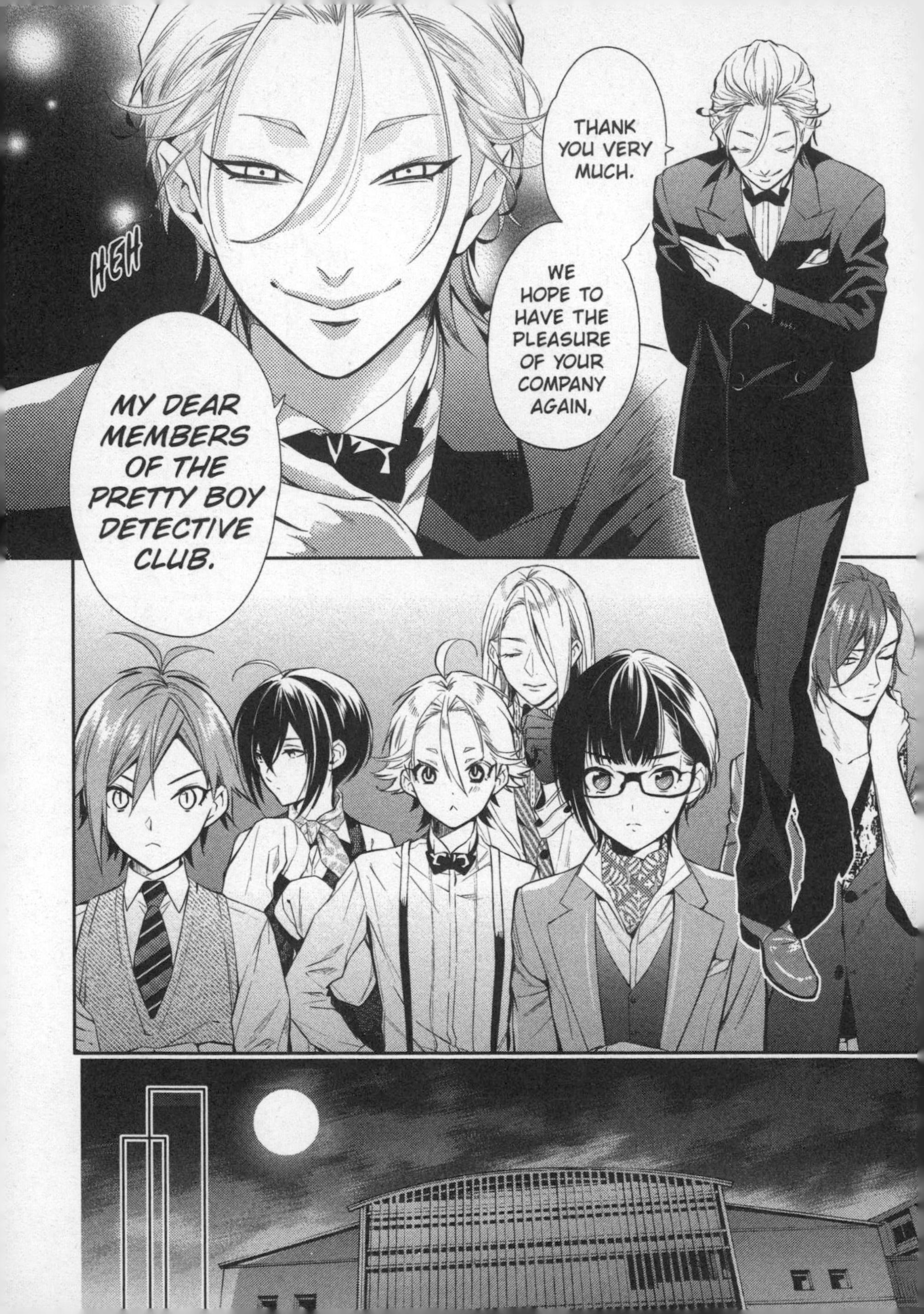
THANK YOU VERY MUCH.
WE HOPE TO HAVE THE PLEASURE OF YOUR COMPANY AGAIN,
HEH
MY DEAR MEMBERS OF THE PRETTY BOY DETECTIVE CLUB.

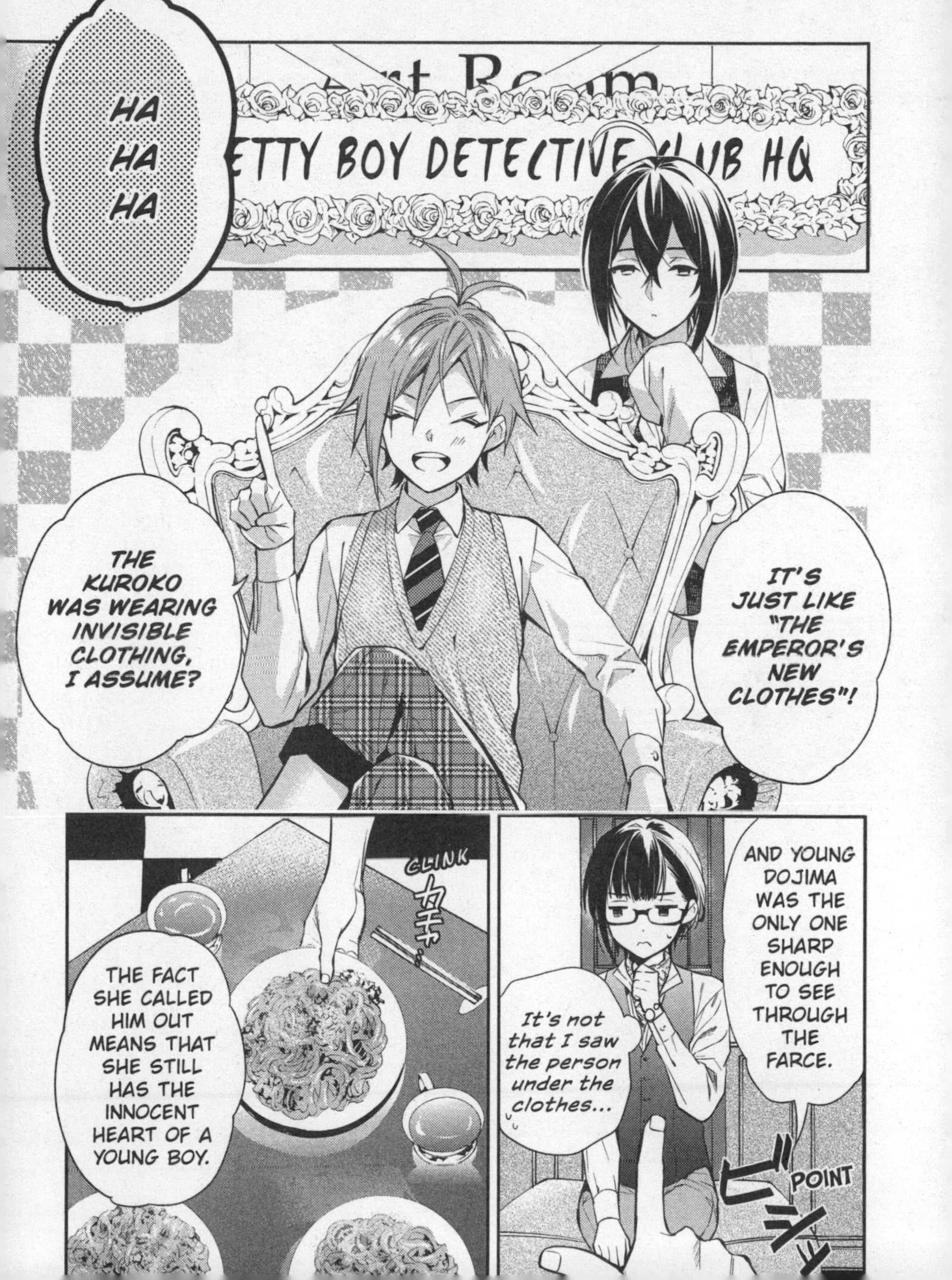
ETTY BOY DETECTIVE
UB HQ
HA HA HA
IT'S JUST LIKE "THE EMPEROR'S NEW CLOTHES"!
THE KUROKO WAS WEARING INVISIBLE CLOTHING, I ASSUME?
AND YOUNG DOJIMA WAS THE ONLY ONE SHARP ENOUGH TO SEE THROUGH THE FARCE.
It's not that I saw the person under the clothes...
POINT
CLINK
THE FACT SHE CALLED HIM OUT MEANS THAT SHE STILL HAS THE INNOCENT HEART OF A YOUNG BOY.

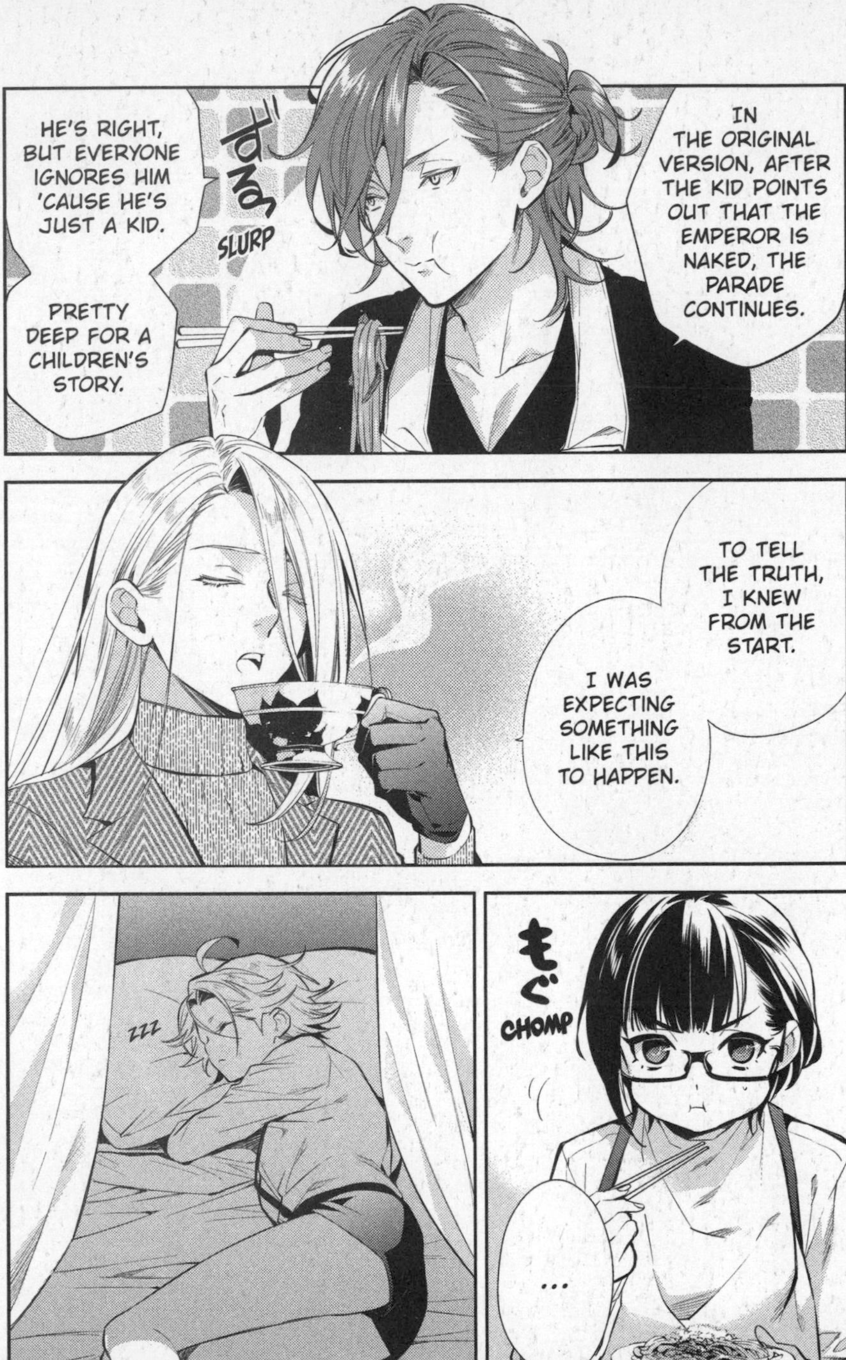
IN THE ORIGINAL VERSION, AFTER THE KID POINTS OUT THAT THE EMPEROR IS NAKED, THE PARADE CONTINUES.
ずる
SLURP
HE'S RIGHT, BUT EVERYONE IGNORES HIM 'CAUSE HE'S JUST A KID.
PRETTY DEEP FOR A CHILDREN'S STORY.
TO TELL THE TRUTH, I KNEW FROM THE START.
I WAS EXPECTING SOMETHING LIKE THIS TO HAPPEN.
もぐ
CHOMP
...
ZZZ

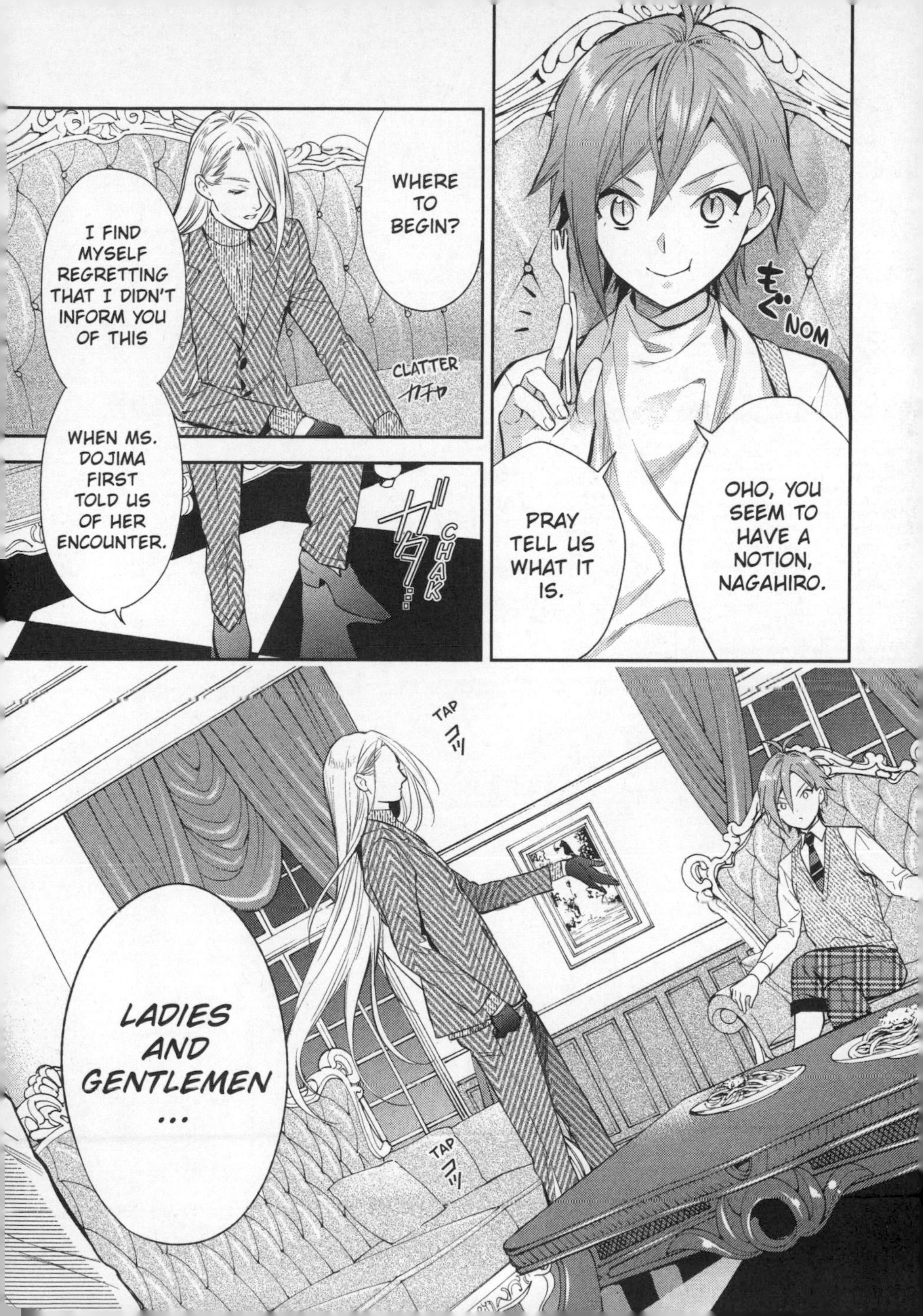
もぐ NOM
OHO, YOU SEEM TO HAVE A NOTION, NAGAHIRO.
PRAY TELL US WHAT IT IS.
WHERE TO BEGIN?
I FIND MYSELF REGRETTING THAT I DIDN'T INFORM YOU OF THIS
CLATTER カチャ
WHEN MS. DOJIMA FIRST TOLD US OF HER ENCOUNTER.
ガタ… CHAK
TAP コッ
LADIES AND GENTLEMEN ...
TAP コッ

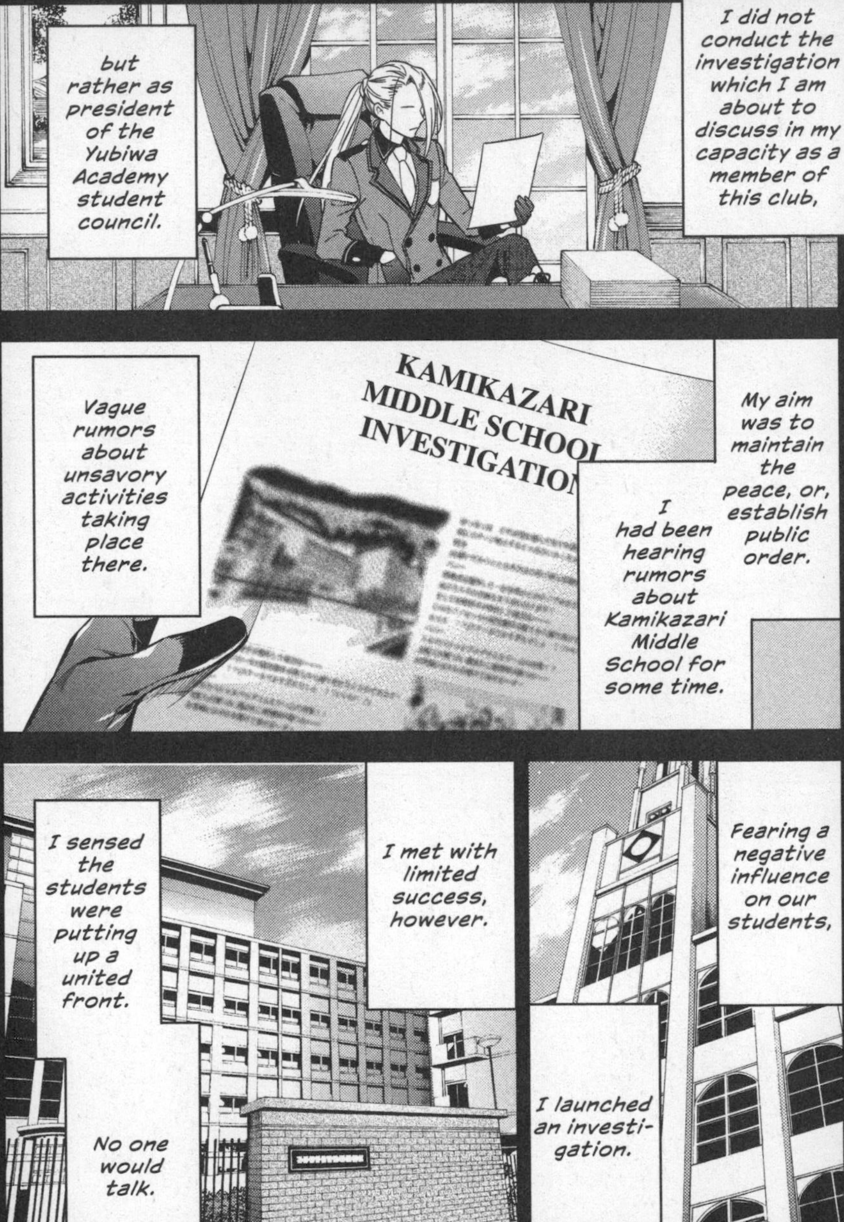
I did not conduct the investigation which I am about to discuss in my capacity as a member of this club,
but rather as president of the Yubiwa Academy student council.
My aim was to maintain the peace, or, establish public order.
I had been hearing rumors about Kamikazari Middle School for some time.
KAMIKAZARI MIDDLE SCHOOL INVESTIGATIO
Vague rumors about unsavory activities taking place there.
Fearing a negative influence on our students,
I launched an investi-gation.
I met with limited success, however.
I sensed the students were putting up a united front.
No one would talk.

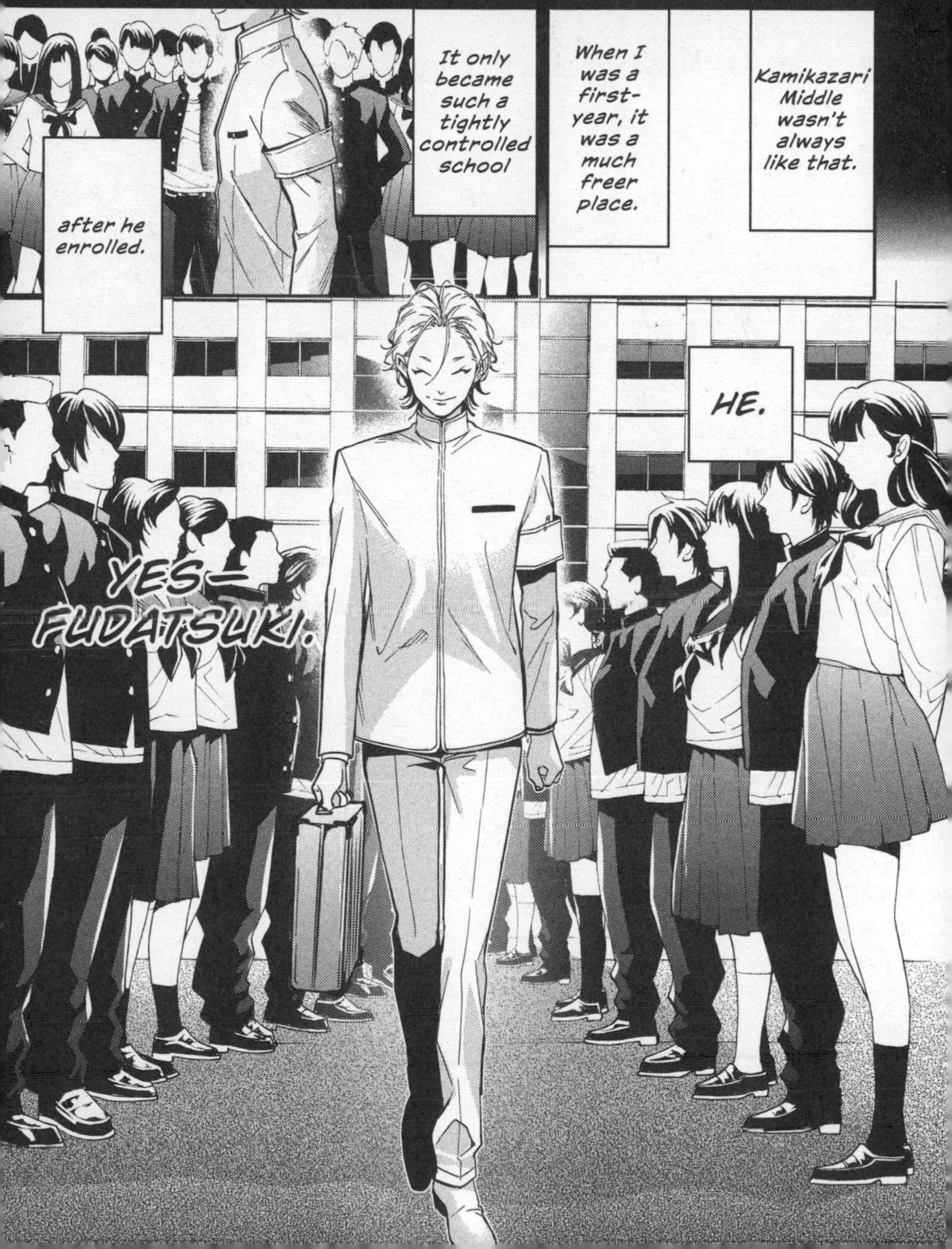
Kamikazari Middle wasn't always like that.
When I was a first-year, it was a much freer place.
It only became such a tightly controlled school
after he enrolled.
HE.
YES— FUDATSUKI.

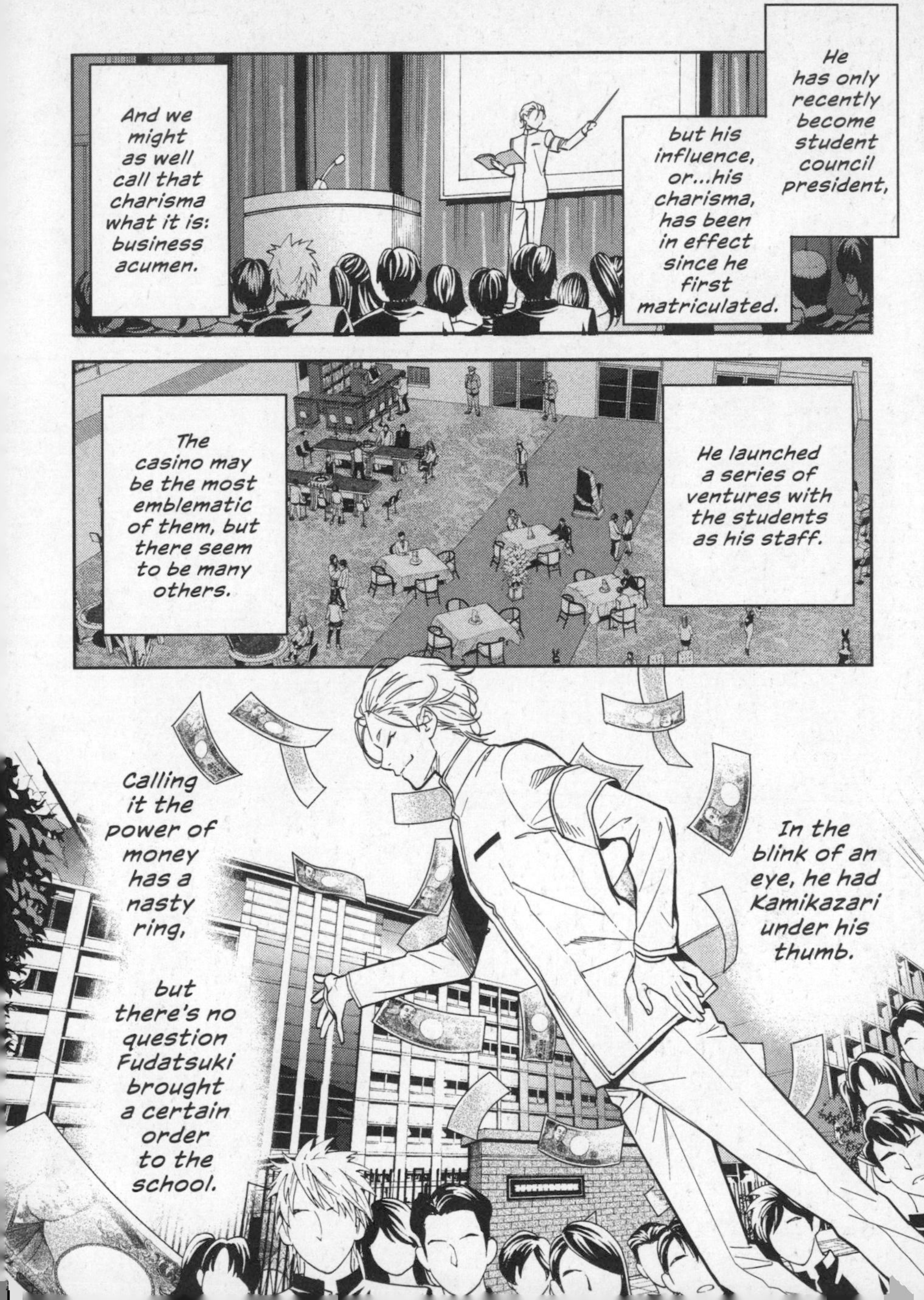
He has only recently become student council president,
but his influence, or...his charisma, has been in effect since he first matriculated.
And we might as well call that charisma what it is: business acumen.
He launched a series of ventures with the students as his staff.
The casino may be the most emblematic of them, but there seem to be many others.
In the blink of an eye, he had Kamikazari under his thumb.
Calling it the power of money has a nasty ring,
but there's no question Fudatsuki brought a certain order to the school.

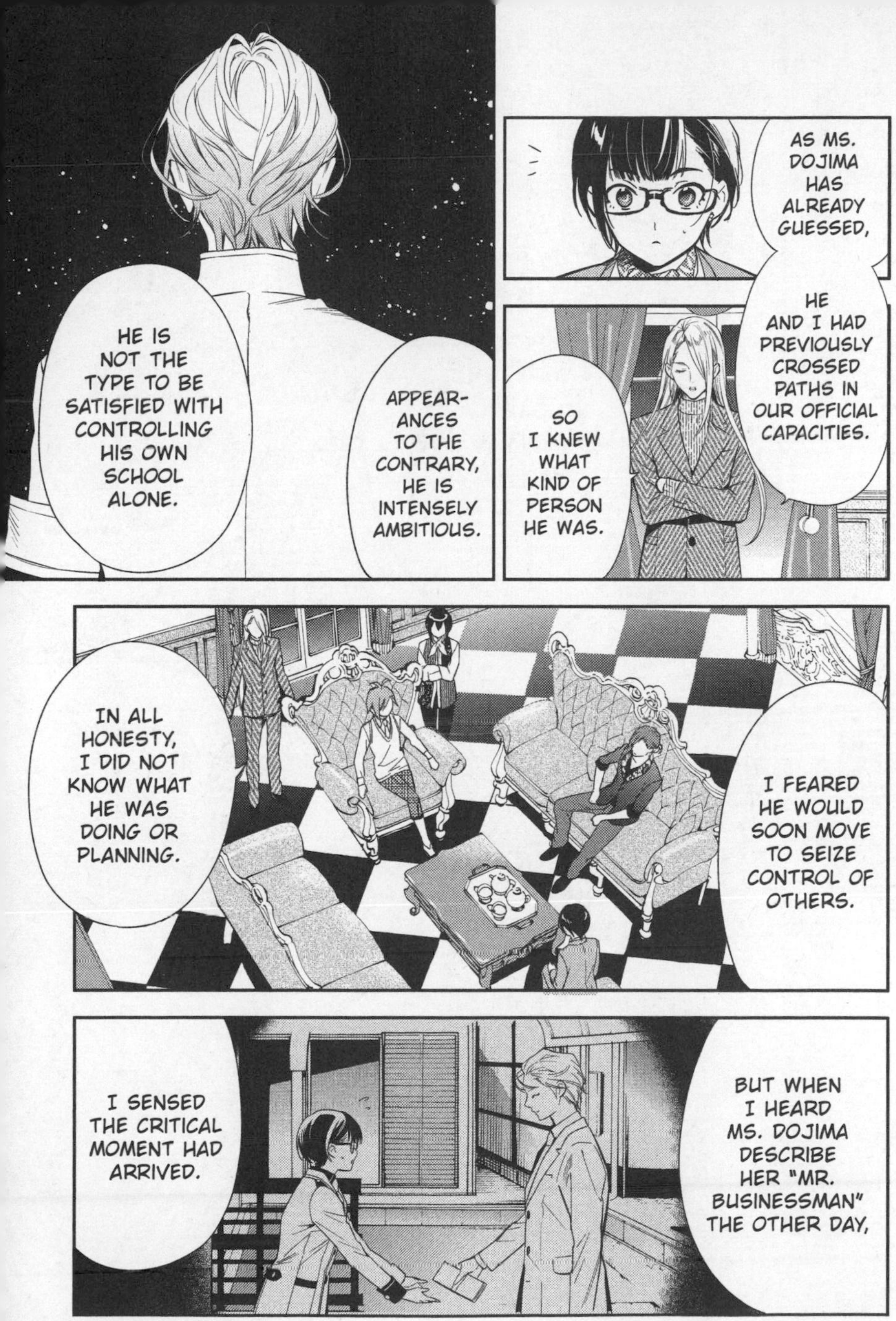
AS MS. DOJIMA HAS ALREADY GUESSED,
HE AND I HAD PREVIOUSLY CROSSED PATHS IN OUR OFFICIAL CAPACITIES.
SO I KNEW WHAT KIND OF PERSON HE WAS.
APPEAR-ANCES TO THE CONTRARY, HE IS INTENSELY AMBITIOUS.
HE IS NOT THE TYPE TO BE SATISFIED WITH CONTROLLING HIS OWN SCHOOL ALONE.
I FEARED HE WOULD SOON MOVE TO SEIZE CONTROL OF OTHERS.
IN ALL HONESTY, I DID NOT KNOW WHAT HE WAS DOING OR PLANNING.
BUT WHEN I HEARD MS. DOJIMA DESCRIBE HER "MR. BUSINESSMAN" THE OTHER DAY,
I SENSED THE CRITICAL MOMENT HAD ARRIVED.

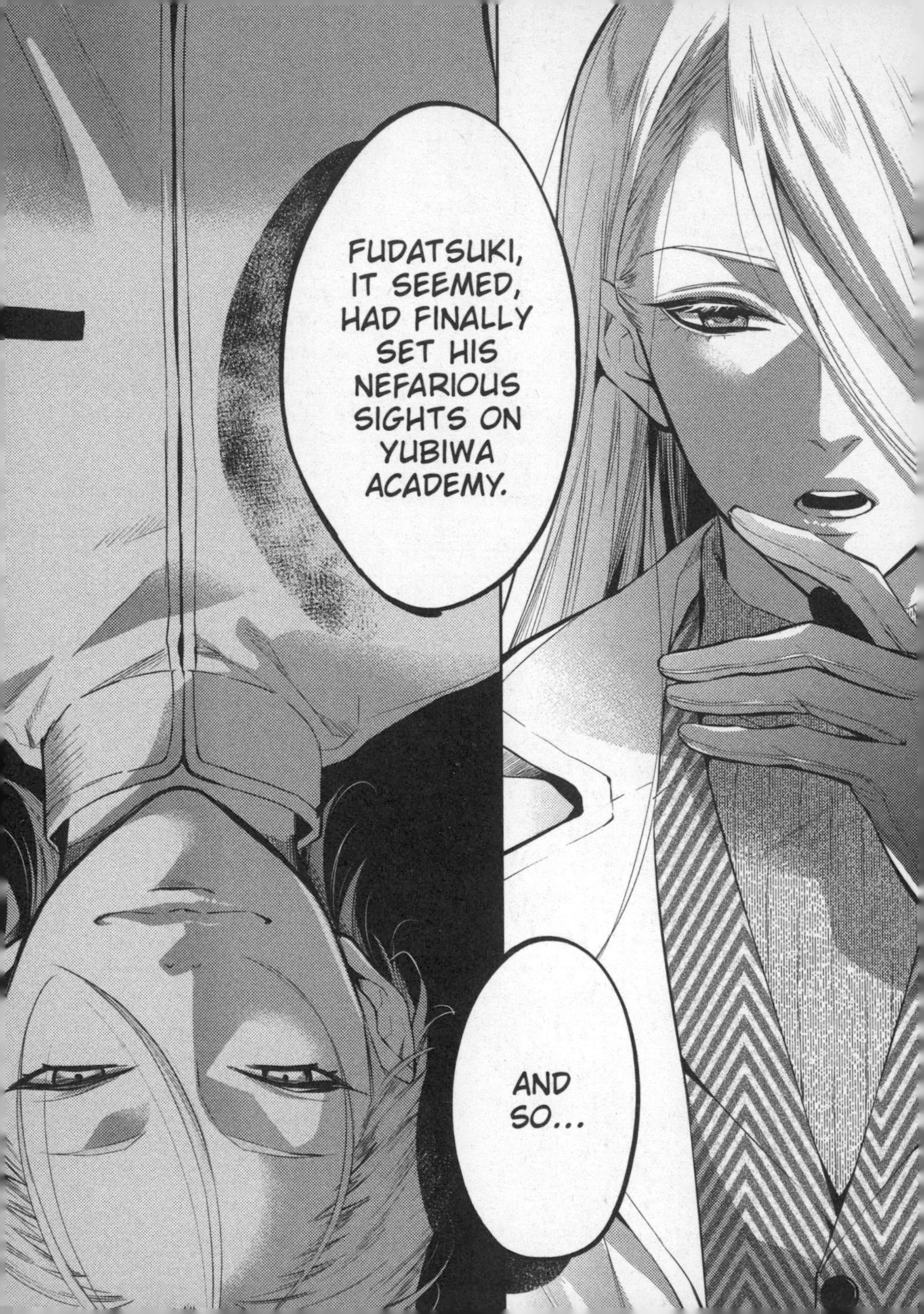
FUDATSUKI, IT SEEMED, HAD FINALLY SET HIS NEFARIOUS SIGHTS ON YUBIWA ACADEMY.
AND SO...

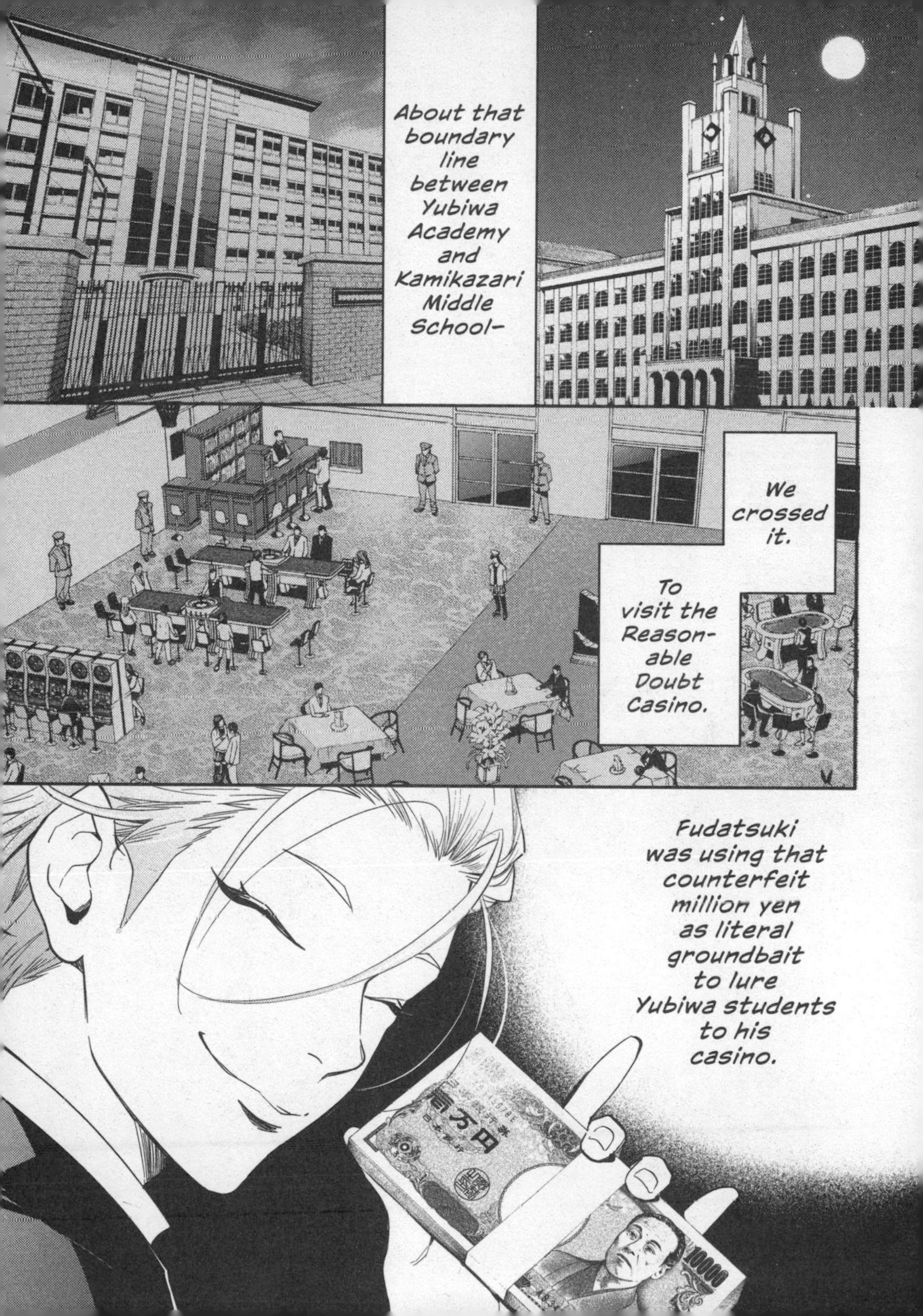
About that boundary line between Yubiwa Academy and Kamikazari Middle School-
We crossed it.
To visit the Reasonable Doubt Casino.
Fudatsuki was using that counterfeit million yen as literal groundbait to lure Yubiwa students to his casino.

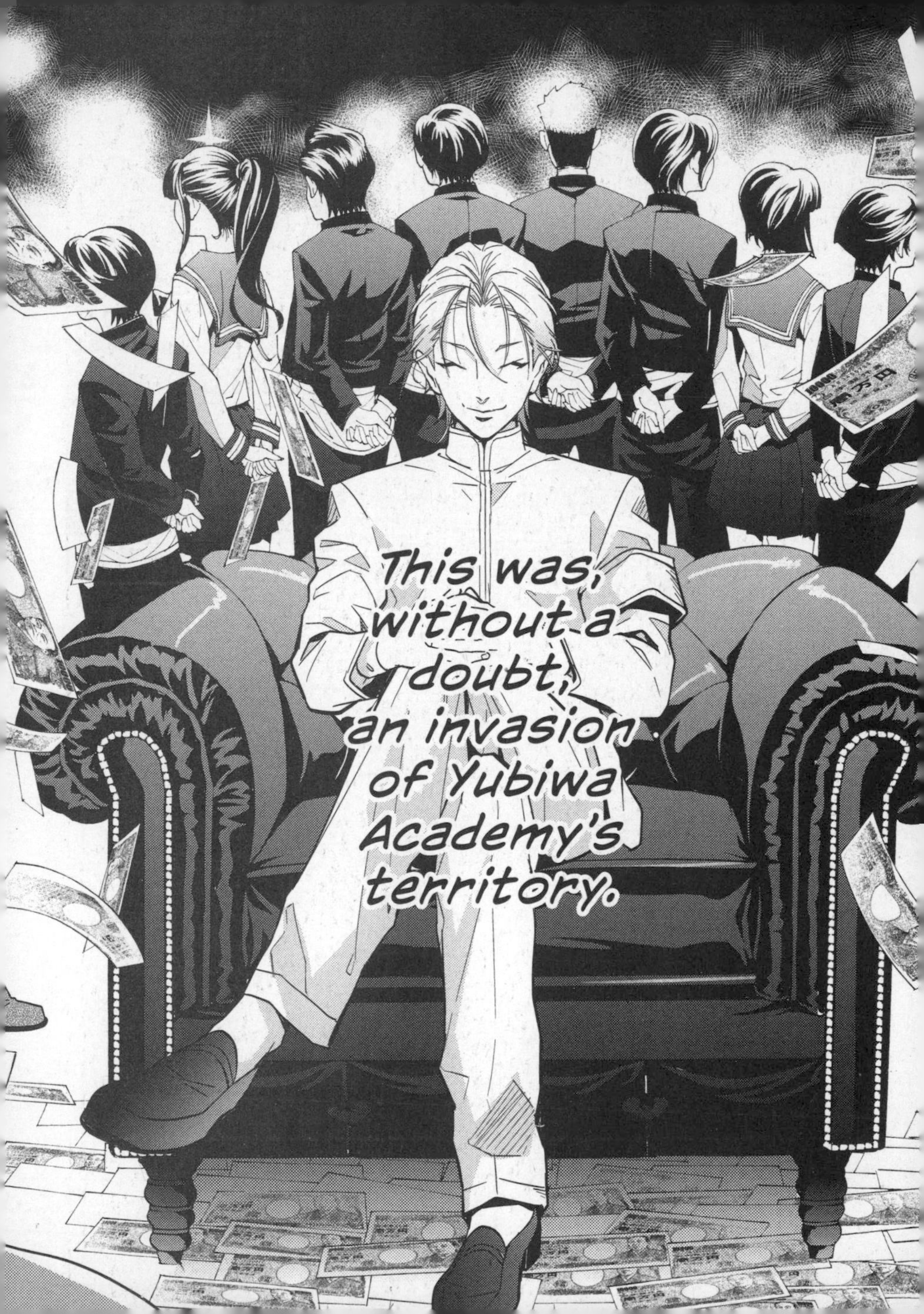
This was, without a doubt, an invasion of Yubiwa Academy's territory.

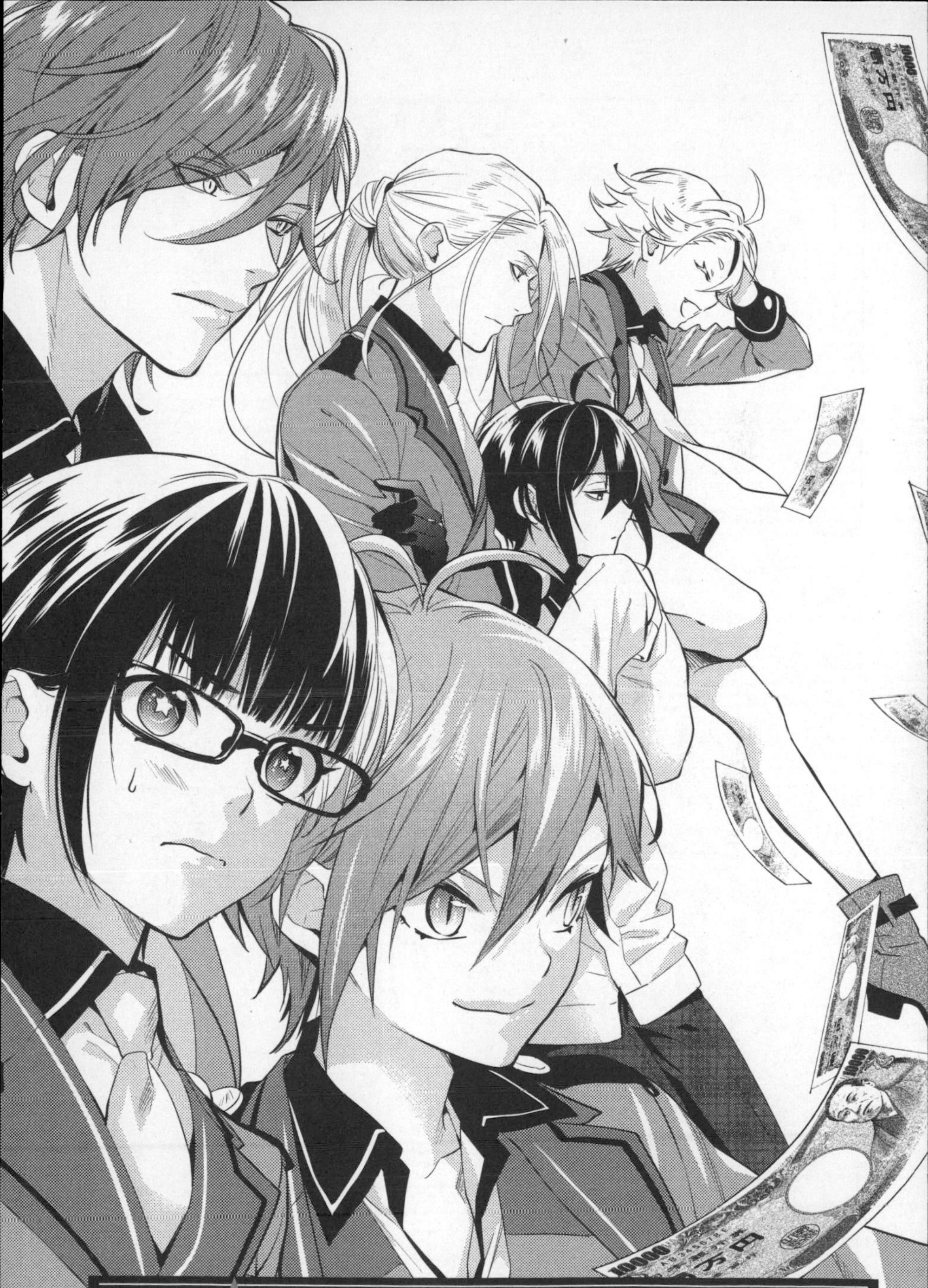

FILE ★ The Swindler, the Vanishing Man, and the Pretty Boys 4

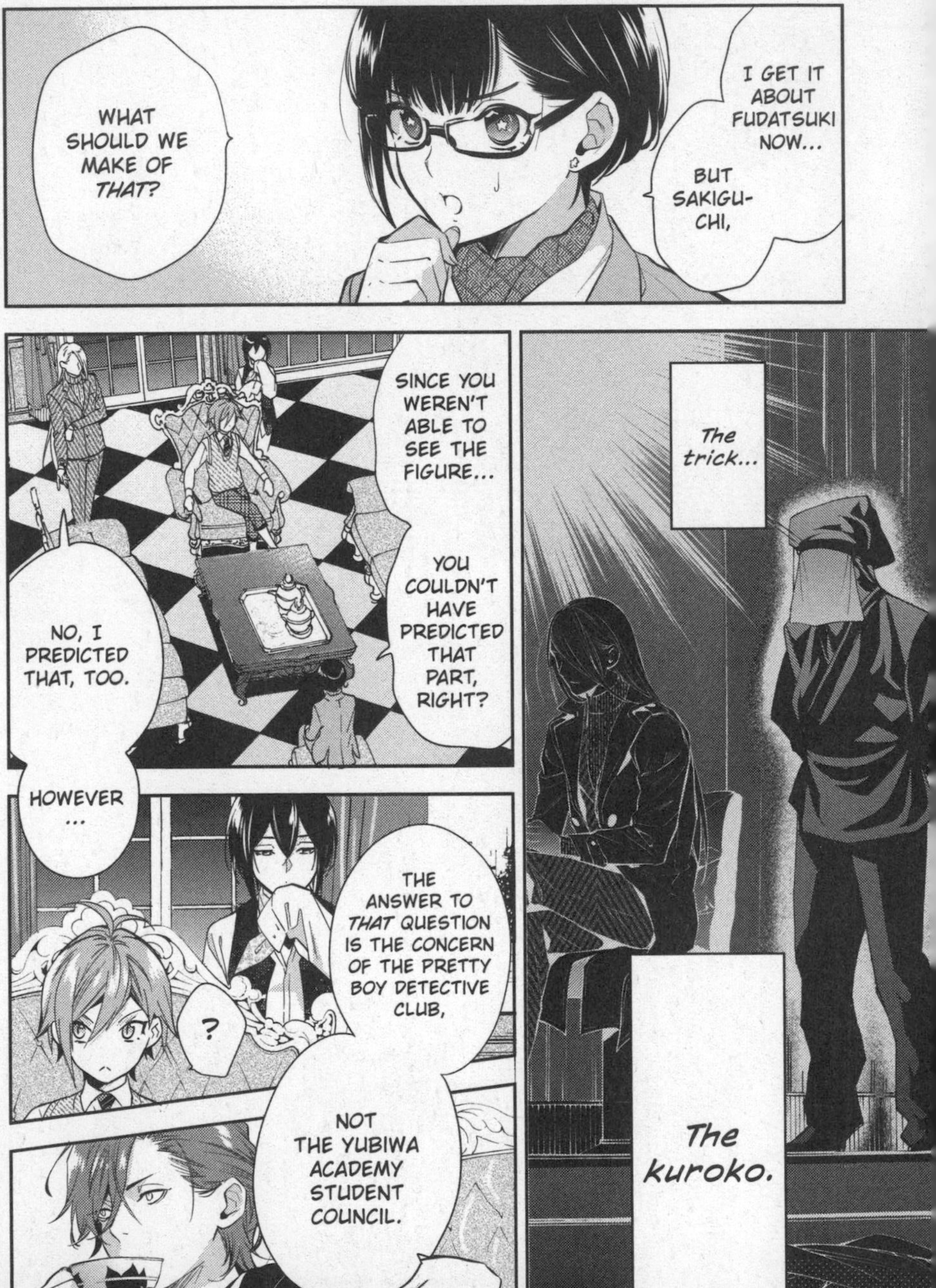
I GET IT ABOUT FUDATSUKI NOW...
BUT SAKIGU-CHI,
WHAT SHOULD WE MAKE OF *THAT?*
The trick...
The kuroko.
SINCE YOU WEREN'T ABLE TO SEE THE FIGURE...
YOU COULDN'T HAVE PREDICTED THAT PART, RIGHT?
NO, I PREDICTED THAT, TOO.
HOWEVER...
THE ANSWER TO *THAT* QUESTION IS THE CONCERN OF THE PRETTY BOY DETECTIVE CLUB,
?
NOT THE YUBIWA ACADEMY STUDENT COUNCIL.

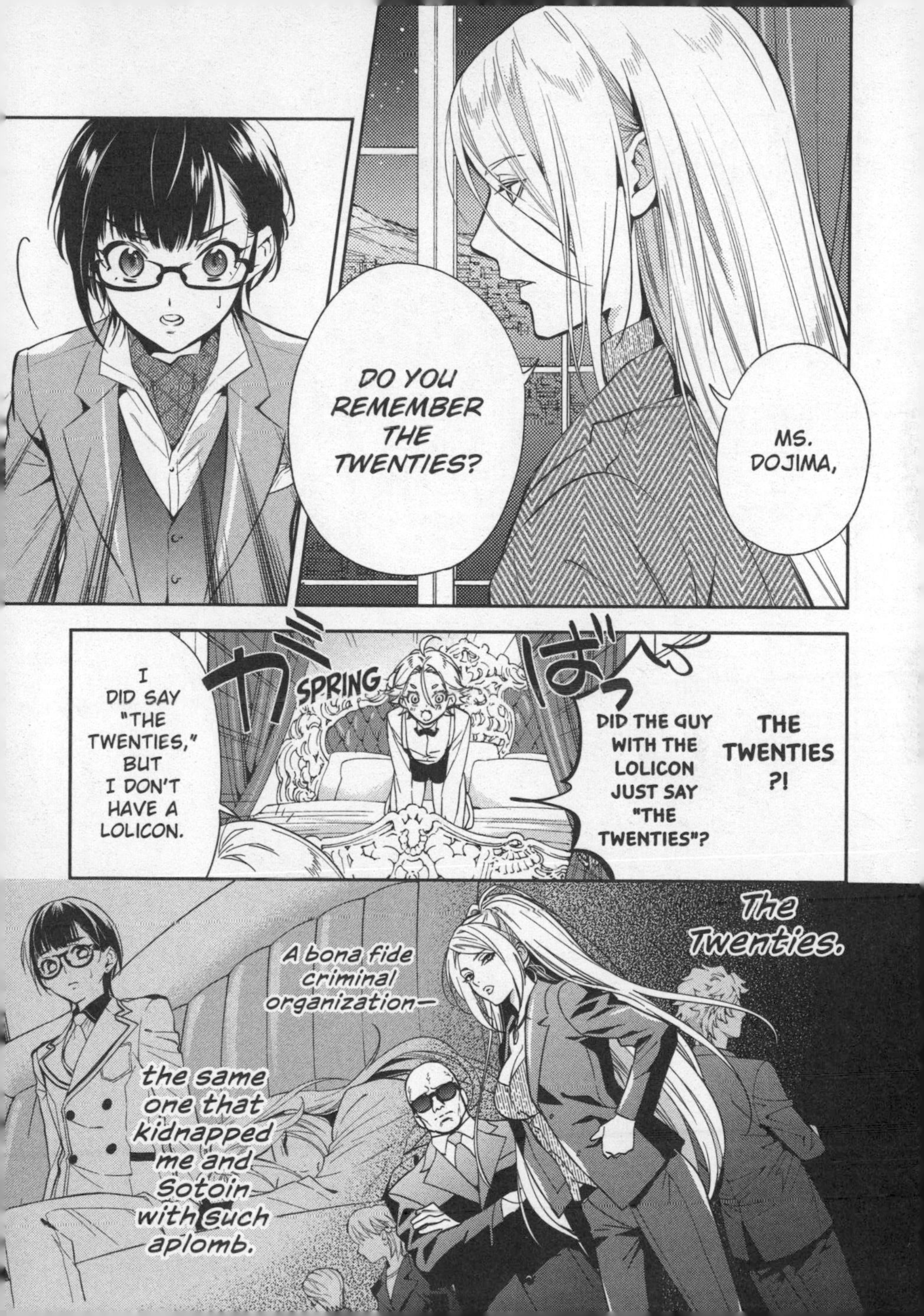
MS. DOJIMA,
DO YOU REMEMBER THE TWENTIES?
THE TWENTIES ?!
DID THE GUY WITH THE LOLICON JUST SAY "THE TWENTIES"?
SPRING
I DID SAY "THE TWENTIES," BUT I DON'T HAVE A LOLICON.
The Twenties.
A bona fide criminal organization—
the same one that kidnapped me and Sotoin with such aplomb.

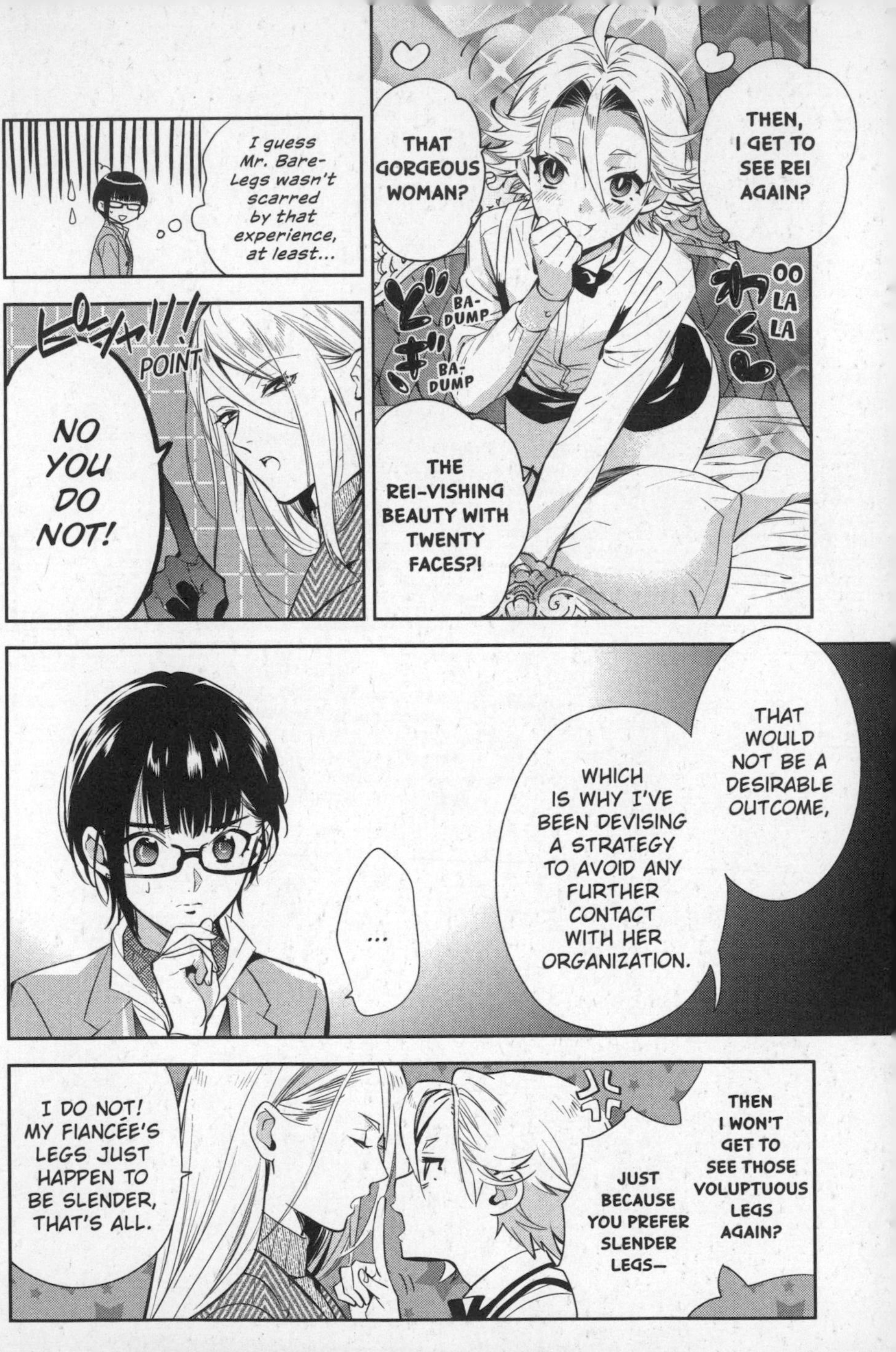
THEN, I GET TO SEE REI AGAIN?
THAT GORGEOUS WOMAN?
OO LA LA
BA-DUMP
BA-DUMP
THE REI-VISHING BEAUTY WITH TWENTY FACES?!
I guess Mr. Bare-Legs wasn't scarred by that experience, at least...
POINT
NO YOU DO NOT!
THAT WOULD NOT BE A DESIRABLE OUTCOME,
WHICH IS WHY I'VE BEEN DEVISING A STRATEGY TO AVOID ANY FURTHER CONTACT WITH HER ORGANIZATION.
...
THEN I WON'T GET TO SEE THOSE VOLUPTUOUS LEGS AGAIN?
JUST BECAUSE YOU PREFER SLENDER LEGS—
I DO NOT! MY FIANCÉE'S LEGS JUST HAPPEN TO BE SLENDER, THAT'S ALL.

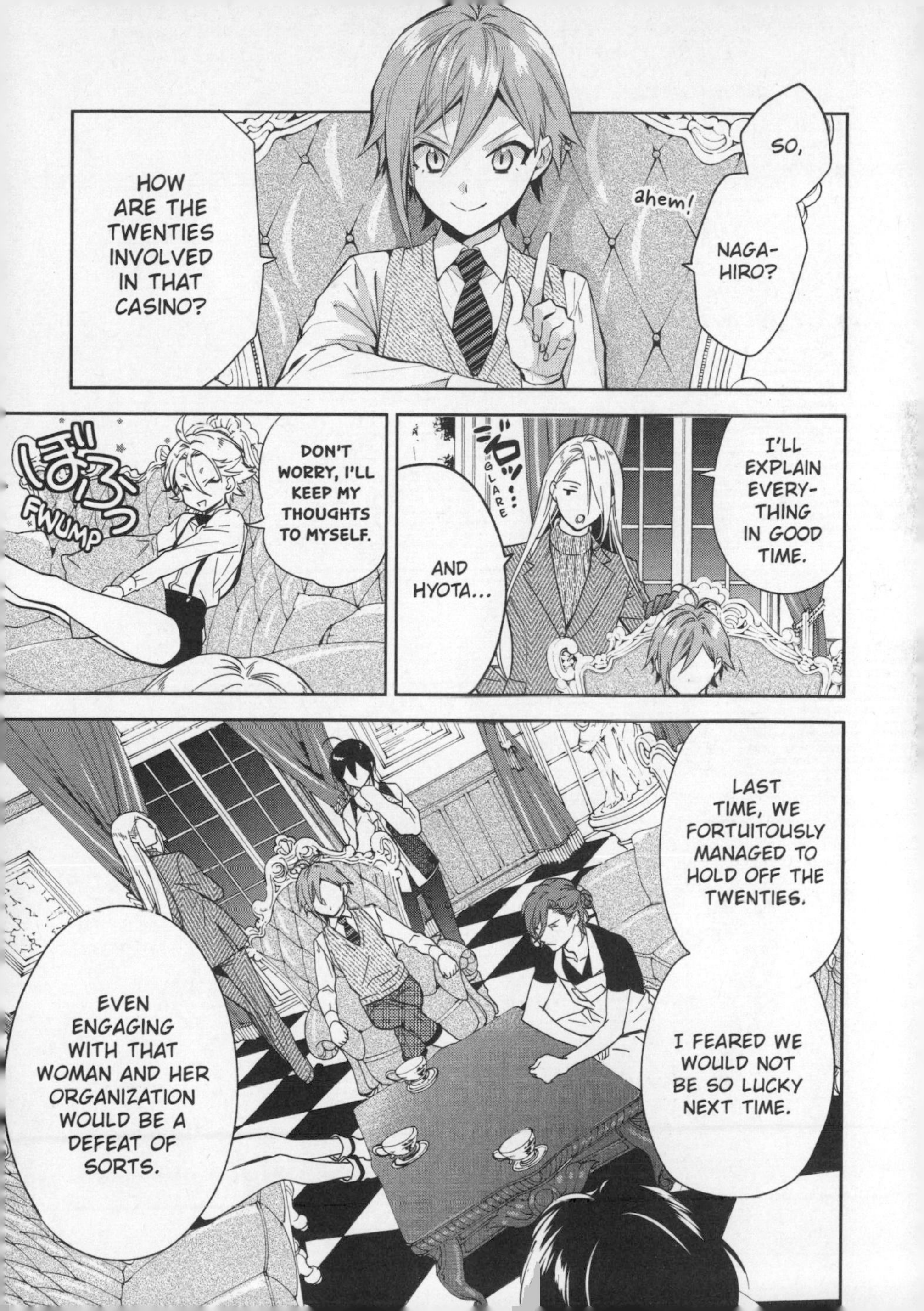
SO,
ahem!
NAGA-HIRO?
HOW ARE THE TWENTIES INVOLVED IN THAT CASINO?
I'LL EXPLAIN EVERY-THING IN GOOD TIME.
ジロッ
GLARE
AND HYOTA...
DON'T WORRY, I'LL KEEP MY THOUGHTS TO MYSELF.
ぼふっ
FWUMP
LAST TIME, WE FORTUITOUSLY MANAGED TO HOLD OFF THE TWENTIES.
I FEARED WE WOULD NOT BE SO LUCKY NEXT TIME.
EVEN ENGAGING WITH THAT WOMAN AND HER ORGANIZATION WOULD BE A DEFEAT OF SORTS.

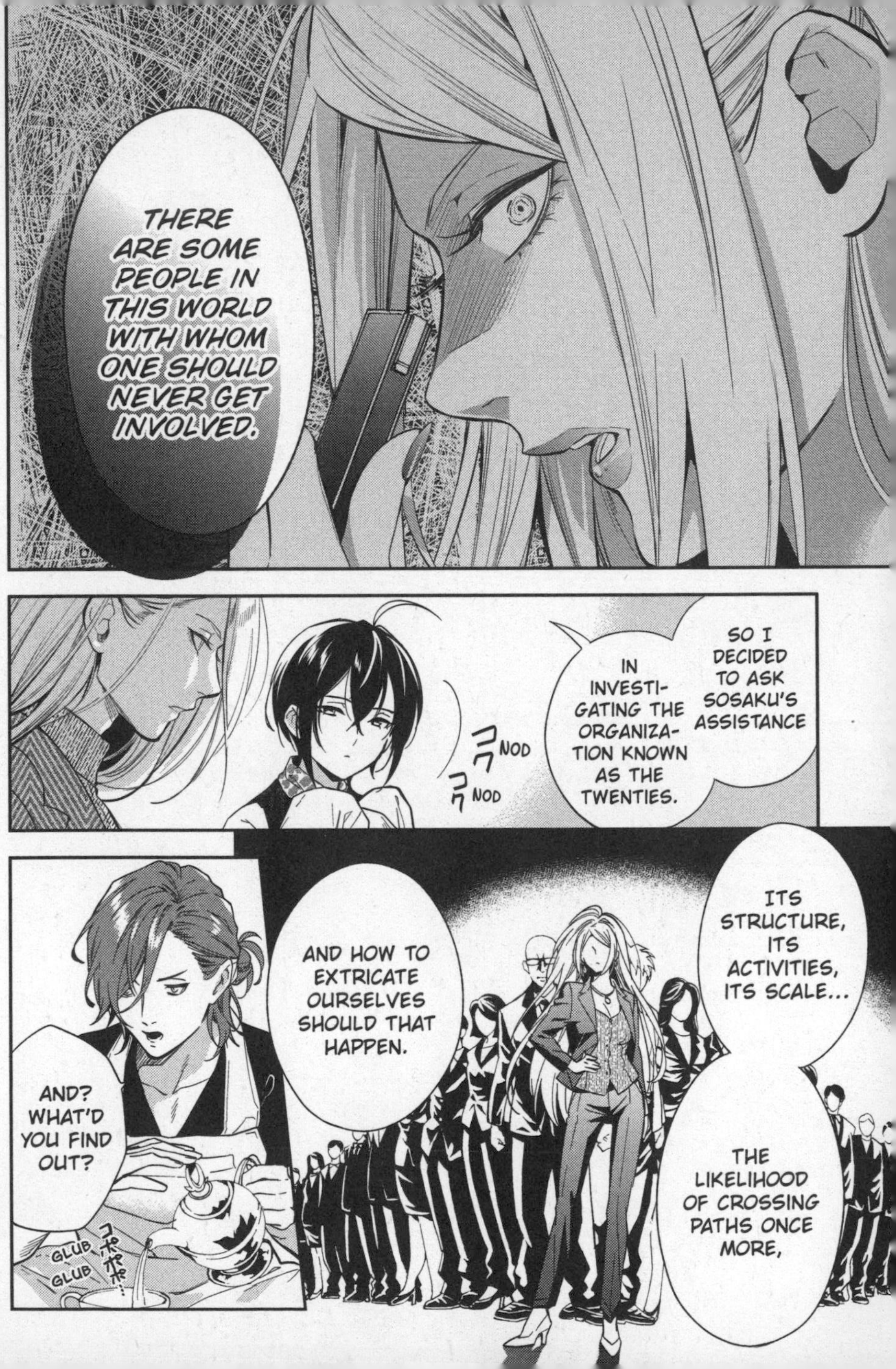
THERE ARE SOME PEOPLE IN THIS WORLD WITH WHOM ONE SHOULD NEVER GET INVOLVED.
SO I DECIDED TO ASK SOSAKU'S ASSISTANCE
IN INVESTIGATING THE ORGANIZATION KNOWN AS THE TWENTIES.
NOD
NOD
ITS STRUCTURE, ITS ACTIVITIES, ITS SCALE...
THE LIKELIHOOD OF CROSSING PATHS ONCE MORE,
AND HOW TO EXTRICATE OURSELVES SHOULD THAT HAPPEN.
AND? WHAT'D YOU FIND OUT?
GLUB GLUB

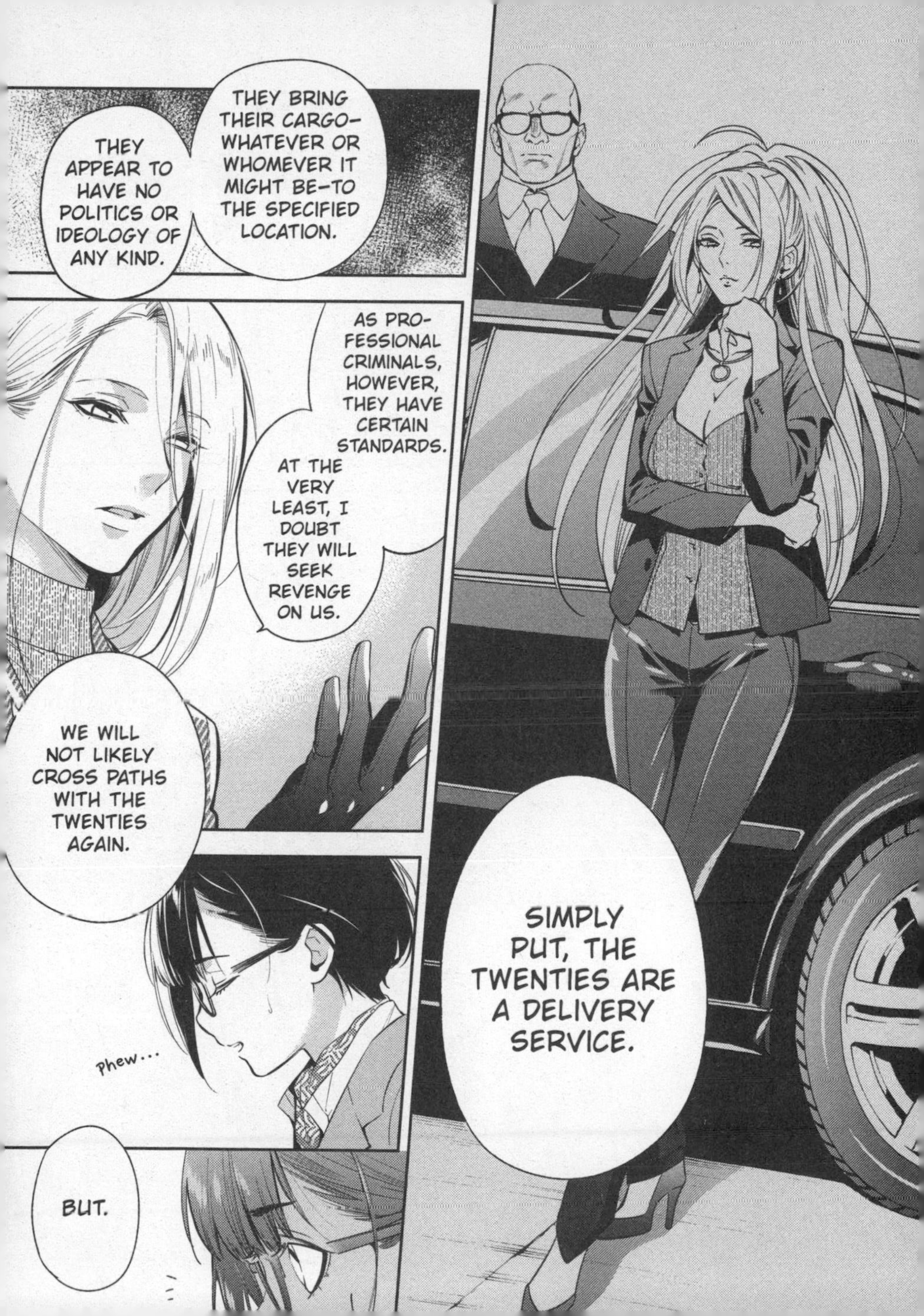
SIMPLY PUT, THE TWENTIES ARE A DELIVERY SERVICE.
THEY BRING THEIR CARGO—WHATEVER OR WHOMEVER IT MIGHT BE—TO THE SPECIFIED LOCATION.
THEY APPEAR TO HAVE NO POLITICS OR IDEOLOGY OF ANY KIND.
AS PROFESSIONAL CRIMINALS, HOWEVER, THEY HAVE CERTAIN STANDARDS.
AT THE VERY LEAST, I DOUBT THEY WILL SEEK REVENGE ON US.
WE WILL NOT LIKELY CROSS PATHS WITH THE TWENTIES AGAIN.
Phew...
BUT.

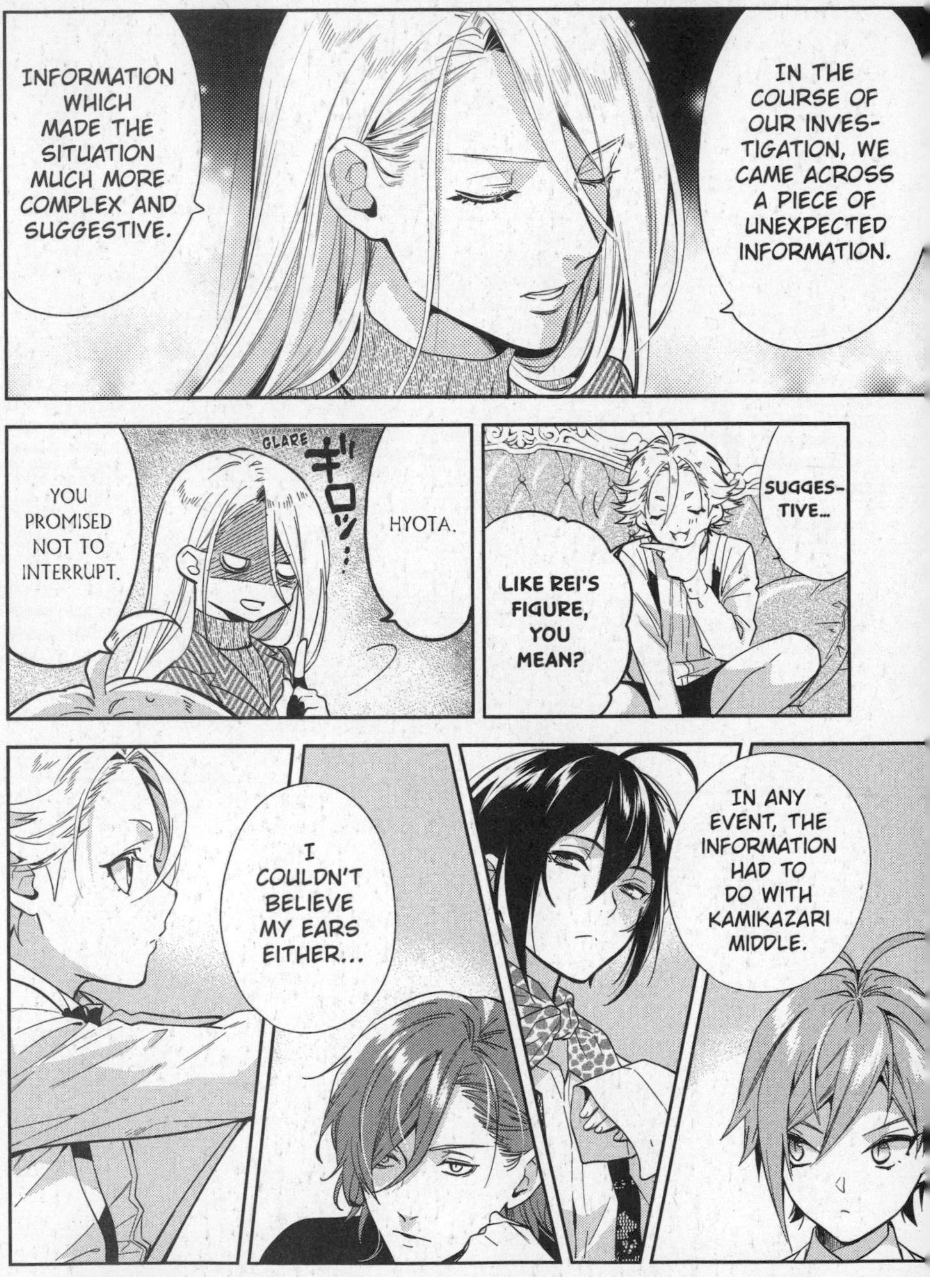
IN THE COURSE OF OUR INVES-TIGATION, WE CAME ACROSS A PIECE OF UNEXPECTED INFORMATION.
INFORMATION WHICH MADE THE SITUATION MUCH MORE COMPLEX AND SUGGESTIVE.
SUGGES-TIVE...
LIKE REI'S FIGURE, YOU MEAN?
HYOTA.
GLARE
ギロッ
YOU PROMISED NOT TO INTERRUPT.
IN ANY EVENT, THE INFORMATION HAD TO DO WITH KAMIKAZARI MIDDLE.
I COULDN'T BELIEVE MY EARS EITHER...

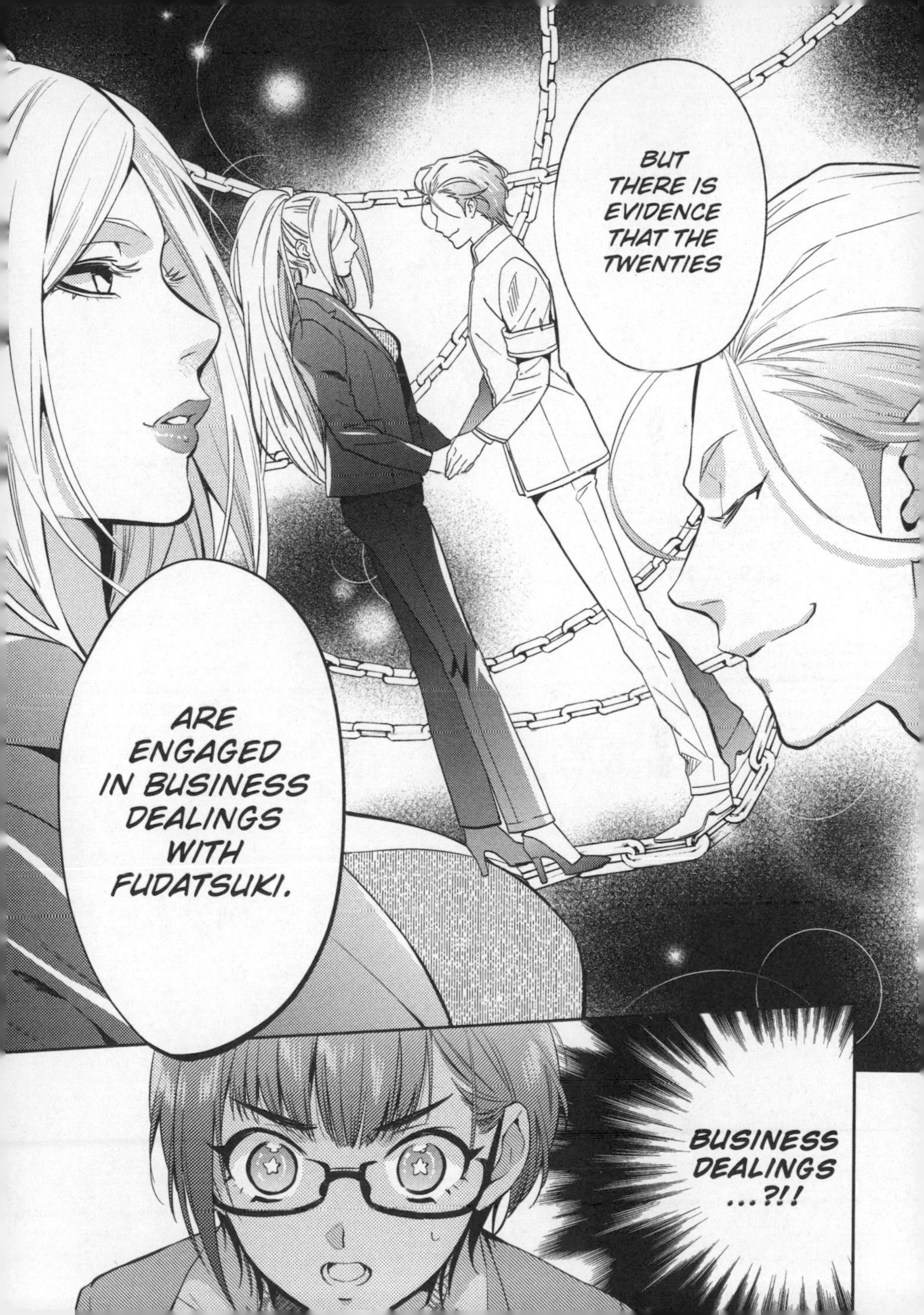
BUT THERE IS EVIDENCE THAT THE TWENTIES
ARE ENGAGED IN BUSINESS DEALINGS WITH FUDATSUKI.
BUSINESS DEALINGS ...?!!

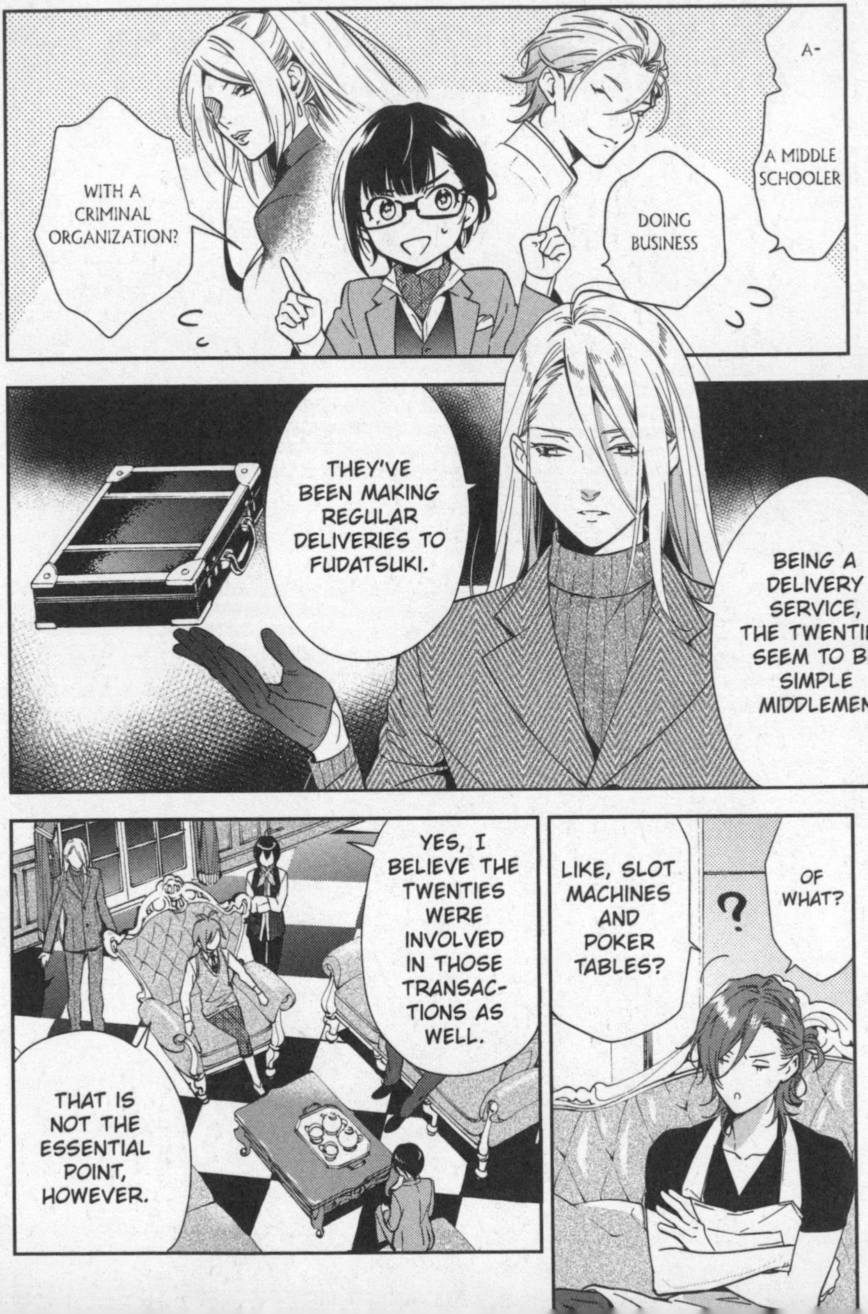
A-
A MIDDLE SCHOOLER
DOING BUSINESS
WITH A CRIMINAL ORGANIZATION?
THEY'VE BEEN MAKING REGULAR DELIVERIES TO FUDATSUKI.
BEING A DELIVERY SERVICE, THE TWENTIES SEEM TO BE SIMPLE MIDDLEMEN.
OF WHAT?
LIKE, SLOT MACHINES AND POKER TABLES?
YES, I BELIEVE THE TWENTIES WERE INVOLVED IN THOSE TRANSAC-TIONS AS WELL.
THAT IS NOT THE ESSENTIAL POINT, HOWEVER.

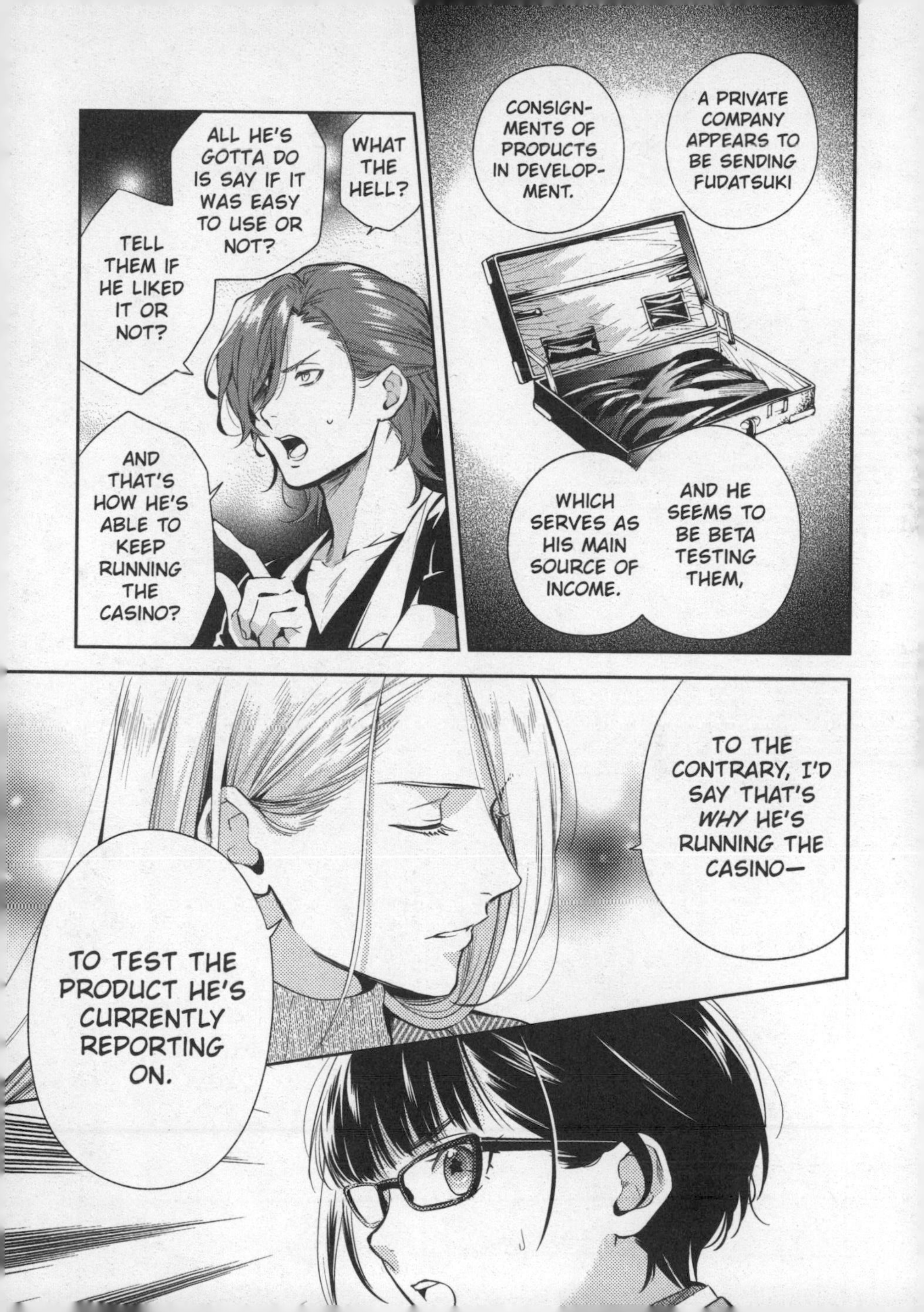
A PRIVATE COMPANY APPEARS TO BE SENDING FUDATSUKI
CONSIGNMENTS OF PRODUCTS IN DEVELOPMENT.
AND HE SEEMS TO BE BETA TESTING THEM,
WHICH SERVES AS HIS MAIN SOURCE OF INCOME.
WHAT THE HELL?
ALL HE'S GOTTA DO IS SAY IF IT WAS EASY TO USE OR NOT?
TELL THEM IF HE LIKED IT OR NOT?
AND THAT'S HOW HE'S ABLE TO KEEP RUNNING THE CASINO?
TO THE CONTRARY, I'D SAY THAT'S *WHY* HE'S RUNNING THE CASINO—
TO TEST THE PRODUCT HE'S CURRENTLY REPORTING ON.

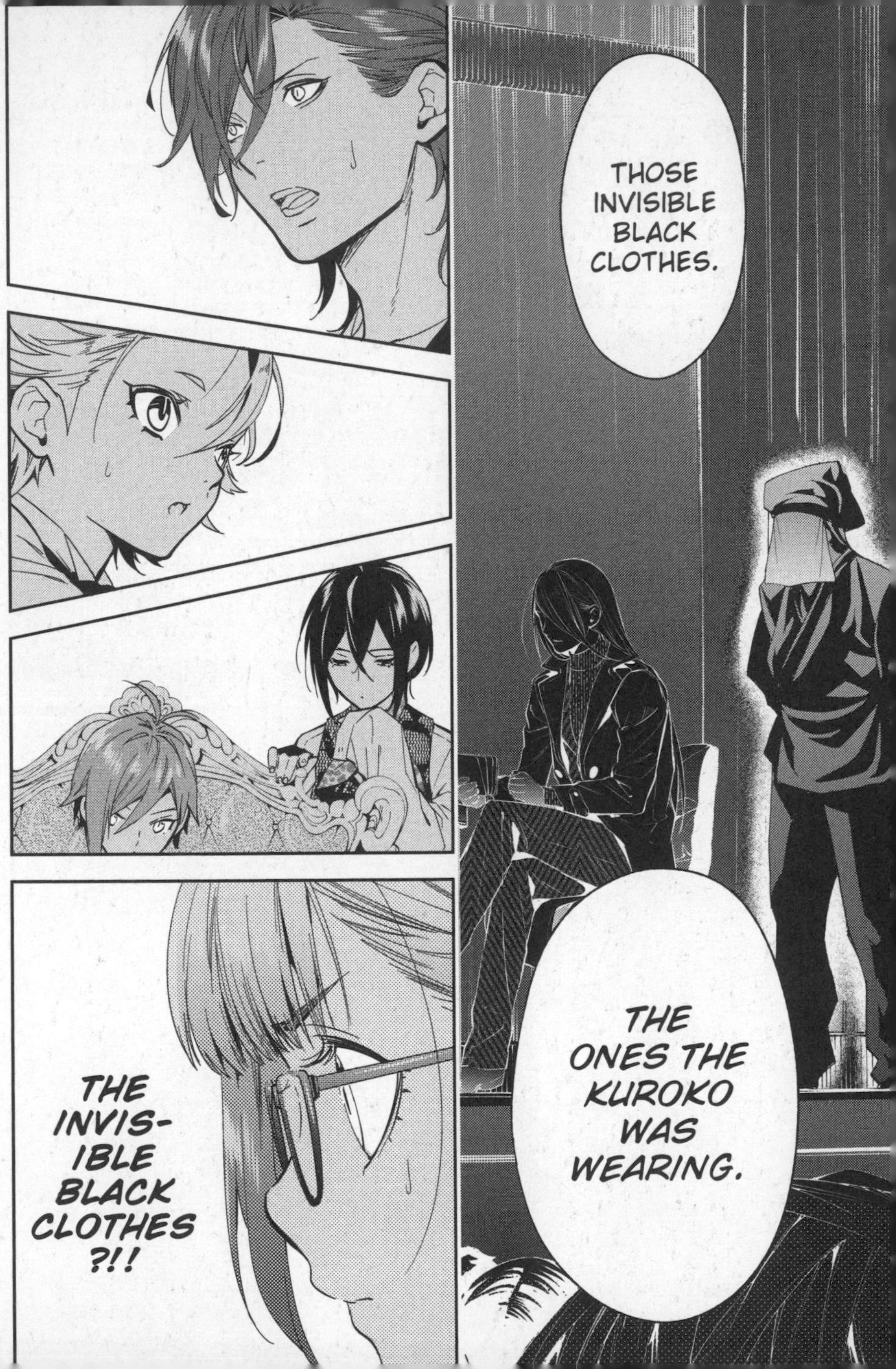
THOSE INVISIBLE BLACK CLOTHES.
THE ONES THE KUROKO WAS WEARING.
THE INVIS-IBLE BLACK CLOTHES ?!!

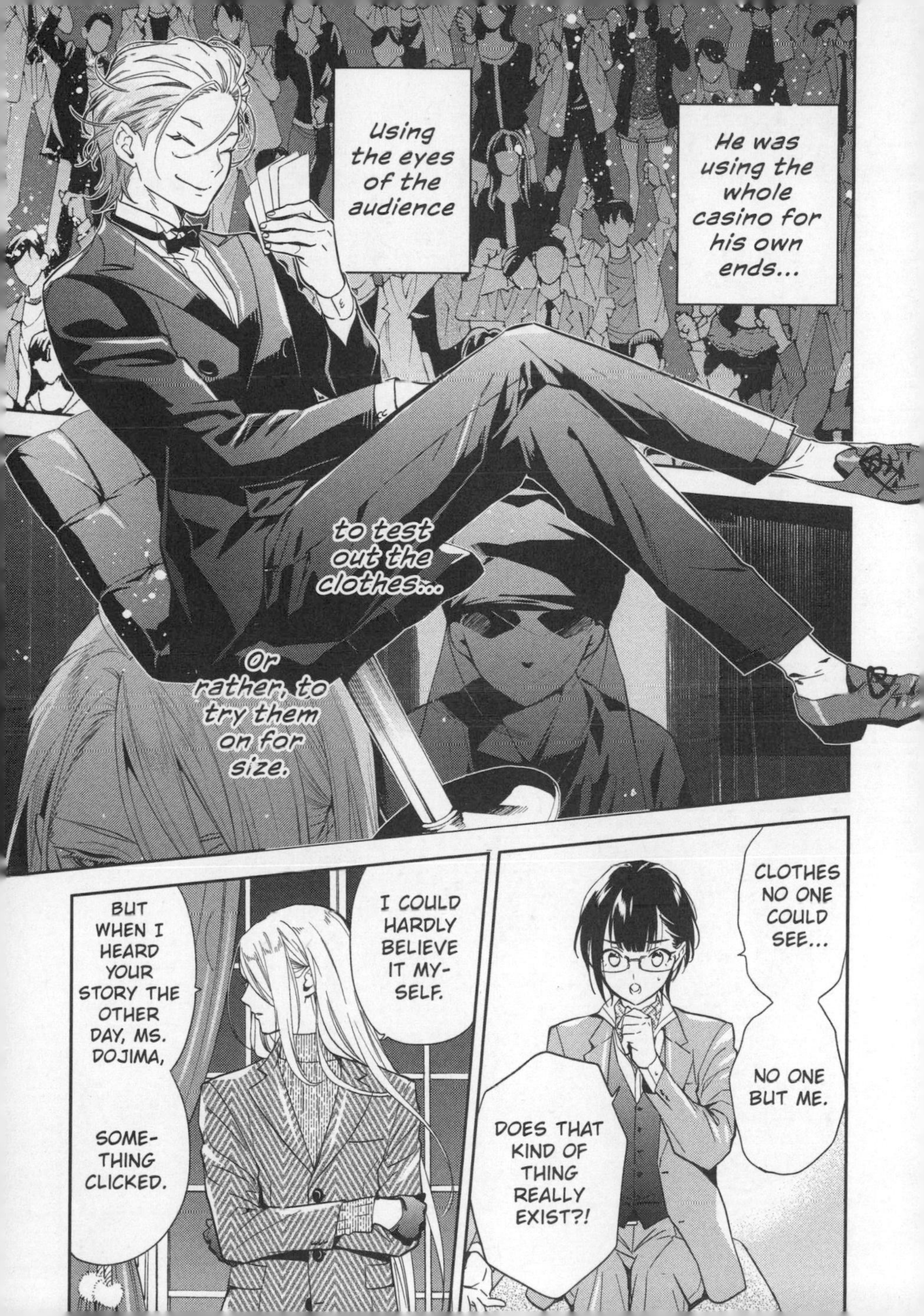
He was using the whole casino for his own ends...
Using the eyes of the audience
to test out the clothes...
Or rather, to try them on for size.
CLOTHES NO ONE COULD SEE...
NO ONE BUT ME.
DOES THAT KIND OF THING REALLY EXIST?!
I COULD HARDLY BELIEVE IT MY-SELF.
BUT WHEN I HEARD YOUR STORY THE OTHER DAY, MS. DOJIMA,
SOME-THING CLICKED.

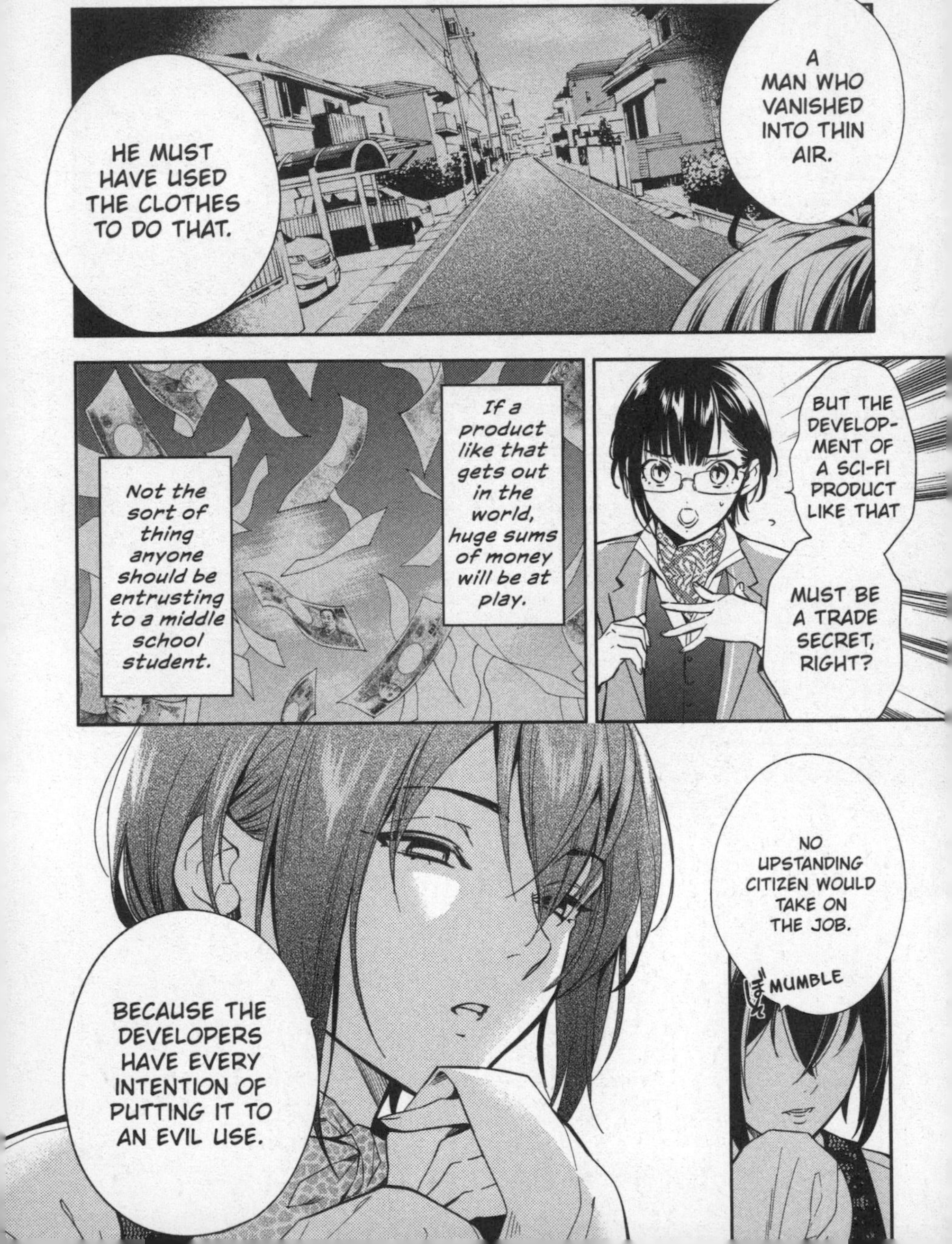
A MAN WHO VANISHED INTO THIN AIR.
HE MUST HAVE USED THE CLOTHES TO DO THAT.
BUT THE DEVELOP-MENT OF A SCI-FI PRODUCT LIKE THAT
MUST BE A TRADE SECRET, RIGHT?
If a product like that gets out in the world, huge sums of money will be at play.
Not the sort of thing anyone should be entrusting to a middle school student.
NO UPSTANDING CITIZEN WOULD TAKE ON THE JOB.
MUMBLE
BECAUSE THE DEVELOPERS HAVE EVERY INTENTION OF PUTTING IT TO AN EVIL USE.

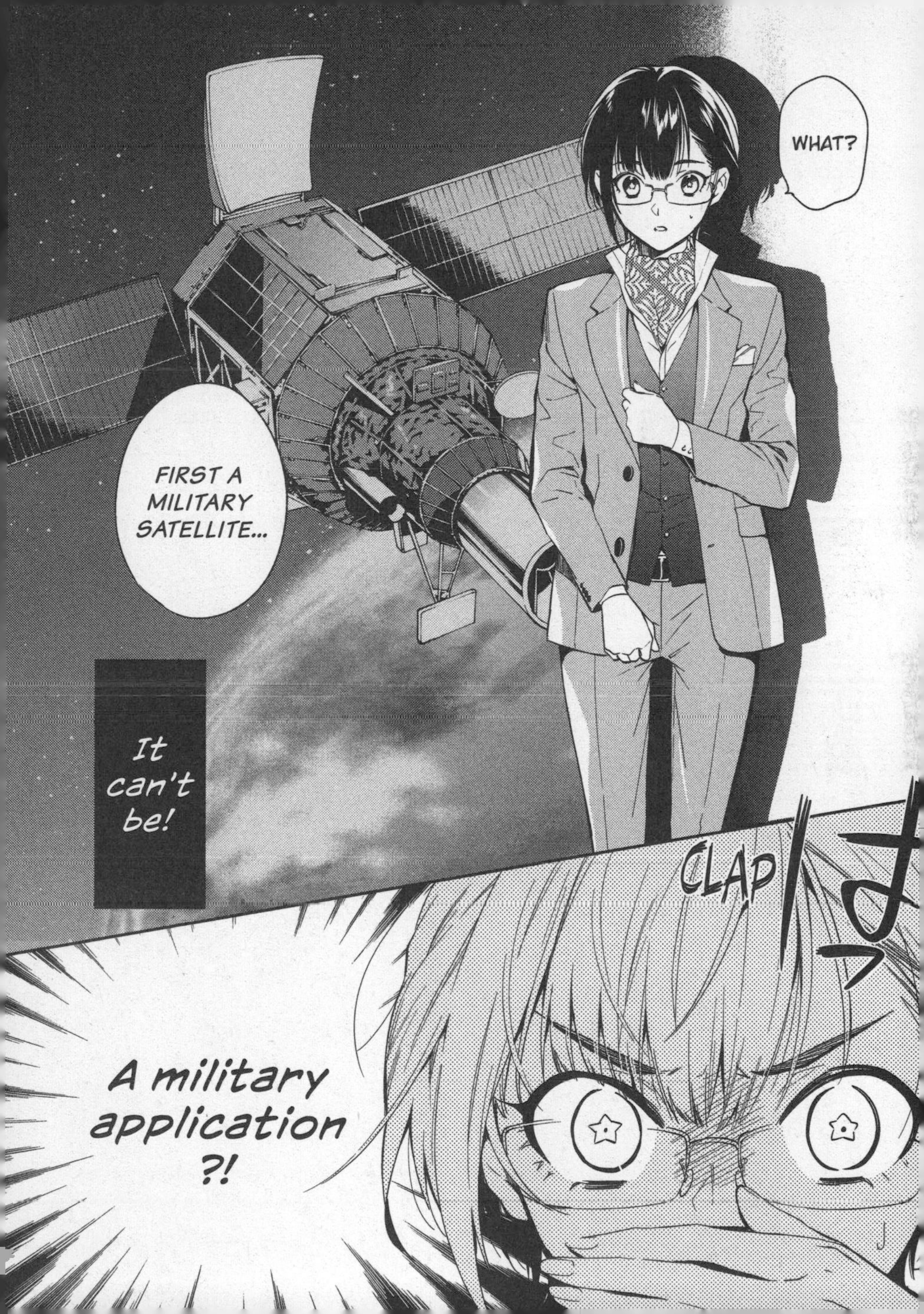
WHAT?
FIRST A MILITARY SATELLITE...
It can't be!
CLAP
A military application ?!

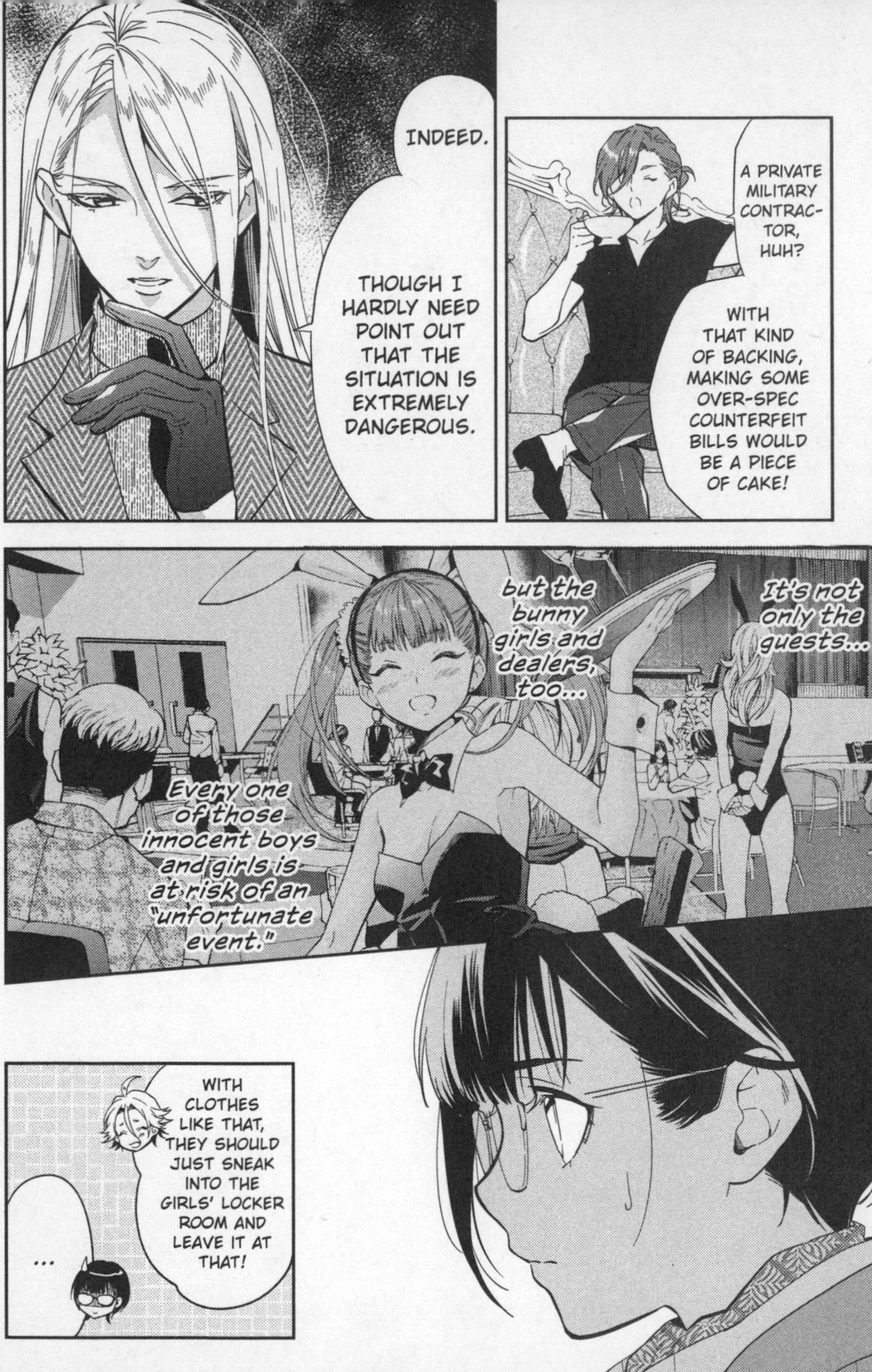
A PRIVATE MILITARY CONTRACTOR, HUH?
WITH THAT KIND OF BACKING, MAKING SOME OVER-SPEC COUNTERFEIT BILLS WOULD BE A PIECE OF CAKE!
INDEED.
THOUGH I HARDLY NEED POINT OUT THAT THE SITUATION IS EXTREMELY DANGEROUS.
It's not only the guests...
but the bunny girls and dealers, too...
Every one of those innocent boys and girls is at risk of an "unfortunate event."
WITH CLOTHES LIKE THAT, THEY SHOULD JUST SNEAK INTO THE GIRLS' LOCKER ROOM AND LEAVE IT AT THAT!
...

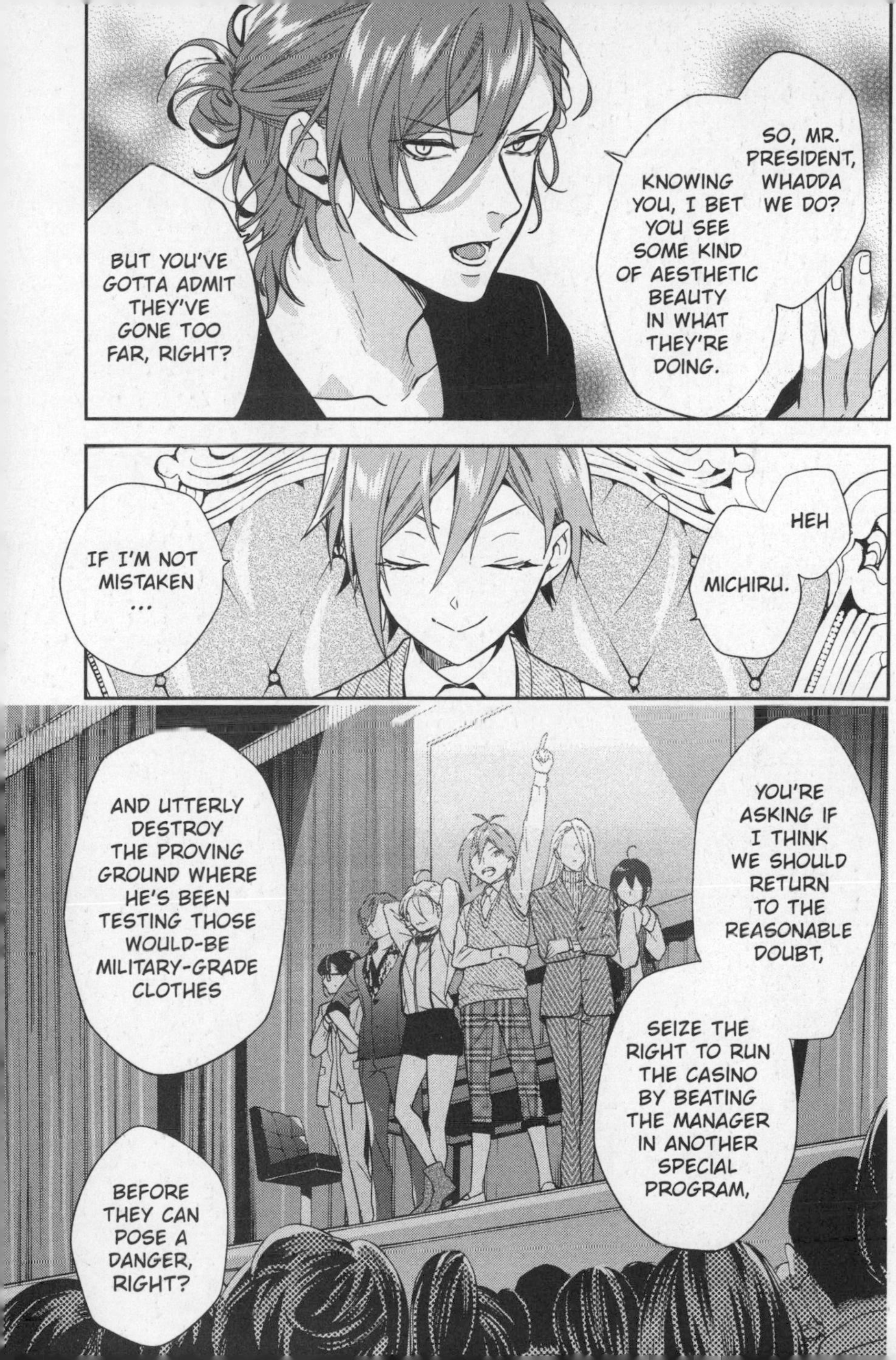
SO, MR. PRESIDENT, WHADDA WE DO?
KNOWING YOU, I BET YOU SEE SOME KIND OF AESTHETIC BEAUTY IN WHAT THEY'RE DOING.
BUT YOU'VE GOTTA ADMIT THEY'VE GONE TOO FAR, RIGHT?
HEH
MICHIRU.
IF I'M NOT MISTAKEN ...
YOU'RE ASKING IF I THINK WE SHOULD RETURN TO THE REASONABLE DOUBT,
SEIZE THE RIGHT TO RUN THE CASINO BY BEATING THE MANAGER IN ANOTHER SPECIAL PROGRAM,
AND UTTERLY DESTROY THE PROVING GROUND WHERE HE'S BEEN TESTING THOSE WOULD-BE MILITARY-GRADE CLOTHES
BEFORE THEY CAN POSE A DANGER, RIGHT?

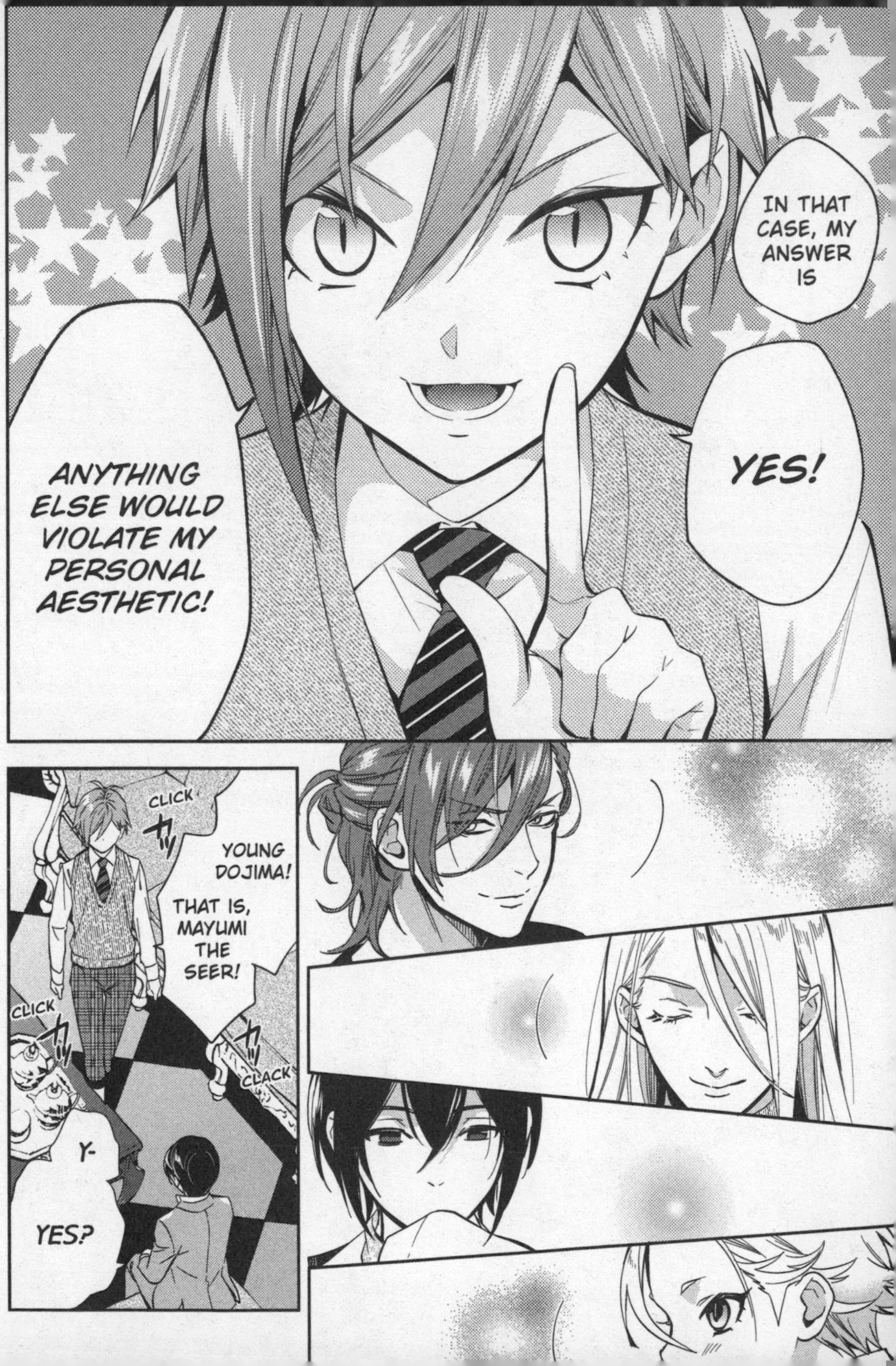
IN THAT CASE, MY ANSWER IS
YES!
ANYTHING ELSE WOULD VIOLATE MY PERSONAL AESTHETIC!
CLICK
YOUNG DOJIMA!
THAT IS, MAYUMI THE SEER!
CLICK
CLACK
Y-
YES?

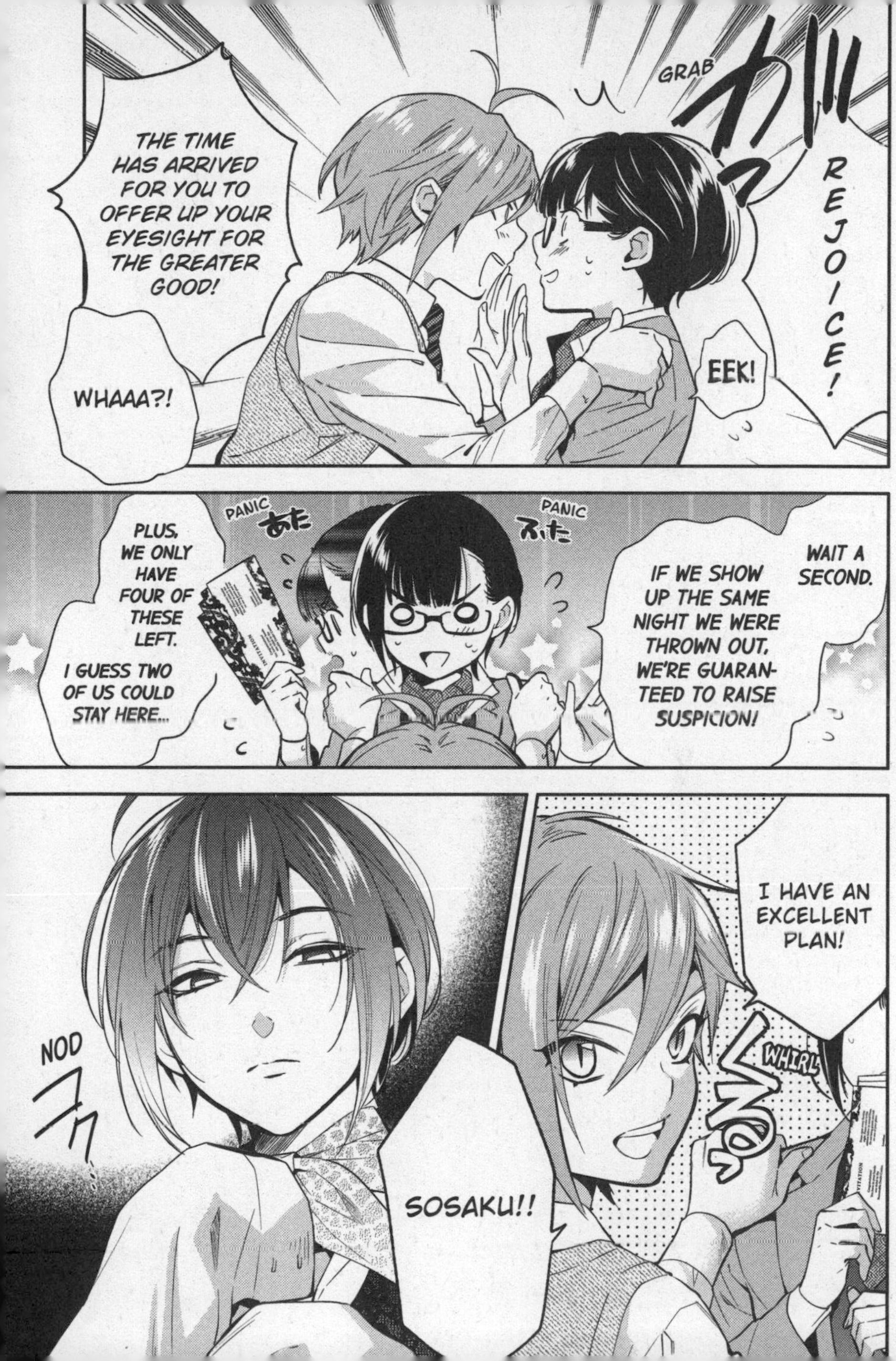
GRAB
REJOICE!
THE TIME HAS ARRIVED FOR YOU TO OFFER UP YOUR EYESIGHT FOR THE GREATER GOOD!
EEK!
WHAAA?!
WAIT A SECOND.
IF WE SHOW UP THE SAME NIGHT WE WERE THROWN OUT, WE'RE GUARANTEED TO RAISE SUSPICION!
PANIC
PANIC
PLUS, WE ONLY HAVE FOUR OF THESE LEFT.
I GUESS TWO OF US COULD STAY HERE...
I HAVE AN EXCELLENT PLAN!
WHIRL
SOSAKU!!
NOD

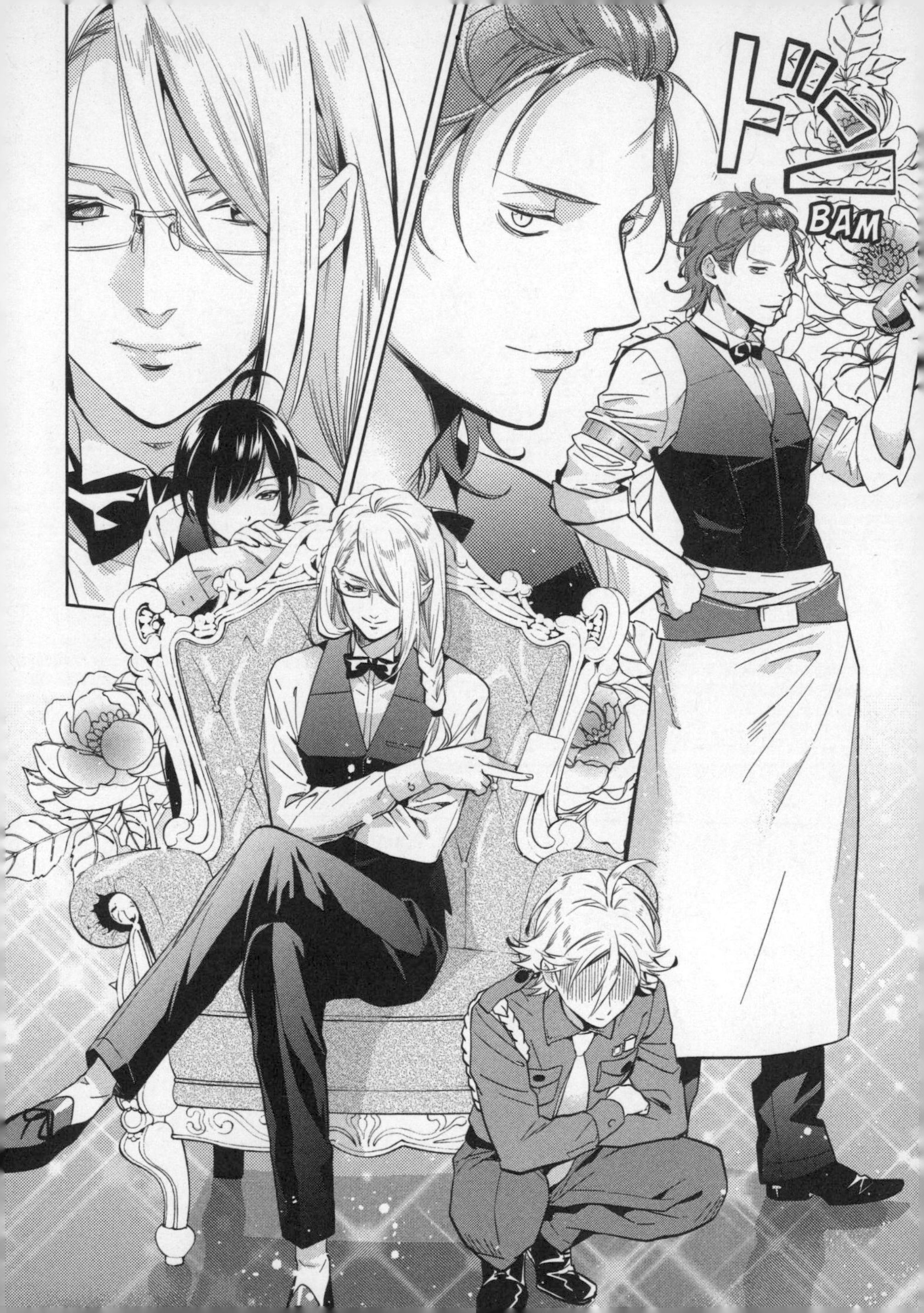
ドン
BAM

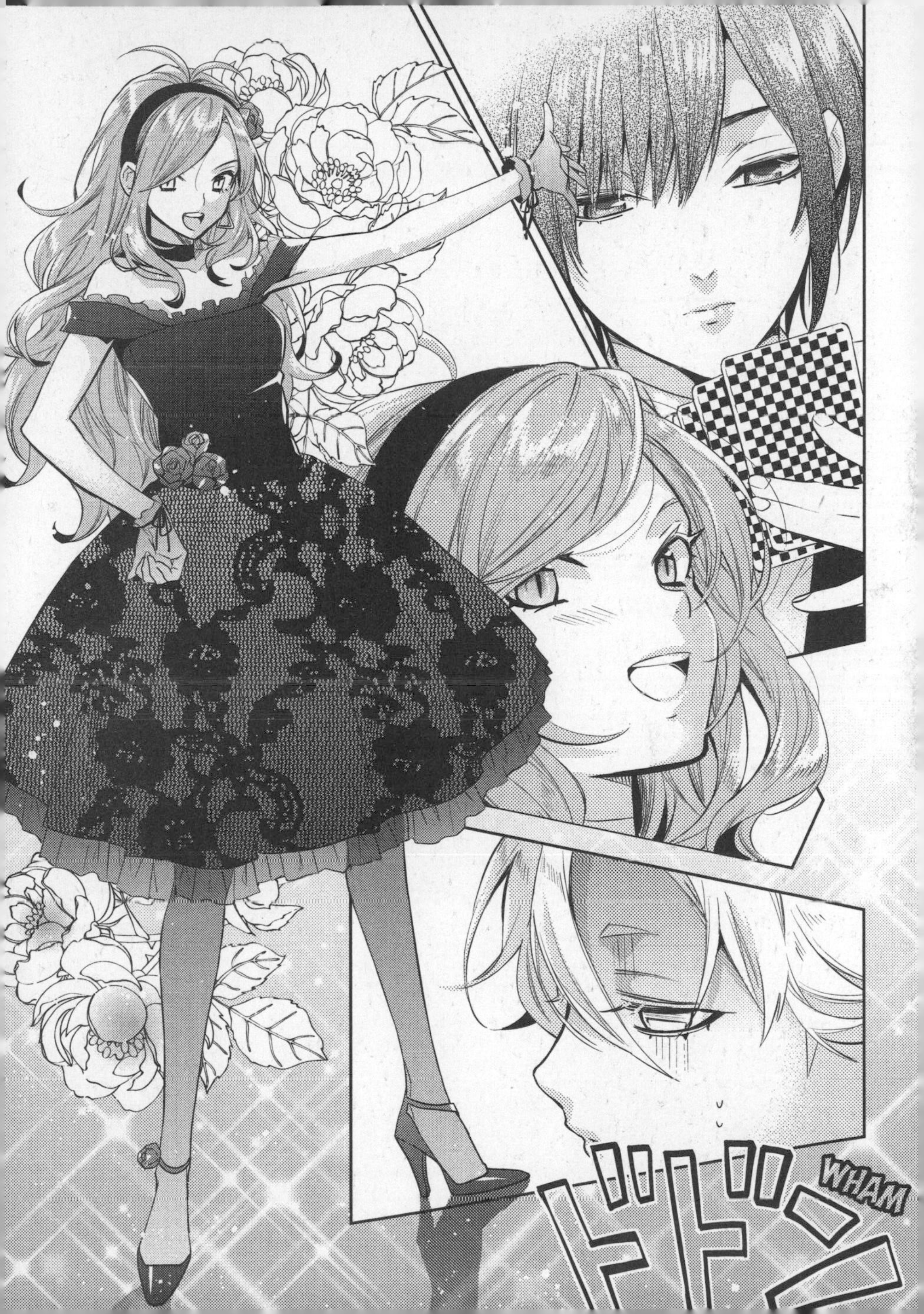
ドドーン
WHAM

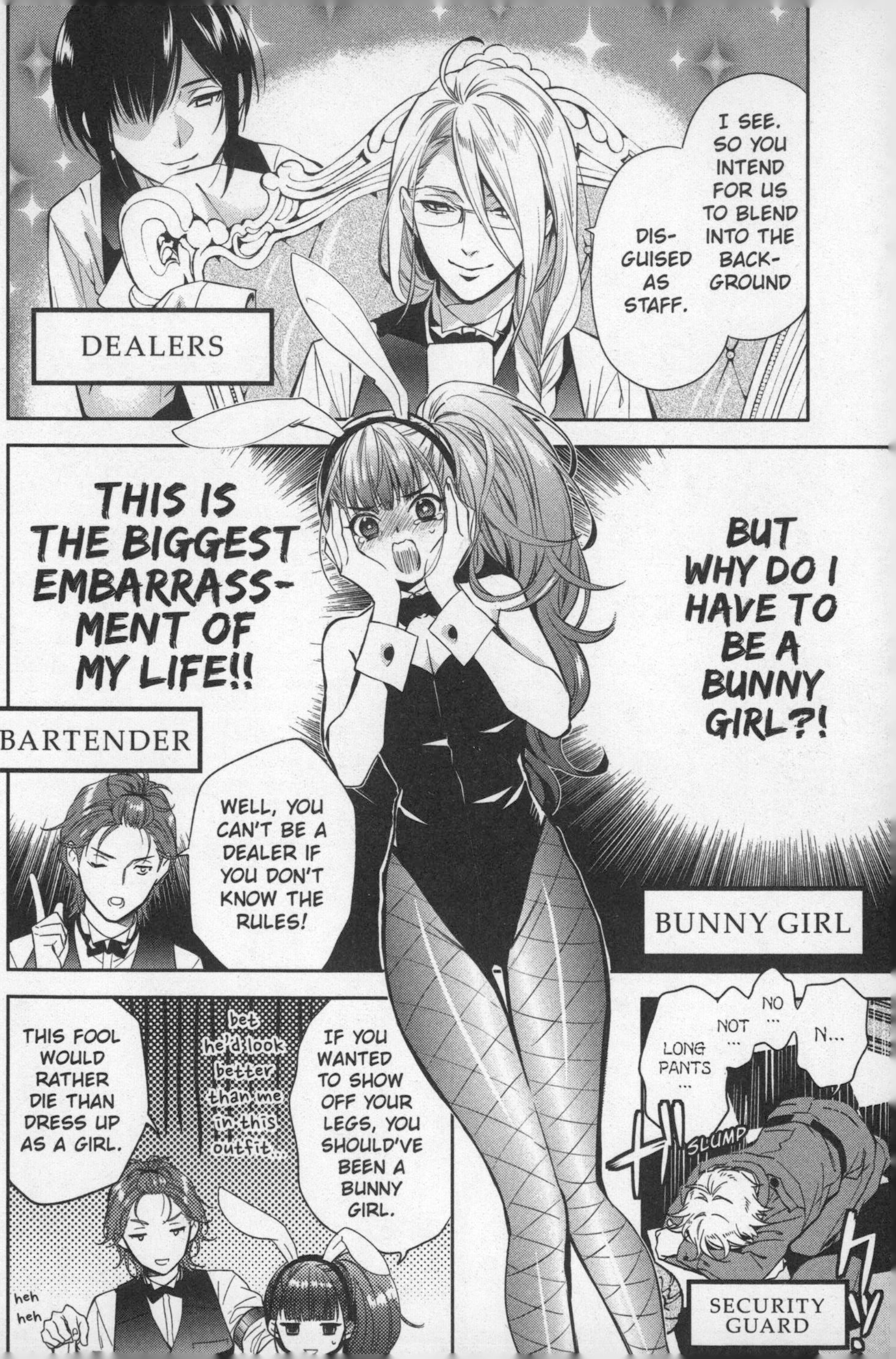
I SEE. SO YOU INTEND FOR US TO BLEND INTO THE BACKGROUND
DIS-GUISED AS STAFF.
DEALERS
BUT WHY DO I HAVE TO BE A BUNNY GIRL?!
BUNNY GIRL
THIS IS THE BIGGEST EMBARRASS-MENT OF MY LIFE!!
BARTENDER
WELL, YOU CAN'T BE A DEALER IF YOU DON'T KNOW THE RULES!
N...
NO ...
NOT ...
LONG PANTS ...
SLUMP
SECURITY GUARD
IF YOU WANTED TO SHOW OFF YOUR LEGS, YOU SHOULD'VE BEEN A BUNNY GIRL.
bet he'd look better than me in this outfit...
THIS FOOL WOULD RATHER DIE THAN DRESS UP AS A GIRL.
heh heh

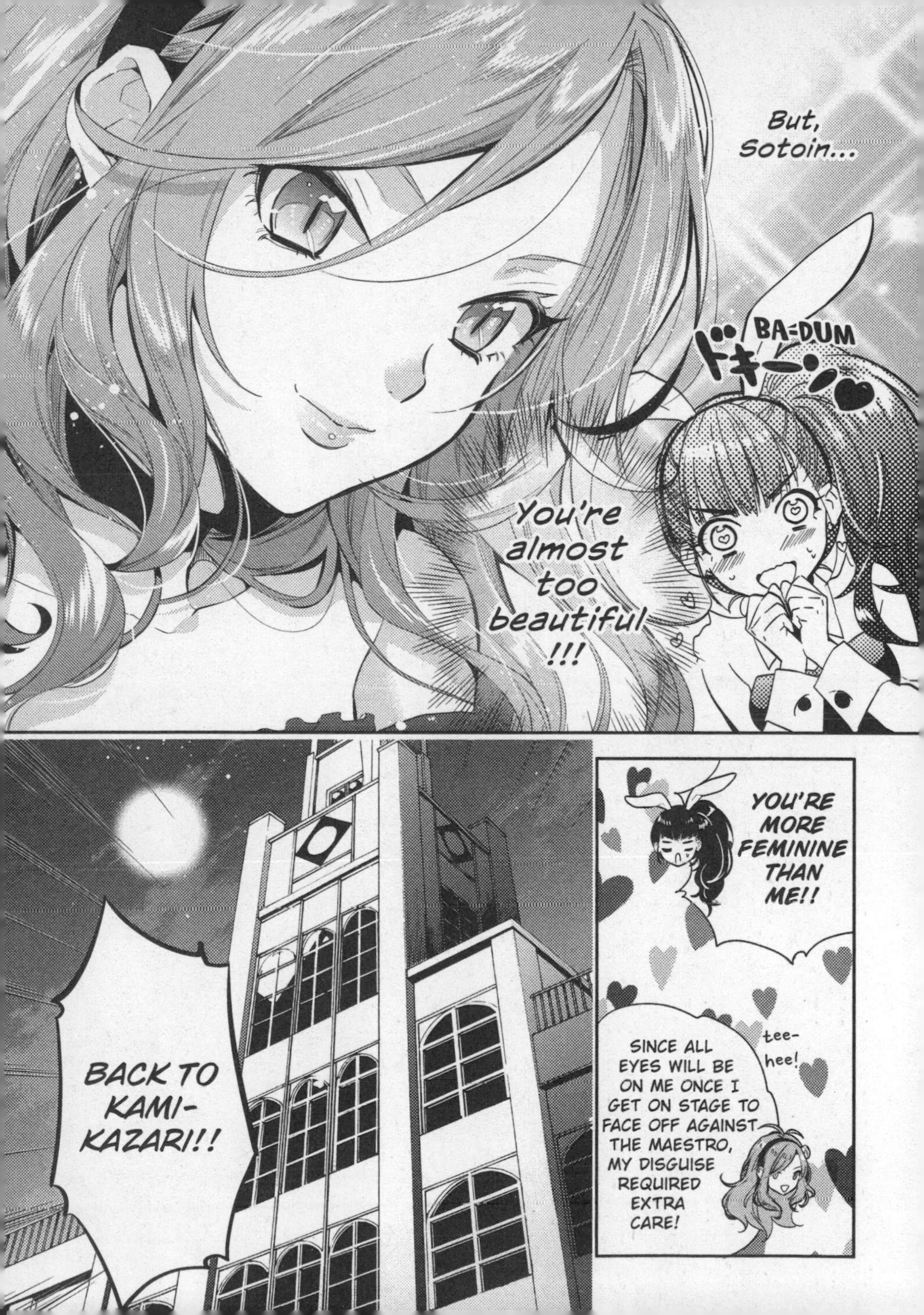
But, Sotoin...
BA-DUM
ドキーン
You're almost too beautiful!!!
YOU'RE MORE FEMININE THAN ME!!
SINCE ALL EYES WILL BE ON ME ONCE I GET ON STAGE TO FACE OFF AGAINST THE MAESTRO, MY DISGUISE REQUIRED EXTRA CARE!
tee-hee!
BACK TO KAMI-KAZARI!!

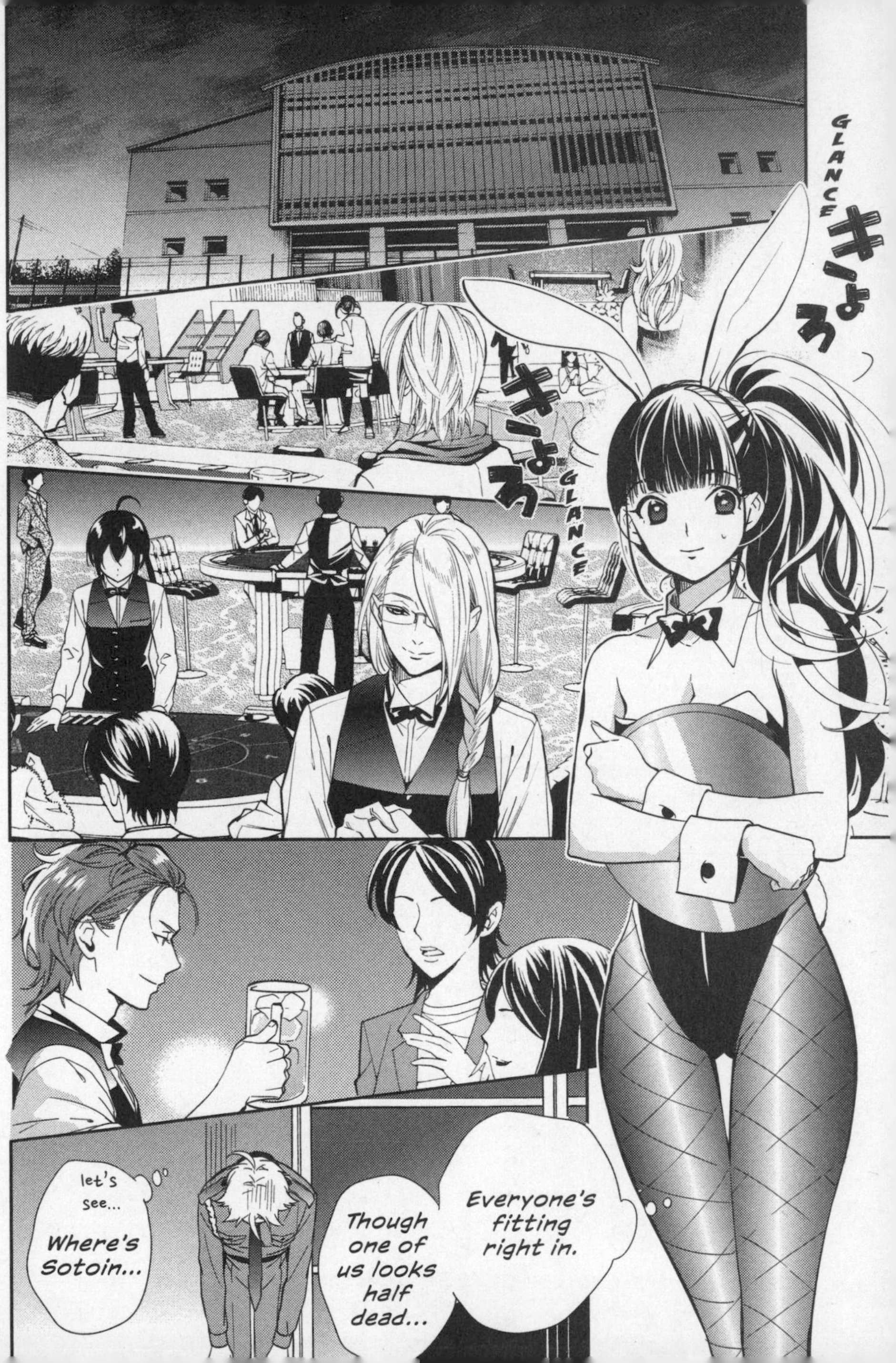
GLANCE
キょろ
キょろ
GLANCE
Everyone's fitting right in.
Though one of us looks half dead...
let's see...
Where's Sotoin...

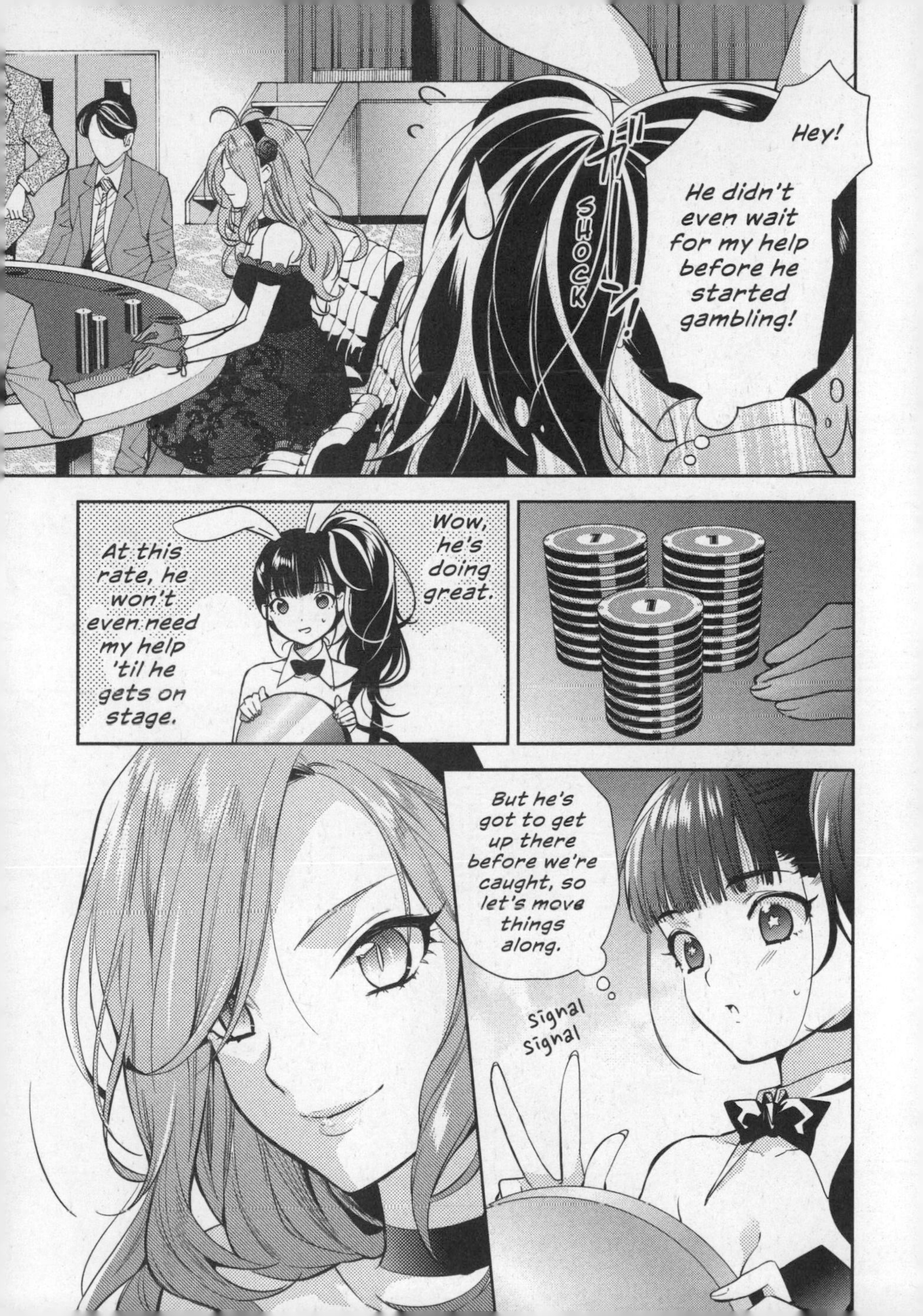
Hey!
He didn't even wait for my help before he started gambling!
SHOCK
Wow, he's doing great.
At this rate, he won't even need my help 'til he gets on stage.
But he's got to get up there before we're caught, so let's move things along.
Signal signal

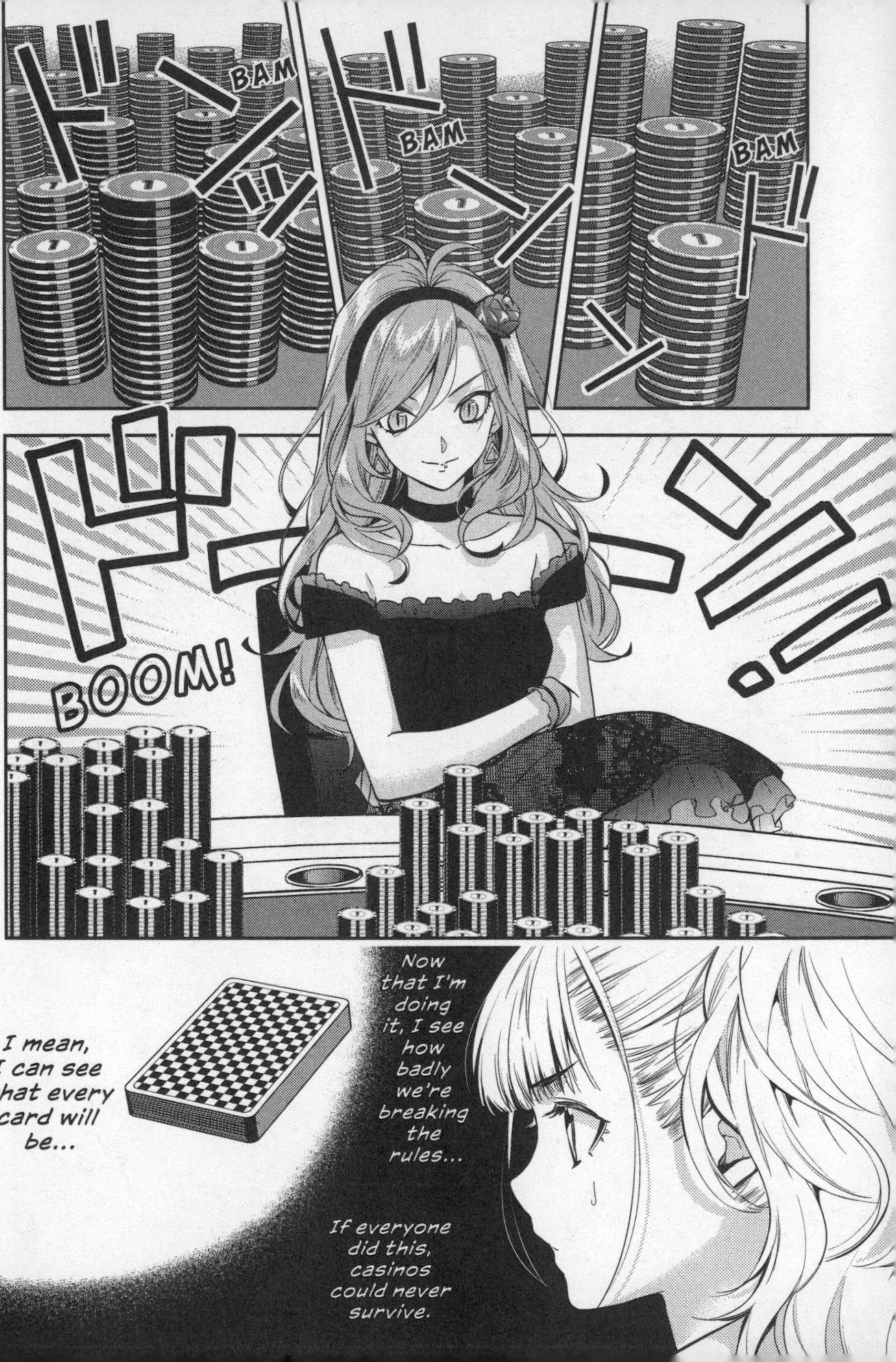
BAM
BAM
BAM
BOOM!
Now that I'm doing it, I see how badly we're breaking the rules...
I mean, I can see what every card will be...
If everyone did this, casinos could never survive.

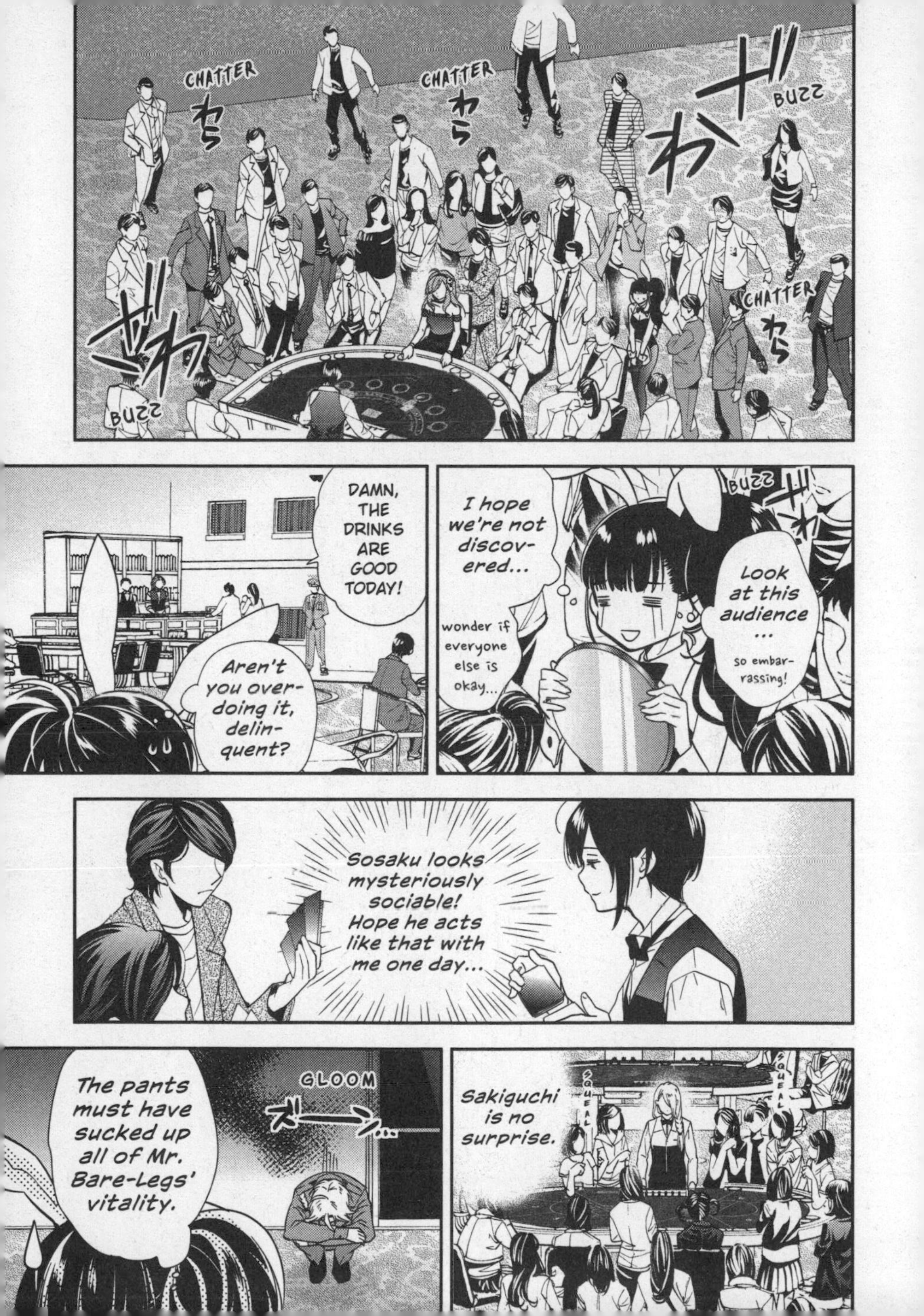
CHATTER
CHATTER
BUZZ
CHATTER
BUZZ
BUZZ
I hope we're not discovered...
wonder if everyone else is okay...
Look at this audience ...
so embarrassing!
DAMN, THE DRINKS ARE GOOD TODAY!
Aren't you overdoing it, delinquent?
Sosaku looks mysteriously sociable! Hope he acts like that with me one day...
SQUEAL
SQUEAL
Sakiguchi is no surprise.
GLOOM
The pants must have sucked up all of Mr. Bare-Legs' vitality.

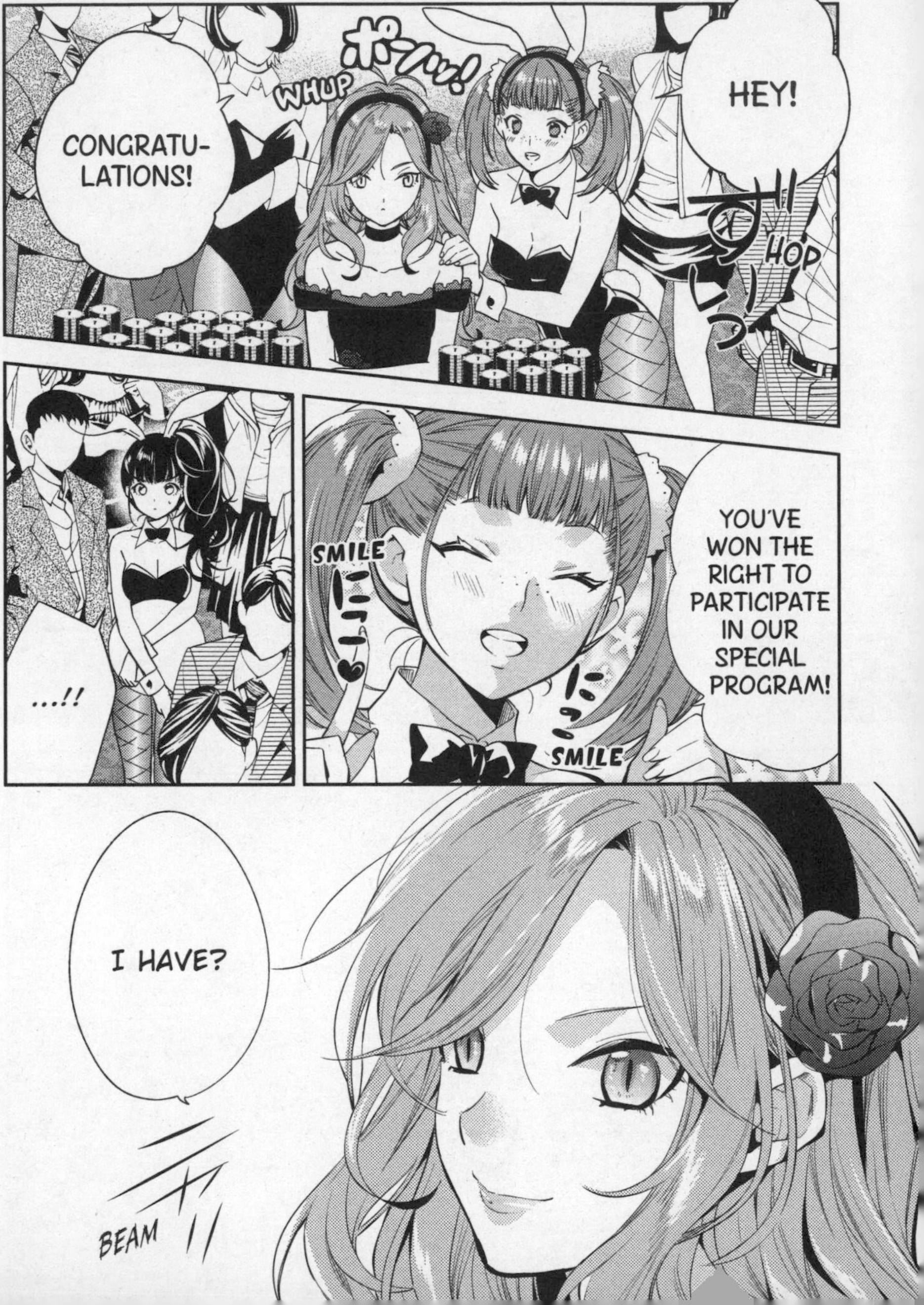
HEY!
WHUP
CONGRATU-
LATIONS!
HOP
YOU'VE WON THE RIGHT TO PARTICIPATE IN OUR SPECIAL PROGRAM!
SMILE
SMILE
...!!
I HAVE?
BEAM

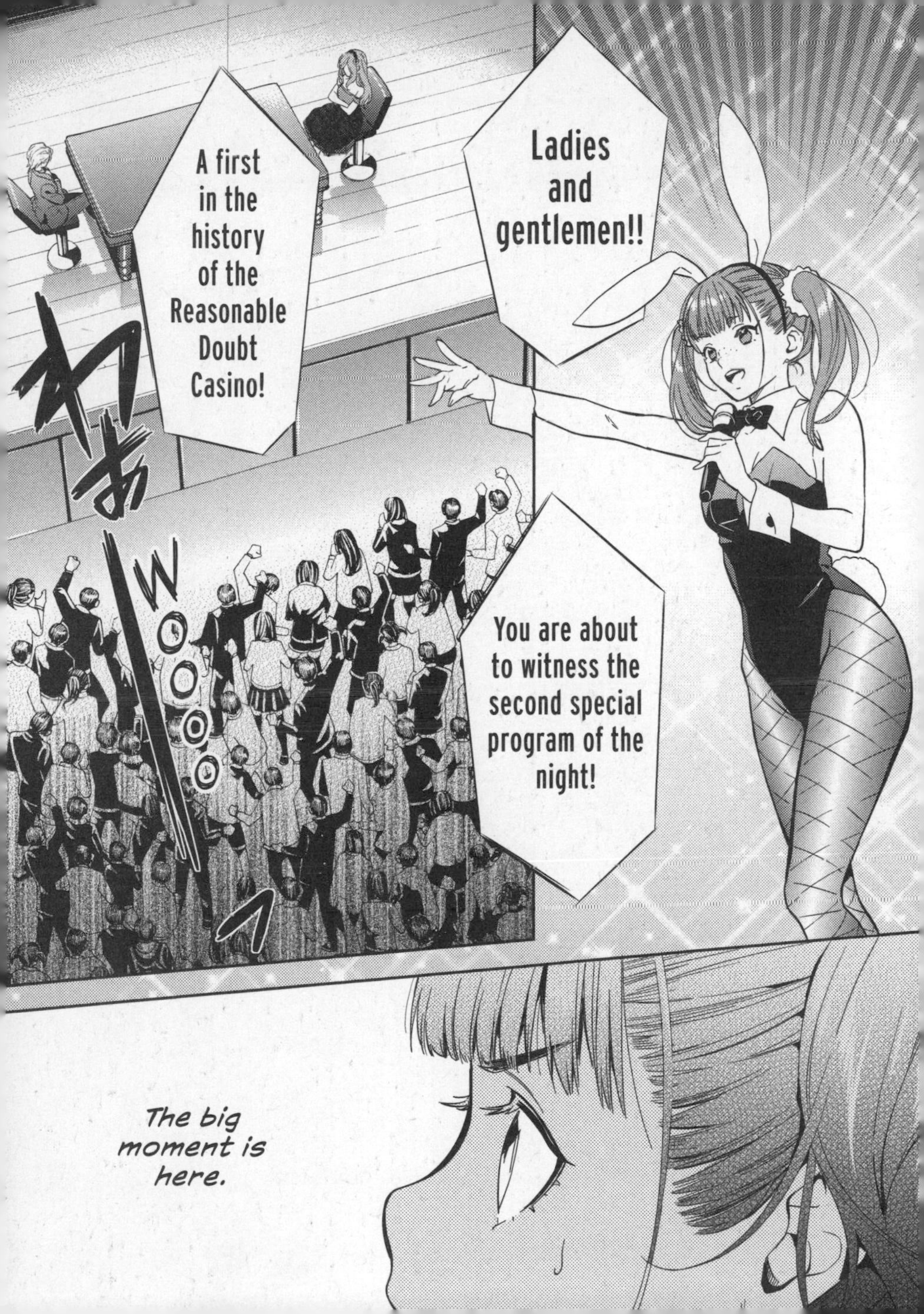
Ladies and gentlemen!!
A first in the history of the Reasonable Doubt Casino!
You are about to witness the second special program of the night!
わあ
WOOOO
The big moment is here.

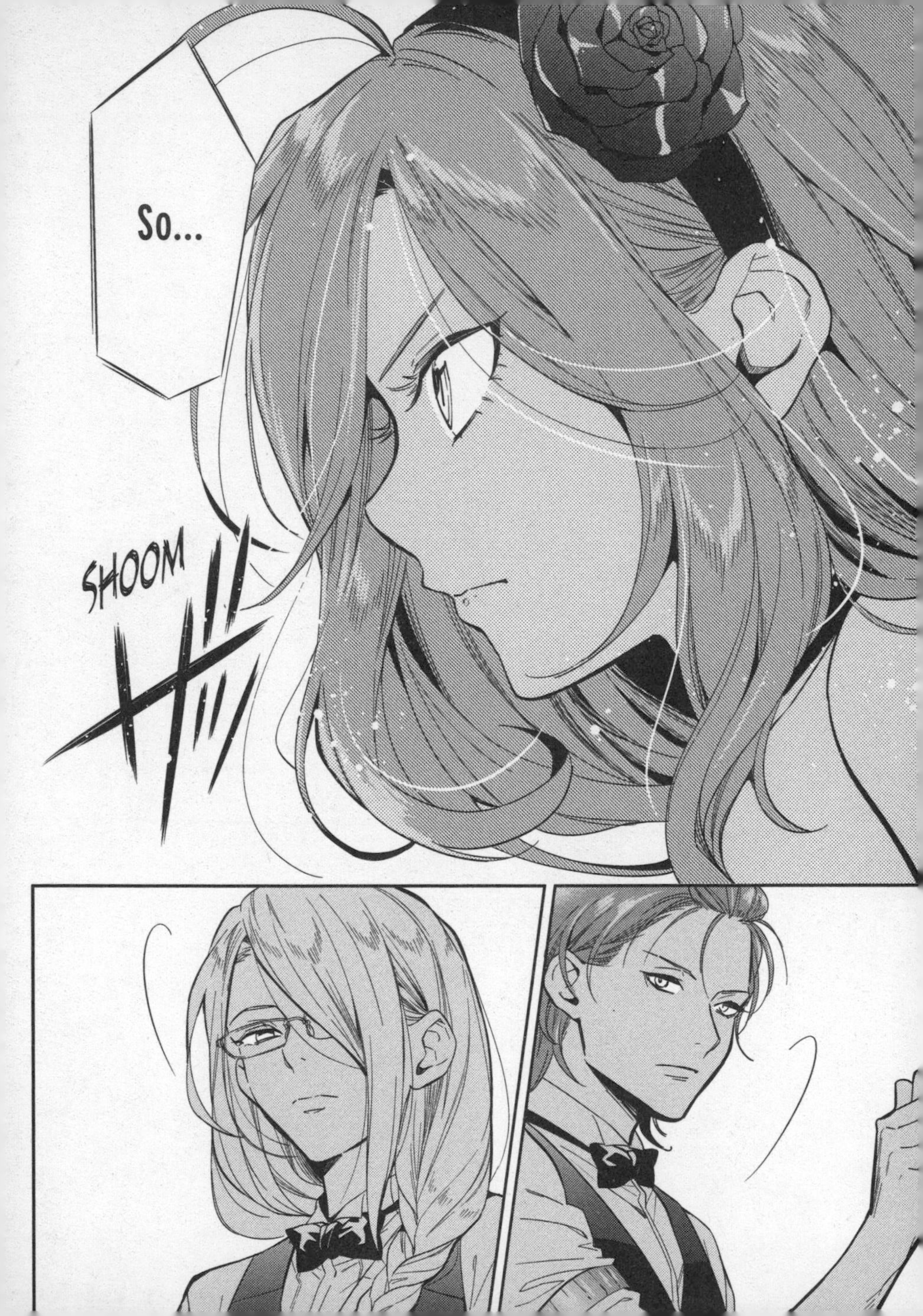
So...
SHOOM

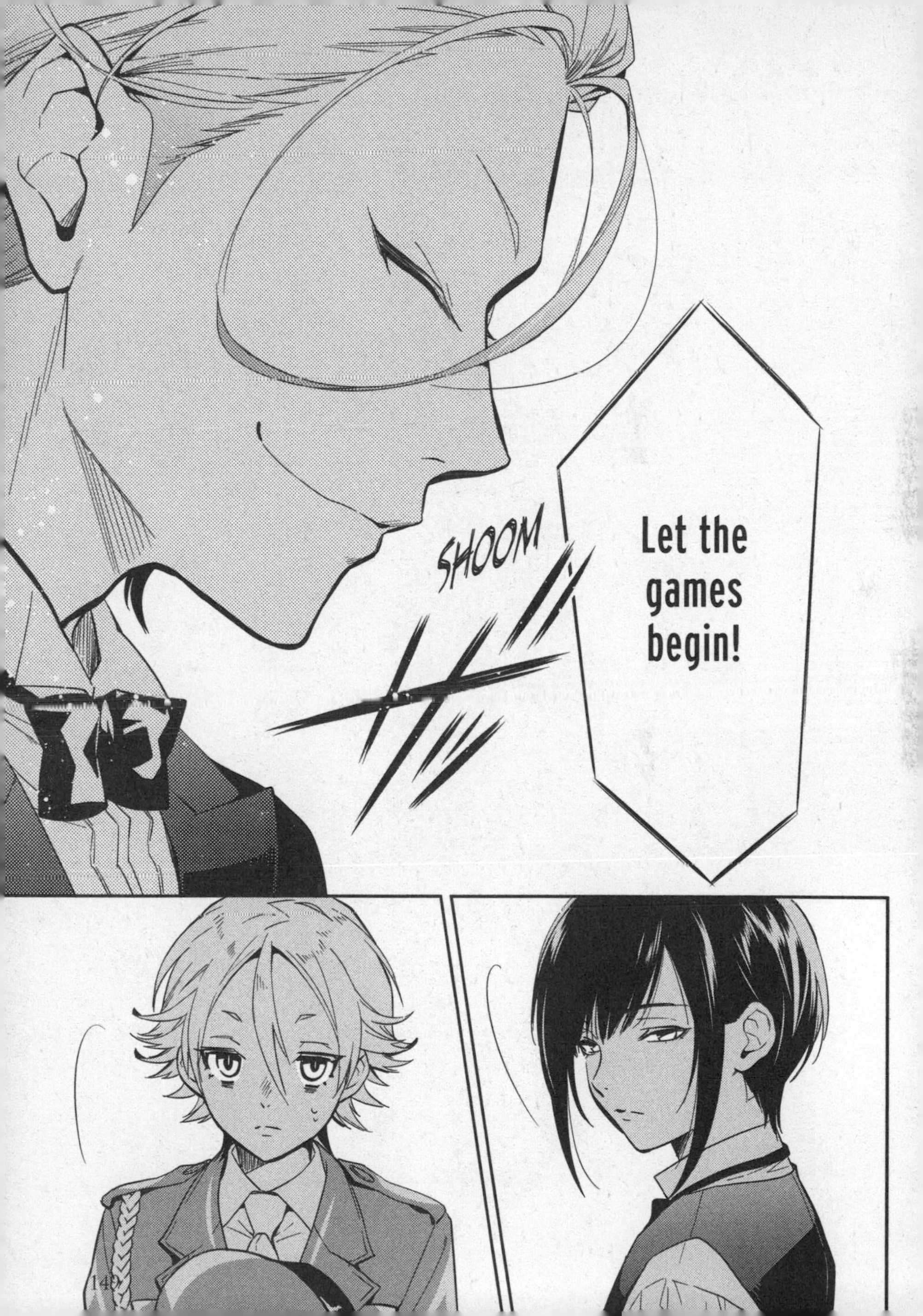
Let the games begin!
SHOOM

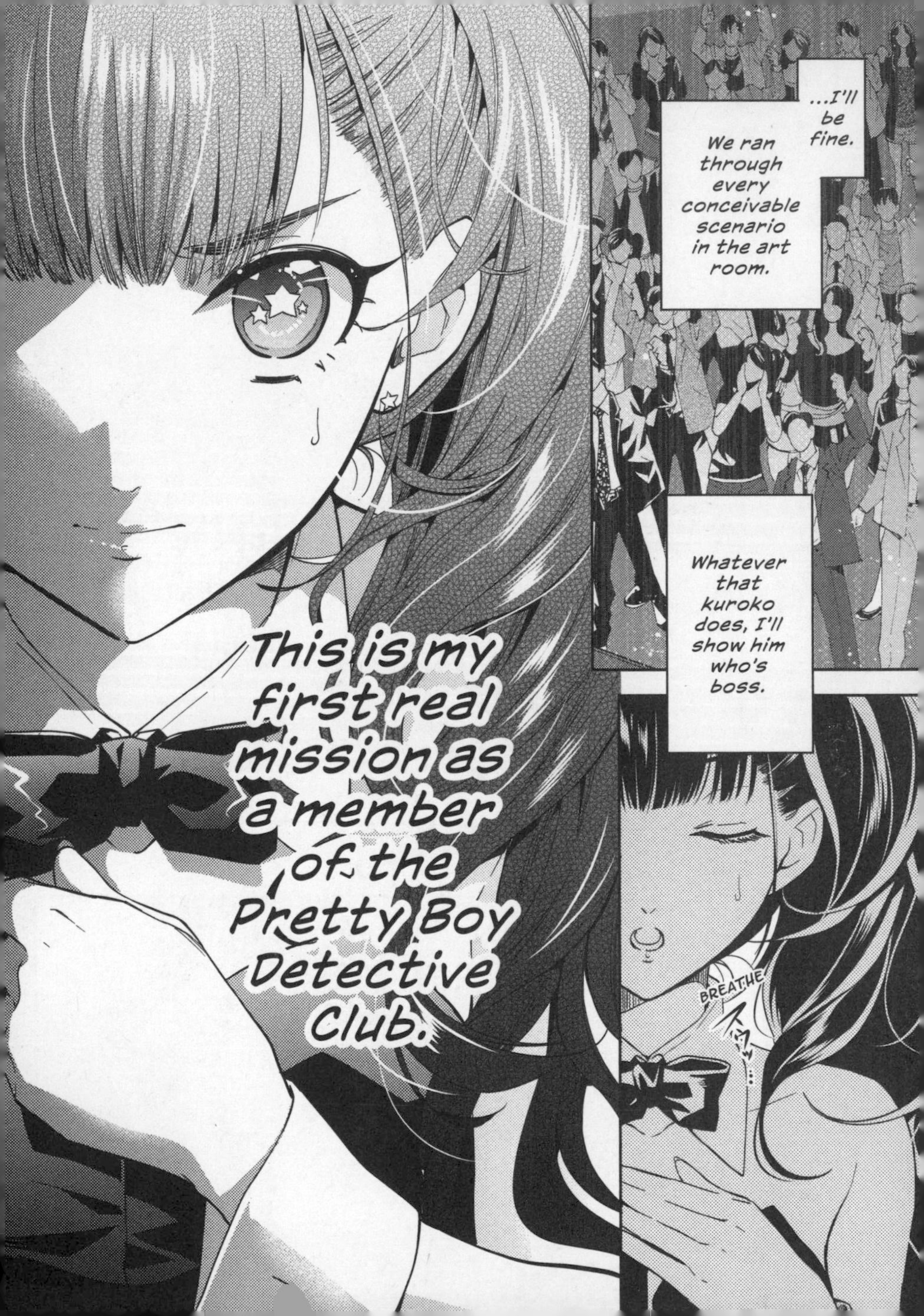
...I'll be fine.
We ran through every conceivable scenario in the art room.
Whatever that kuroko does, I'll show him who's boss.
BREATHE
This is my first real mission as a member of the Pretty Boy Detective Club.

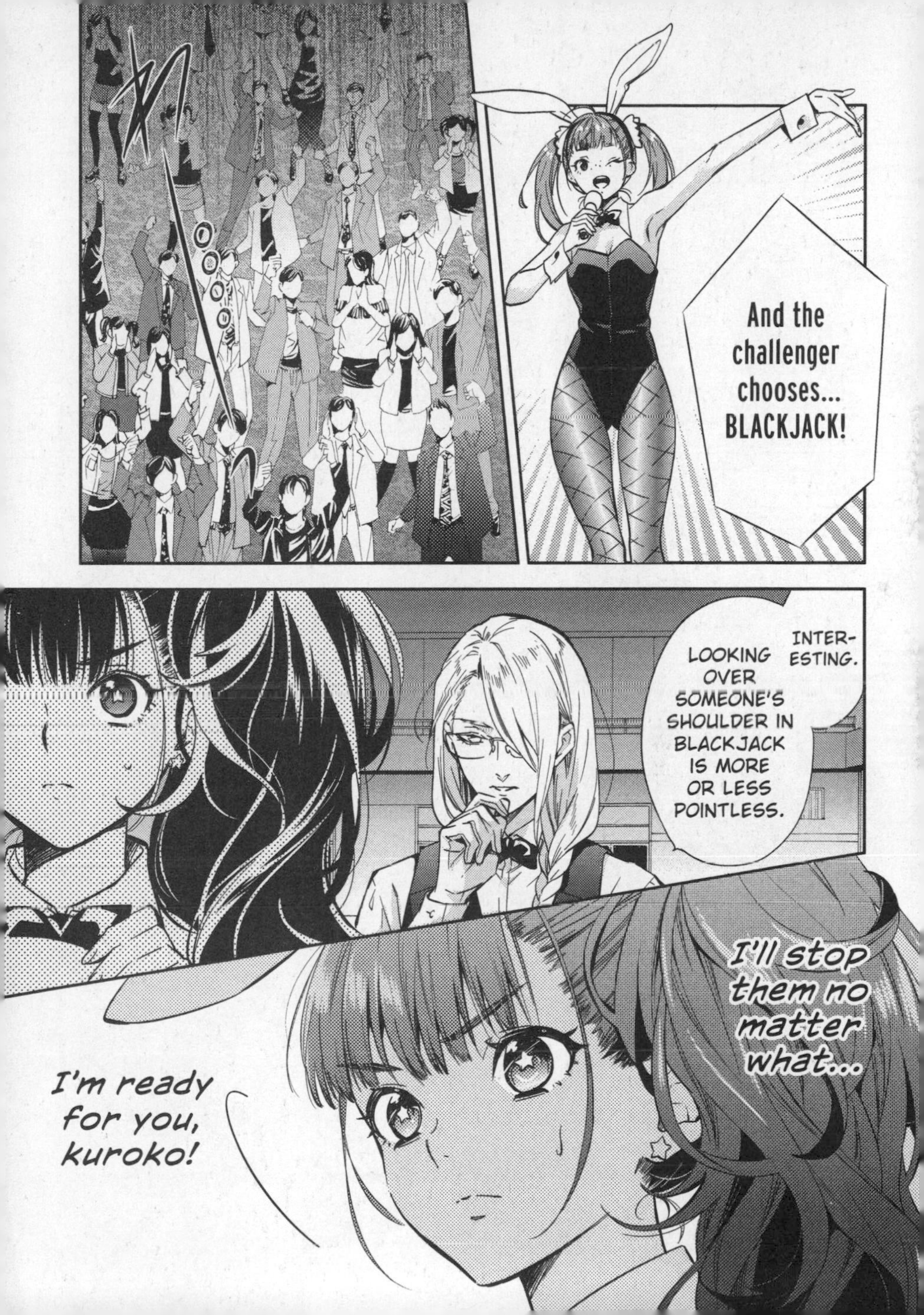
And the challenger chooses... BLACKJACK!
INTER-ESTING. LOOKING OVER SOMEONE'S SHOULDER IN BLACKJACK IS MORE OR LESS POINTLESS.
I'll stop them no matter what...
I'm ready for you, kuroko!

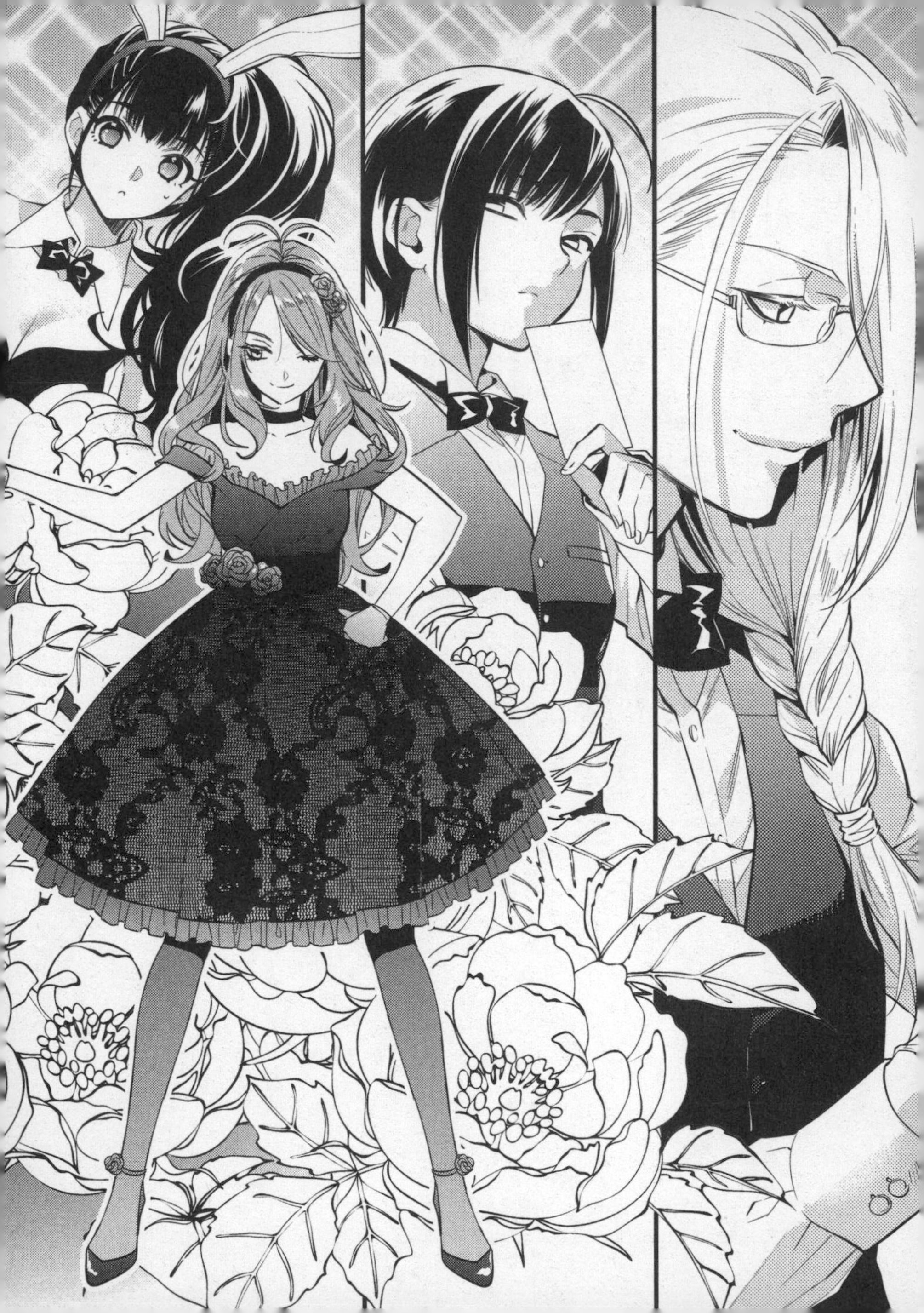

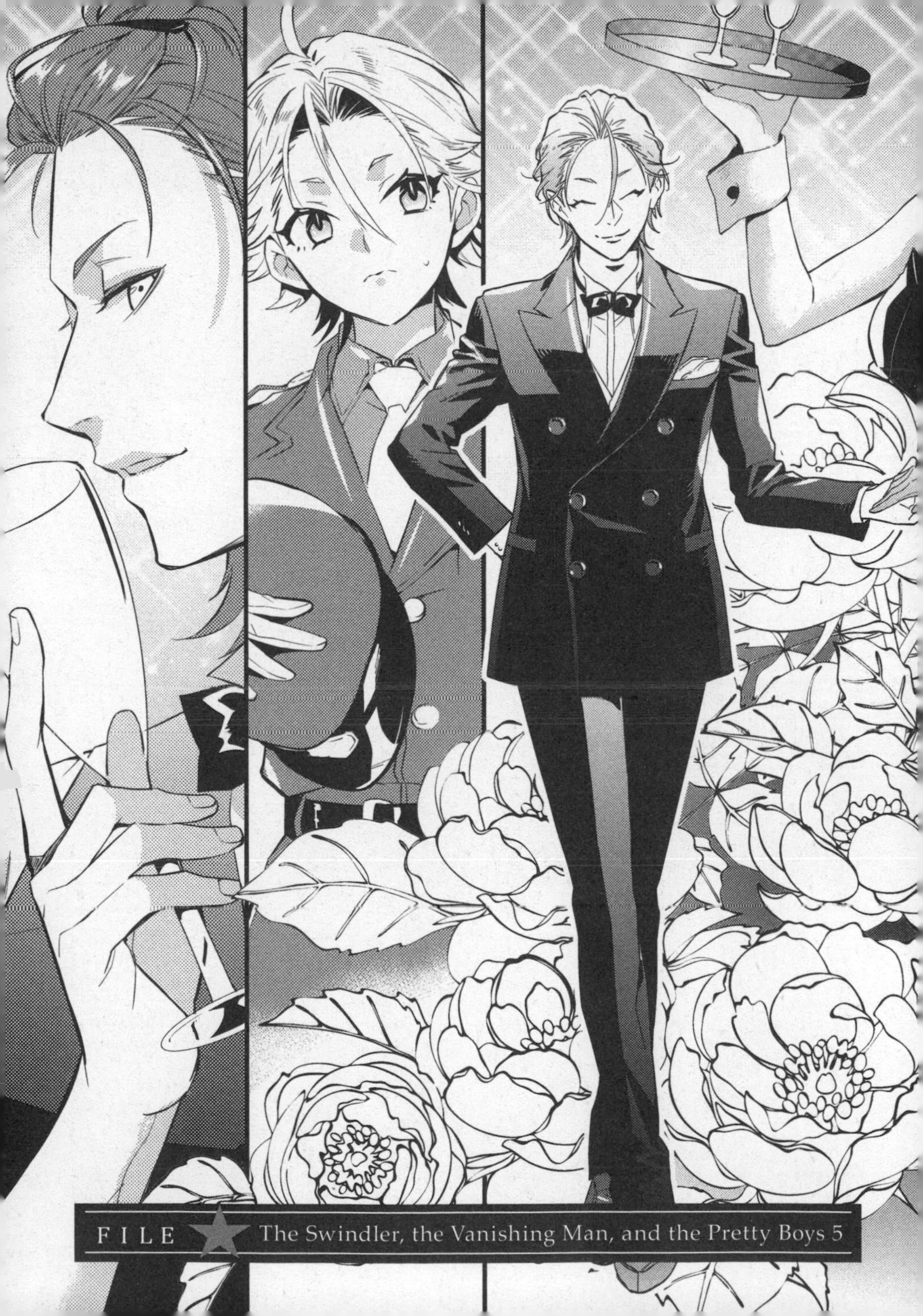

FILE ★ The Swindler, the Vanishing Man, and the Pretty Boys 5

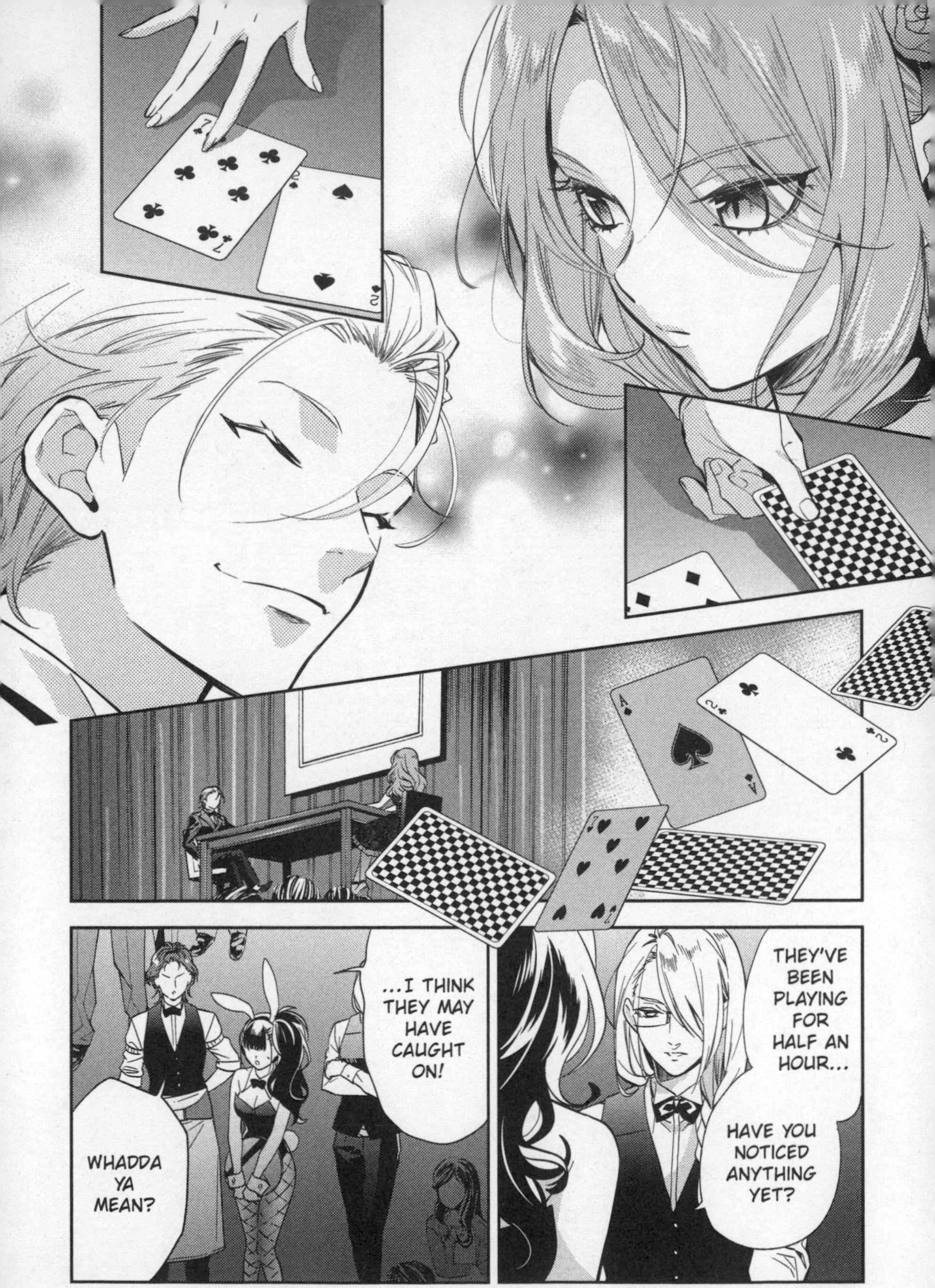
THEY'VE BEEN PLAYING FOR HALF AN HOUR...
HAVE YOU NOTICED ANYTHING YET?
...I THINK THEY MAY HAVE CAUGHT ON!
WHADDA YA MEAN?

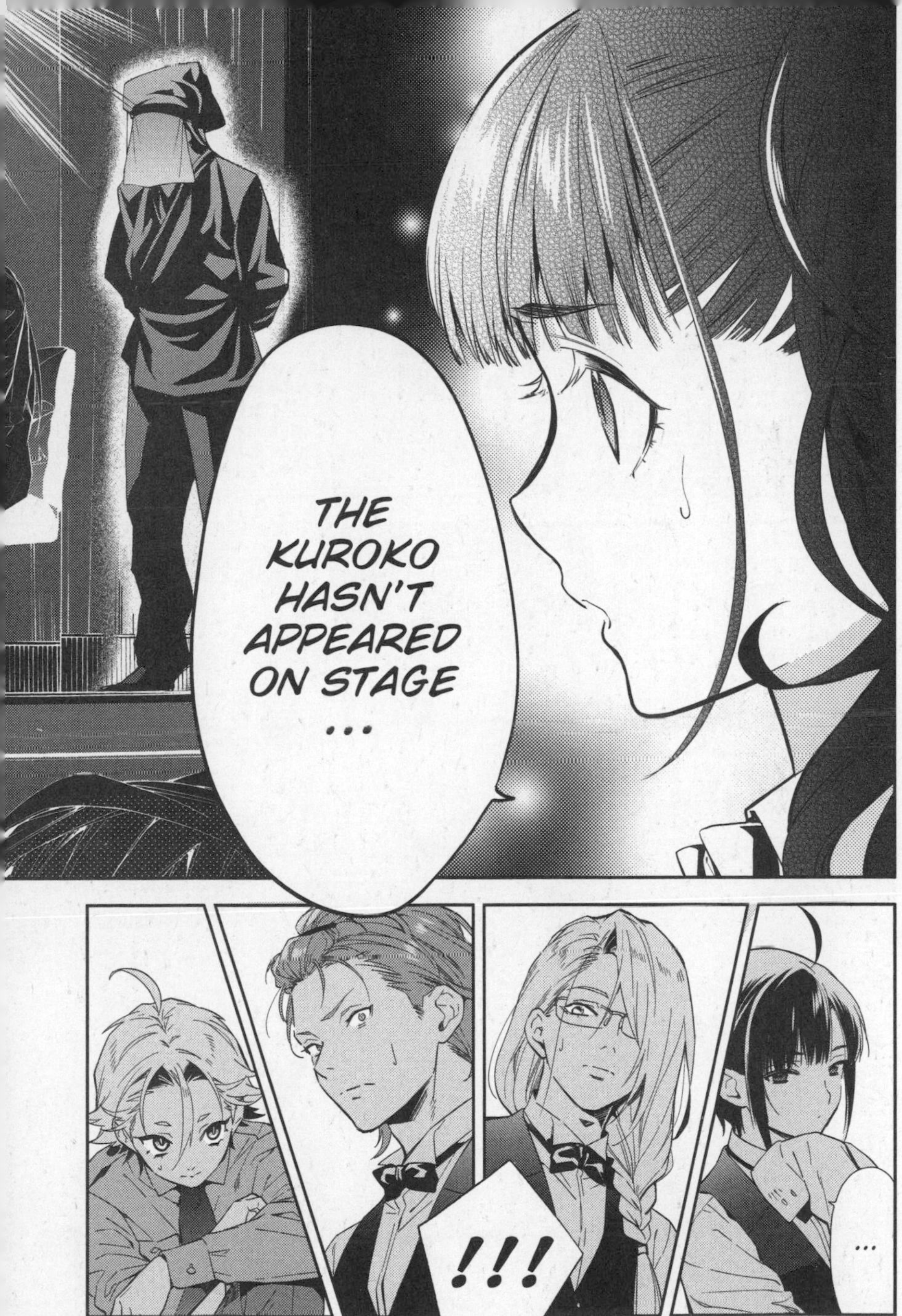
THE KUROKO HASN'T APPEARED ON STAGE ...
...
!!!

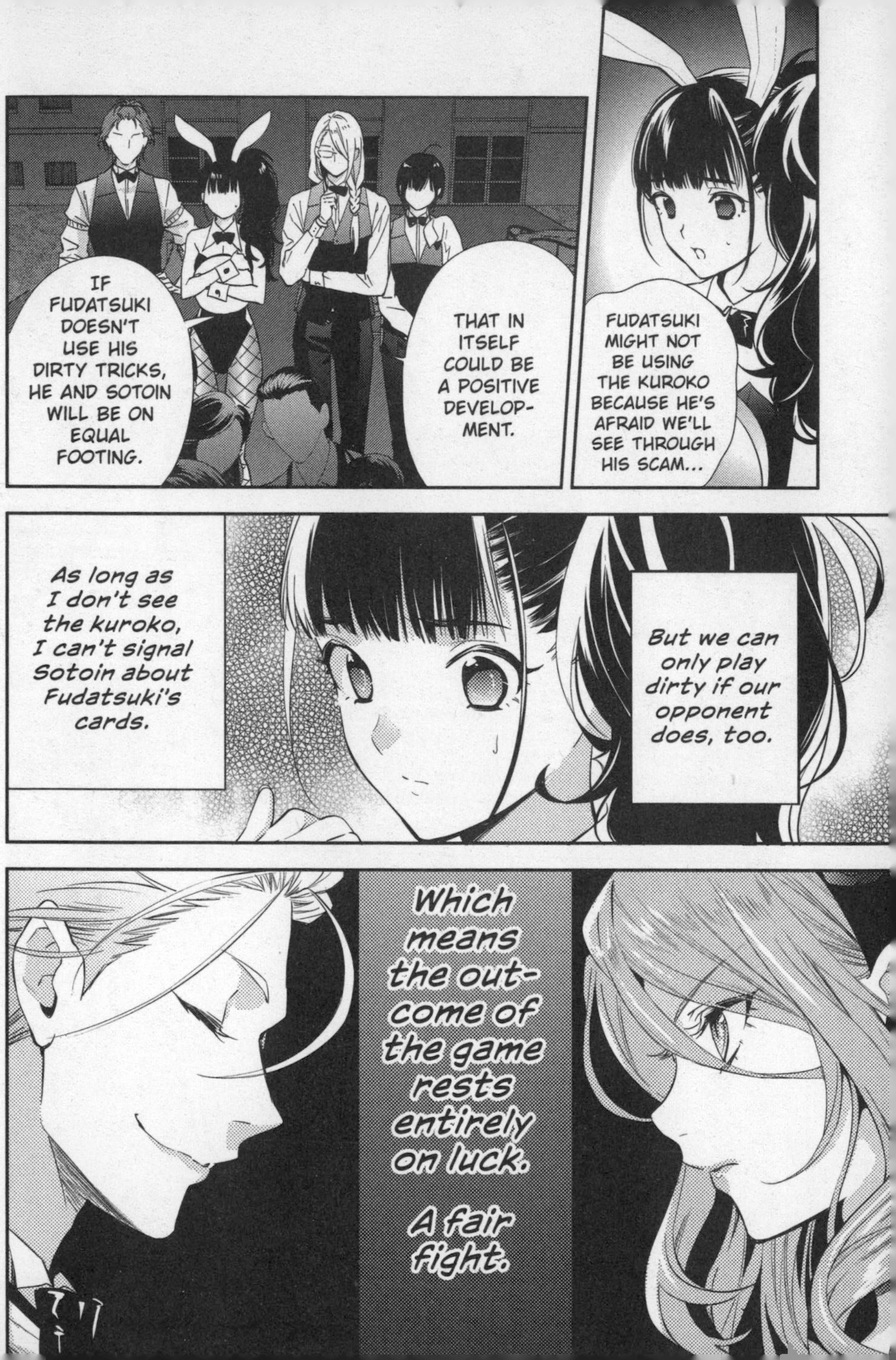
FUDATSUKI MIGHT NOT BE USING THE KUROKO BECAUSE HE'S AFRAID WE'LL SEE THROUGH HIS SCAM...
THAT IN ITSELF COULD BE A POSITIVE DEVELOP-MENT.
IF FUDATSUKI DOESN'T USE HIS DIRTY TRICKS, HE AND SOTOIN WILL BE ON EQUAL FOOTING.
As long as I don't see the kuroko, I can't signal Sotoin about Fudatsuki's cards.
But we can only play dirty if our opponent does, too.
Which means the out-come of the game rests entirely on luck.
A fair fight.

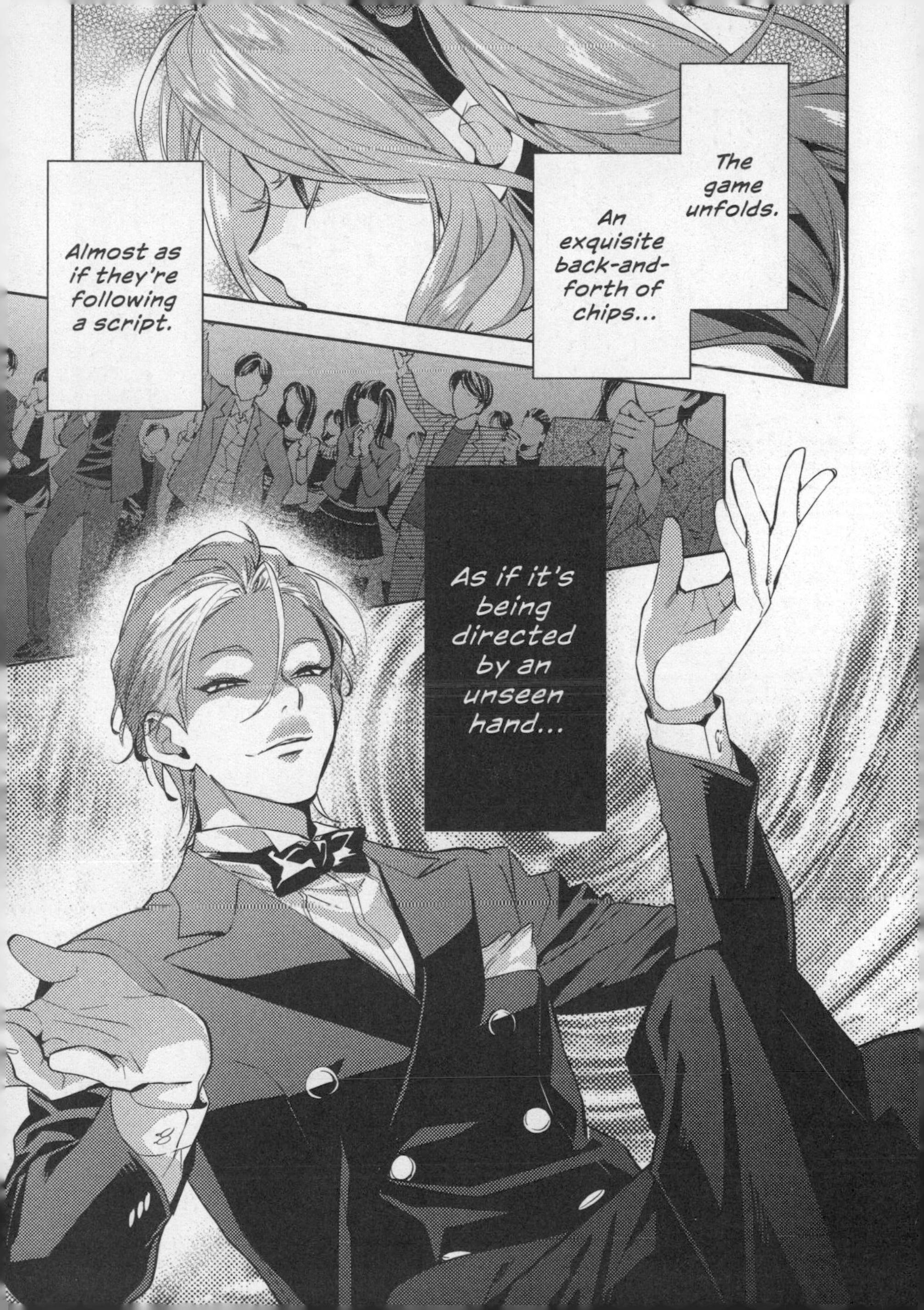
The game unfolds.
An exquisite back-and-forth of chips...
Almost as if they're following a script.
As if it's being directed by an unseen hand...

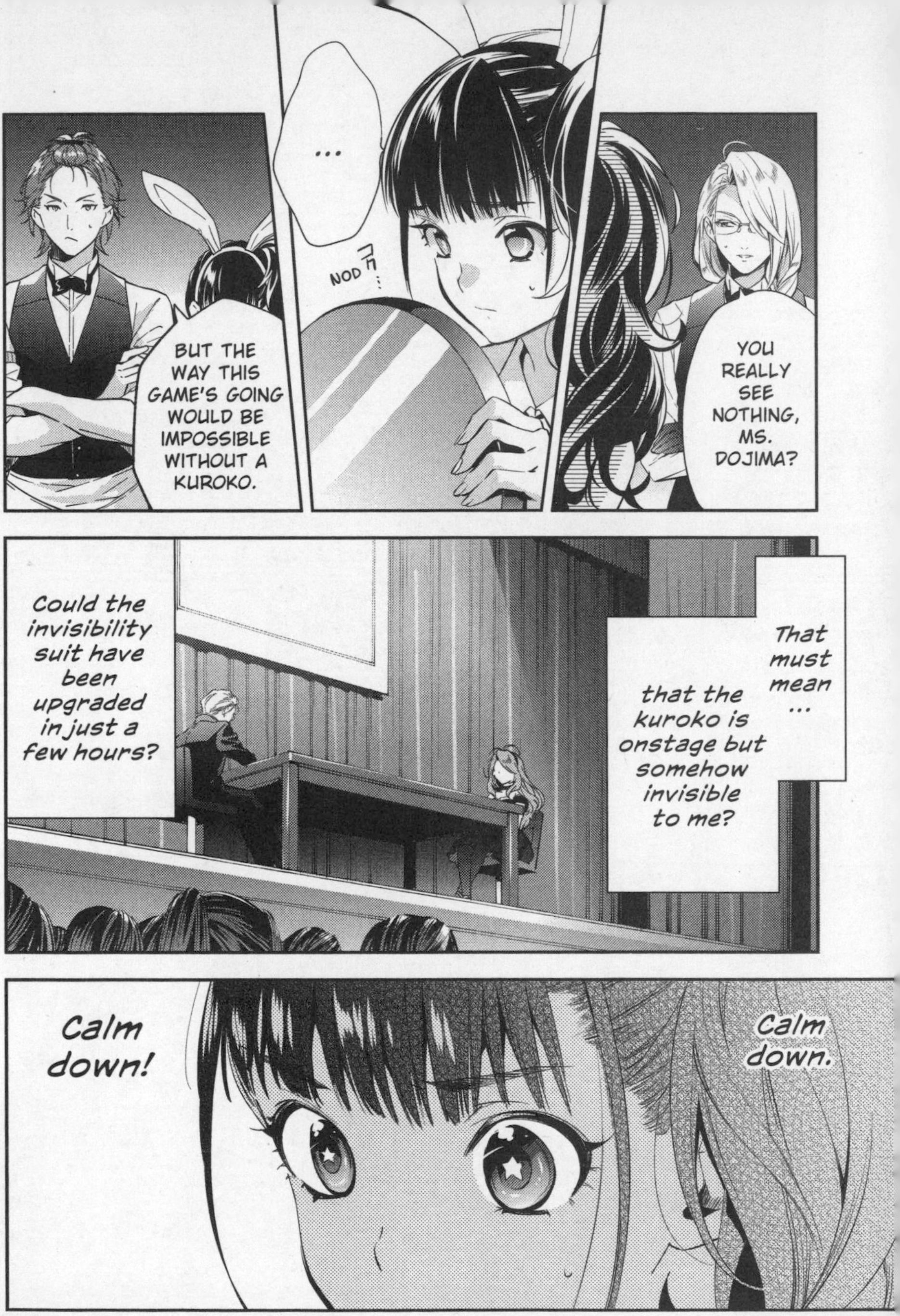
YOU REALLY SEE NOTHING, MS. DOJIMA?
...
NOD
BUT THE WAY THIS GAME'S GOING WOULD BE IMPOSSIBLE WITHOUT A KUROKO.
That must mean ...
that the kuroko is onstage but somehow invisible to me?
Could the invisibility suit have been upgraded in just a few hours?
Calm down.
Calm down!

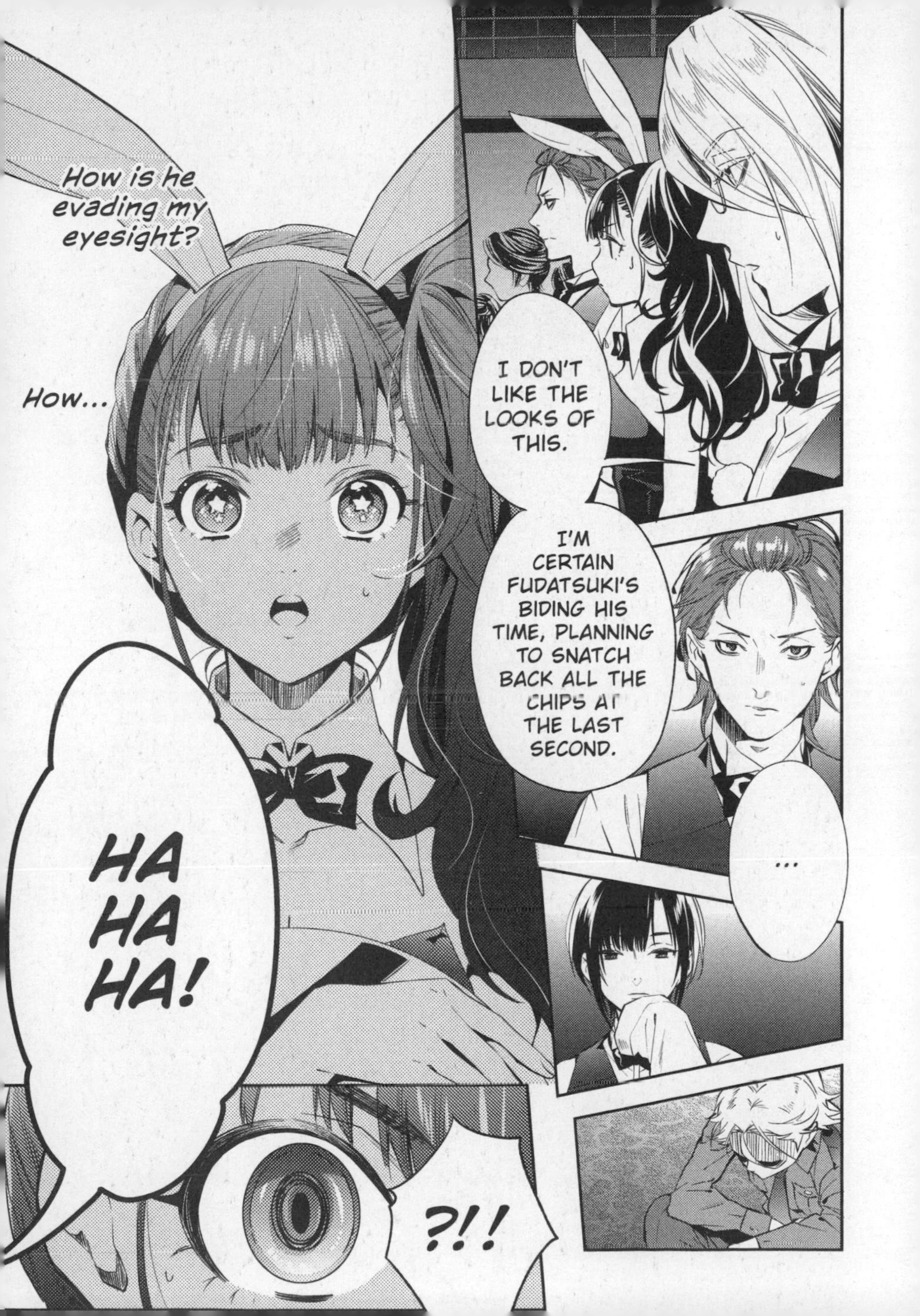
I DON'T LIKE THE LOOKS OF THIS.
I'M CERTAIN FUDATSUKI'S BIDING HIS TIME, PLANNING TO SNATCH BACK ALL THE CHIPS AT THE LAST SECOND.
...
How is he evading my eyesight?
How...
HA HA HA!
?!!

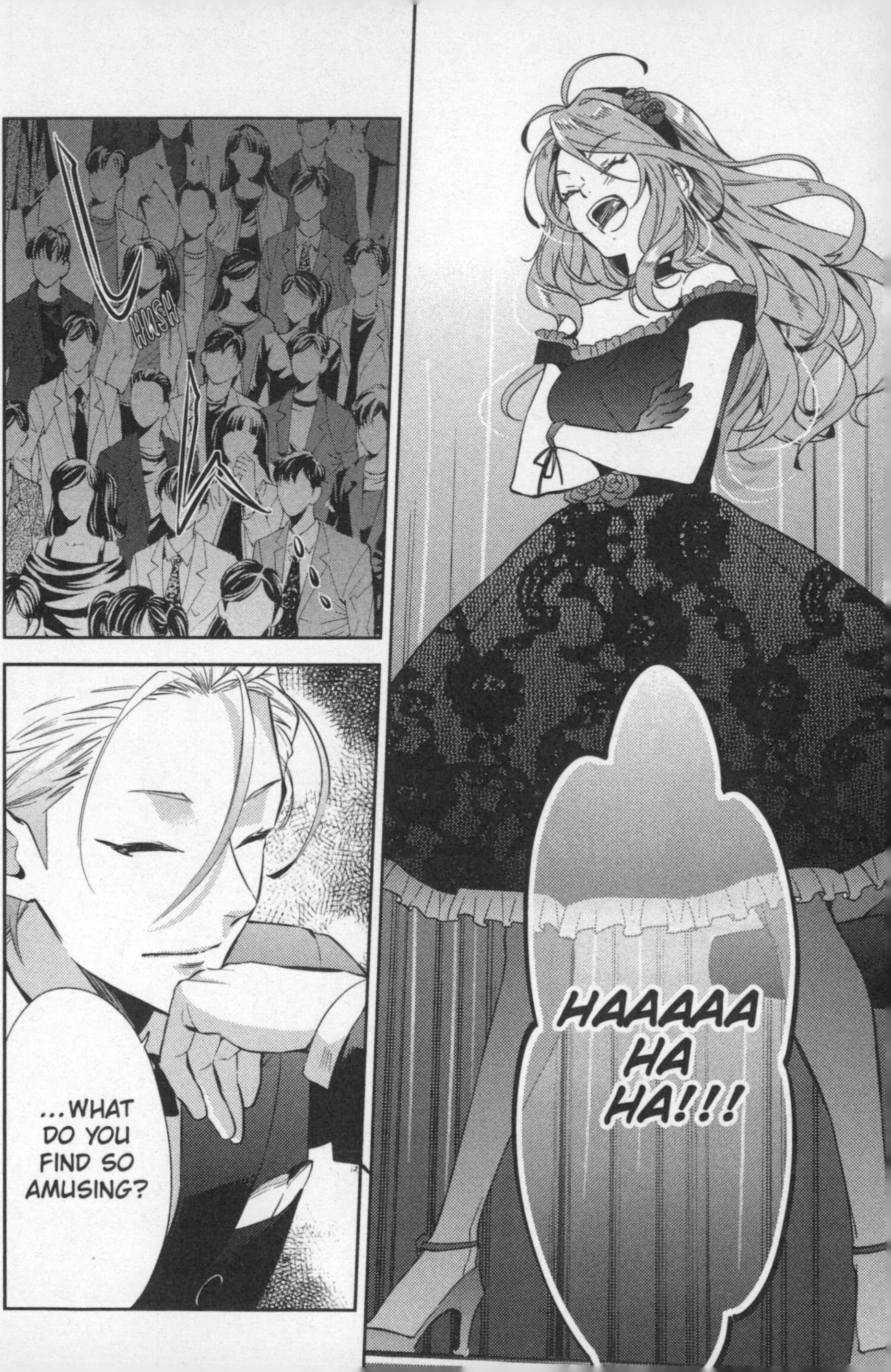
HAAAAA HA HA!!!
HUSH
...WHAT DO YOU FIND SO AMUSING?

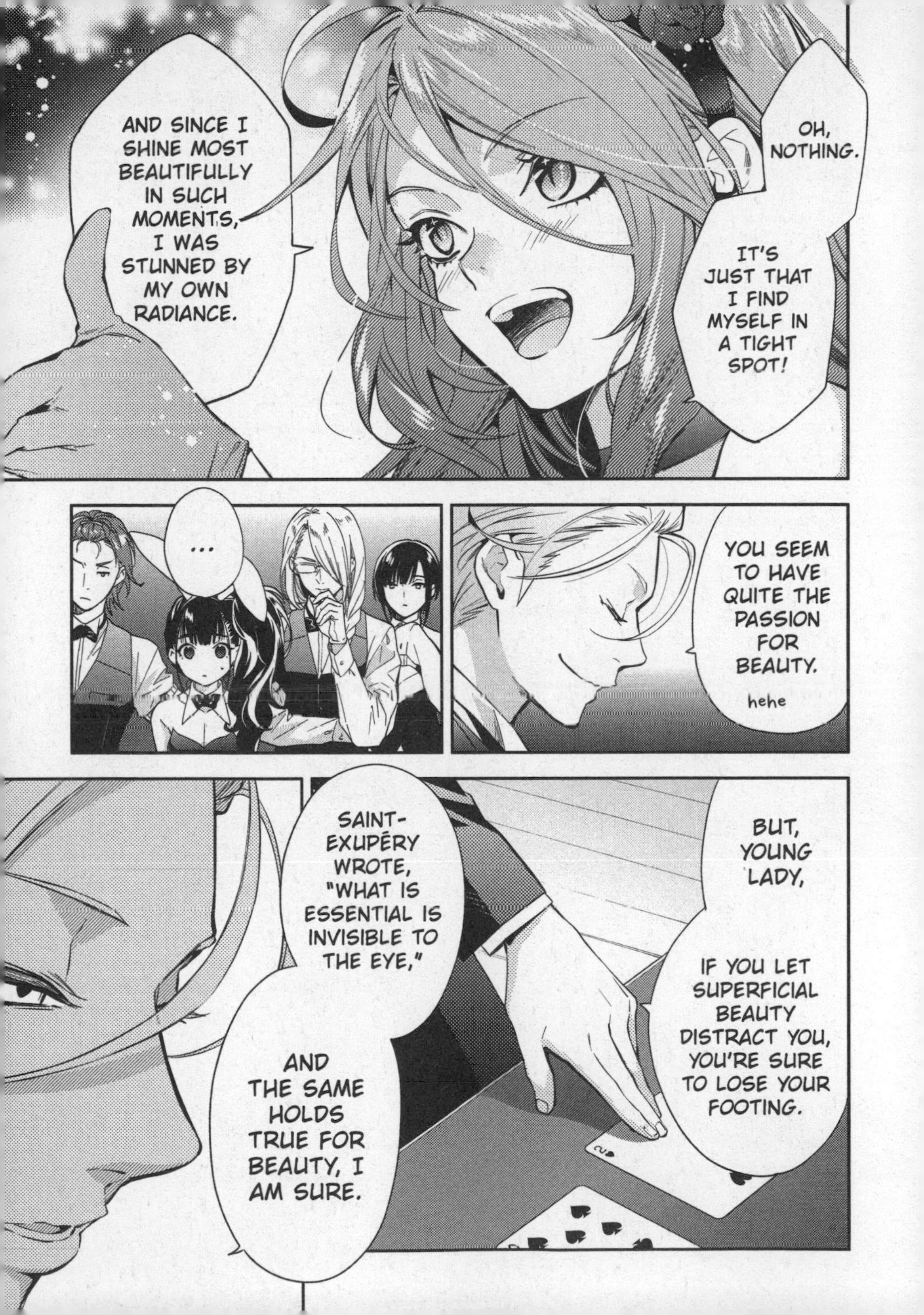
OH, NOTHING.
IT'S JUST THAT I FIND MYSELF IN A TIGHT SPOT!
AND SINCE I SHINE MOST BEAUTIFULLY IN SUCH MOMENTS, I WAS STUNNED BY MY OWN RADIANCE.
YOU SEEM TO HAVE QUITE THE PASSION FOR BEAUTY.
hehe
...
BUT, YOUNG LADY,
IF YOU LET SUPERFICIAL BEAUTY DISTRACT YOU, YOU'RE SURE TO LOSE YOUR FOOTING.
SAINT-EXUPÉRY WROTE, "WHAT IS ESSENTIAL IS INVISIBLE TO THE EYE,"
AND THE SAME HOLDS TRUE FOR BEAUTY, I AM SURE.

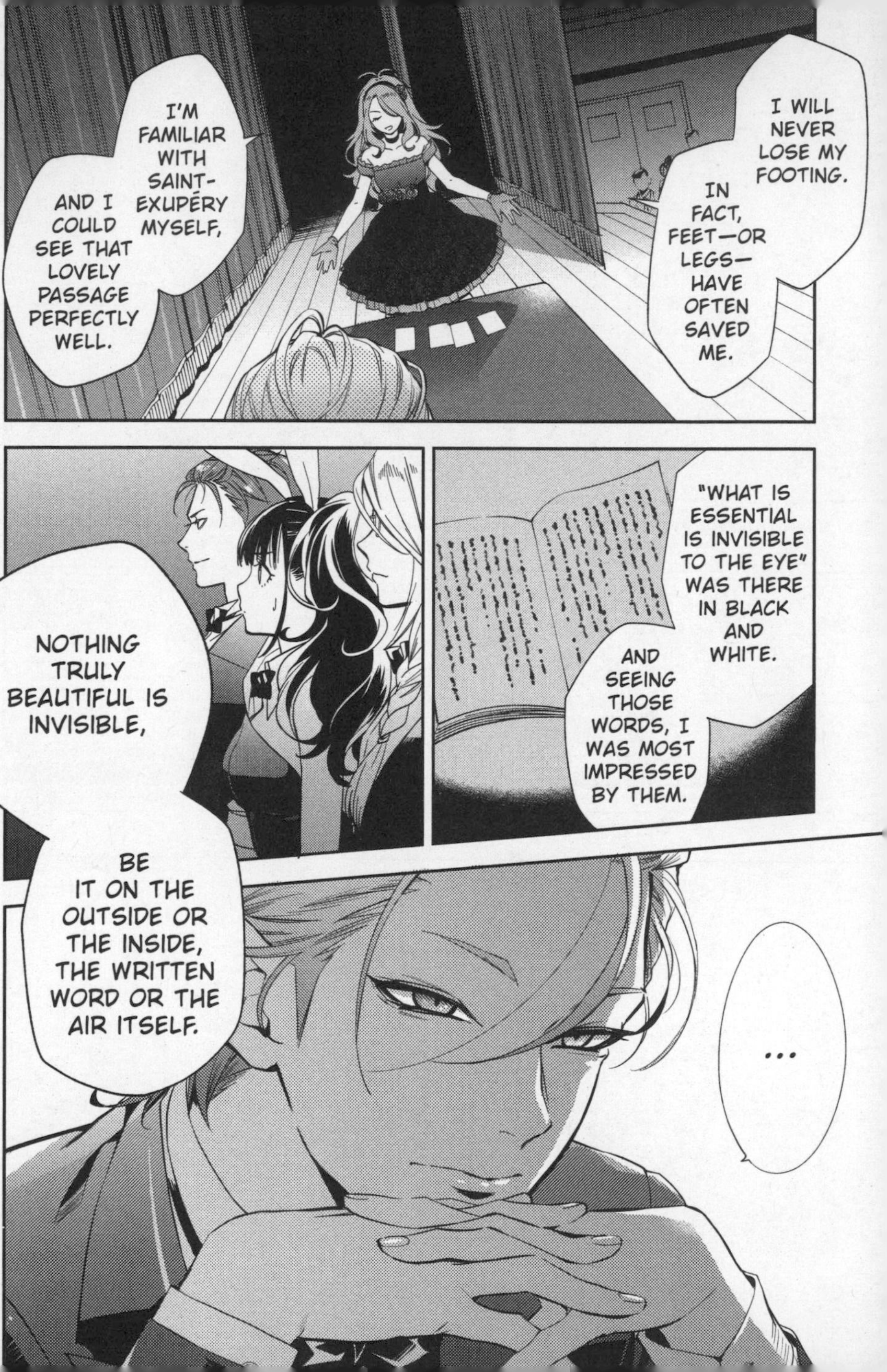
I WILL NEVER LOSE MY FOOTING.
IN FACT, FEET—OR LEGS—HAVE OFTEN SAVED ME.
I'M FAMILIAR WITH SAINT-EXUPÉRY MYSELF,
AND I COULD SEE THAT LOVELY PASSAGE PERFECTLY WELL.
"WHAT IS ESSENTIAL IS INVISIBLE TO THE EYE" WAS THERE IN BLACK AND WHITE.
AND SEEING THOSE WORDS, I WAS MOST IMPRESSED BY THEM.
NOTHING TRULY BEAUTIFUL IS INVISIBLE,
BE IT ON THE OUTSIDE OR THE INSIDE, THE WRITTEN WORD OR THE AIR ITSELF.
...

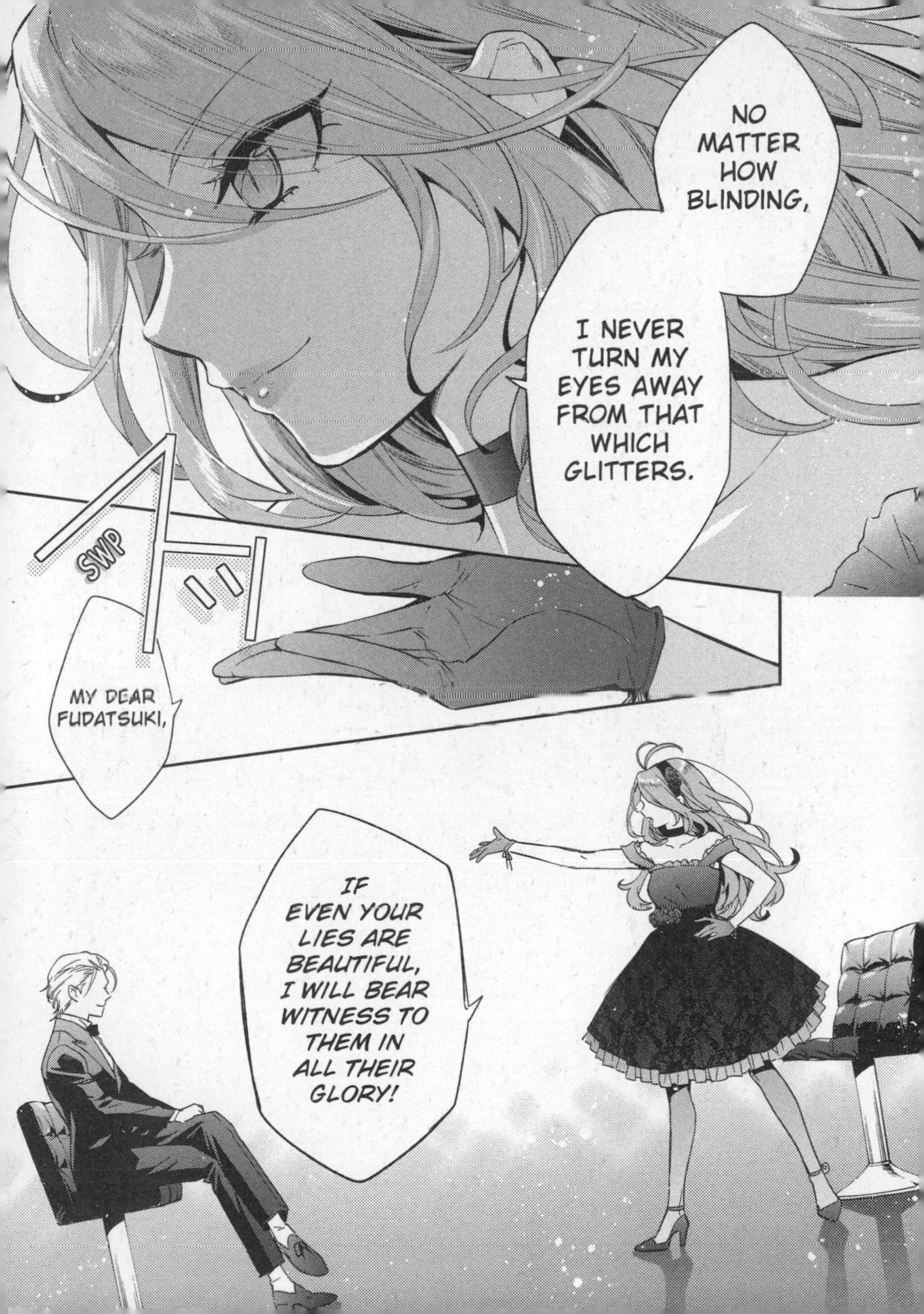
NO MATTER HOW BLINDING,
I NEVER TURN MY EYES AWAY FROM THAT WHICH GLITTERS.
SWP
MY DEAR FUDATSUKI,
IF EVEN YOUR LIES ARE BEAUTIFUL, I WILL BEAR WITNESS TO THEM IN ALL THEIR GLORY!

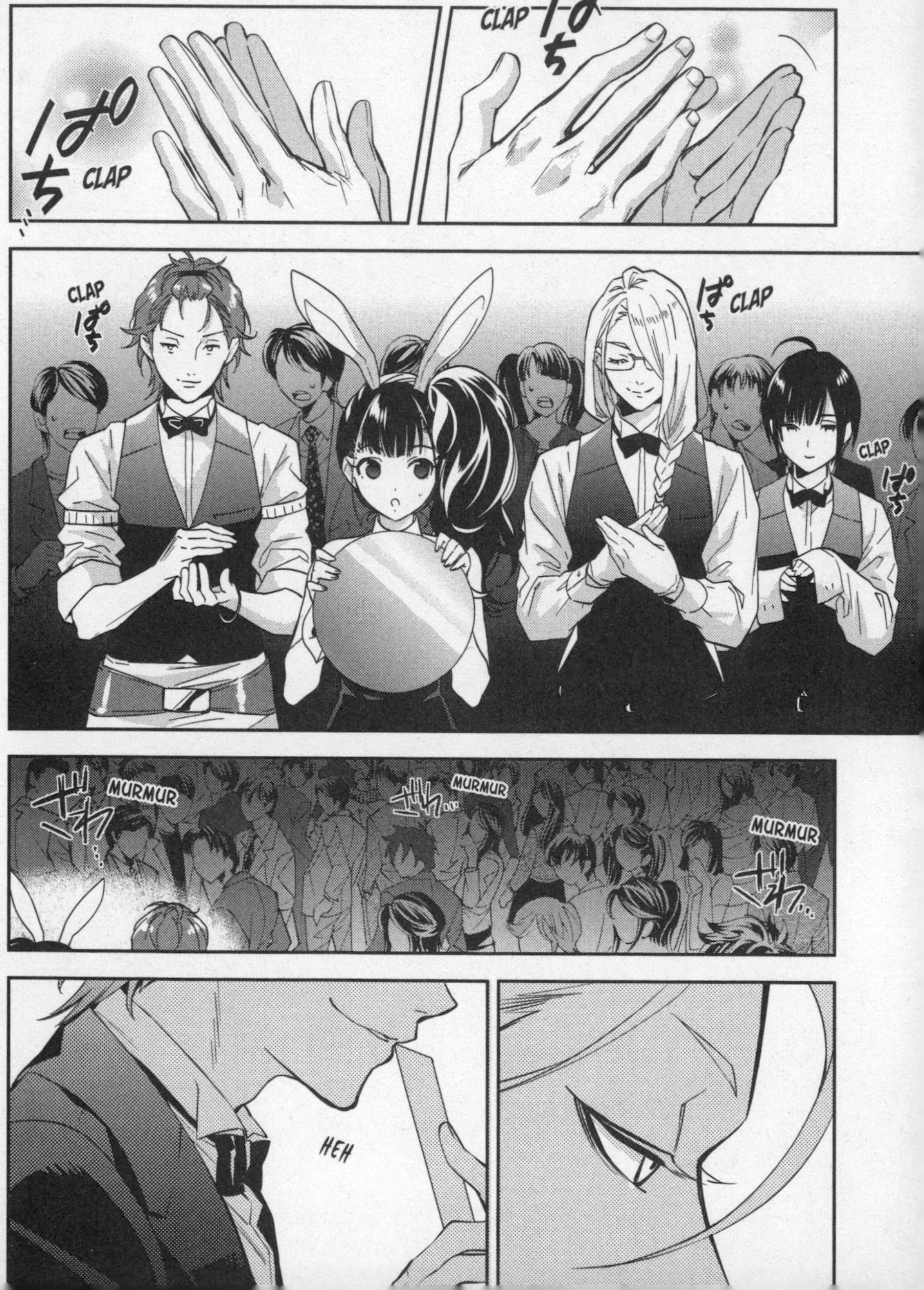
CLAP
ぱち
ぱち
CLAP
CLAP
ぱち
ぱち
CLAP
CLAP
ぱち
MURMUR
ざわ…
ざわ…
MURMUR
ざわ…
MURMUR
HEH

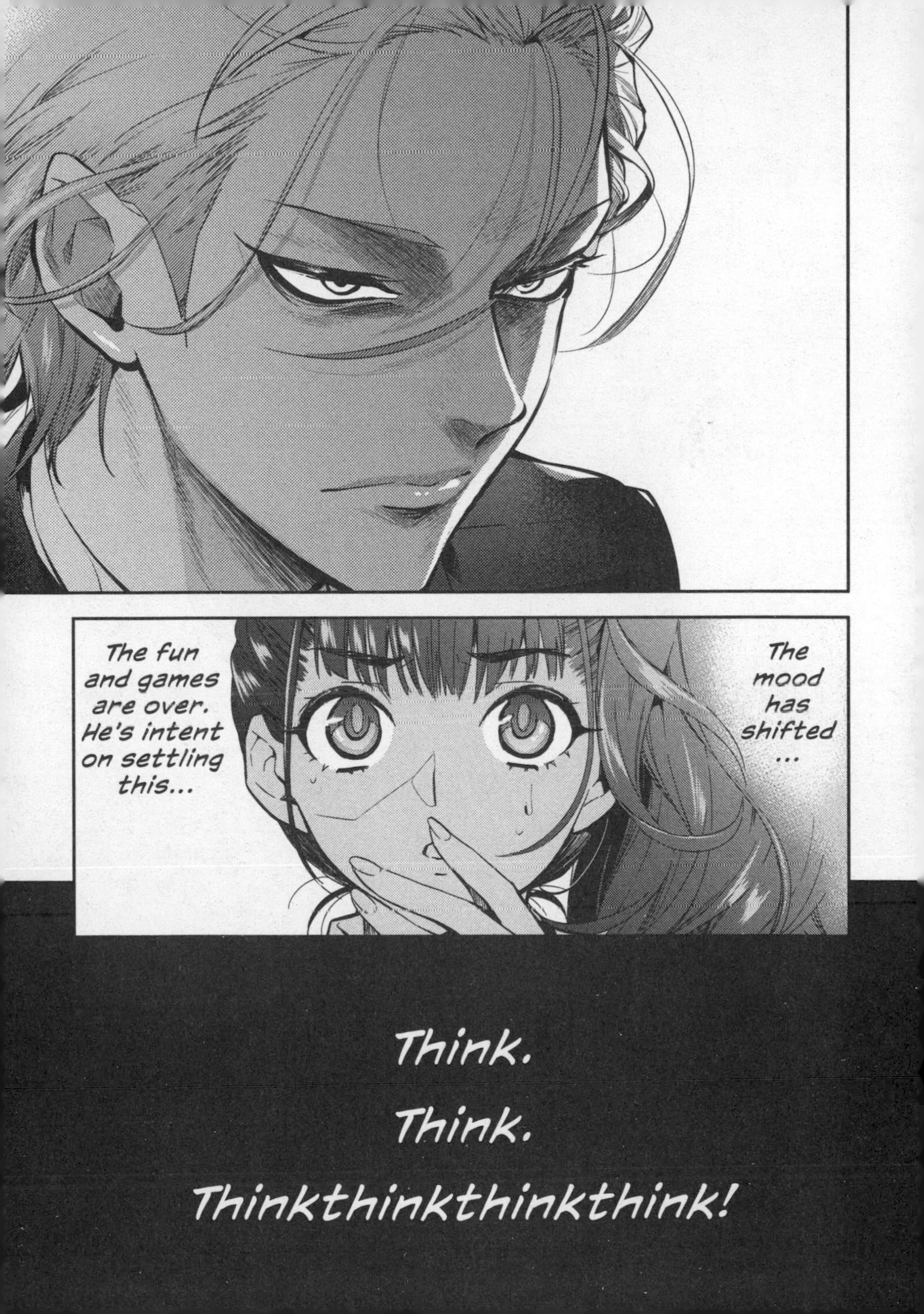
The mood has shifted ...
The fun and games are over. He's intent on settling this...
Think.
Think.
Thinkthinkthinkthink!

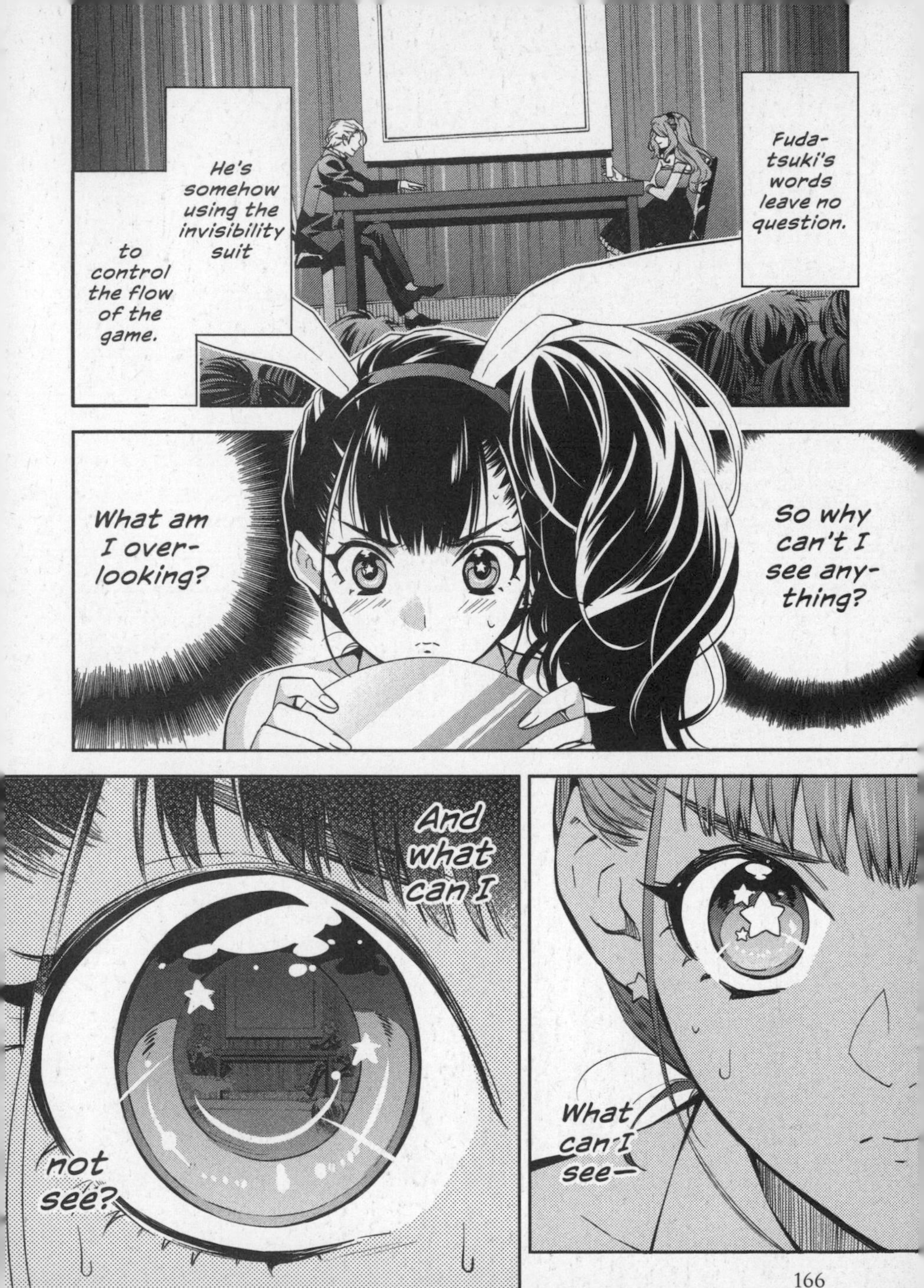
Fuda-tsuki's words leave no question.
He's somehow using the invisibility suit to control the flow of the game.
So why can't I see anything?
What am I overlooking?
What can I see—
And what can I not see?

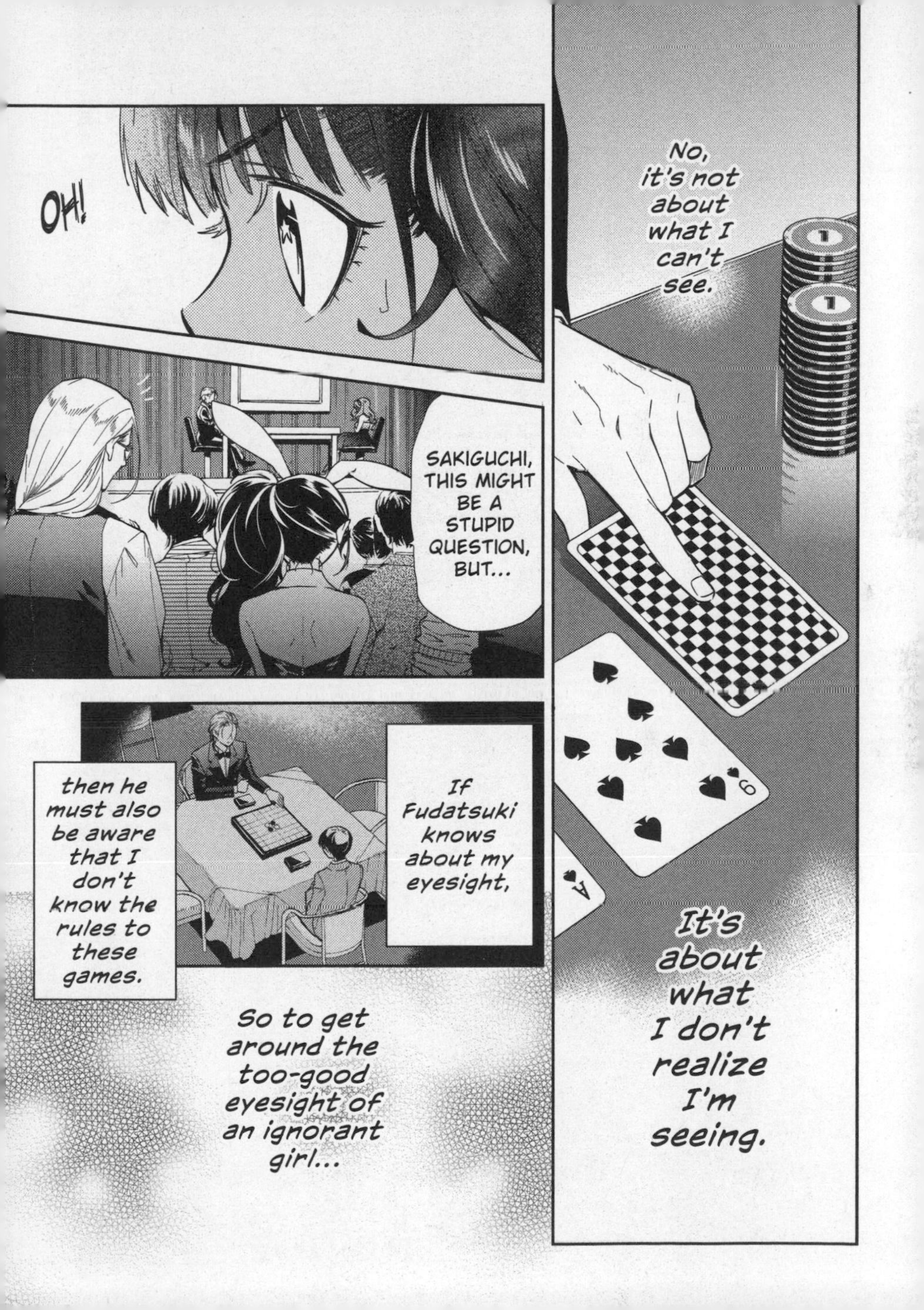
No, it's not about what I can't see.
It's about what I don't realize I'm seeing.
OH!
SAKIGUCHI, THIS MIGHT BE A STUPID QUESTION, BUT...
If Fudatsuki knows about my eyesight,
then he must also be aware that I don't know the rules to these games.
So to get around the too-good eyesight of an ignorant girl...

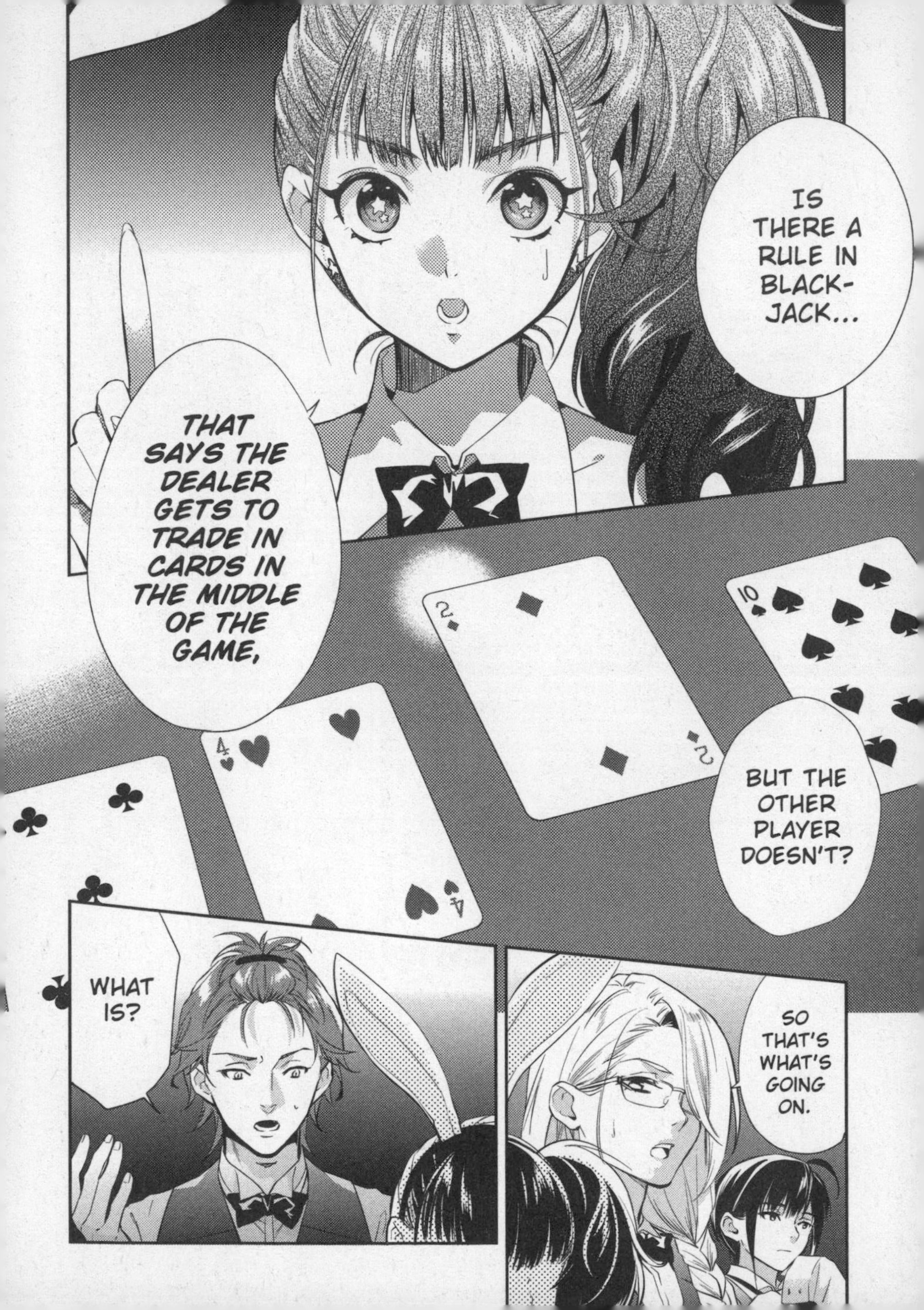
IS THERE A RULE IN BLACK-JACK...
THAT SAYS THE DEALER GETS TO TRADE IN CARDS IN THE MIDDLE OF THE GAME,
BUT THE OTHER PLAYER DOESN'T?
SO THAT'S WHAT'S GOING ON.
WHAT IS?

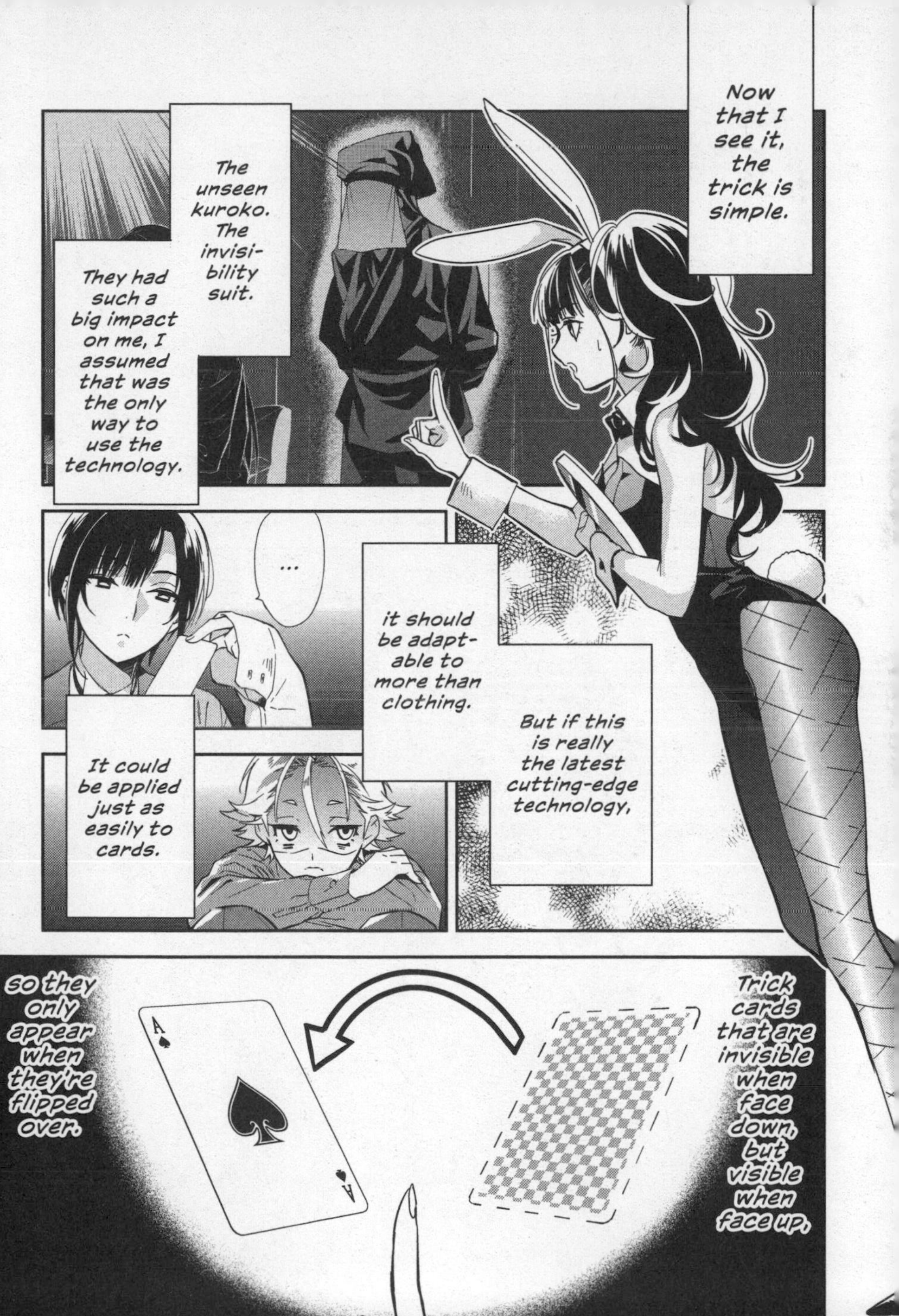

Now that I see it, the trick is simple.
The unseen kuroko. The invisibility suit.
They had such a big impact on me, I assumed that was the only way to use the technology.
But if this is really the latest cutting-edge technology,
it should be adaptable to more than clothing.
...
It could be applied just as easily to cards.
Trick cards that are invisible when face down, but visible when face up,
so they only appear when they're flipped over.

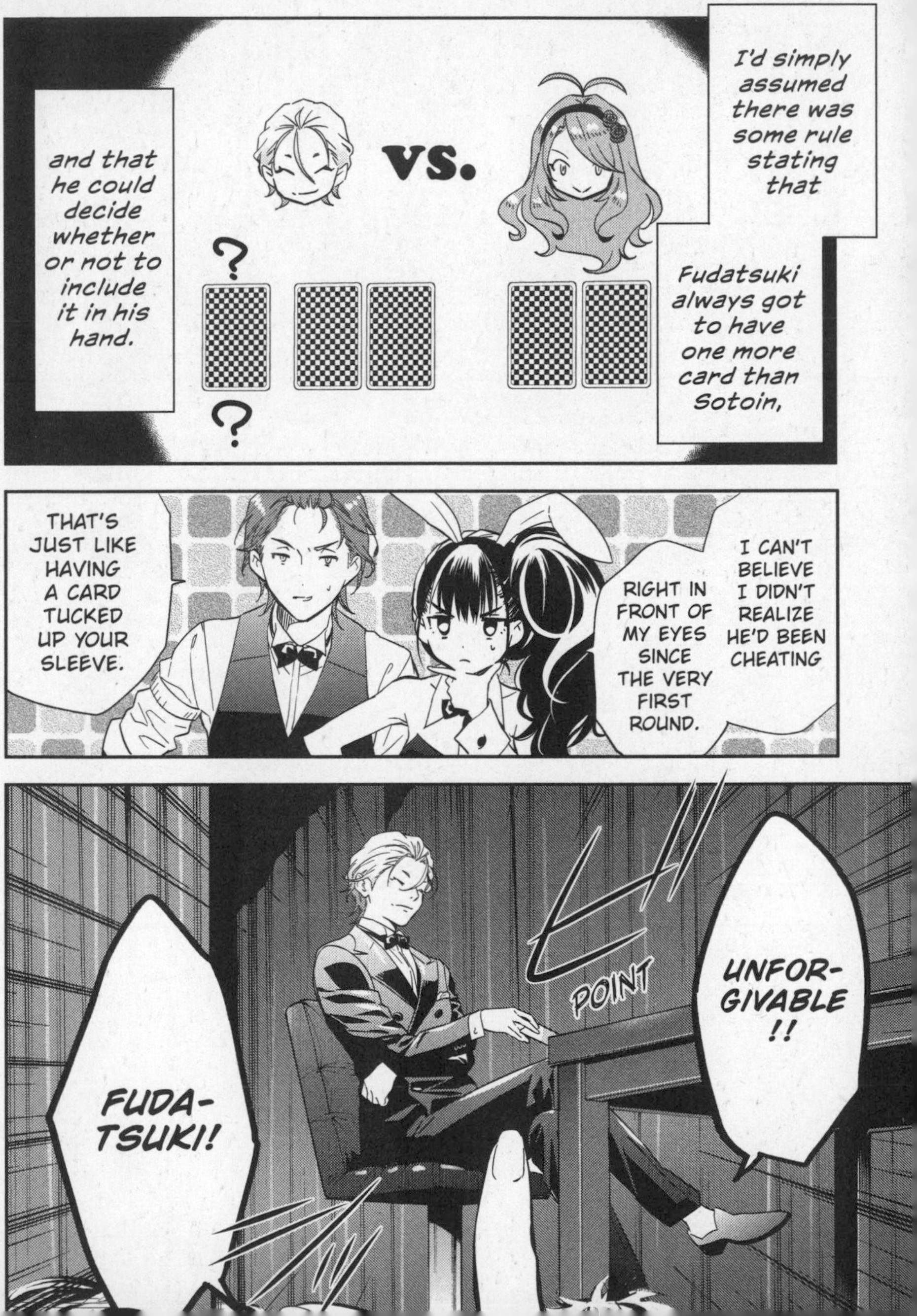
I'd simply assumed there was some rule stating that
Fudatsuki always got to have one more card than Sotoin,
and that he could decide whether or not to include it in his hand.
VS.
? ?
I CAN'T BELIEVE I DIDN'T REALIZE HE'D BEEN CHEATING
RIGHT IN FRONT OF MY EYES SINCE THE VERY FIRST ROUND.
THAT'S JUST LIKE HAVING A CARD TUCKED UP YOUR SLEEVE.
UNFORGIVABLE!!
POINT
FUDATSUKI!

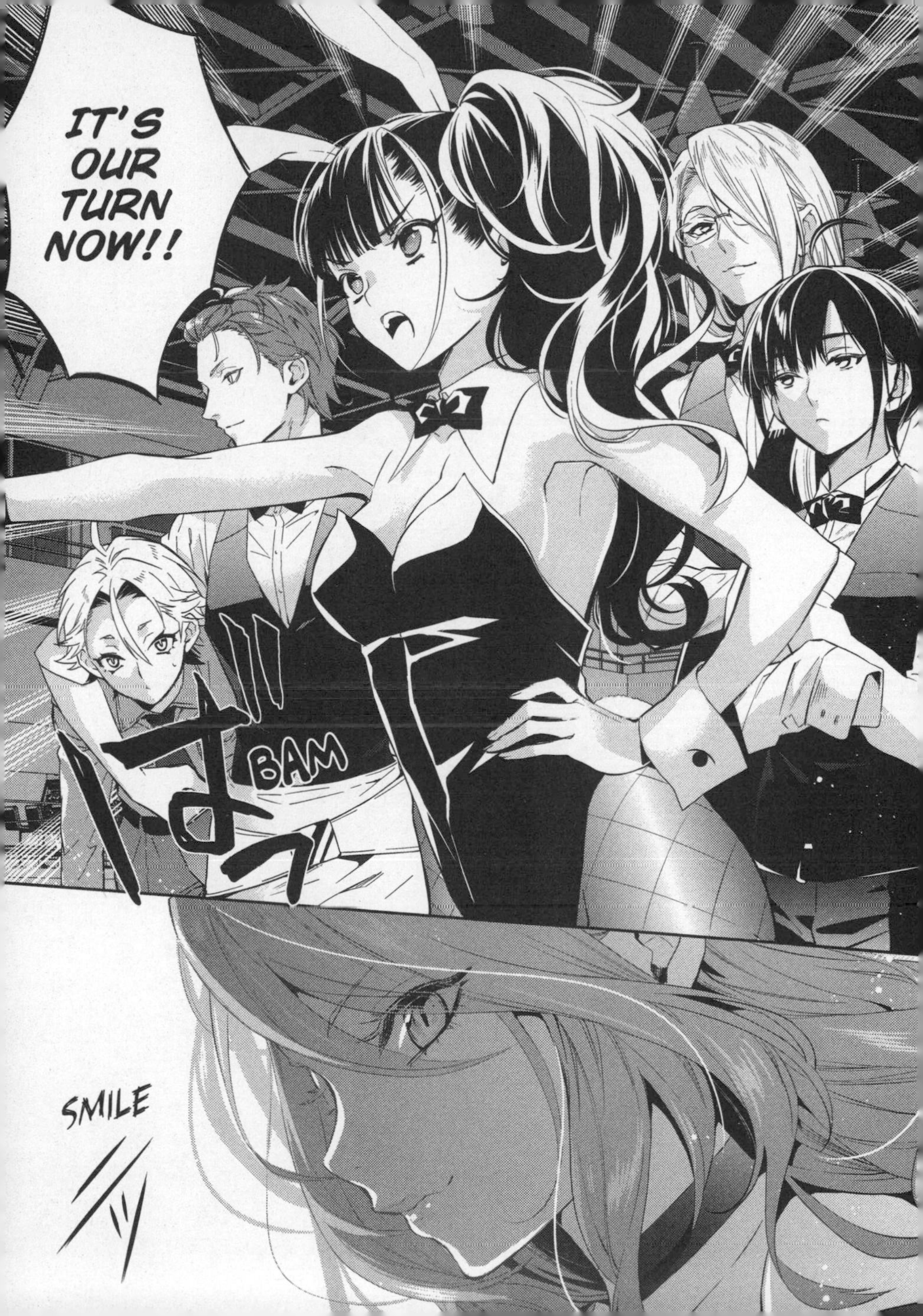
IT'S OUR TURN NOW!!
BAM
SMILE

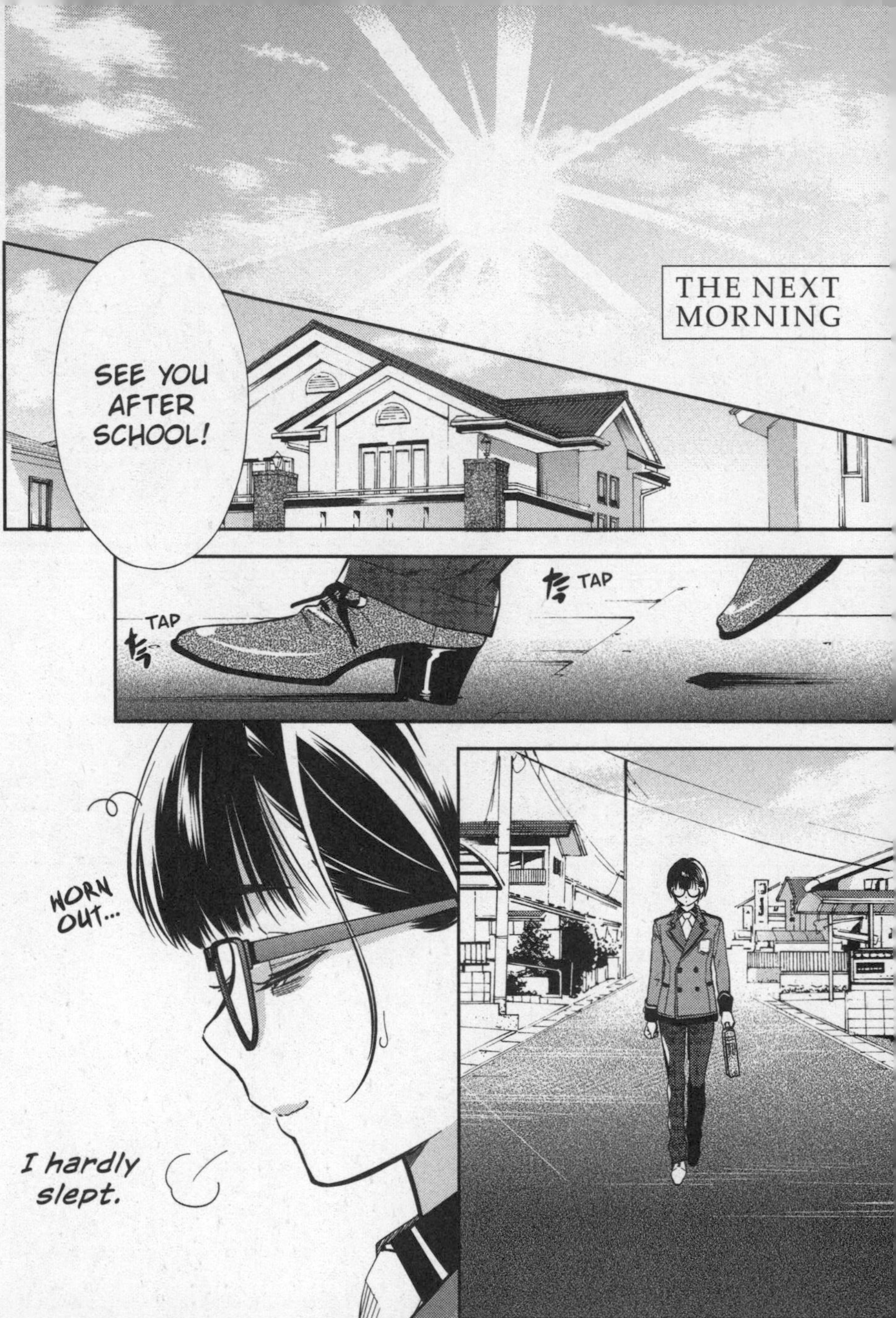
THE NEXT MORNING
SEE YOU AFTER SCHOOL!
TAP
TAP
WORN OUT...
I hardly slept.

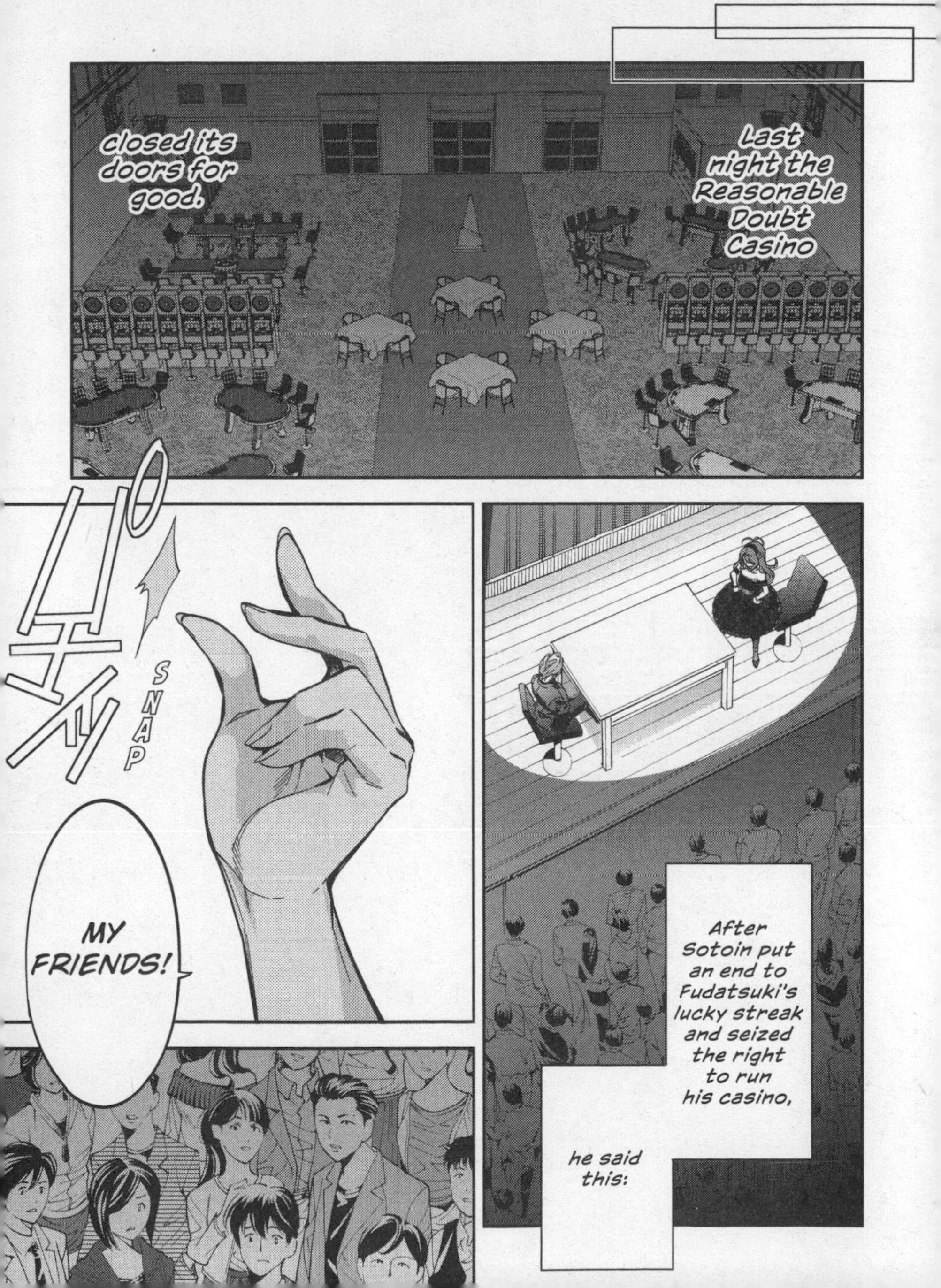

Last night the Reasonable Doubt Casino
closed its doors for good.
After Sotoin put an end to Fudatsuki's lucky streak and seized the right to run his casino,
he said this:
SNAP
MY FRIENDS!

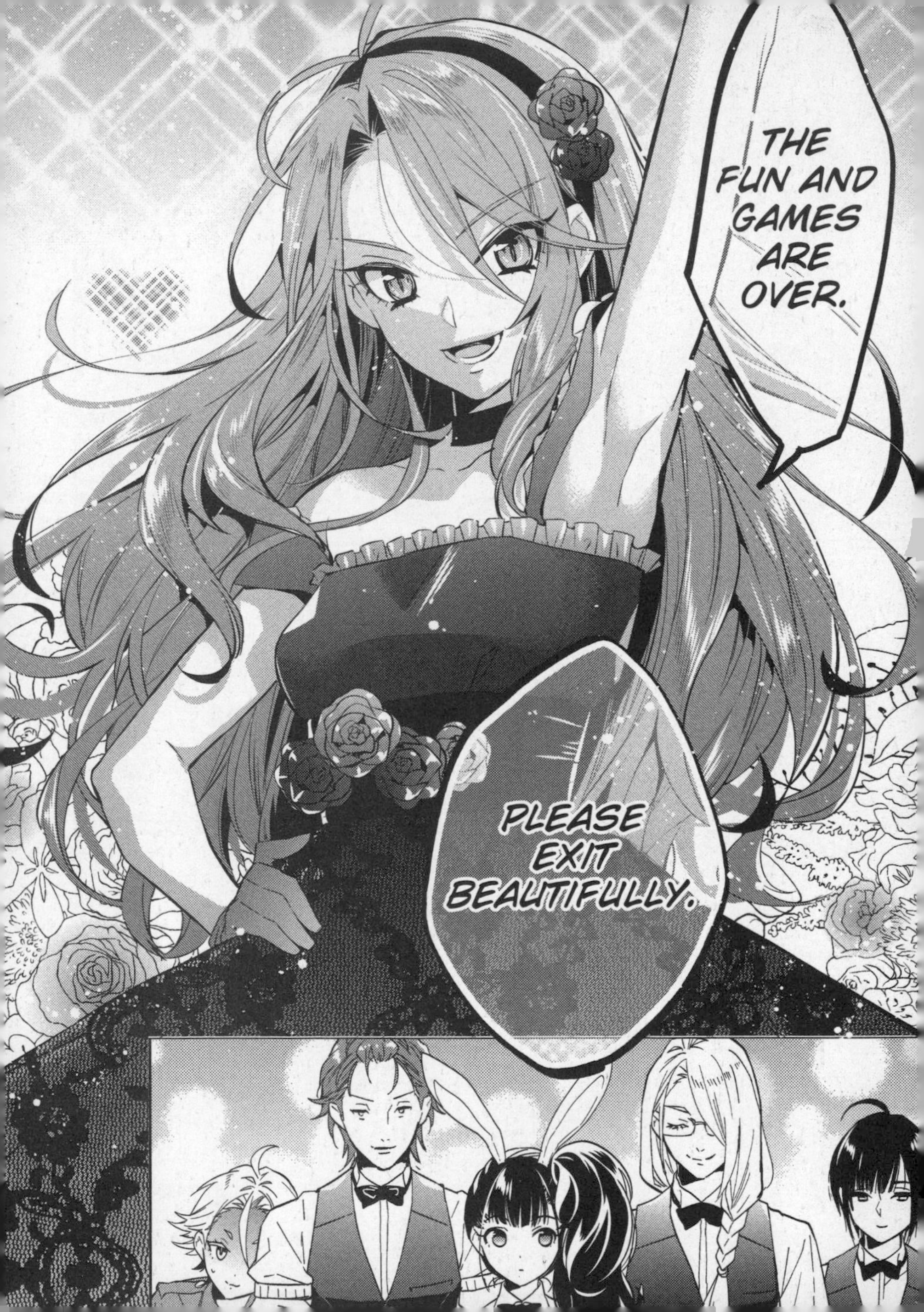
THE FUN AND GAMES ARE OVER.
PLEASE EXIT BEAUTIFULLY.

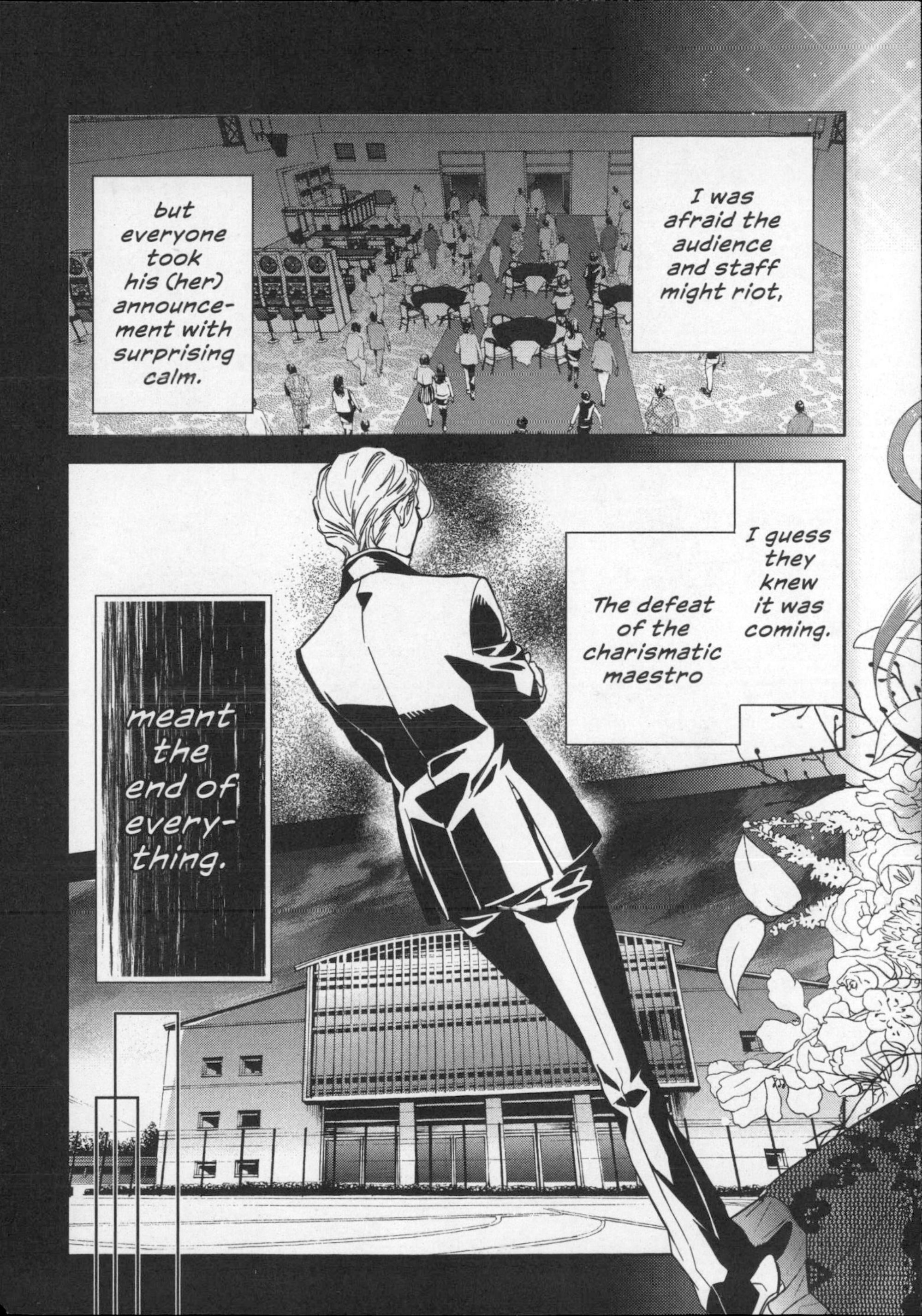
I was afraid the audience and staff might riot,
but everyone took his (her) announcement with surprising calm.
I guess they knew it was coming.
The defeat of the charismatic maestro
meant the end of everything.

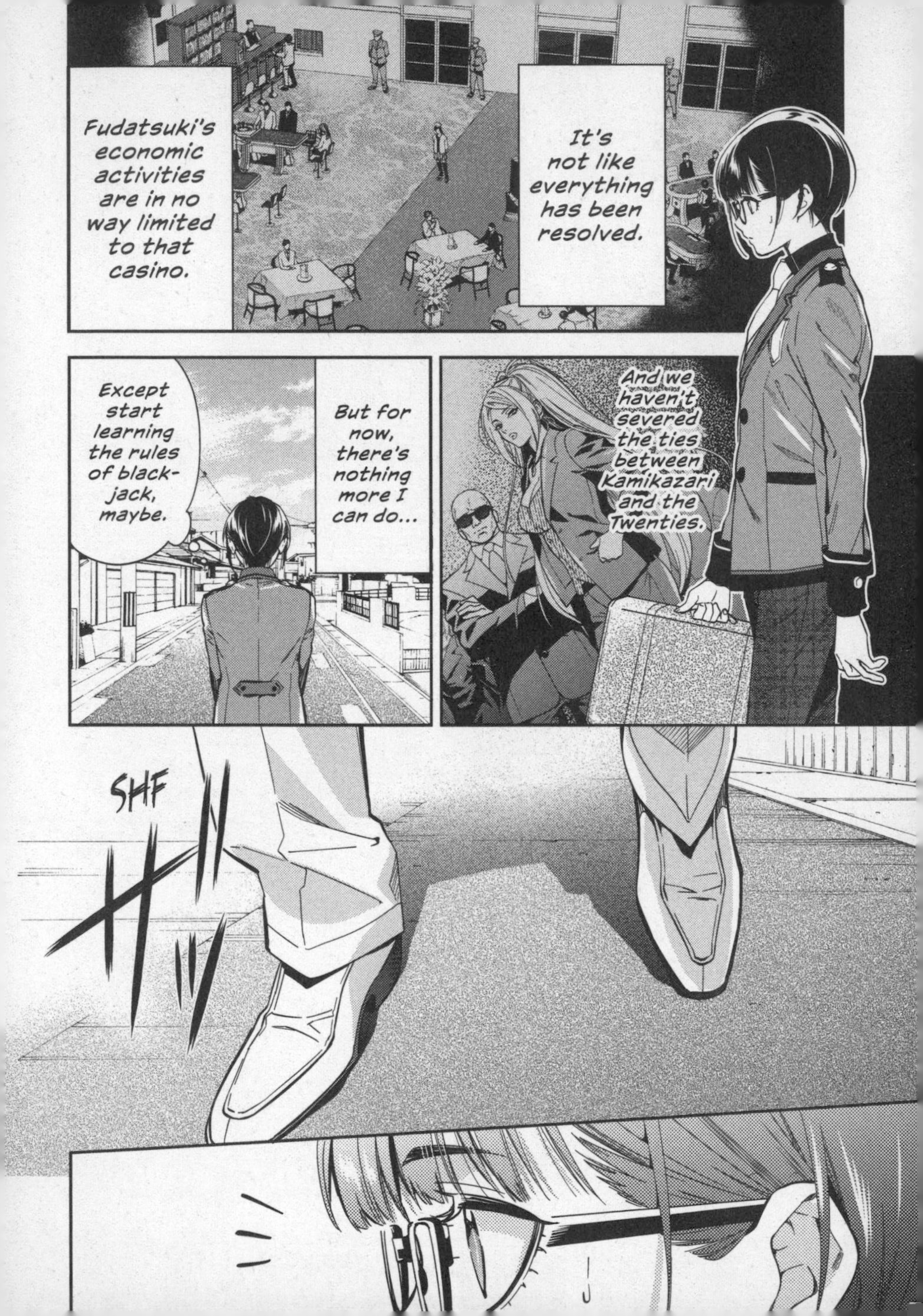
It's not like everything has been resolved.
Fudatsuki's economic activities are in no way limited to that casino.
And we haven't severed the ties between Kamikazari and the Twenties.
But for now, there's nothing more I can do...
Except start learning the rules of black-jack, maybe.
SHF

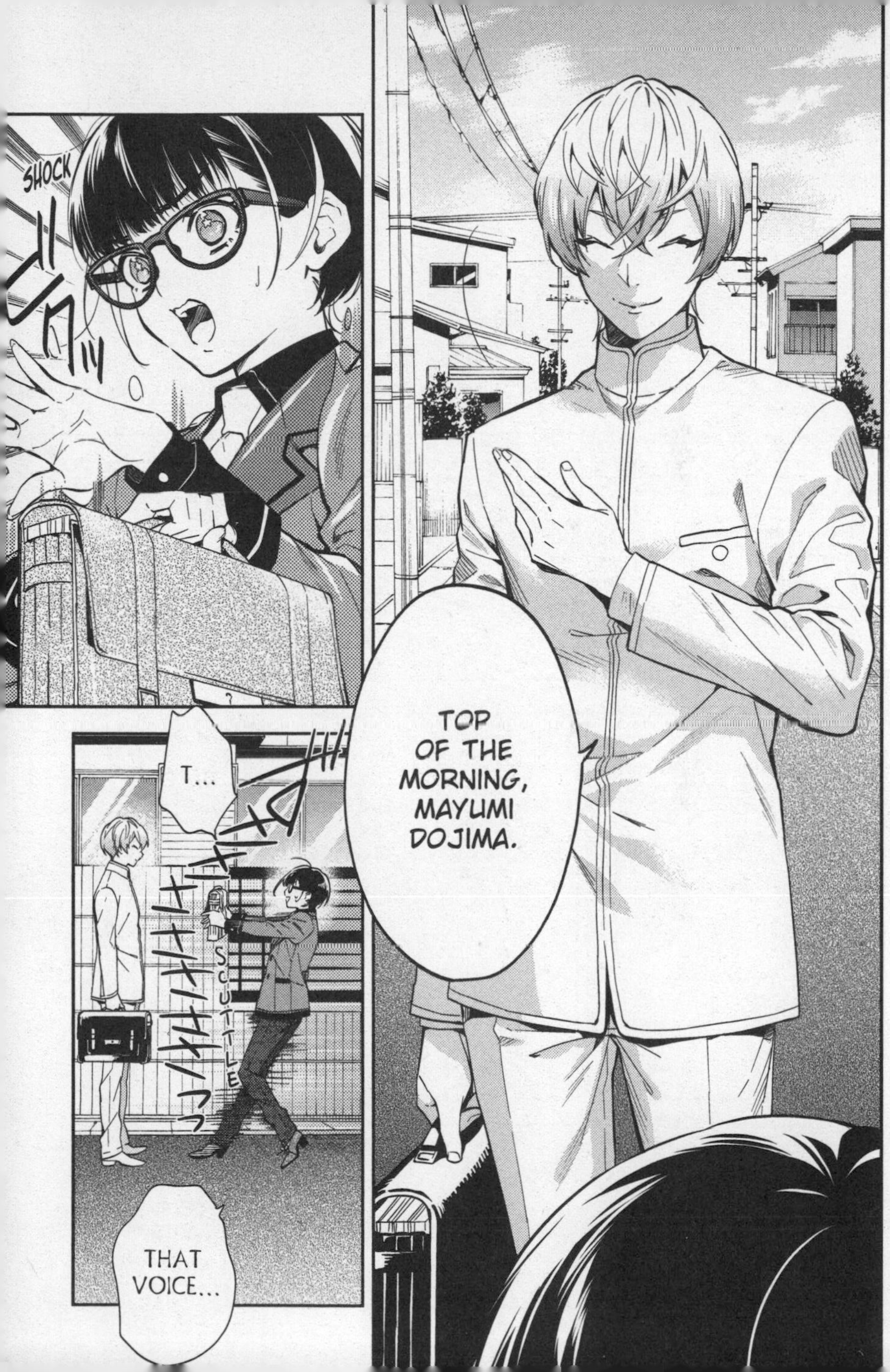
TOP OF THE MORNING, MAYUMI DOJIMA.
SHOCK
T...
SCUTTLE
THAT VOICE...

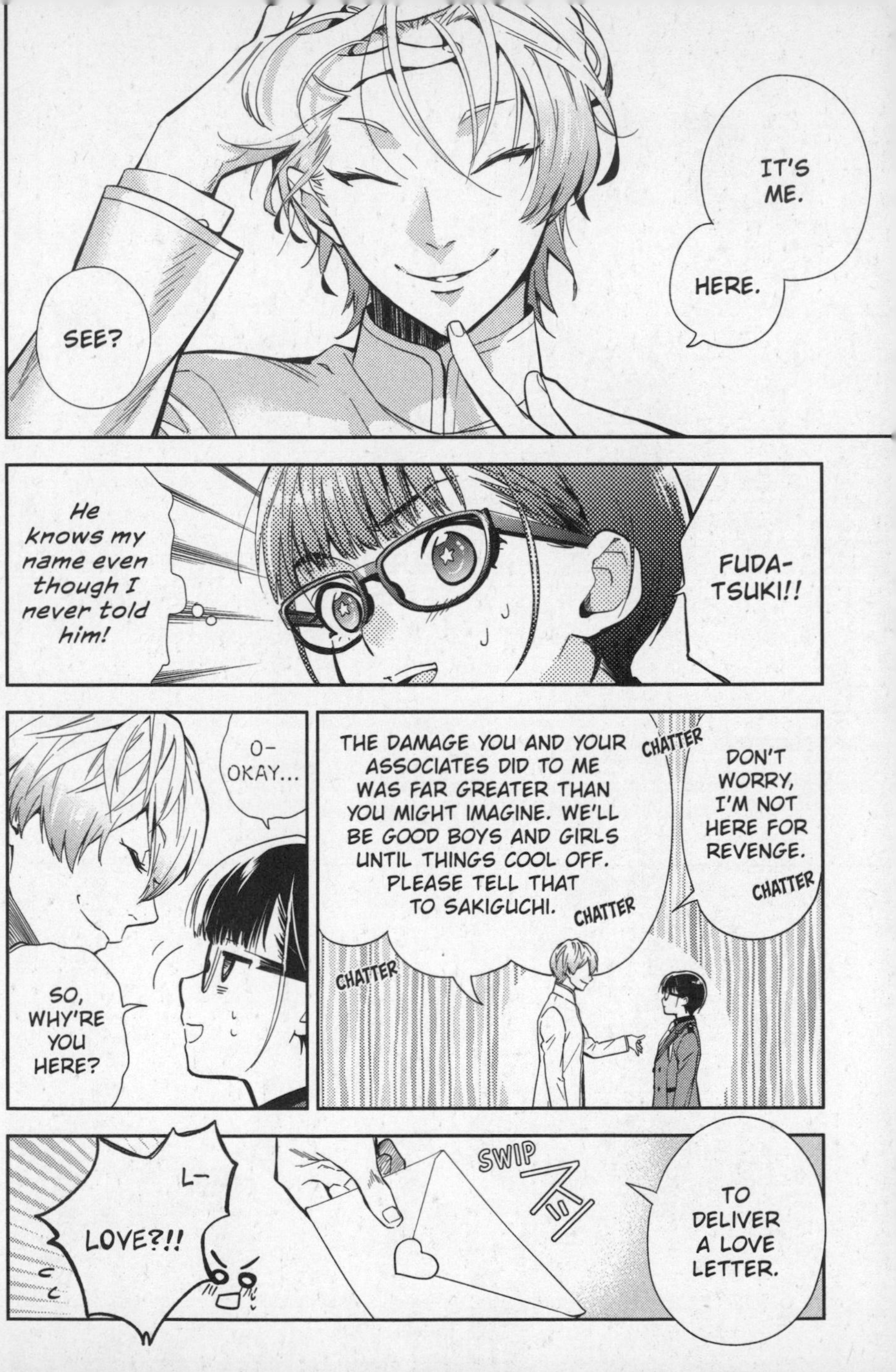
IT'S ME.
HERE.
SEE?
FUDA-TSUKI!!
He knows my name even though I never told him!
DON'T WORRY, I'M NOT HERE FOR REVENGE.
CHATTER
CHATTER
THE DAMAGE YOU AND YOUR ASSOCIATES DID TO ME WAS FAR GREATER THAN YOU MIGHT IMAGINE. WE'LL BE GOOD BOYS AND GIRLS UNTIL THINGS COOL OFF. PLEASE TELL THAT TO SAKIGUCHI.
CHATTER
CHATTER
O-OKAY...
SO, WHY'RE YOU HERE?
TO DELIVER A LOVE LETTER.
SWIP
L-
LOVE?!!

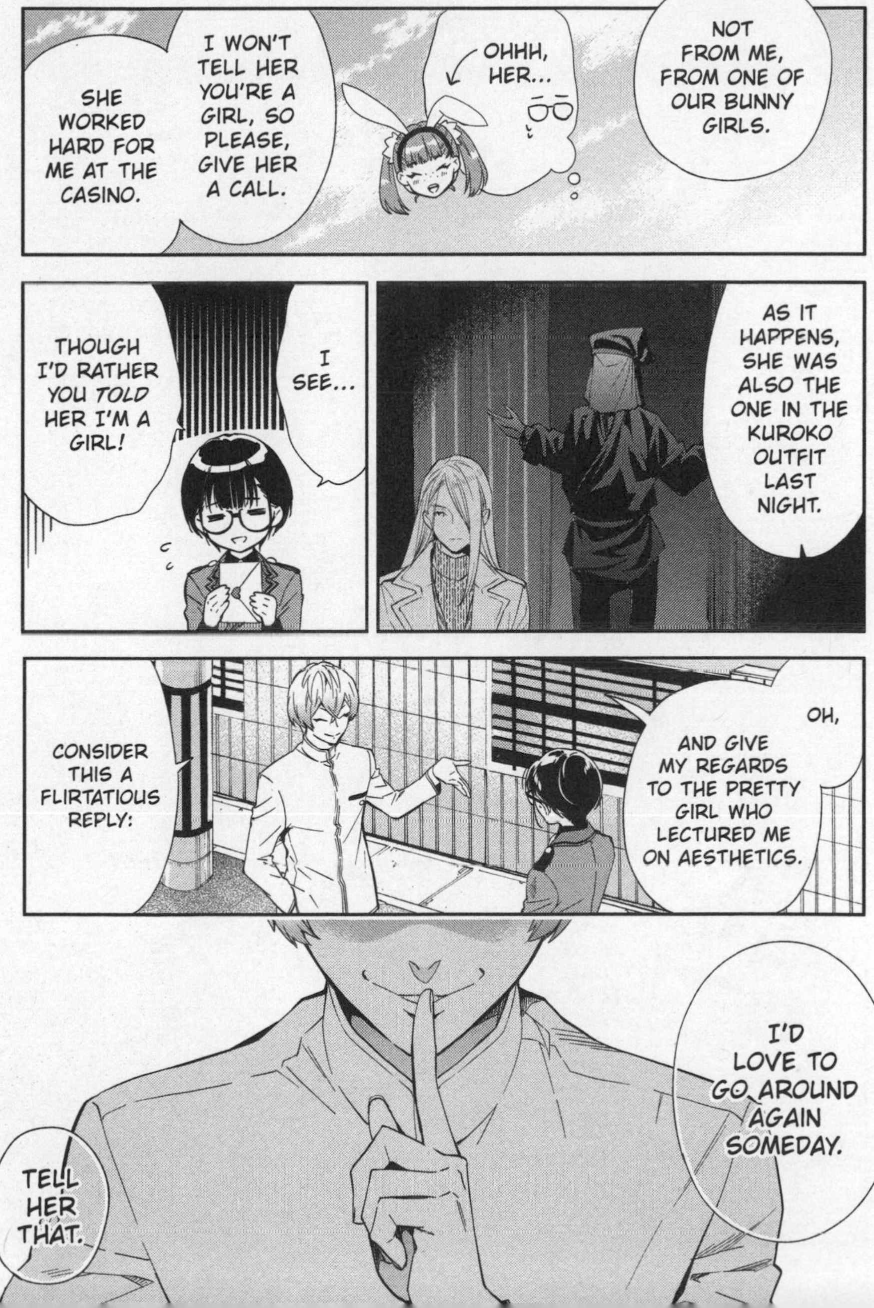
NOT FROM ME, FROM ONE OF OUR BUNNY GIRLS.
OHHH, HER...
I WON'T TELL HER YOU'RE A GIRL, SO PLEASE, GIVE HER A CALL.
SHE WORKED HARD FOR ME AT THE CASINO.
AS IT HAPPENS, SHE WAS ALSO THE ONE IN THE KUROKO OUTFIT LAST NIGHT.
I SEE...
THOUGH I'D RATHER YOU *TOLD* HER I'M A GIRL!
OH, AND GIVE MY REGARDS TO THE PRETTY GIRL WHO LECTURED ME ON AESTHETICS.
CONSIDER THIS A FLIRTATIOUS REPLY:
I'D LOVE TO GO AROUND AGAIN SOMEDAY.
TELL HER THAT.

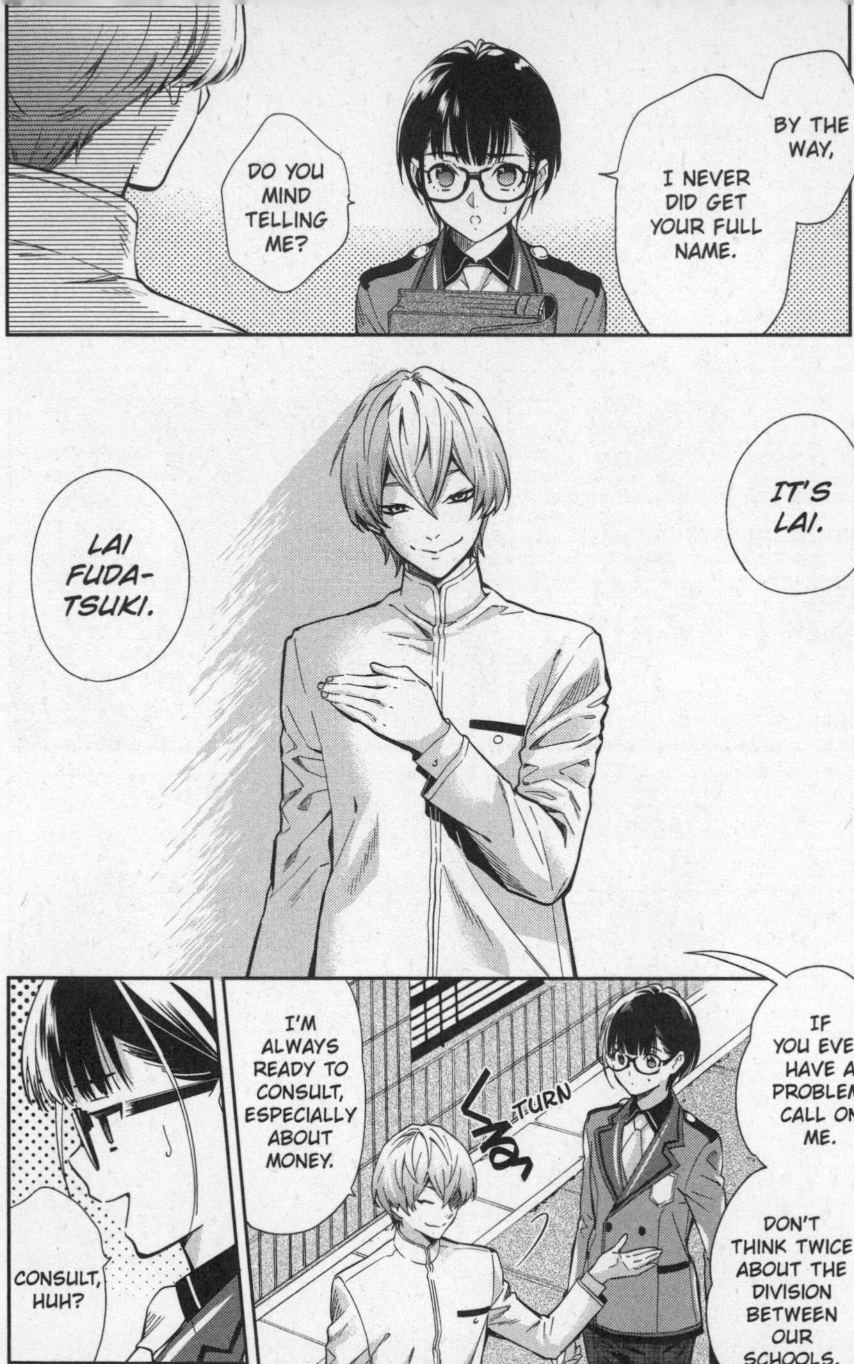
BY THE WAY, I NEVER DID GET YOUR FULL NAME.
DO YOU MIND TELLING ME?
IT'S LAI.
LAI FUDA-TSUKI.
IF YOU EVER HAVE A PROBLEM, CALL ON ME.
DON'T THINK TWICE ABOUT THE DIVISION BETWEEN OUR SCHOOLS.
TURN
I'M ALWAYS READY TO CONSULT, ESPECIALLY ABOUT MONEY.
CONSULT, HUH?

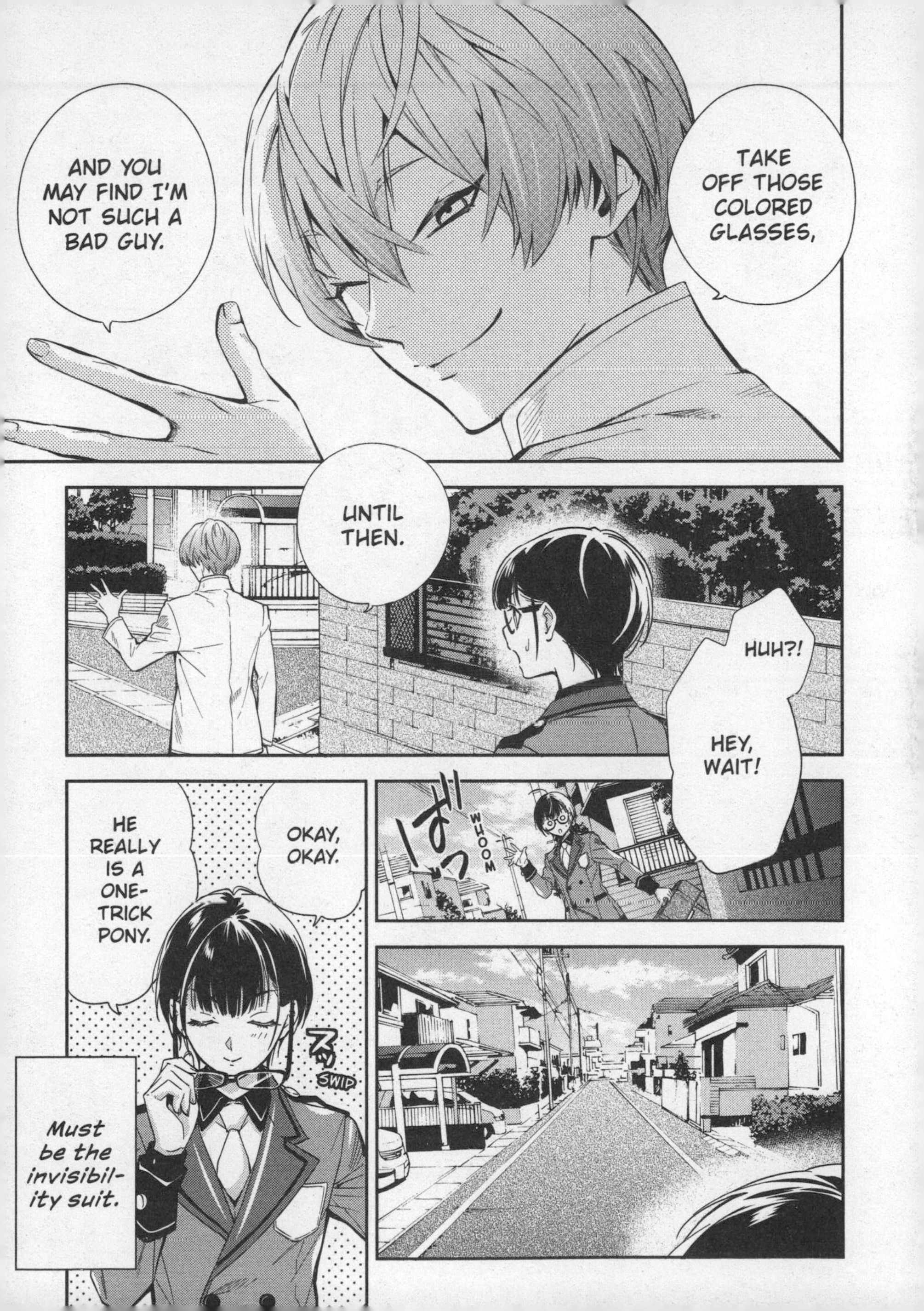
TAKE OFF THOSE COLORED GLASSES,
AND YOU MAY FIND I'M NOT SUCH A BAD GUY.
UNTIL THEN.
HUH?!
HEY, WAIT!
WHOOM
OKAY, OKAY.
HE REALLY IS A ONE-TRICK PONY.
SWIP
Must be the invisibility suit.

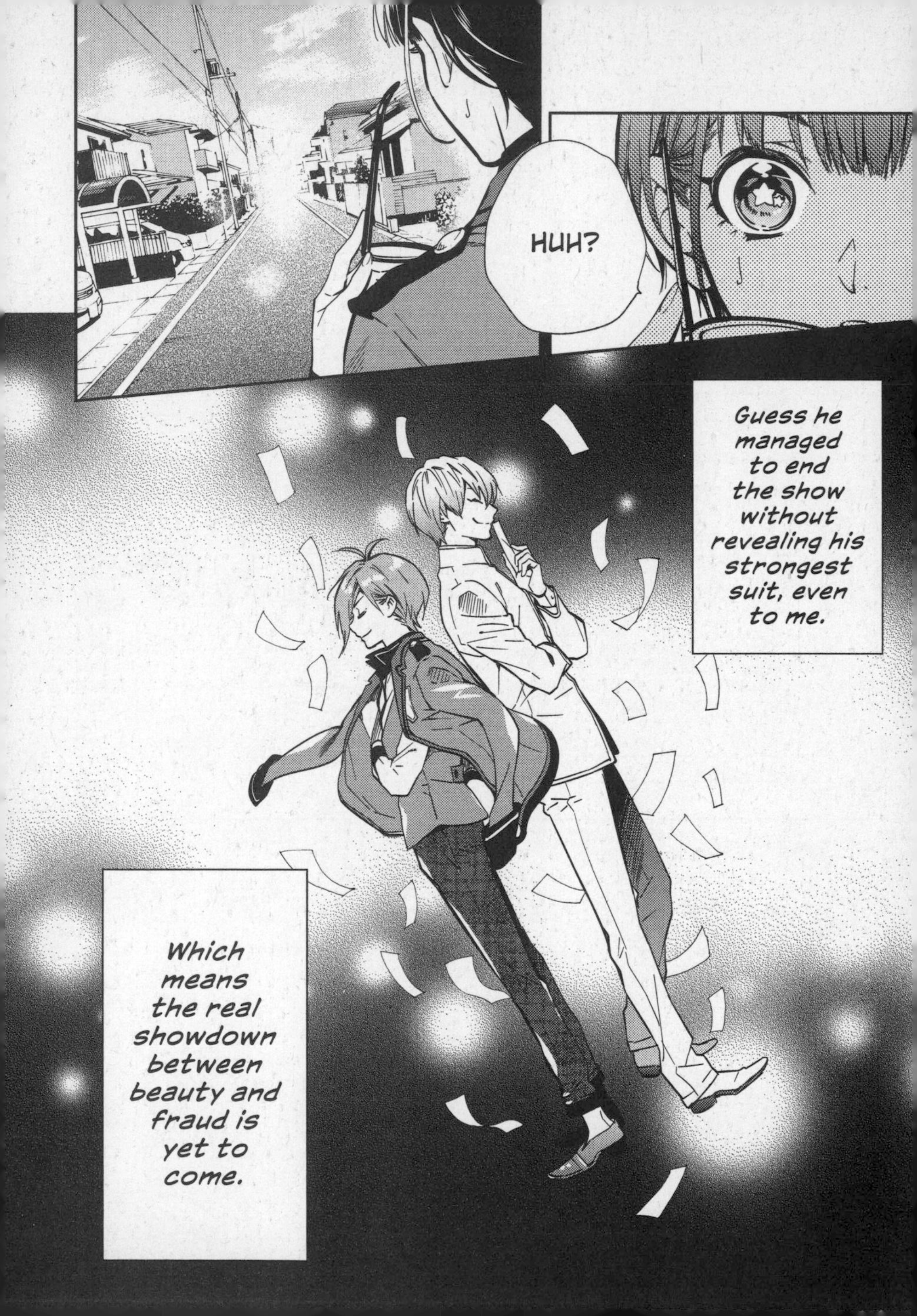
HUH?
Guess he managed to end the show without revealing his strongest suit, even to me.
Which means the real showdown between beauty and fraud is yet to come.

PRETTY BOY

DETECTIVE CLUB!!

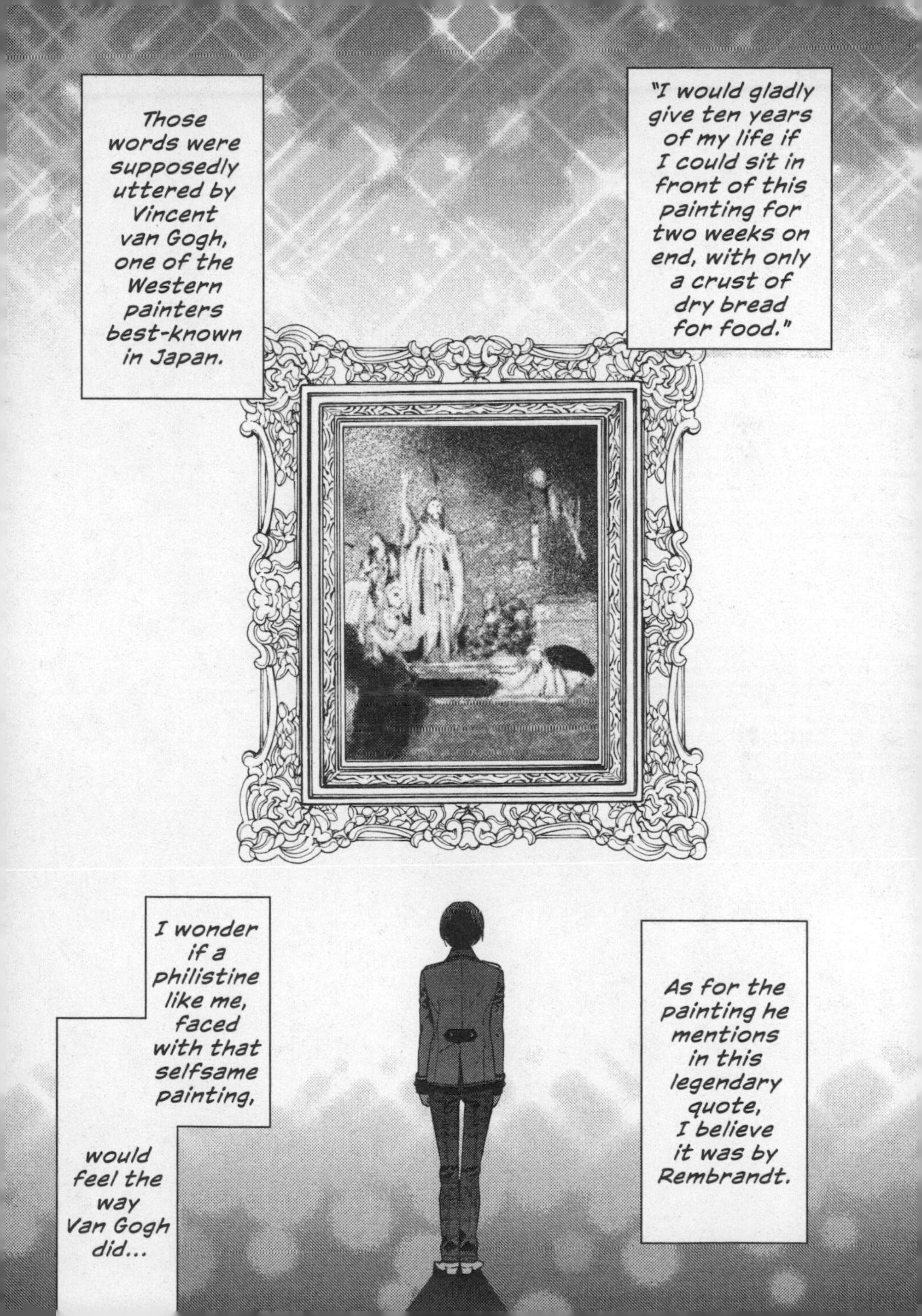
"I would gladly give ten years of my life if I could sit in front of this painting for two weeks on end, with only a crust of dry bread for food."
Those words were supposedly uttered by Vincent van Gogh, one of the Western painters best-known in Japan.
As for the painting he mentions in this legendary quote, I believe it was by Rembrandt.
I wonder if a philistine like me, faced with that selfsame painting,
would feel the way Van Gogh did...

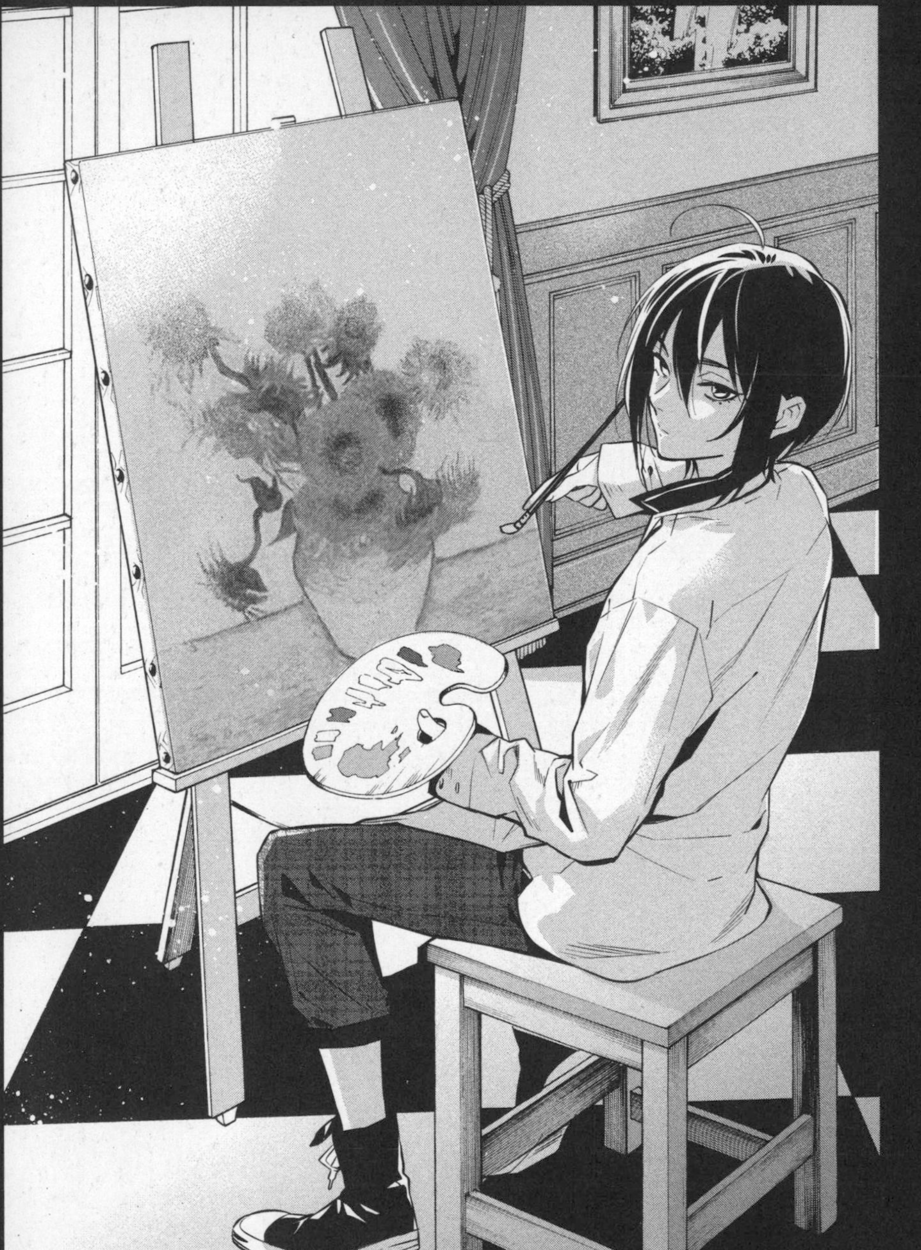

FILE ★ The Pretty Boy in the Attic 1

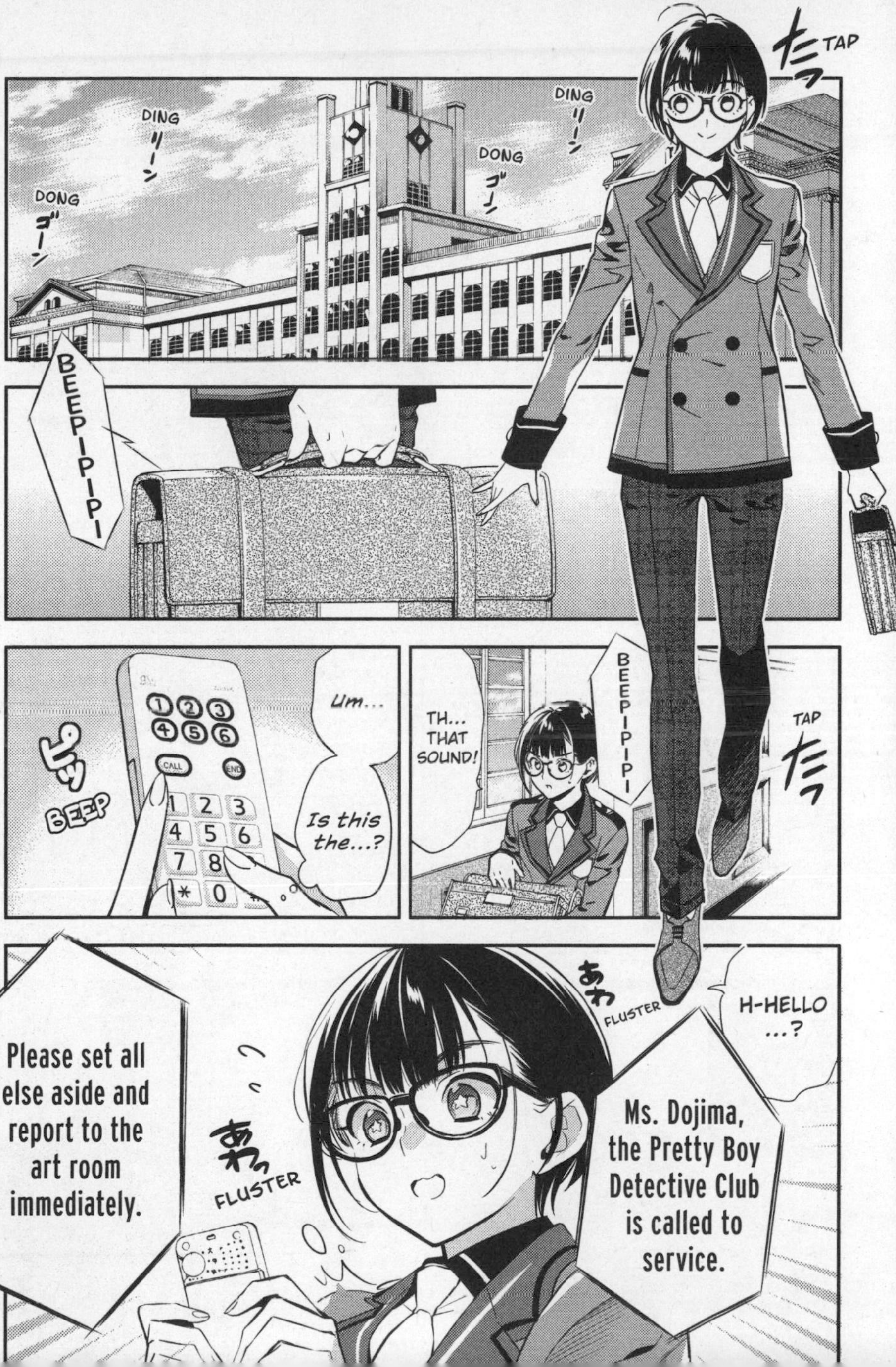
TAP
DING
DONG
DING
DONG
BEEPIPIPI
BEEPIPIPI
TH... THAT SOUND!
TAP
Um...
Is this the...?
BEEP
H-HELLO ...?
FLUSTER
Ms. Dojima, the Pretty Boy Detective Club is called to service.
FLUSTER
Please set all else aside and report to the art room immediately.

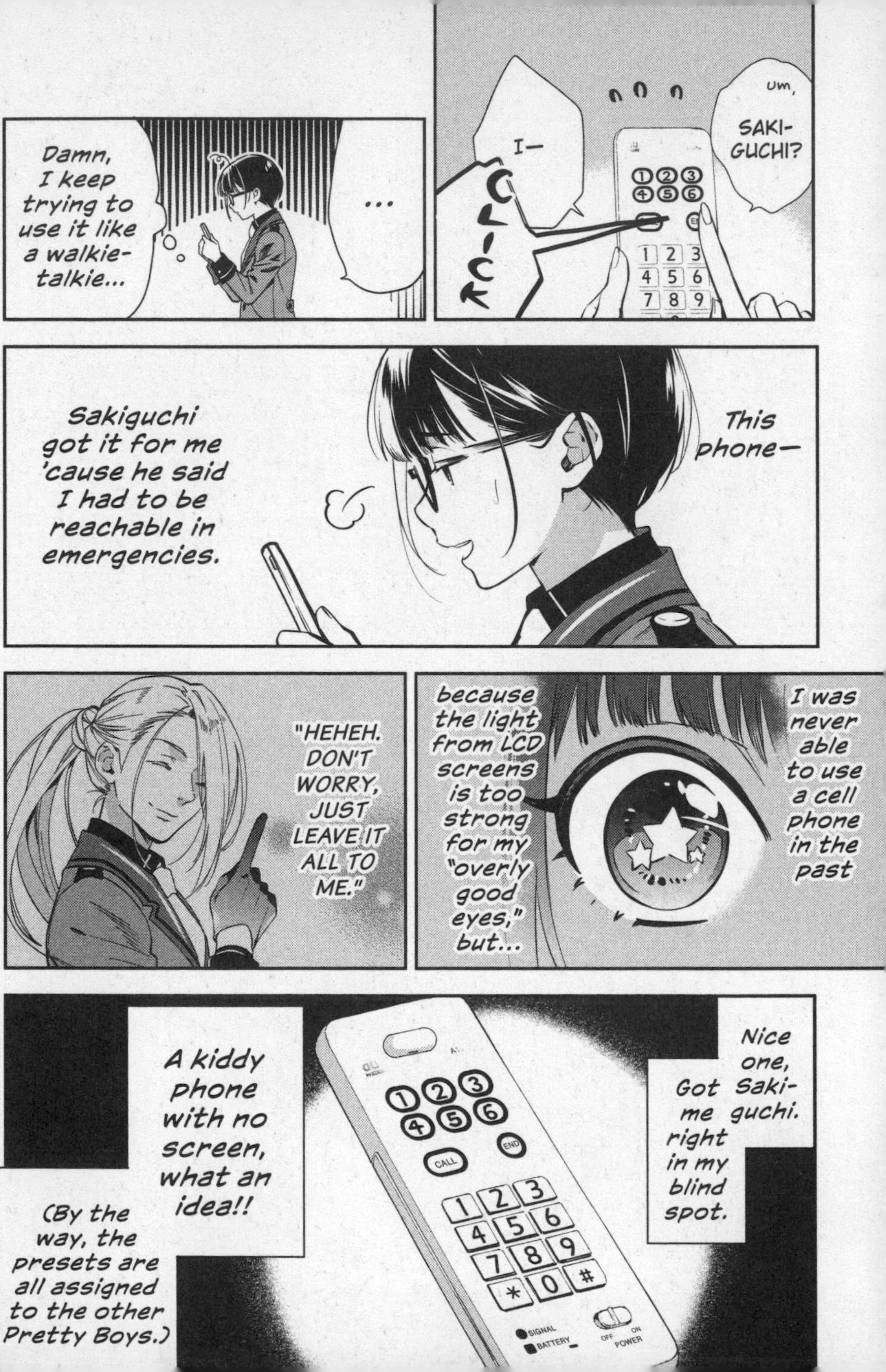
Um, SAKI-GUCHI?
I—
CLICK
...
Damn, I keep trying to use it like a walkie-talkie...
This phone—
Sakiguchi got it for me 'cause he said I had to be reachable in emergencies.
I was never able to use a cell phone in the past
because the light from LCD screens is too strong for my "overly good eyes," but...
"HEHEH. DON'T WORRY, JUST LEAVE IT ALL TO ME."
Nice one, Saki-guchi.
Got me right in my blind spot.
A kiddy phone with no screen, what an idea!!
(By the way, the presets are all assigned to the other Pretty Boys.)
CALL
END
SIGNAL
BATTERY
OFF ON POWER

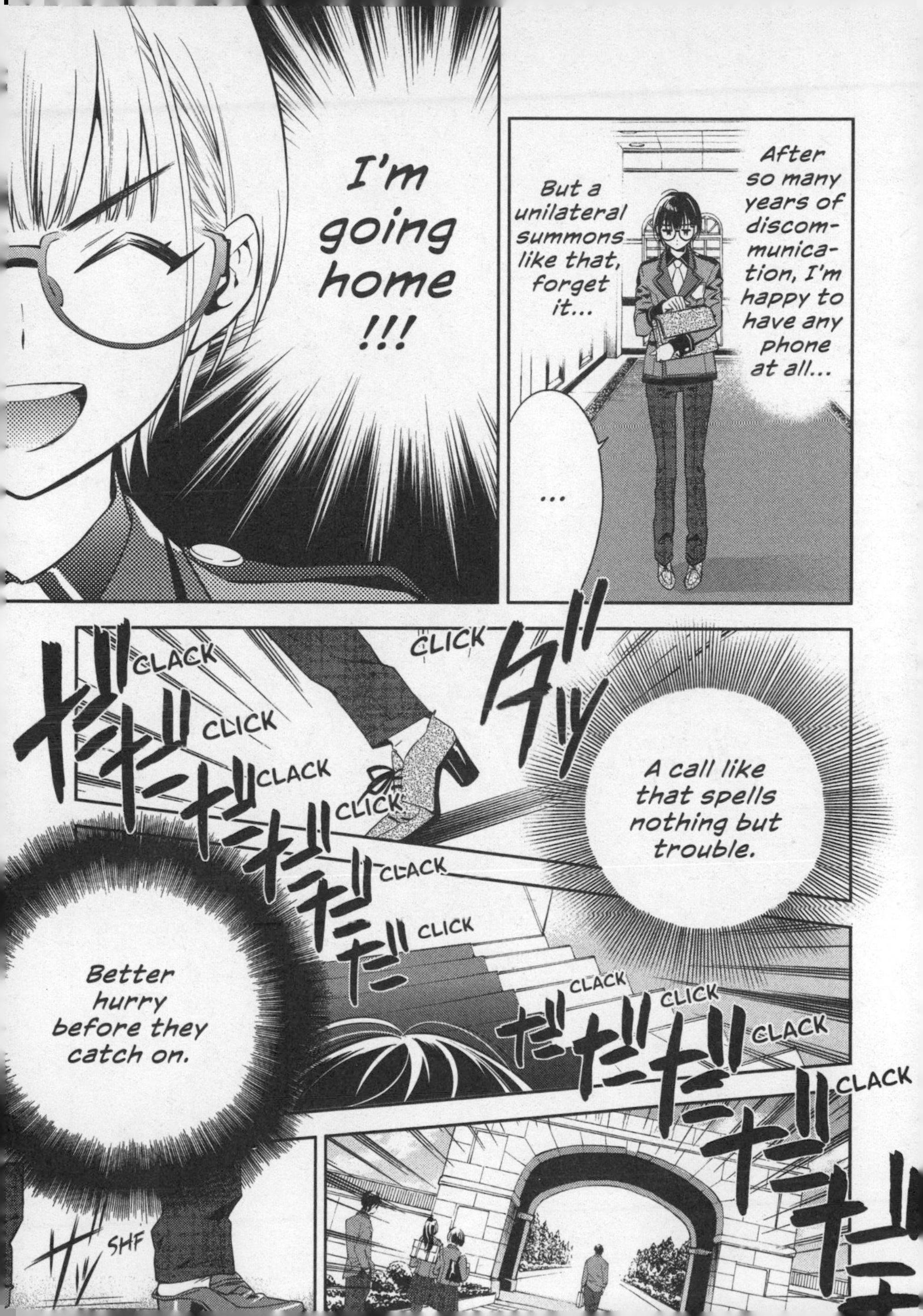
After so many years of discom-munica-tion, I'm happy to have any phone at all...
But a unilateral summons like that, forget it...
...
I'm going home!!!
CLICK
CLACK
CLICK
CLACK
CLICK
CLACK
CLICK
A call like that spells nothing but trouble.
CLACK
CLICK
CLACK
CLACK
Better hurry before they catch on.
SHF

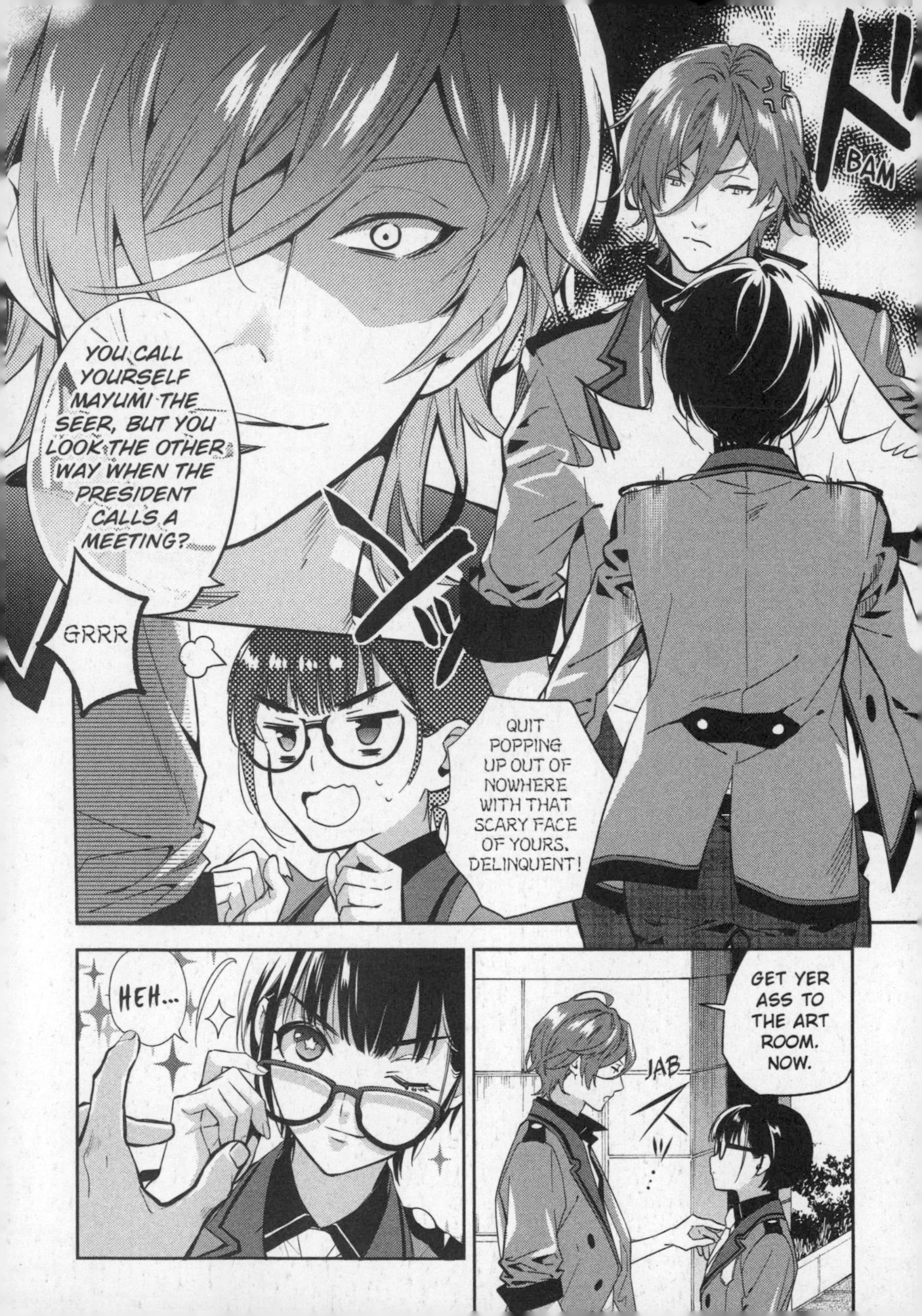
BAM
YOU CALL YOURSELF MAYUMI THE SEER, BUT YOU LOOK THE OTHER WAY WHEN THE PRESIDENT CALLS A MEETING?
GRRR
QUIT POPPING UP OUT OF NOWHERE WITH THAT SCARY FACE OF YOURS, DELINQUENT!
GET YER ASS TO THE ART ROOM. NOW.
JAB
HEH...

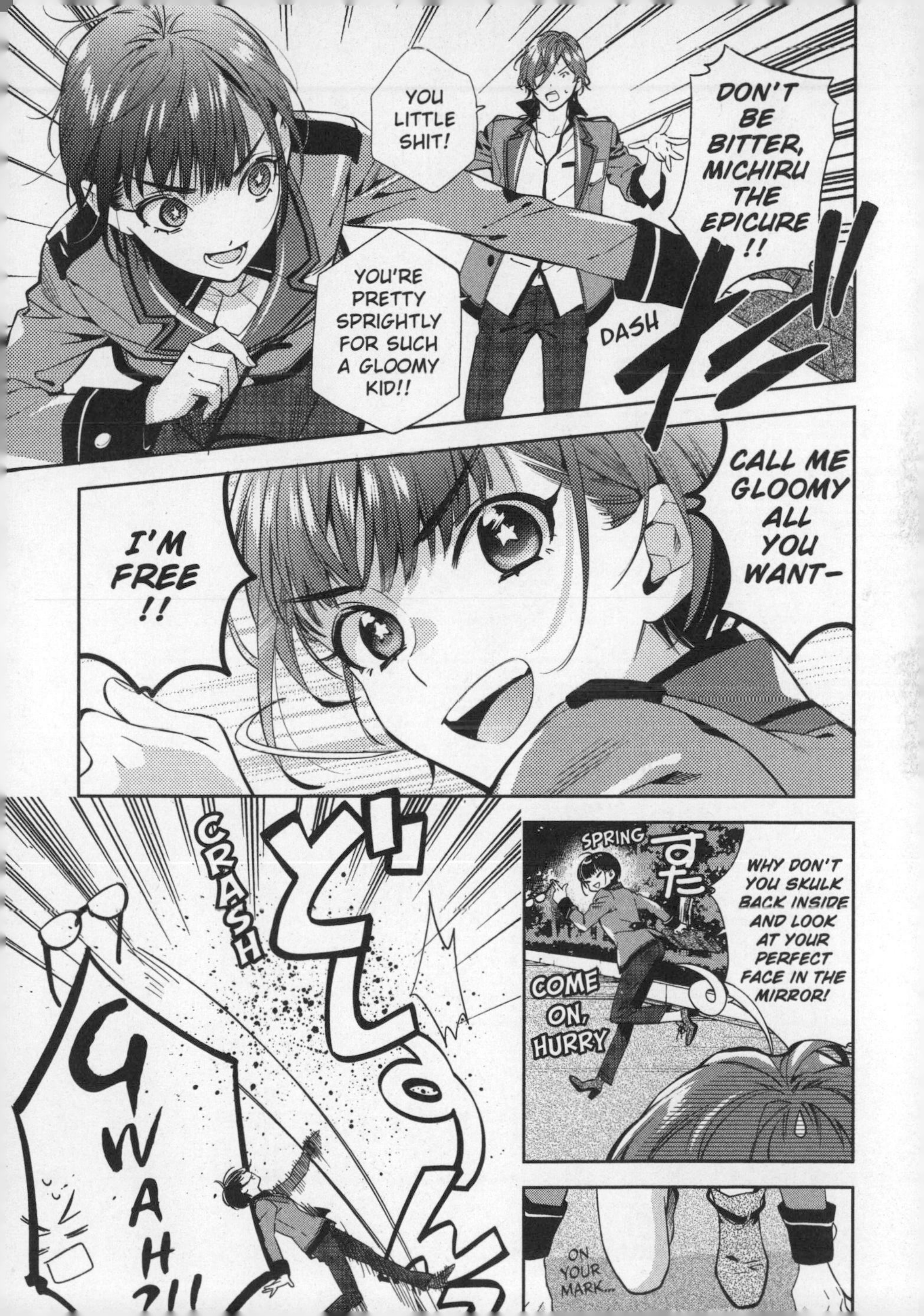
DON'T BE BITTER, MICHIRU THE EPICURE!!
YOU LITTLE SHIT!
DASH
YOU'RE PRETTY SPRIGHTLY FOR SUCH A GLOOMY KID!!
CALL ME GLOOMY ALL YOU WANT—
I'M FREE!!
SPRING
すた
WHY DON'T YOU SKULK BACK INSIDE AND LOOK AT YOUR PERFECT FACE IN THE MIRROR!
COME ON, HURRY
ON YOUR MARK...
CRASH
GWAH?!!

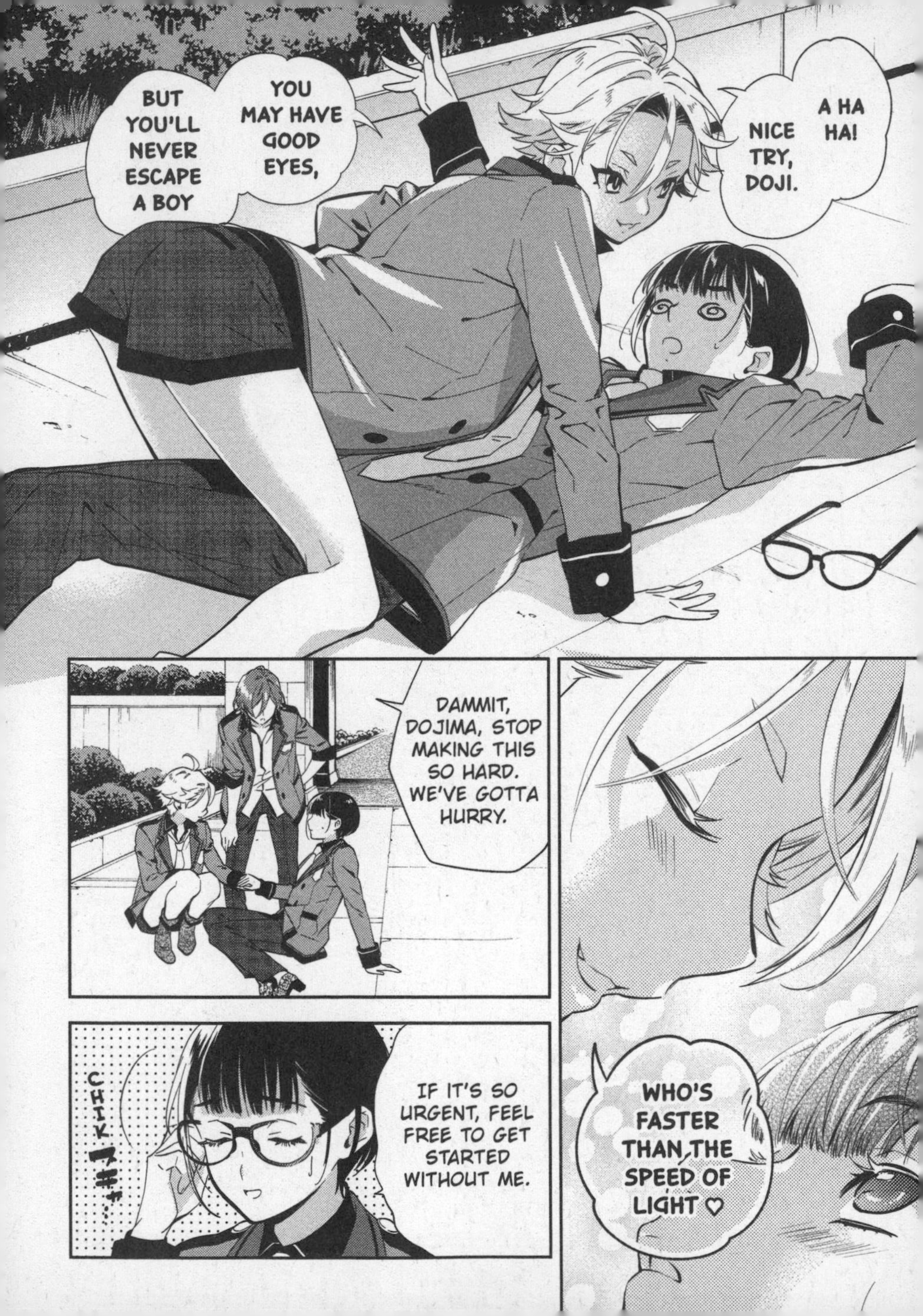
A HA HA!
NICE TRY, DOJI.
YOU MAY HAVE GOOD EYES,
BUT YOU'LL NEVER ESCAPE A BOY
WHO'S FASTER THAN THE SPEED OF LIGHT ♡
DAMMIT, DOJIMA, STOP MAKING THIS SO HARD. WE'VE GOTTA HURRY.
IF IT'S SO URGENT, FEEL FREE TO GET STARTED WITHOUT ME.
CHIK

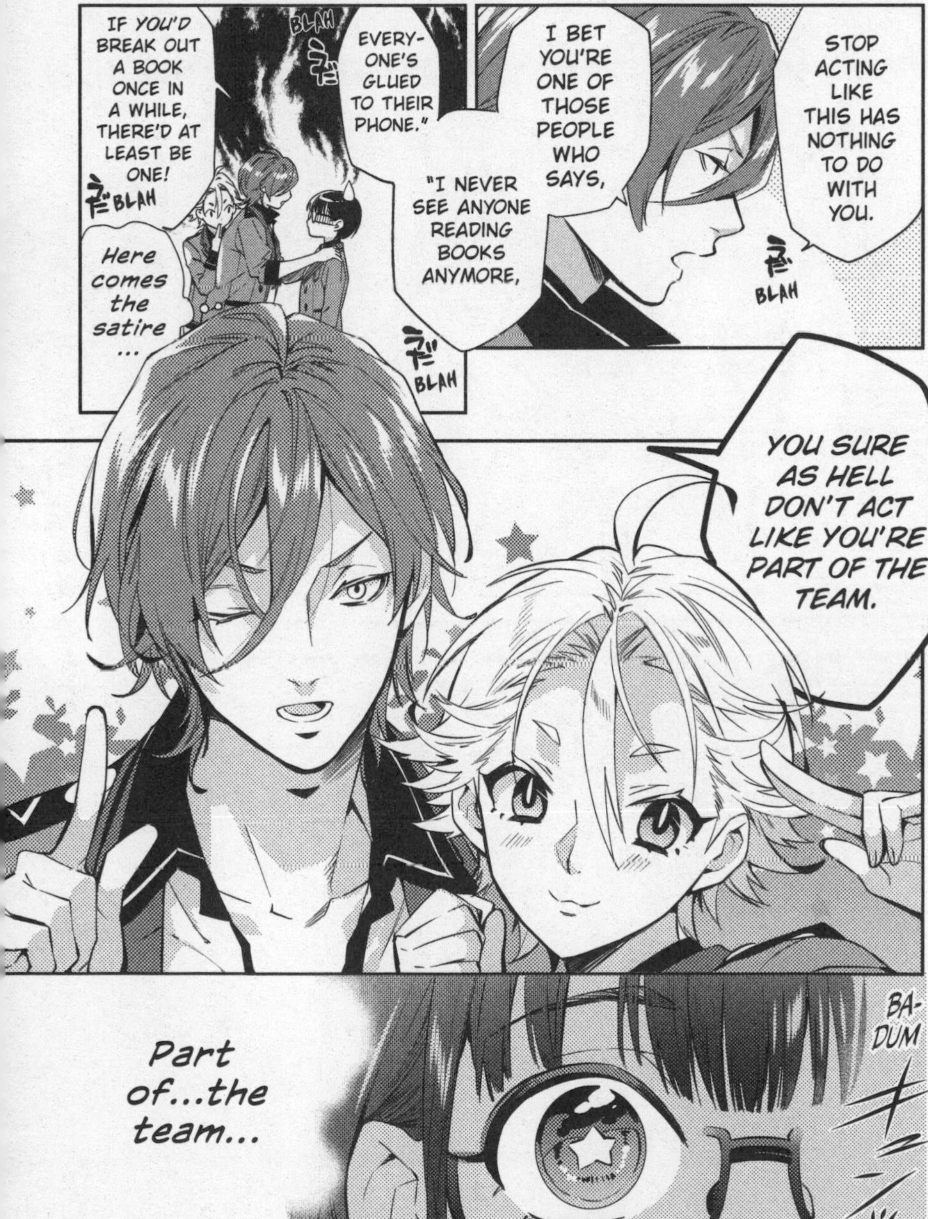

STOP ACTING LIKE THIS HAS NOTHING TO DO WITH YOU.
BLAH
I BET YOU'RE ONE OF THOSE PEOPLE WHO SAYS,
"I NEVER SEE ANYONE READING BOOKS ANYMORE,
EVERYONE'S GLUED TO THEIR PHONE."
BLAH
IF YOU'D BREAK OUT A BOOK ONCE IN A WHILE, THERE'D AT LEAST BE ONE!
BLAH
BLAH
Here comes the satire...
YOU SURE AS HELL DON'T ACT LIKE YOU'RE PART OF THE TEAM.
BA-DUM
Part of...the team...

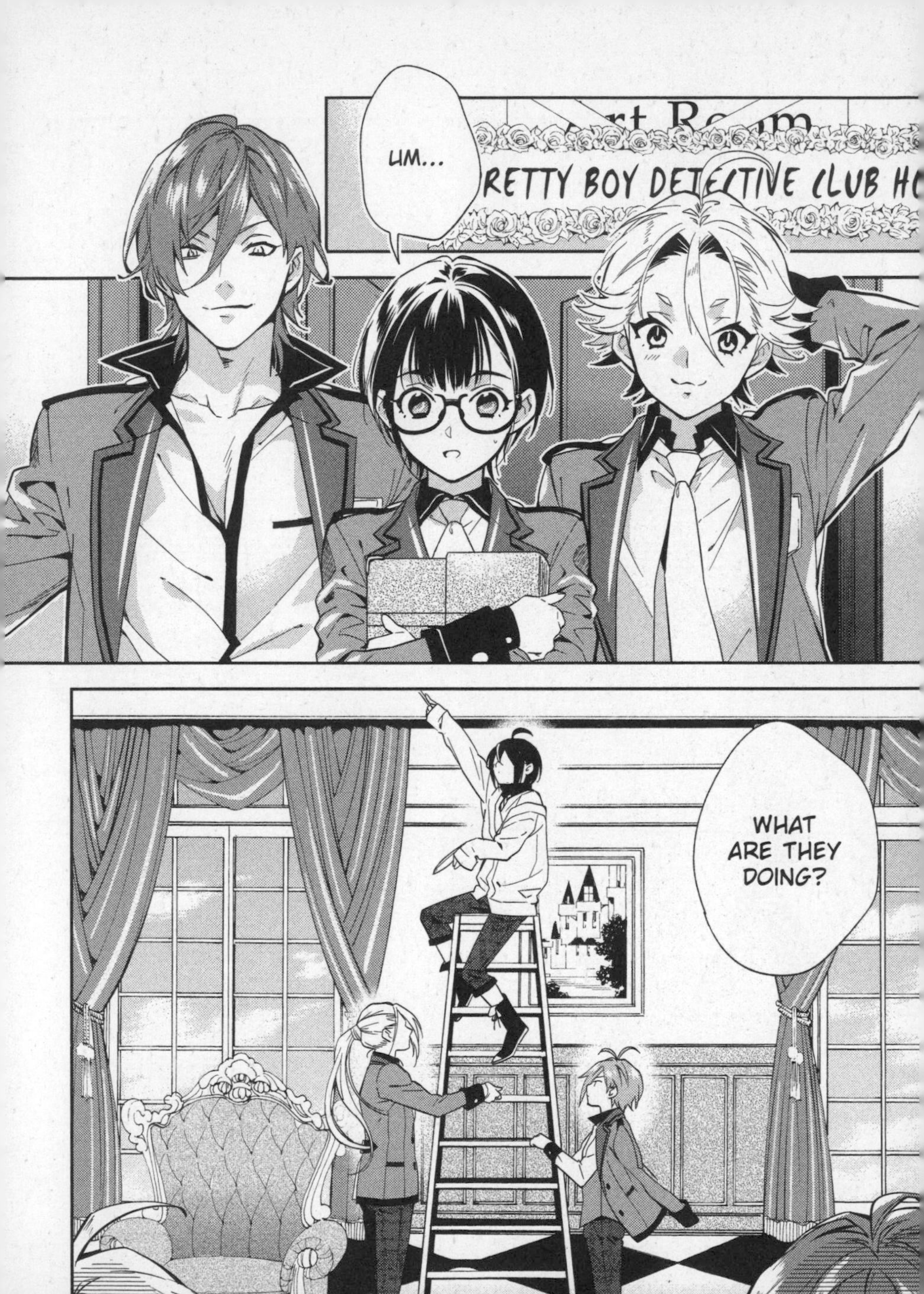
UM...
WHAT ARE THEY DOING?

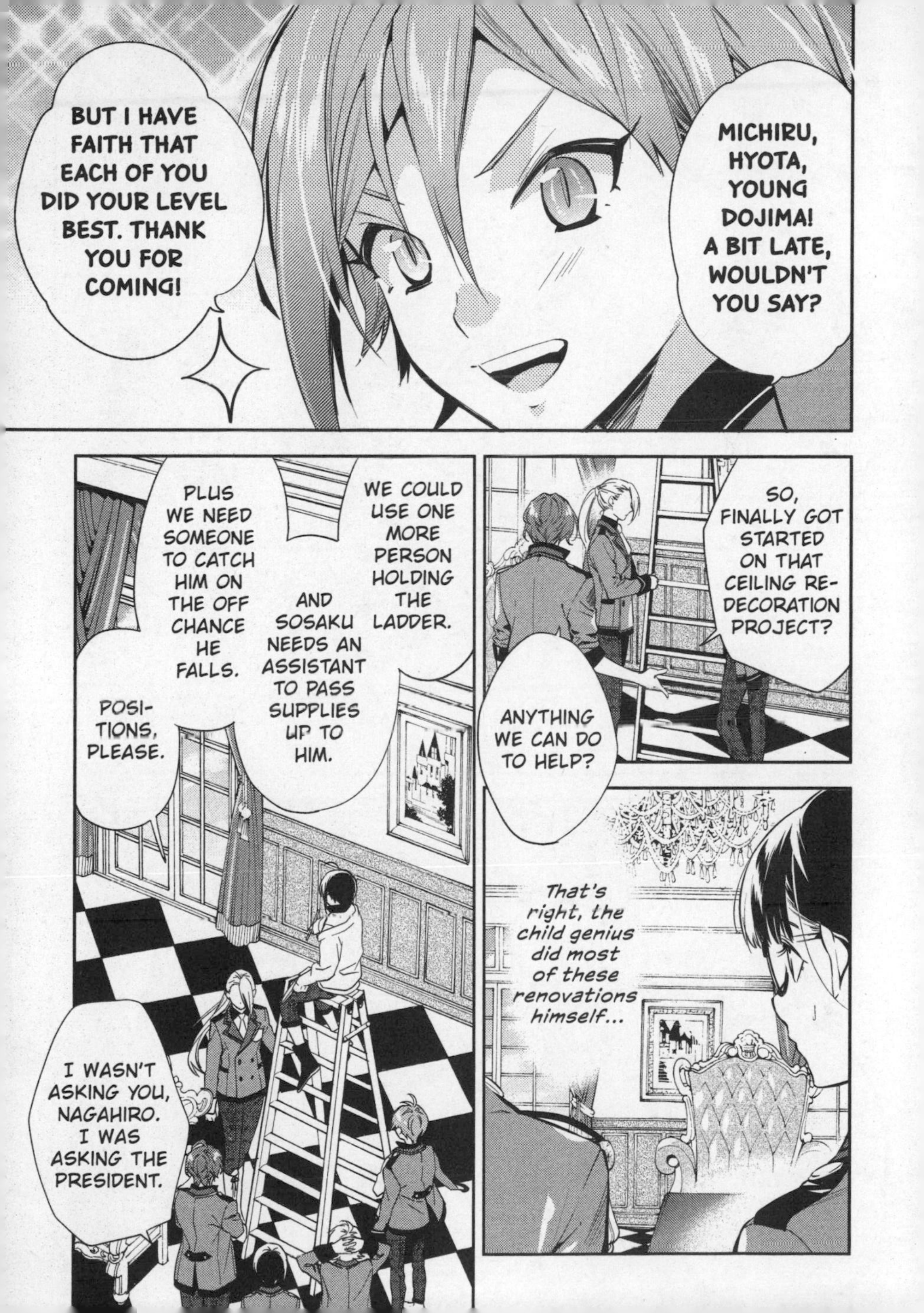
MICHIRU, HYOTA, YOUNG DOJIMA! A BIT LATE, WOULDN'T YOU SAY?
BUT I HAVE FAITH THAT EACH OF YOU DID YOUR LEVEL BEST. THANK YOU FOR COMING!
SO, FINALLY GOT STARTED ON THAT CEILING RE-DECORATION PROJECT?
ANYTHING WE CAN DO TO HELP?
That's right, the child genius did most of these renovations himself...
WE COULD USE ONE MORE PERSON HOLDING THE LADDER.
PLUS WE NEED SOMEONE TO CATCH HIM ON THE OFF CHANCE HE FALLS.
AND SOSAKU NEEDS AN ASSISTANT TO PASS SUPPLIES UP TO HIM.
POSITIONS, PLEASE.
I WASN'T ASKING YOU, NAGAHIRO. I WAS ASKING THE PRESIDENT.

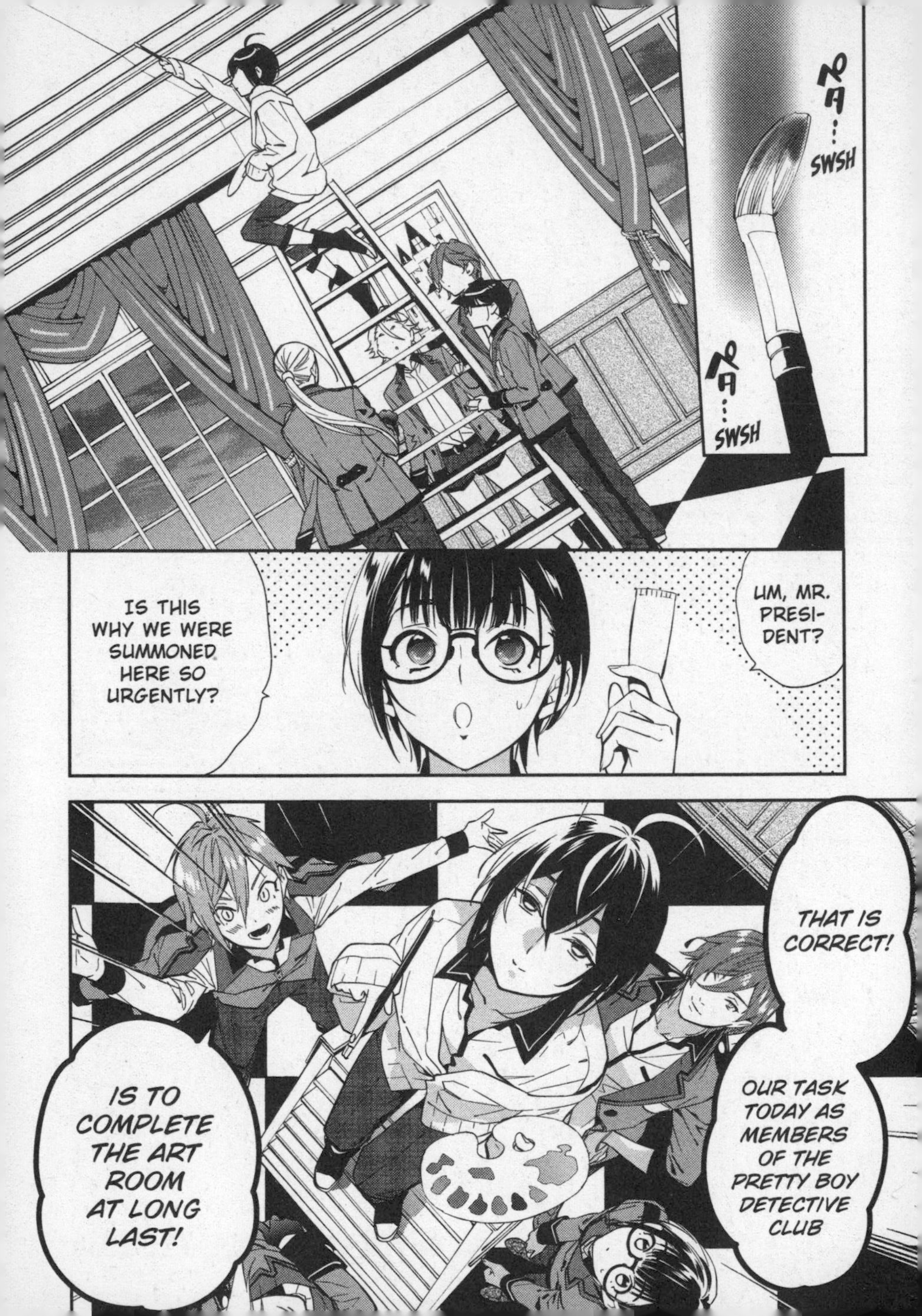
ペタ…
SWSH
ペタ…
SWSH
UM, MR. PRESI-DENT?
IS THIS WHY WE WERE SUMMONED HERE SO URGENTLY?
THAT IS CORRECT!
OUR TASK TODAY AS MEMBERS OF THE PRETTY BOY DETECTIVE CLUB
IS TO COMPLETE THE ART ROOM AT LONG LAST!

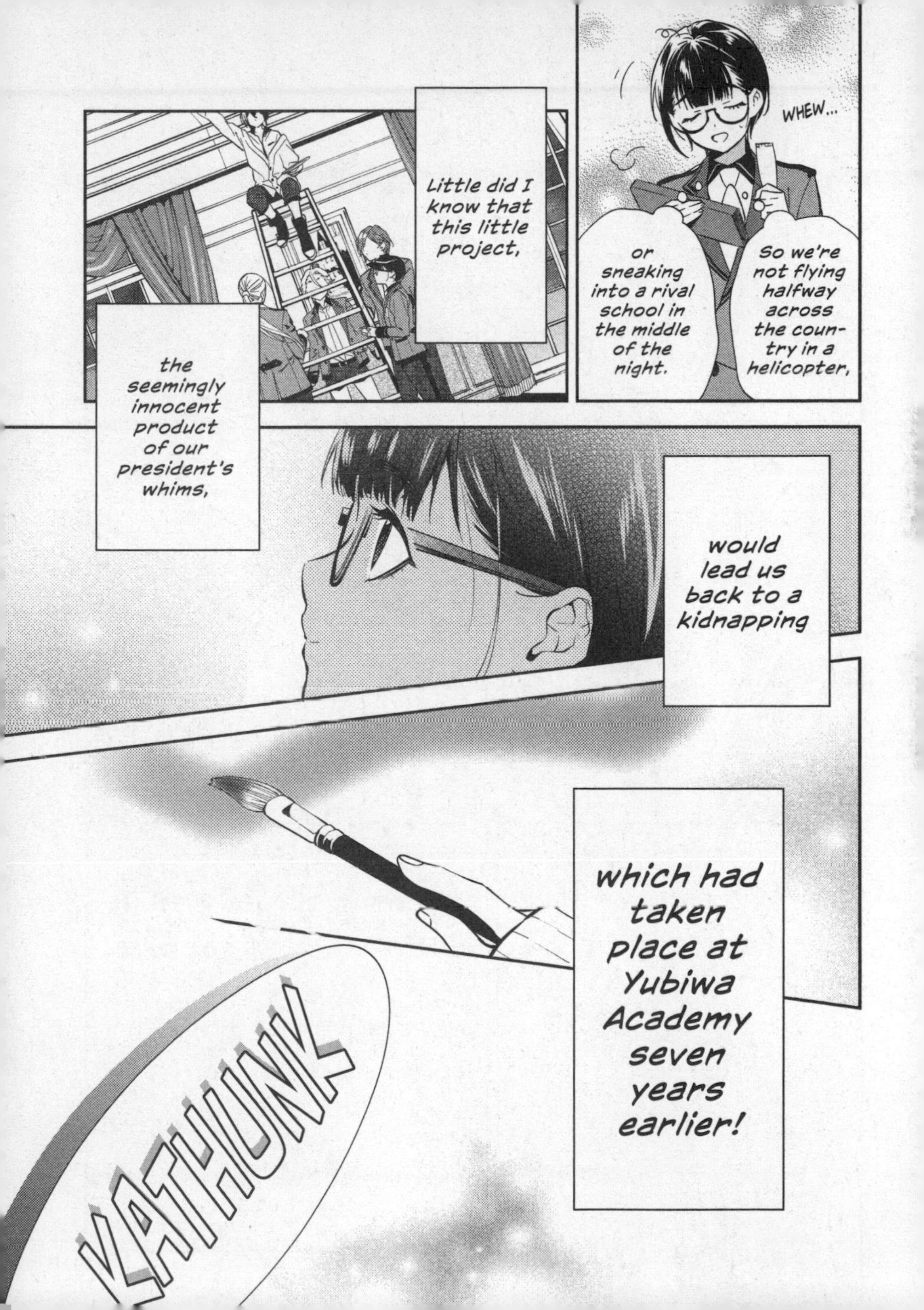

WHEW...
So we're not flying halfway across the country in a helicopter,
or sneaking into a rival school in the middle of the night.
Little did I know that this little project,
the seemingly innocent product of our president's whims,
would lead us back to a kidnapping
which had taken place at Yubiwa Academy seven years earlier!
KATHUNK

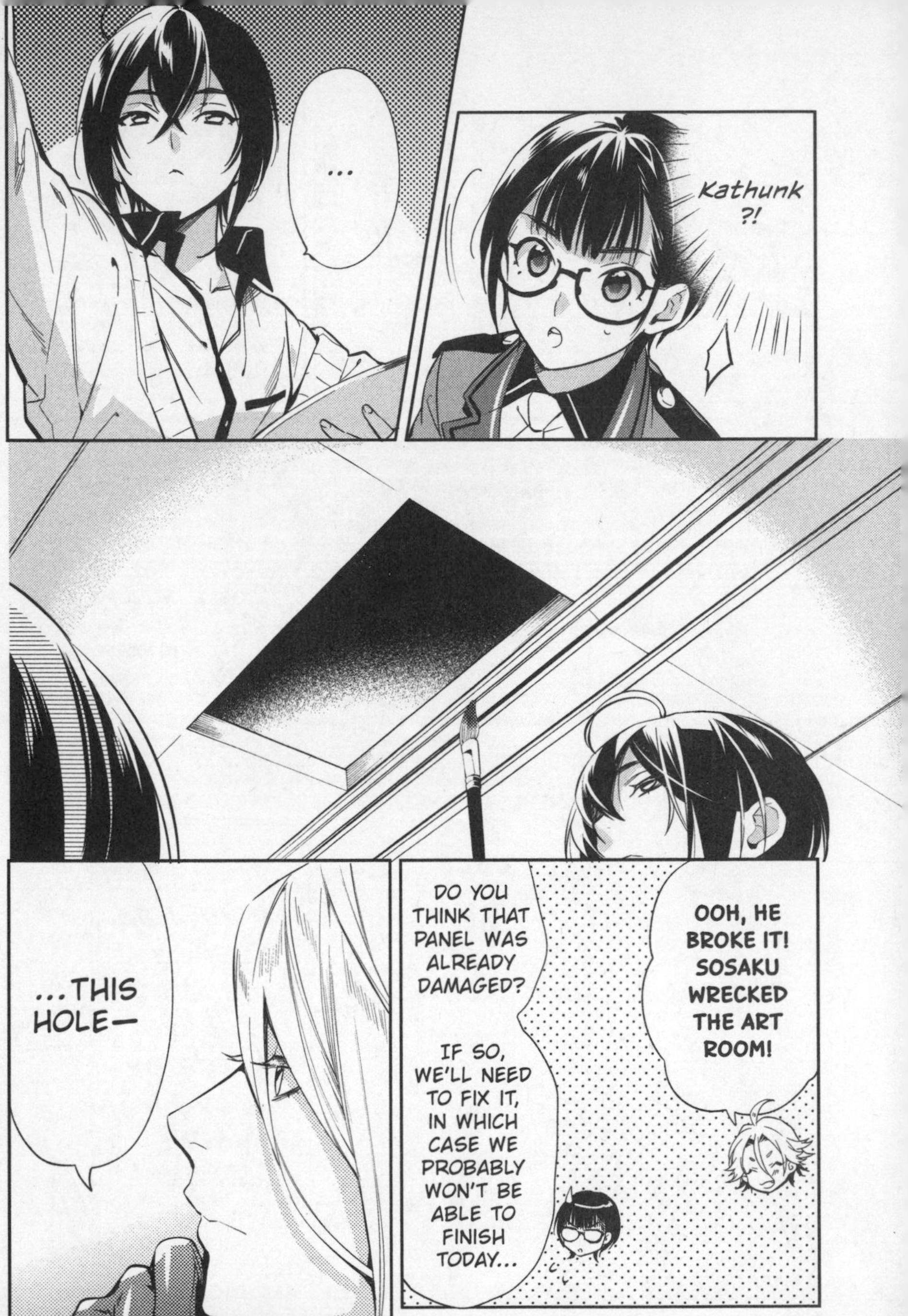
Kathunk
?!
...
OOH, HE BROKE IT! SOSAKU WRECKED THE ART ROOM!
DO YOU THINK THAT PANEL WAS ALREADY DAMAGED?
IF SO, WE'LL NEED TO FIX IT, IN WHICH CASE WE PROBABLY WON'T BE ABLE TO FINISH TODAY...
...THIS HOLE—

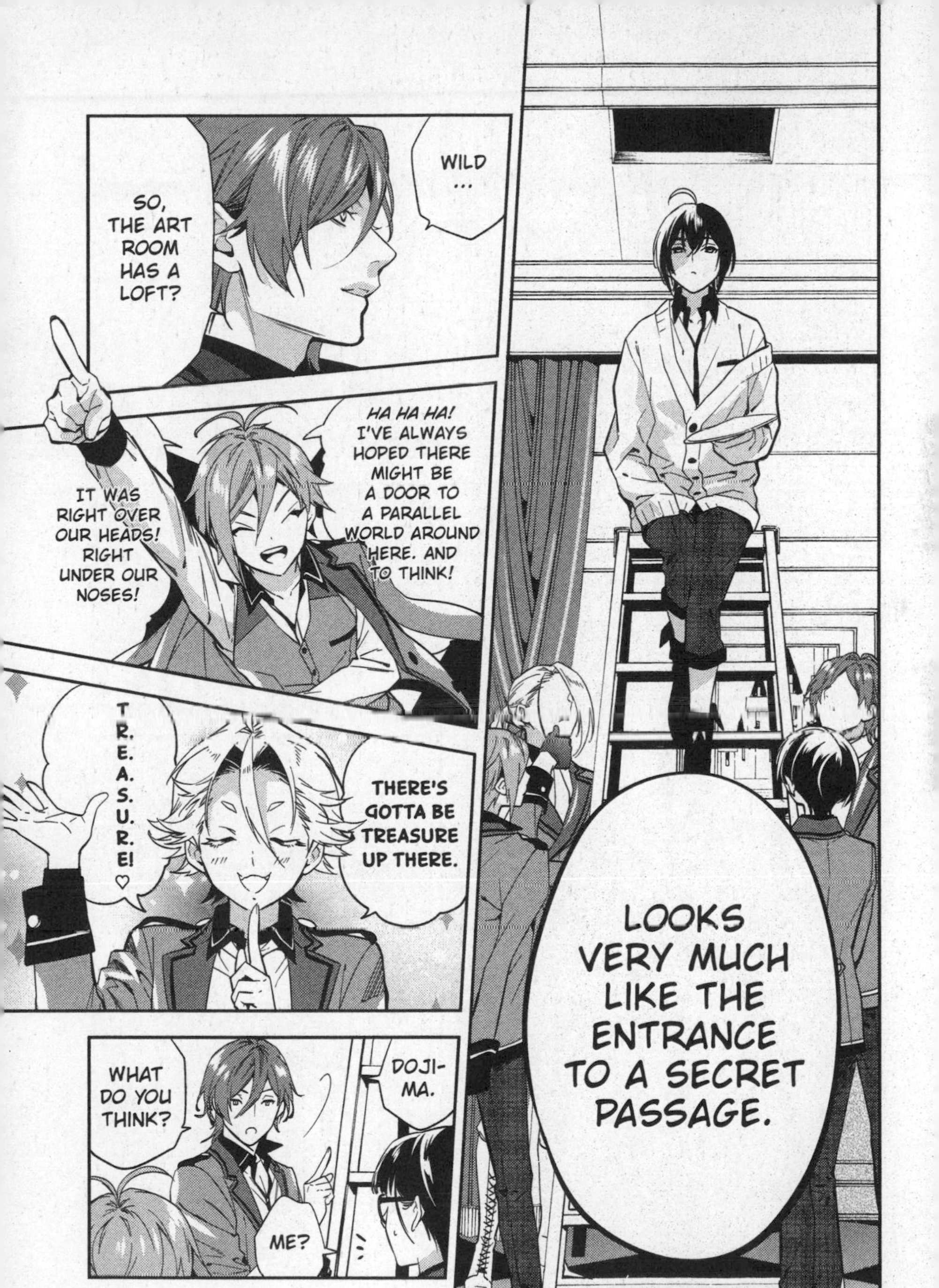
LOOKS VERY MUCH LIKE THE ENTRANCE TO A SECRET PASSAGE.
WILD ...
SO, THE ART ROOM HAS A LOFT?
HA HA HA! I'VE ALWAYS HOPED THERE MIGHT BE A DOOR TO A PARALLEL WORLD AROUND HERE. AND TO THINK!
IT WAS RIGHT OVER OUR HEADS! RIGHT UNDER OUR NOSES!
THERE'S GOTTA BE TREASURE UP THERE.
T.R.E.A.S.U.R.E! ♡
DOJI-MA.
WHAT DO YOU THINK?
ME?

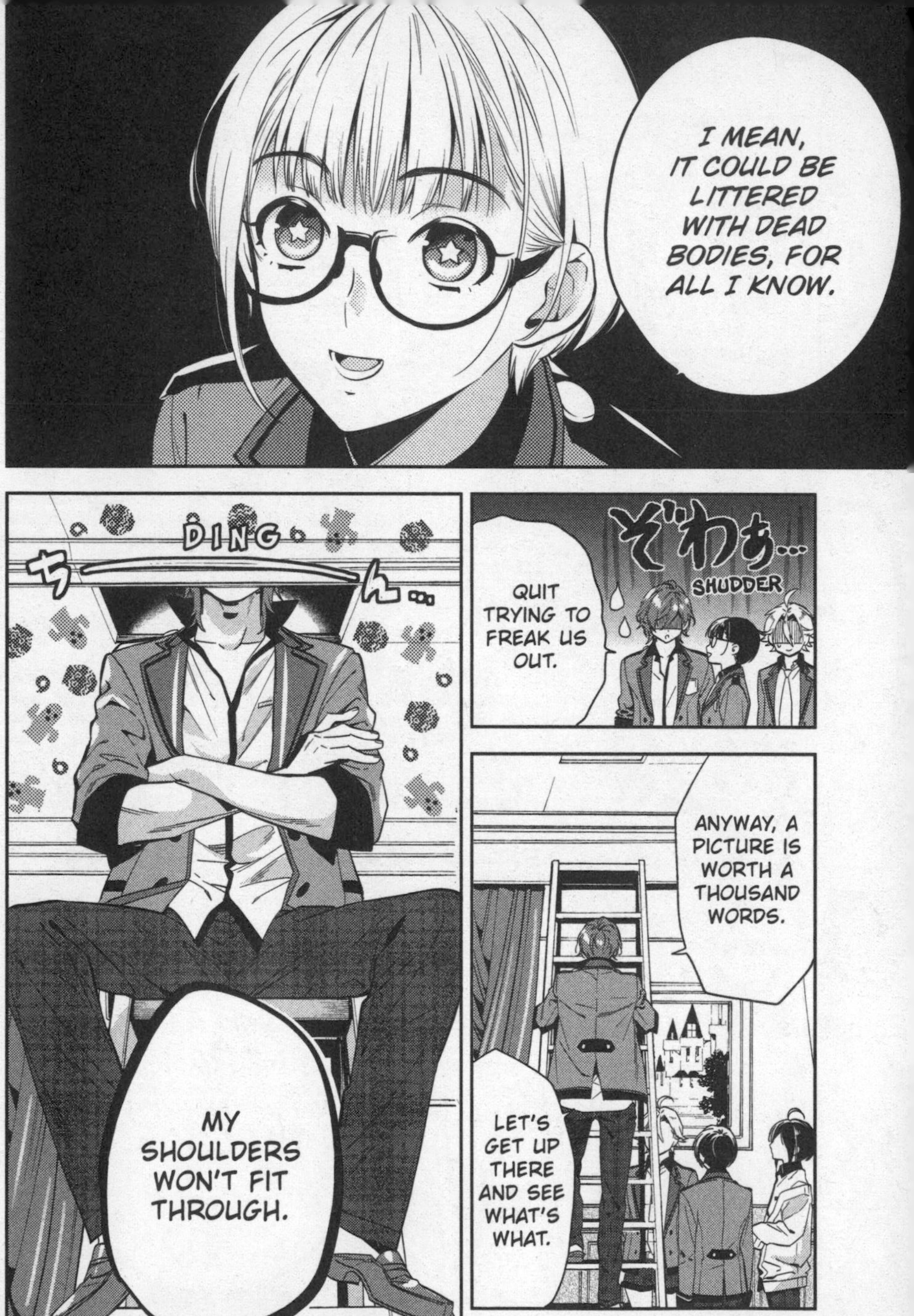
I MEAN, IT COULD BE LITTERED WITH DEAD BODIES, FOR ALL I KNOW.
ぞわぁ…
SHUDDER
QUIT TRYING TO FREAK US OUT.
ANYWAY, A PICTURE IS WORTH A THOUSAND WORDS.
LET'S GET UP THERE AND SEE WHAT'S WHAT.
DING
ち——ん…
MY SHOULDERS WON'T FIT THROUGH.

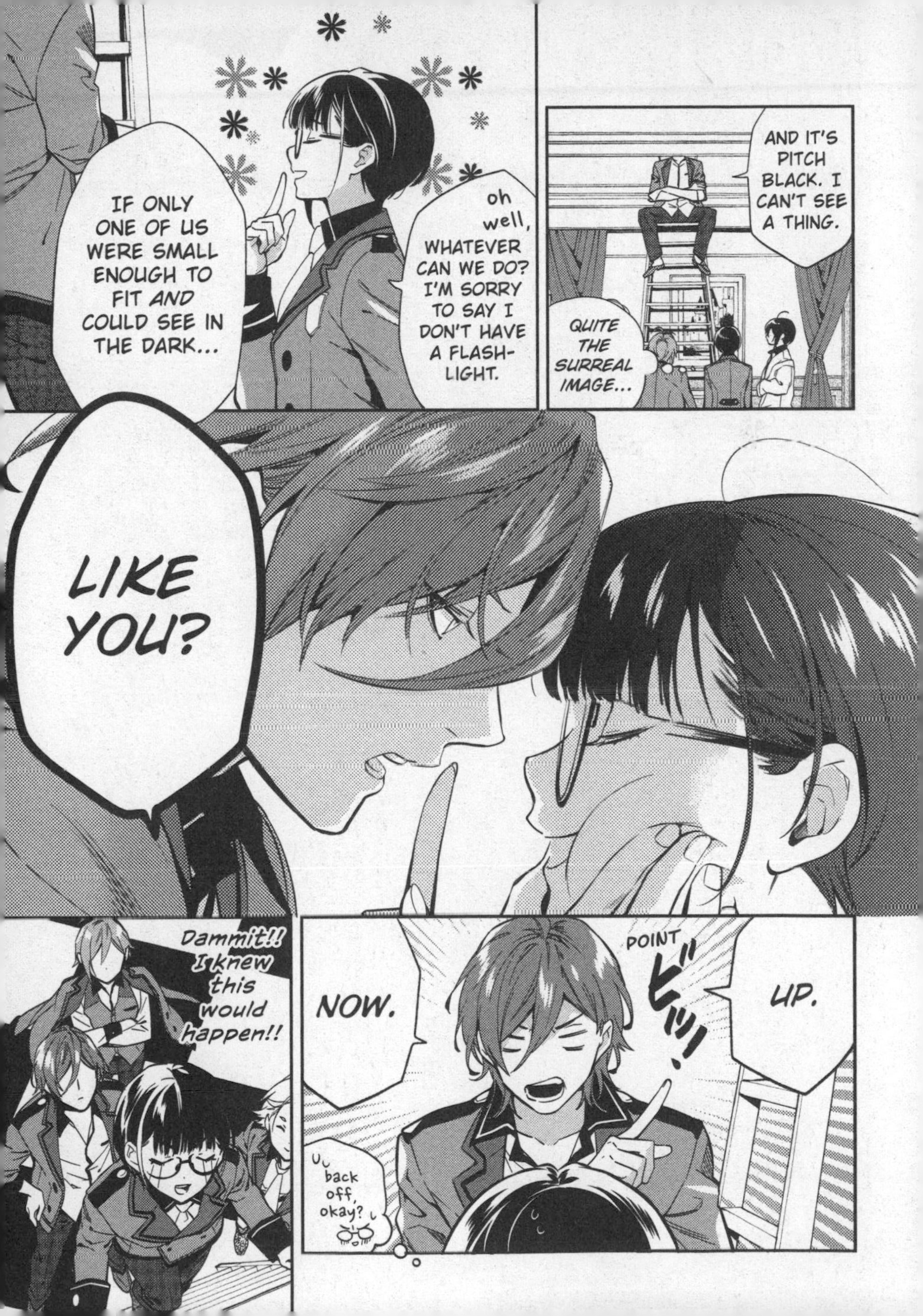
AND IT'S PITCH BLACK. I CAN'T SEE A THING.
QUITE THE SURREAL IMAGE...
oh well, WHATEVER CAN WE DO? I'M SORRY TO SAY I DON'T HAVE A FLASHLIGHT.
IF ONLY ONE OF US WERE SMALL ENOUGH TO FIT AND COULD SEE IN THE DARK...
LIKE YOU?
UP.
POINT
NOW.
back off, okay?
Dammit!! I knew this would happen!!

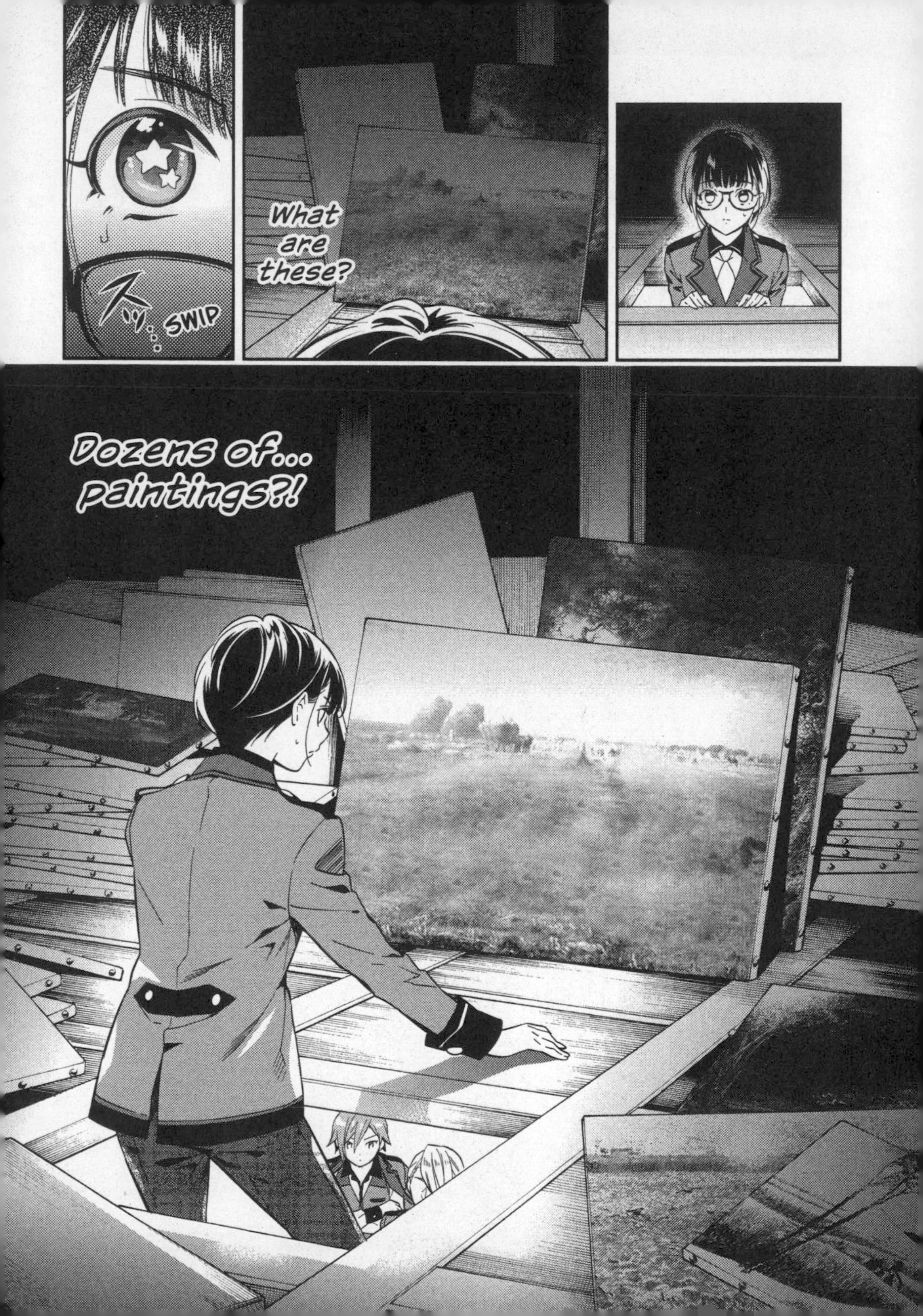
What are these?
スッ
SWIP
Dozens of... paintings?!

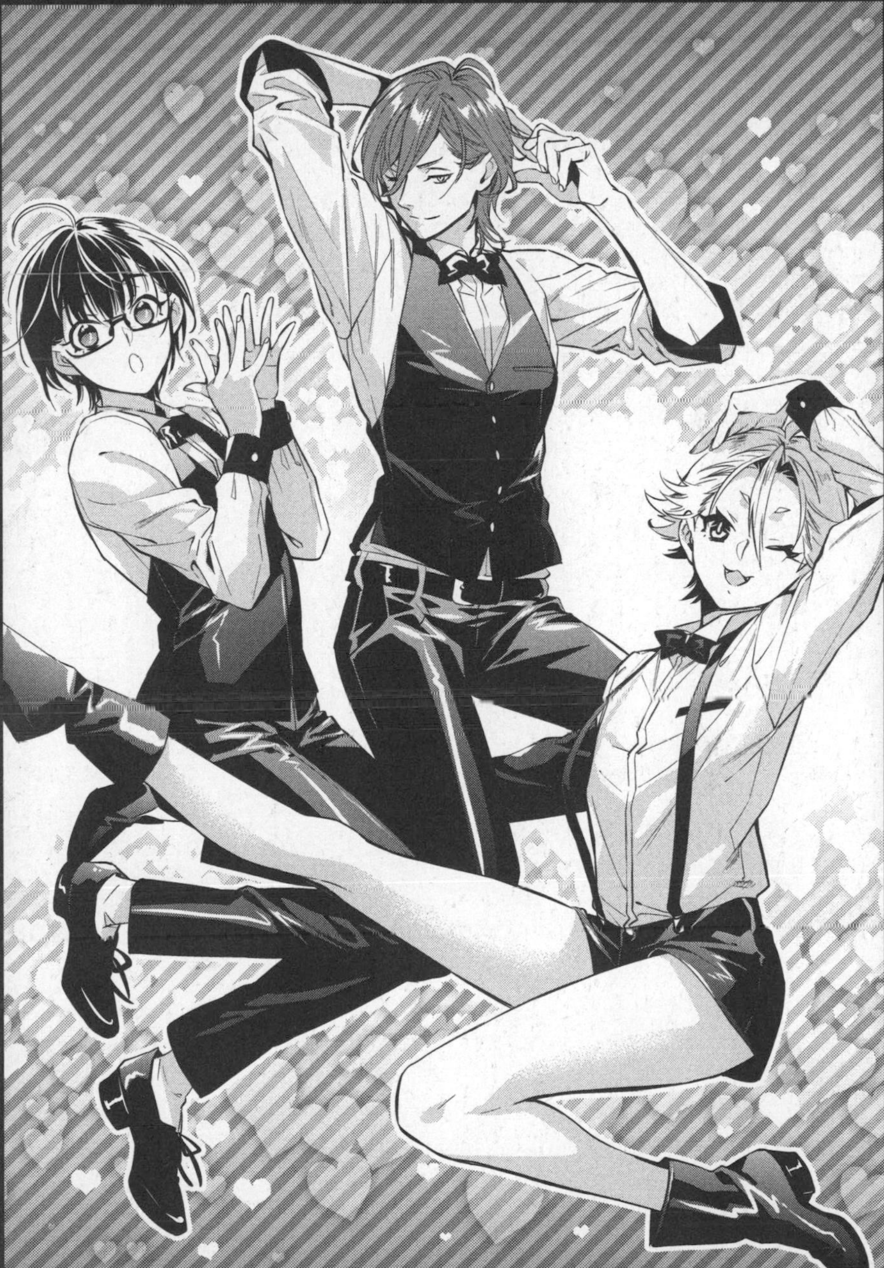

FILE ★ The Pretty Boy in the Attic 2

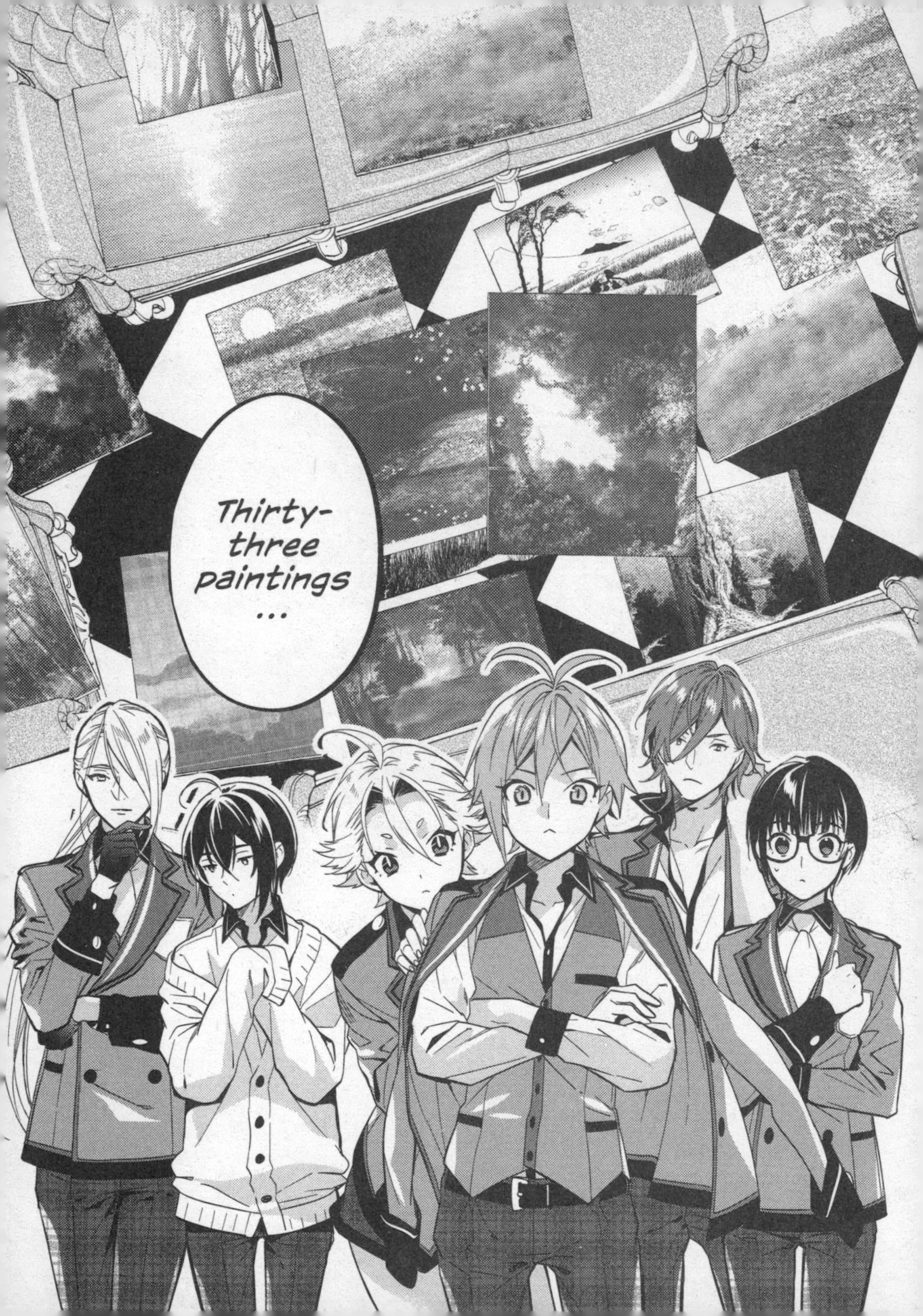
Thirty-three paintings ...

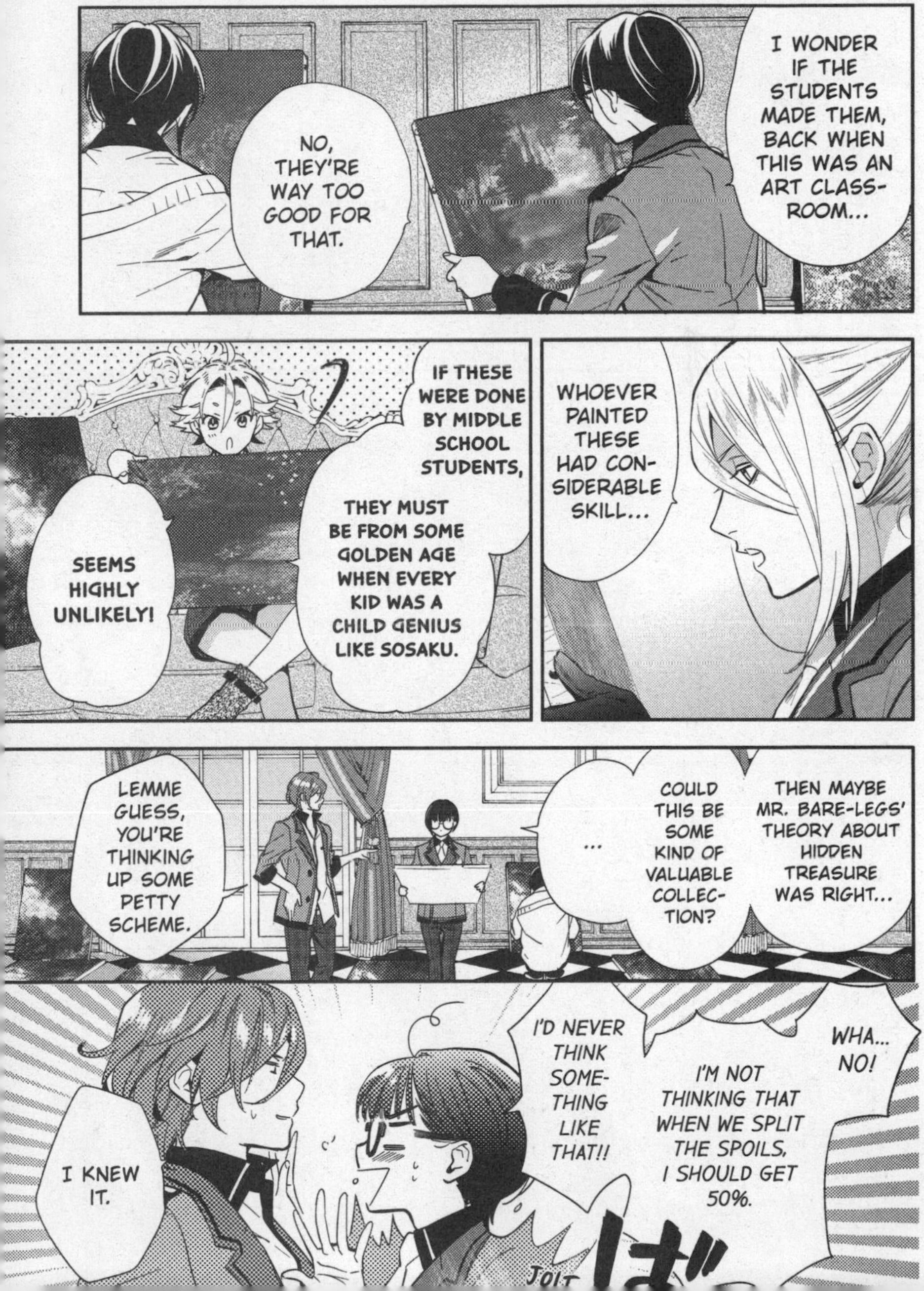
I WONDER IF THE STUDENTS MADE THEM, BACK WHEN THIS WAS AN ART CLASS-ROOM...
NO, THEY'RE WAY TOO GOOD FOR THAT.
WHOEVER PAINTED THESE HAD CON-SIDERABLE SKILL...
IF THESE WERE DONE BY MIDDLE SCHOOL STUDENTS,
THEY MUST BE FROM SOME GOLDEN AGE WHEN EVERY KID WAS A CHILD GENIUS LIKE SOSAKU.
SEEMS HIGHLY UNLIKELY!
THEN MAYBE MR. BARE-LEGS' THEORY ABOUT HIDDEN TREASURE WAS RIGHT...
COULD THIS BE SOME KIND OF VALUABLE COLLEC-TION?
...
LEMME GUESS, YOU'RE THINKING UP SOME PETTY SCHEME.
WHA... NO!
I'M NOT THINKING THAT WHEN WE SPLIT THE SPOILS, I SHOULD GET 50%.
I'D NEVER THINK SOME-THING LIKE THAT!!
I KNEW IT.
JOLT

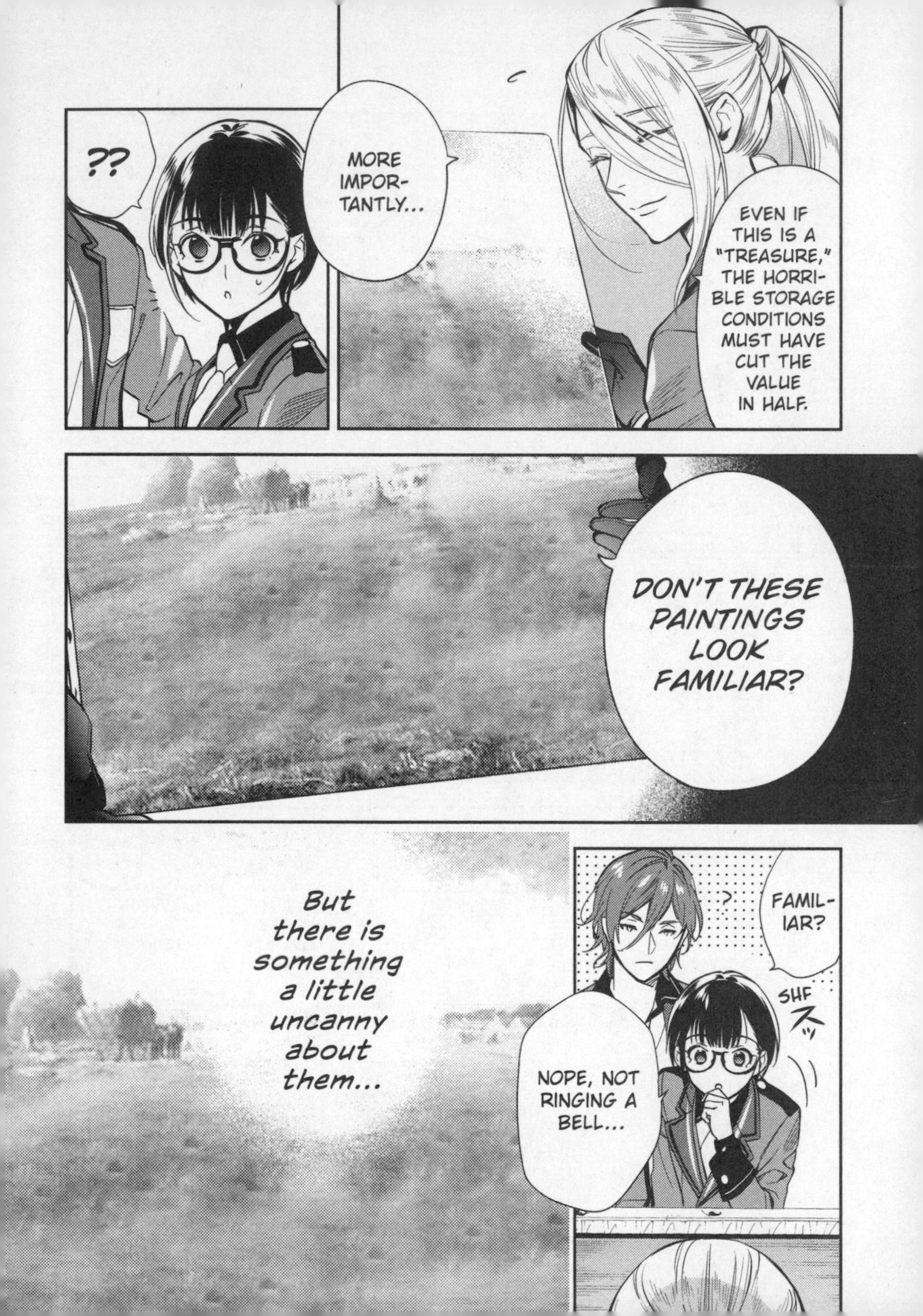
EVEN IF THIS IS A "TREASURE," THE HORRIBLE STORAGE CONDITIONS MUST HAVE CUT THE VALUE IN HALF.
MORE IMPORTANTLY...
??
DON'T THESE PAINTINGS LOOK FAMILIAR?
FAMILIAR?
?
SHF
スッ
NOPE, NOT RINGING A BELL...
But there is something a little uncanny about them...

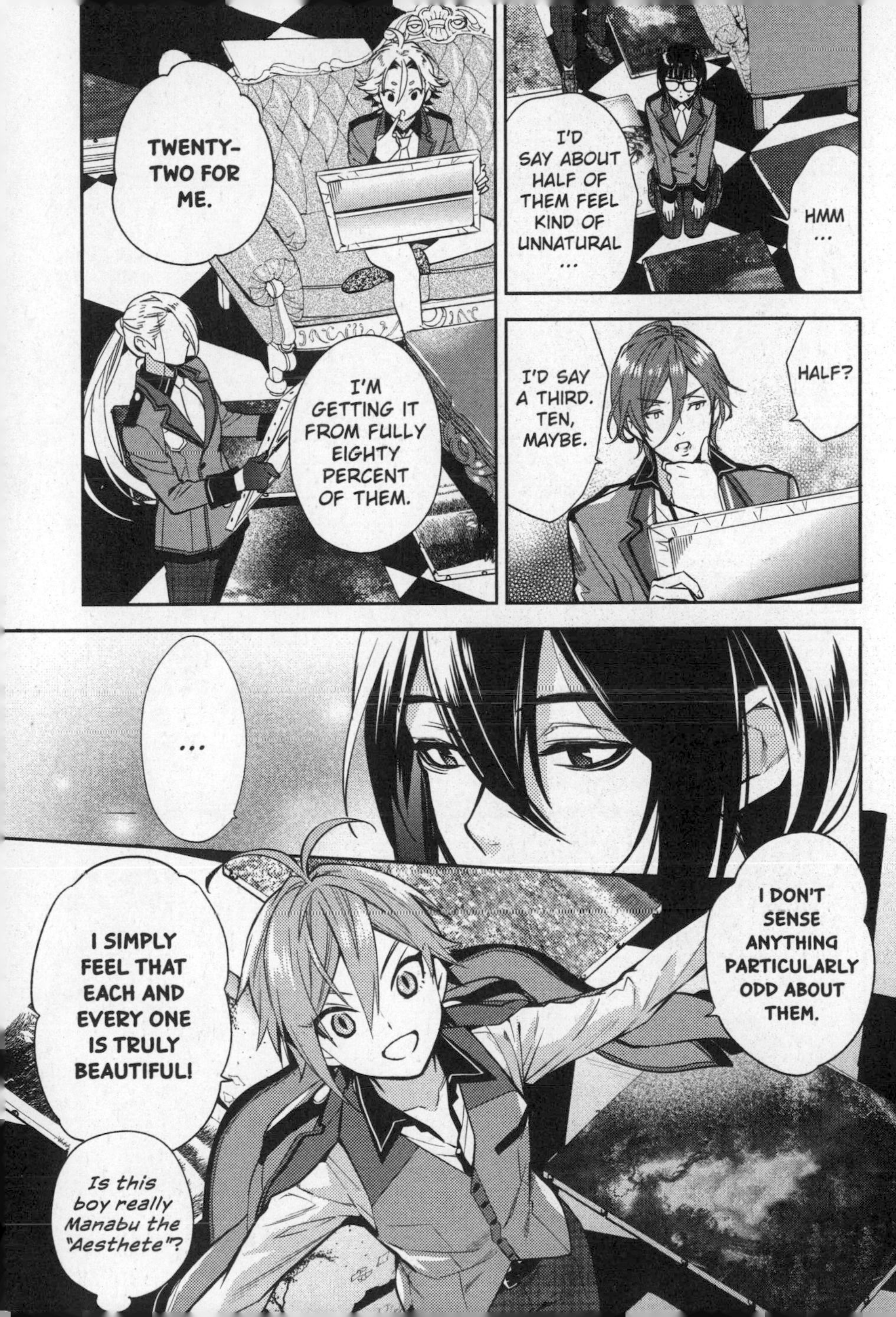
HMM ...
I'D SAY ABOUT HALF OF THEM FEEL KIND OF UNNATURAL ...
HALF?
I'D SAY A THIRD. TEN, MAYBE.
TWENTY-TWO FOR ME.
I'M GETTING IT FROM FULLY EIGHTY PERCENT OF THEM.
...
I DON'T SENSE ANYTHING PARTICULARLY ODD ABOUT THEM.
I SIMPLY FEEL THAT EACH AND EVERY ONE IS TRULY BEAUTIFUL!
Is this boy really Manabu the "Aesthete"?

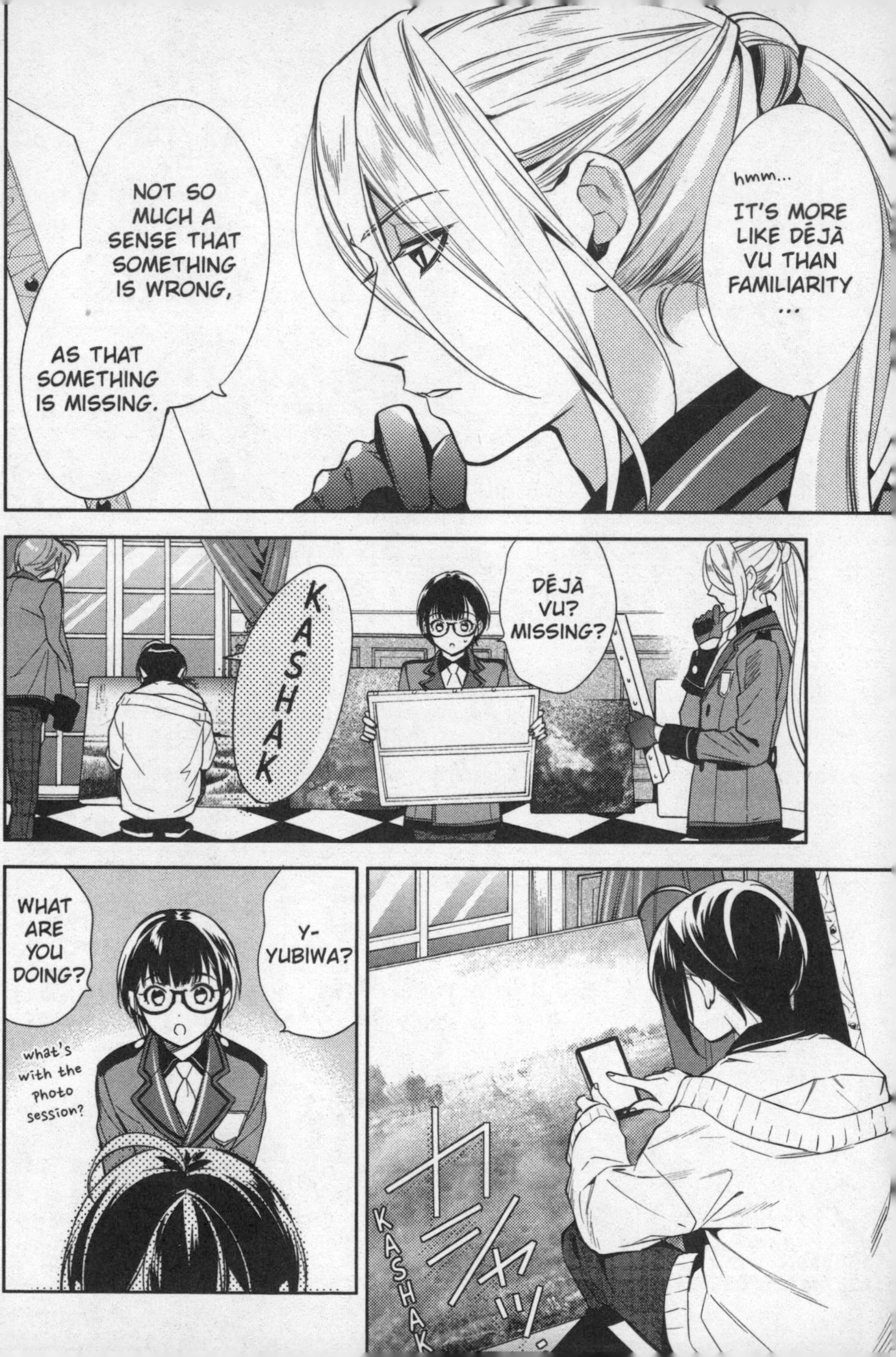
hmm...
IT'S MORE LIKE DÉJÀ VU THAN FAMILIARITY ...
NOT SO MUCH A SENSE THAT SOMETHING IS WRONG,
AS THAT SOMETHING IS MISSING.
DÉJÀ VU? MISSING?
KASHAK
Y-YUBIWA?
WHAT ARE YOU DOING?
what's with the photo session?
KASHAK

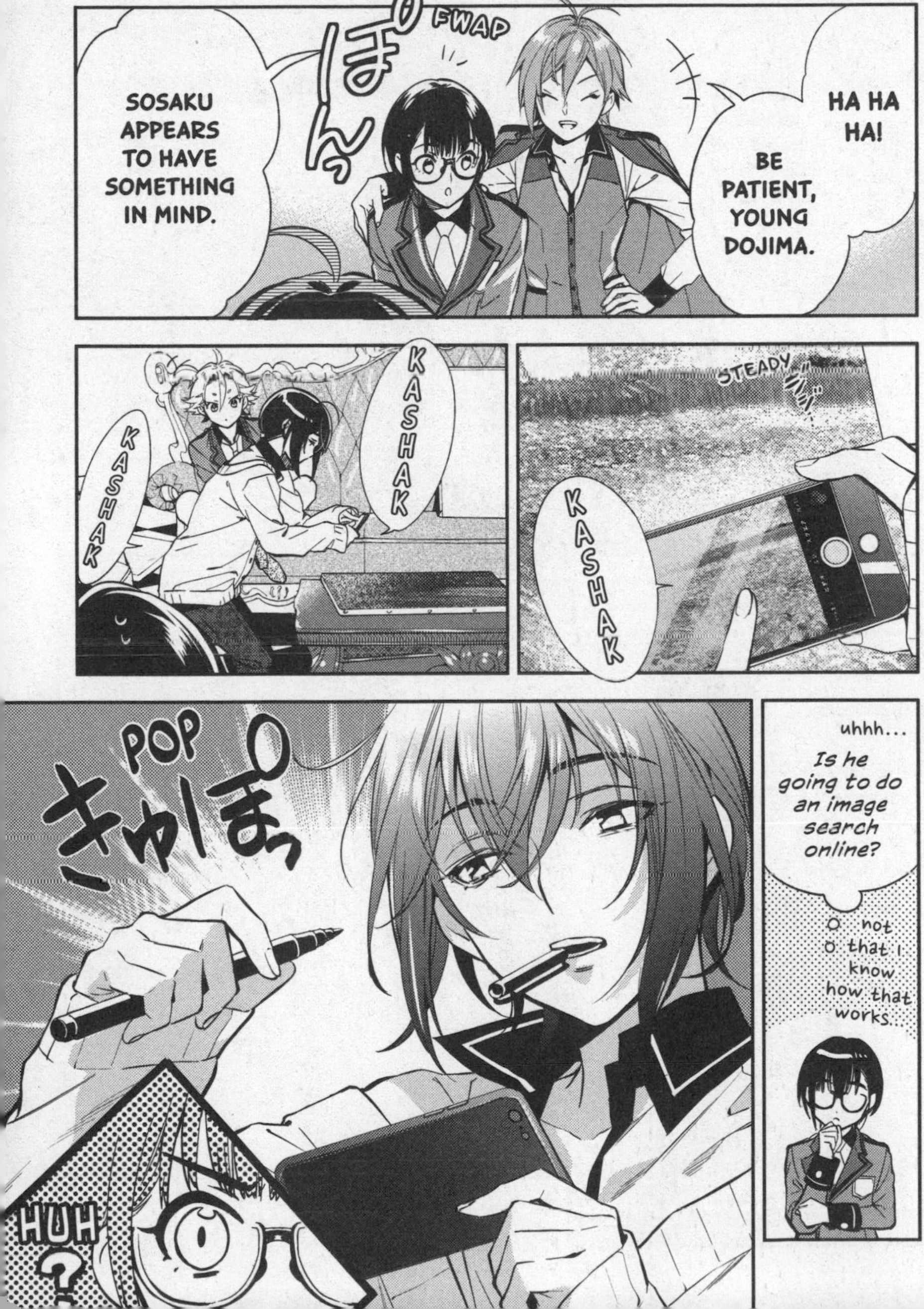
HA HA HA!
BE PATIENT, YOUNG DOJIMA.
FWAP
ぽんっ
SOSAKU APPEARS TO HAVE SOMETHING IN MIND.
STEADY
KASHAK
KASHAK
KASHAK
uhhh...
Is he going to do an image search online?
...not that I know how that works...
POP
きゅぽっ
HUH?

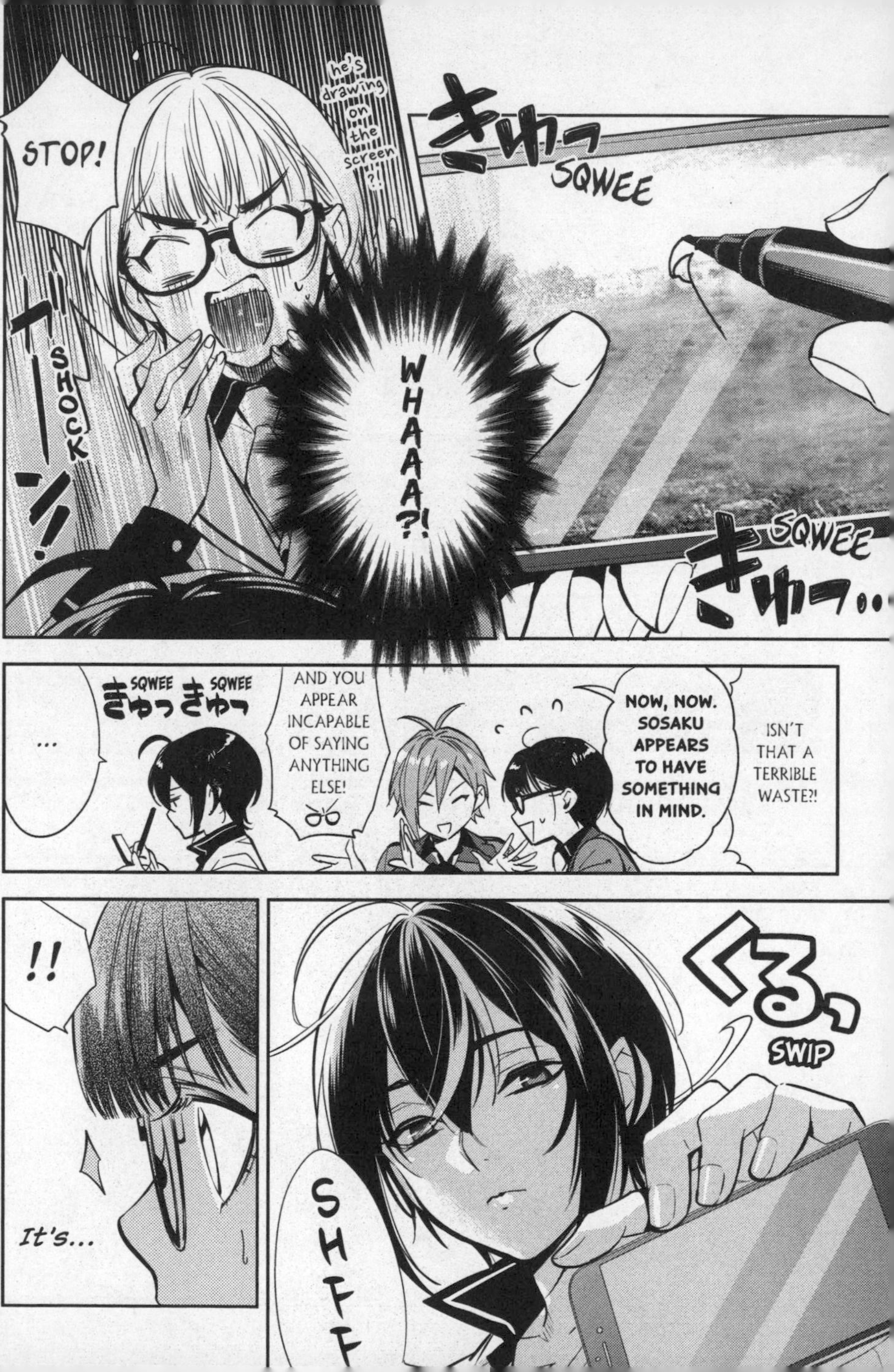
きゅっ
SQWEE
he's drawing on the screen?!
STOP!
WHAAAA?!
SQWEE
きゅっ..
SHOCK
ISN'T THAT A TERRIBLE WASTE?!
NOW, NOW. SOSAKU APPEARS TO HAVE SOMETHING IN MIND.
AND YOU APPEAR INCAPABLE OF SAYING ANYTHING ELSE!
きゅっきゅっ
SQWEE SQWEE
...
くるっ
SWIP
SHFF
!!
It's...

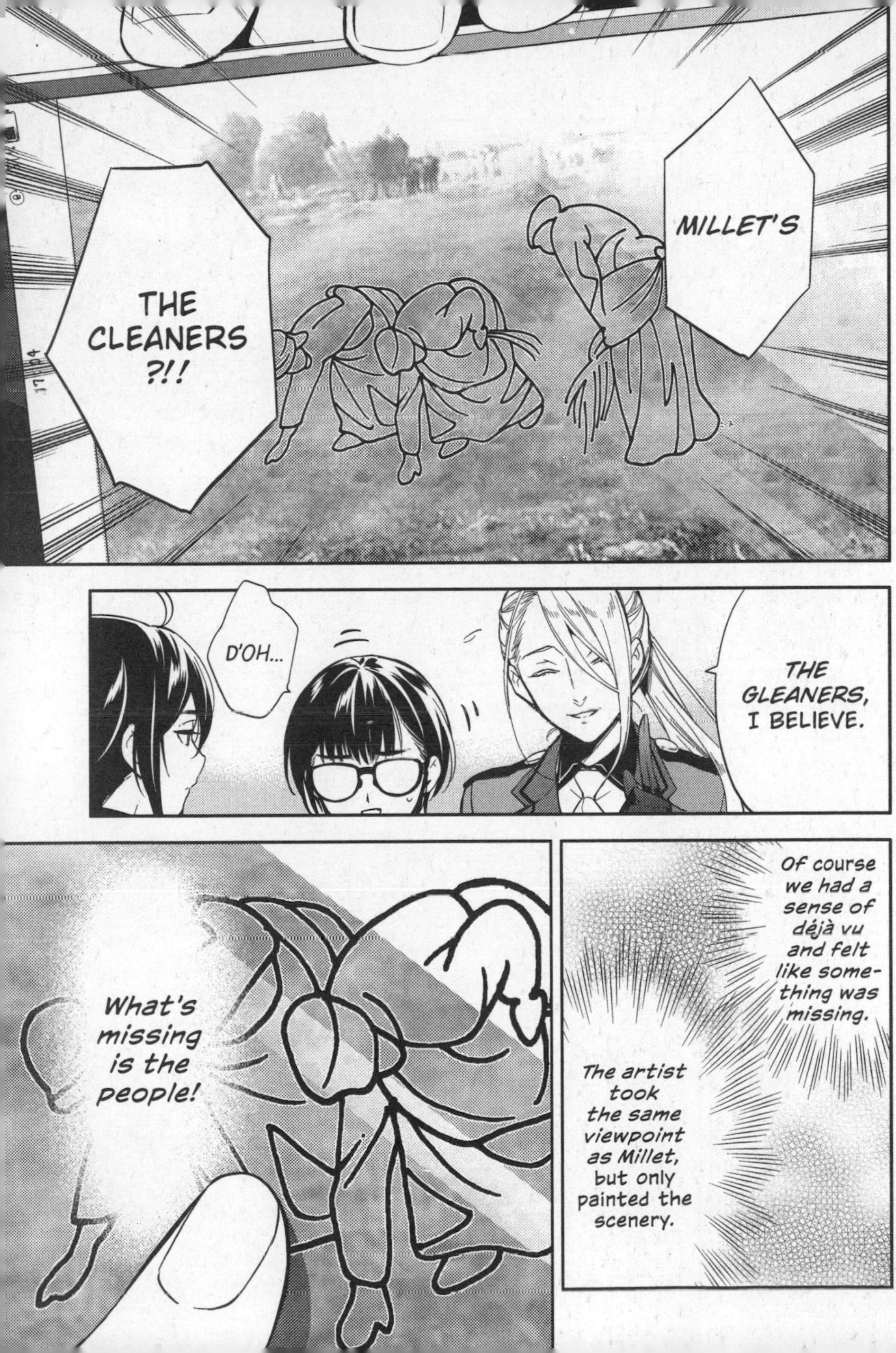
MILLET'S
THE CLEANERS ?!!
THE GLEANERS, I BELIEVE.
D'OH...
Of course we had a sense of déjà vu and felt like something was missing.
The artist took the same viewpoint as Millet, but only painted the scenery.
What's missing is the people!

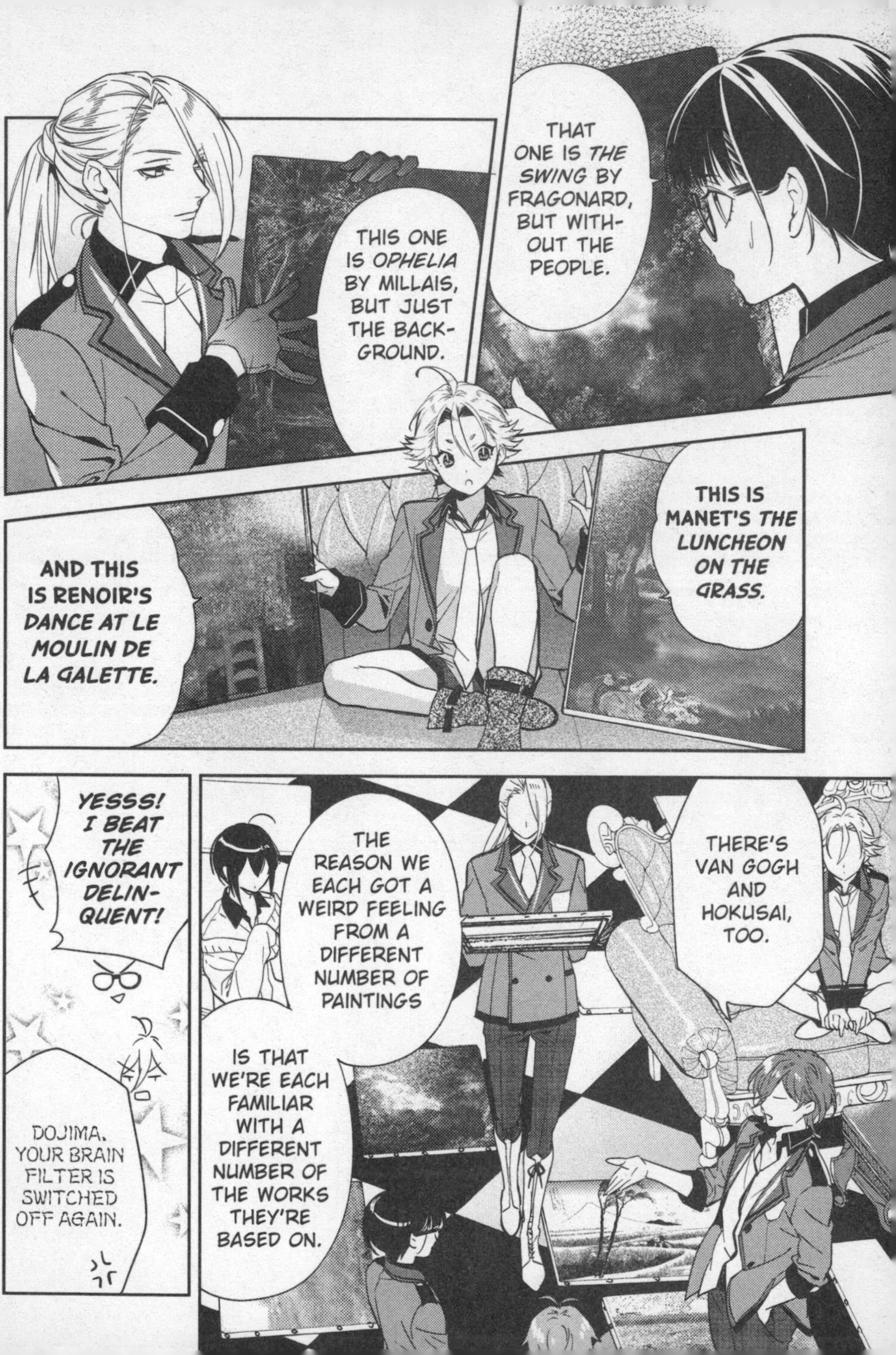
THAT ONE IS THE SWING BY FRAGONARD, BUT WITH-OUT THE PEOPLE.
THIS ONE IS OPHELIA BY MILLAIS, BUT JUST THE BACK-GROUND.
THIS IS MANET'S THE LUNCHEON ON THE GRASS.
AND THIS IS RENOIR'S DANCE AT LE MOULIN DE LA GALETTE.
THERE'S VAN GOGH AND HOKUSAI, TOO.
THE REASON WE EACH GOT A WEIRD FEELING FROM A DIFFERENT NUMBER OF PAINTINGS
IS THAT WE'RE EACH FAMILIAR WITH A DIFFERENT NUMBER OF THE WORKS THEY'RE BASED ON.
YESSS! I BEAT THE IGNORANT DELIN-QUENT!
DOJIMA. YOUR BRAIN FILTER IS SWITCHED OFF AGAIN.

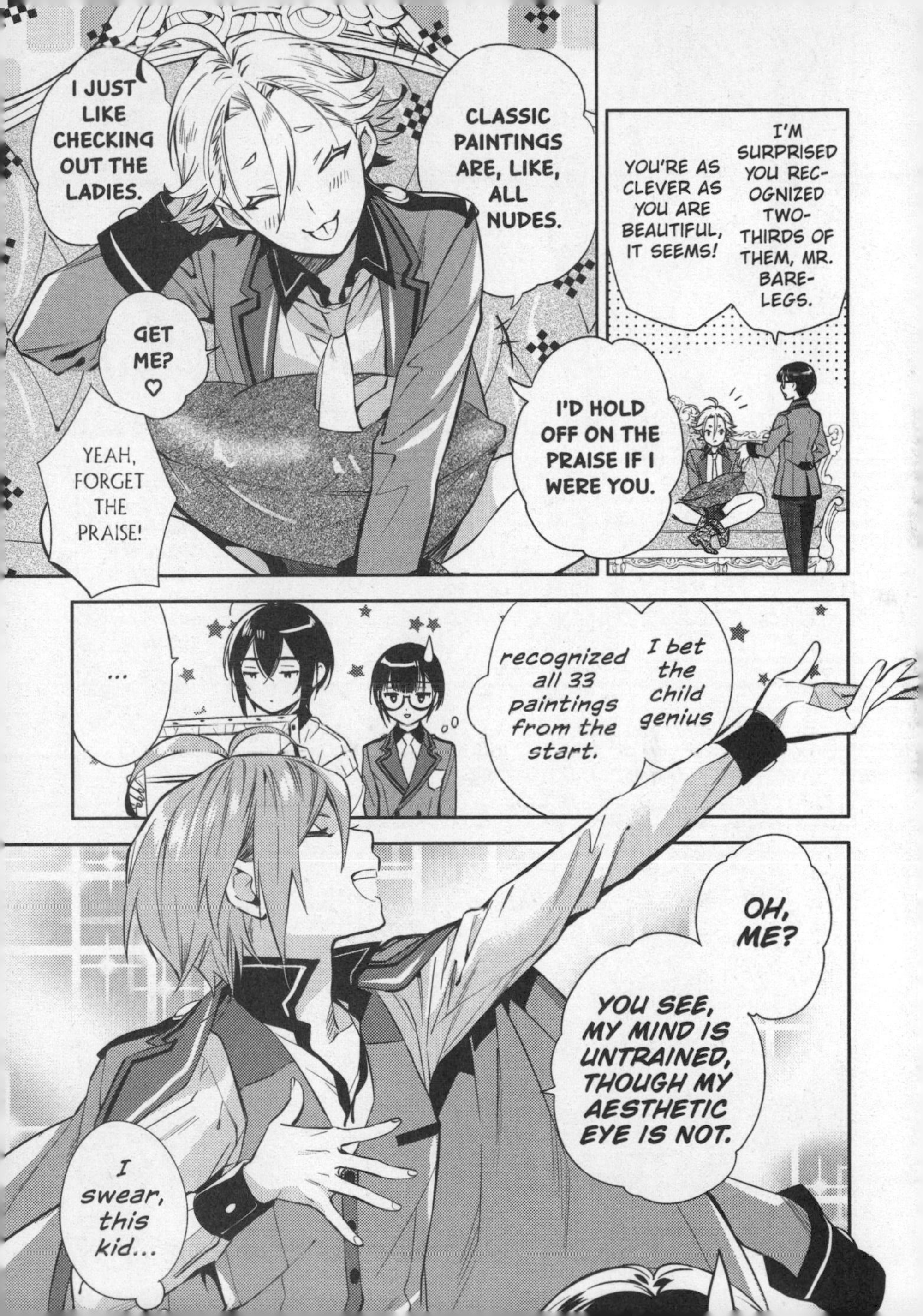
I'M SURPRISED YOU RECOGNIZED TWO-THIRDS OF THEM, MR. BARE-LEGS.
YOU'RE AS CLEVER AS YOU ARE BEAUTIFUL, IT SEEMS!
I'D HOLD OFF ON THE PRAISE IF I WERE YOU.
CLASSIC PAINTINGS ARE, LIKE, ALL NUDES.
I JUST LIKE CHECKING OUT THE LADIES.
GET ME? ♡
YEAH, FORGET THE PRAISE!
I bet the child genius recognized all 33 paintings from the start.
...
OH, ME?
YOU SEE, MY MIND IS UNTRAINED, THOUGH MY AESTHETIC EYE IS NOT.
I swear, this kid...

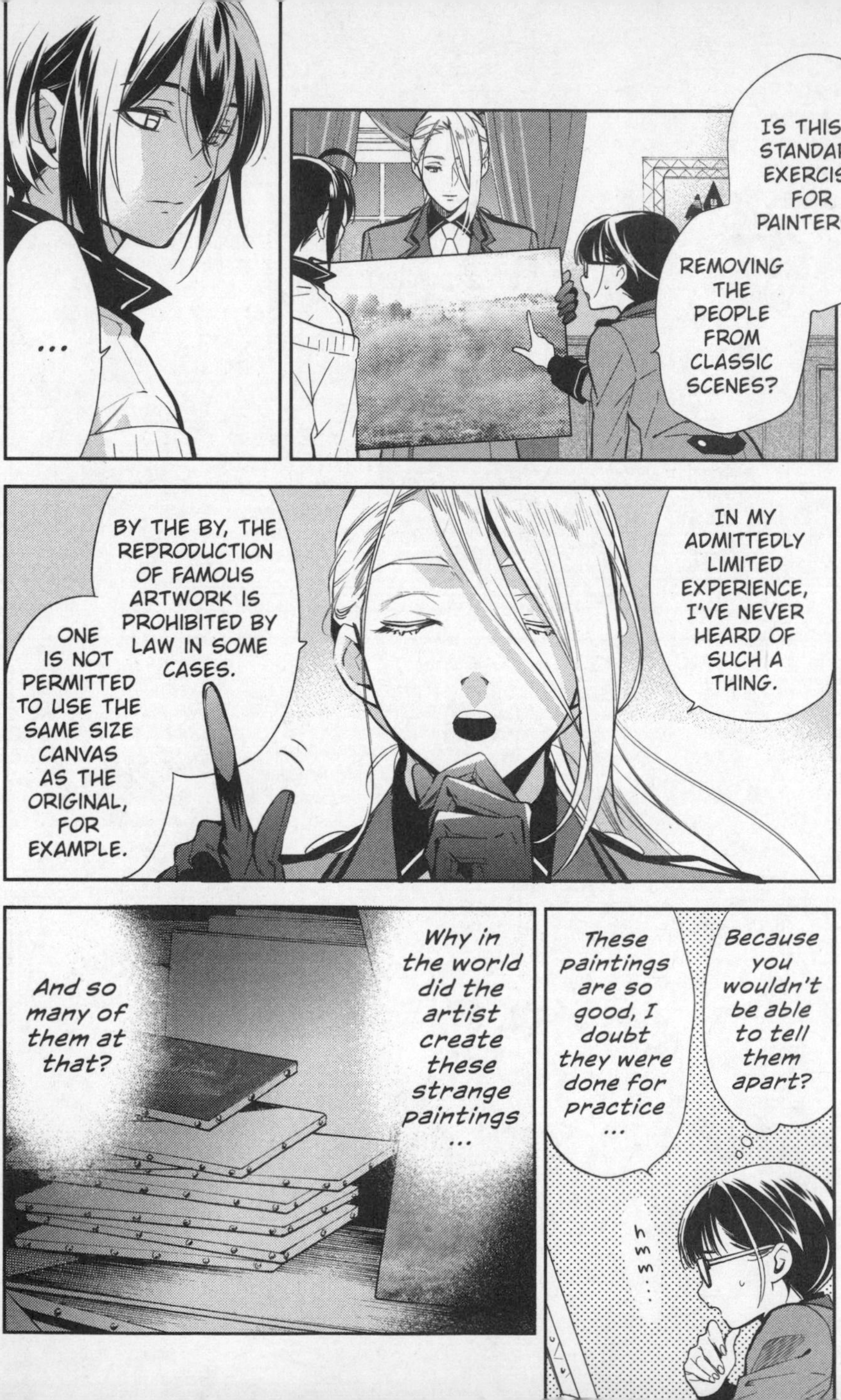
IS THIS A STANDARD EXERCISE FOR PAINTERS?
REMOVING THE PEOPLE FROM CLASSIC SCENES?
...
IN MY ADMITTEDLY LIMITED EXPERIENCE, I'VE NEVER HEARD OF SUCH A THING.
BY THE BY, THE REPRODUCTION OF FAMOUS ARTWORK IS PROHIBITED BY LAW IN SOME CASES.
ONE IS NOT PERMITTED TO USE THE SAME SIZE CANVAS AS THE ORIGINAL, FOR EXAMPLE.
Because you wouldn't be able to tell them apart?
These paintings are so good, I doubt they were done for practice...
hmm...
Why in the world did the artist create these strange paintings...
And so many of them at that?

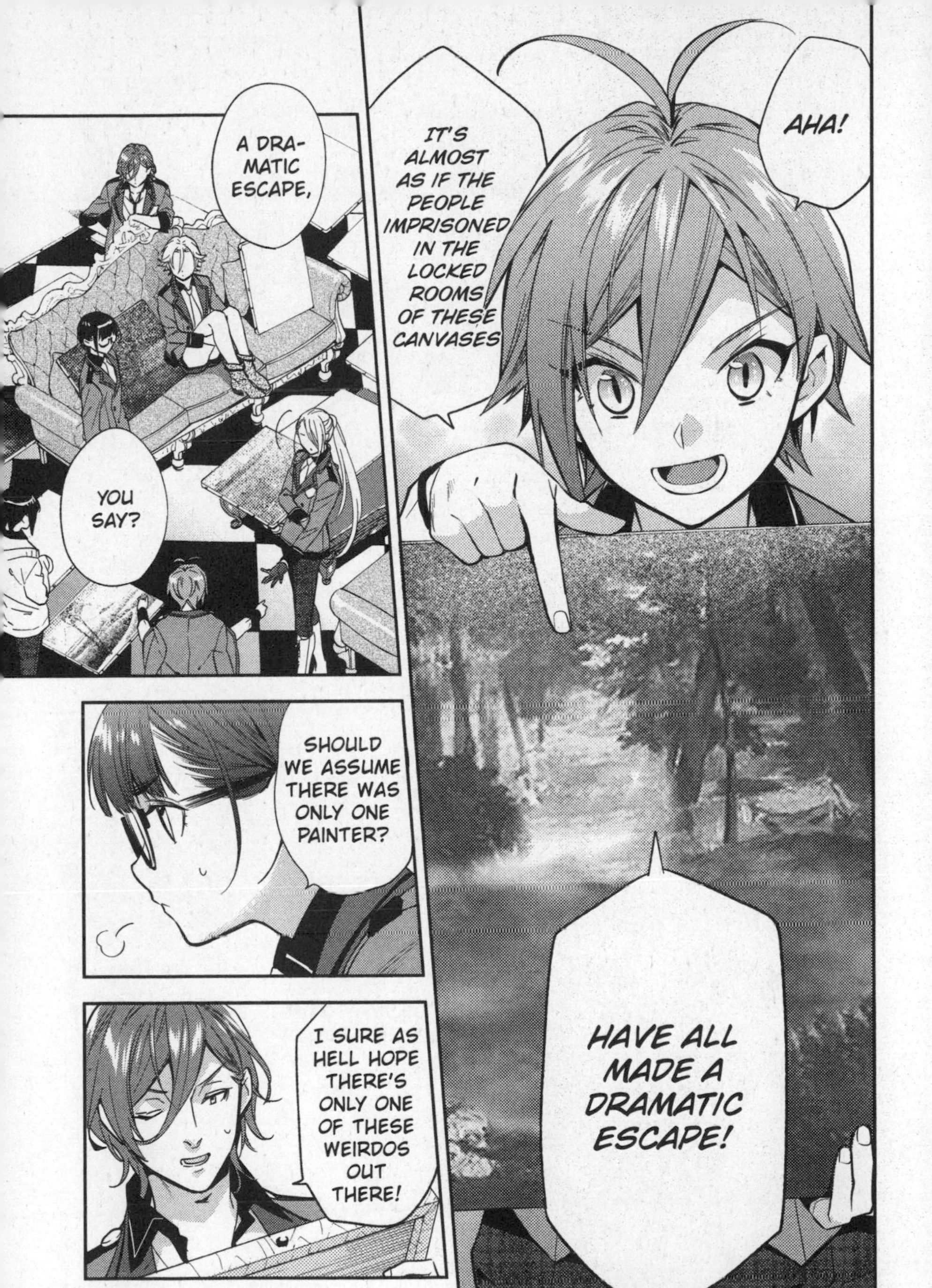
AHA!
IT'S ALMOST AS IF THE PEOPLE IMPRISONED IN THE LOCKED ROOMS OF THESE CANVASES
HAVE ALL MADE A DRAMATIC ESCAPE!
A DRA-MATIC ESCAPE,
YOU SAY?
SHOULD WE ASSUME THERE WAS ONLY ONE PAINTER?
I SURE AS HELL HOPE THERE'S ONLY ONE OF THESE WEIRDOS OUT THERE!

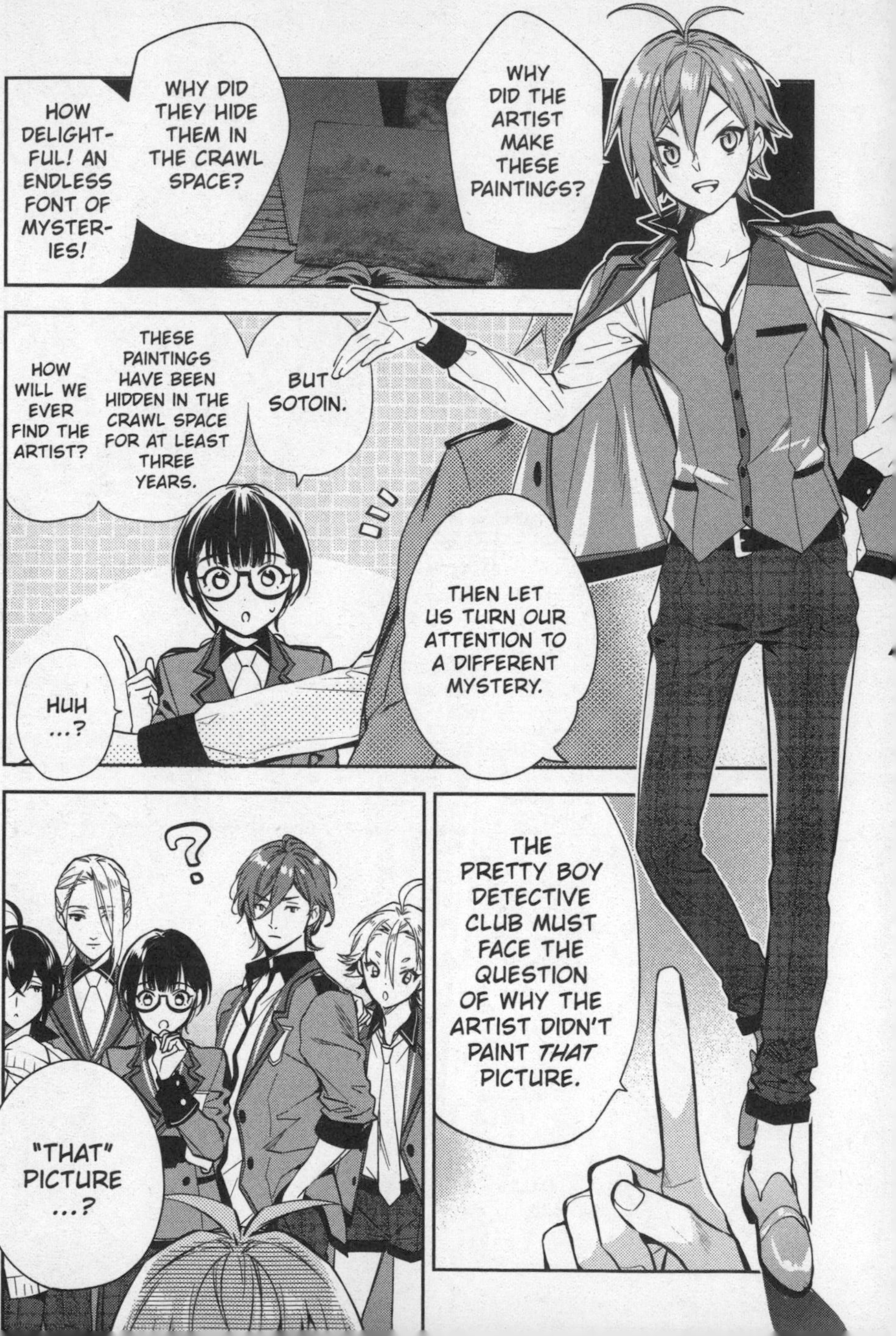
WHY DID THE ARTIST MAKE THESE PAINTINGS?
WHY DID THEY HIDE THEM IN THE CRAWL SPACE?
HOW DELIGHT-FUL! AN ENDLESS FONT OF MYSTER-IES!
BUT SOTOIN.
THESE PAINTINGS HAVE BEEN HIDDEN IN THE CRAWL SPACE FOR AT LEAST THREE YEARS.
HOW WILL WE EVER FIND THE ARTIST?
THEN LET US TURN OUR ATTENTION TO A DIFFERENT MYSTERY.
HUH ...?
THE PRETTY BOY DETECTIVE CLUB MUST FACE THE QUESTION OF WHY THE ARTIST DIDN'T PAINT *THAT* PICTURE.
"THAT" PICTURE ...?

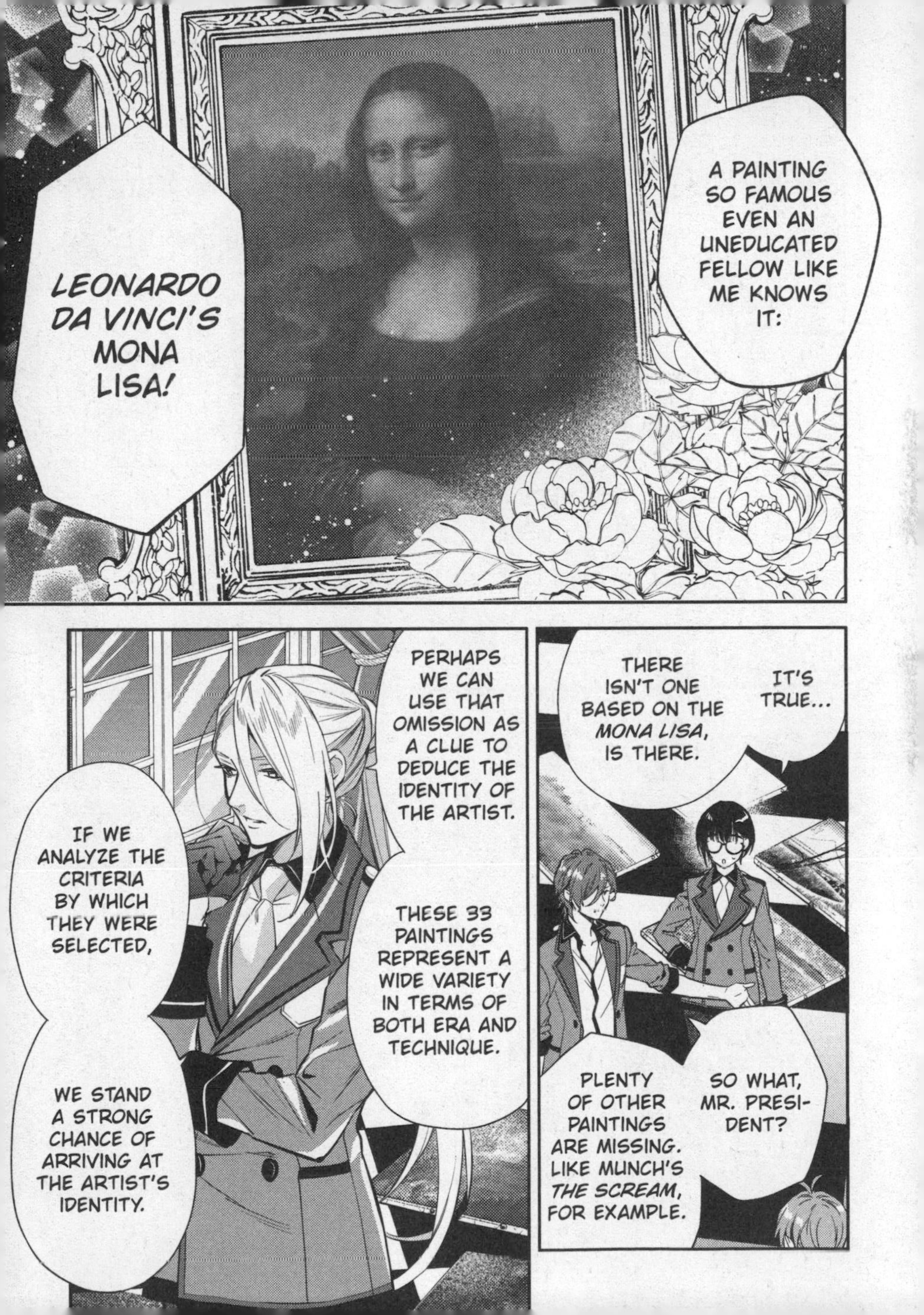
A PAINTING SO FAMOUS EVEN AN UNEDUCATED FELLOW LIKE ME KNOWS IT:
LEONARDO DA VINCI'S MONA LISA!
IT'S TRUE...
THERE ISN'T ONE BASED ON THE *MONA LISA*, IS THERE.
SO WHAT, MR. PRESI-DENT?
PLENTY OF OTHER PAINTINGS ARE MISSING. LIKE MUNCH'S *THE SCREAM*, FOR EXAMPLE.
PERHAPS WE CAN USE THAT OMISSION AS A CLUE TO DEDUCE THE IDENTITY OF THE ARTIST.
THESE 33 PAINTINGS REPRESENT A WIDE VARIETY IN TERMS OF BOTH ERA AND TECHNIQUE.
IF WE ANALYZE THE CRITERIA BY WHICH THEY WERE SELECTED,
WE STAND A STRONG CHANCE OF ARRIVING AT THE ARTIST'S IDENTITY.

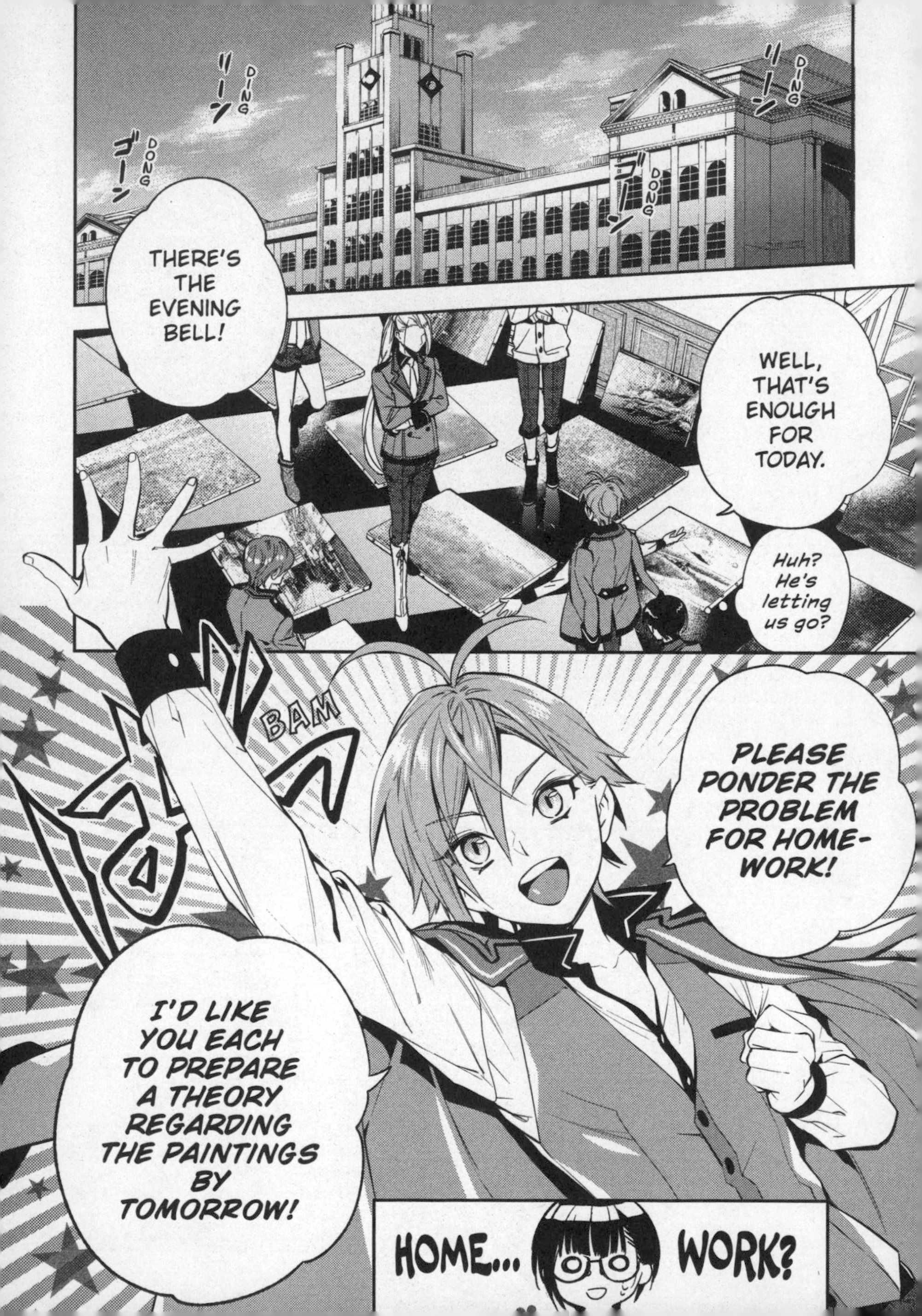
リーン
DING
ゴーン
DONG
リーン
DING
ゴーン
DONG
THERE'S THE EVENING BELL!
WELL, THAT'S ENOUGH FOR TODAY.
Huh? He's letting us go?
BAM
PLEASE PONDER THE PROBLEM FOR HOME-WORK!
I'D LIKE YOU EACH TO PREPARE A THEORY REGARDING THE PAINTINGS BY TOMORROW!
HOME... WORK?

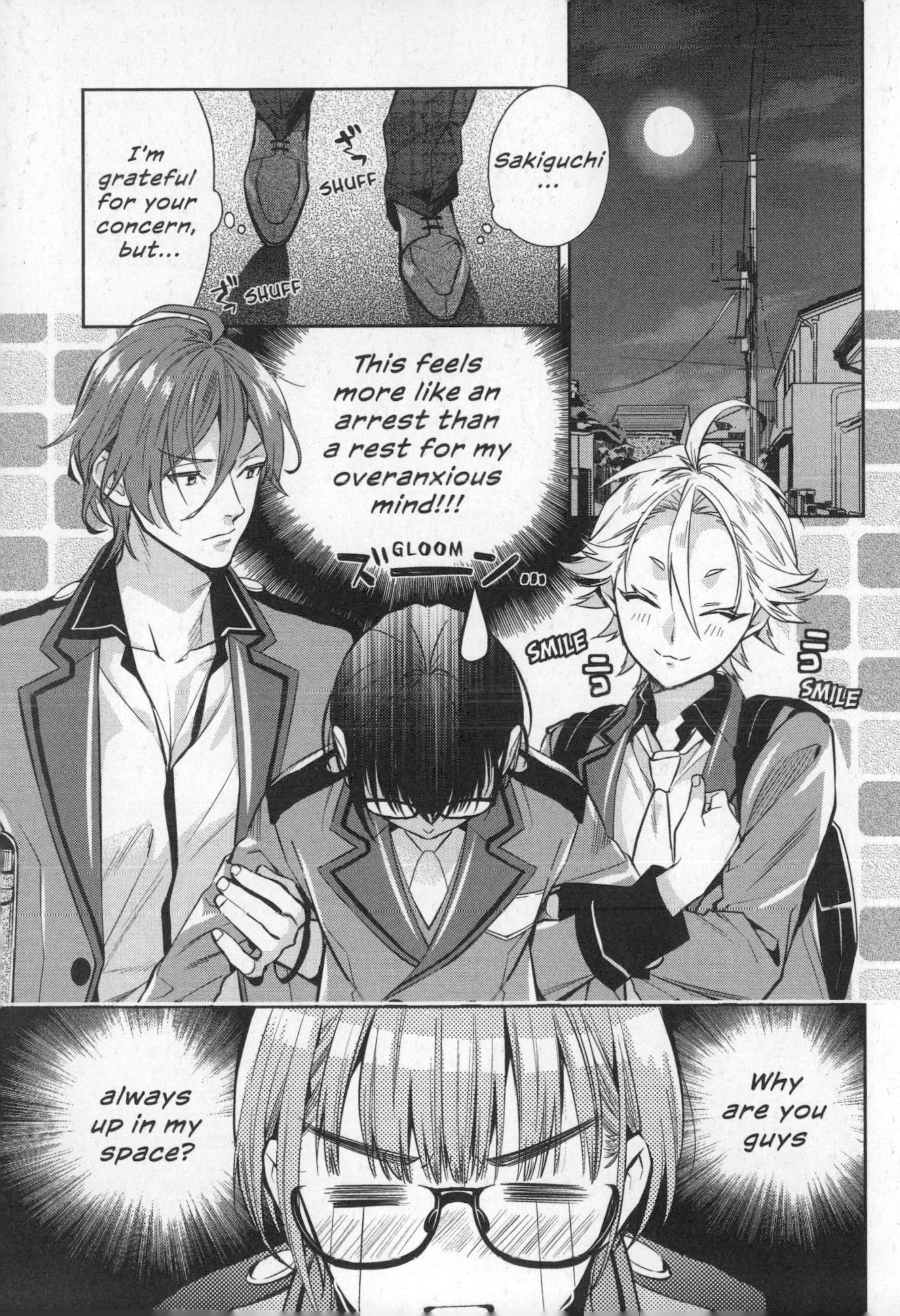

Sakiguchi ...
SHUFF
I'm grateful for your concern, but...
SHUFF
This feels more like an arrest than a rest for my overanxious mind!!!
GLOOM
SMILE
SMILE
Why are you guys
always up in my space?

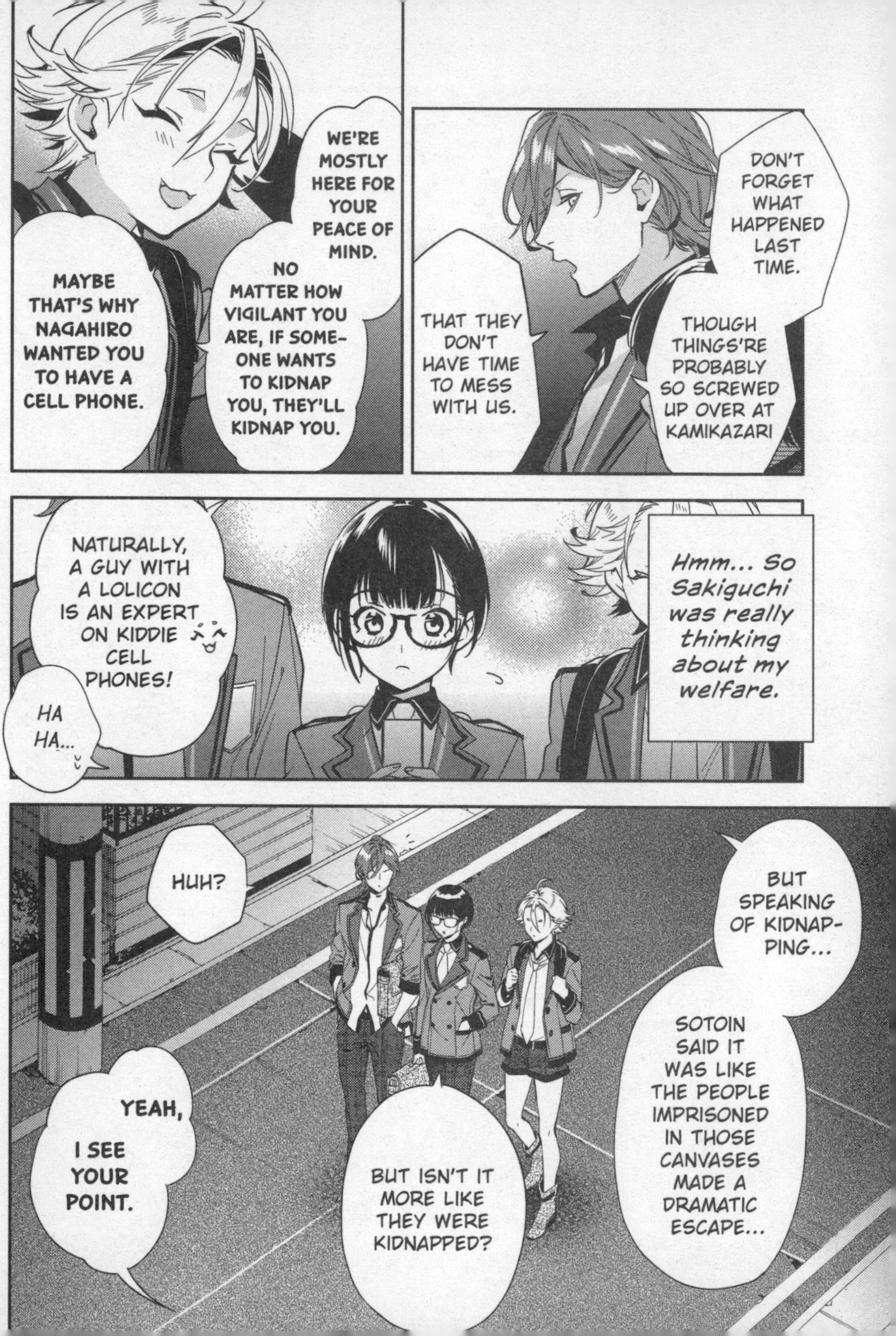
DON'T FORGET WHAT HAPPENED LAST TIME.
THOUGH THINGS'RE PROBABLY SO SCREWED UP OVER AT KAMIKAZARI
THAT THEY DON'T HAVE TIME TO MESS WITH US.
WE'RE MOSTLY HERE FOR YOUR PEACE OF MIND.
NO MATTER HOW VIGILANT YOU ARE, IF SOME-ONE WANTS TO KIDNAP YOU, THEY'LL KIDNAP YOU.
MAYBE THAT'S WHY NAGAHIRO WANTED YOU TO HAVE A CELL PHONE.
Hmm... So Sakiguchi was really thinking about my welfare.
NATURALLY, A GUY WITH A LOLICON IS AN EXPERT ON KIDDIE CELL PHONES!
HA HA...
BUT SPEAKING OF KIDNAP-PING...
SOTOIN SAID IT WAS LIKE THE PEOPLE IMPRISONED IN THOSE CANVASES MADE A DRAMATIC ESCAPE...
HUH?
BUT ISN'T IT MORE LIKE THEY WERE KIDNAPPED?
YEAH, I SEE YOUR POINT.

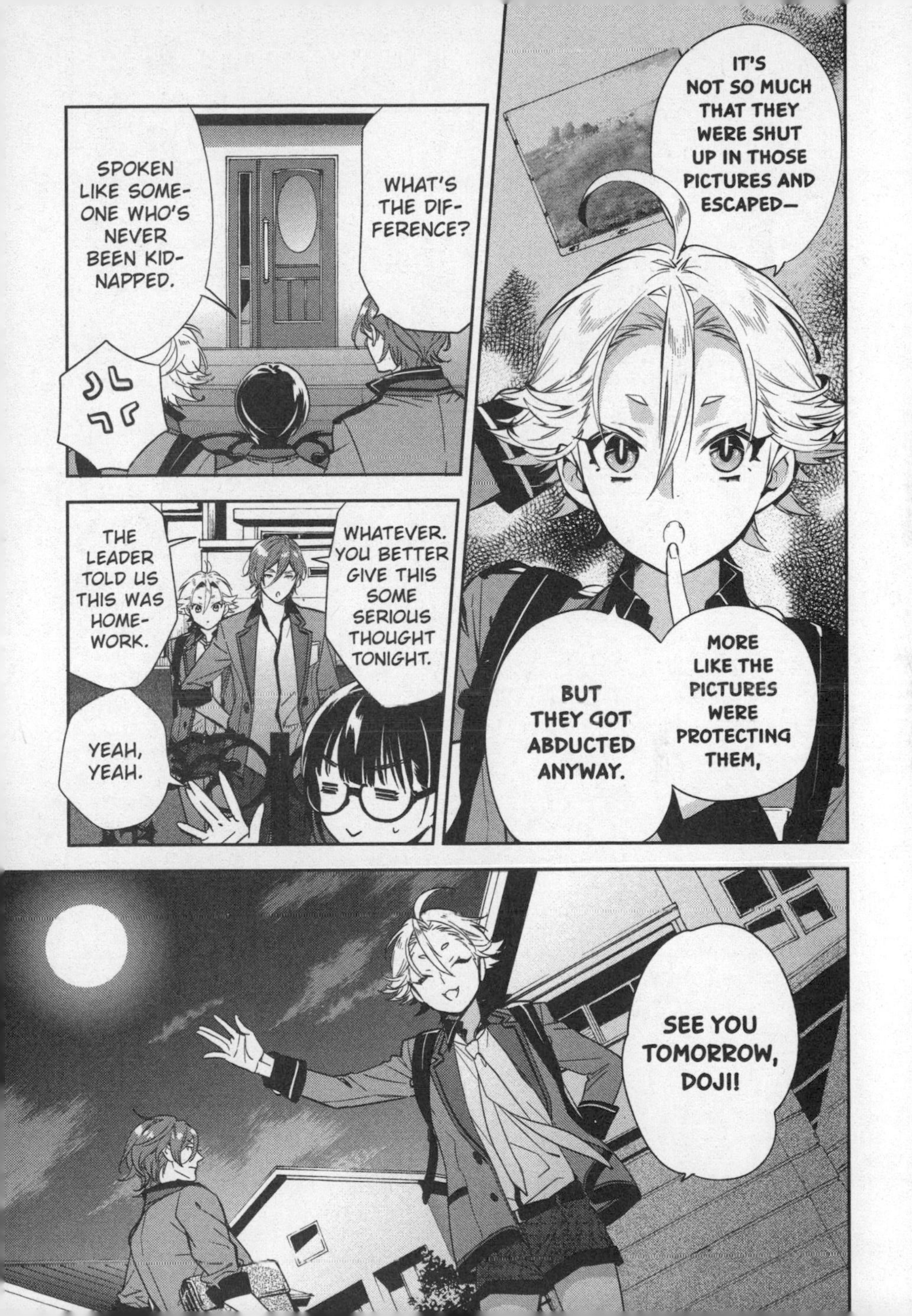
IT'S NOT SO MUCH THAT THEY WERE SHUT UP IN THOSE PICTURES AND ESCAPED—
MORE LIKE THE PICTURES WERE PROTECTING THEM,
BUT THEY GOT ABDUCTED ANYWAY.
WHAT'S THE DIFFERENCE?
SPOKEN LIKE SOMEONE WHO'S NEVER BEEN KIDNAPPED.
WHATEVER. YOU BETTER GIVE THIS SOME SERIOUS THOUGHT TONIGHT.
THE LEADER TOLD US THIS WAS HOMEWORK.
YEAH, YEAH.
SEE YOU TOMORROW, DOJI!!

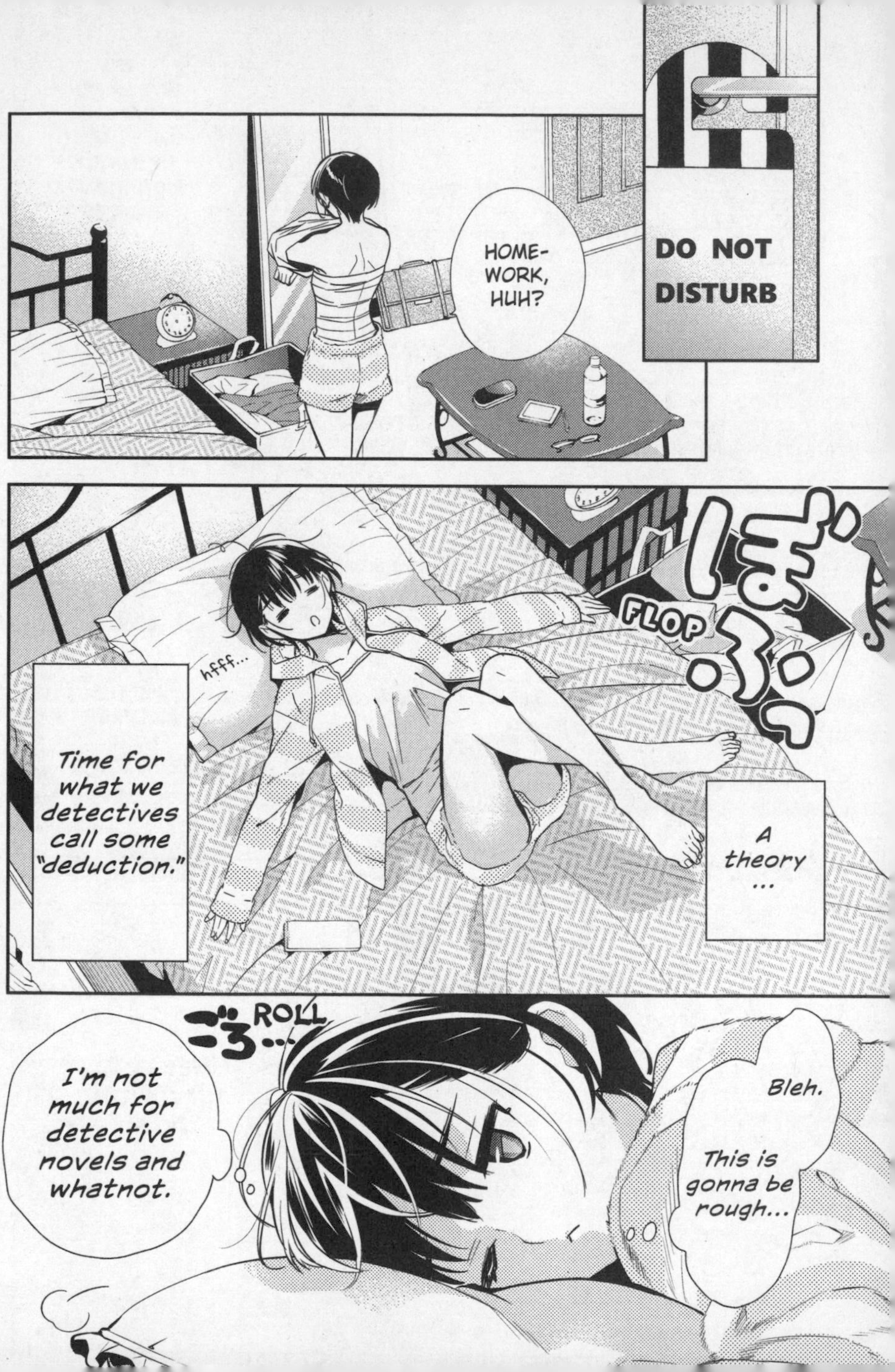

DO NOT DISTURB
HOME-WORK, HUH?
ぼふっ
FLOP
hfff...
Time for what we detectives call some "deduction."
A theory ...
ごろ…
ROLL
Bleh.
This is gonna be rough...
I'm not much for detective novels and whatnot.

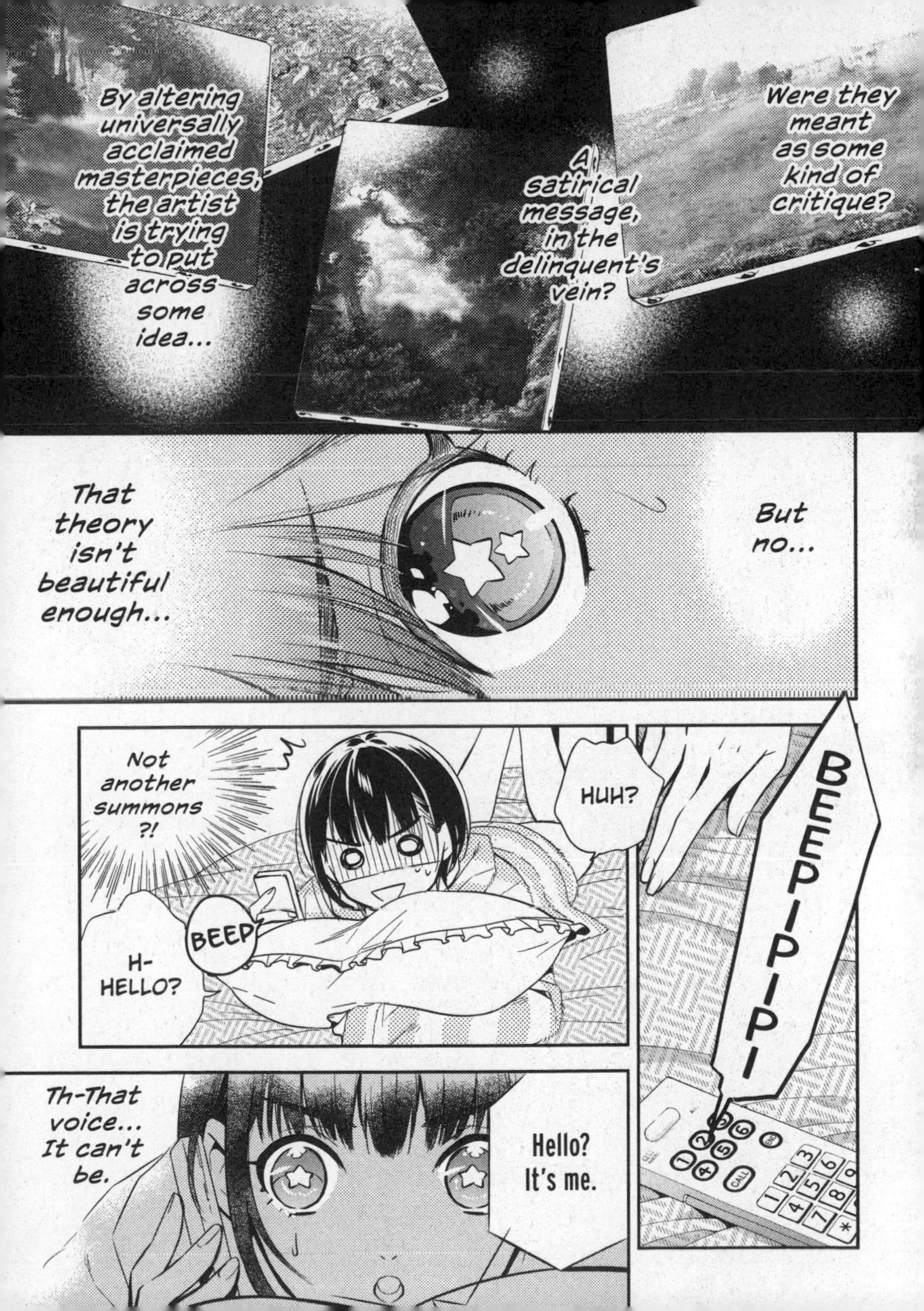
Were they meant as some kind of critique?
A satirical message, in the delinquent's vein?
By altering universally acclaimed masterpieces, the artist is trying to put across some idea...
But no...
That theory isn't beautiful enough...
BEEPIPIPI
HUH?
Not another summons?!
BEEP
H-HELLO?
Hello? It's me.
Th-That voice... It can't be.

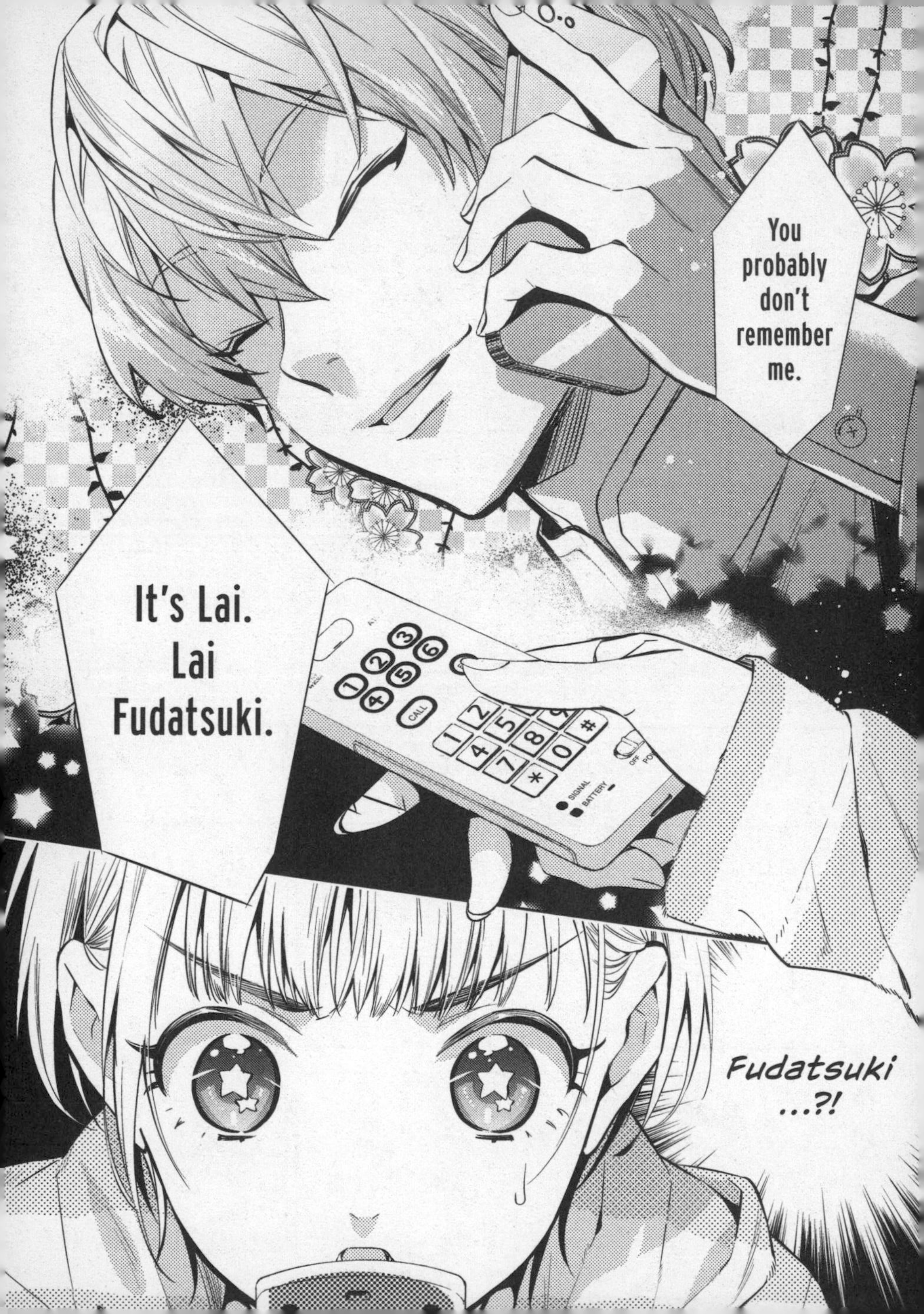
You probably don't remember me.
It's Lai. Lai Fudatsuki.
Fudatsuki ...?!

PRETTY BOY

————DETECTIVE CLUB!!

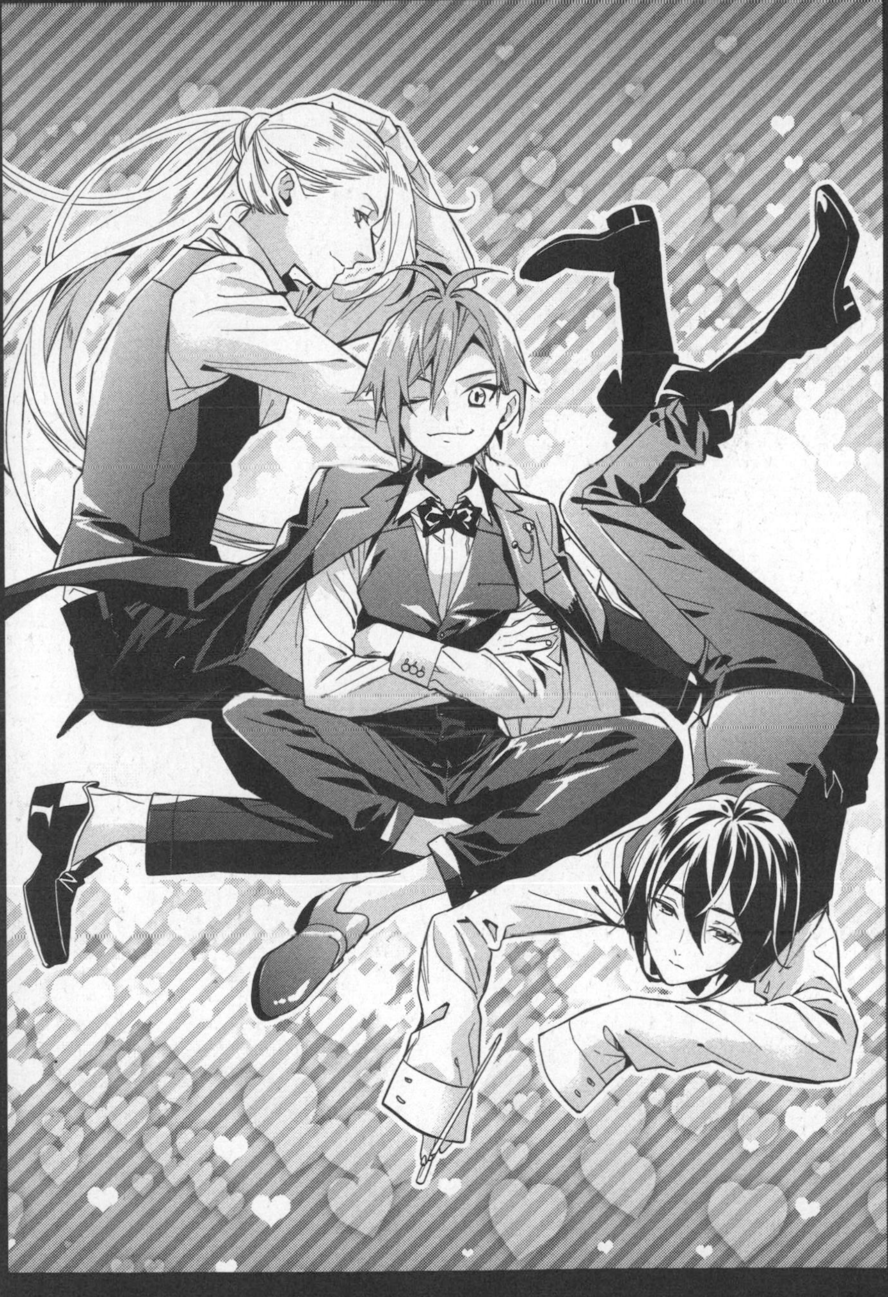

FILE ★ The Pretty Boy in the Attic 3

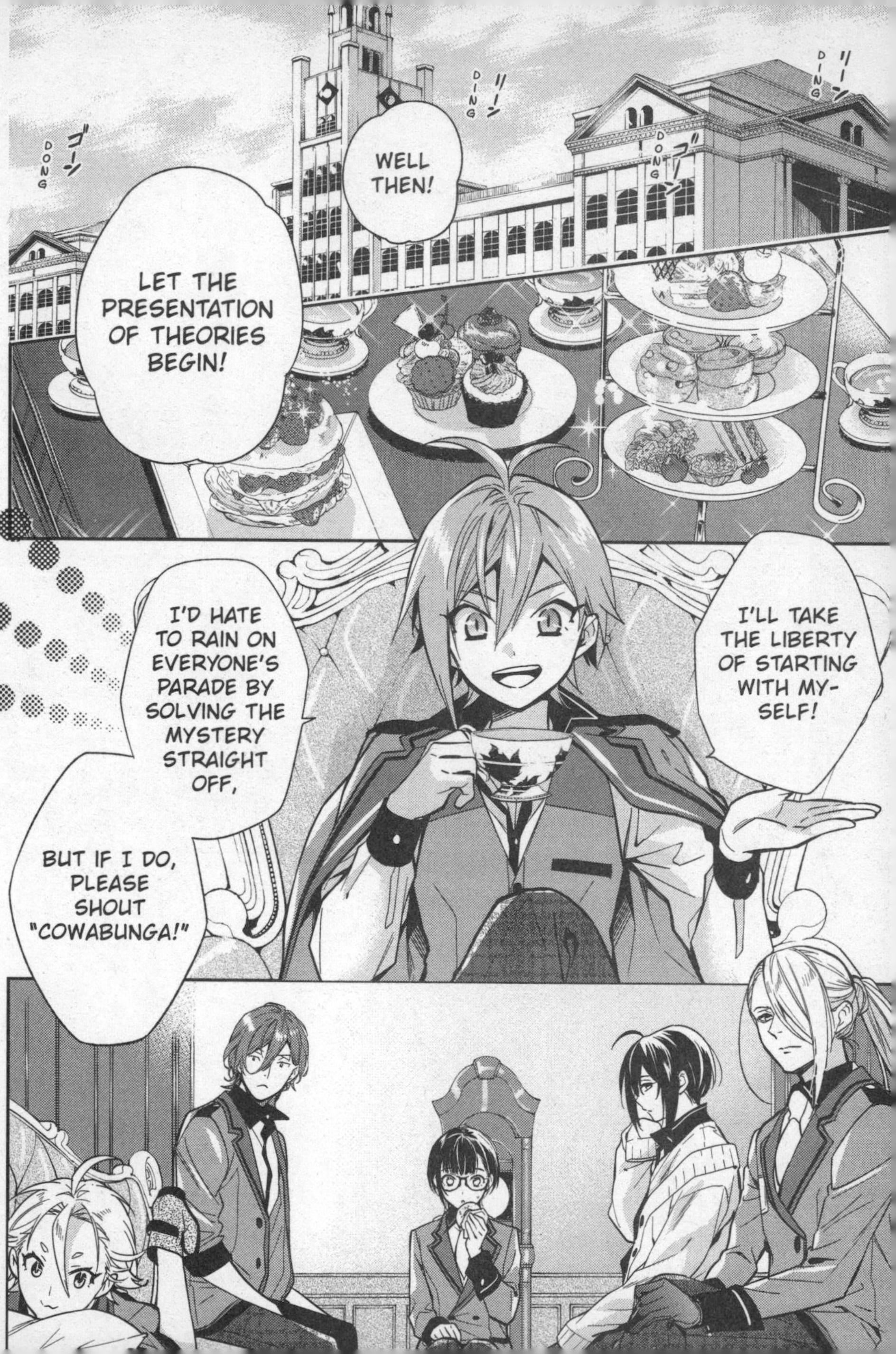
DING
DING
DONG
DONG
WELL THEN!
LET THE PRESENTATION OF THEORIES BEGIN!
I'LL TAKE THE LIBERTY OF STARTING WITH MY-SELF!
I'D HATE TO RAIN ON EVERYONE'S PARADE BY SOLVING THE MYSTERY STRAIGHT OFF,
BUT IF I DO, PLEASE SHOUT "COWABUNGA!"

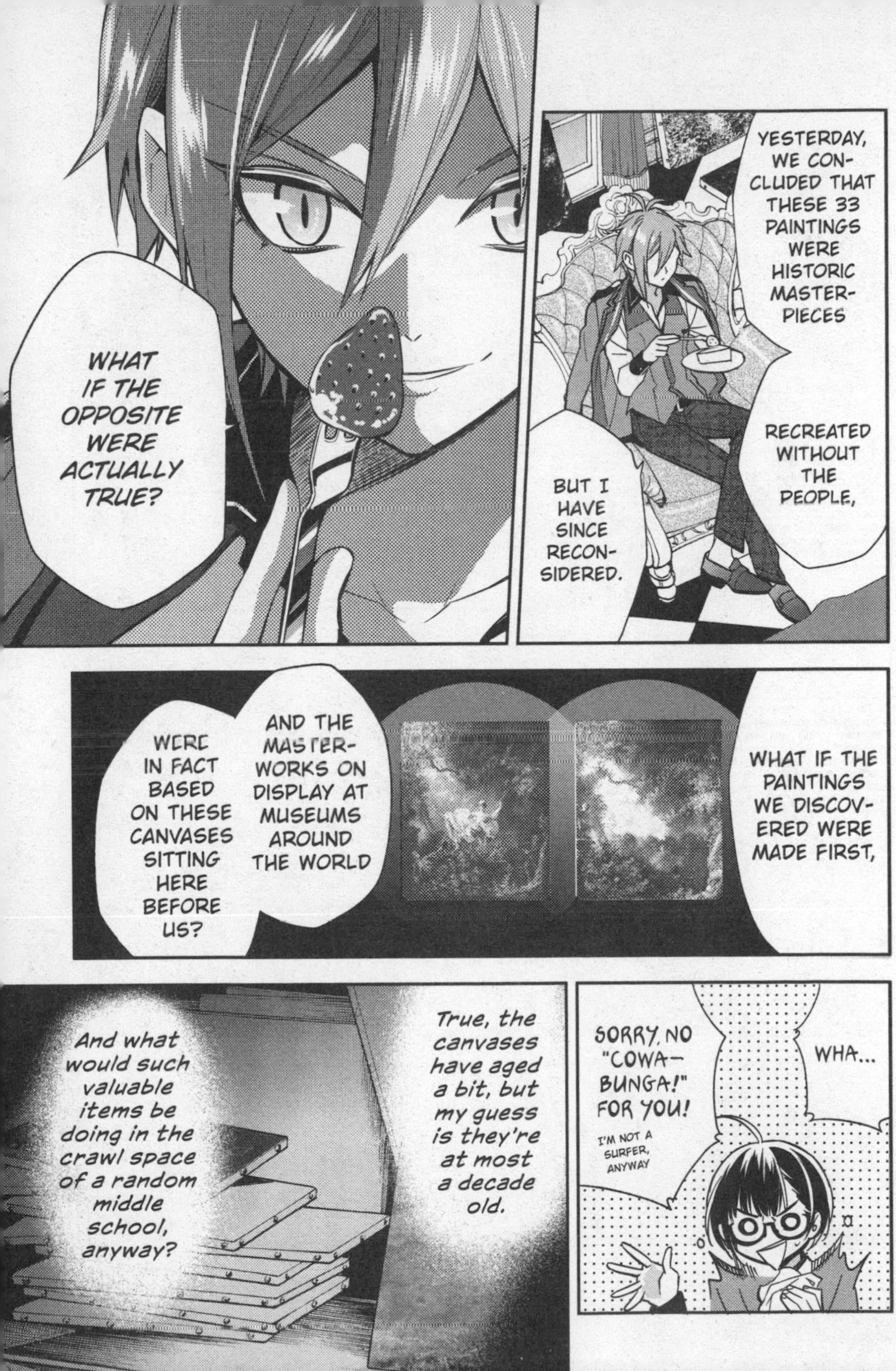
YESTERDAY, WE CONCLUDED THAT THESE 33 PAINTINGS WERE HISTORIC MASTERPIECES
RECREATED WITHOUT THE PEOPLE,
BUT I HAVE SINCE RECONSIDERED.
WHAT IF THE OPPOSITE WERE ACTUALLY TRUE?
WHAT IF THE PAINTINGS WE DISCOVERED WERE MADE FIRST,
AND THE MASTERWORKS ON DISPLAY AT MUSEUMS AROUND THE WORLD
WERE IN FACT BASED ON THESE CANVASES SITTING HERE BEFORE US?
WHA...
SORRY, NO "COWABUNGA!" FOR YOU!
I'M NOT A SURFER, ANYWAY
True, the canvases have aged a bit, but my guess is they're at most a decade old.
And what would such valuable items be doing in the crawl space of a random middle school, anyway?

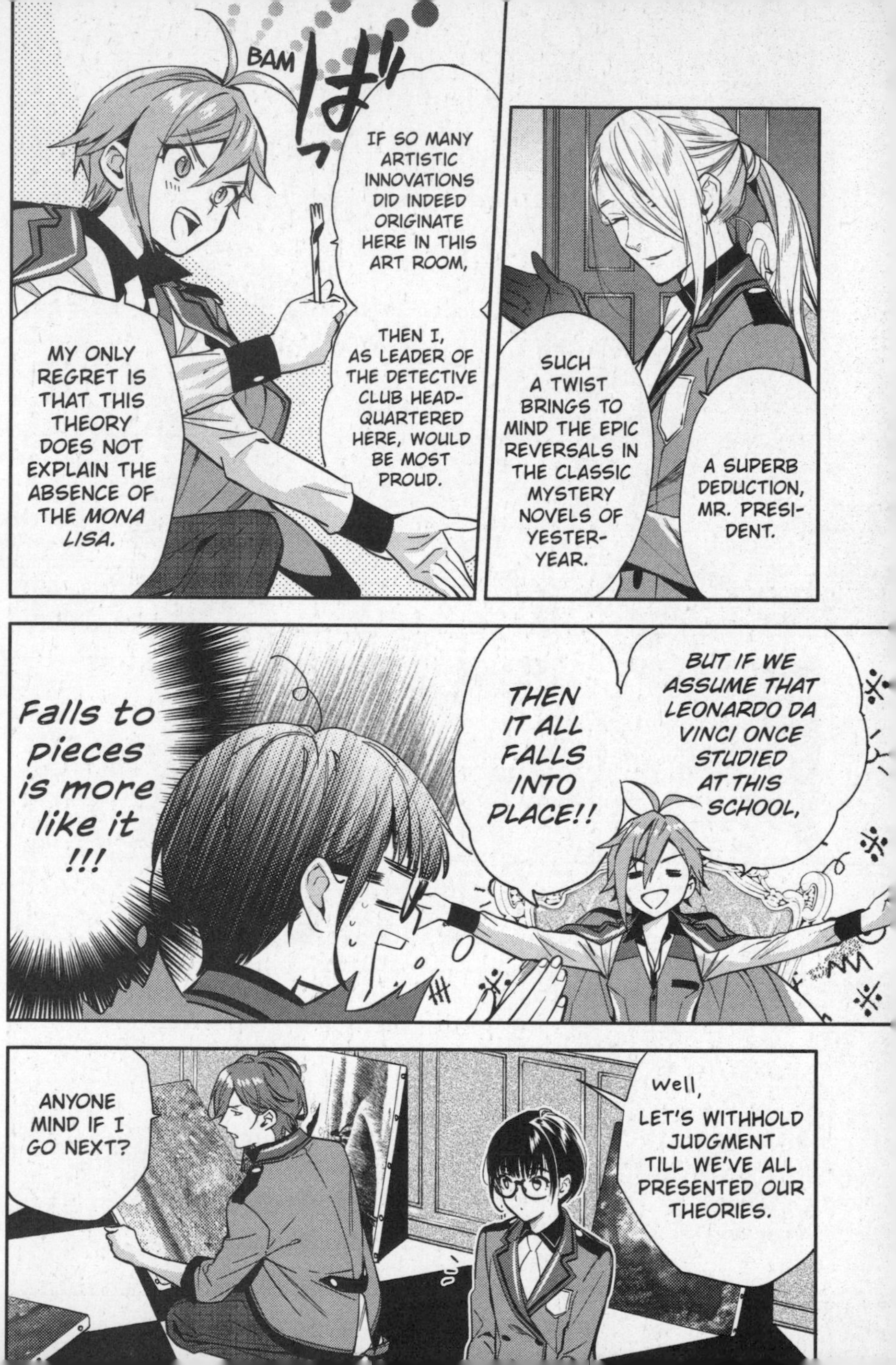
A SUPERB DEDUCTION, MR. PRESIDENT.
SUCH A TWIST BRINGS TO MIND THE EPIC REVERSALS IN THE CLASSIC MYSTERY NOVELS OF YESTER-YEAR.
BAM ばっ
IF SO MANY ARTISTIC INNOVATIONS DID INDEED ORIGINATE HERE IN THIS ART ROOM,
THEN I, AS LEADER OF THE DETECTIVE CLUB HEAD-QUARTERED HERE, WOULD BE MOST PROUD.
MY ONLY REGRET IS THAT THIS THEORY DOES NOT EXPLAIN THE ABSENCE OF THE *MONA LISA*.
BUT IF WE ASSUME THAT LEONARDO DA VINCI ONCE STUDIED AT THIS SCHOOL,
THEN IT ALL FALLS INTO PLACE!!
Falls to pieces is more like it !!!
Well, LET'S WITHHOLD JUDGMENT TILL WE'VE ALL PRESENTED OUR THEORIES.
ANYONE MIND IF I GO NEXT?

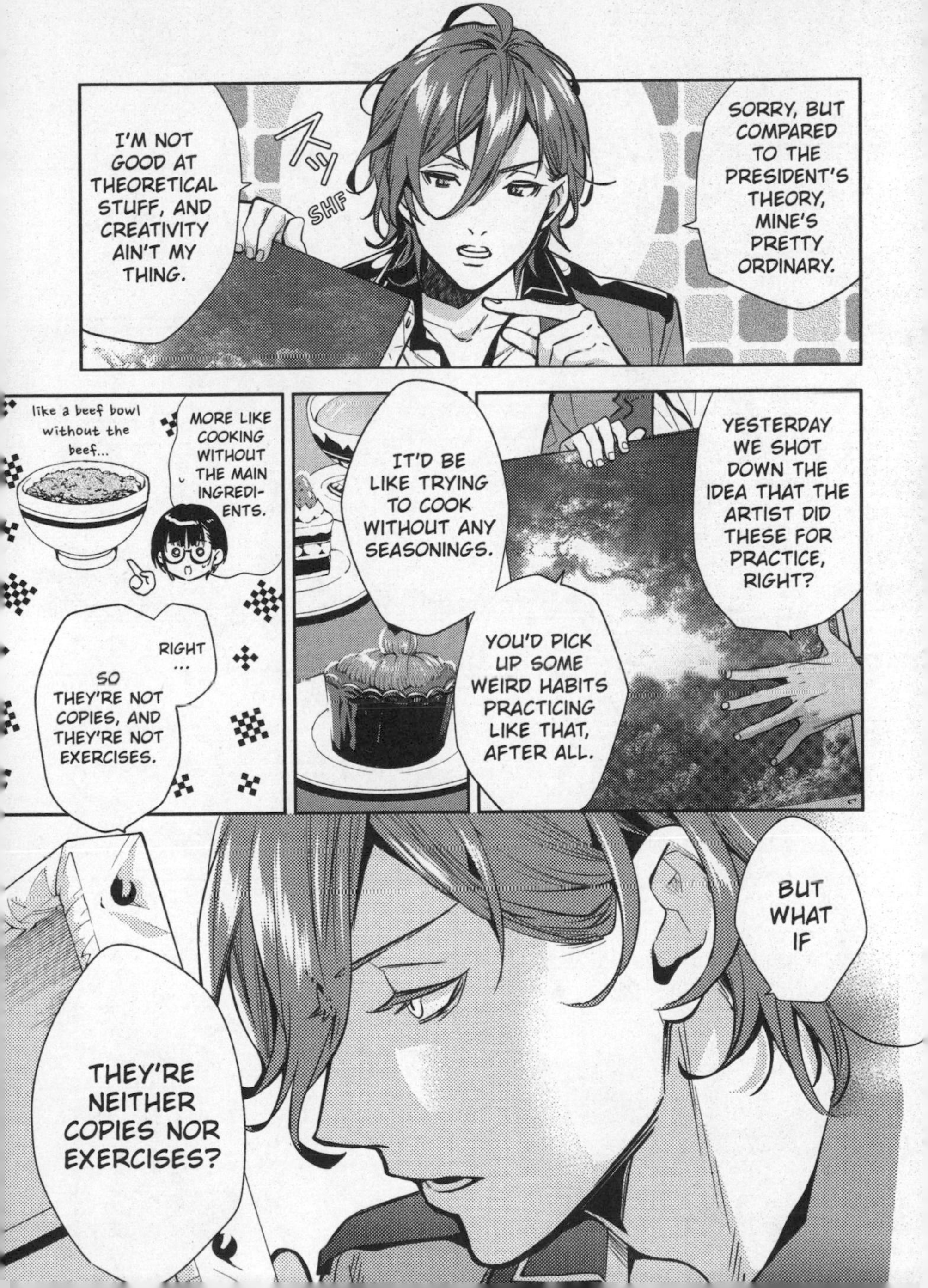
SORRY, BUT COMPARED TO THE PRESIDENT'S THEORY, MINE'S PRETTY ORDINARY.
SHF
I'M NOT GOOD AT THEORETICAL STUFF, AND CREATIVITY AIN'T MY THING.
YESTERDAY WE SHOT DOWN THE IDEA THAT THE ARTIST DID THESE FOR PRACTICE, RIGHT?
IT'D BE LIKE TRYING TO COOK WITHOUT ANY SEASONINGS.
YOU'D PICK UP SOME WEIRD HABITS PRACTICING LIKE THAT, AFTER ALL.
MORE LIKE COOKING WITHOUT THE MAIN INGREDI-ENTS.
like a beef bowl without the beef...
RIGHT...
SO THEY'RE NOT COPIES, AND THEY'RE NOT EXERCISES.
BUT WHAT IF
THEY'RE NEITHER COPIES NOR EXERCISES?

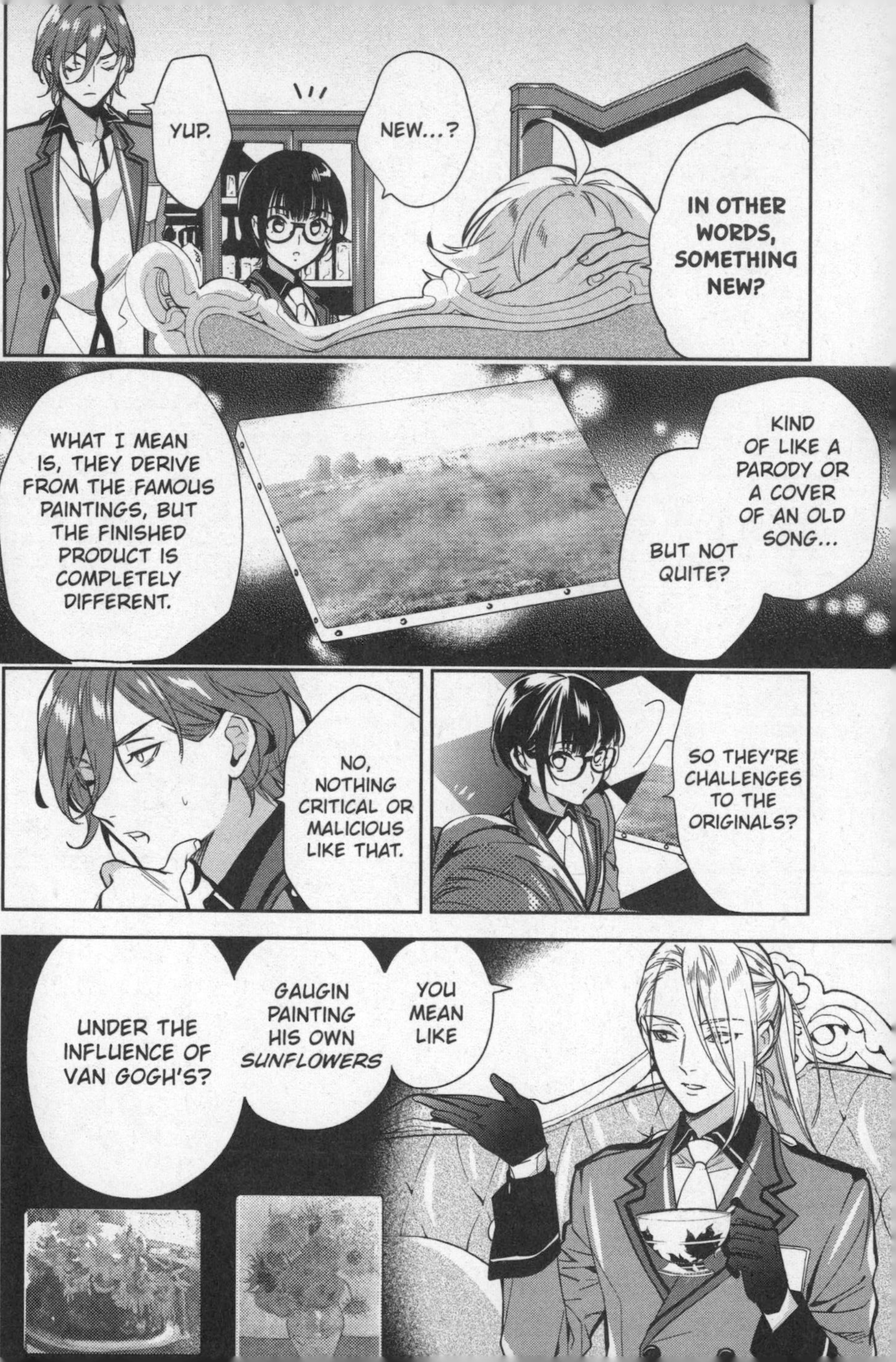
IN OTHER WORDS, SOMETHING NEW?
NEW...?
YUP.
KIND OF LIKE A PARODY OR A COVER OF AN OLD SONG...
BUT NOT QUITE?
WHAT I MEAN IS, THEY DERIVE FROM THE FAMOUS PAINTINGS, BUT THE FINISHED PRODUCT IS COMPLETELY DIFFERENT.
SO THEY'RE CHALLENGES TO THE ORIGINALS?
NO, NOTHING CRITICAL OR MALICIOUS LIKE THAT.
YOU MEAN LIKE
GAUGIN PAINTING HIS OWN *SUNFLOWERS*
UNDER THE INFLUENCE OF VAN GOGH'S?

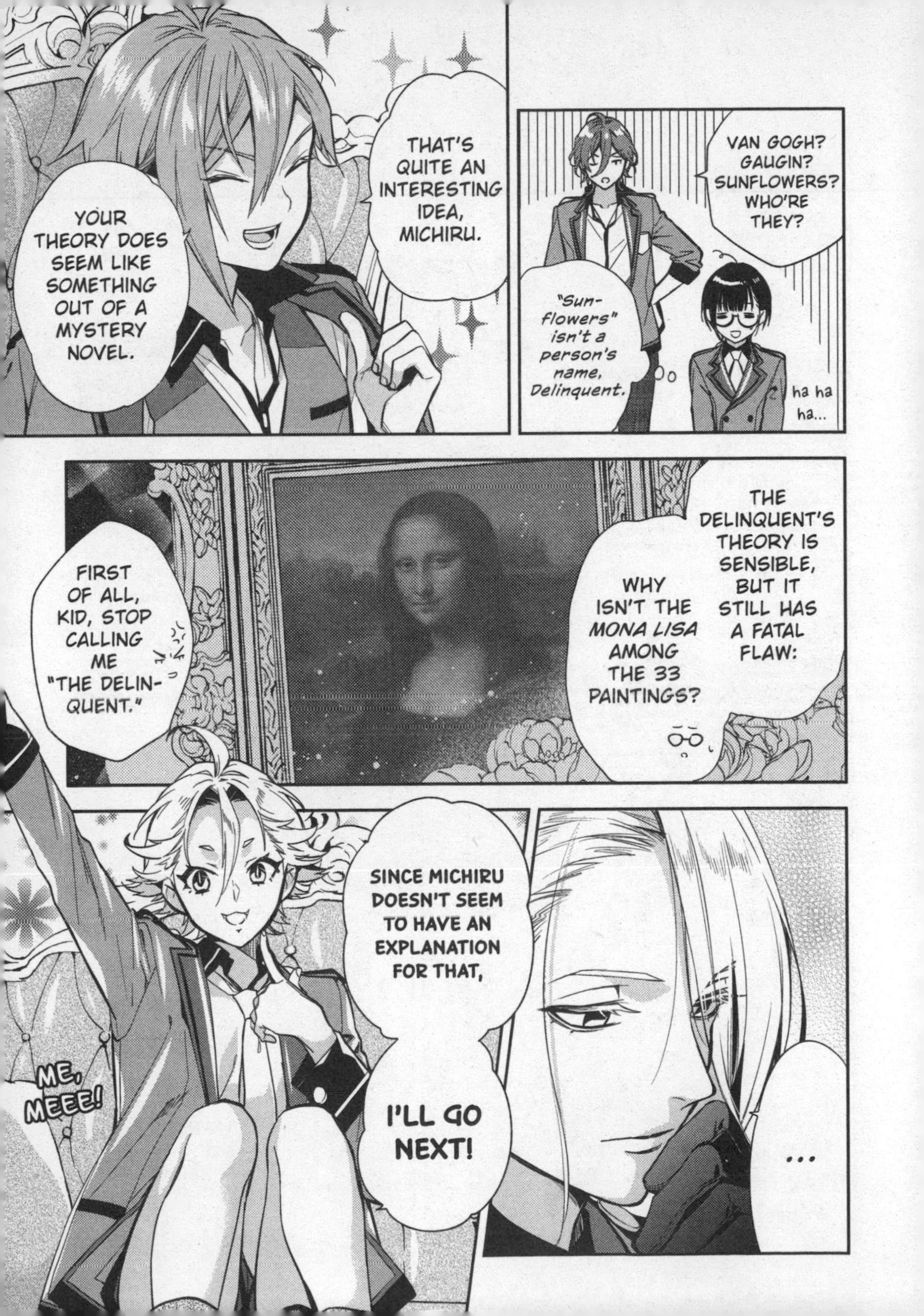
VAN GOGH? GAUGIN? SUNFLOWERS? WHO'RE THEY?
"Sun-flowers" isn't a person's name, Delinquent.
ha ha ha...
THAT'S QUITE AN INTERESTING IDEA, MICHIRU.
YOUR THEORY DOES SEEM LIKE SOMETHING OUT OF A MYSTERY NOVEL.
THE DELINQUENT'S THEORY IS SENSIBLE, BUT IT STILL HAS A FATAL FLAW:
WHY ISN'T THE *MONA LISA* AMONG THE 33 PAINTINGS?
FIRST OF ALL, KID, STOP CALLING ME "THE DELIN-QUENT."
...
SINCE MICHIRU DOESN'T SEEM TO HAVE AN EXPLANATION FOR THAT,
ME, MEEE!
I'LL GO NEXT!

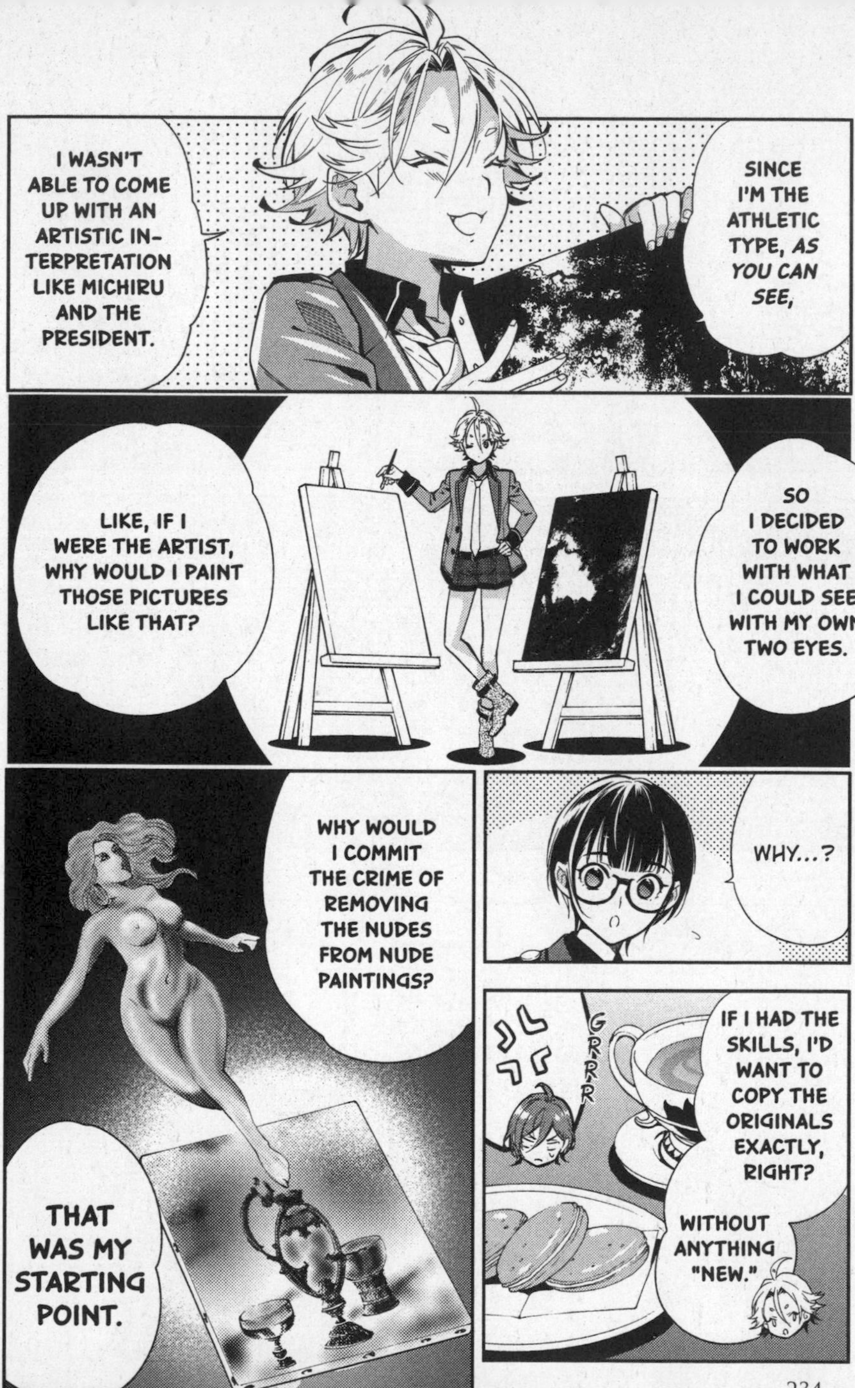
SINCE I'M THE ATHLETIC TYPE, AS YOU CAN SEE,
I WASN'T ABLE TO COME UP WITH AN ARTISTIC IN-TERPRETATION LIKE MICHIRU AND THE PRESIDENT.
SO I DECIDED TO WORK WITH WHAT I COULD SEE WITH MY OWN TWO EYES.
LIKE, IF I WERE THE ARTIST, WHY WOULD I PAINT THOSE PICTURES LIKE THAT?
WHY...?
IF I HAD THE SKILLS, I'D WANT TO COPY THE ORIGINALS EXACTLY, RIGHT?
GRRRR
WITHOUT ANYTHING "NEW."
WHY WOULD I COMMIT THE CRIME OF REMOVING THE NUDES FROM NUDE PAINTINGS?
THAT WAS MY STARTING POINT.

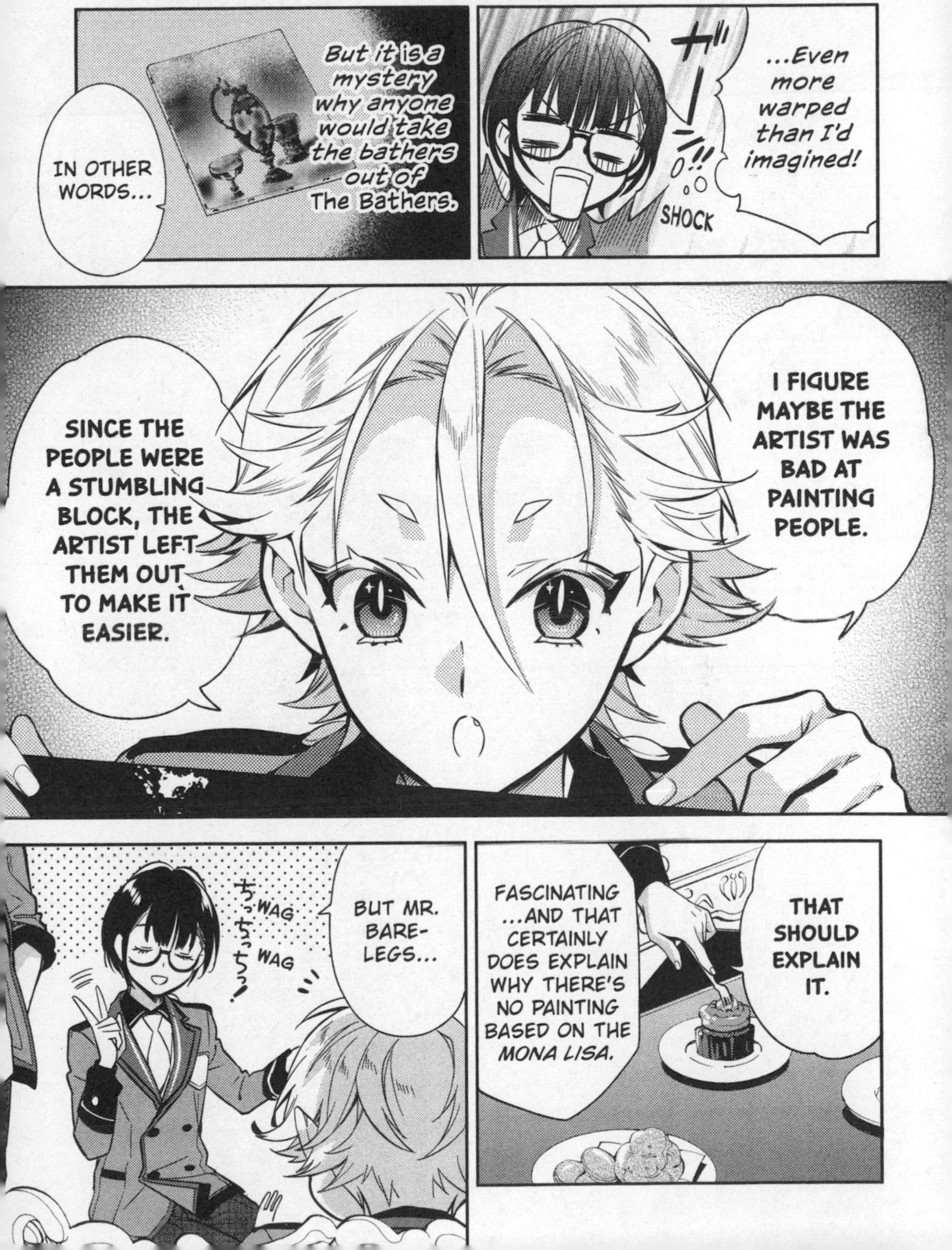
...Even more warped than I'd imagined!
SHOCK
But it is a mystery why anyone would take the bathers out of The Bathers.
IN OTHER WORDS...
I FIGURE MAYBE THE ARTIST WAS BAD AT PAINTING PEOPLE.
SINCE THE PEOPLE WERE A STUMBLING BLOCK, THE ARTIST LEFT THEM OUT TO MAKE IT EASIER.
THAT SHOULD EXPLAIN IT.
FASCINATING ...AND THAT CERTAINLY DOES EXPLAIN WHY THERE'S NO PAINTING BASED ON THE *MONA LISA*.
BUT MR. BARE-LEGS...
WAG
WAG

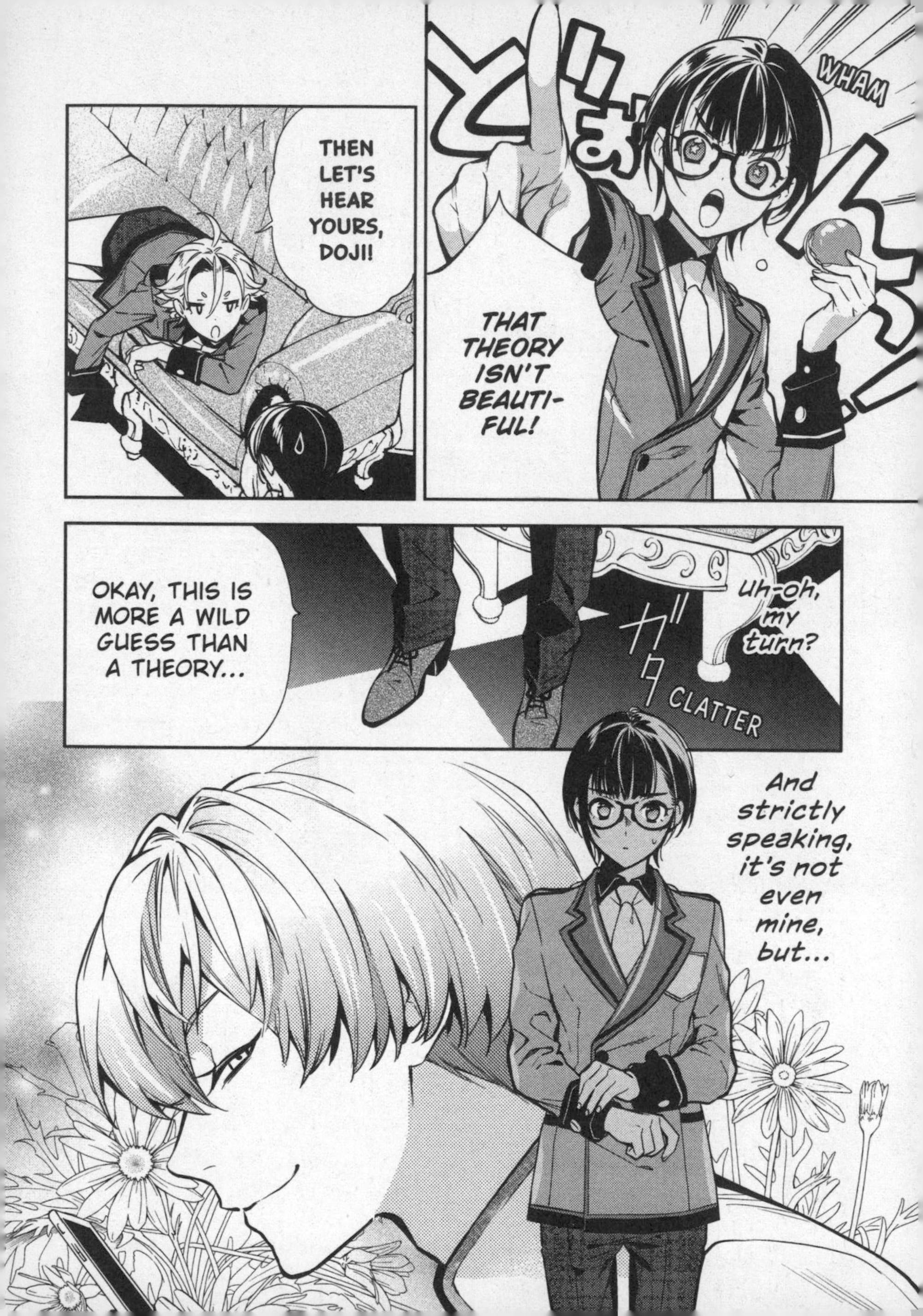
WHAM
THAT THEORY ISN'T BEAUTIFUL!
THEN LET'S HEAR YOURS, DOJI!
uh-oh, my turn?
ガタ
CLATTER
OKAY, THIS IS MORE A WILD GUESS THAN A THEORY...
And strictly speaking, it's not even mine, but...

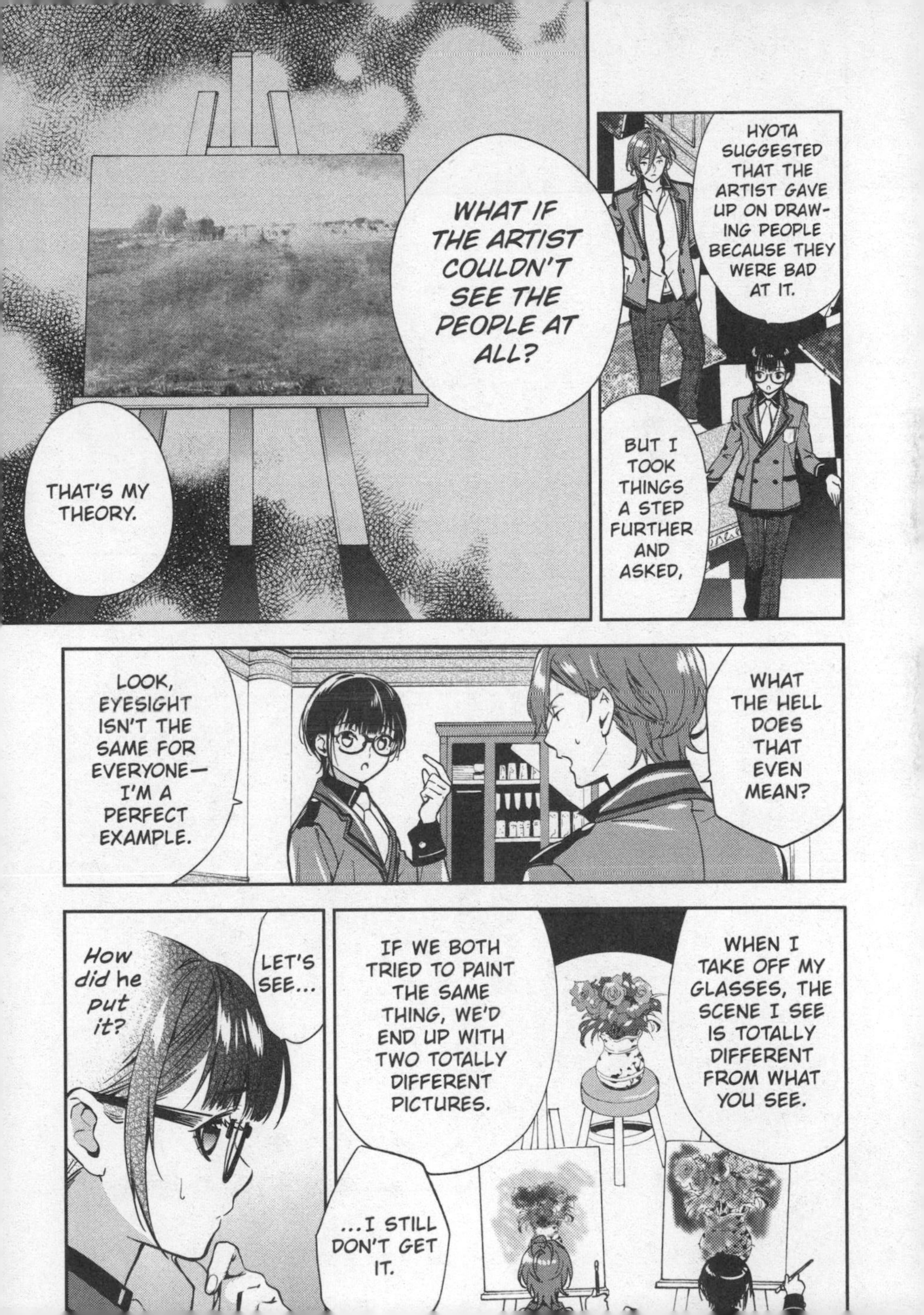
HYOTA SUGGESTED THAT THE ARTIST GAVE UP ON DRAW-ING PEOPLE BECAUSE THEY WERE BAD AT IT.
BUT I TOOK THINGS A STEP FURTHER AND ASKED,
WHAT IF THE ARTIST COULDN'T SEE THE PEOPLE AT ALL?
THAT'S MY THEORY.
WHAT THE HELL DOES THAT EVEN MEAN?
LOOK, EYESIGHT ISN'T THE SAME FOR EVERYONE— I'M A PERFECT EXAMPLE.
WHEN I TAKE OFF MY GLASSES, THE SCENE I SEE IS TOTALLY DIFFERENT FROM WHAT YOU SEE.
IF WE BOTH TRIED TO PAINT THE SAME THING, WE'D END UP WITH TWO TOTALLY DIFFERENT PICTURES.
...I STILL DON'T GET IT.
LET'S SEE...
How did he put it?

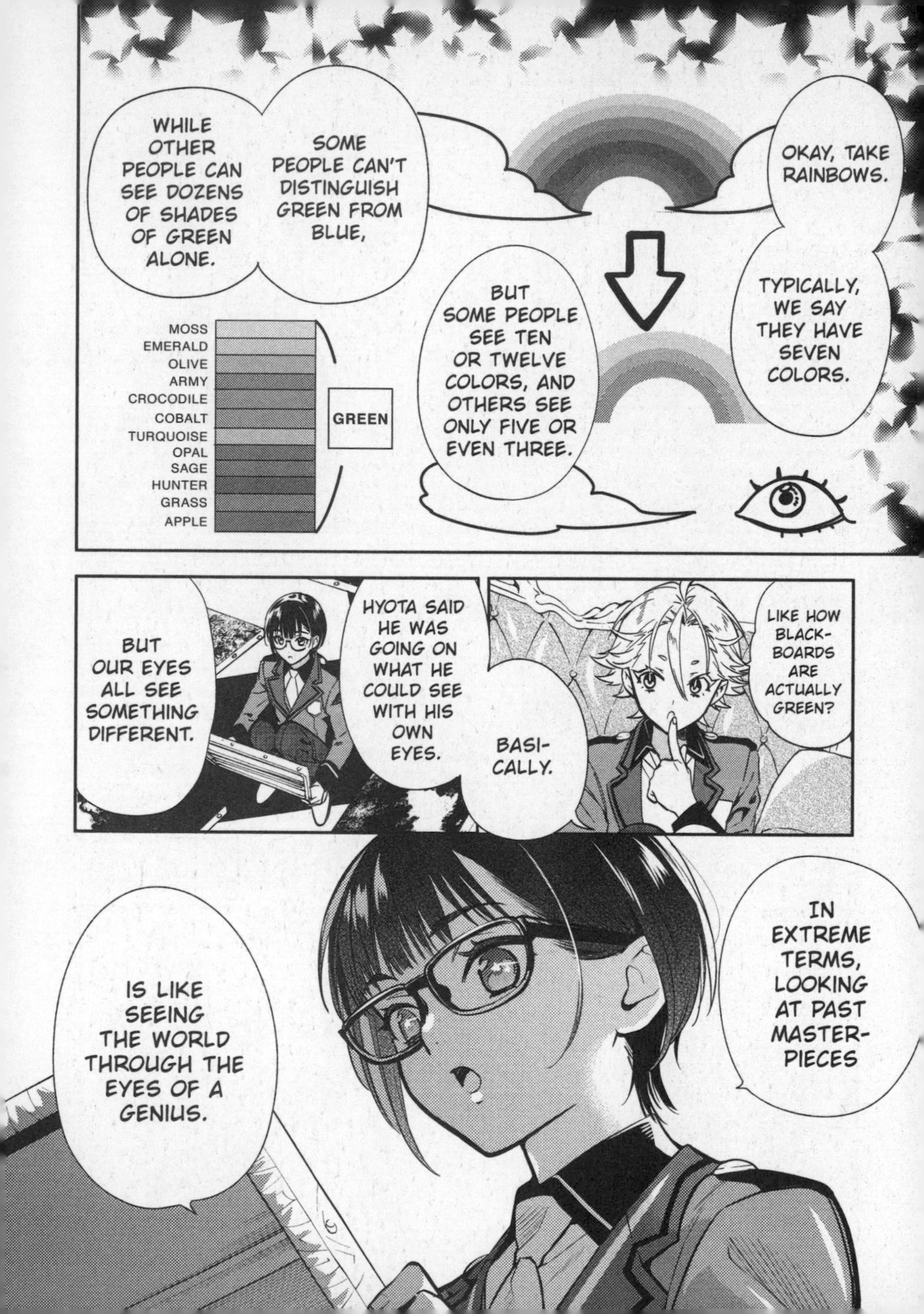
OKAY, TAKE RAINBOWS.
TYPICALLY, WE SAY THEY HAVE SEVEN COLORS.
BUT SOME PEOPLE SEE TEN OR TWELVE COLORS, AND OTHERS SEE ONLY FIVE OR EVEN THREE.
SOME PEOPLE CAN'T DISTINGUISH GREEN FROM BLUE,
WHILE OTHER PEOPLE CAN SEE DOZENS OF SHADES OF GREEN ALONE.
MOSS
EMERALD
OLIVE
ARMY
CROCODILE
COBALT
TURQUOISE
OPAL
SAGE
HUNTER
GRASS
APPLE
GREEN
LIKE HOW BLACK-BOARDS ARE ACTUALLY GREEN?
BASI-CALLY.
HYOTA SAID HE WAS GOING ON WHAT HE COULD SEE WITH HIS OWN EYES.
BUT OUR EYES ALL SEE SOMETHING DIFFERENT.
IN EXTREME TERMS, LOOKING AT PAST MASTER-PIECES
IS LIKE SEEING THE WORLD THROUGH THE EYES OF A GENIUS.

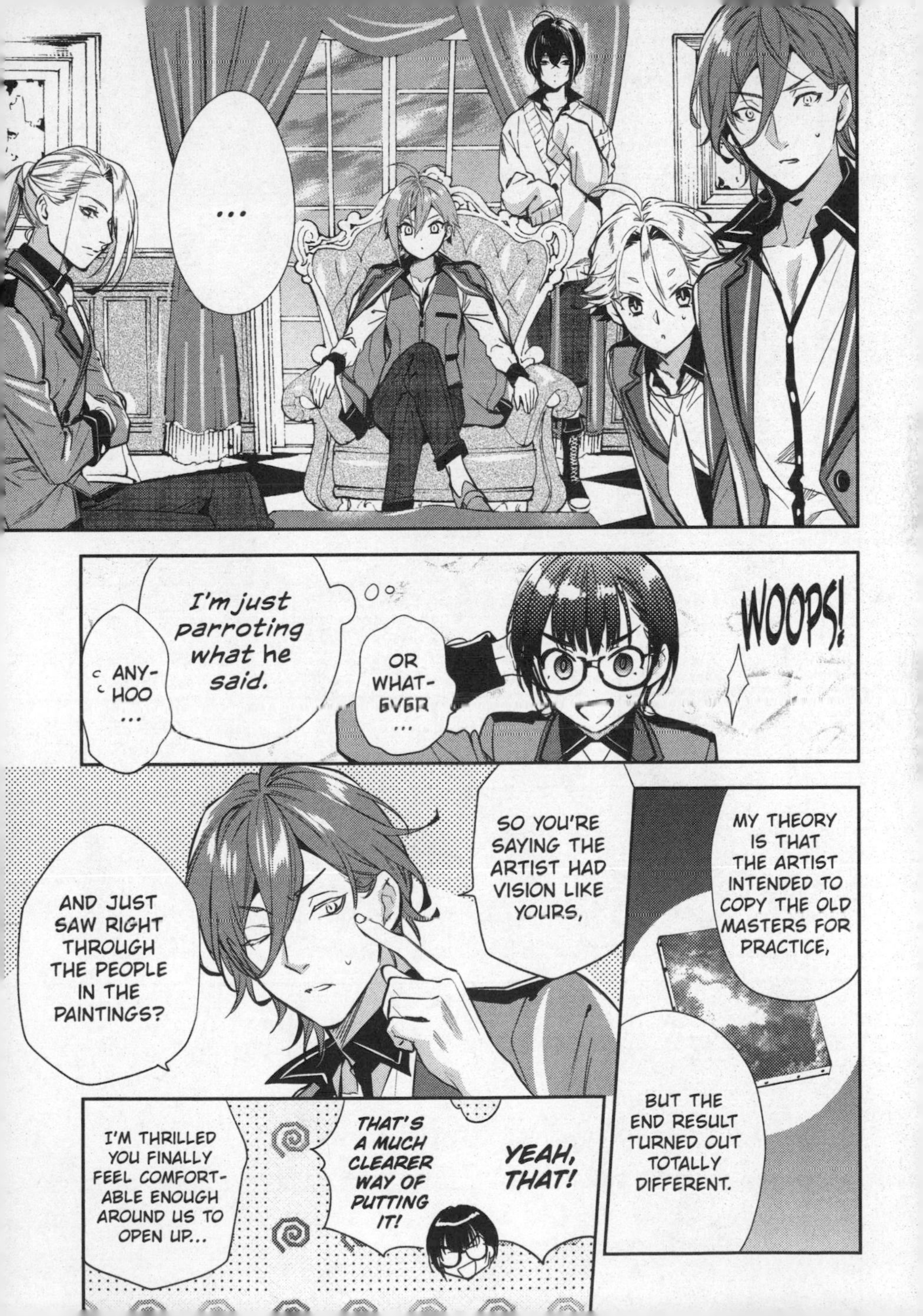
...
WOOPS!
OR WHAT-EVER ...
I'm just parroting what he said.
ANY-HOO ...
MY THEORY IS THAT THE ARTIST INTENDED TO COPY THE OLD MASTERS FOR PRACTICE,
BUT THE END RESULT TURNED OUT TOTALLY DIFFERENT.
SO YOU'RE SAYING THE ARTIST HAD VISION LIKE YOURS,
AND JUST SAW RIGHT THROUGH THE PEOPLE IN THE PAINTINGS?
YEAH, THAT!
THAT'S A MUCH CLEARER WAY OF PUTTING IT!
I'M THRILLED YOU FINALLY FEEL COMFORT-ABLE ENOUGH AROUND US TO OPEN UP...

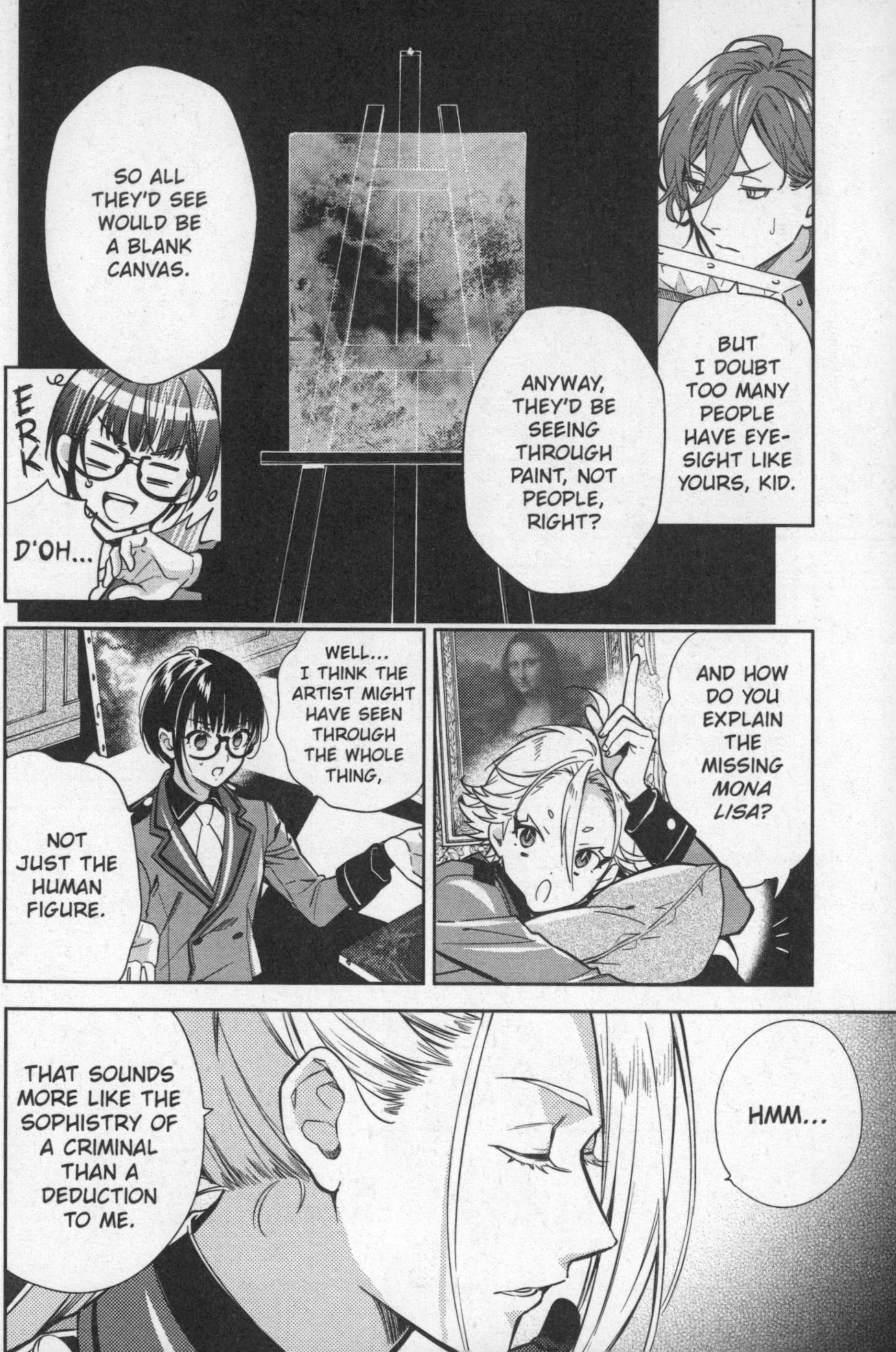
SO ALL THEY'D SEE WOULD BE A BLANK CANVAS.
BUT I DOUBT TOO MANY PEOPLE HAVE EYE-SIGHT LIKE YOURS, KID.
ANYWAY, THEY'D BE SEEING THROUGH PAINT, NOT PEOPLE, RIGHT?
ERK
D'OH...
AND HOW DO YOU EXPLAIN THE MISSING *MONA LISA*?
WELL... I THINK THE ARTIST MIGHT HAVE SEEN THROUGH THE WHOLE THING,
NOT JUST THE HUMAN FIGURE.
HMM...
THAT SOUNDS MORE LIKE THE SOPHISTRY OF A CRIMINAL THAN A DEDUCTION TO ME.

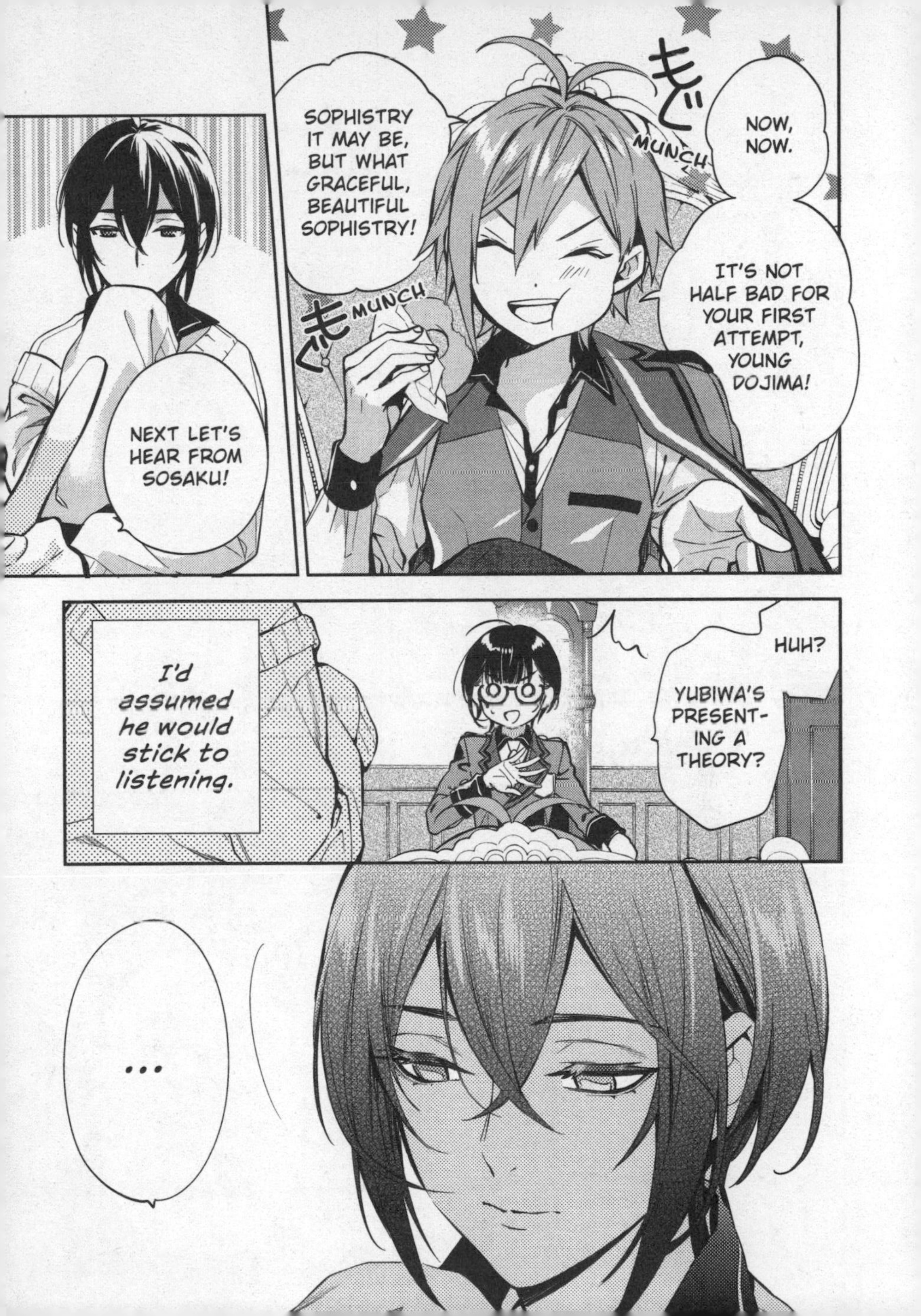
NOW, NOW.
もぐ
MUNCH
IT'S NOT HALF BAD FOR YOUR FIRST ATTEMPT, YOUNG DOJIMA!
SOPHISTRY IT MAY BE, BUT WHAT GRACEFUL, BEAUTIFUL SOPHISTRY!
もぐ
MUNCH
NEXT LET'S HEAR FROM SOSAKU!
HUH?
YUBIWA'S PRESENT-ING A THEORY?
I'd assumed he would stick to listening.
...

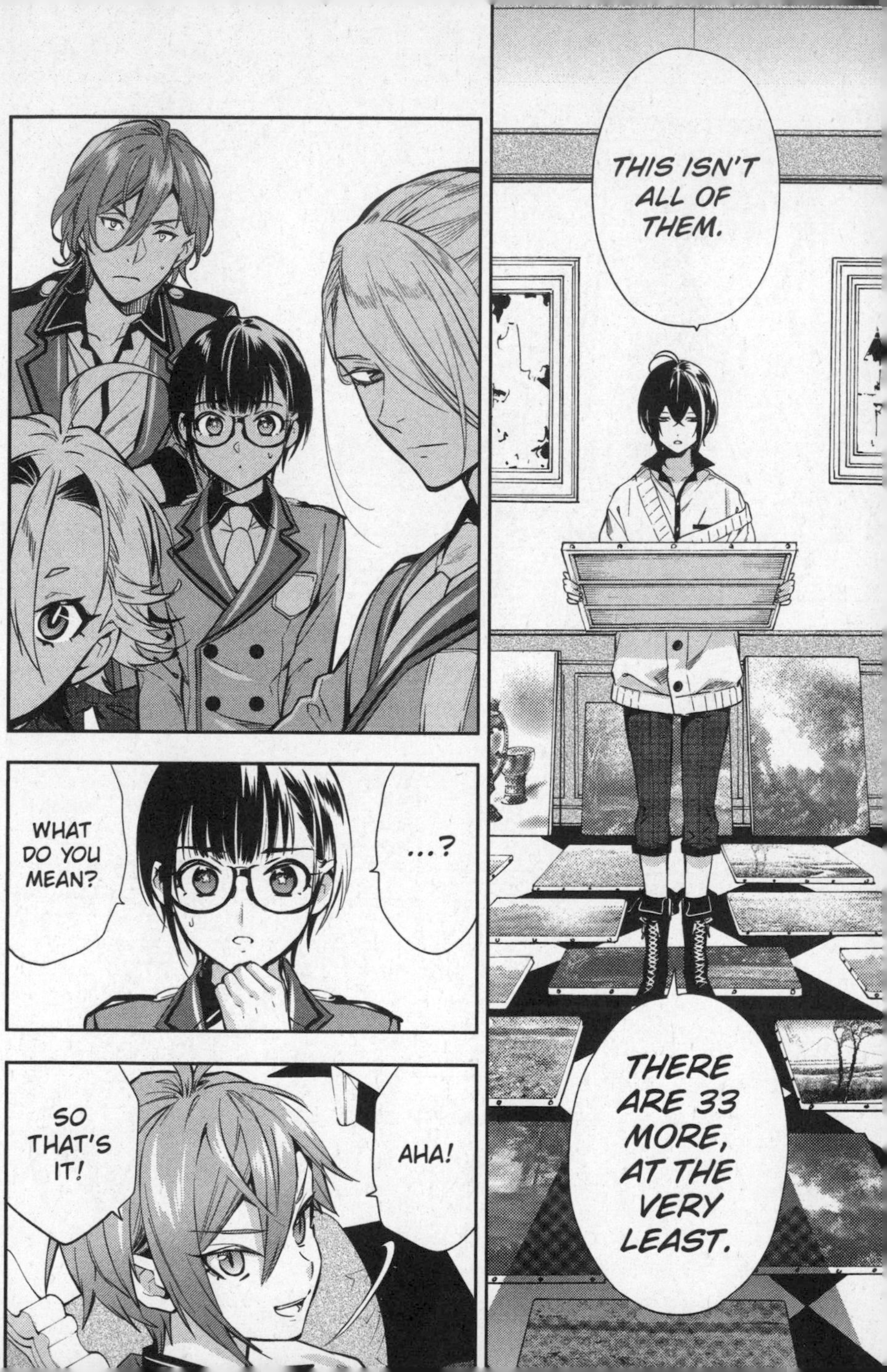
THIS ISN'T ALL OF THEM.
THERE ARE 33 MORE, AT THE VERY LEAST.
...?
WHAT DO YOU MEAN?
AHA!
SO THAT'S IT!

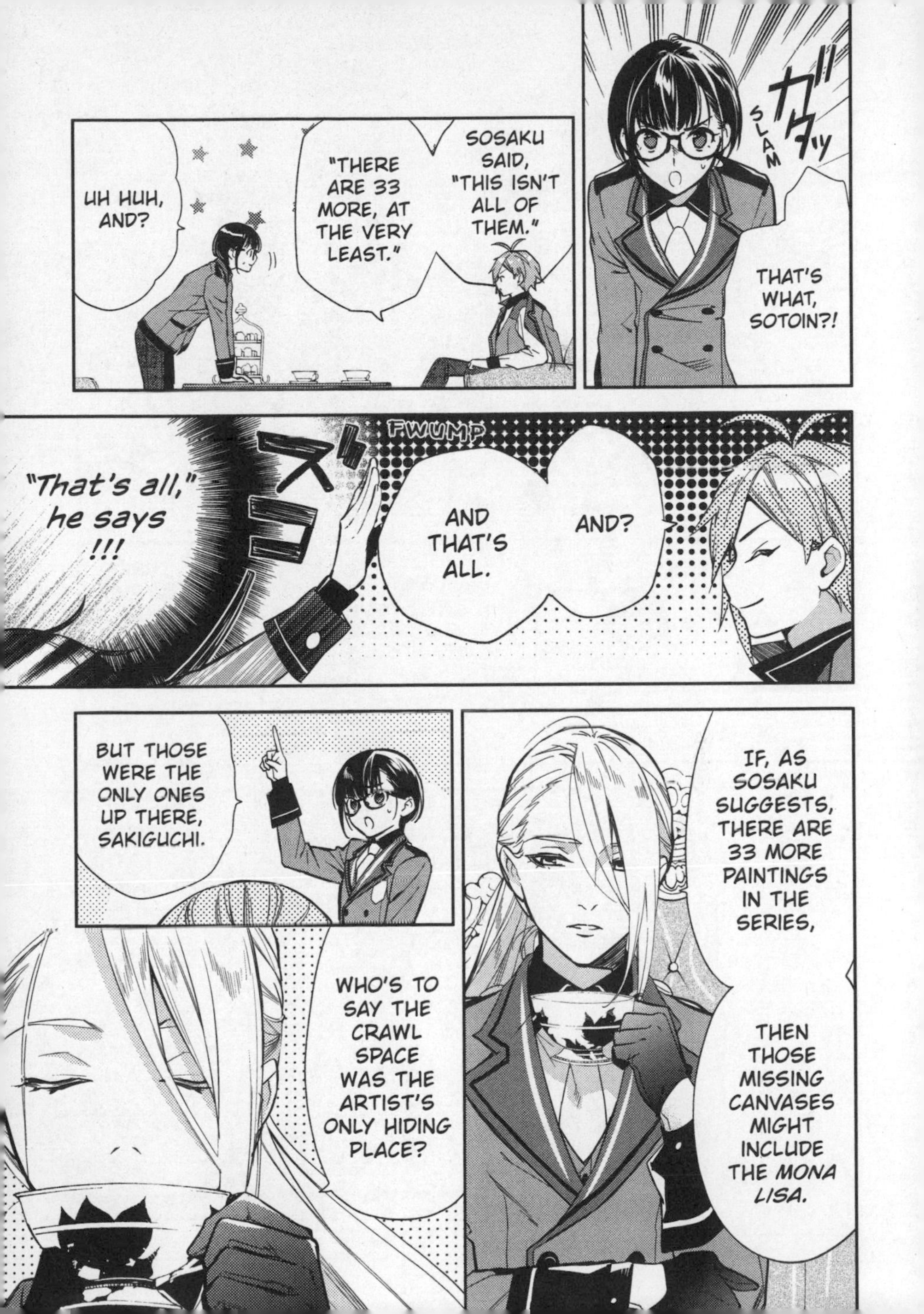
SLAM
THAT'S WHAT, SOTOIN?!
SOSAKU SAID, "THIS ISN'T ALL OF THEM."
"THERE ARE 33 MORE, AT THE VERY LEAST."
UH HUH, AND?
FWUMP
AND?
AND THAT'S ALL.
"That's all," he says !!!
IF, AS SOSAKU SUGGESTS, THERE ARE 33 MORE PAINTINGS IN THE SERIES,
THEN THOSE MISSING CANVASES MIGHT INCLUDE THE *MONA LISA*.
BUT THOSE WERE THE ONLY ONES UP THERE, SAKIGUCHI.
WHO'S TO SAY THE CRAWL SPACE WAS THE ARTIST'S ONLY HIDING PLACE?

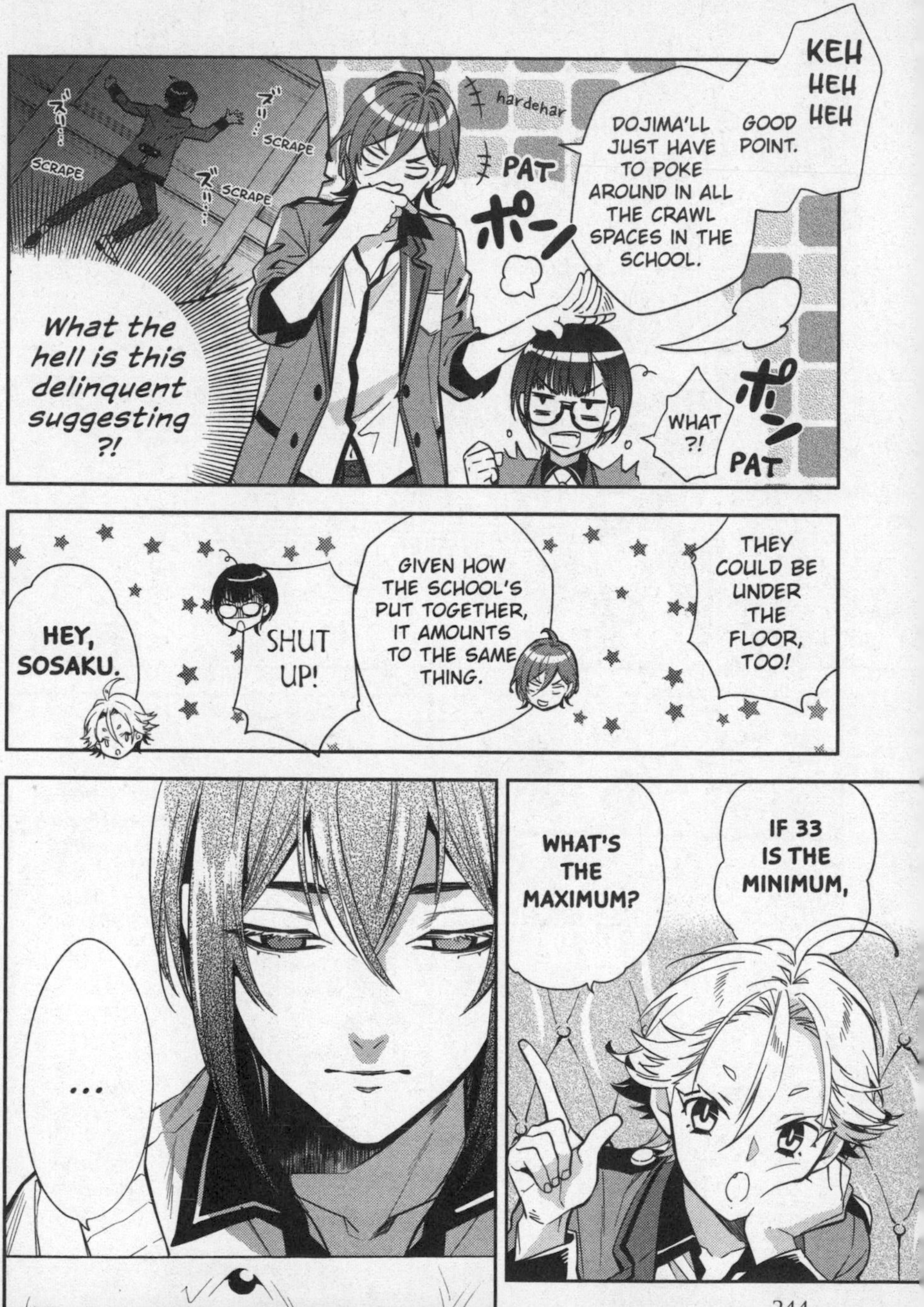
KEH HEH HEH
GOOD POINT.
DOJIMA'LL JUST HAVE TO POKE AROUND IN ALL THE CRAWL SPACES IN THE SCHOOL.
hardehar
PAT
WHAT ?!
PAT
SCRAPE
SCRAPE
SCRAPE
What the hell is this delinquent suggesting ?!
THEY COULD BE UNDER THE FLOOR, TOO!
GIVEN HOW THE SCHOOL'S PUT TOGETHER, IT AMOUNTS TO THE SAME THING.
SHUT UP!
HEY, SOSAKU.
IF 33 IS THE MINIMUM,
WHAT'S THE MAXIMUM?
...

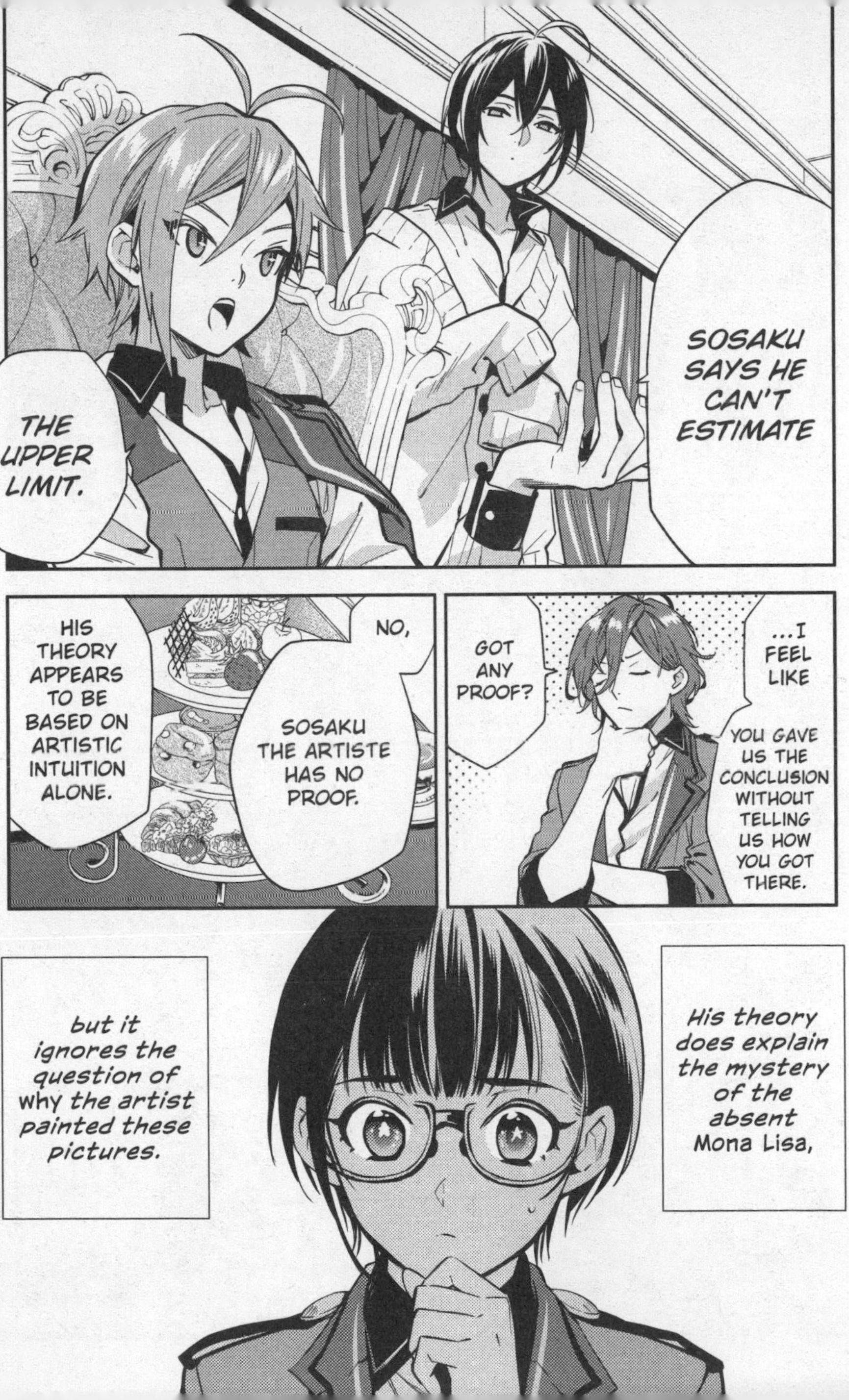
SOSAKU SAYS HE CAN'T ESTIMATE
THE UPPER LIMIT.
...I FEEL LIKE
YOU GAVE US THE CONCLUSION WITHOUT TELLING US HOW YOU GOT THERE.
GOT ANY PROOF?
NO,
SOSAKU THE ARTISTE HAS NO PROOF.
HIS THEORY APPEARS TO BE BASED ON ARTISTIC INTUITION ALONE.
His theory does explain the mystery of the absent Mona Lisa,
but it ignores the question of why the artist painted these pictures.

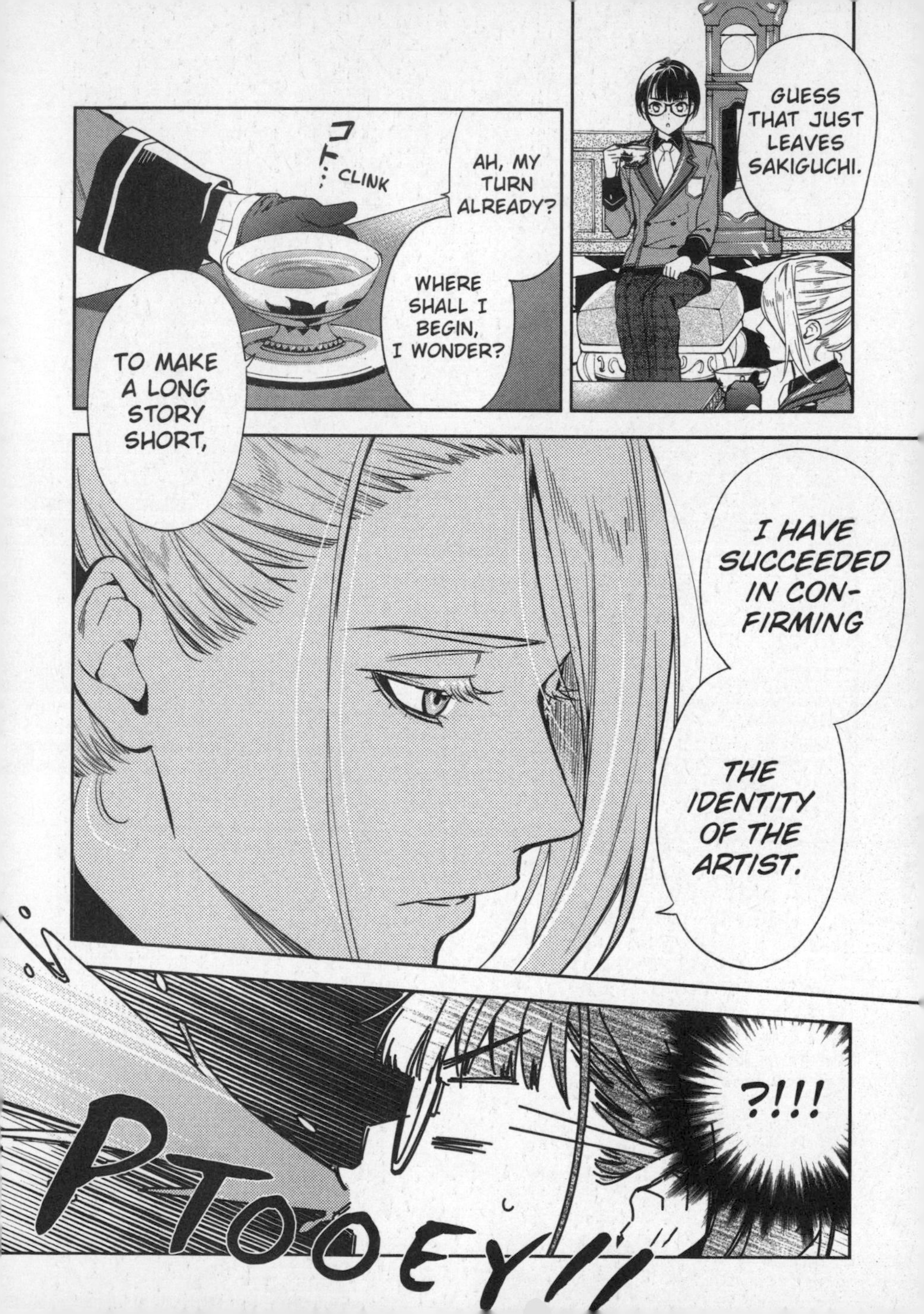
GUESS THAT JUST LEAVES SAKIGUCHI.
AH, MY TURN ALREADY?
コト… CLINK
WHERE SHALL I BEGIN, I WONDER?
TO MAKE A LONG STORY SHORT,
I HAVE SUCCEEDED IN CON-FIRMING
THE IDENTITY OF THE ARTIST.
?!!!
PTOOEY!!!

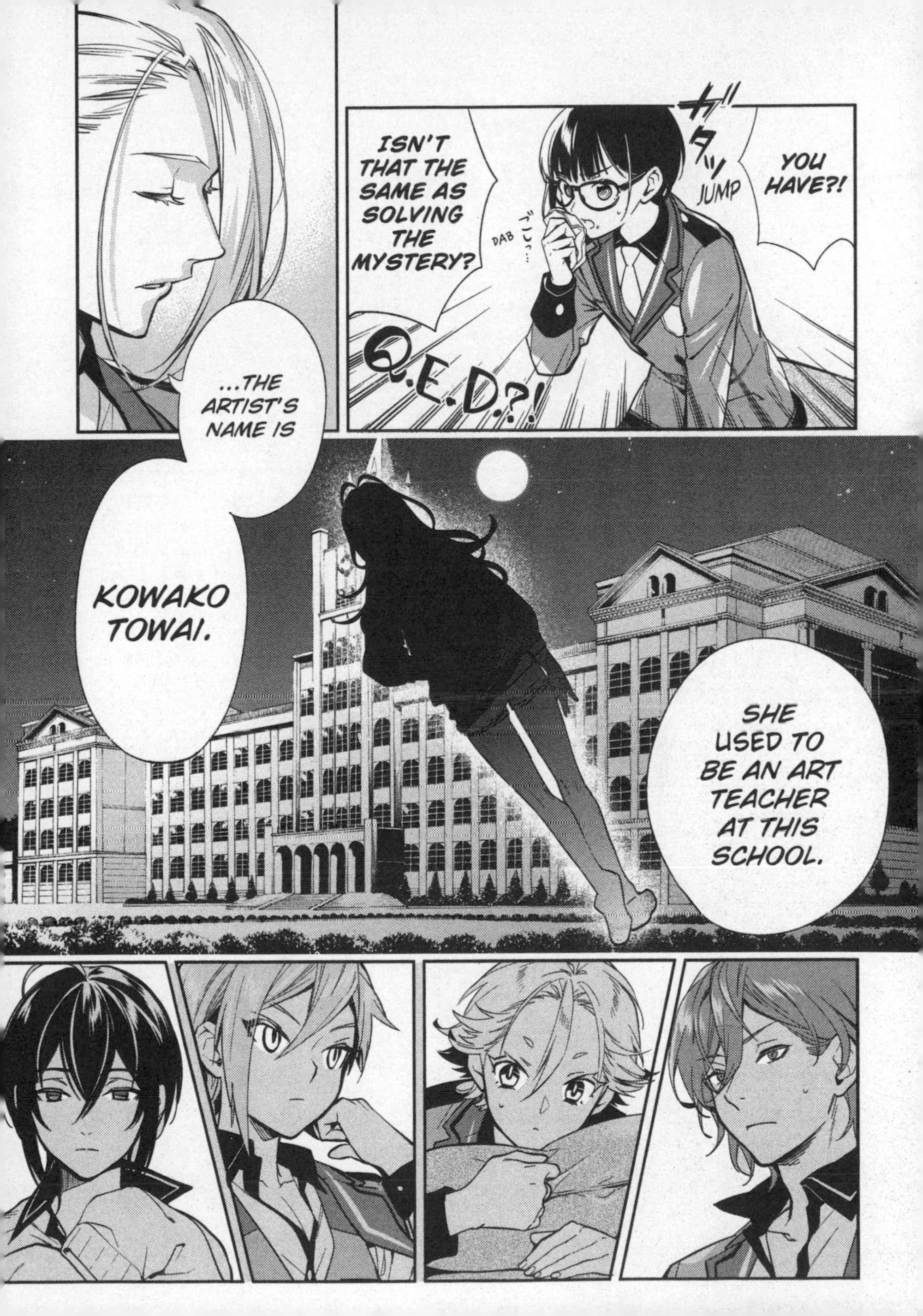

YOU HAVE?!
JUMP
ISN'T THAT THE SAME AS SOLVING THE MYSTERY?
DAB
Q.E.D.?!
...THE ARTIST'S NAME IS
KOWAKO TOWAI.
SHE USED TO BE AN ART TEACHER AT THIS SCHOOL.

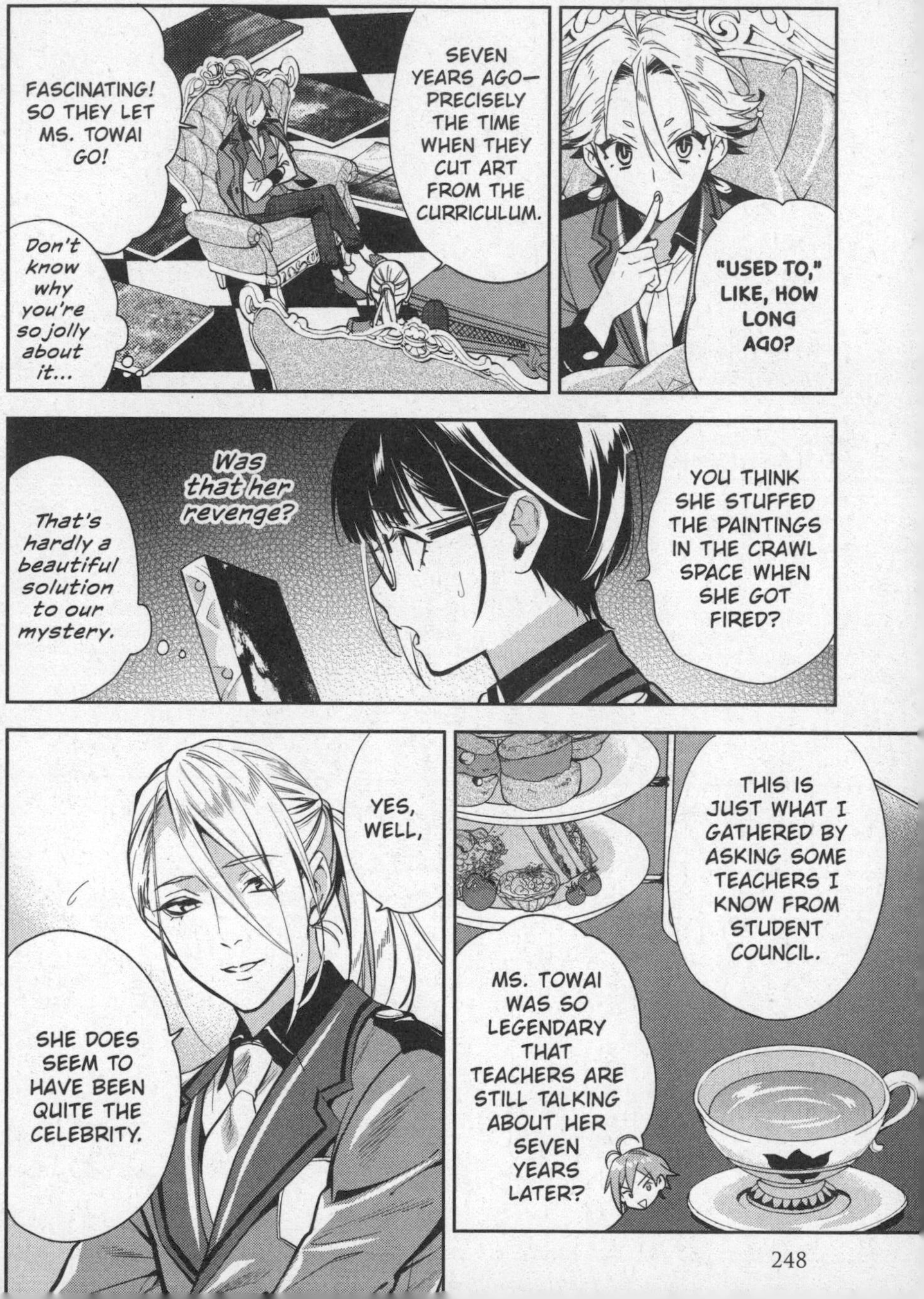
"USED TO," LIKE, HOW LONG AGO?
SEVEN YEARS AGO—PRECISELY THE TIME WHEN THEY CUT ART FROM THE CURRICULUM.
FASCINATING! SO THEY LET MS. TOWAI GO!
Don't know why you're so jolly about it...
YOU THINK SHE STUFFED THE PAINTINGS IN THE CRAWL SPACE WHEN SHE GOT FIRED?
Was that her revenge?
That's hardly a beautiful solution to our mystery.
THIS IS JUST WHAT I GATHERED BY ASKING SOME TEACHERS I KNOW FROM STUDENT COUNCIL.
MS. TOWAI WAS SO LEGENDARY THAT TEACHERS ARE STILL TALKING ABOUT HER SEVEN YEARS LATER?
YES, WELL,
SHE DOES SEEM TO HAVE BEEN QUITE THE CELEBRITY.

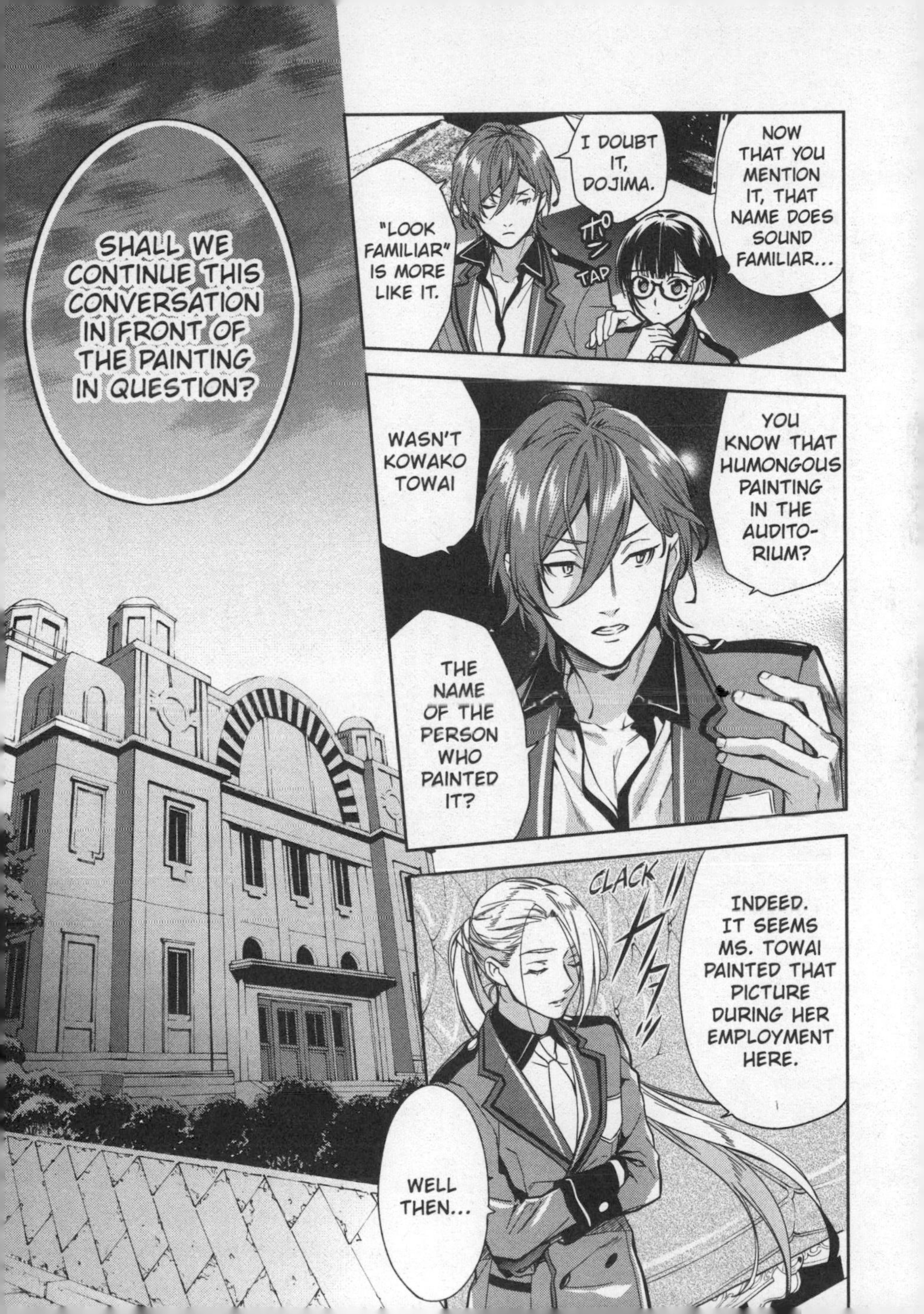
NOW THAT YOU MENTION IT, THAT NAME DOES SOUND FAMILIAR...
I DOUBT IT, DOJIMA.
TAP
"LOOK FAMILIAR" IS MORE LIKE IT.
YOU KNOW THAT HUMONGOUS PAINTING IN THE AUDITO-RIUM?
WASN'T KOWAKO TOWAI
THE NAME OF THE PERSON WHO PAINTED IT?
CLACK
INDEED. IT SEEMS MS. TOWAI PAINTED THAT PICTURE DURING HER EMPLOYMENT HERE.
WELL THEN...
SHALL WE CONTINUE THIS CONVERSATION IN FRONT OF THE PAINTING IN QUESTION?

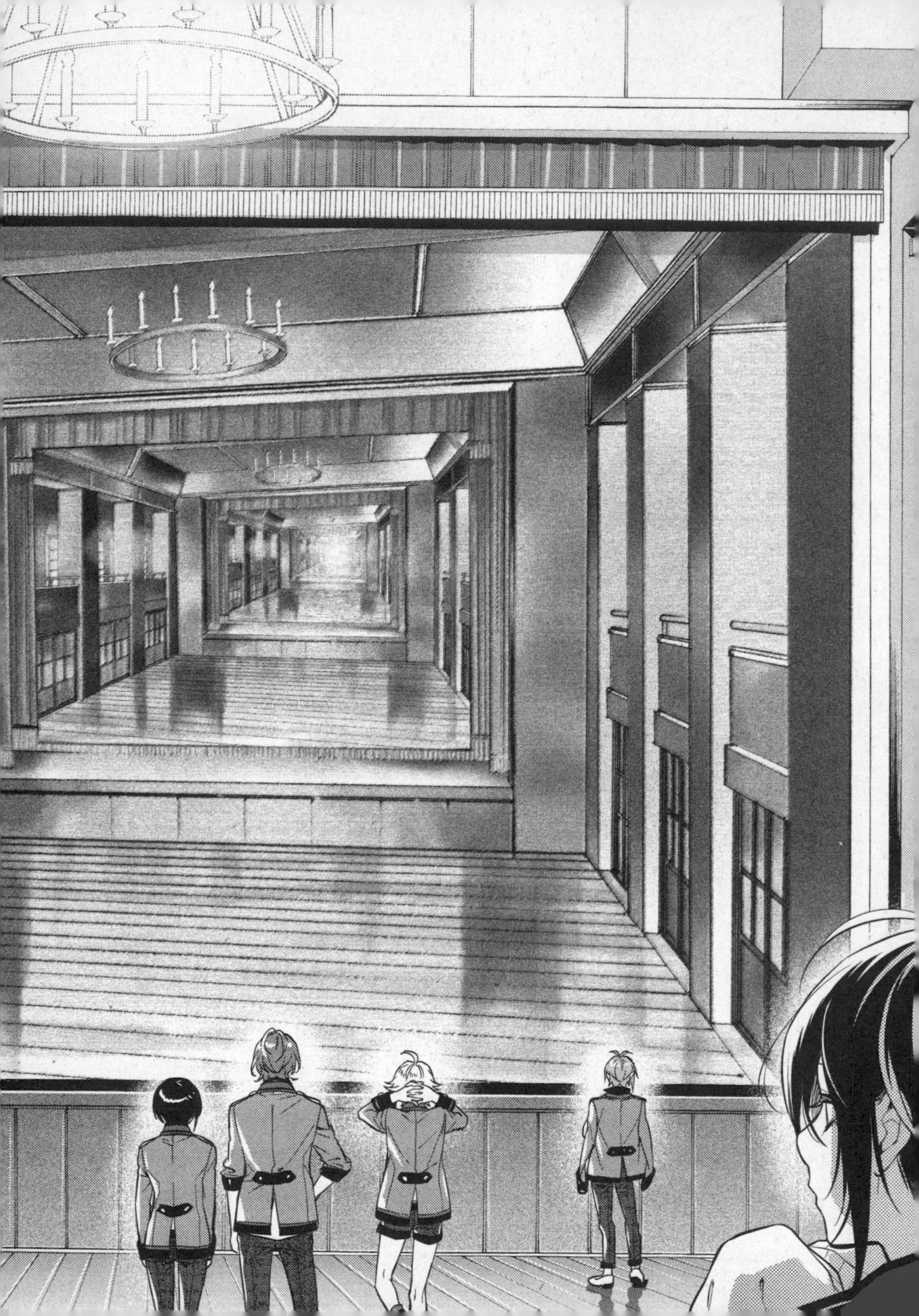

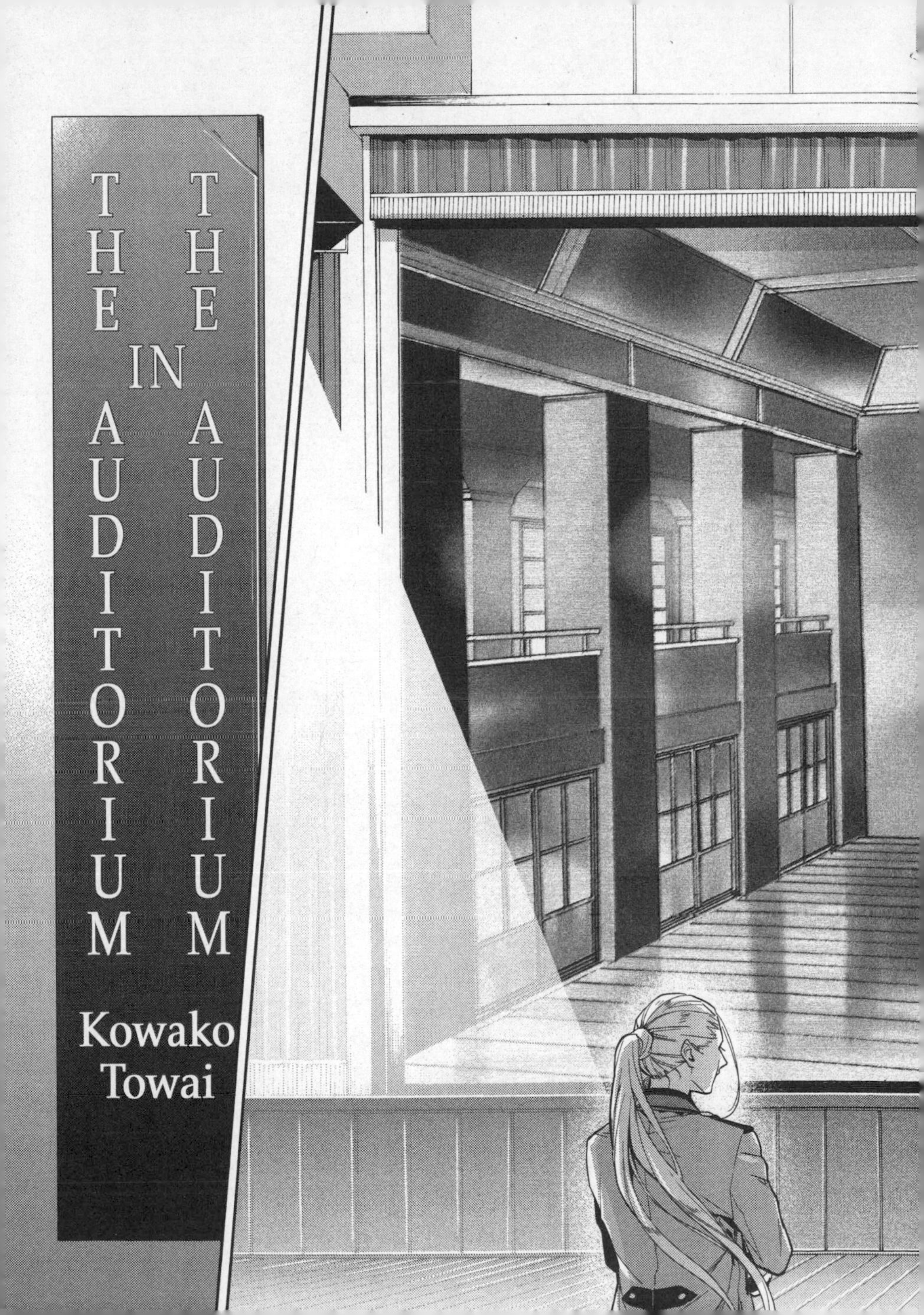
THE AUDITORIUM IN THE AUDITORIUM
Kowako Towai

PRETTY BOY

DETECTIVE CLUB!!

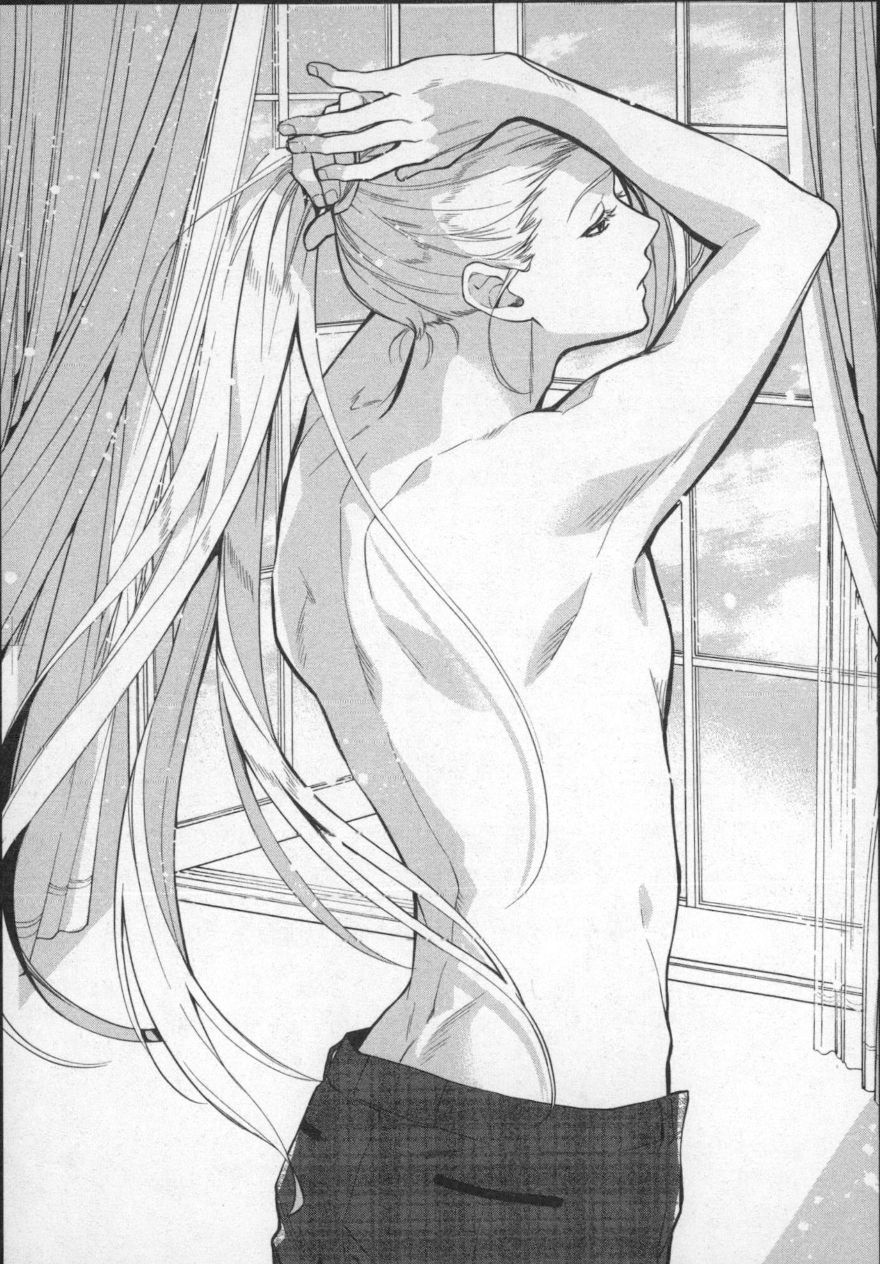

FILE ★ The Pretty Boy in the Attic 4

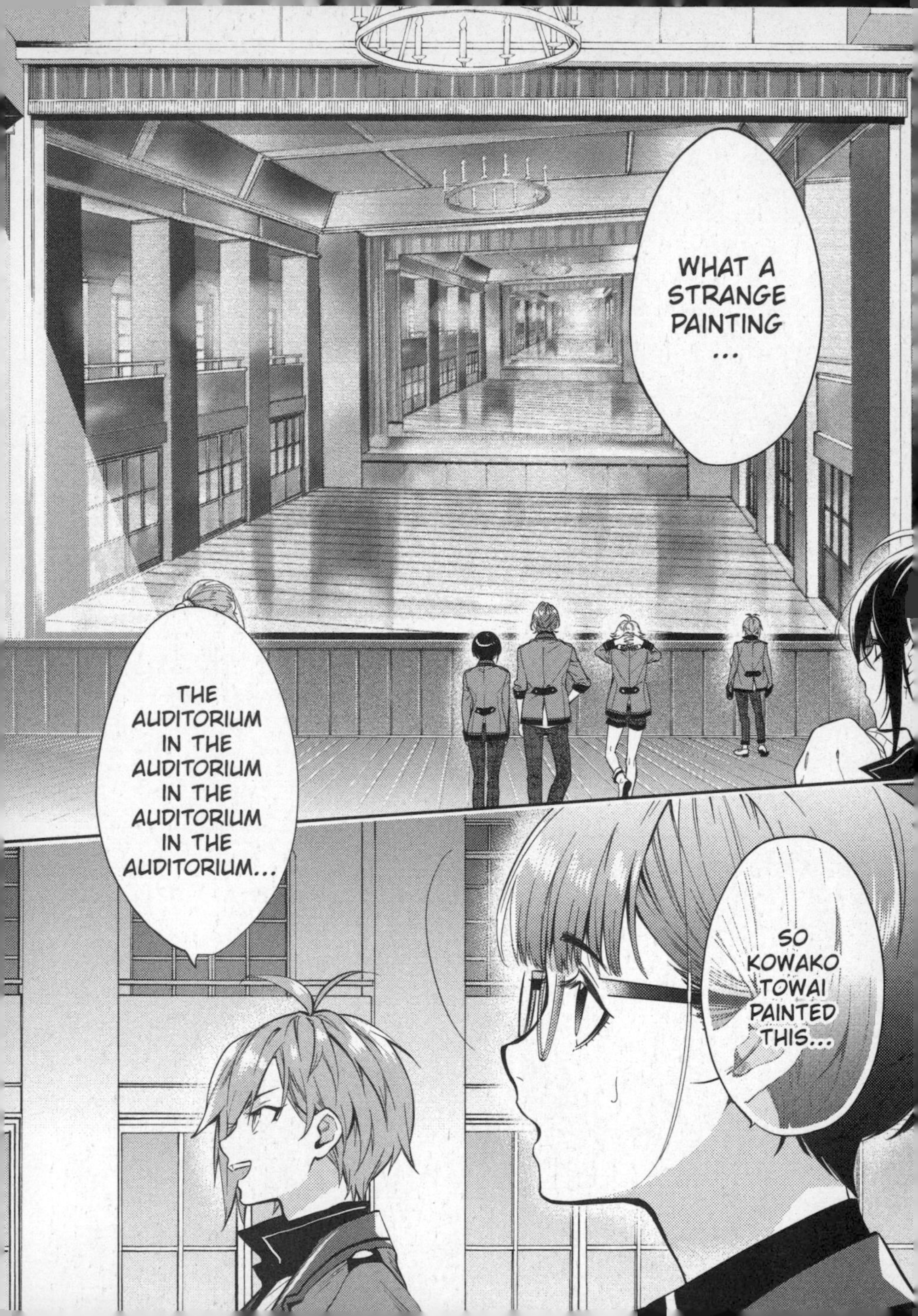
WHAT A STRANGE PAINTING ...
THE AUDITORIUM IN THE AUDITORIUM IN THE AUDITORIUM IN THE AUDITORIUM...
SO KOWAKO TOWAI PAINTED THIS...

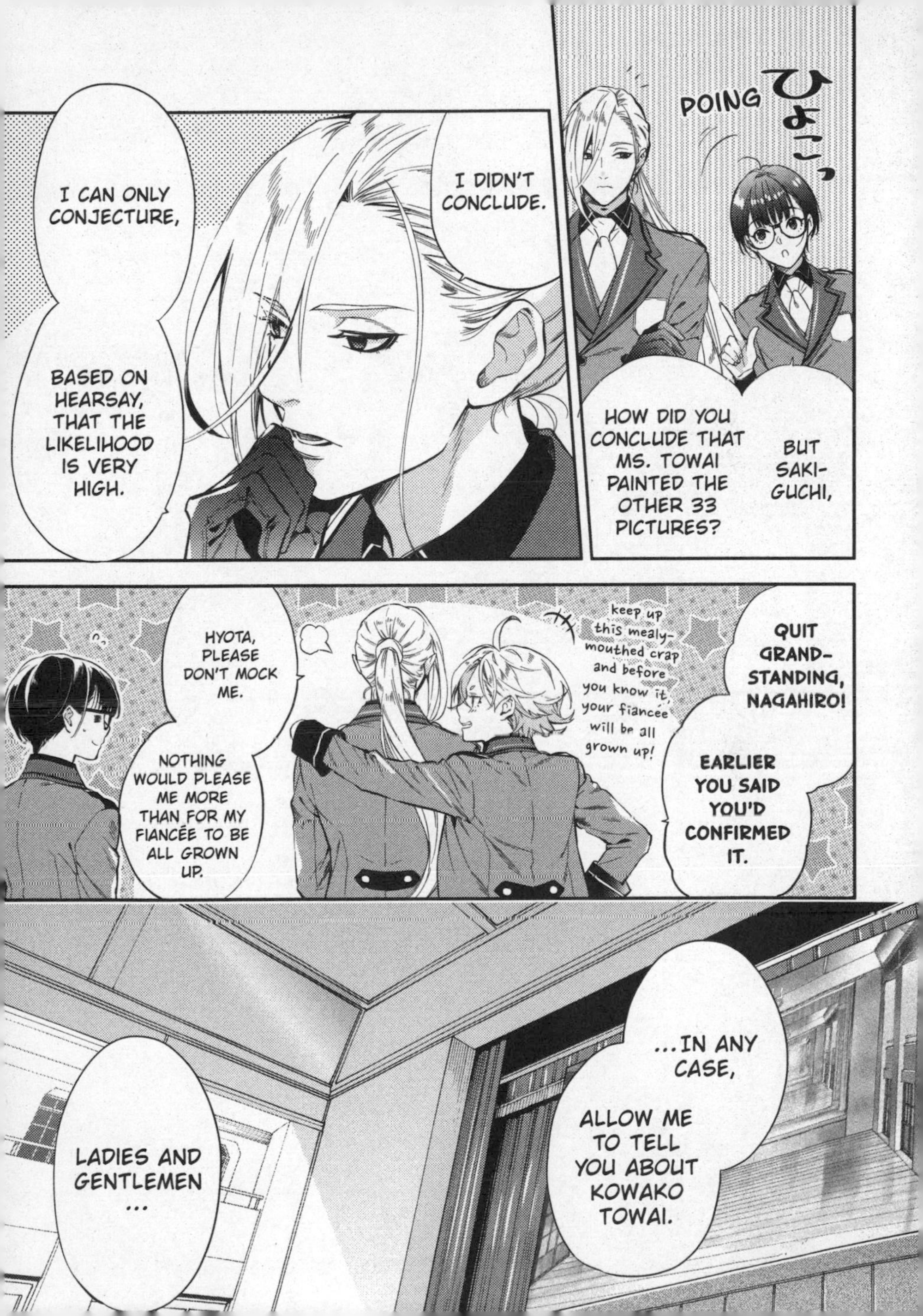
POING
ひょこっ
BUT SAKI-GUCHI,
HOW DID YOU CONCLUDE THAT MS. TOWAI PAINTED THE OTHER 33 PICTURES?
I DIDN'T CONCLUDE.
I CAN ONLY CONJECTURE,
BASED ON HEARSAY, THAT THE LIKELIHOOD IS VERY HIGH.
QUIT GRAND-STANDING, NAGAHIRO!
EARLIER YOU SAID YOU'D CONFIRMED IT.
keep up this mealy-mouthed crap and before you know it, your fiancée will be all grown up!
HYOTA, PLEASE DON'T MOCK ME.
NOTHING WOULD PLEASE ME MORE THAN FOR MY FIANCÉE TO BE ALL GROWN UP.
...IN ANY CASE,
ALLOW ME TO TELL YOU ABOUT KOWAKO TOWAI.
LADIES AND GENTLEMEN ...

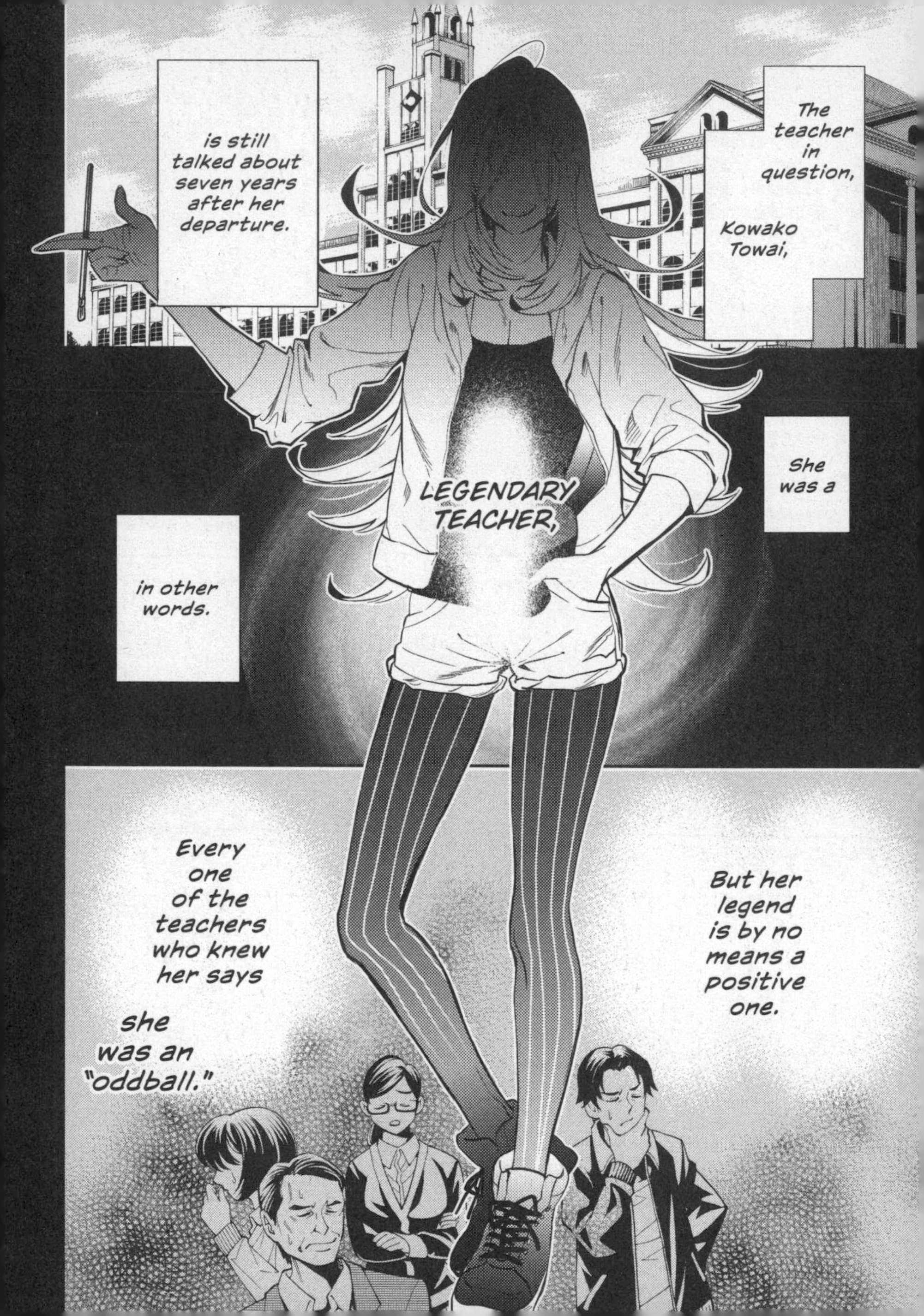
The teacher in question,
Kowako Towai,
is still talked about seven years after her departure.
She was a
LEGENDARY TEACHER,
in other words.
But her legend is by no means a positive one.
Every one of the teachers who knew her says
she was an "oddball."

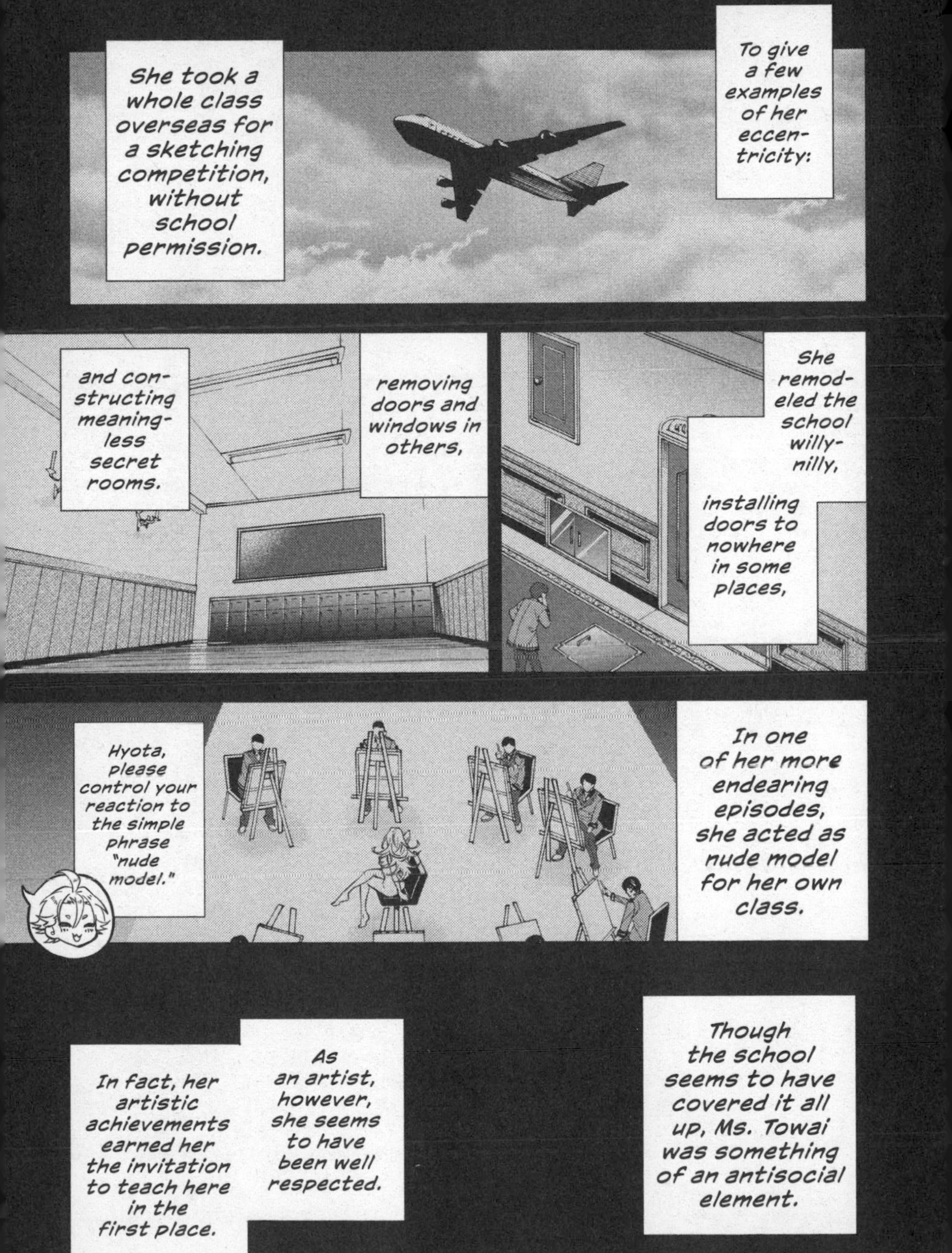
To give a few examples of her eccentricity:
She took a whole class overseas for a sketching competition, without school permission.
She remodeled the school willy-nilly,
installing doors to nowhere in some places,
removing doors and windows in others,
and constructing meaningless secret rooms.
In one of her more endearing episodes, she acted as nude model for her own class.
Hyota, please control your reaction to the simple phrase "nude model."
Though the school seems to have covered it all up, Ms. Towai was something of an antisocial element.
As an artist, however, she seems to have been well respected.
In fact, her artistic achievements earned her the invitation to teach here in the first place.

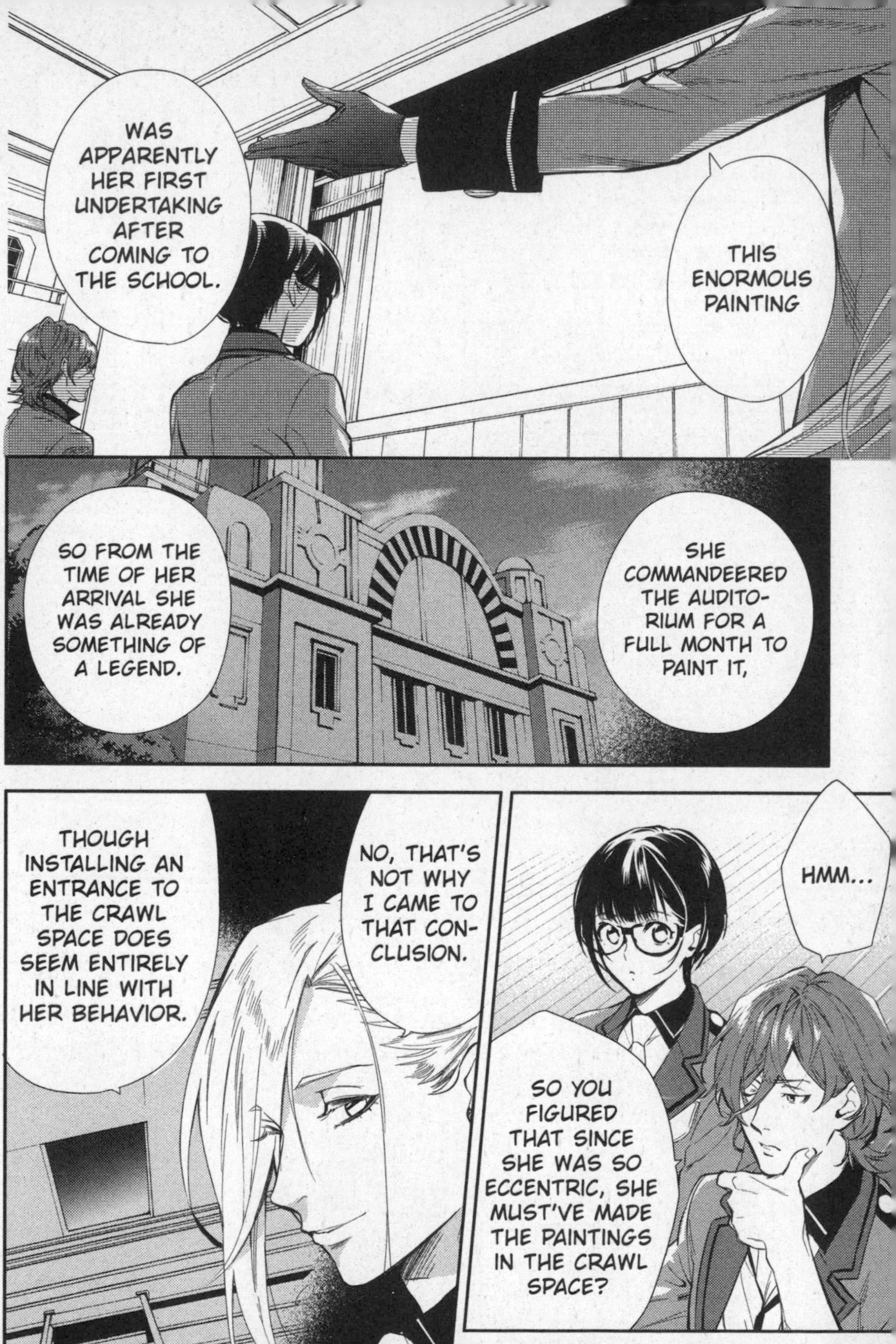
THIS ENORMOUS PAINTING
WAS APPARENTLY HER FIRST UNDERTAKING AFTER COMING TO THE SCHOOL.
SHE COMMANDEERED THE AUDITO-RIUM FOR A FULL MONTH TO PAINT IT,
SO FROM THE TIME OF HER ARRIVAL SHE WAS ALREADY SOMETHING OF A LEGEND.
HMM...
SO YOU FIGURED THAT SINCE SHE WAS SO ECCENTRIC, SHE MUST'VE MADE THE PAINTINGS IN THE CRAWL SPACE?
NO, THAT'S NOT WHY I CAME TO THAT CON-CLUSION.
THOUGH INSTALLING AN ENTRANCE TO THE CRAWL SPACE DOES SEEM ENTIRELY IN LINE WITH HER BEHAVIOR.

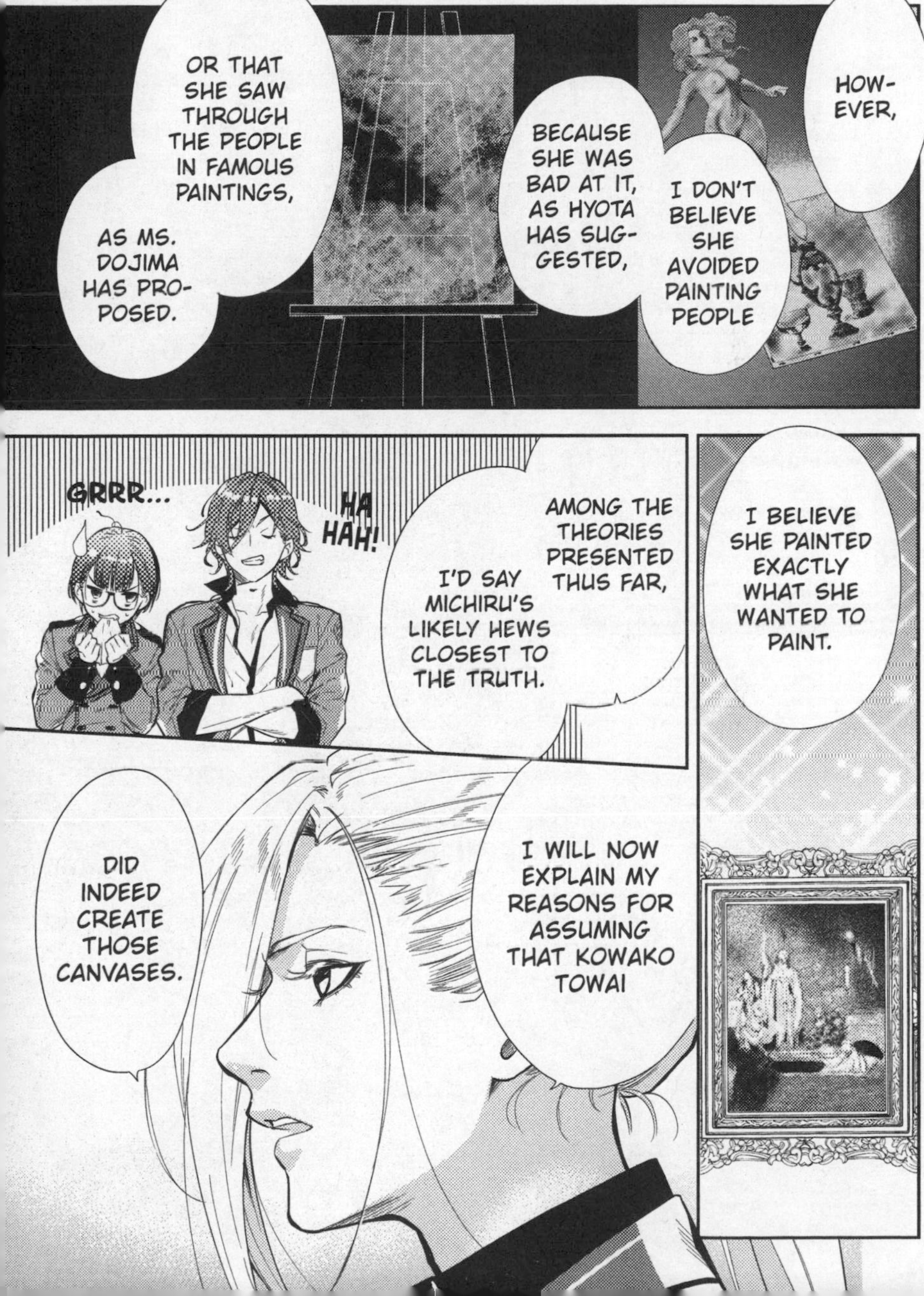
HOW-EVER,
I DON'T BELIEVE SHE AVOIDED PAINTING PEOPLE
BECAUSE SHE WAS BAD AT IT, AS HYOTA HAS SUG-GESTED,
OR THAT SHE SAW THROUGH THE PEOPLE IN FAMOUS PAINTINGS,
AS MS. DOJIMA HAS PRO-POSED.
I BELIEVE SHE PAINTED EXACTLY WHAT SHE WANTED TO PAINT.
AMONG THE THEORIES PRESENTED THUS FAR,
I'D SAY MICHIRU'S LIKELY HEWS CLOSEST TO THE TRUTH.
HA HAH!
GRRR...
I WILL NOW EXPLAIN MY REASONS FOR ASSUMING THAT KOWAKO TOWAI
DID INDEED CREATE THOSE CANVASES.

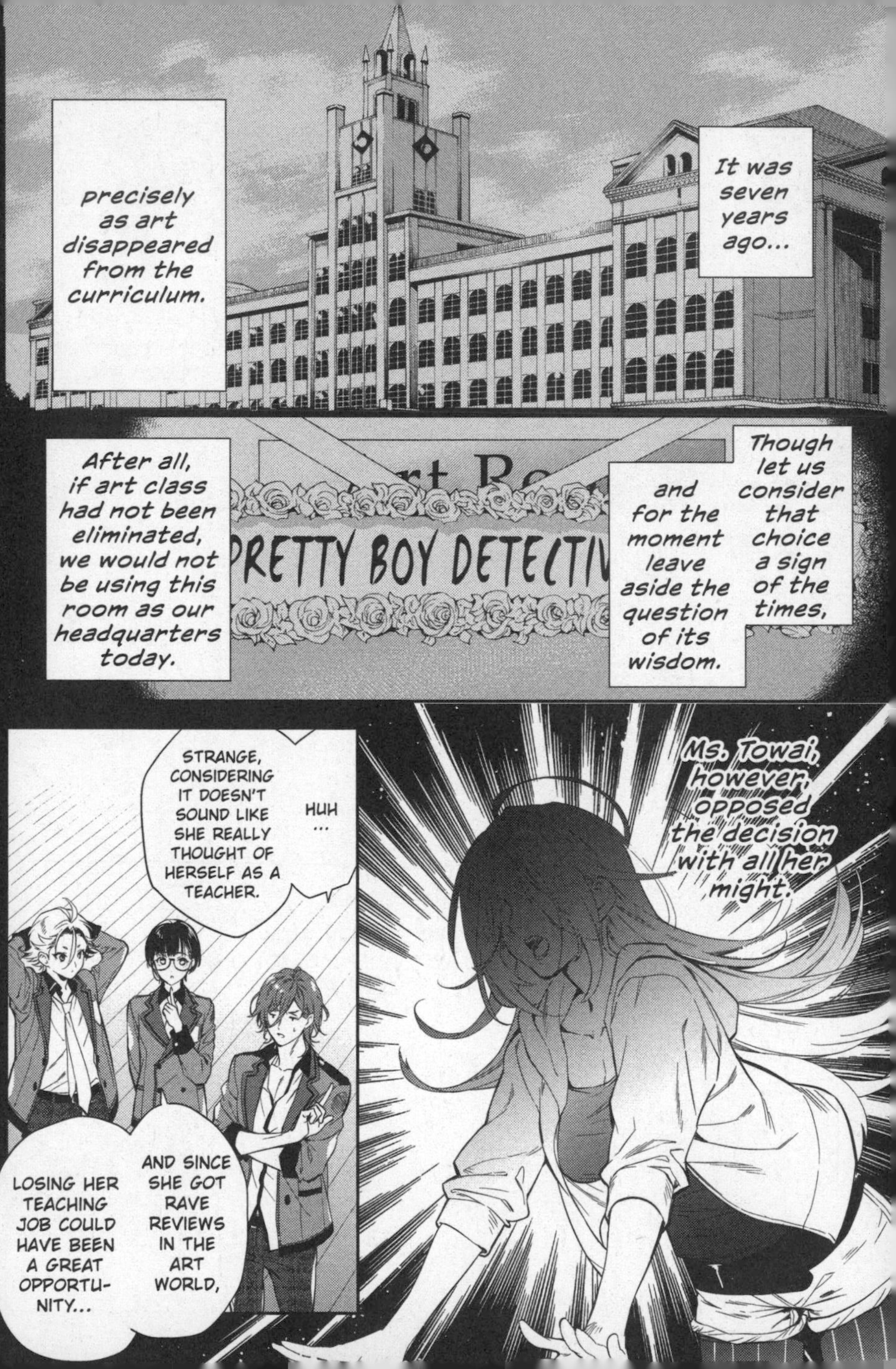
It was seven years ago...
precisely as art disappeared from the curriculum.
Though let us consider that choice a sign of the times,
and for the moment leave aside the question of its wisdom.
PRETTY BOY DETECTIV
After all, if art class had not been eliminated, we would not be using this room as our headquarters today.
Ms. Towai, however, opposed the decision with all her might.
HUH ...
STRANGE, CONSIDERING IT DOESN'T SOUND LIKE SHE REALLY THOUGHT OF HERSELF AS A TEACHER.
AND SINCE SHE GOT RAVE REVIEWS IN THE ART WORLD,
LOSING HER TEACHING JOB COULD HAVE BEEN A GREAT OPPORTU-NITY...

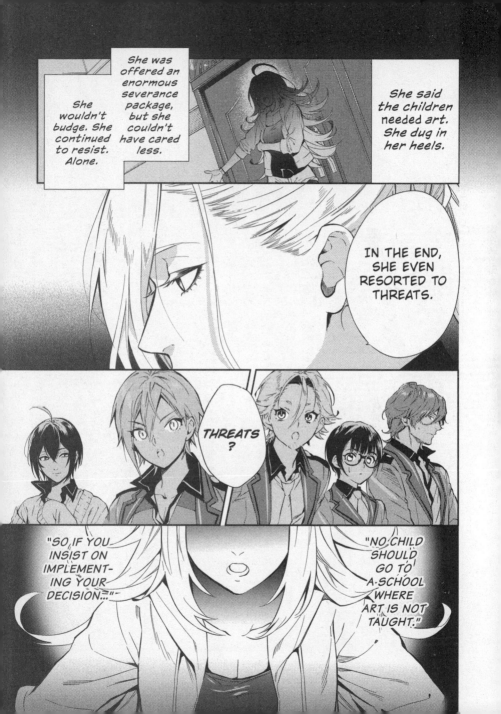

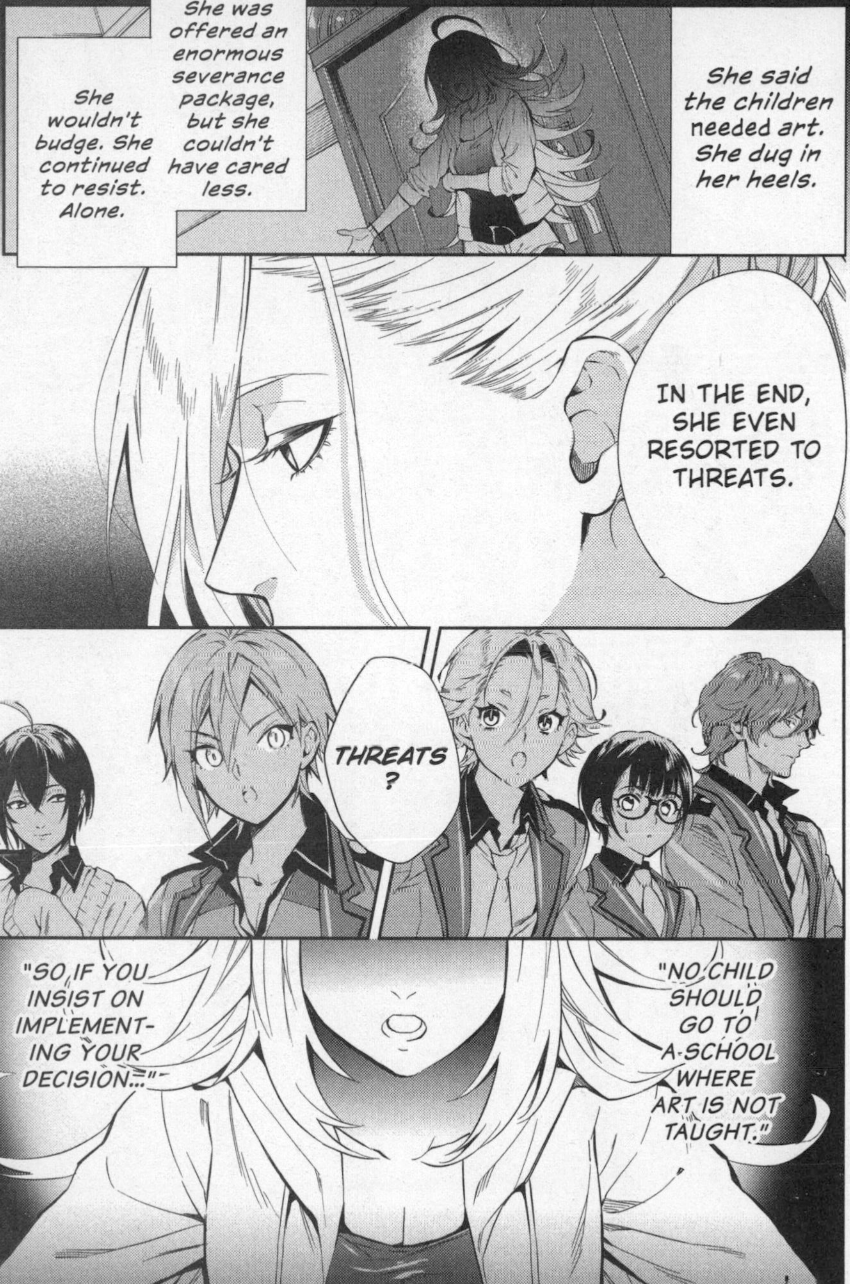
She said the children needed art. She dug in her heels.
She was offered an enormous severance package, but she couldn't have cared less.
She wouldn't budge. She continued to resist. Alone.
IN THE END, SHE EVEN RESORTED TO THREATS.
THREATS?
"NO CHILD SHOULD GO TO A SCHOOL WHERE ART IS NOT TAUGHT."
"SO IF YOU INSIST ON IMPLEMENT-ING YOUR DECISION..."

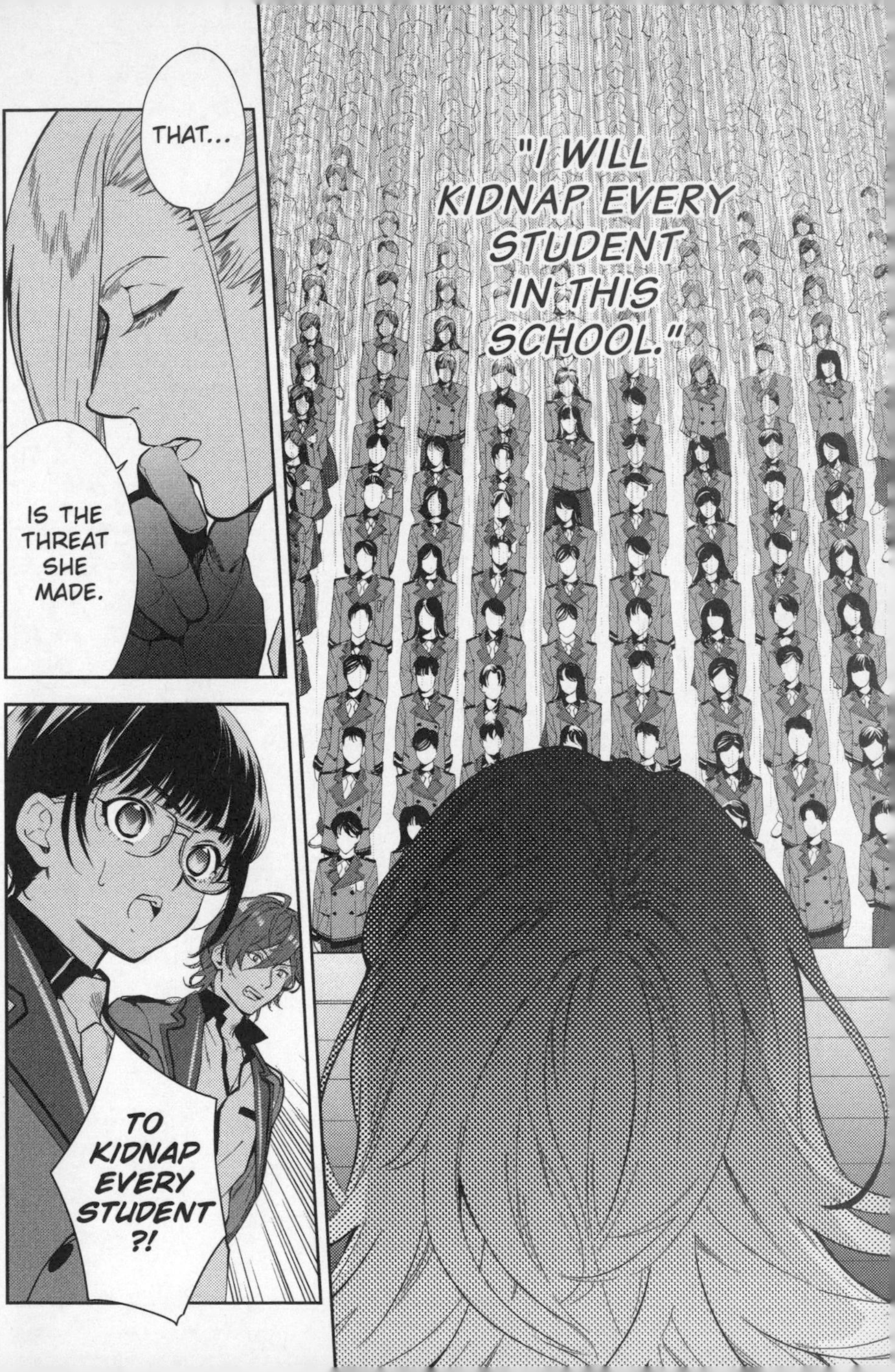
"I WILL KIDNAP EVERY STUDENT IN THIS SCHOOL."
THAT...
IS THE THREAT SHE MADE.
TO KIDNAP EVERY STUDENT?!

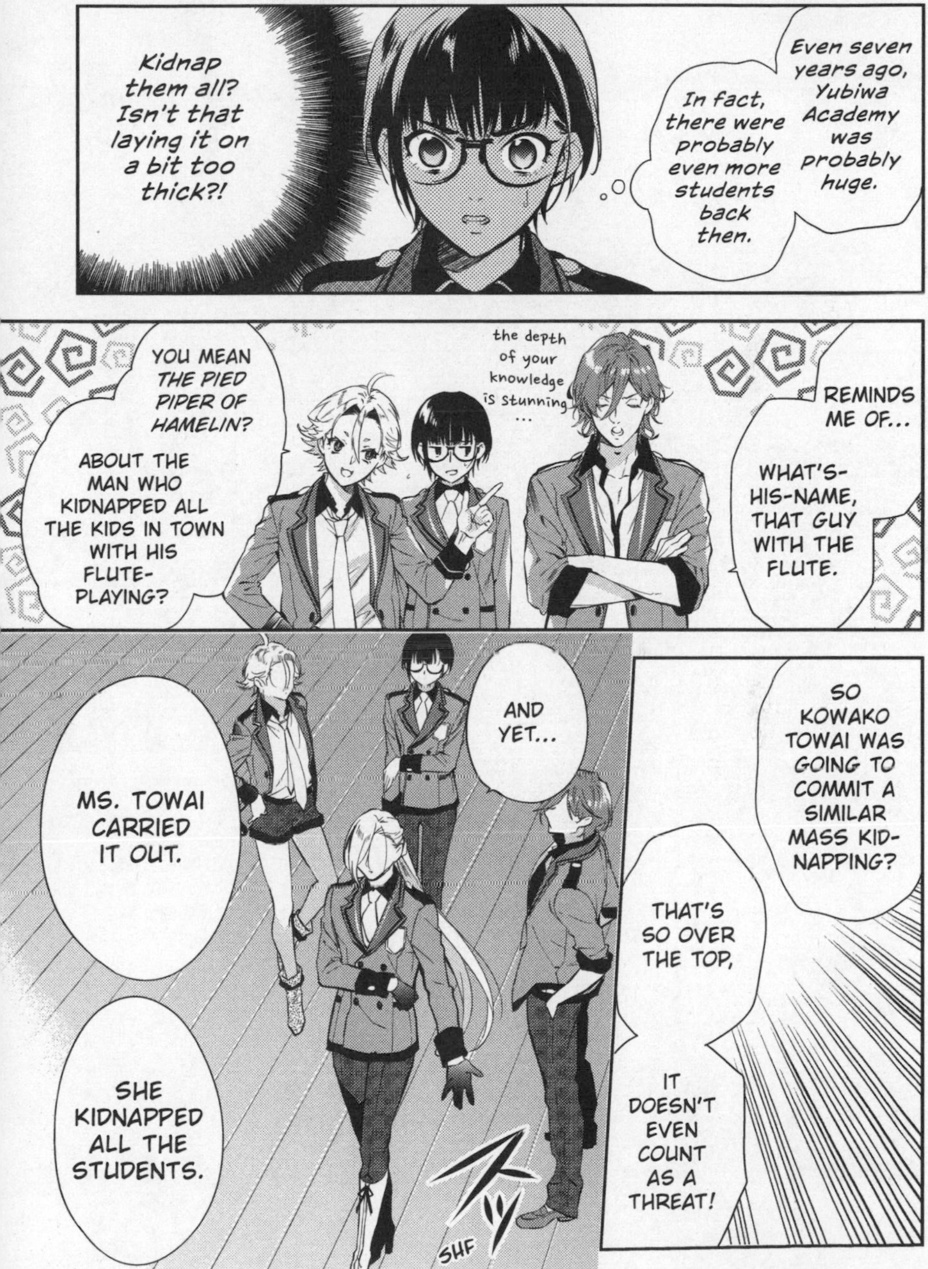
Even seven years ago, Yubiwa Academy was probably huge.
In fact, there were probably even more students back then.
Kidnap them all? Isn't that laying it on a bit too thick?!
REMINDS ME OF...
WHAT'S-HIS-NAME, THAT GUY WITH THE FLUTE.
the depth of your knowledge is stunning...
YOU MEAN THE PIED PIPER OF HAMELIN?
ABOUT THE MAN WHO KIDNAPPED ALL THE KIDS IN TOWN WITH HIS FLUTE-PLAYING?
SO KOWAKO TOWAI WAS GOING TO COMMIT A SIMILAR MASS KID-NAPPING?
THAT'S SO OVER THE TOP,
IT DOESN'T EVEN COUNT AS A THREAT!
AND YET...
MS. TOWAI CARRIED IT OUT.
SHE KIDNAPPED ALL THE STUDENTS.
SHF

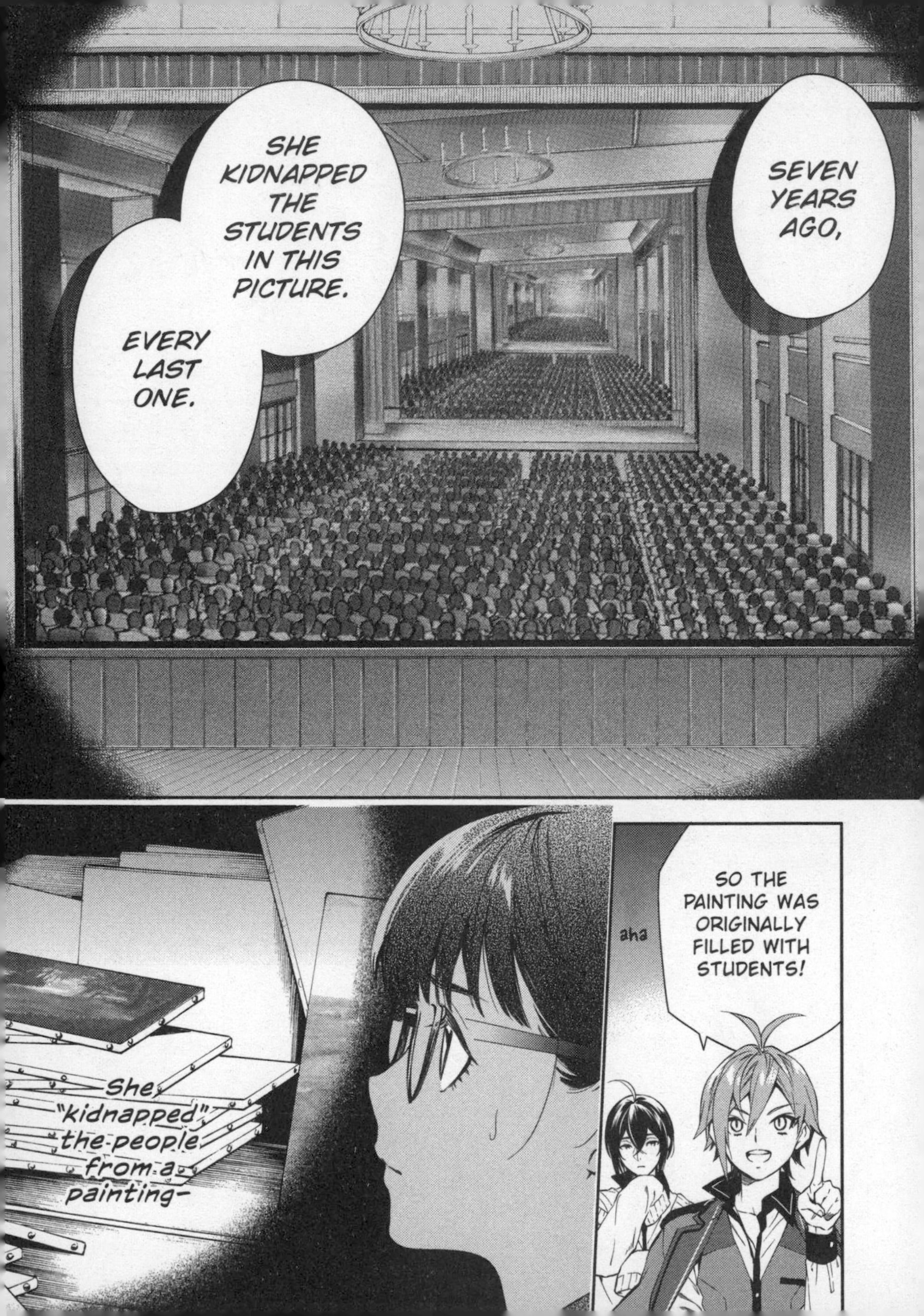
SEVEN YEARS AGO,
SHE KIDNAPPED THE STUDENTS IN THIS PICTURE.
EVERY LAST ONE.
SO THE PAINTING WAS ORIGINALLY FILLED WITH STUDENTS!
aha
She "kidnapped" the people from a painting-

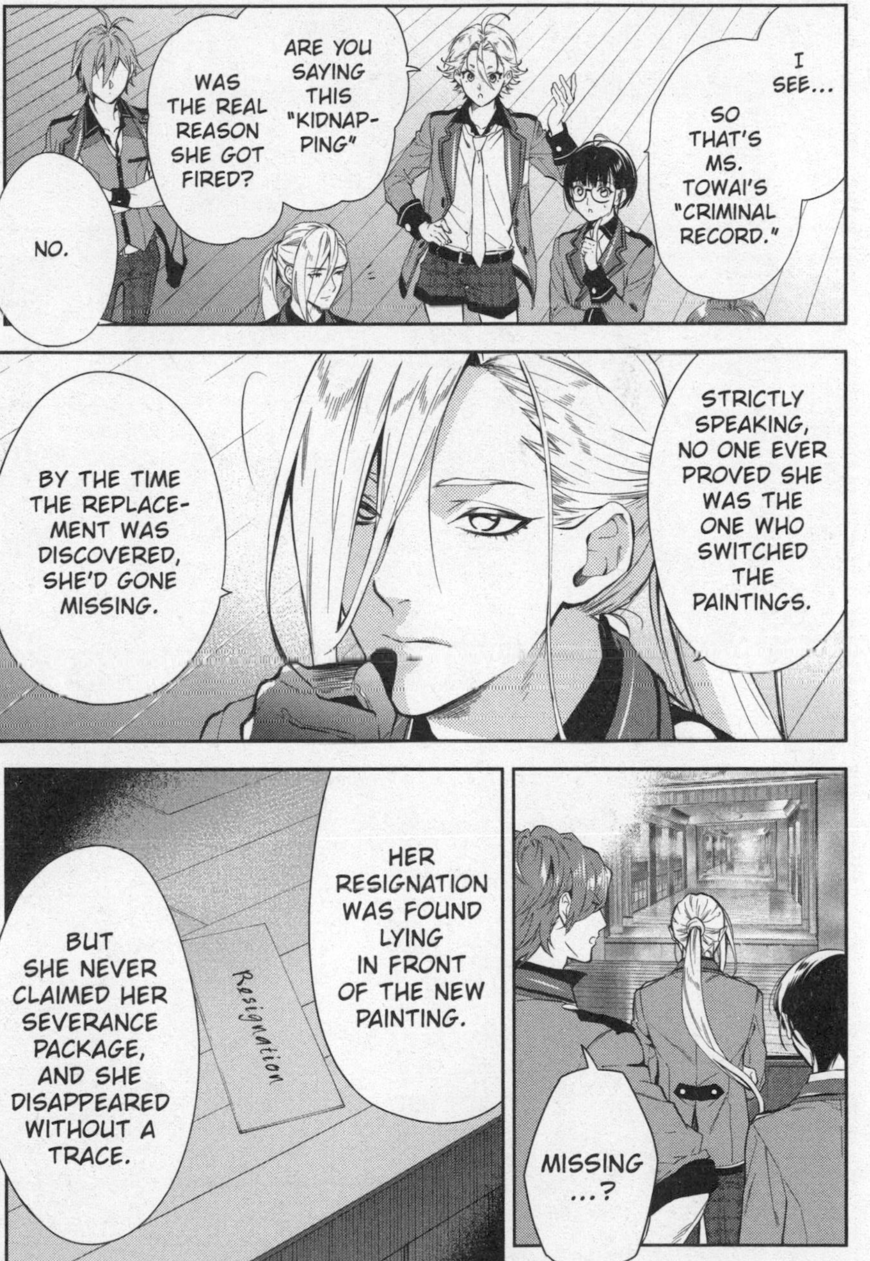
I SEE... SO THAT'S MS. TOWAI'S "CRIMINAL RECORD."
ARE YOU SAYING THIS "KIDNAP-PING"
WAS THE REAL REASON SHE GOT FIRED?
NO.
STRICTLY SPEAKING, NO ONE EVER PROVED SHE WAS THE ONE WHO SWITCHED THE PAINTINGS.
BY THE TIME THE REPLACE-MENT WAS DISCOVERED, SHE'D GONE MISSING.
MISSING ...?
HER RESIGNATION WAS FOUND LYING IN FRONT OF THE NEW PAINTING.
BUT SHE NEVER CLAIMED HER SEVERANCE PACKAGE, AND SHE DISAPPEARED WITHOUT A TRACE.
Resignation

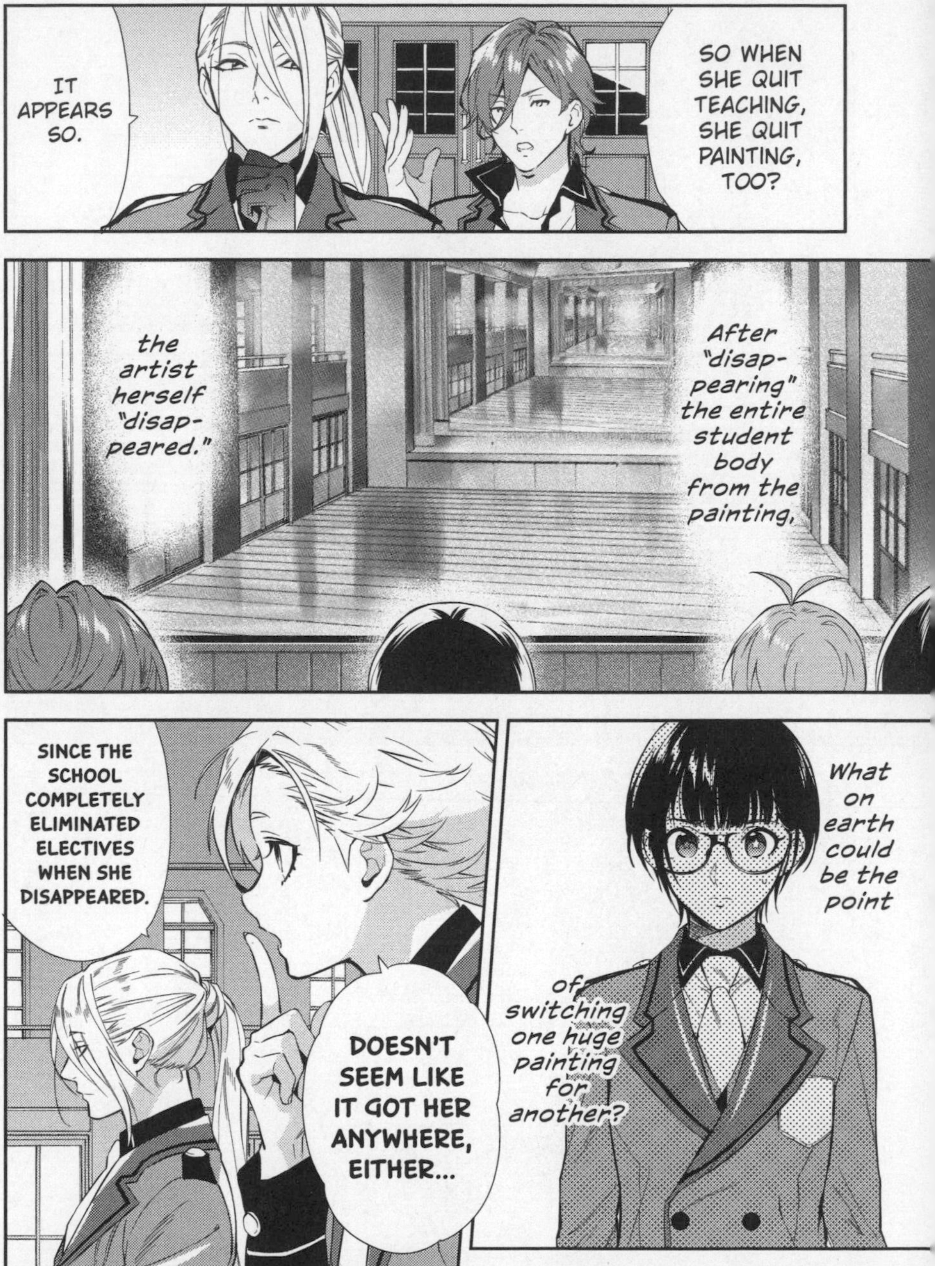
SO WHEN SHE QUIT TEACHING, SHE QUIT PAINTING, TOO?
IT APPEARS SO.
After "disap-pearing" the entire student body from the painting,
the artist herself "disap-peared."
What on earth could be the point
of switching one huge painting for another?
SINCE THE SCHOOL COMPLETELY ELIMINATED ELECTIVES WHEN SHE DISAPPEARED.
DOESN'T SEEM LIKE IT GOT HER ANYWHERE, EITHER...

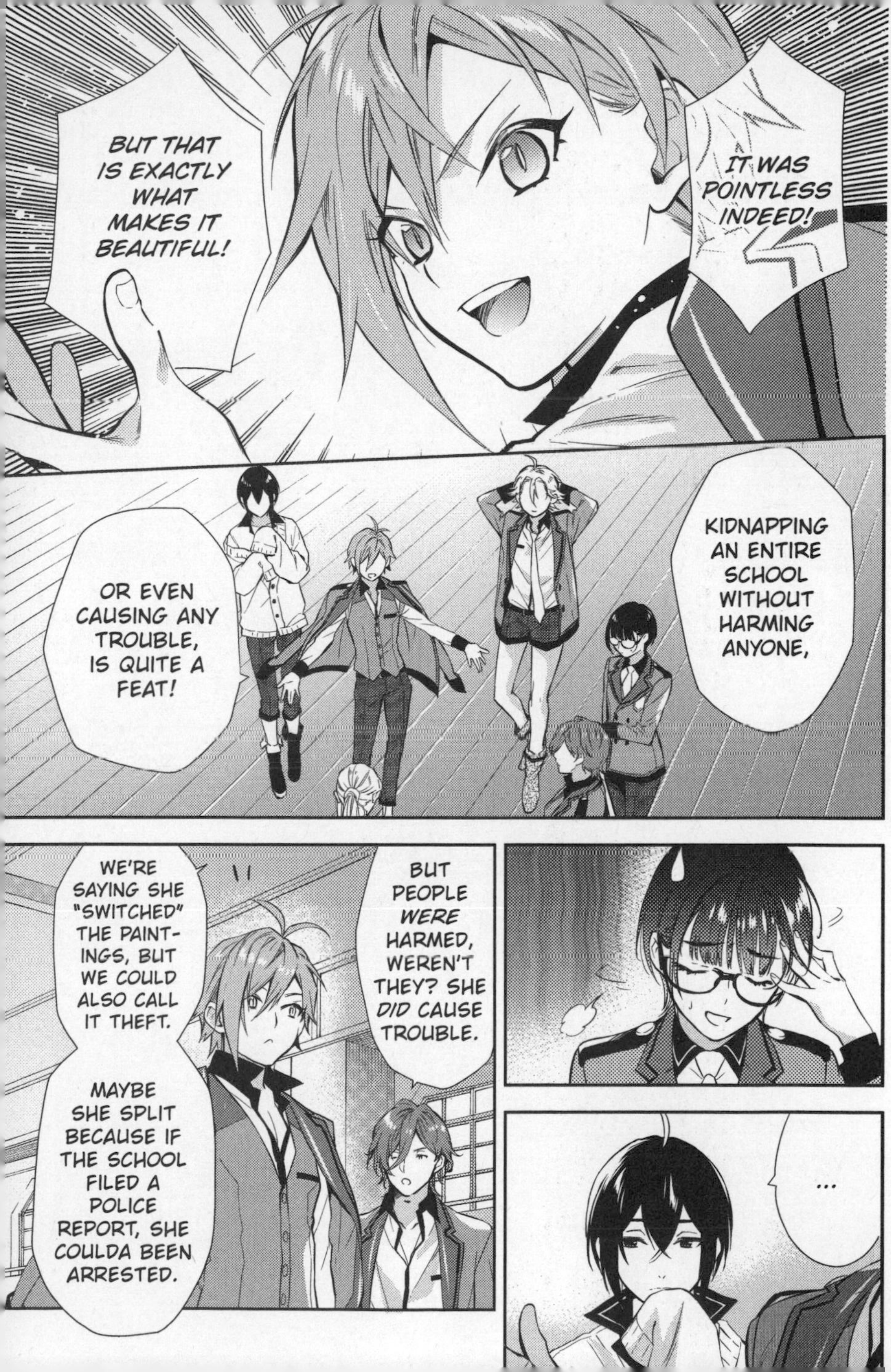
IT WAS POINTLESS INDEED!
BUT THAT IS EXACTLY WHAT MAKES IT BEAUTIFUL!
KIDNAPPING AN ENTIRE SCHOOL WITHOUT HARMING ANYONE,
OR EVEN CAUSING ANY TROUBLE, IS QUITE A FEAT!
...
BUT PEOPLE *WERE* HARMED, WEREN'T THEY? SHE *DID* CAUSE TROUBLE.
WE'RE SAYING SHE "SWITCHED" THE PAINT-INGS, BUT WE COULD ALSO CALL IT THEFT.
MAYBE SHE SPLIT BECAUSE IF THE SCHOOL FILED A POLICE REPORT, SHE COULDA BEEN ARRESTED.

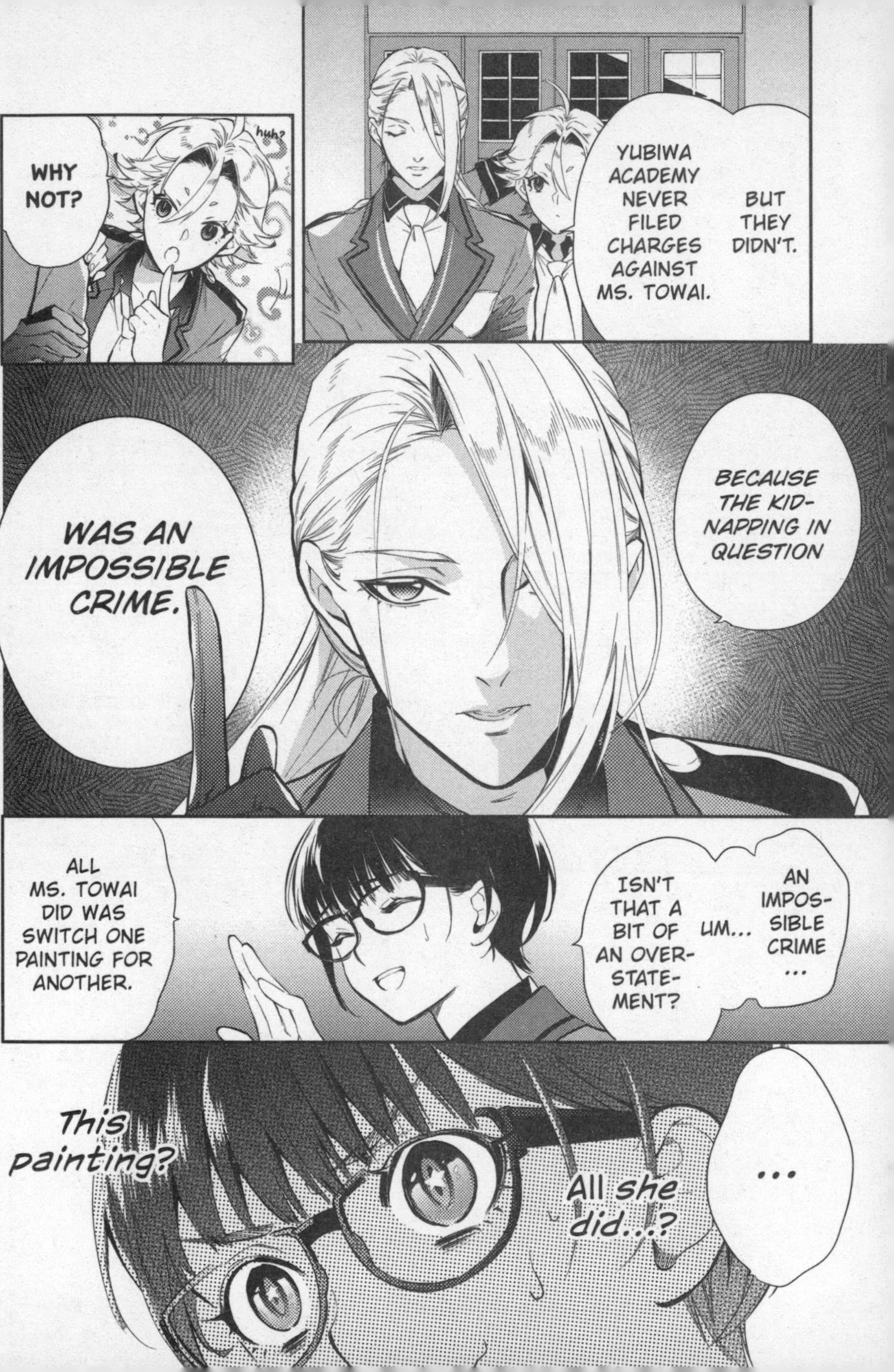
BUT THEY DIDN'T.
YUBIWA ACADEMY NEVER FILED CHARGES AGAINST MS. TOWAI.
huh?
WHY NOT?
BECAUSE THE KID-NAPPING IN QUESTION
WAS AN IMPOSSIBLE CRIME.
AN IMPOS-SIBLE CRIME ...
UM...
ISN'T THAT A BIT OF AN OVER-STATE-MENT?
ALL MS. TOWAI DID WAS SWITCH ONE PAINTING FOR ANOTHER.
...
All she did...?
This painting?

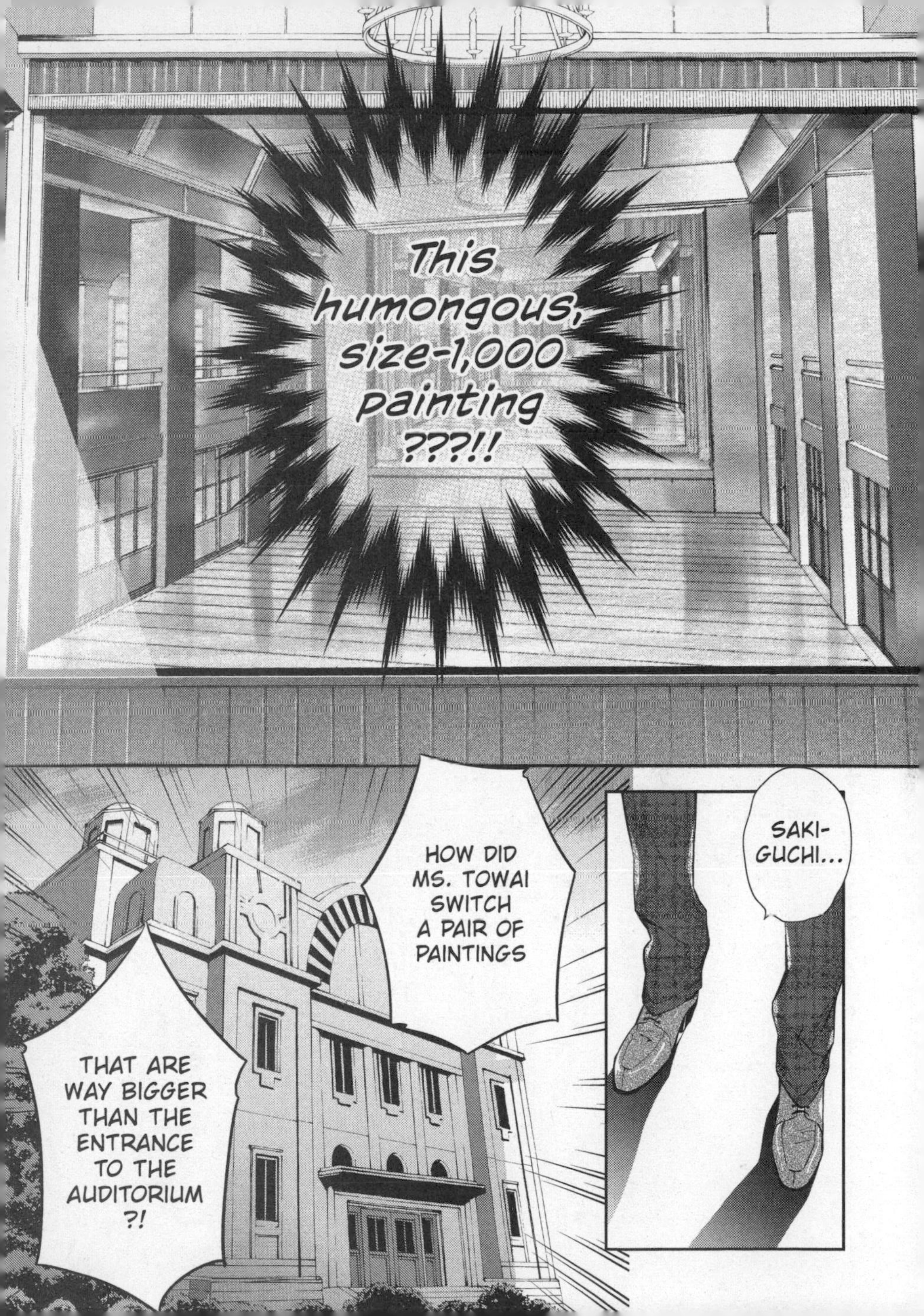
This humongous, size-1,000 painting ???!!
SAKI-GUCHI...
HOW DID MS. TOWAI SWITCH A PAIR OF PAINTINGS
THAT ARE WAY BIGGER THAN THE ENTRANCE TO THE AUDITORIUM ?!

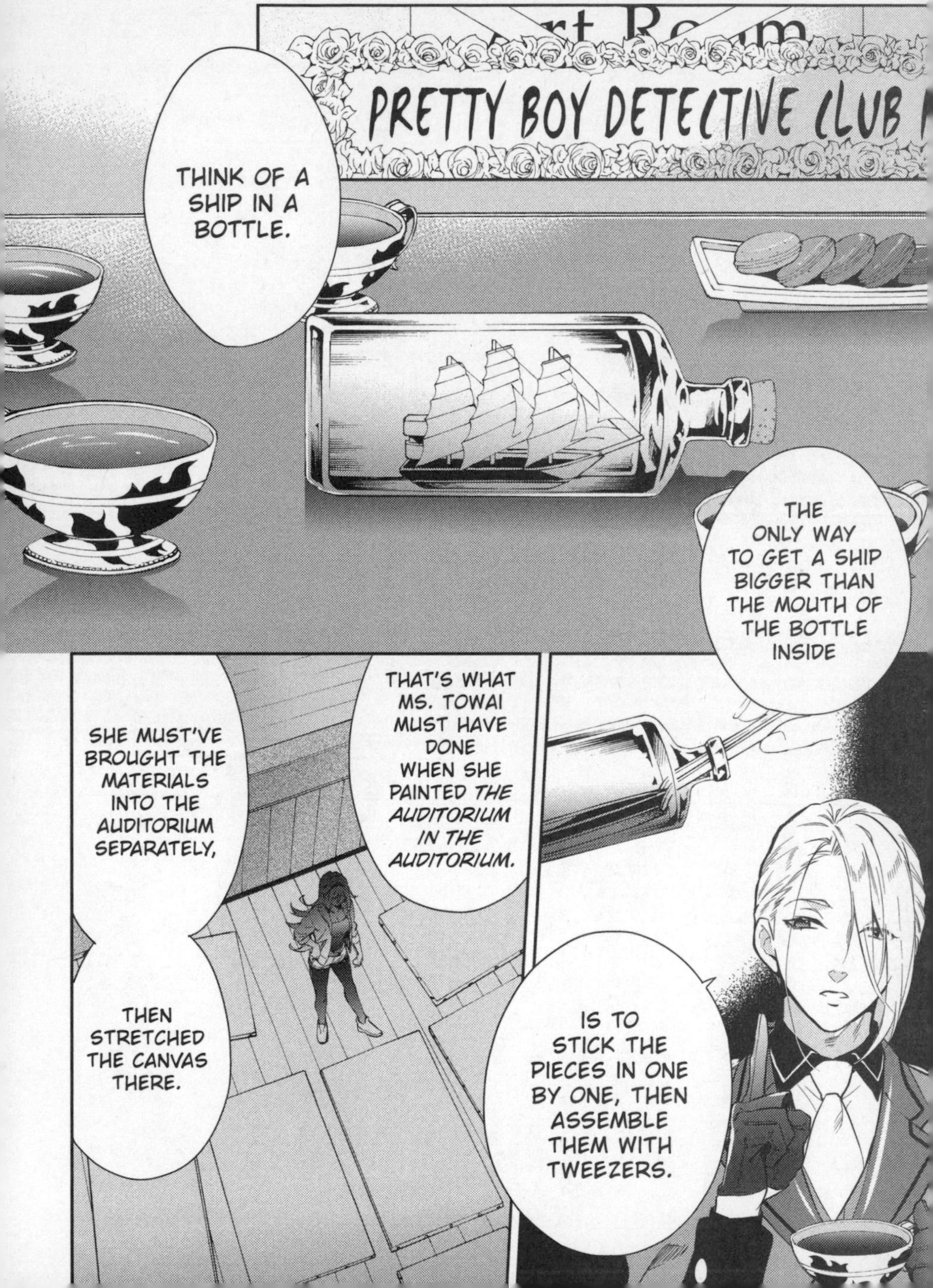
PRETTY BOY DETECTIVE CLUB
THINK OF A SHIP IN A BOTTLE.
THE ONLY WAY TO GET A SHIP BIGGER THAN THE MOUTH OF THE BOTTLE INSIDE
IS TO STICK THE PIECES IN ONE BY ONE, THEN ASSEMBLE THEM WITH TWEEZERS.
THAT'S WHAT MS. TOWAI MUST HAVE DONE WHEN SHE PAINTED *THE AUDITORIUM IN THE AUDITORIUM.*
SHE MUST'VE BROUGHT THE MATERIALS INTO THE AUDITORIUM SEPARATELY,
THEN STRETCHED THE CANVAS THERE.

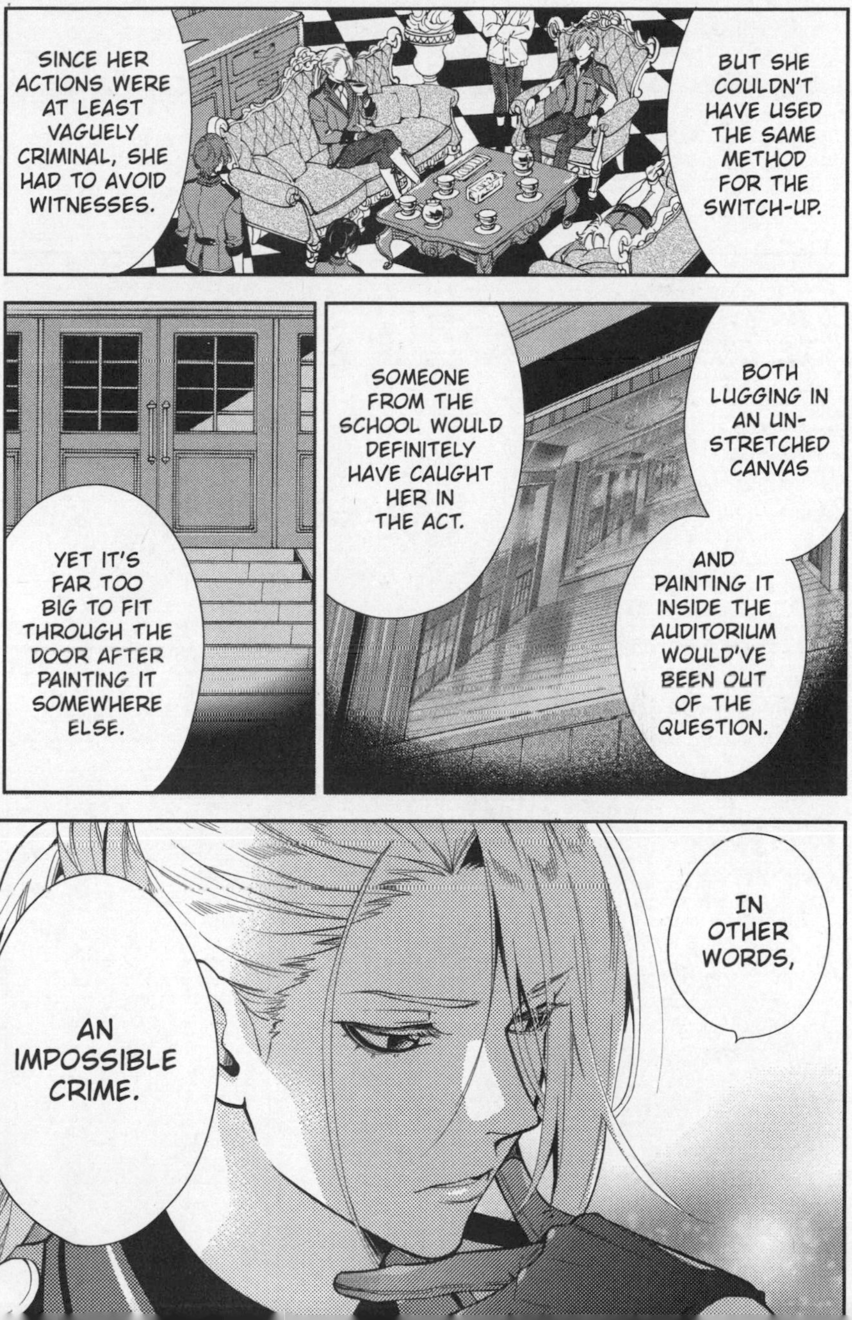
BUT SHE COULDN'T HAVE USED THE SAME METHOD FOR THE SWITCH-UP.
SINCE HER ACTIONS WERE AT LEAST VAGUELY CRIMINAL, SHE HAD TO AVOID WITNESSES.
BOTH LUGGING IN AN UN-STRETCHED CANVAS
AND PAINTING IT INSIDE THE AUDITORIUM WOULD'VE BEEN OUT OF THE QUESTION.
SOMEONE FROM THE SCHOOL WOULD DEFINITELY HAVE CAUGHT HER IN THE ACT.
YET IT'S FAR TOO BIG TO FIT THROUGH THE DOOR AFTER PAINTING IT SOMEWHERE ELSE.
IN OTHER WORDS,
AN IMPOSSIBLE CRIME.

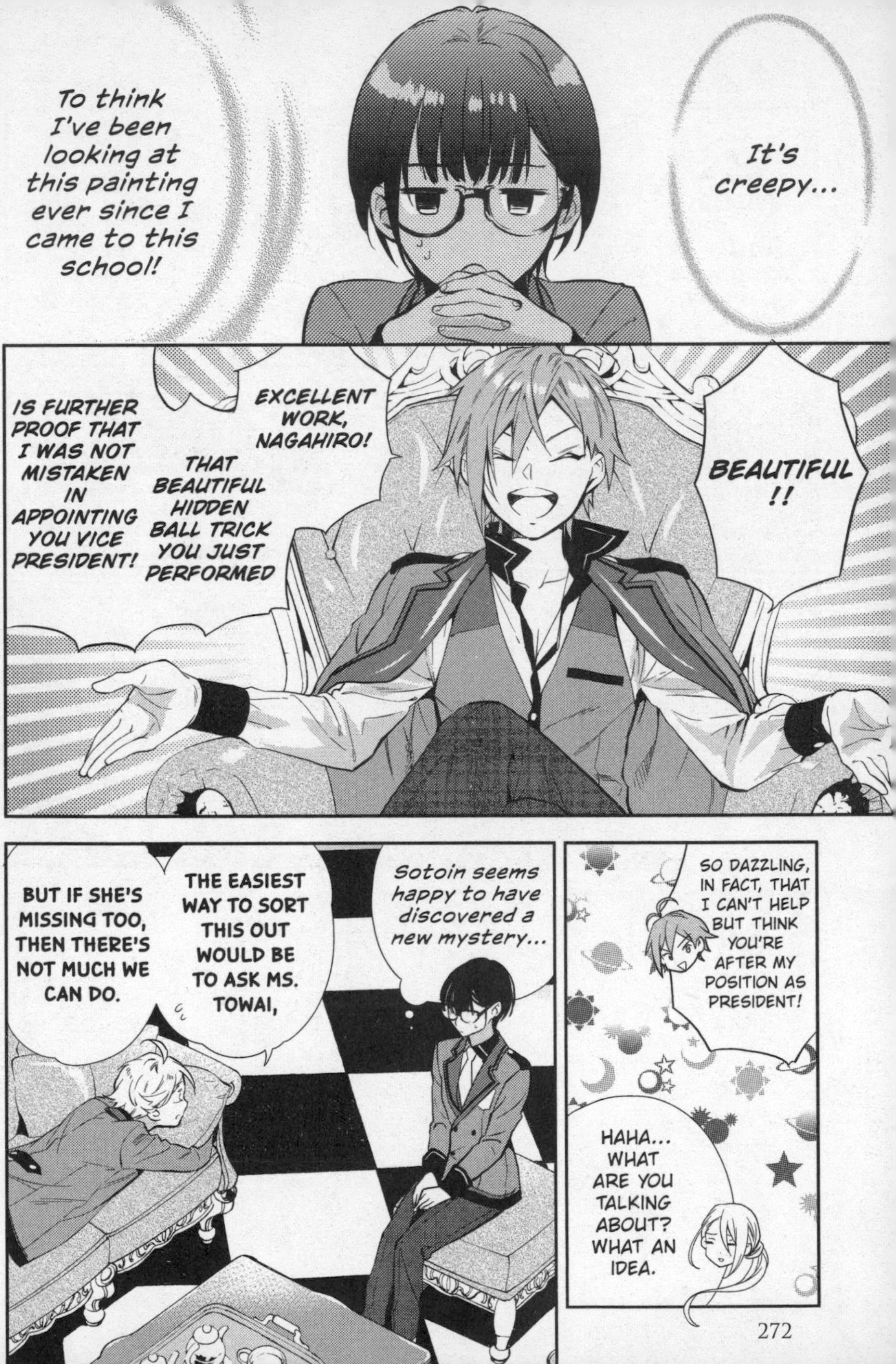
To think I've been looking at this painting ever since I came to this school!
It's creepy...
BEAUTIFUL!!
EXCELLENT WORK, NAGAHIRO!
THAT BEAUTIFUL HIDDEN BALL TRICK YOU JUST PERFORMED
IS FURTHER PROOF THAT I WAS NOT MISTAKEN IN APPOINTING YOU VICE PRESIDENT!
SO DAZZLING, IN FACT, THAT I CAN'T HELP BUT THINK YOU'RE AFTER MY POSITION AS PRESIDENT!
HAHA... WHAT ARE YOU TALKING ABOUT? WHAT AN IDEA.
Sotoin seems happy to have discovered a new mystery...
THE EASIEST WAY TO SORT THIS OUT WOULD BE TO ASK MS. TOWAI,
BUT IF SHE'S MISSING TOO, THEN THERE'S NOT MUCH WE CAN DO.

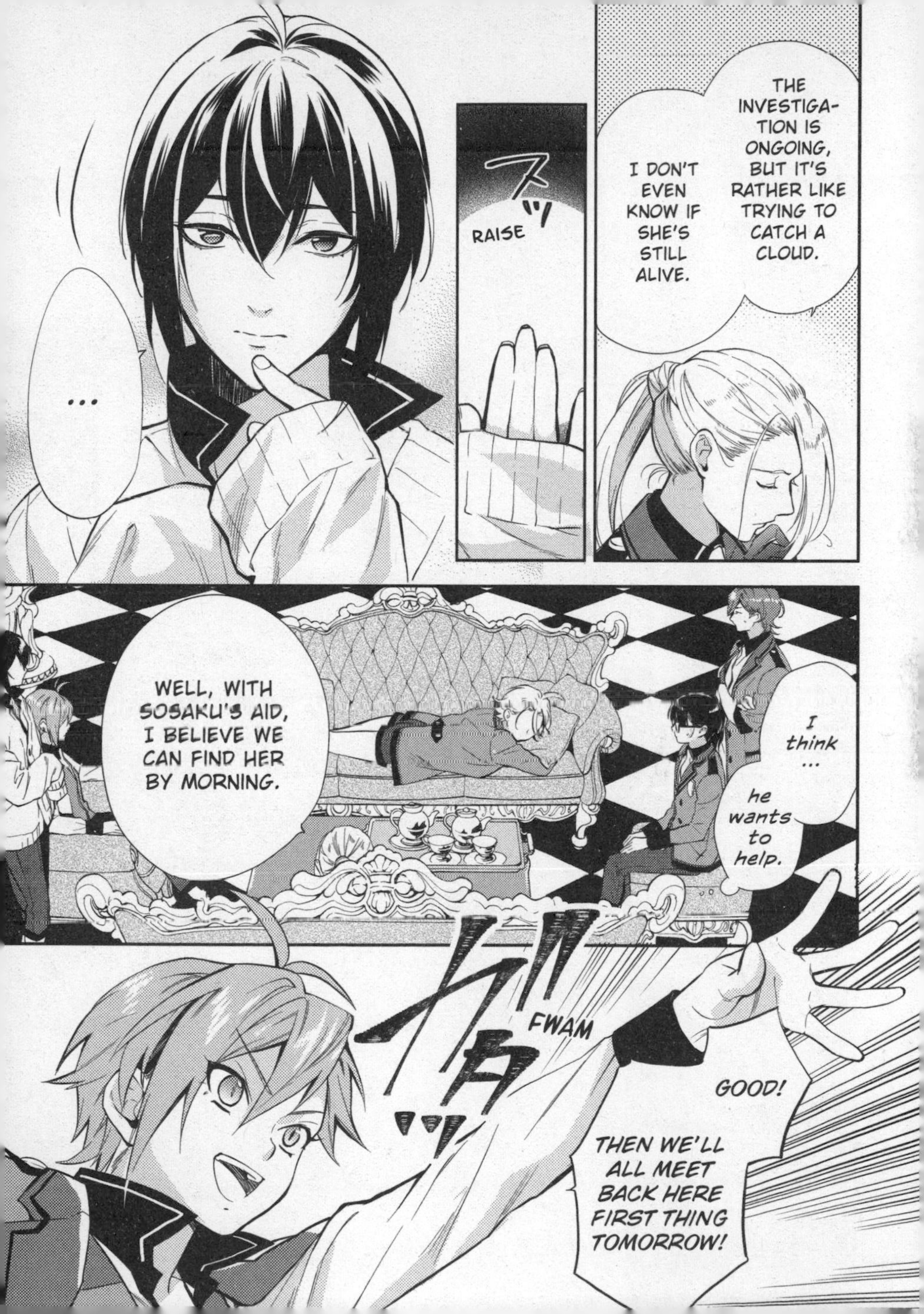
THE INVESTIGATION IS ONGOING, BUT IT'S RATHER LIKE TRYING TO CATCH A CLOUD.
I DON'T EVEN KNOW IF SHE'S STILL ALIVE.
スッ
RAISE
...
I think... he wants to help.
WELL, WITH SOSAKU'S AID, I BELIEVE WE CAN FIND HER BY MORNING.
GOOD!
THEN WE'LL ALL MEET BACK HERE FIRST THING TOMORROW!
FWAM

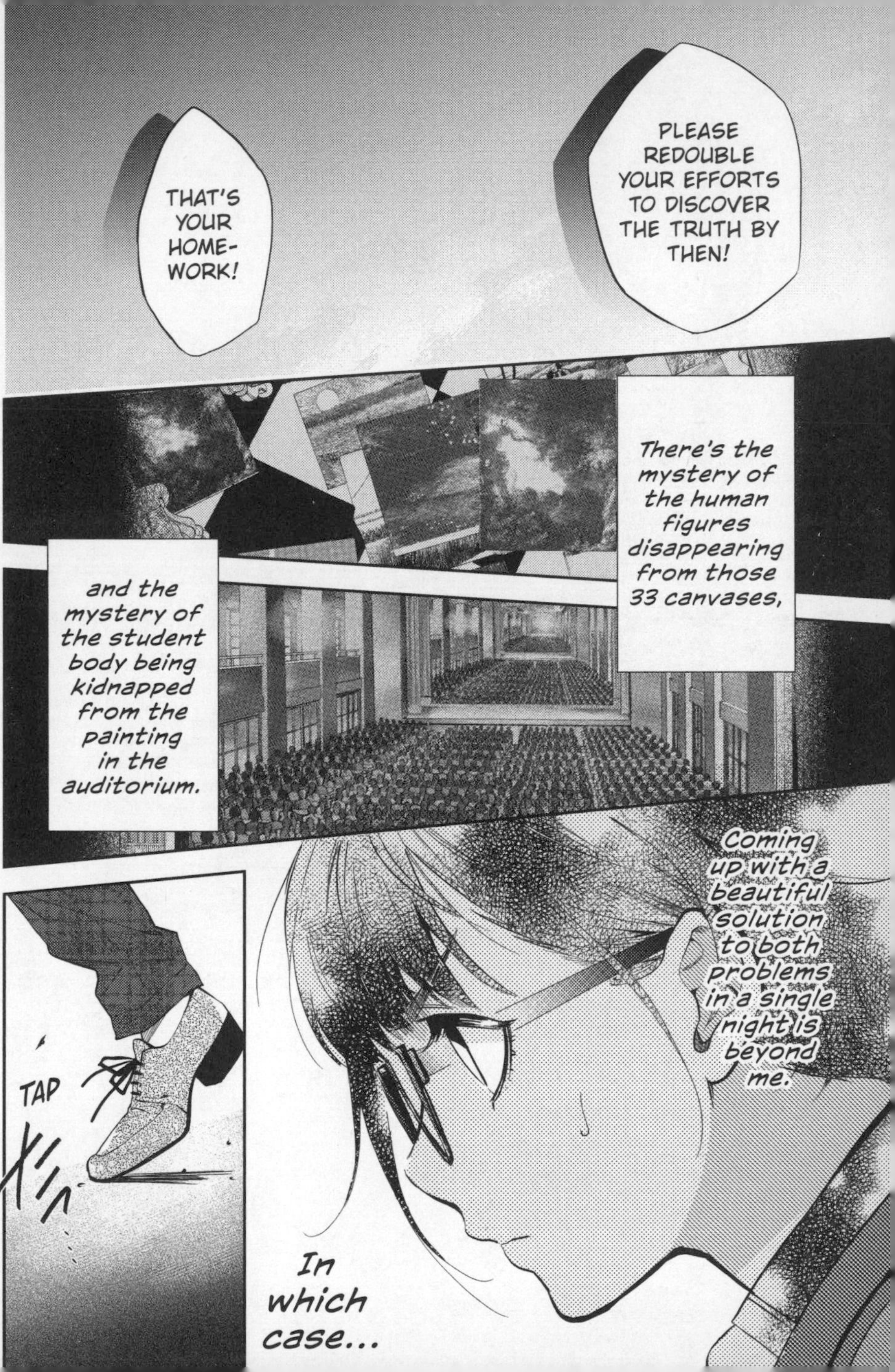
PLEASE REDOUBLE YOUR EFFORTS TO DISCOVER THE TRUTH BY THEN!
THAT'S YOUR HOME-WORK!
There's the mystery of the human figures disappearing from those 33 canvases,
and the mystery of the student body being kidnapped from the painting in the auditorium.
Coming up with a beautiful solution to both problems in a single night is beyond me.
In which case...
TAP

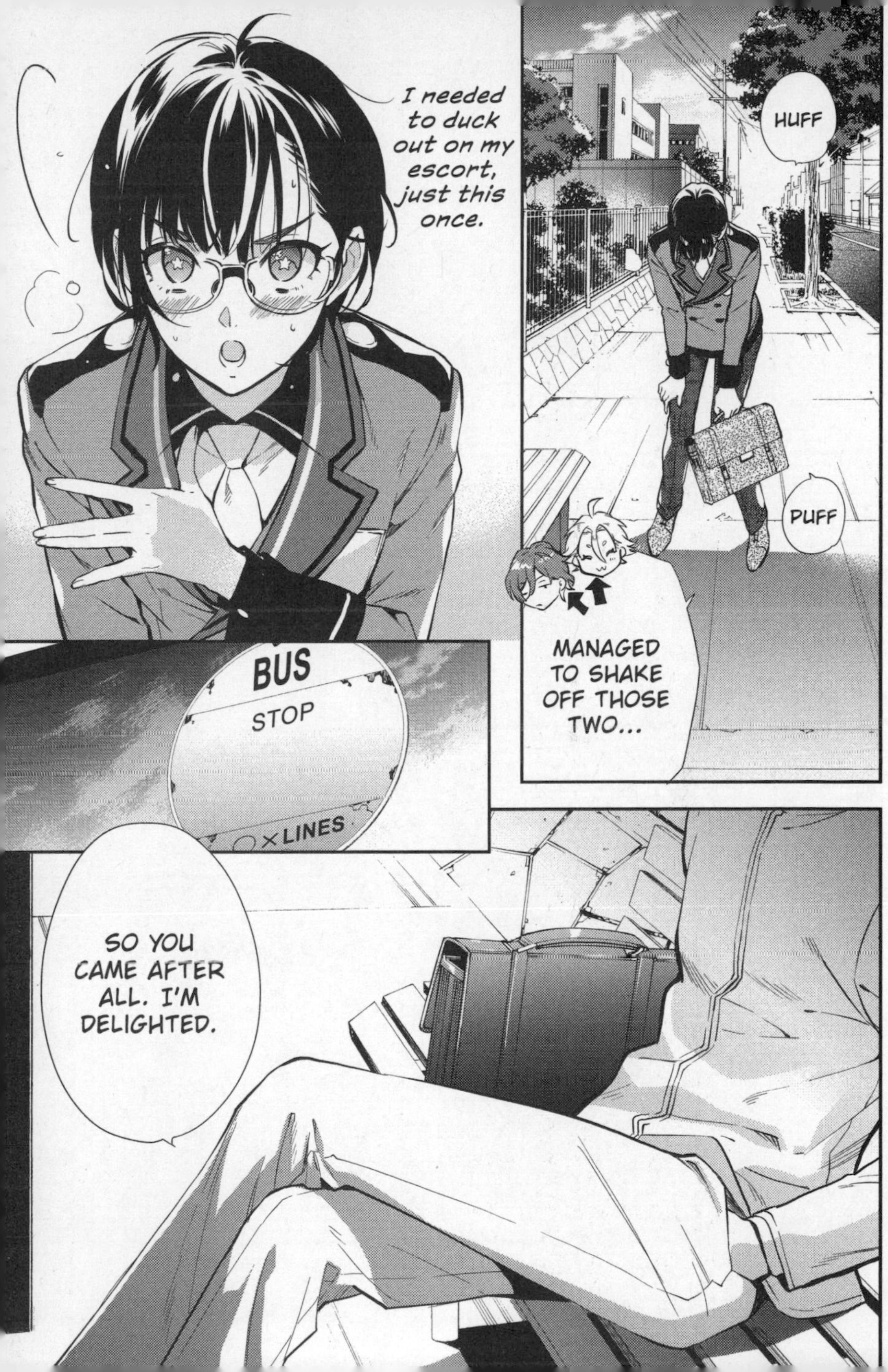
HUFF
PUFF
MANAGED TO SHAKE OFF THOSE TWO...
I needed to duck out on my escort, just this once.
BUS
STOP
○×LINES
SO YOU CAME AFTER ALL. I'M DELIGHTED.

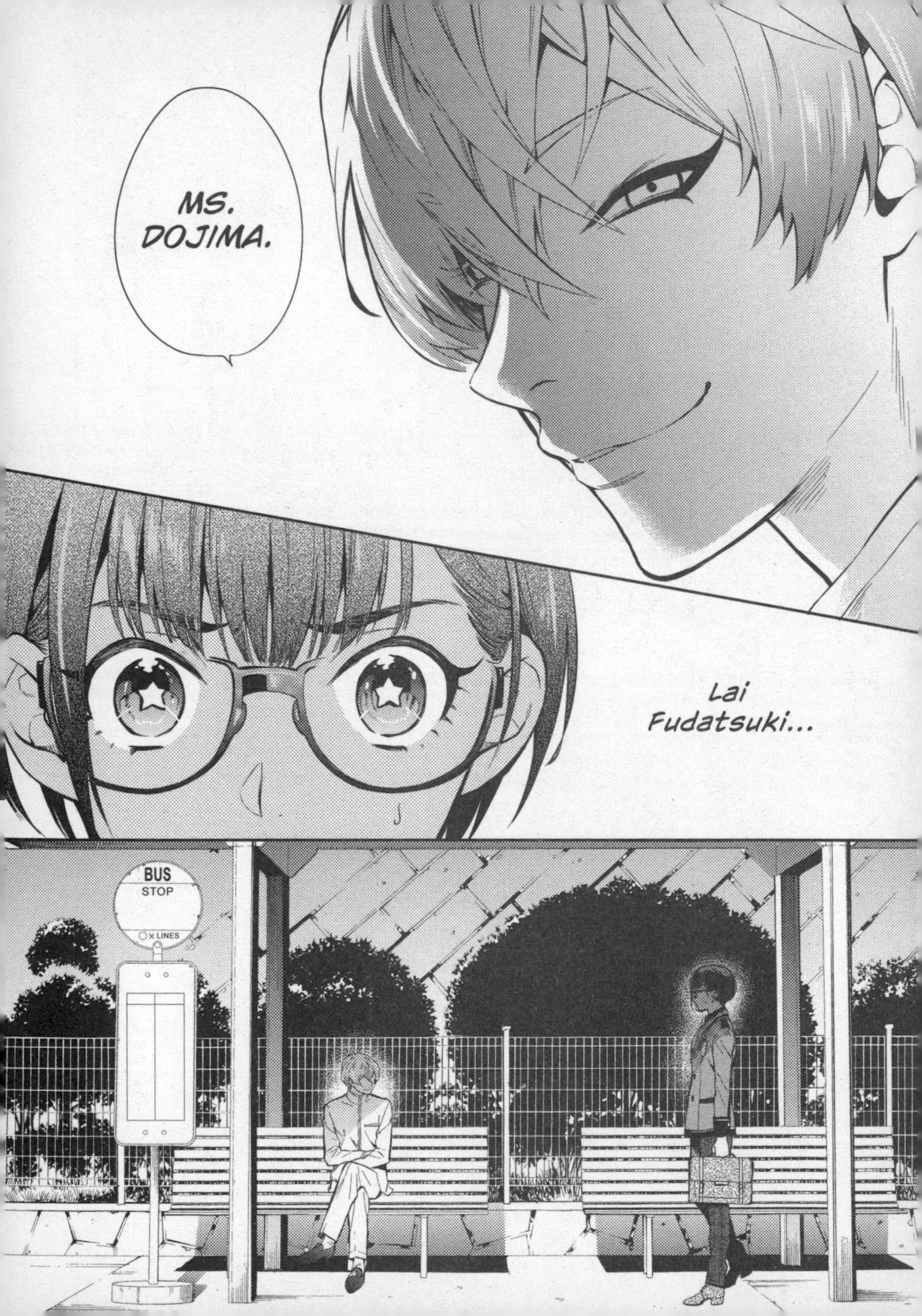
MS. DOJIMA.
Lai Fudatsuki...
BUS STOP
○×LINES

PRETTY BOY

DETECTIVE CLUB!!

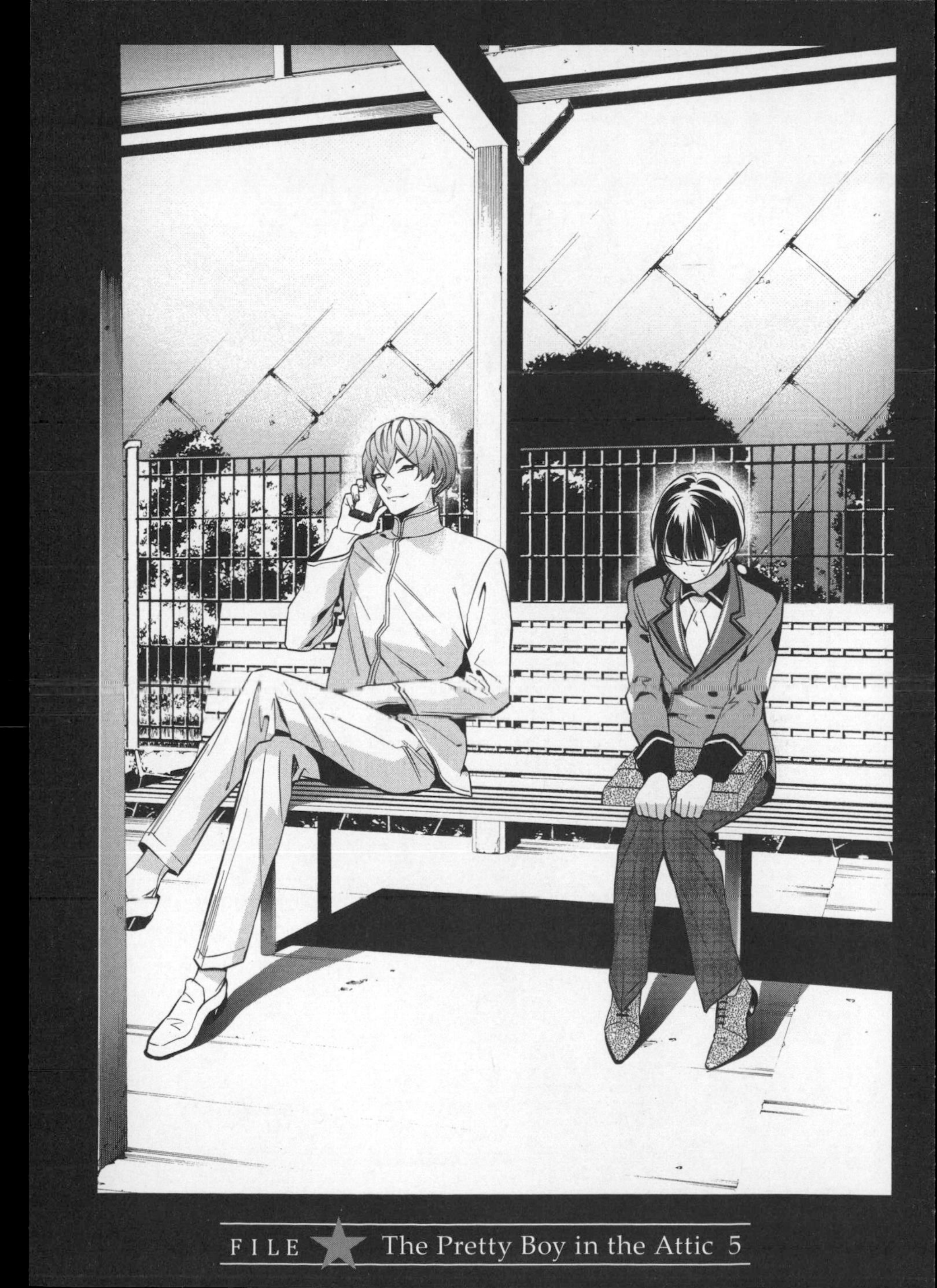

FILE ★ The Pretty Boy in the Attic 5

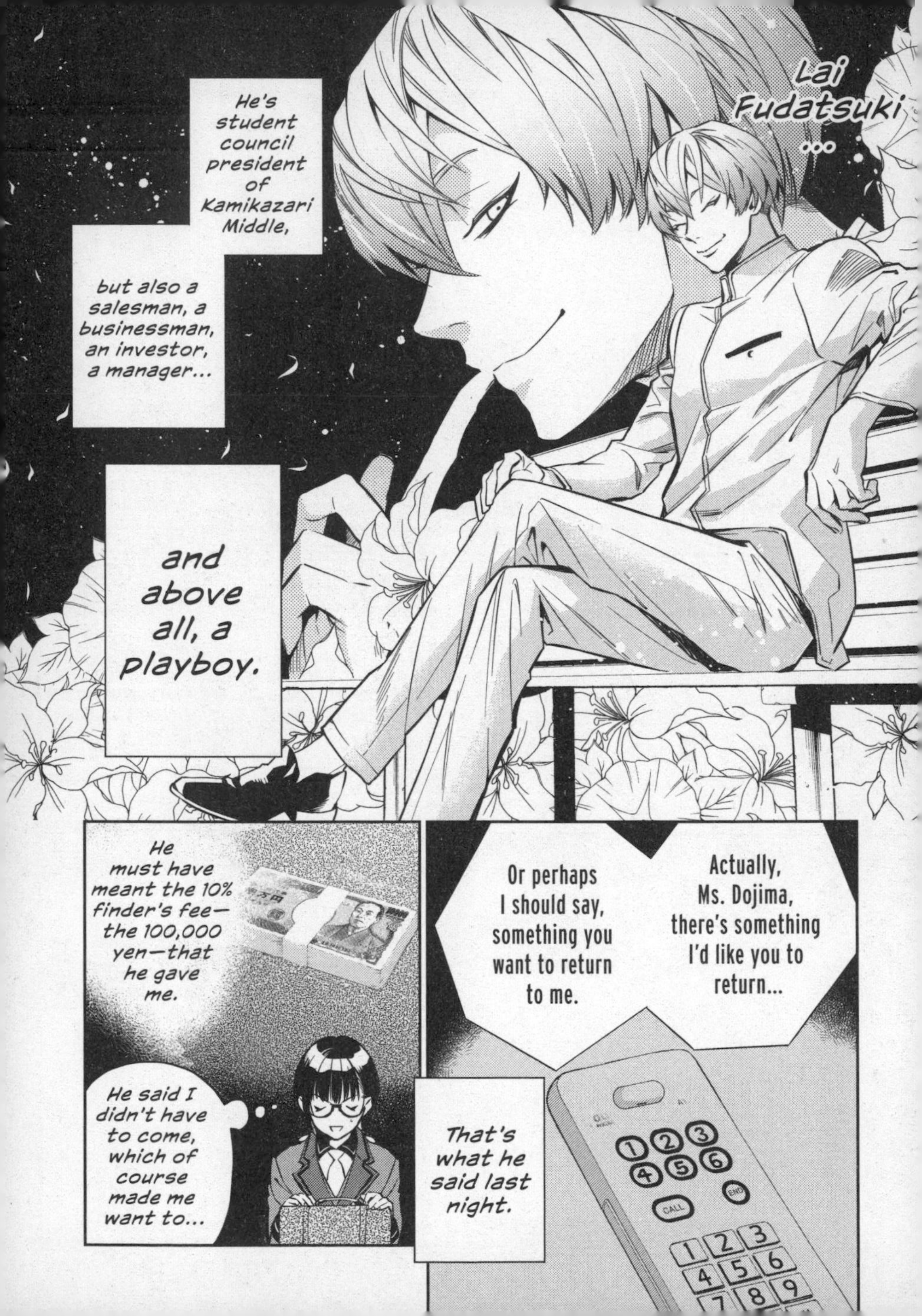
Lai Fudatsuki...
He's student council president of Kamikazari Middle,
but also a salesman, a businessman, an investor, a manager...
and above all, a playboy.
Actually, Ms. Dojima, there's something I'd like you to return...
Or perhaps I should say, something you want to return to me.
That's what he said last night.
He must have meant the 10% finder's fee—the 100,000 yen—that he gave me.
He said I didn't have to come, which of course made me want to...

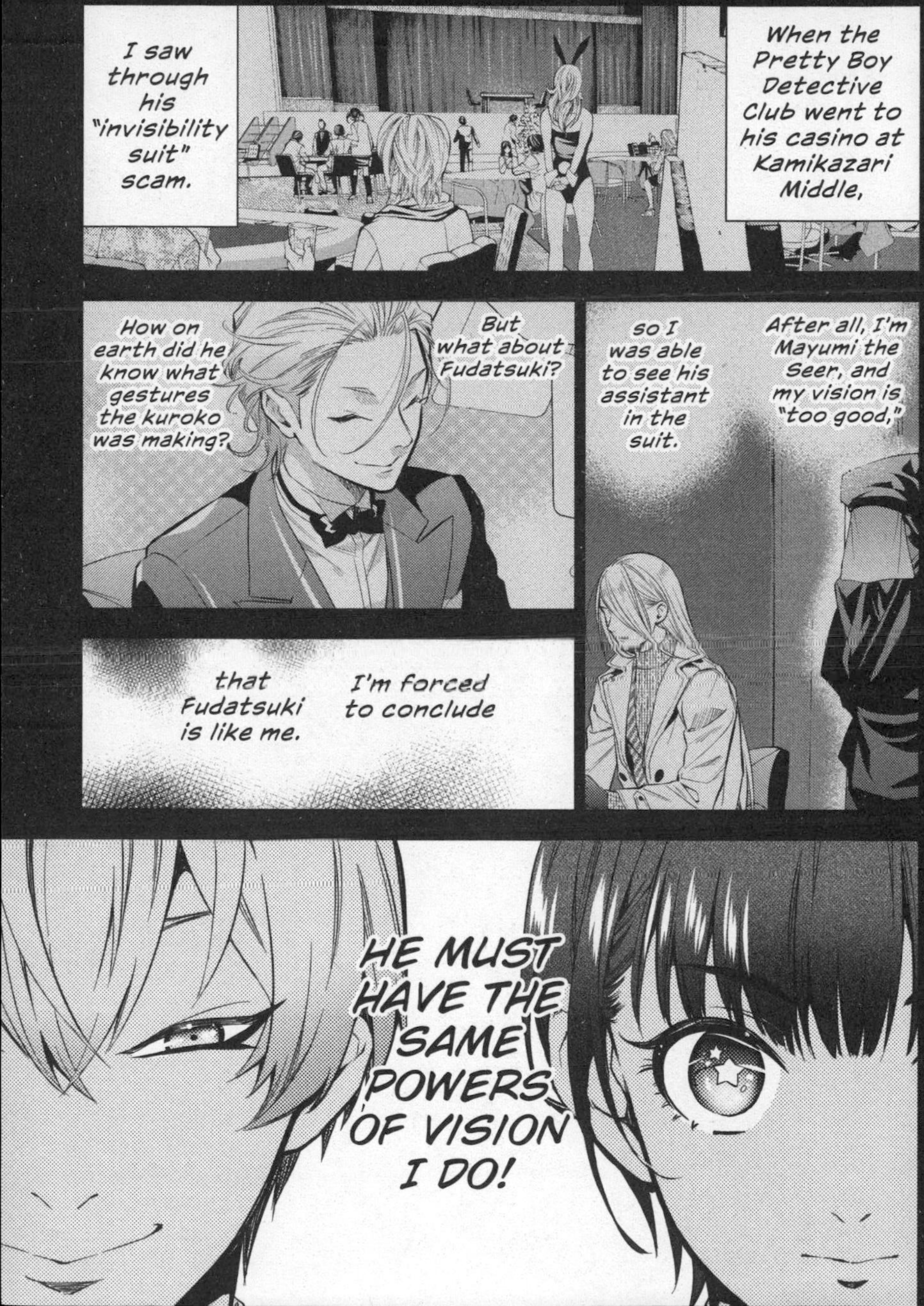
When the Pretty Boy Detective Club went to his casino at Kamikazari Middle,
I saw through his "invisibility suit" scam.
After all, I'm Mayumi the Seer, and my vision is "too good,"
so I was able to see his assistant in the suit.
But what about Fudatsuki?
How on earth did he know what gestures the kuroko was making?
I'm forced to conclude
that Fudatsuki is like me.
HE MUST HAVE THE SAME POWERS OF VISION I DO!

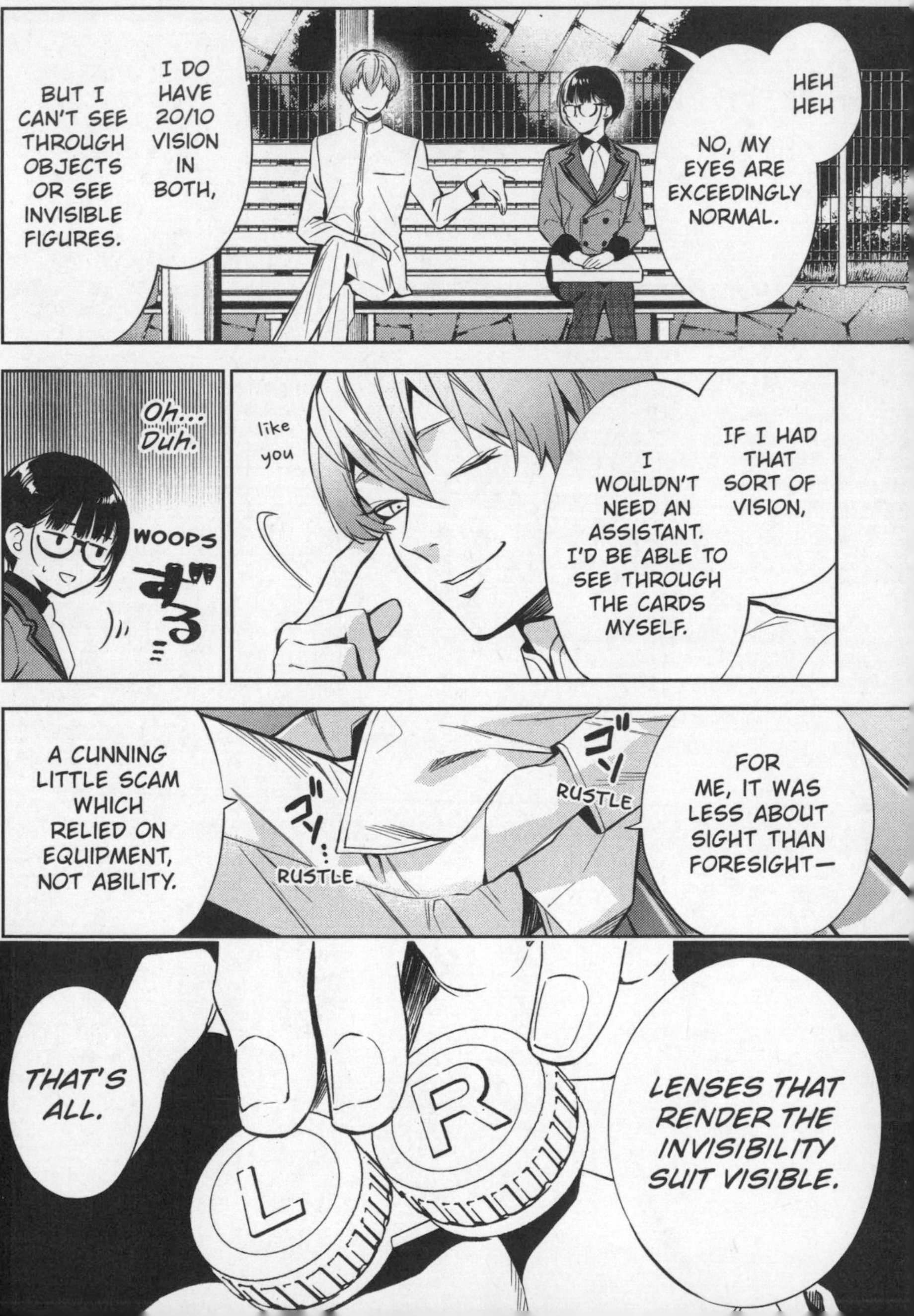
HEH HEH
NO, MY EYES ARE EXCEEDINGLY NORMAL.
I DO HAVE 20/10 VISION IN BOTH,
BUT I CAN'T SEE THROUGH OBJECTS OR SEE INVISIBLE FIGURES.
IF I HAD THAT SORT OF VISION,
I WOULDN'T NEED AN ASSISTANT. I'D BE ABLE TO SEE THROUGH THE CARDS MYSELF.
like you
Oh... Duh.
WOOPS
ずる
FOR ME, IT WAS LESS ABOUT SIGHT THAN FORESIGHT—
RUSTLE
RUSTLE
A CUNNING LITTLE SCAM WHICH RELIED ON EQUIPMENT, NOT ABILITY.
LENSES THAT RENDER THE INVISIBILITY SUIT VISIBLE.
R
L
THAT'S ALL.

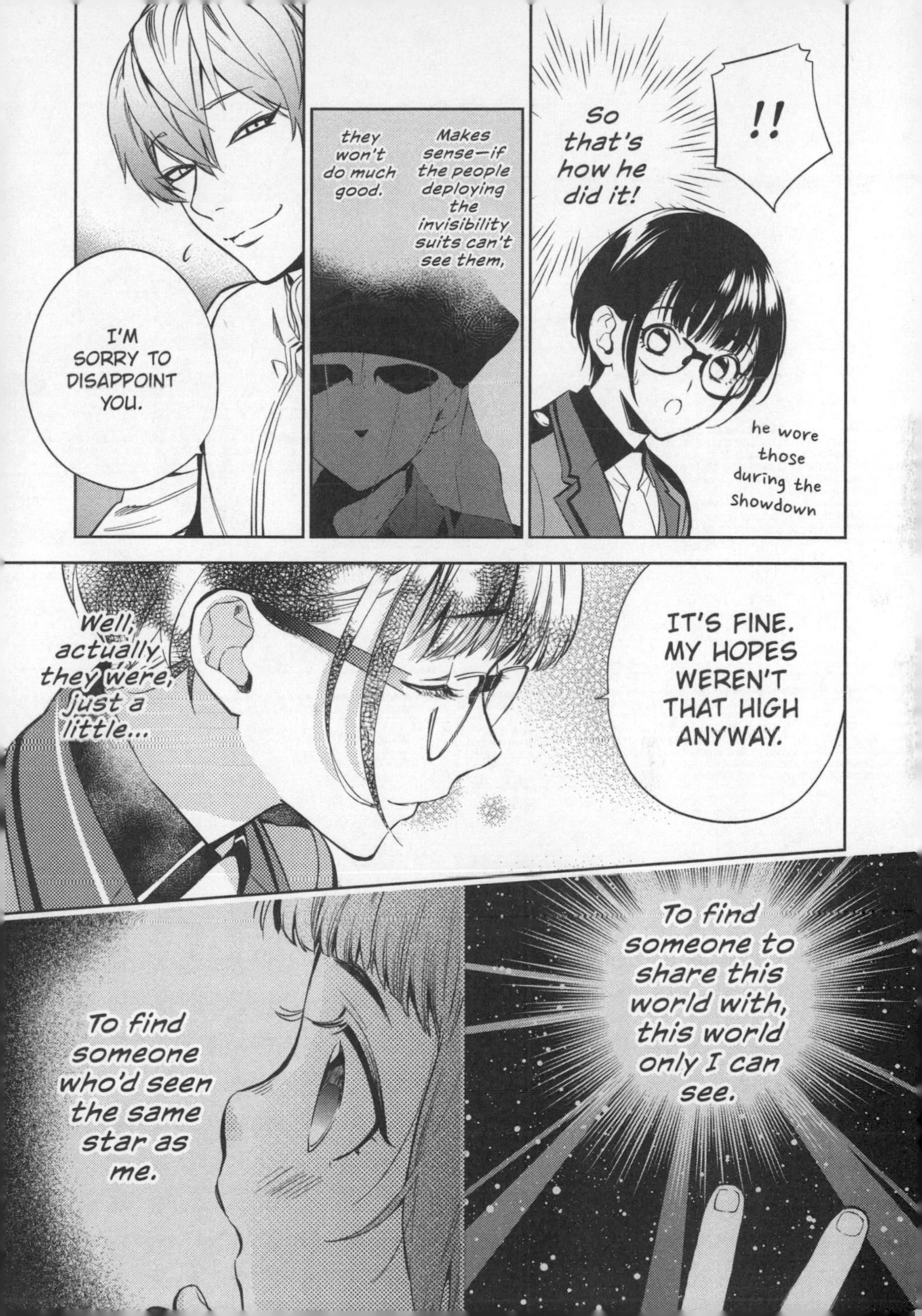
!!
So that's how he did it!
he wore those during the Showdown
Makes sense—if the people deploying the invisibility suits can't see them,
they won't do much good.
I'M SORRY TO DISAPPOINT YOU.
IT'S FINE. MY HOPES WEREN'T THAT HIGH ANYWAY.
Well, actually they were, just a little...
To find someone to share this world with, this world only I can see.
To find someone who'd seen the same star as me.

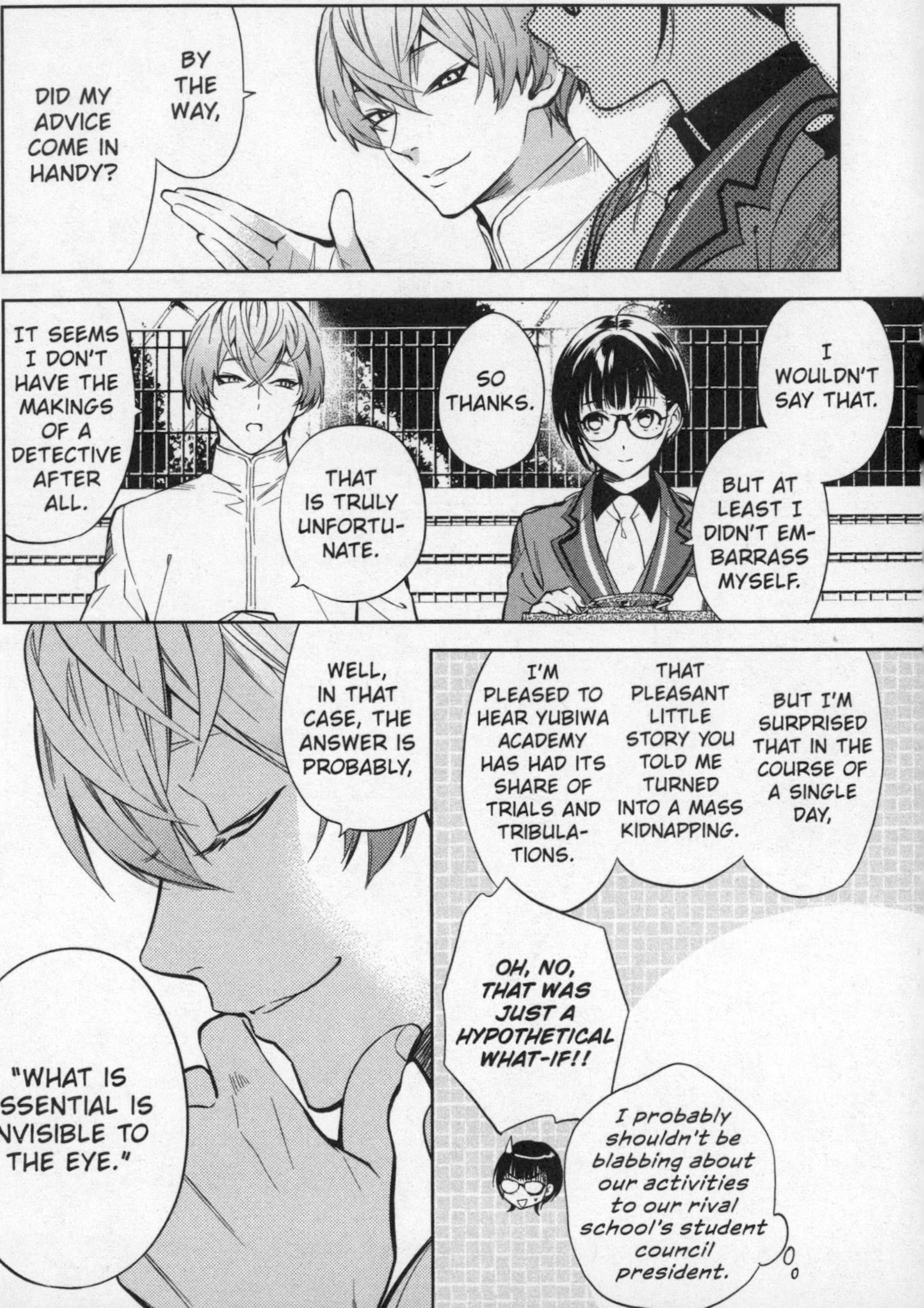
BY THE WAY,
DID MY ADVICE COME IN HANDY?
I WOULDN'T SAY THAT.
BUT AT LEAST I DIDN'T EMBARRASS MYSELF.
SO THANKS.
IT SEEMS I DON'T HAVE THE MAKINGS OF A DETECTIVE AFTER ALL.
THAT IS TRULY UNFORTUNATE.
BUT I'M SURPRISED THAT IN THE COURSE OF A SINGLE DAY,
THAT PLEASANT LITTLE STORY YOU TOLD ME TURNED INTO A MASS KIDNAPPING.
I'M PLEASED TO HEAR YUBIWA ACADEMY HAS HAD ITS SHARE OF TRIALS AND TRIBULATIONS.
OH, NO, THAT WAS JUST A HYPOTHETICAL WHAT-IF!!
I probably shouldn't be blabbing about our activities to our rival school's student council president.
WELL, IN THAT CASE, THE ANSWER IS PROBABLY,
"WHAT IS ESSENTIAL IS INVISIBLE TO THE EYE."

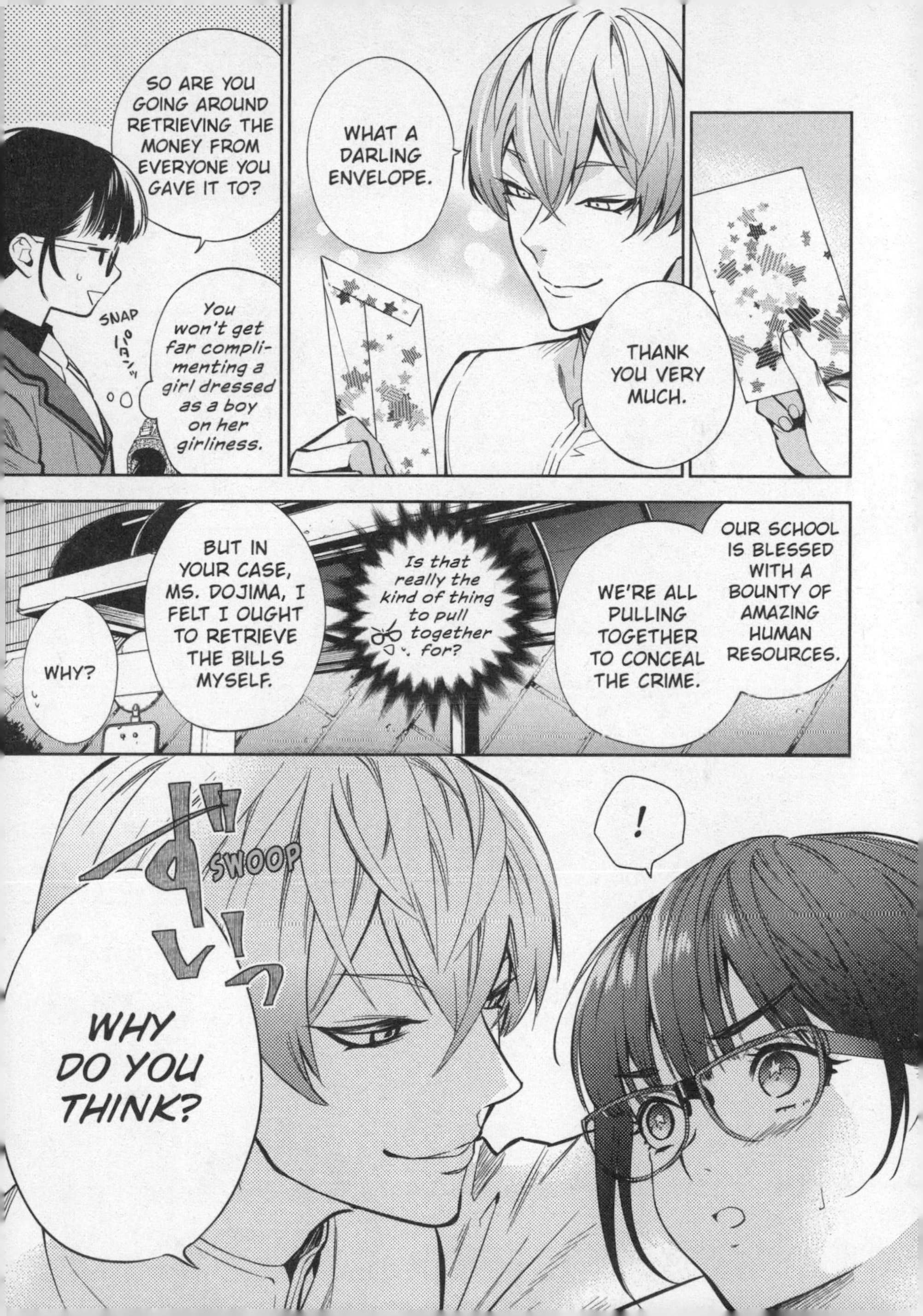
THANK YOU VERY MUCH.
WHAT A DARLING ENVELOPE.
SO ARE YOU GOING AROUND RETRIEVING THE MONEY FROM EVERYONE YOU GAVE IT TO?
SNAP
You won't get far compli-menting a girl dressed as a boy on her girliness.
OUR SCHOOL IS BLESSED WITH A BOUNTY OF AMAZING HUMAN RESOURCES.
WE'RE ALL PULLING TOGETHER TO CONCEAL THE CRIME.
Is that really the kind of thing to pull together for?
BUT IN YOUR CASE, MS. DOJIMA, I FELT I OUGHT TO RETRIEVE THE BILLS MYSELF.
WHY?
!
SWOOP
WHY DO YOU THINK?

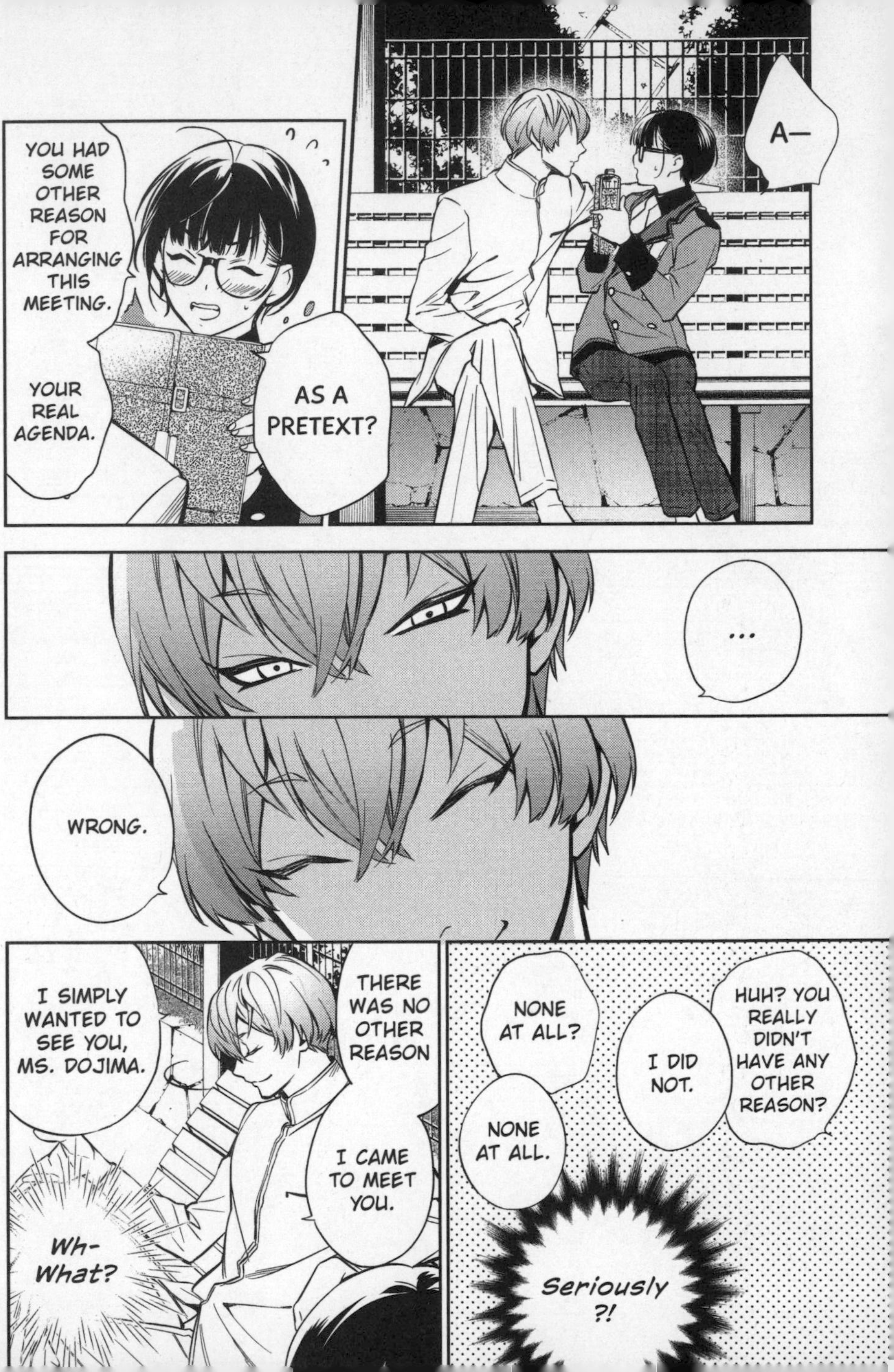
A—
YOU HAD SOME OTHER REASON FOR ARRANGING THIS MEETING.
AS A PRETEXT?
YOUR REAL AGENDA.
...
WRONG.
HUH? YOU REALLY DIDN'T HAVE ANY OTHER REASON?
I DID NOT.
NONE AT ALL?
NONE AT ALL.
Seriously ?!
THERE WAS NO OTHER REASON
I SIMPLY WANTED TO SEE YOU, MS. DOJIMA.
I CAME TO MEET YOU.
Wh- What?

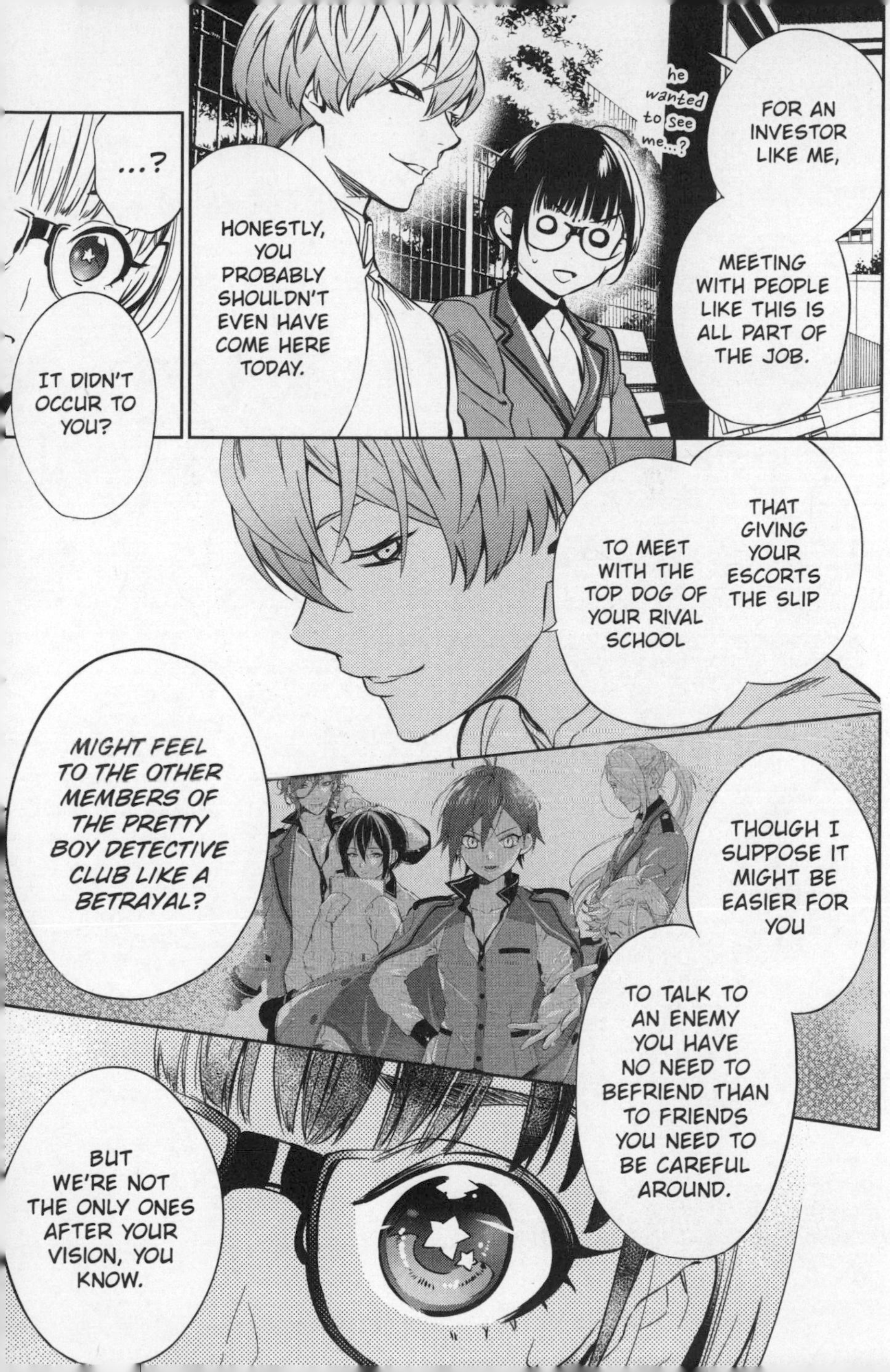
FOR AN INVESTOR LIKE ME,
he wanted to see me...?
MEETING WITH PEOPLE LIKE THIS IS ALL PART OF THE JOB.
HONESTLY, YOU PROBABLY SHOULDN'T EVEN HAVE COME HERE TODAY.
...?
IT DIDN'T OCCUR TO YOU?
THAT GIVING YOUR ESCORTS THE SLIP
TO MEET WITH THE TOP DOG OF YOUR RIVAL SCHOOL
MIGHT FEEL TO THE OTHER MEMBERS OF THE PRETTY BOY DETECTIVE CLUB LIKE A BETRAYAL?
THOUGH I SUPPOSE IT MIGHT BE EASIER FOR YOU
TO TALK TO AN ENEMY YOU HAVE NO NEED TO BEFRIEND THAN TO FRIENDS YOU NEED TO BE CAREFUL AROUND.
BUT WE'RE NOT THE ONLY ONES AFTER YOUR VISION, YOU KNOW.

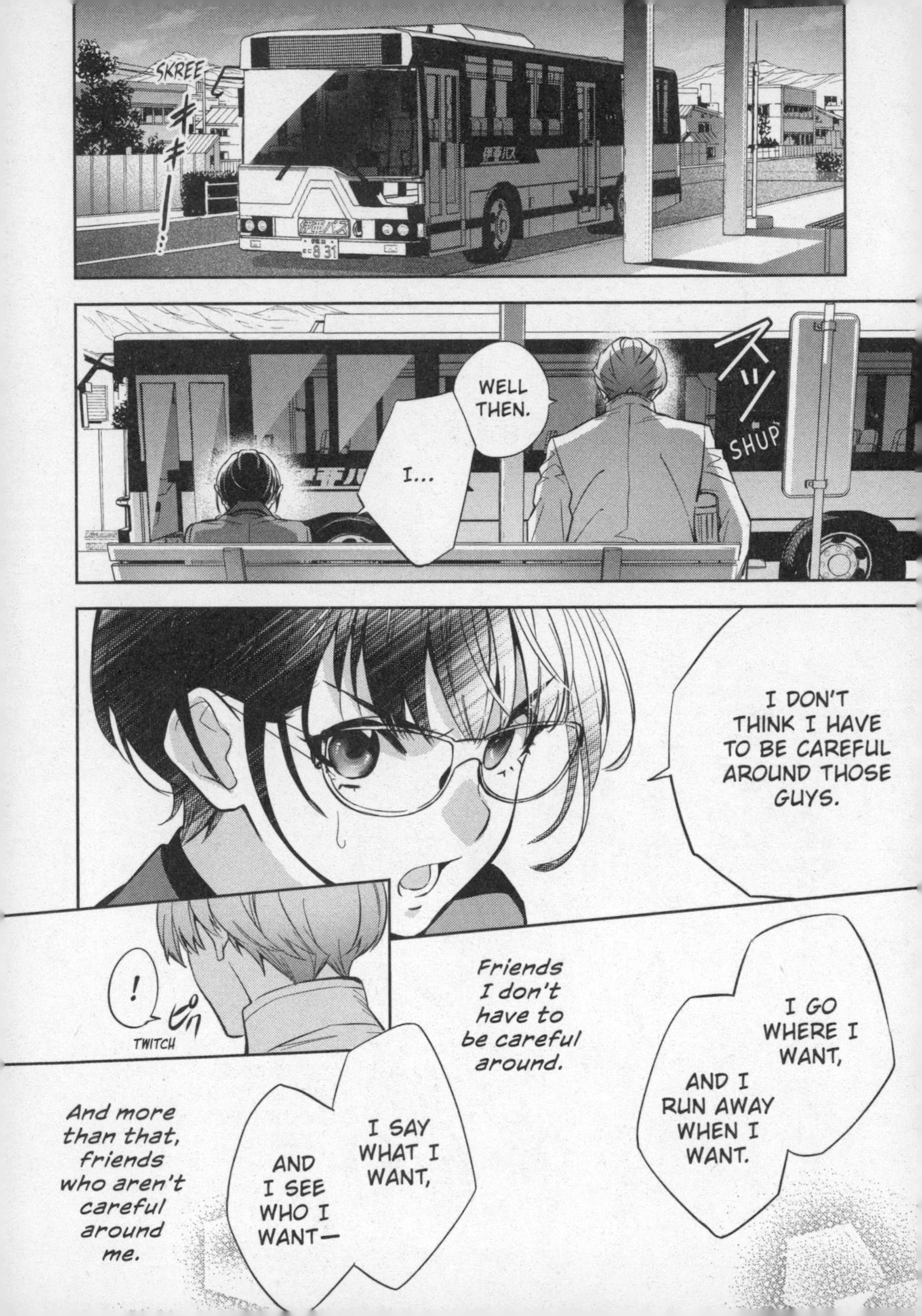
SKREE
キキー!!
スッ
SHUP
WELL THEN.
I...
I DON'T THINK I HAVE TO BE CAREFUL AROUND THOSE GUYS.
!
ピク
TWITCH
I GO WHERE I WANT,
AND I RUN AWAY WHEN I WANT.
Friends I don't have to be careful around.
I SAY WHAT I WANT,
AND I SEE WHO I WANT—
And more than that, friends who aren't careful around me.

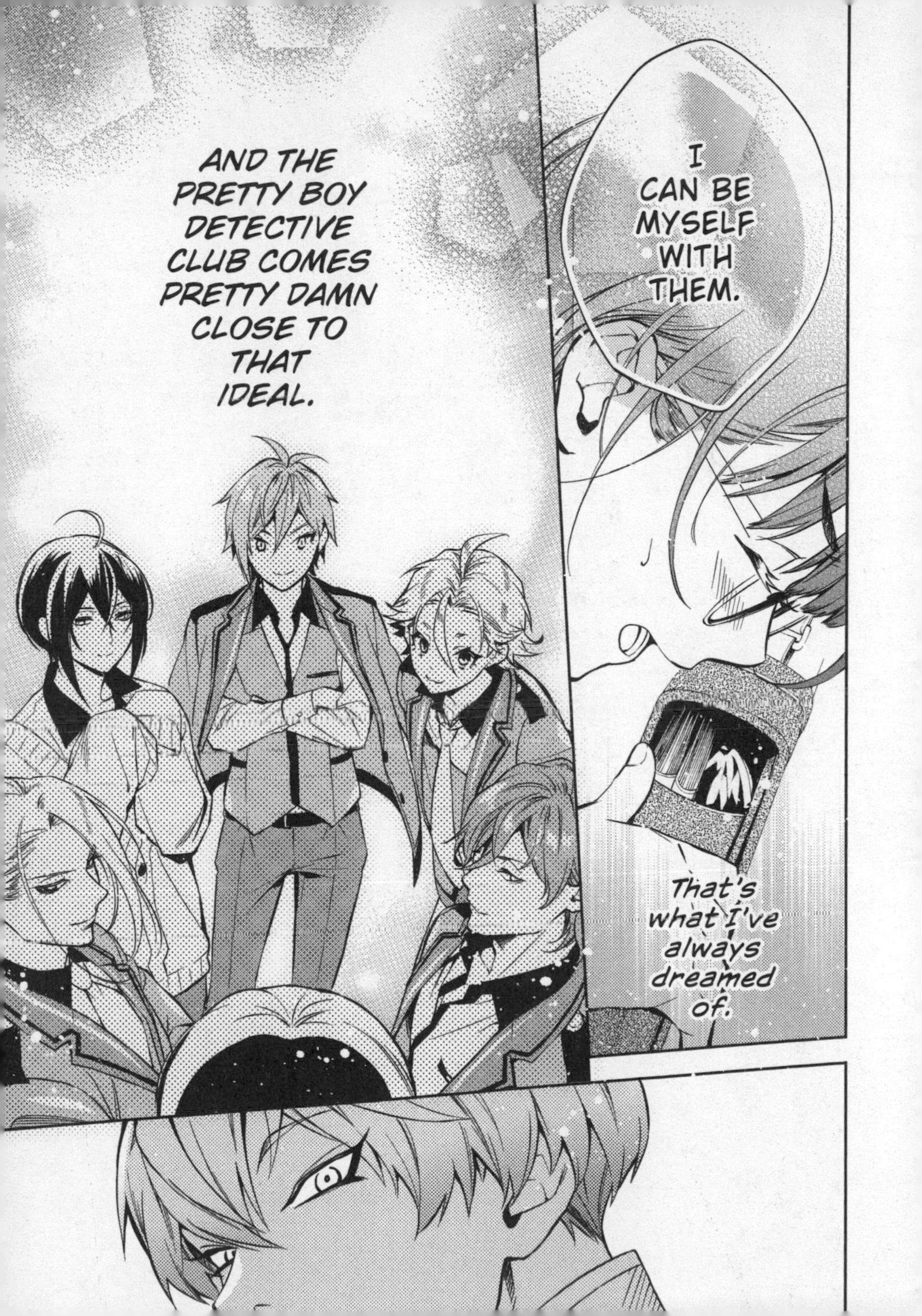
I CAN BE MYSELF WITH THEM.
That's what I've always dreamed of.
AND THE PRETTY BOY DETECTIVE CLUB COMES PRETTY DAMN CLOSE TO THAT IDEAL.

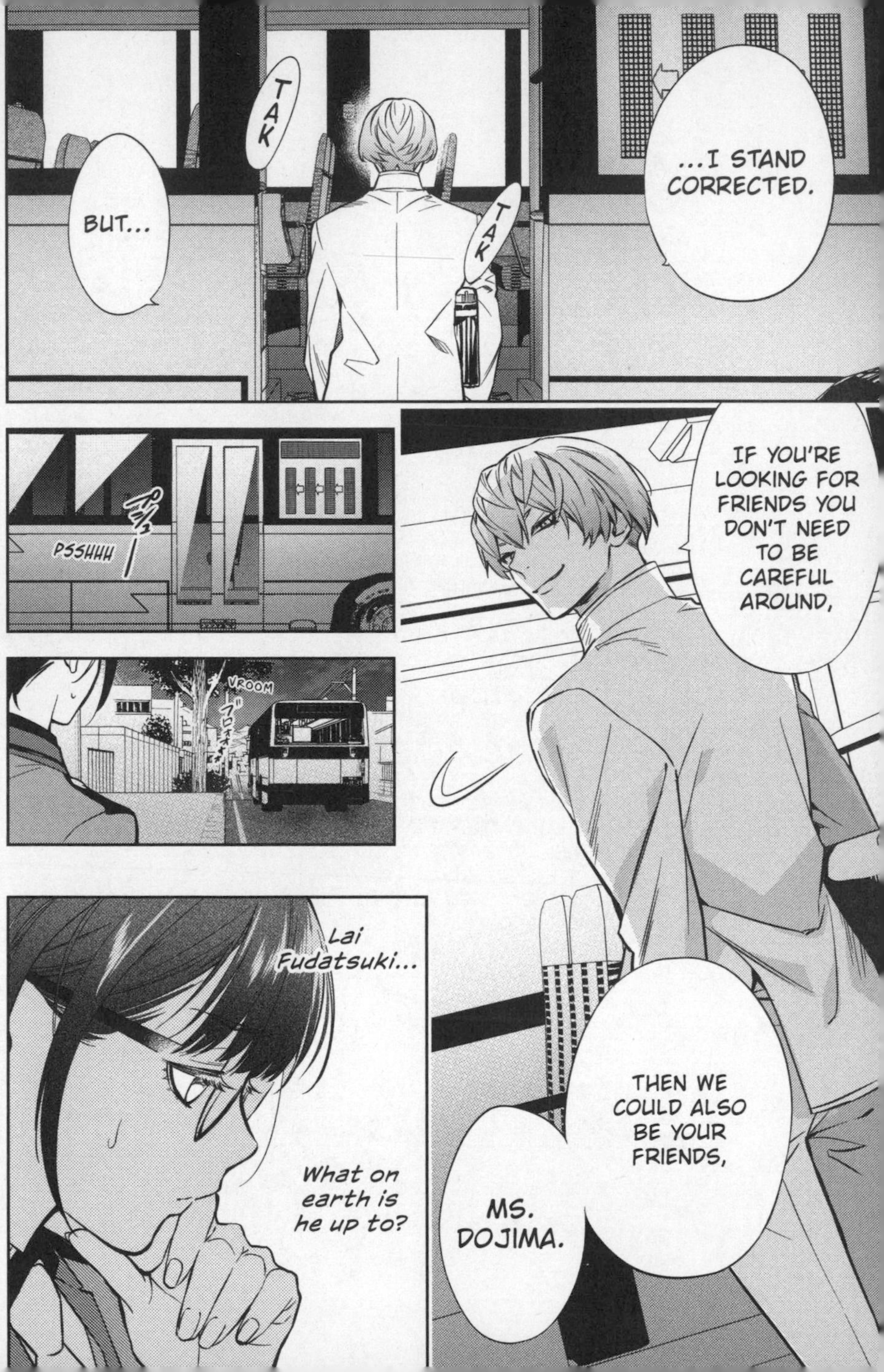
...I STAND CORRECTED.
TAK
TAK
BUT...
IF YOU'RE LOOKING FOR FRIENDS YOU DON'T NEED TO BE CAREFUL AROUND,
THEN WE COULD ALSO BE YOUR FRIENDS,
MS. DOJIMA.
PSSHHH
VROOM
Lai Fudatsuki...
What on earth is he up to?

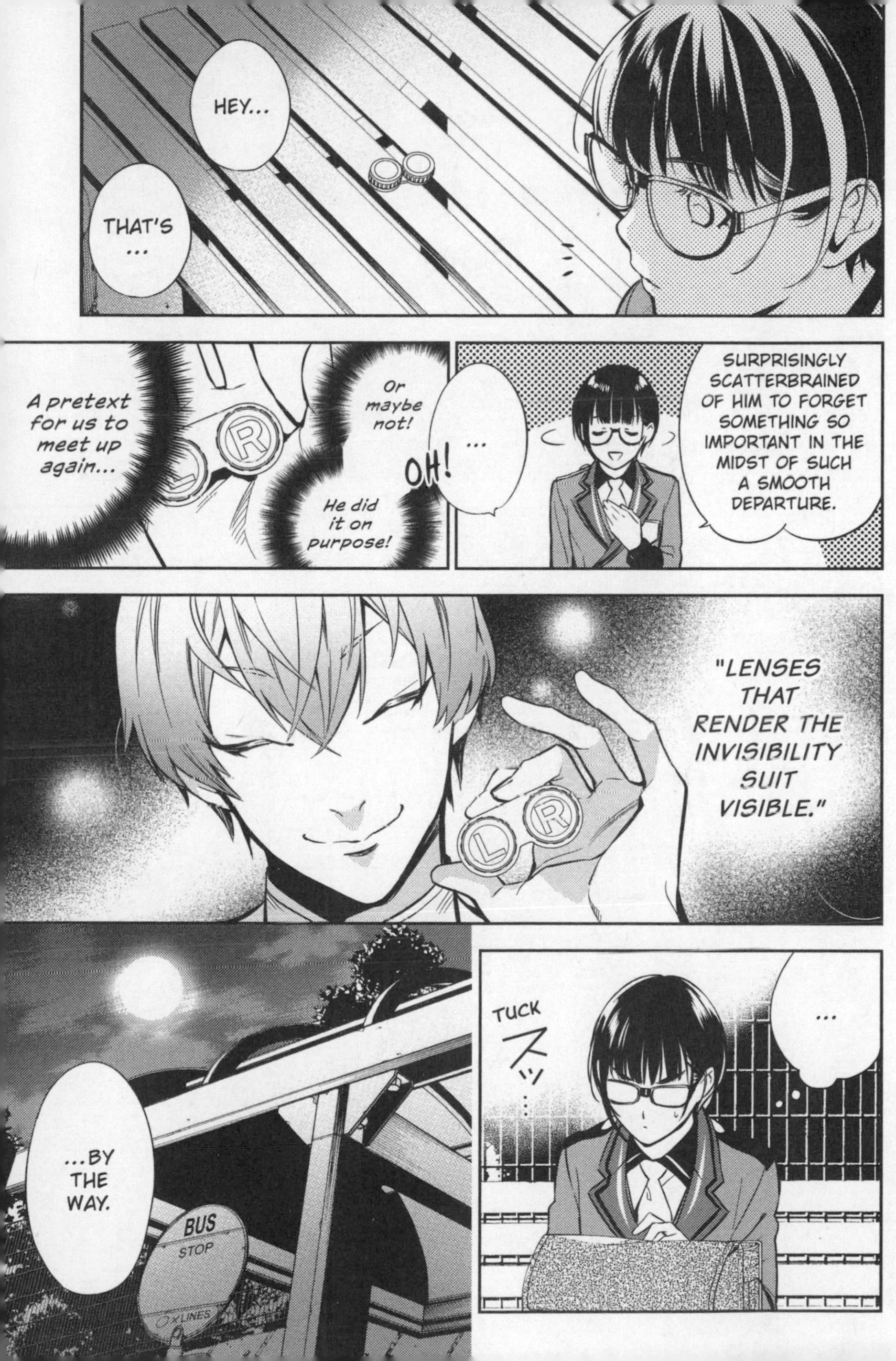
HEY...
THAT'S...
SURPRISINGLY SCATTERBRAINED OF HIM TO FORGET SOMETHING SO IMPORTANT IN THE MIDST OF SUCH A SMOOTH DEPARTURE.
...
OH!
Or maybe not!
He did it on purpose!
A pretext for us to meet up again...
"LENSES THAT RENDER THE INVISIBILITY SUIT VISIBLE."
...
TUCK
スッ...
...BY THE WAY.
BUS STOP

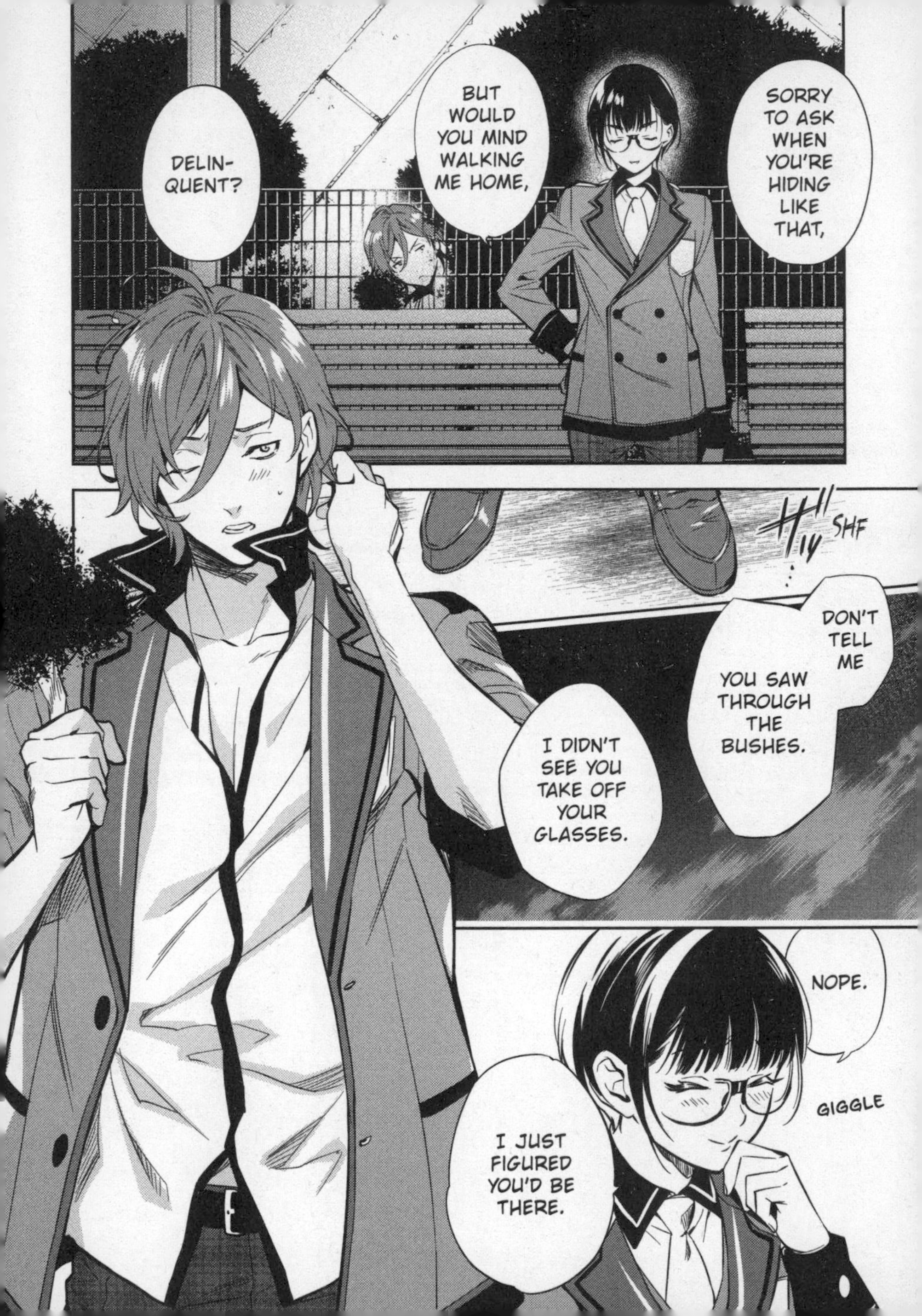

SORRY TO ASK WHEN YOU'RE HIDING LIKE THAT,
BUT WOULD YOU MIND WALKING ME HOME,
DELIN-QUENT?
SHF
DON'T TELL ME
YOU SAW THROUGH THE BUSHES.
I DIDN'T SEE YOU TAKE OFF YOUR GLASSES.
NOPE.
GIGGLE
I JUST FIGURED YOU'D BE THERE.

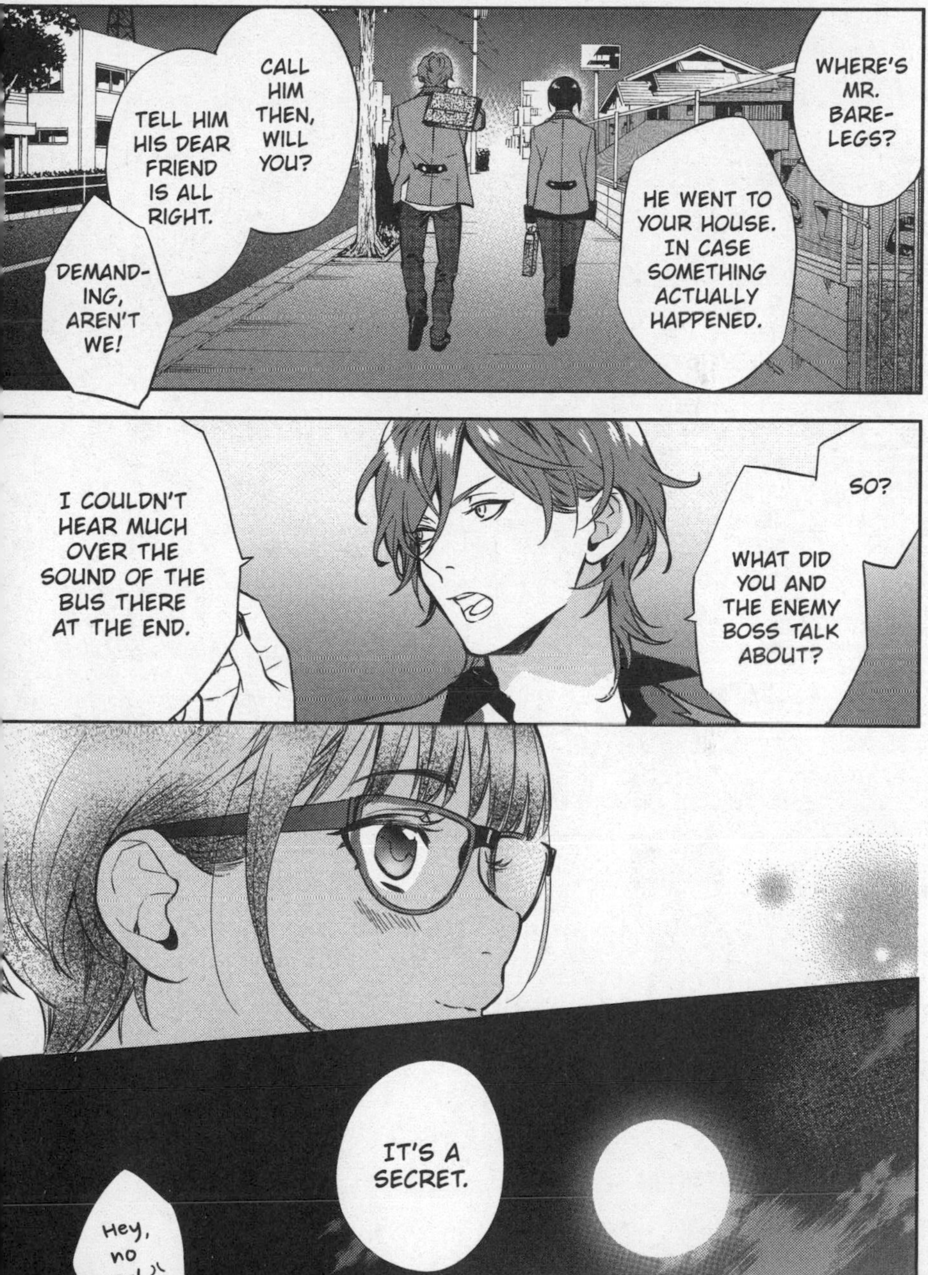
WHERE'S MR. BARE-LEGS?
HE WENT TO YOUR HOUSE. IN CASE SOMETHING ACTUALLY HAPPENED.
CALL HIM THEN, WILL YOU?
TELL HIM HIS DEAR FRIEND IS ALL RIGHT.
DEMAND-ING, AREN'T WE!
SO?
WHAT DID YOU AND THE ENEMY BOSS TALK ABOUT?
I COULDN'T HEAR MUCH OVER THE SOUND OF THE BUS THERE AT THE END.
IT'S A SECRET.
Hey, no fair!

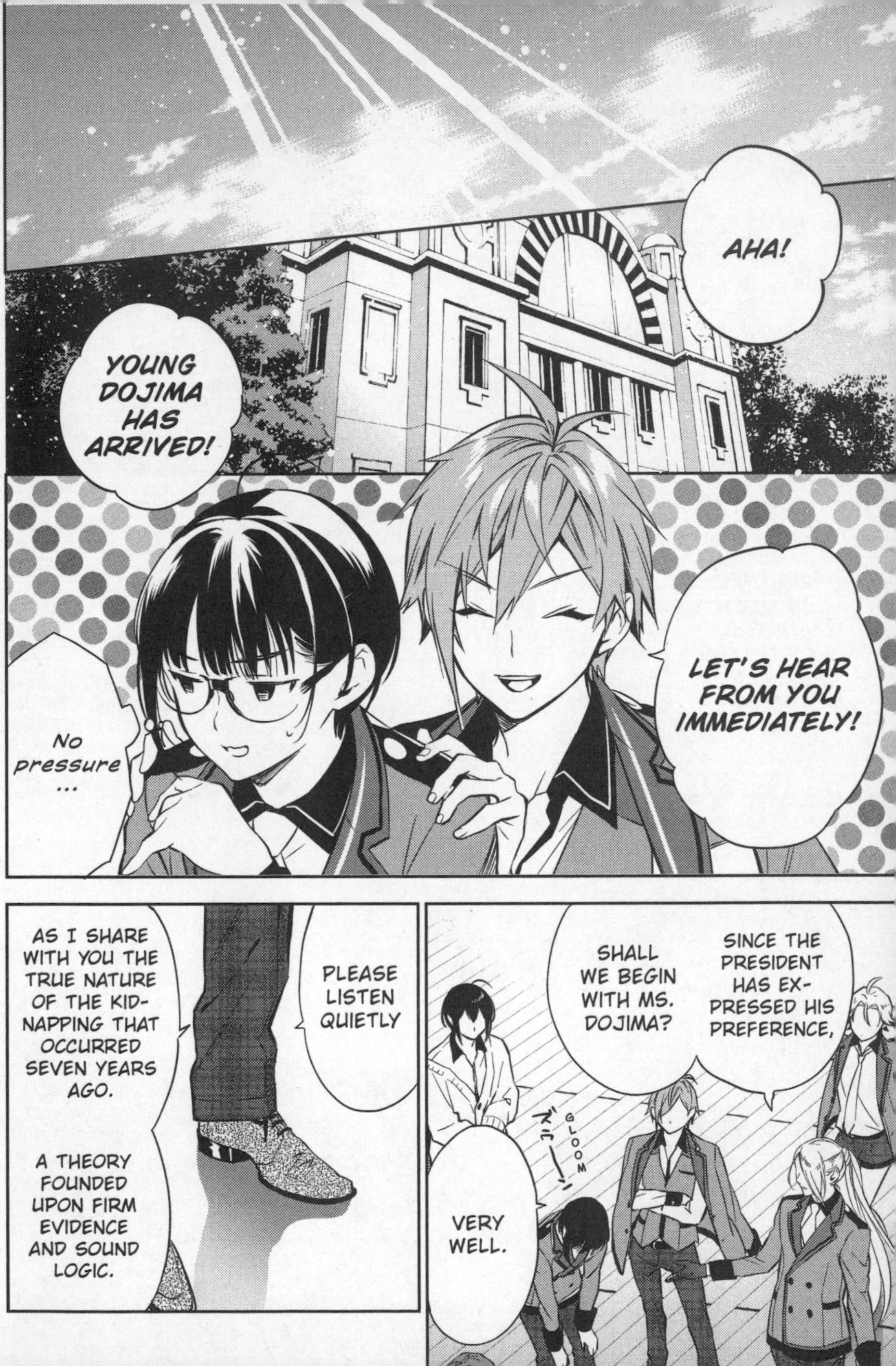
AHA!
YOUNG DOJIMA HAS ARRIVED!
LET'S HEAR FROM YOU IMMEDIATELY!
No pressure ...
SINCE THE PRESIDENT HAS EX- PRESSED HIS PREFERENCE,
SHALL WE BEGIN WITH MS. DOJIMA?
GLOOM
VERY WELL.
PLEASE LISTEN QUIETLY
AS I SHARE WITH YOU THE TRUE NATURE OF THE KID- NAPPING THAT OCCURRED SEVEN YEARS AGO.
A THEORY FOUNDED UPON FIRM EVIDENCE AND SOUND LOGIC.

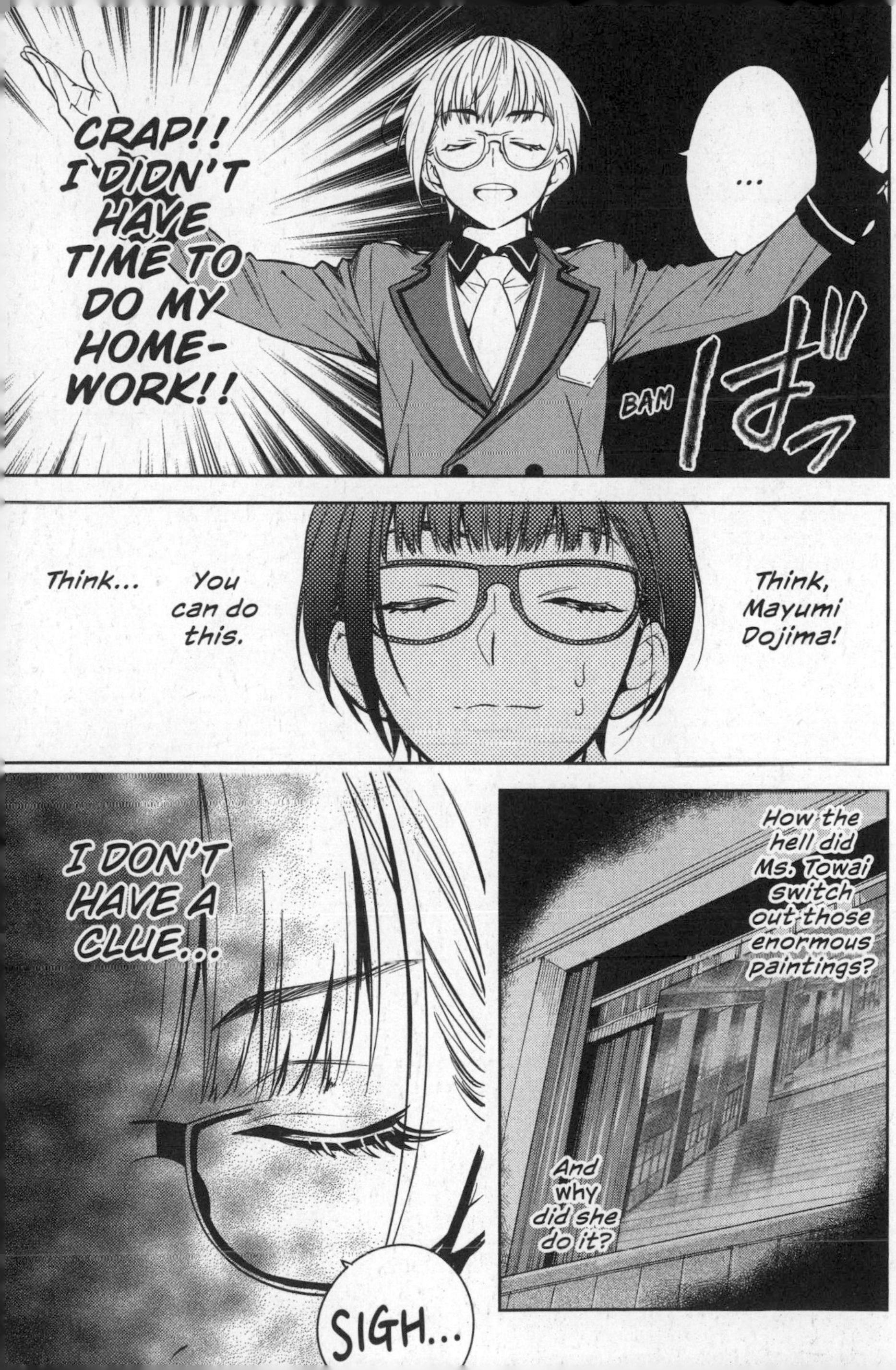
...
CRAP!! I DIDN'T HAVE TIME TO DO MY HOMEWORK!!
BAM
ばっ
Think, Mayumi Dojima!
You can do this.
Think...
How the hell did Ms. Towai switch out those enormous paintings?
And why did she do it?
I DON'T HAVE A CLUE...
SIGH...

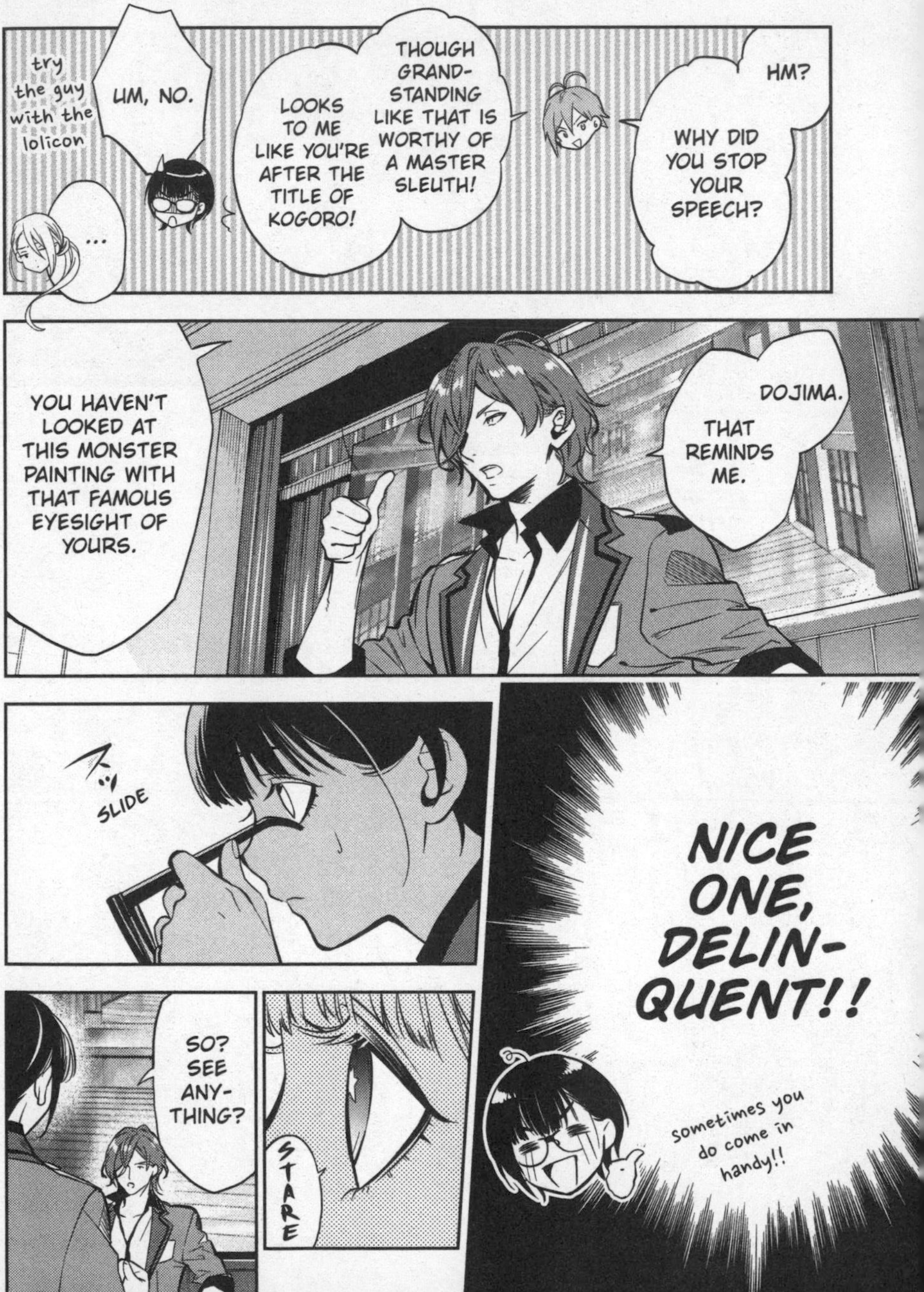
HM?
WHY DID YOU STOP YOUR SPEECH?
THOUGH GRAND-STANDING LIKE THAT IS WORTHY OF A MASTER SLEUTH!
LOOKS TO ME LIKE YOU'RE AFTER THE TITLE OF KOGORO!
UM, NO.
try the guy with the lolicon
...
DOJIMA.
THAT REMINDS ME.
YOU HAVEN'T LOOKED AT THIS MONSTER PAINTING WITH THAT FAMOUS EYESIGHT OF YOURS.
NICE ONE, DELIN-QUENT!!
Sometimes you do come in handy!!
SLIDE
STARE
SO? SEE ANY-THING?

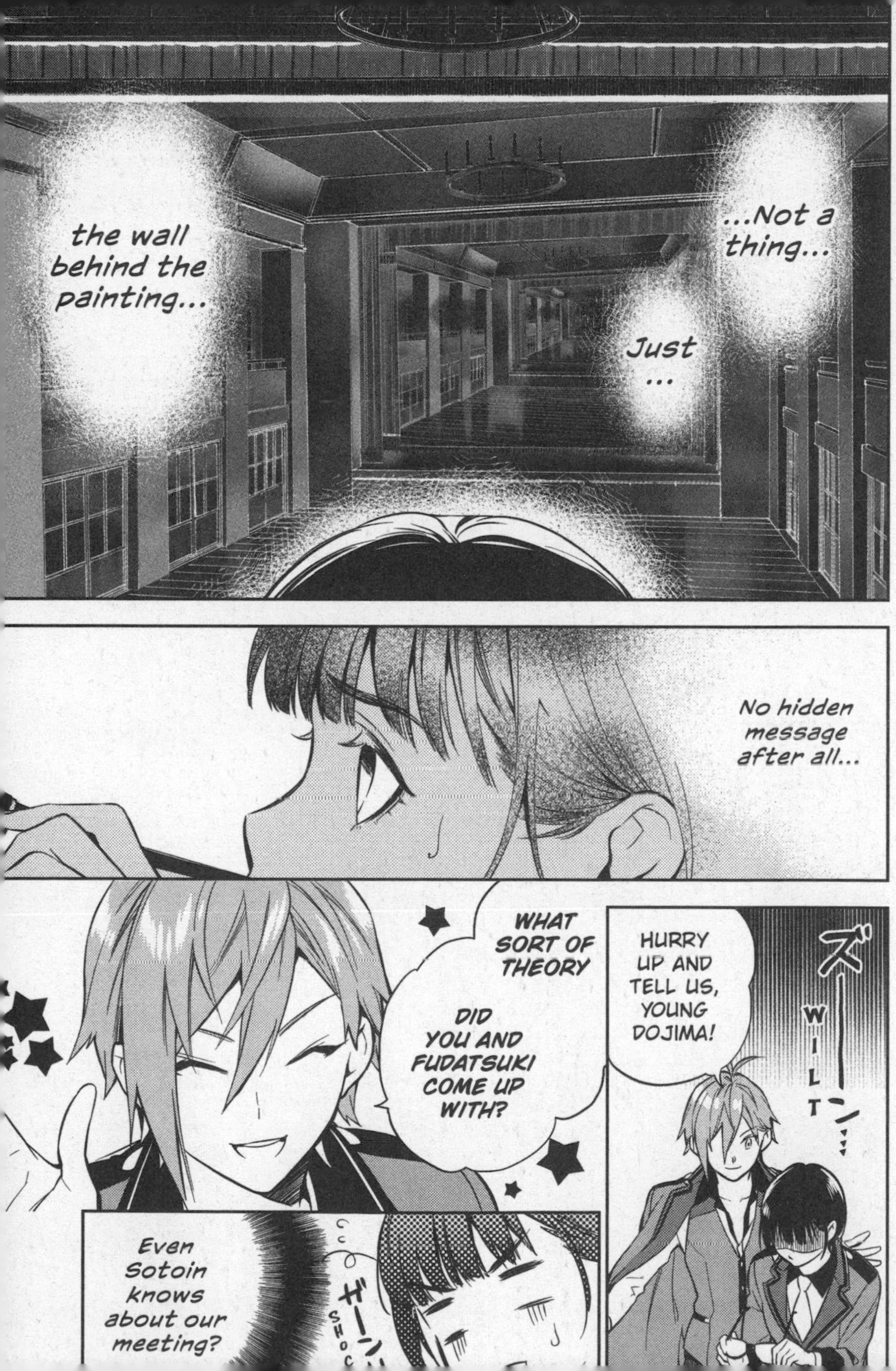

...Not a thing...
Just ...
the wall behind the painting...
No hidden message after all...
ズー
WILT
HURRY UP AND TELL US, YOUNG DOJIMA!
WHAT SORT OF THEORY
DID YOU AND FUDATSUKI COME UP WITH?
Even Sotoin knows about our meeting?

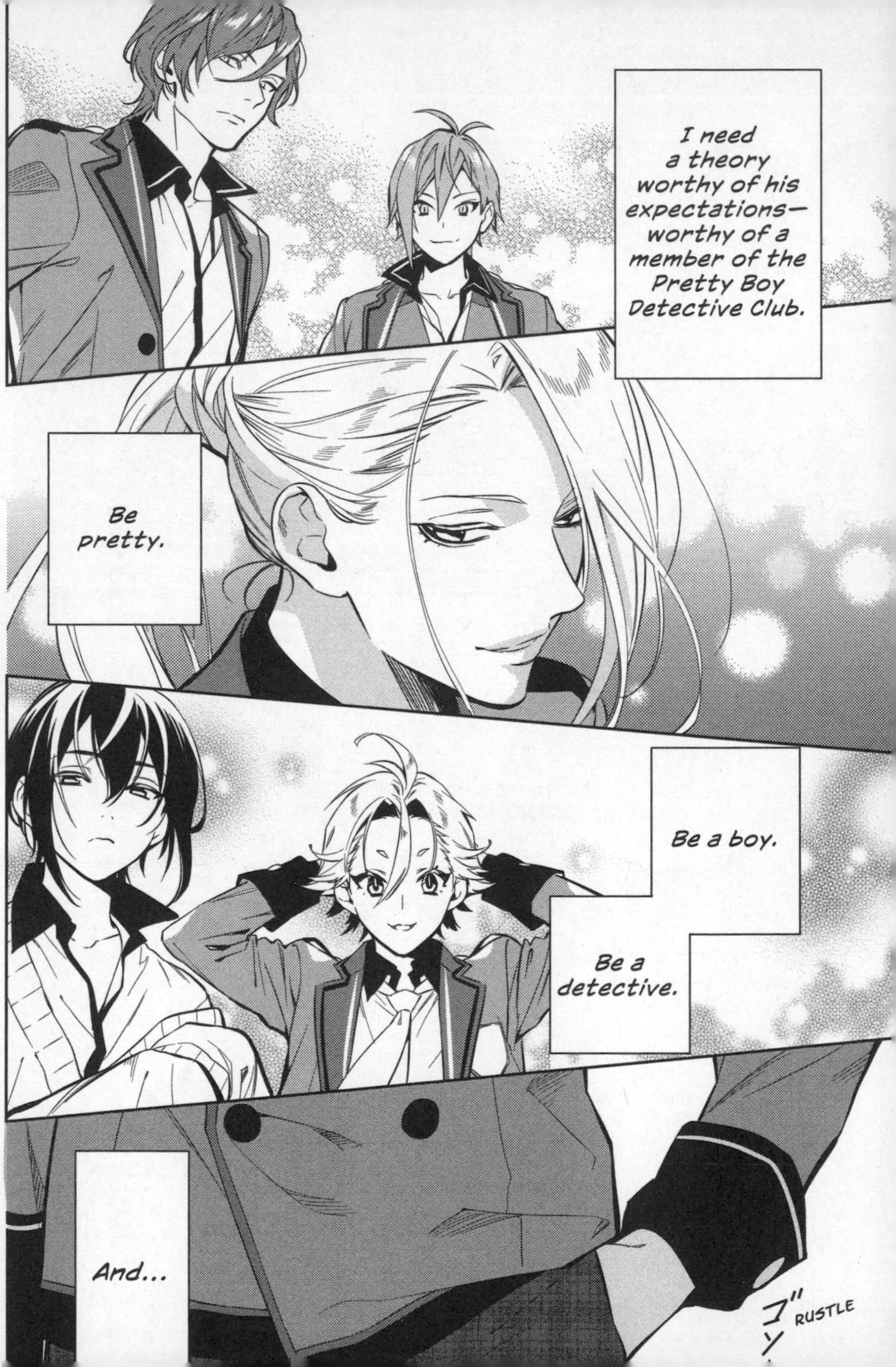
I need a theory worthy of his expectations—worthy of a member of the Pretty Boy Detective Club.
Be pretty.
Be a boy.
Be a detective.
And...
RUSTLE

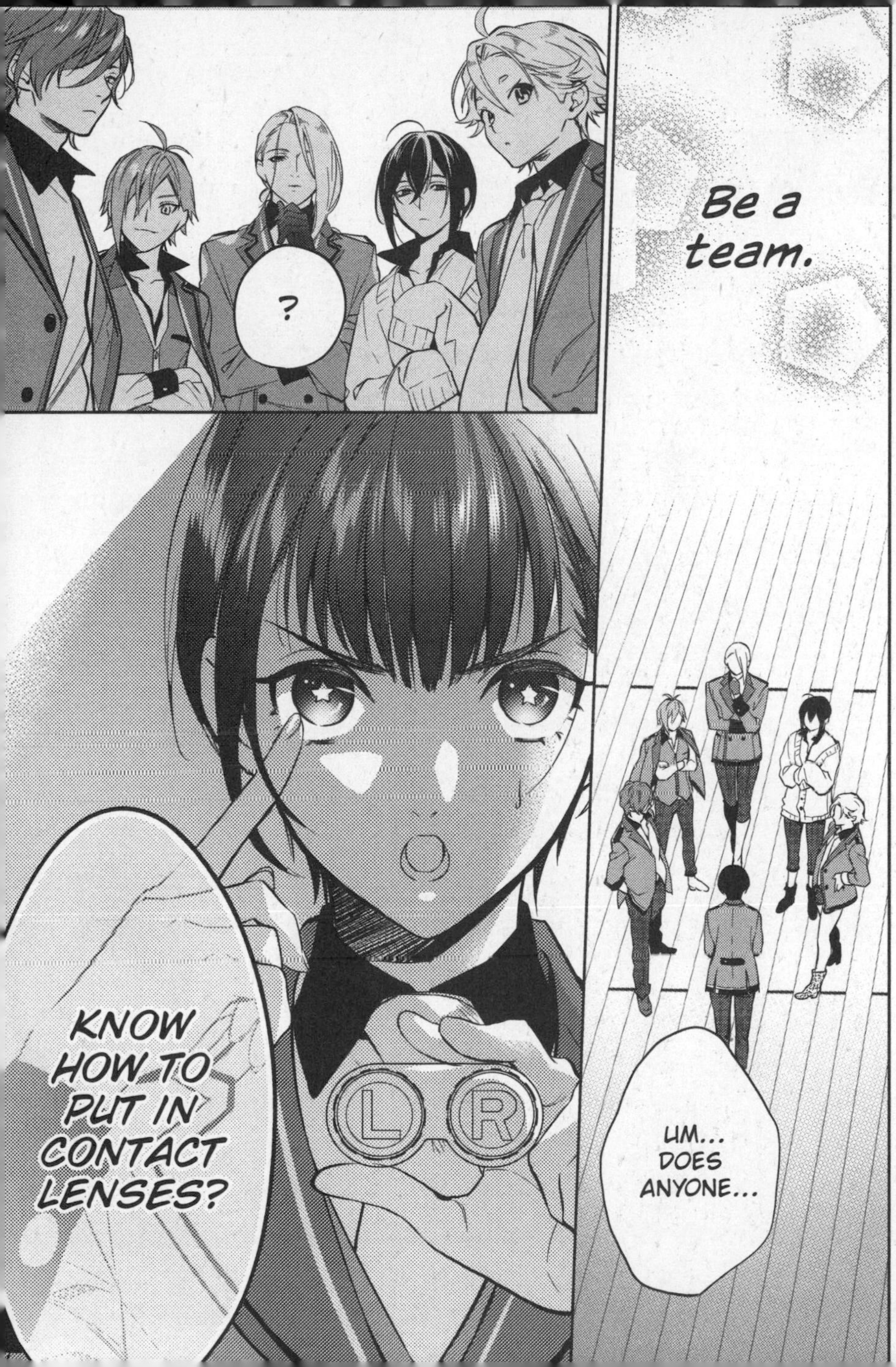
Be a team.
?
UM... DOES ANYONE...
KNOW HOW TO PUT IN CONTACT LENSES?

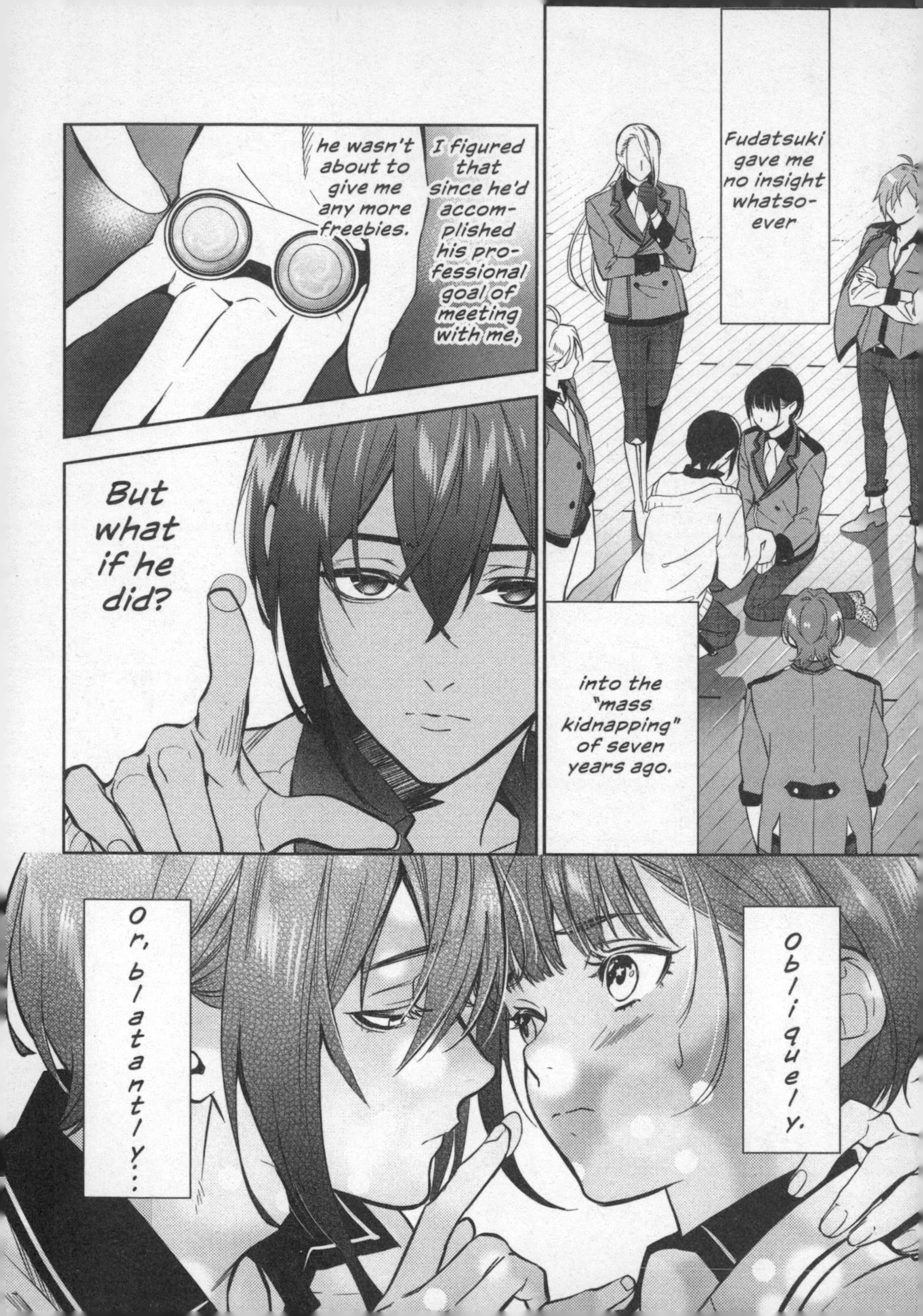

Fudatsuki gave me no insight whatso-ever
into the "mass kidnapping" of seven years ago.
I figured that since he'd accom-plished his pro-fessional goal of meeting with me,
he wasn't about to give me any more freebies.
But what if he did?
Obliquely.
Or, blatantly...

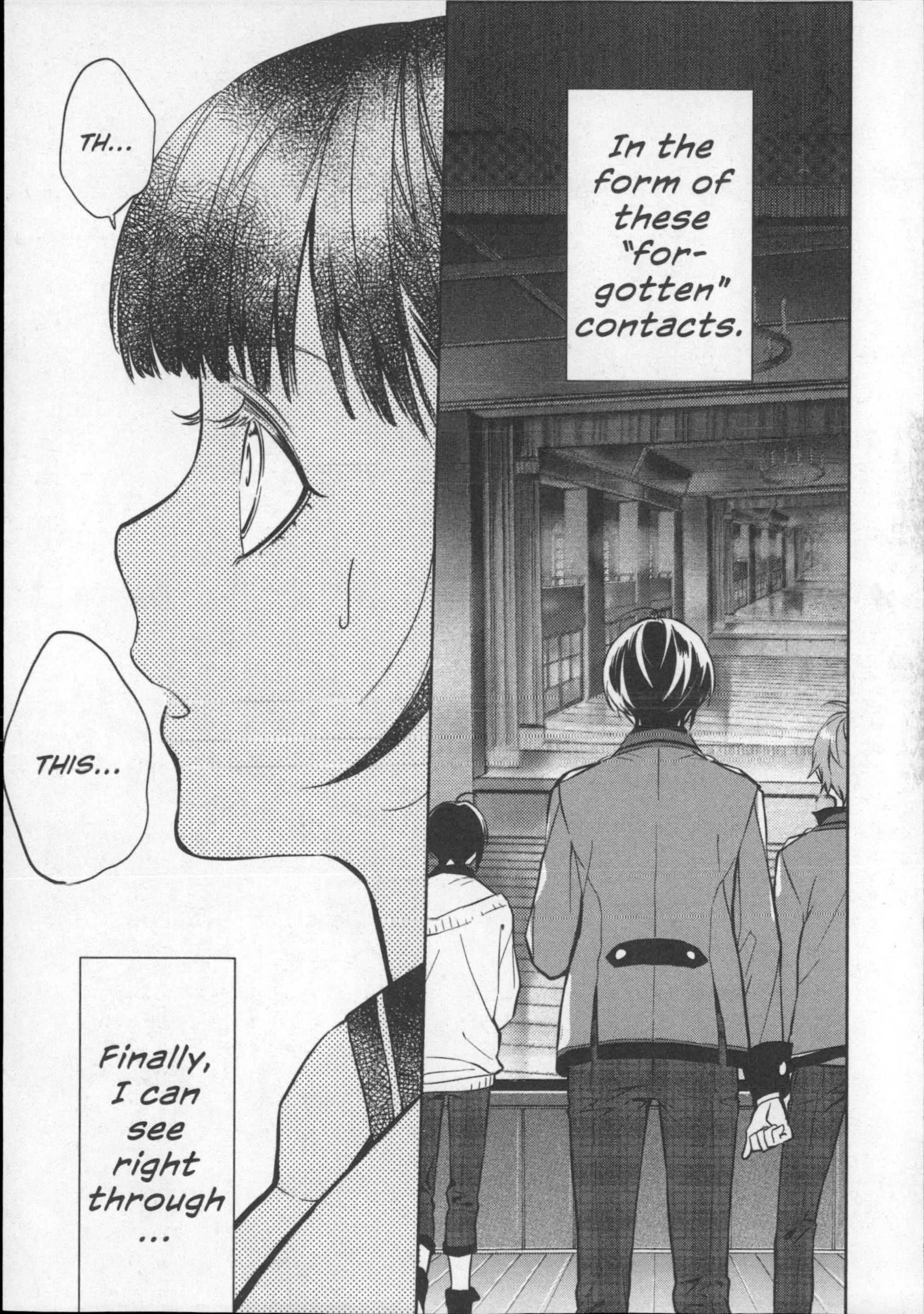
In the form of these "for-gotten" contacts.
TH...
THIS...
Finally, I can see right through ...

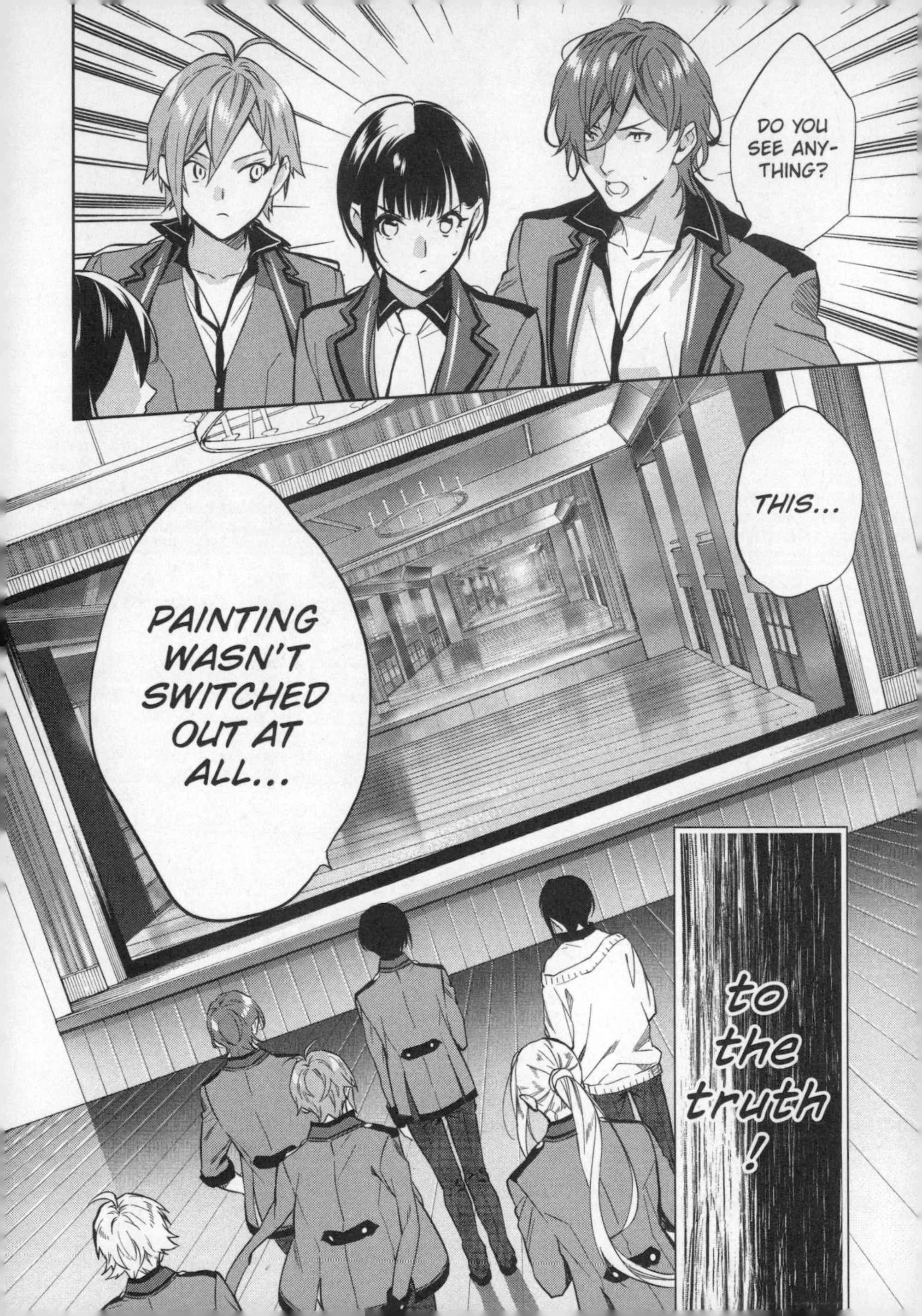
DO YOU SEE ANY-THING?
THIS...
PAINTING WASN'T SWITCHED OUT AT ALL...
to the truth!

PRETTY BOY

DETECTIVE CLUB!!

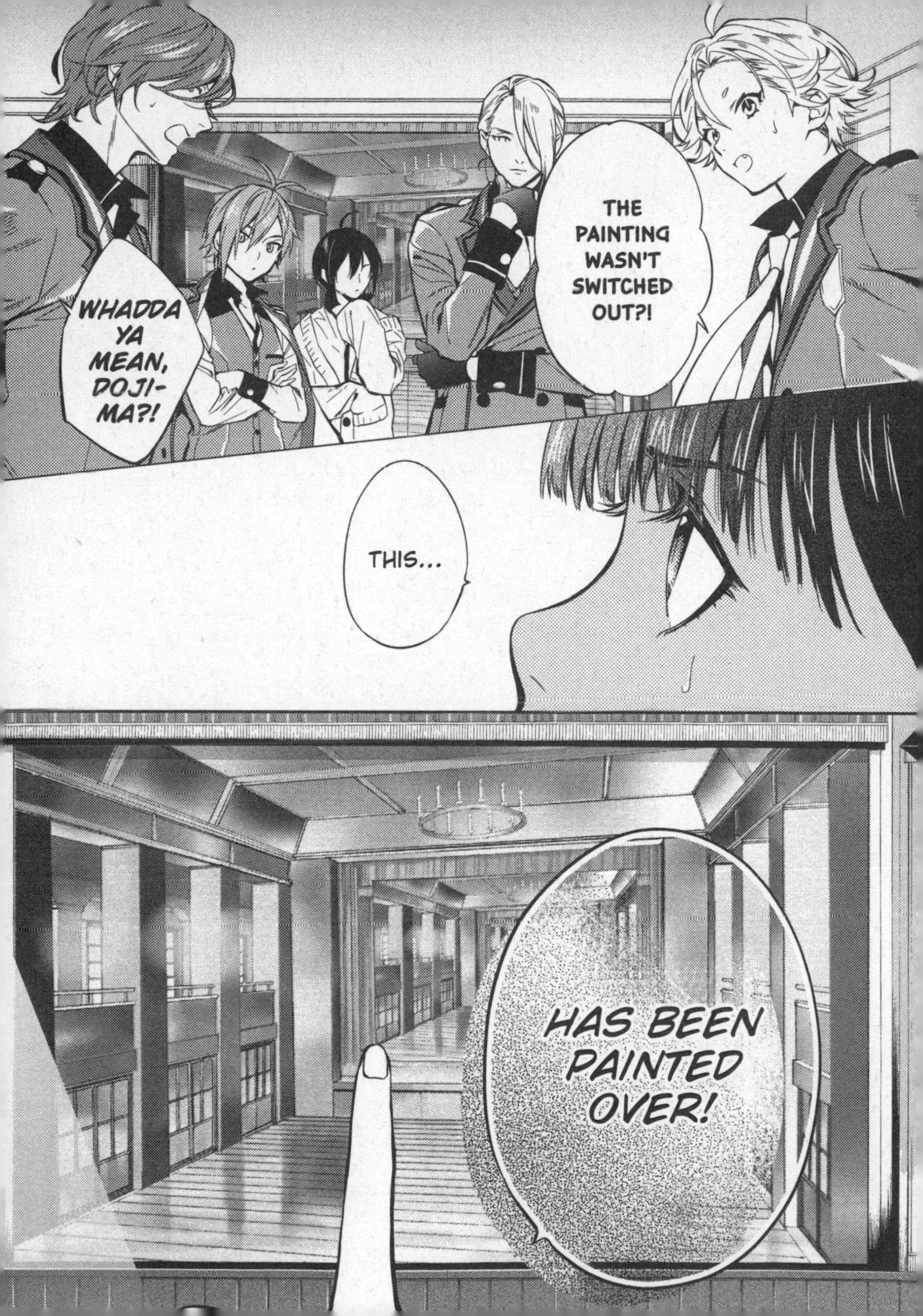
THE PAINTING WASN'T SWITCHED OUT?!
WHADDA YA MEAN, DOJIMA?!
THIS...
HAS BEEN PAINTED OVER!

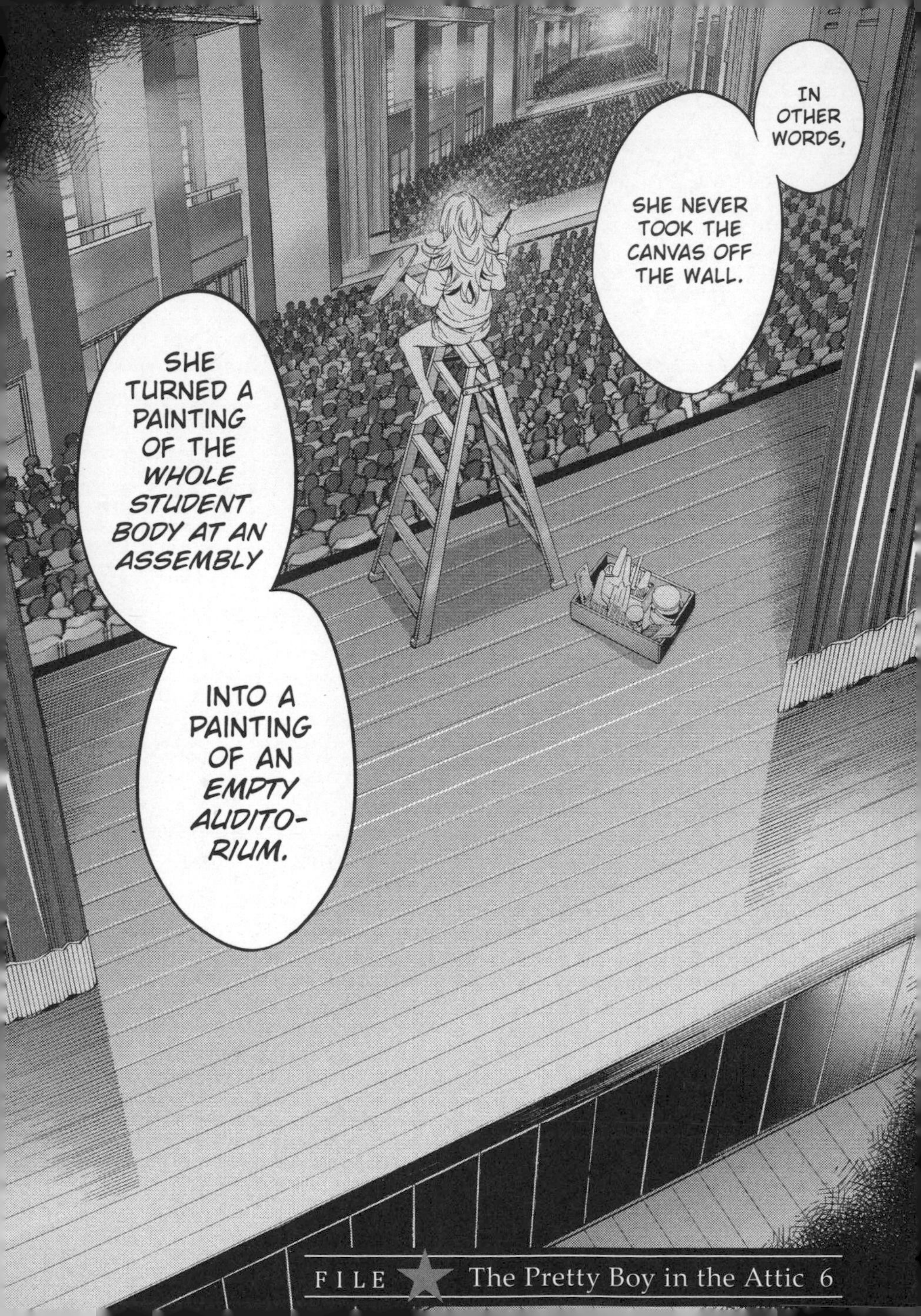
IN OTHER WORDS,
SHE NEVER TOOK THE CANVAS OFF THE WALL.
SHE TURNED A PAINTING OF THE *WHOLE STUDENT BODY AT AN ASSEMBLY*
INTO A PAINTING OF AN *EMPTY AUDITO-RIUM.*

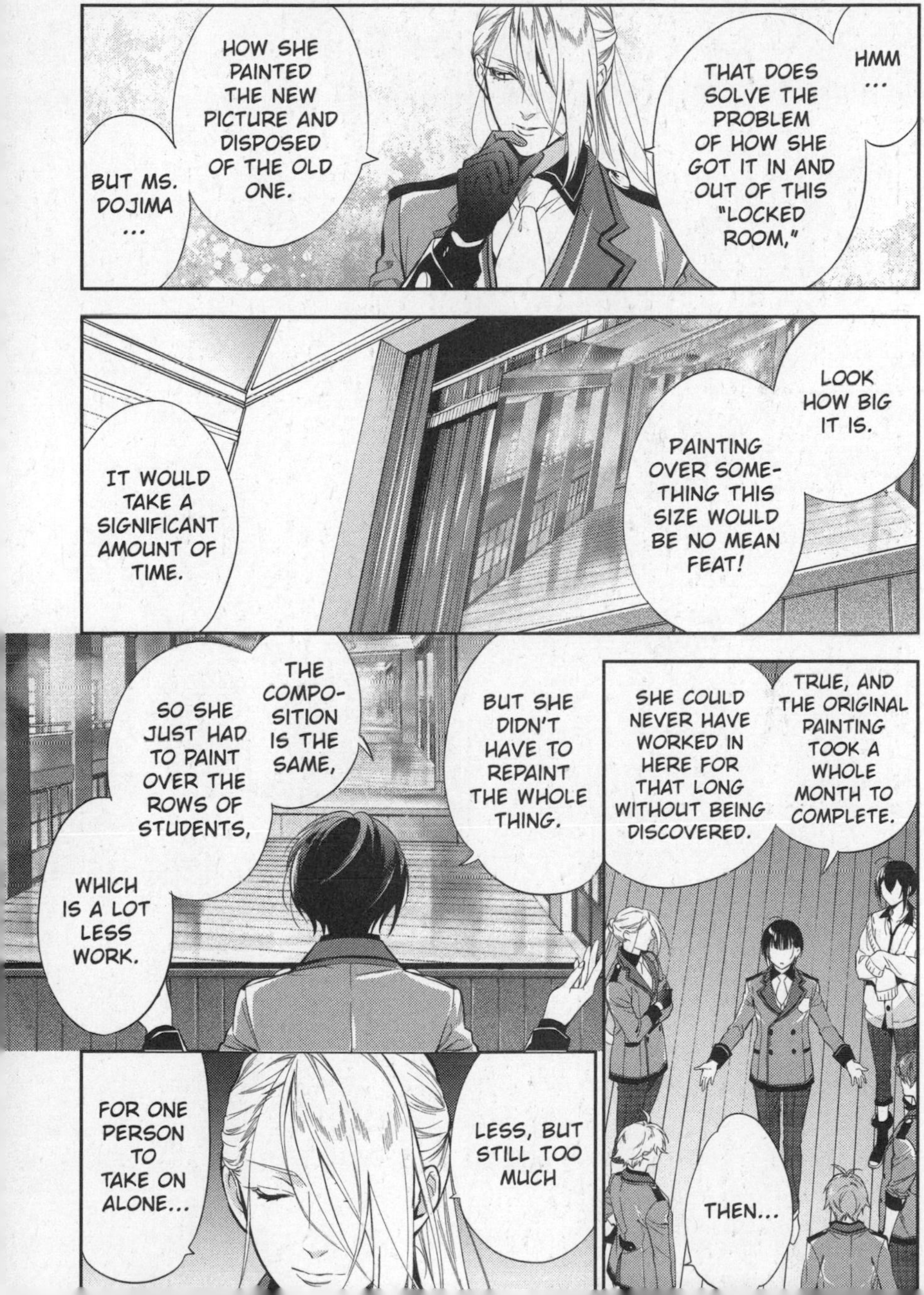
HMM ...
THAT DOES SOLVE THE PROBLEM OF HOW SHE GOT IT IN AND OUT OF THIS "LOCKED ROOM,"
HOW SHE PAINTED THE NEW PICTURE AND DISPOSED OF THE OLD ONE.
BUT MS. DOJIMA ...
LOOK HOW BIG IT IS.
PAINTING OVER SOME-THING THIS SIZE WOULD BE NO MEAN FEAT!
IT WOULD TAKE A SIGNIFICANT AMOUNT OF TIME.
TRUE, AND THE ORIGINAL PAINTING TOOK A WHOLE MONTH TO COMPLETE.
SHE COULD NEVER HAVE WORKED IN HERE FOR THAT LONG WITHOUT BEING DISCOVERED.
THEN...
BUT SHE DIDN'T HAVE TO REPAINT THE WHOLE THING.
THE COMPO-SITION IS THE SAME,
SO SHE JUST HAD TO PAINT OVER THE ROWS OF STUDENTS,
WHICH IS A LOT LESS WORK.
LESS, BUT STILL TOO MUCH
FOR ONE PERSON TO TAKE ON ALONE...

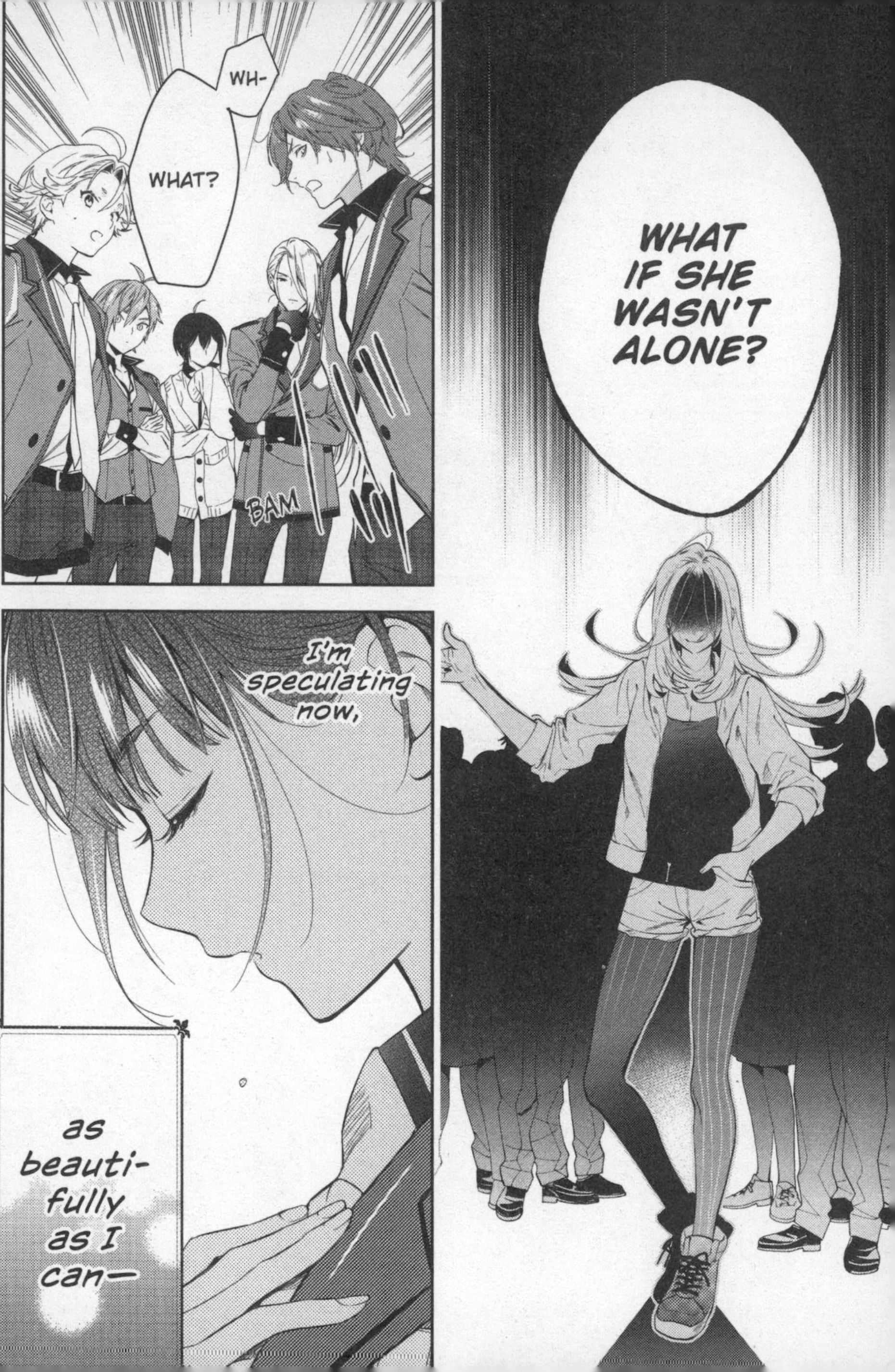
WHAT IF SHE WASN'T ALONE?
WH-
WHAT?
BAM
I'm speculating now,
as beautifully as I can—

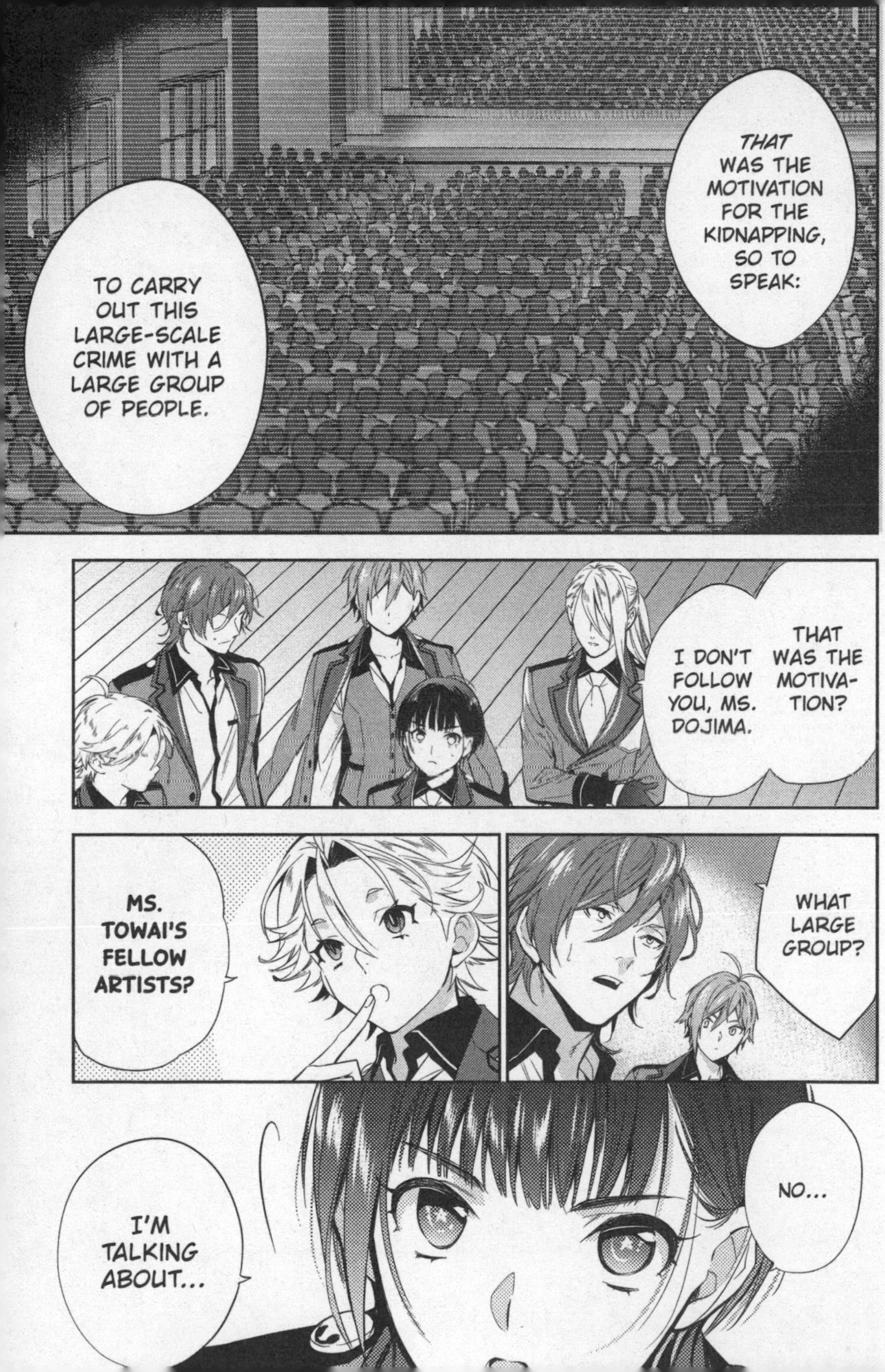
THAT WAS THE MOTIVATION FOR THE KIDNAPPING, SO TO SPEAK:
TO CARRY OUT THIS LARGE-SCALE CRIME WITH A LARGE GROUP OF PEOPLE.
THAT WAS THE MOTIVA-TION?
I DON'T FOLLOW YOU, MS. DOJIMA.
WHAT LARGE GROUP?
MS. TOWAI'S FELLOW ARTISTS?
NO...
I'M TALKING ABOUT...

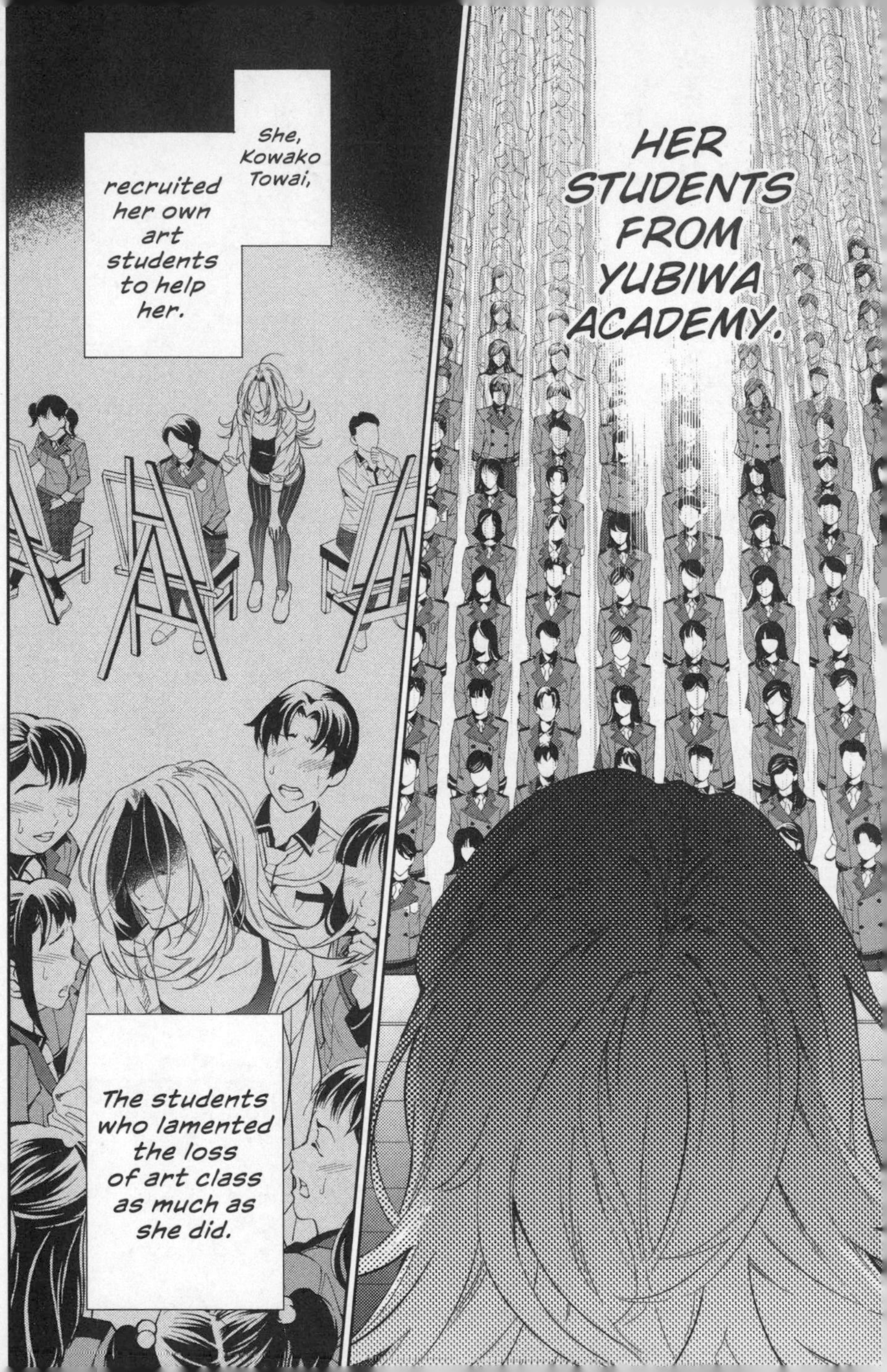
HER STUDENTS FROM YUBIWA ACADEMY.
She, Kowako Towai,
recruited her own art students to help her.
The students who lamented the loss of art class as much as she did.

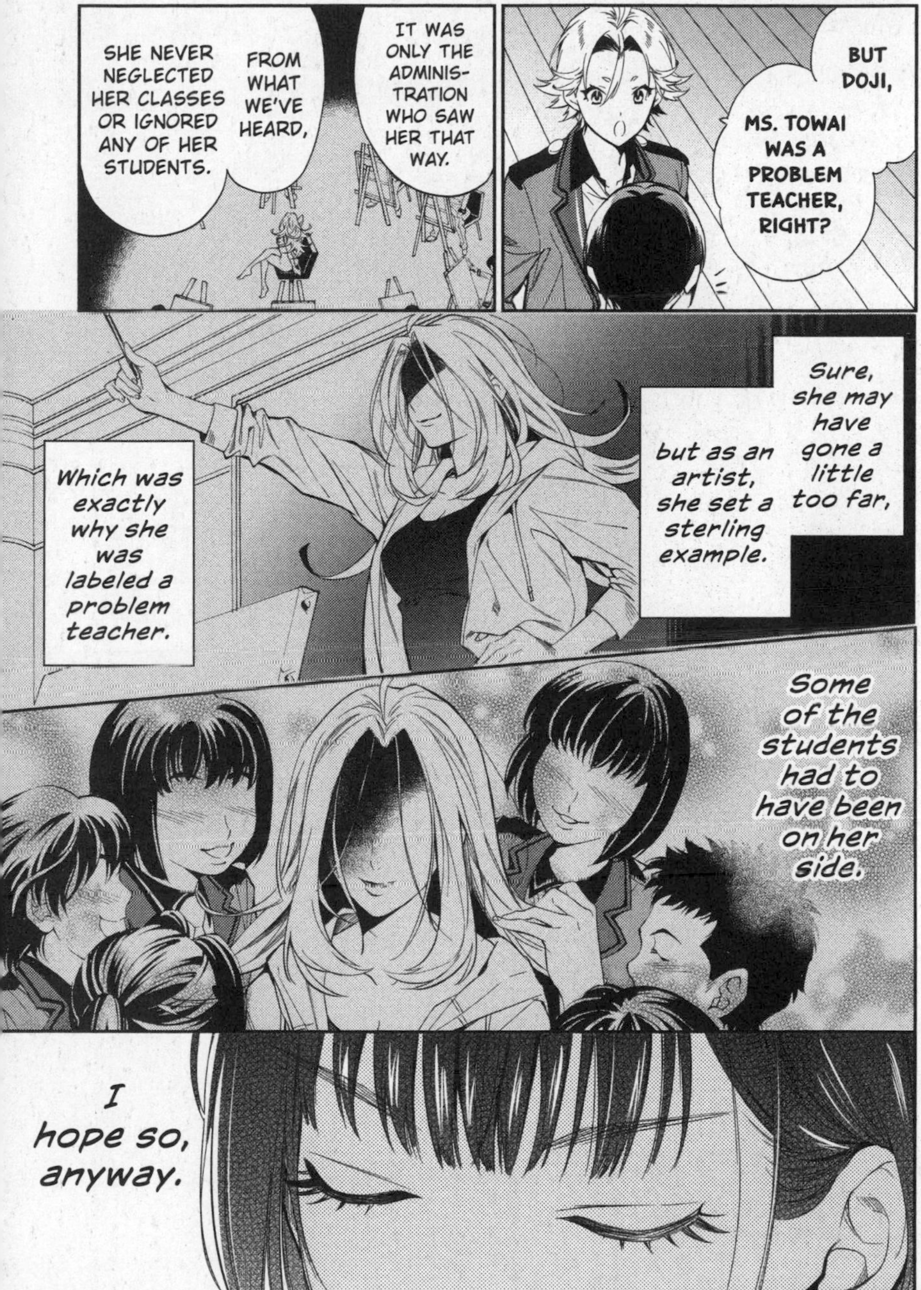
BUT DOJI,
MS. TOWAI WAS A PROBLEM TEACHER, RIGHT?
IT WAS ONLY THE ADMINIS-TRATION WHO SAW HER THAT WAY.
FROM WHAT WE'VE HEARD,
SHE NEVER NEGLECTED HER CLASSES OR IGNORED ANY OF HER STUDENTS.
Sure, she may have gone a little too far,
but as an artist, she set a sterling example.
Which was exactly why she was labeled a problem teacher.
Some of the students had to have been on her side.
I hope so, anyway.

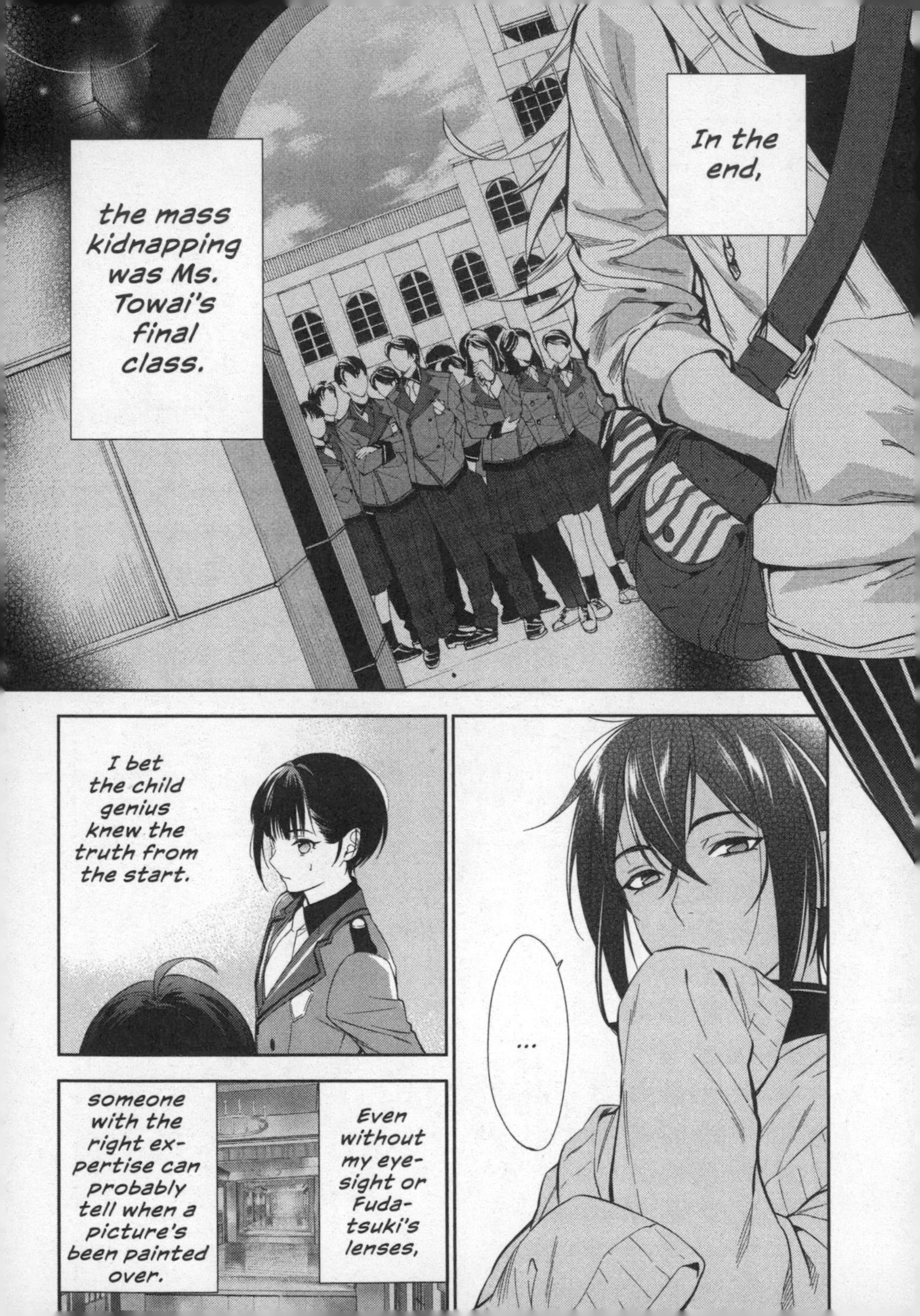
In the end,
the mass kidnapping was Ms. Towai's final class.
...
I bet the child genius knew the truth from the start.
Even without my eye-sight or Fuda-tsuki's lenses,
someone with the right ex-pertise can probably tell when a picture's been painted over.

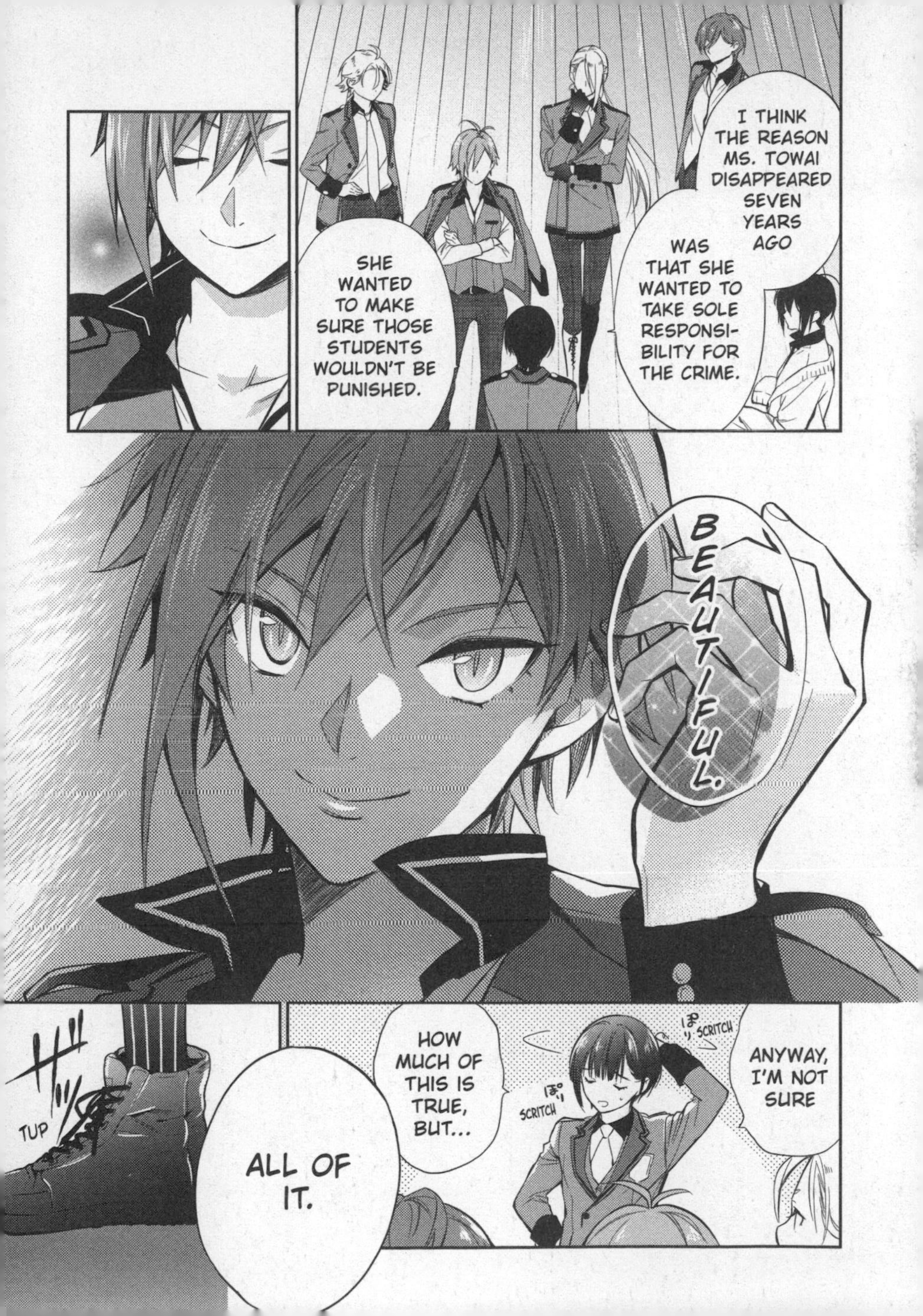
I THINK THE REASON MS. TOWAI DISAPPEARED SEVEN YEARS AGO
WAS THAT SHE WANTED TO TAKE SOLE RESPONSIBILITY FOR THE CRIME.
SHE WANTED TO MAKE SURE THOSE STUDENTS WOULDN'T BE PUNISHED.
BEAUTIFUL.
ANYWAY, I'M NOT SURE
ぽり SCRITCH
ぽり SCRITCH
HOW MUCH OF THIS IS TRUE, BUT...
ALL OF IT.
TUP

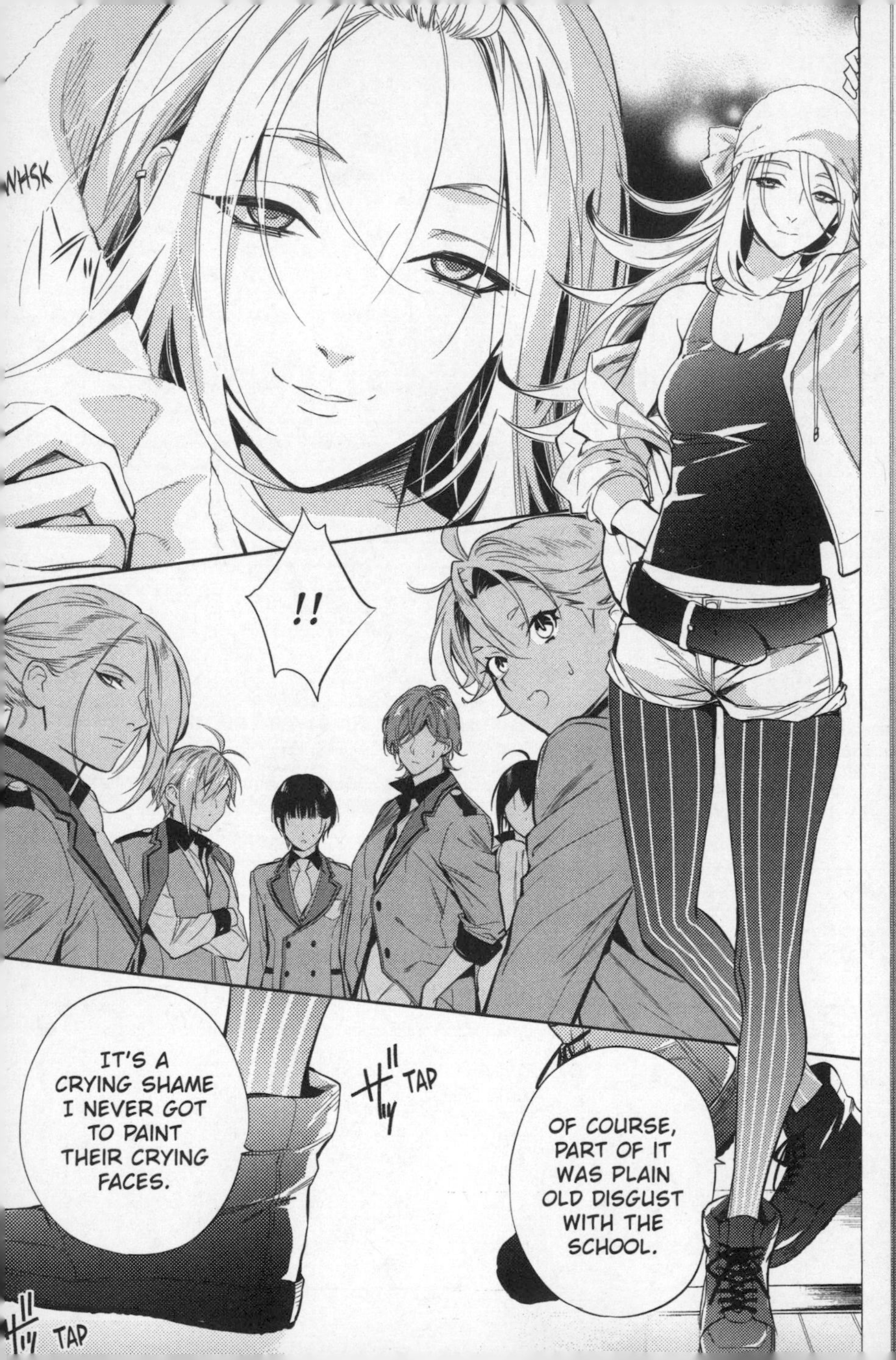
WHSK
!!
OF COURSE, PART OF IT WAS PLAIN OLD DISGUST WITH THE SCHOOL.
TAP
IT'S A CRYING SHAME I NEVER GOT TO PAINT THEIR CRYING FACES.
TAP

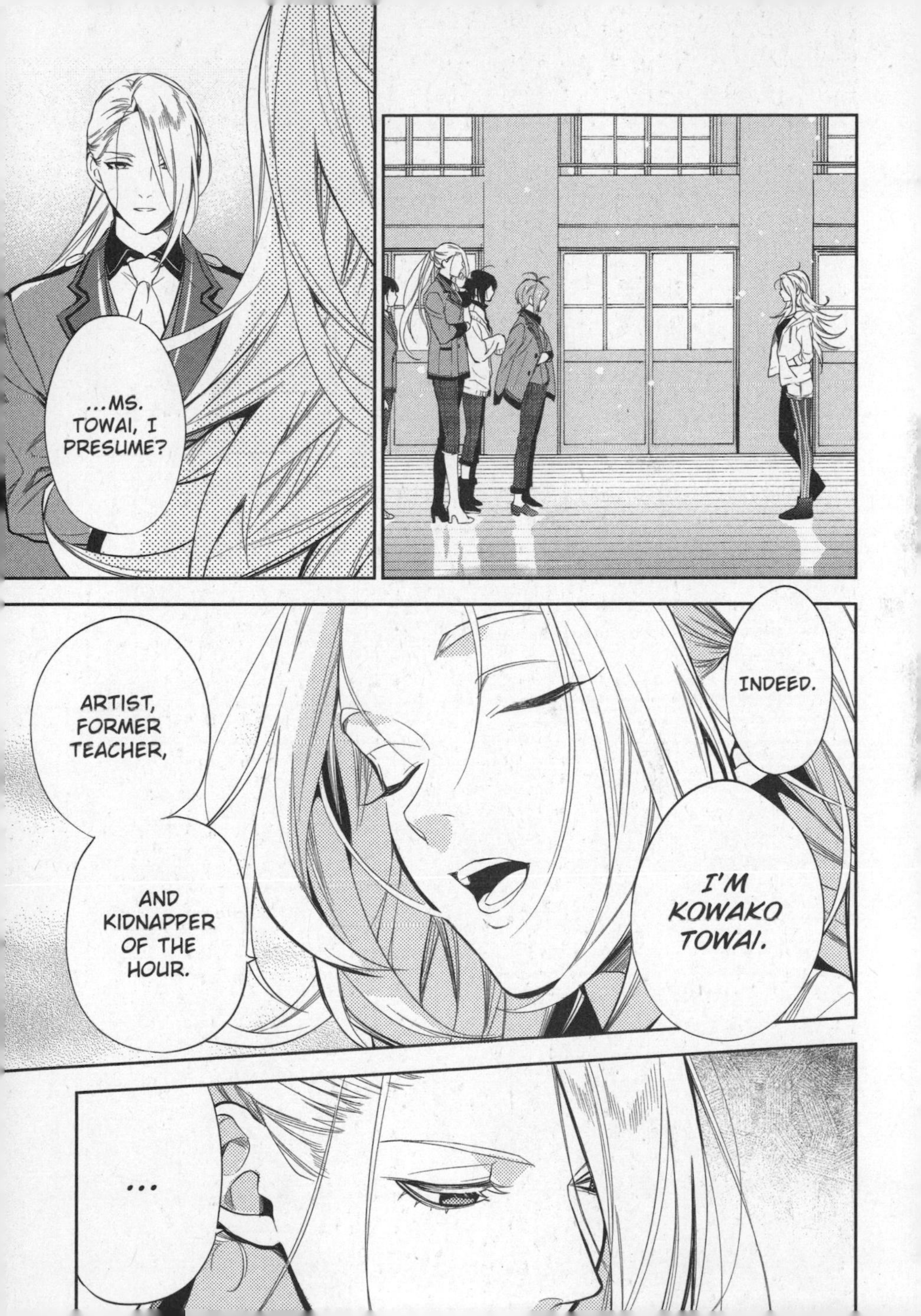
...MS. TOWAI, I PRESUME?
INDEED.
I'M KOWAKO TOWAI.
ARTIST, FORMER TEACHER,
AND KIDNAPPER OF THE HOUR.
...

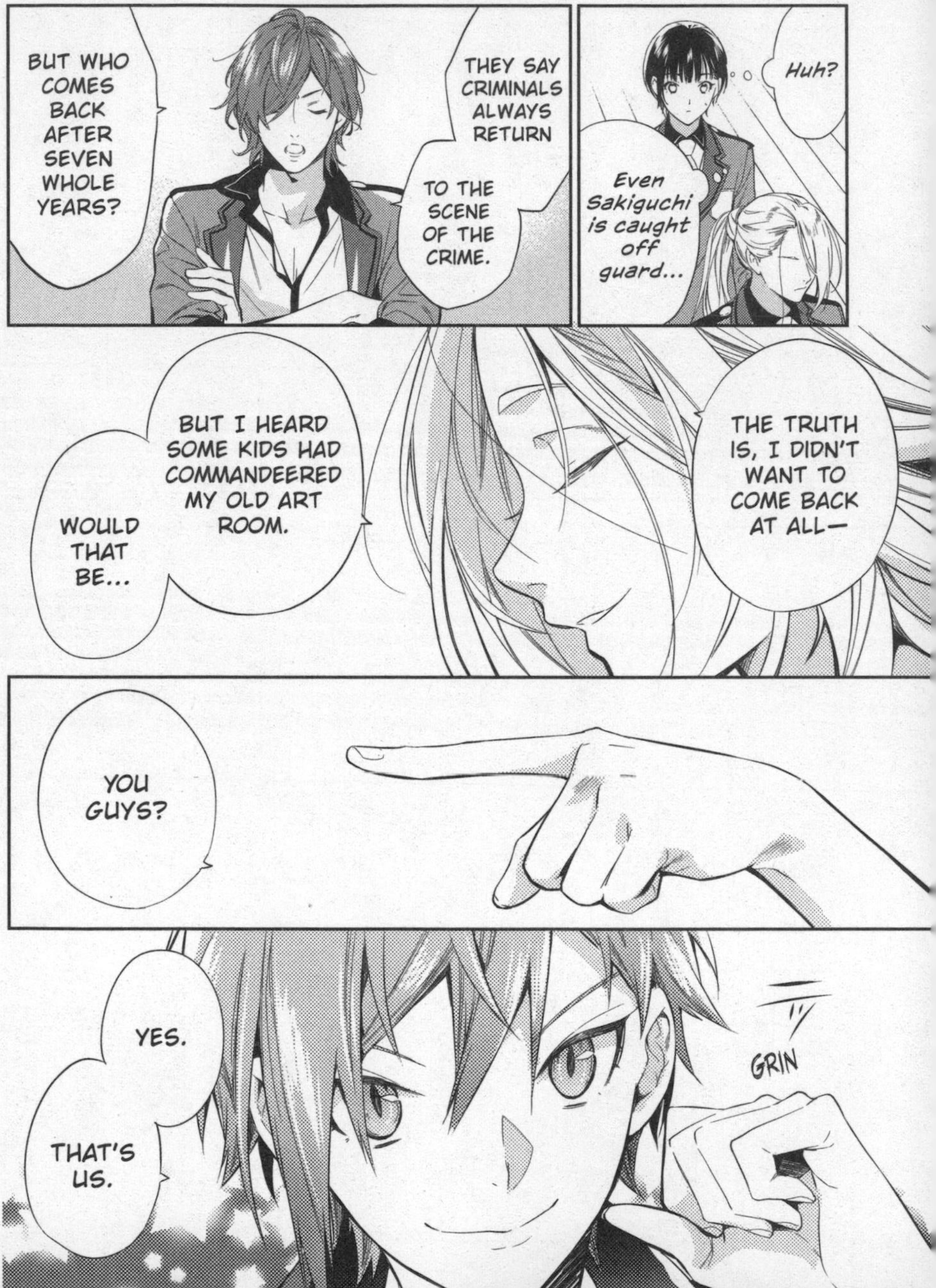
Huh?
Even Sakiguchi is caught off guard...
THEY SAY CRIMINALS ALWAYS RETURN
TO THE SCENE OF THE CRIME.
BUT WHO COMES BACK AFTER SEVEN WHOLE YEARS?
THE TRUTH IS, I DIDN'T WANT TO COME BACK AT ALL—
BUT I HEARD SOME KIDS HAD COMMANDEERED MY OLD ART ROOM.
WOULD THAT BE...
YOU GUYS?
GRIN
YES.
THAT'S US.

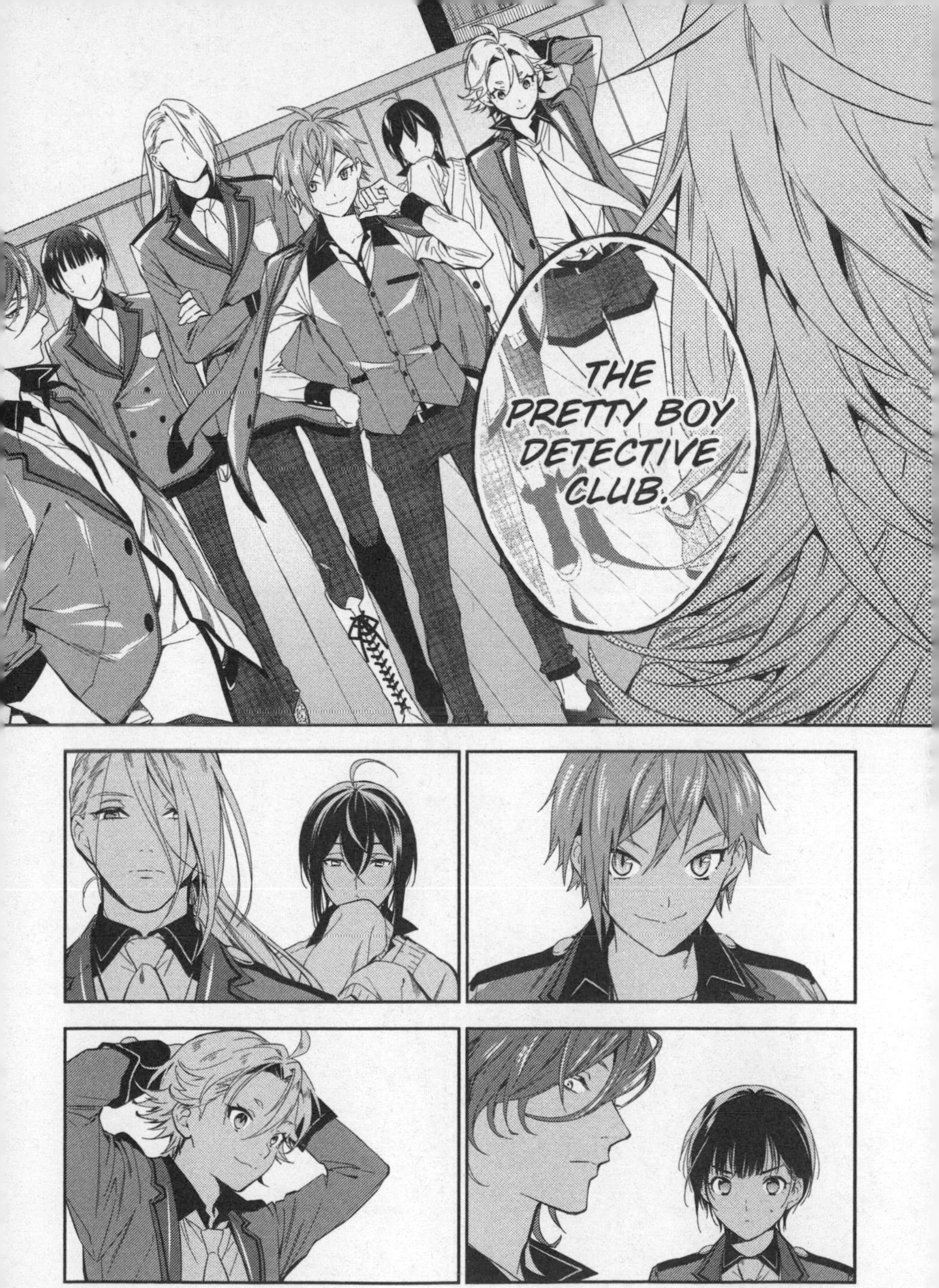
THE PRETTY BOY DETECTIVE CLUB.

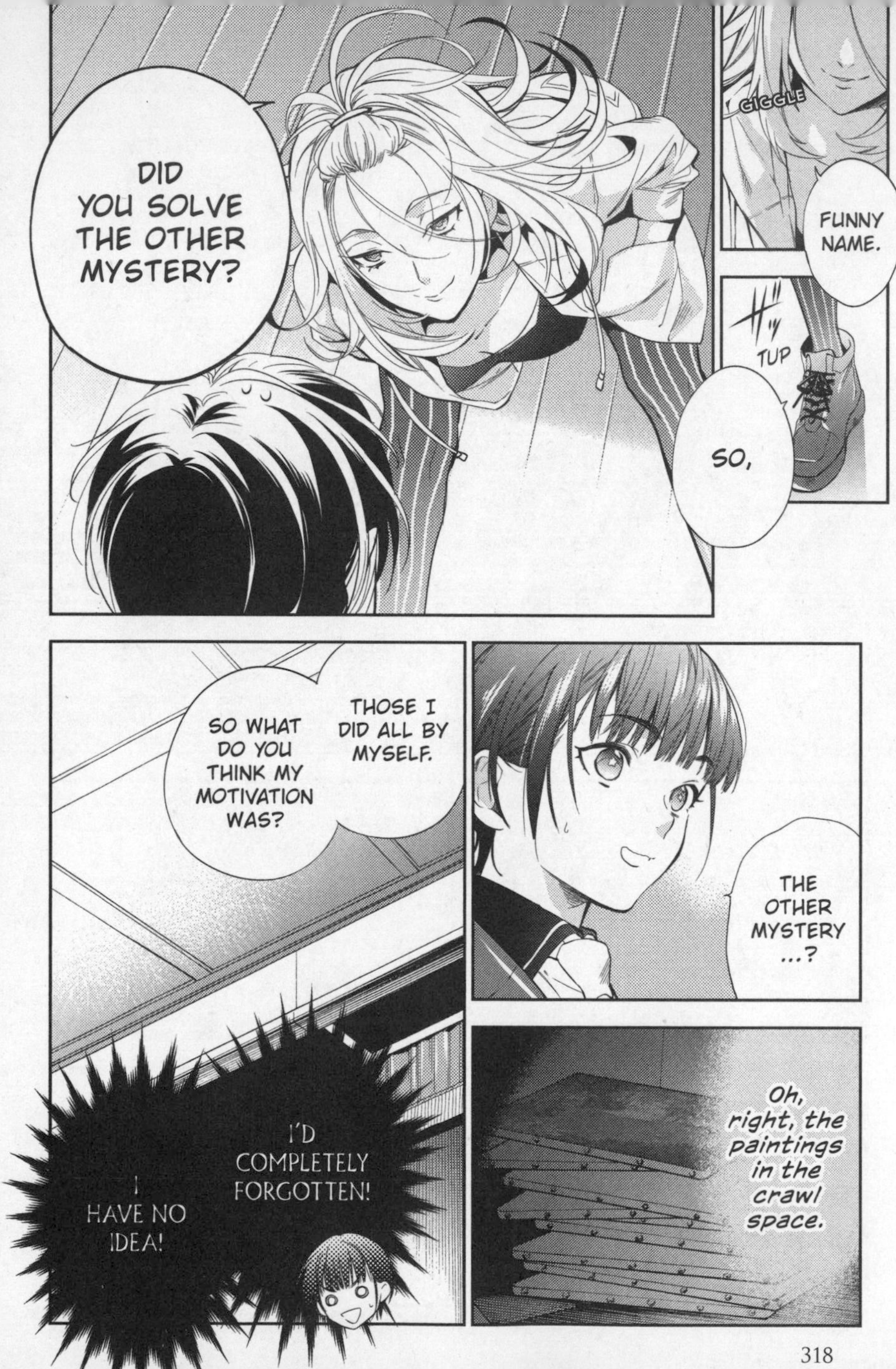
GIGGLE
FUNNY NAME.
ザッ
TUP
SO,
DID YOU SOLVE THE OTHER MYSTERY?
THE OTHER MYSTERY ...?
Oh, right, the paintings in the crawl space.
THOSE I DID ALL BY MYSELF.
SO WHAT DO YOU THINK MY MOTIVATION WAS?
I'D COMPLETELY FORGOTTEN!
I HAVE NO IDEA!

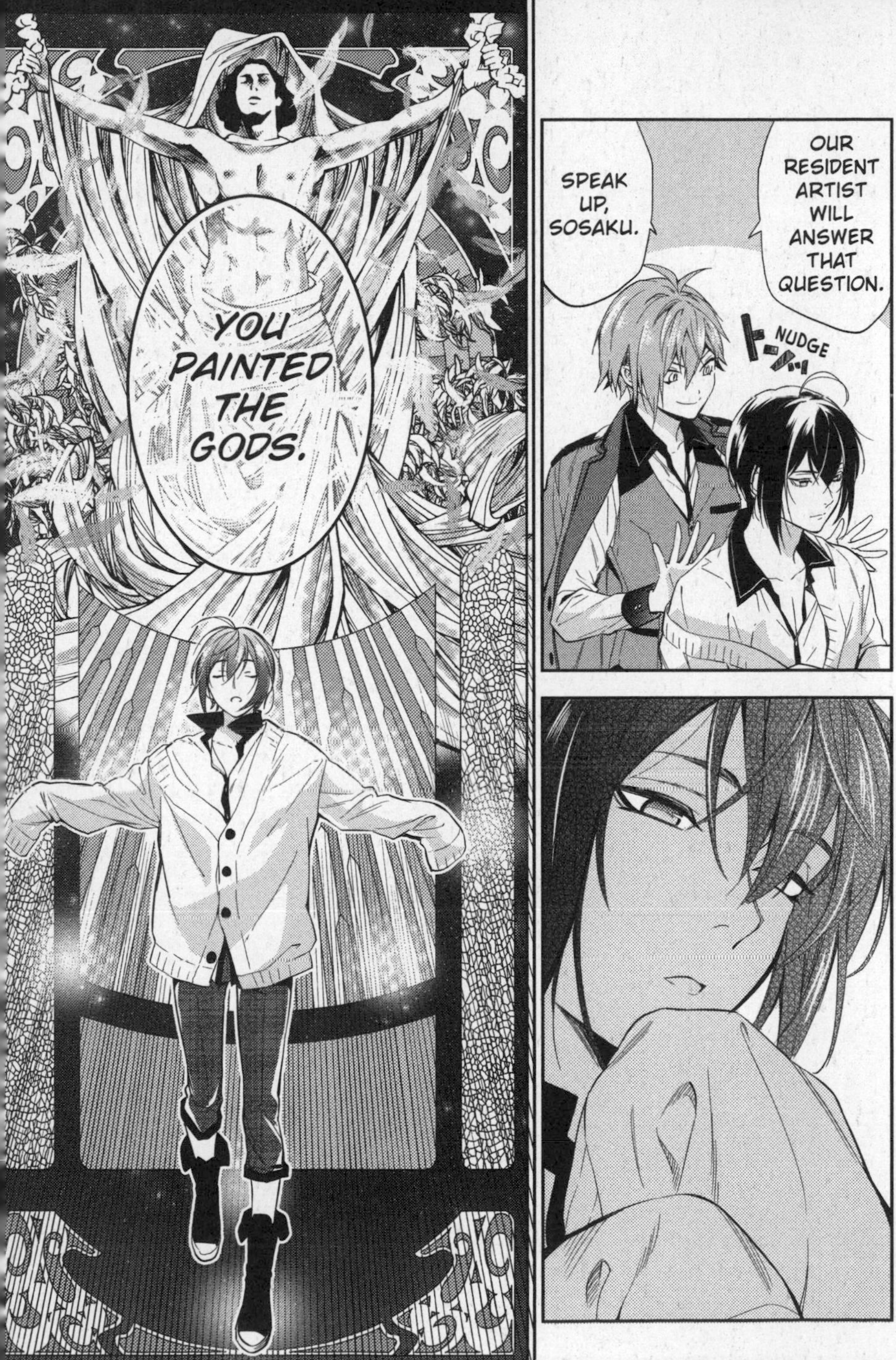
OUR RESIDENT ARTIST WILL ANSWER THAT QUESTION.
SPEAK UP, SOSAKU.
NUDGE
YOU PAINTED THE GODS.

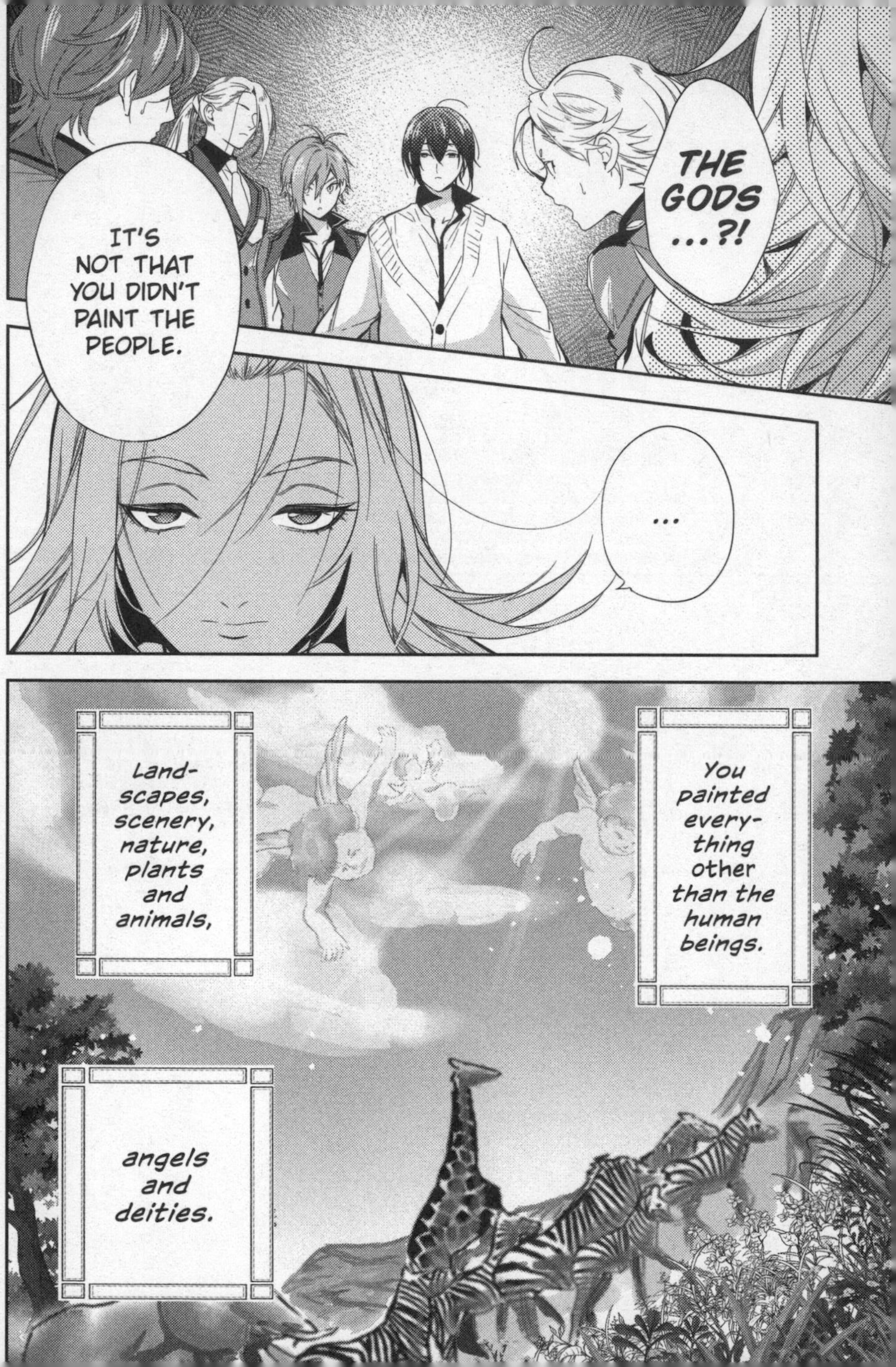
THE GODS ...?!
IT'S NOT THAT YOU DIDN'T PAINT THE PEOPLE.
...
You painted every-thing other than the human beings.
Land-scapes, scenery, nature, plants and animals,
angels and deities.

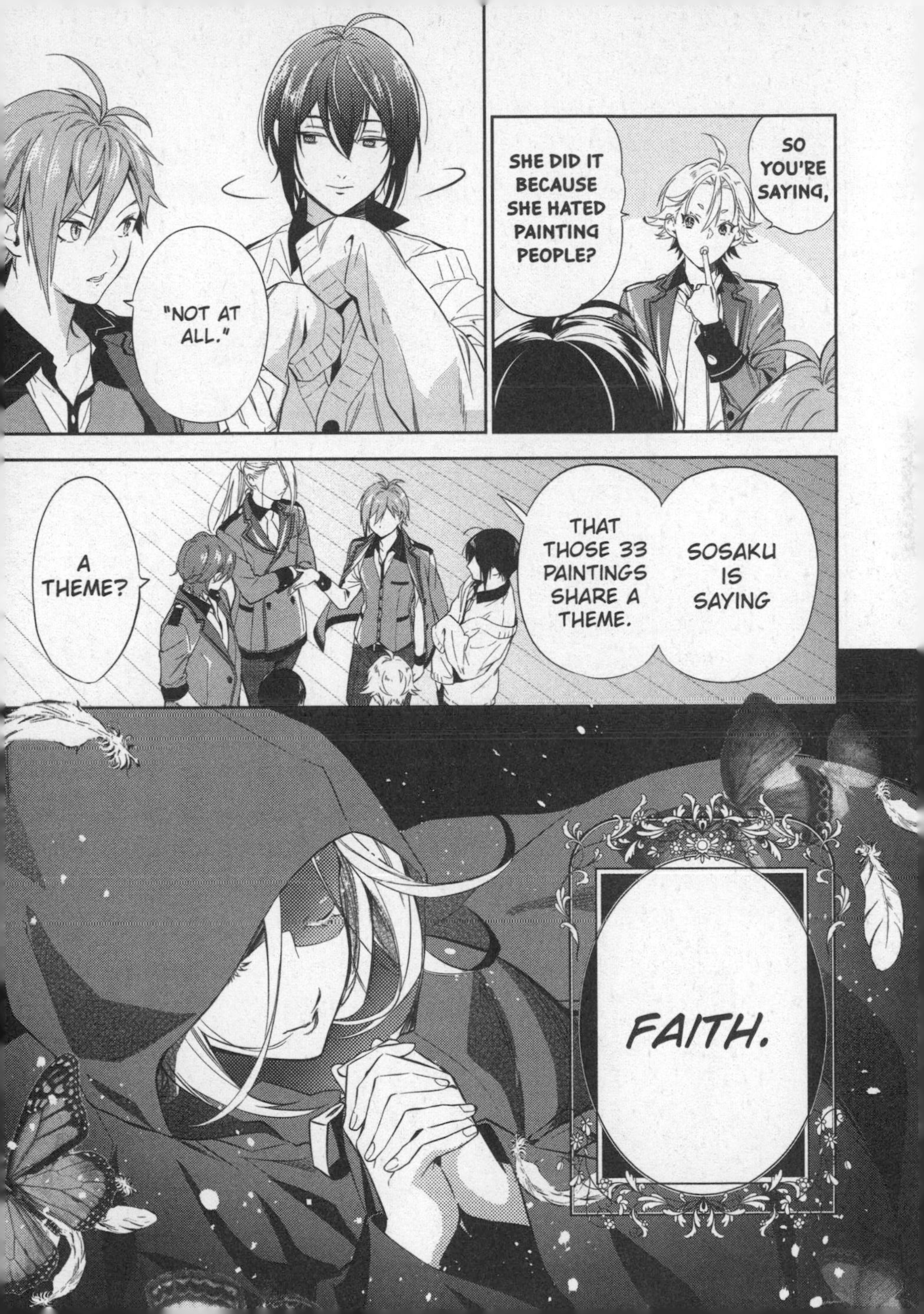
SO YOU'RE SAYING,
SHE DID IT BECAUSE SHE HATED PAINTING PEOPLE?
"NOT AT ALL."
SOSAKU IS SAYING
THAT THOSE 33 PAINTINGS SHARE A THEME.
A THEME?
FAITH.

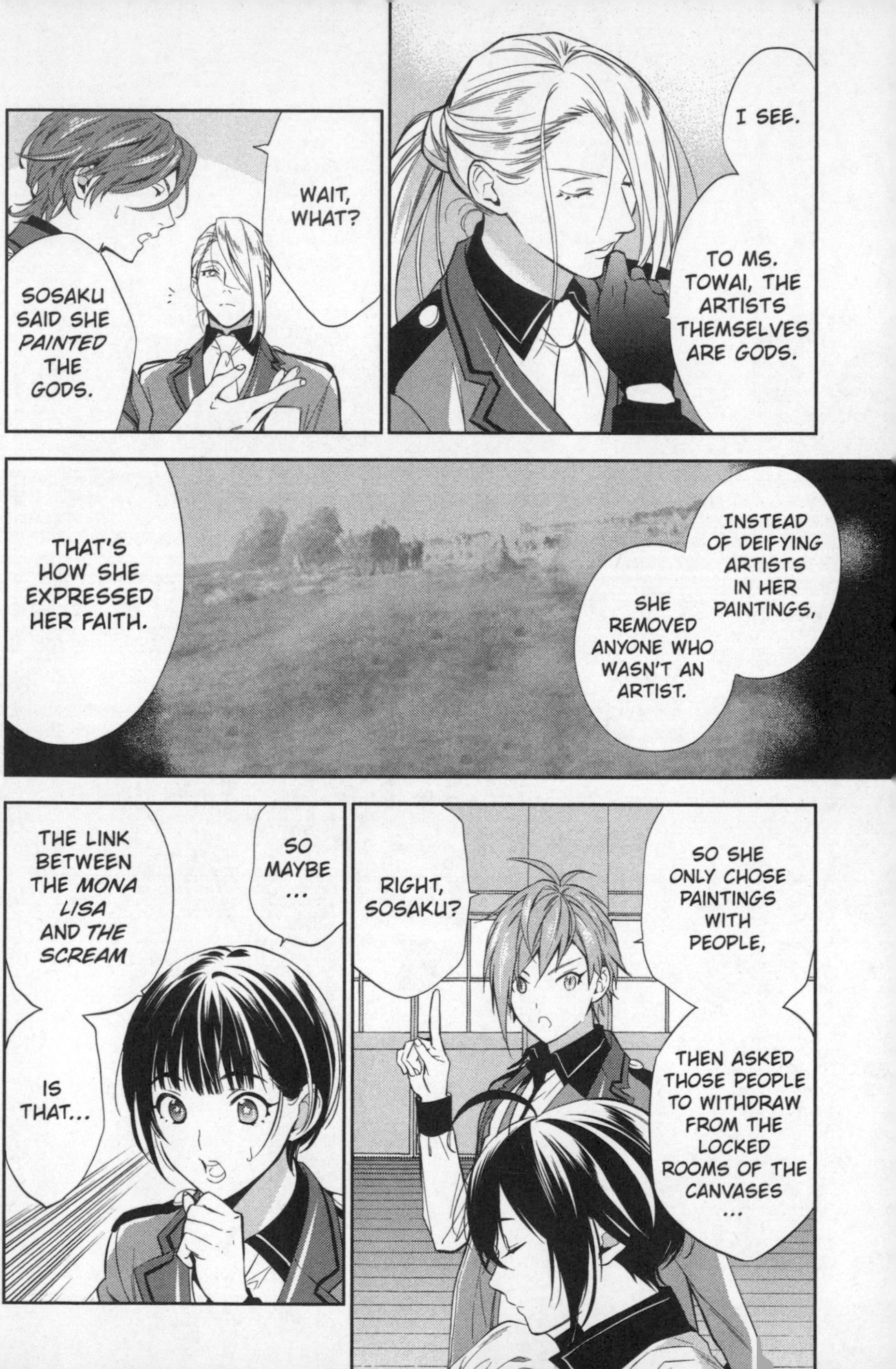
I SEE.
TO MS. TOWAI, THE ARTISTS THEMSELVES ARE GODS.
WAIT, WHAT?
SOSAKU SAID SHE *PAINTED* THE GODS.
INSTEAD OF DEIFYING ARTISTS IN HER PAINTINGS,
SHE REMOVED ANYONE WHO WASN'T AN ARTIST.
THAT'S HOW SHE EXPRESSED HER FAITH.
SO SHE ONLY CHOSE PAINTINGS WITH PEOPLE,
THEN ASKED THOSE PEOPLE TO WITHDRAW FROM THE LOCKED ROOMS OF THE CANVASES...
RIGHT, SOSAKU?
SO MAYBE...
THE LINK BETWEEN THE *MONA LISA* AND *THE SCREAM*
IS THAT...

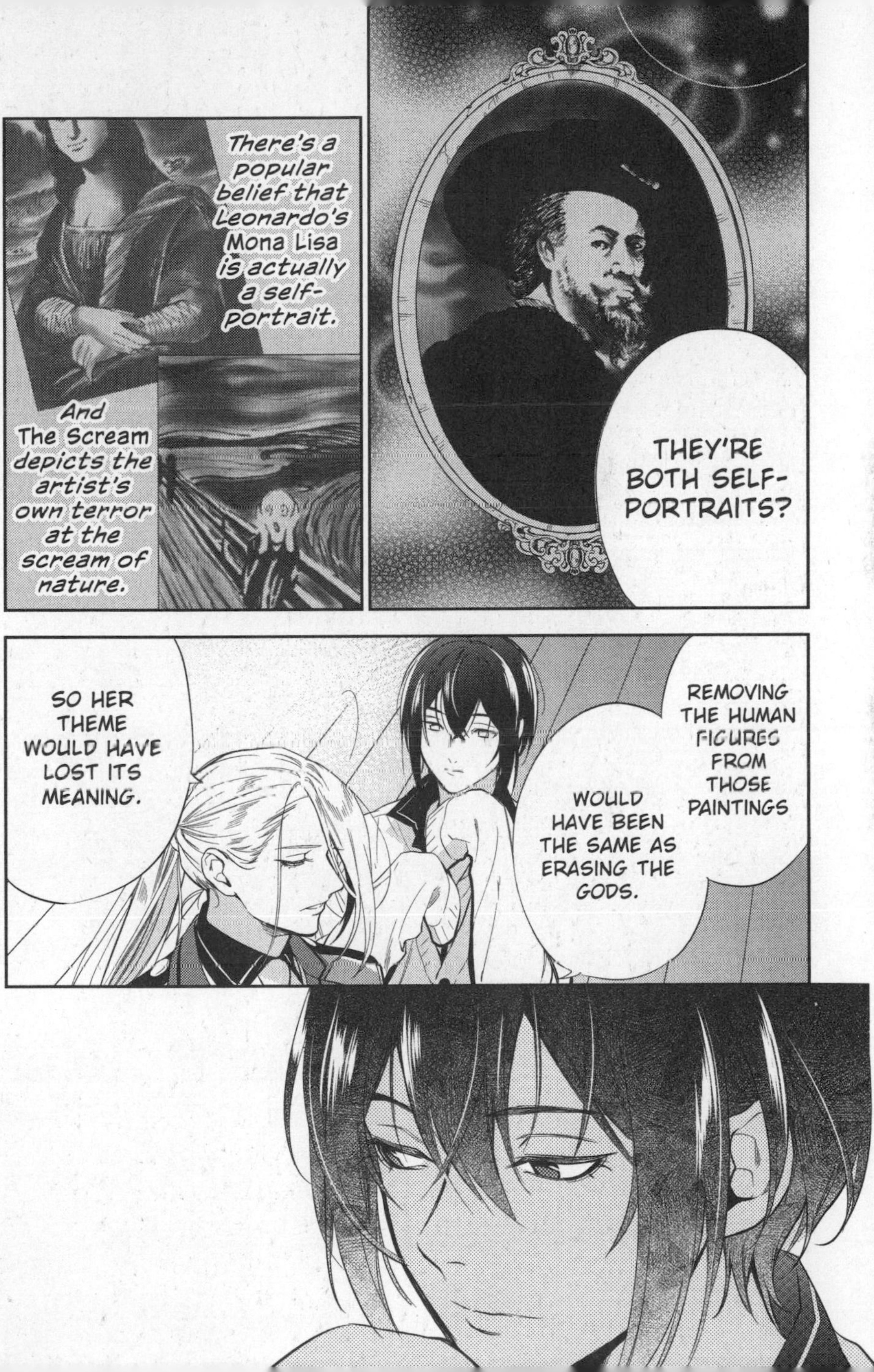
THEY'RE BOTH SELF-PORTRAITS?
There's a popular belief that Leonardo's Mona Lisa is actually a self-portrait.
And The Scream depicts the artist's own terror at the scream of nature.
REMOVING THE HUMAN FIGURES FROM THOSE PAINTINGS
WOULD HAVE BEEN THE SAME AS ERASING THE GODS.
SO HER THEME WOULD HAVE LOST ITS MEANING.

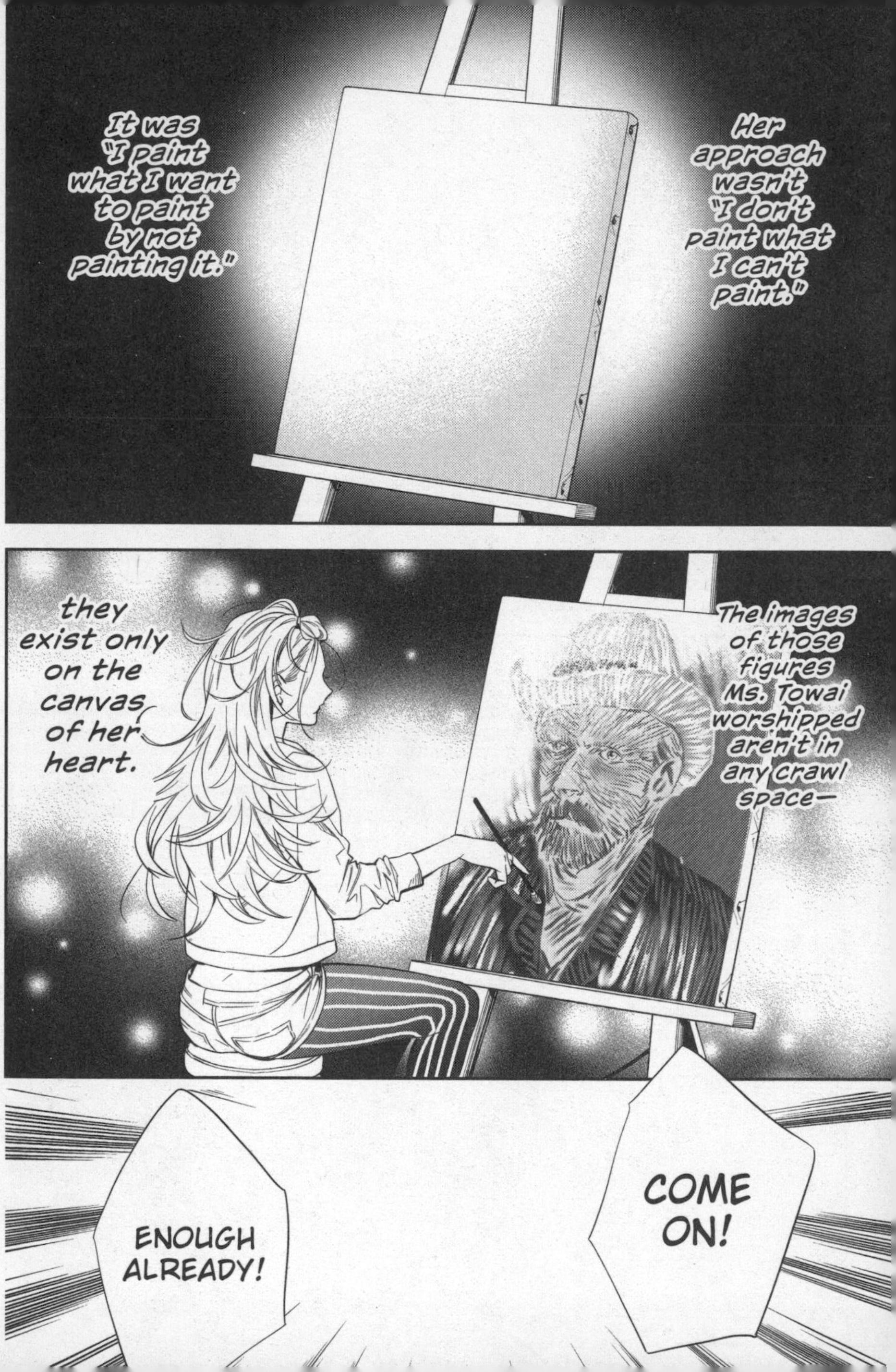
Her approach wasn't "I don't paint what I can't paint."
It was "I paint what I want to paint by not painting it."
The images of those figures Ms. Towai worshipped aren't in any crawl space—
they exist only on the canvas of her heart.
COME ON!
ENOUGH ALREADY!

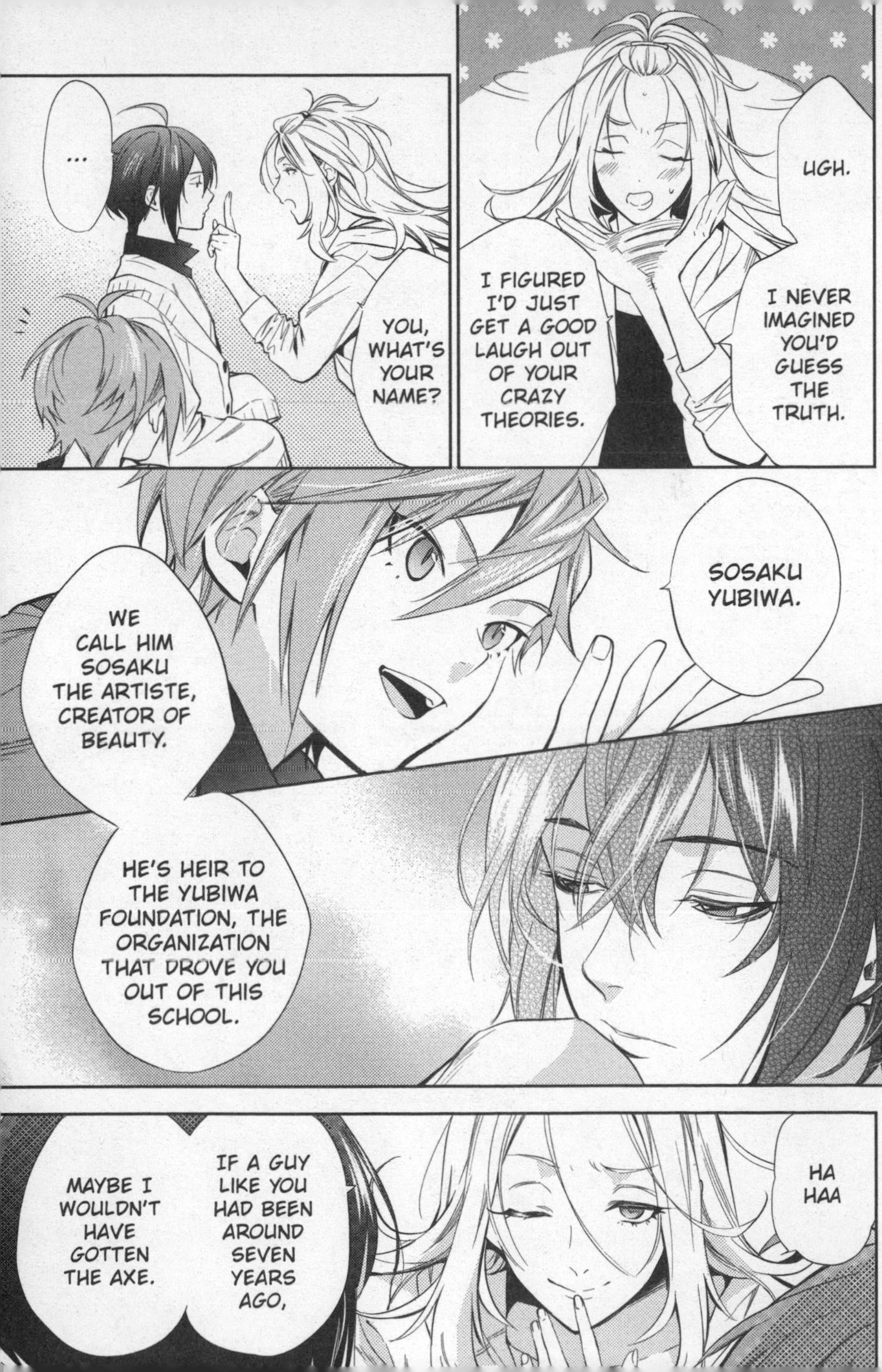
UGH.
I NEVER IMAGINED YOU'D GUESS THE TRUTH.
I FIGURED I'D JUST GET A GOOD LAUGH OUT OF YOUR CRAZY THEORIES.
YOU, WHAT'S YOUR NAME?
...
SOSAKU YUBIWA.
WE CALL HIM SOSAKU THE ARTISTE, CREATOR OF BEAUTY.
HE'S HEIR TO THE YUBIWA FOUNDATION, THE ORGANIZATION THAT DROVE YOU OUT OF THIS SCHOOL.
HA HAA
IF A GUY LIKE YOU HAD BEEN AROUND SEVEN YEARS AGO,
MAYBE I WOULDN'T HAVE GOTTEN THE AXE.

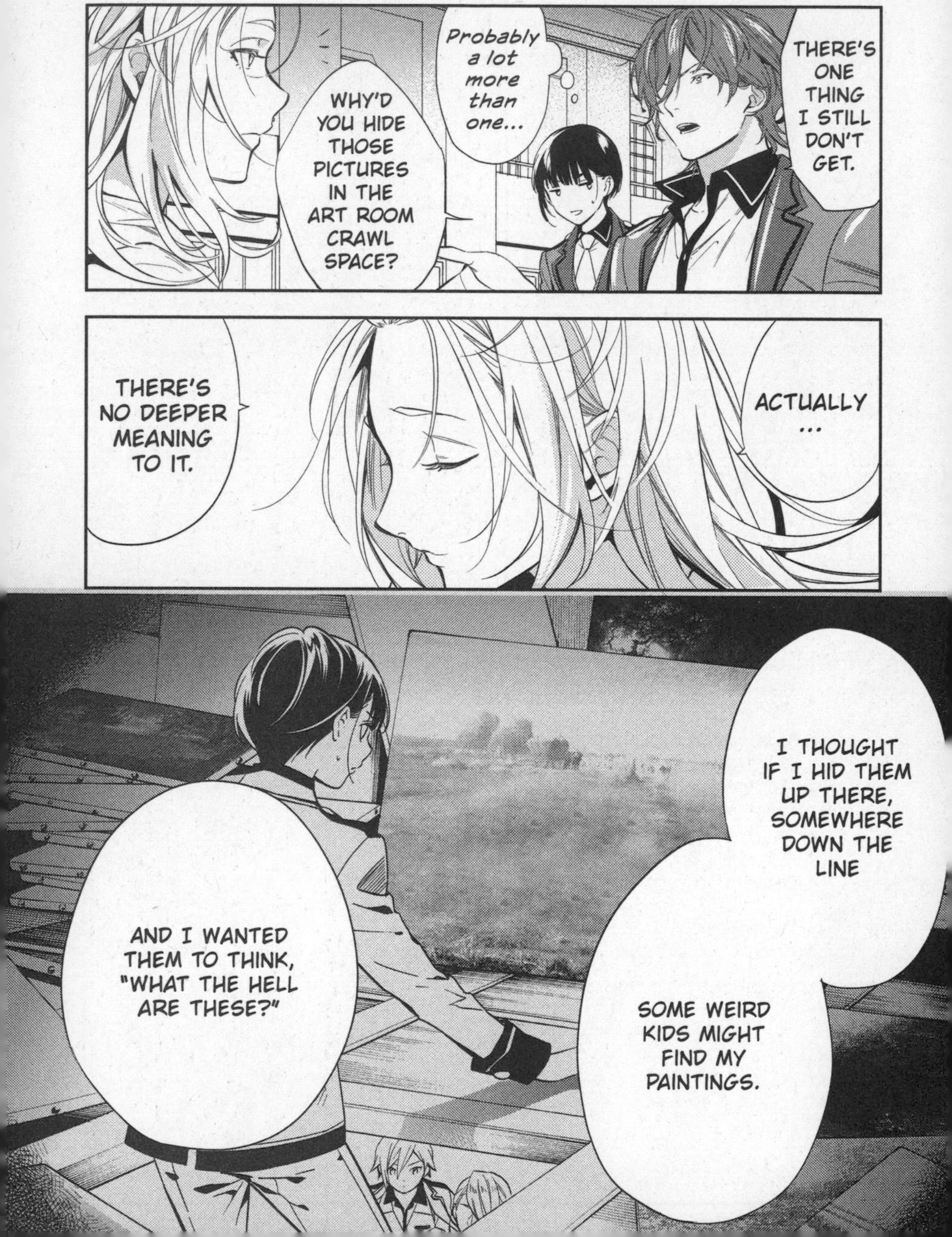
THERE'S ONE THING I STILL DON'T GET.
Probably a lot more than one...
WHY'D YOU HIDE THOSE PICTURES IN THE ART ROOM CRAWL SPACE?
ACTUALLY ...
THERE'S NO DEEPER MEANING TO IT.
I THOUGHT IF I HID THEM UP THERE, SOMEWHERE DOWN THE LINE
SOME WEIRD KIDS MIGHT FIND MY PAINTINGS.
AND I WANTED THEM TO THINK, "WHAT THE HELL ARE THESE?"

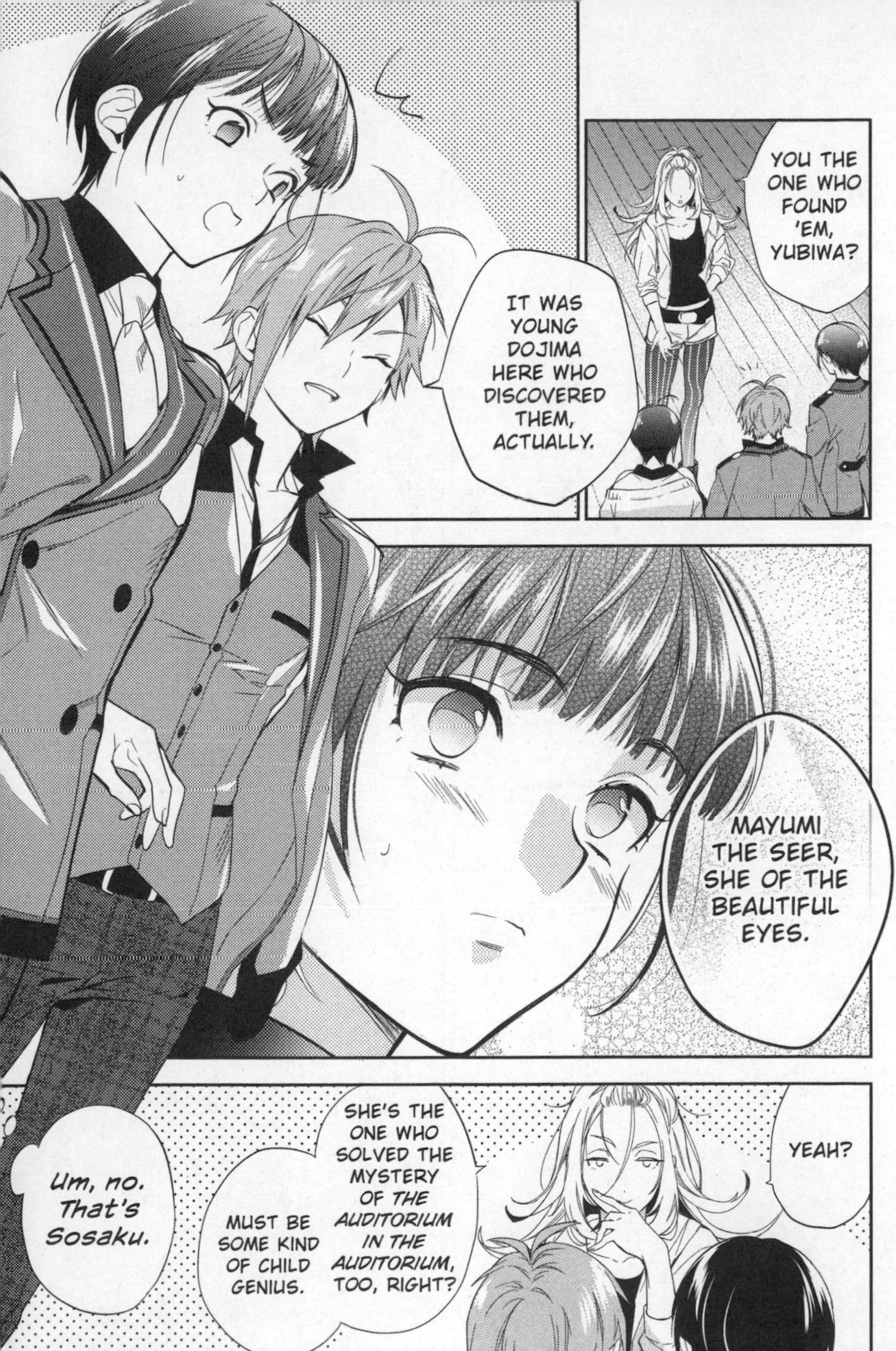
YOU THE ONE WHO FOUND 'EM, YUBIWA?
IT WAS YOUNG DOJIMA HERE WHO DISCOVERED THEM, ACTUALLY.
MAYUMI THE SEER, SHE OF THE BEAUTIFUL EYES.
YEAH?
SHE'S THE ONE WHO SOLVED THE MYSTERY OF *THE AUDITORIUM IN THE AUDITORIUM*, TOO, RIGHT?
MUST BE SOME KIND OF CHILD GENIUS.
Um, no. That's Sosaku.

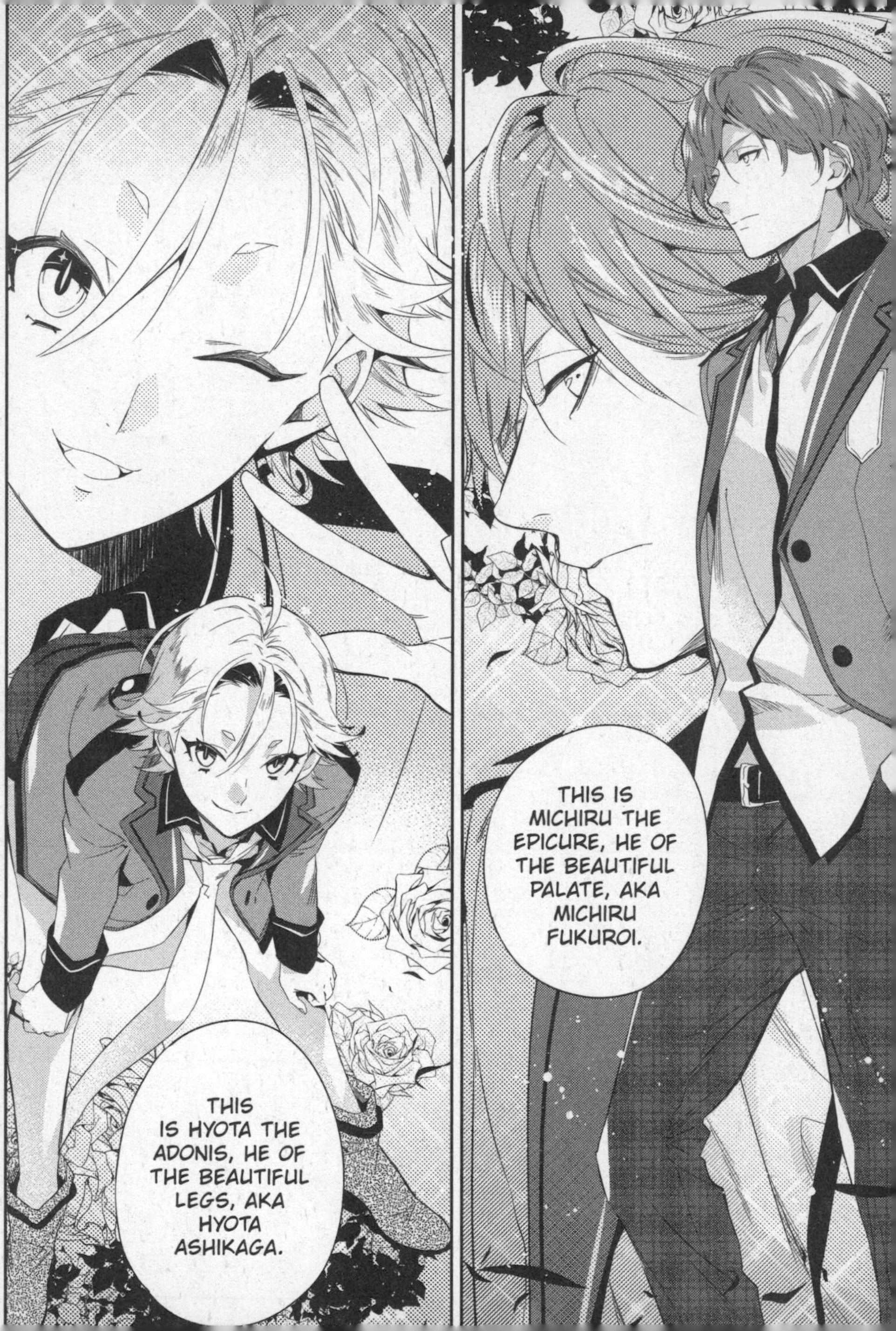
THIS IS MICHIRU THE EPICURE, HE OF THE BEAUTIFUL PALATE, AKA MICHIRU FUKUROI.
THIS IS HYOTA THE ADONIS, HE OF THE BEAUTIFUL LEGS, AKA HYOTA ASHIKAGA.

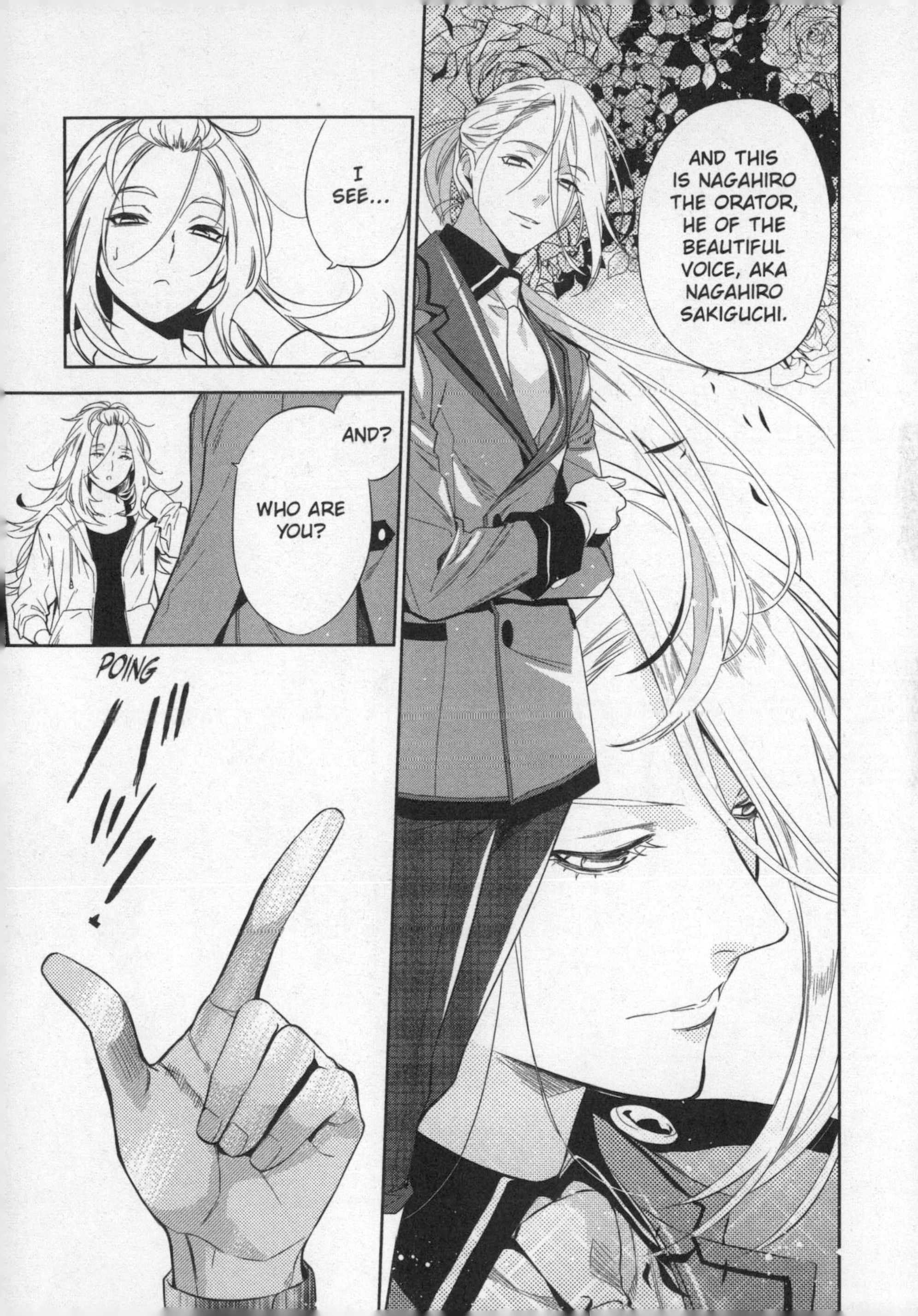
AND THIS IS NAGAHIRO THE ORATOR, HE OF THE BEAUTIFUL VOICE, AKA NAGAHIRO SAKIGUCHI.
I SEE...
AND?
WHO ARE YOU?
POING

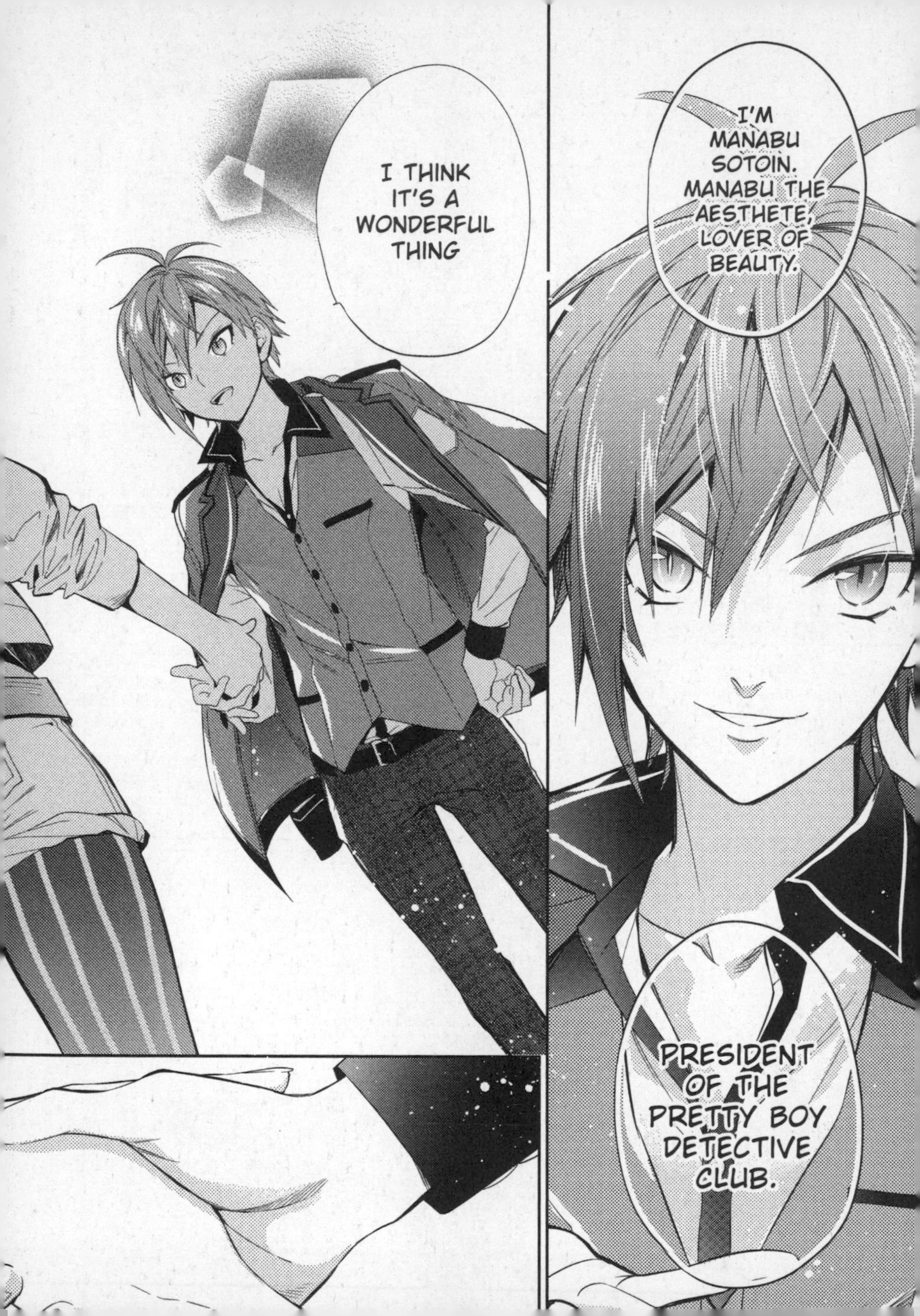
I'M MANABU SOTOIN. MANABU THE AESTHETE, LOVER OF BEAUTY.
PRESIDENT OF THE PRETTY BOY DETECTIVE CLUB.
I THINK IT'S A WONDERFUL THING

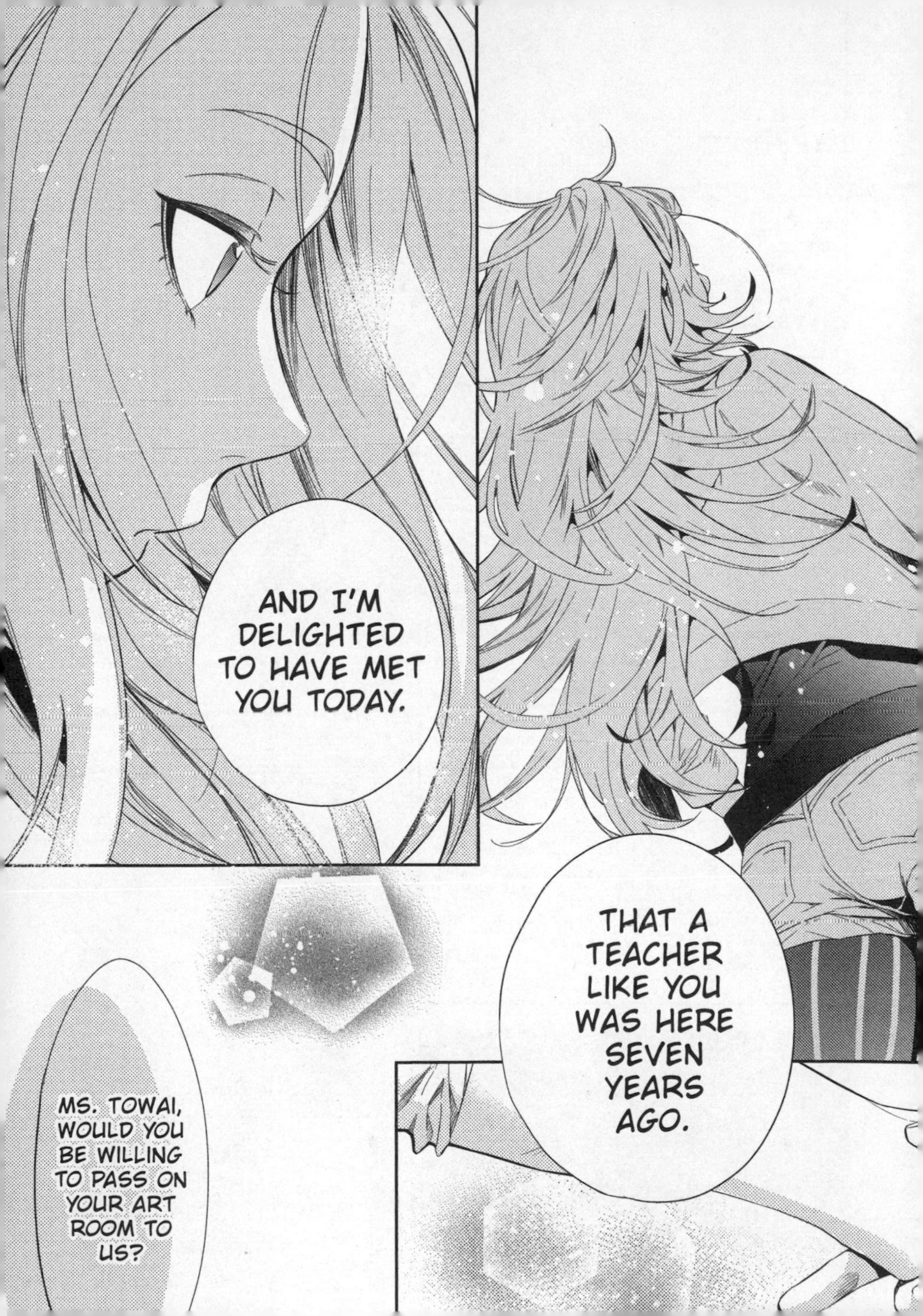
AND I'M DELIGHTED TO HAVE MET YOU TODAY.
THAT A TEACHER LIKE YOU WAS HERE SEVEN YEARS AGO.
MS. TOWAI, WOULD YOU BE WILLING TO PASS ON YOUR ART ROOM TO US?

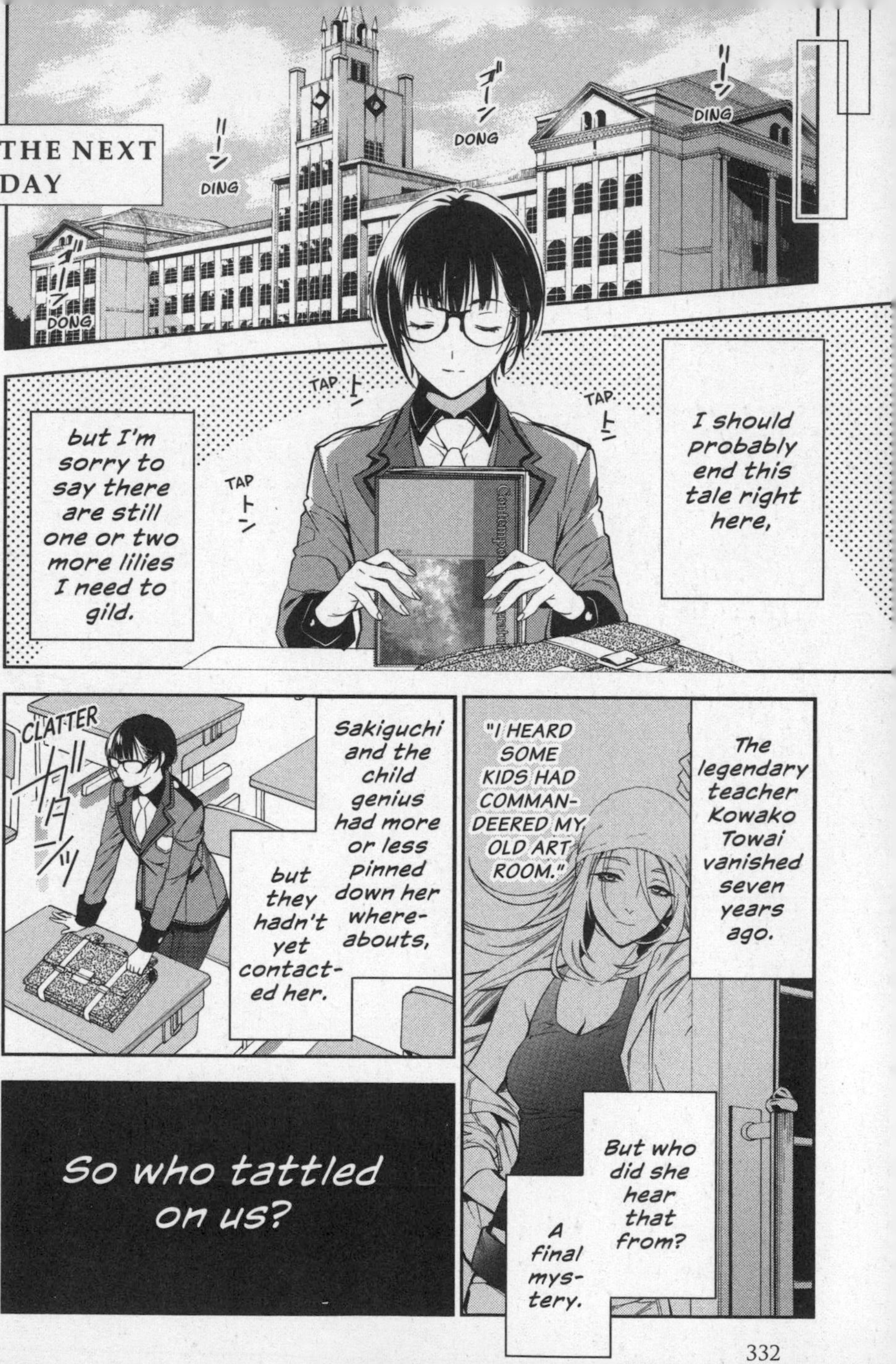
THE NEXT DAY
DING
DONG
DING
DONG
I should probably end this tale right here,
TAP
TAP
TAP
but I'm sorry to say there are still one or two more lilies I need to gild.
The legendary teacher Kowako Towai vanished seven years ago.
"I HEARD SOME KIDS HAD COMMANDEERED MY OLD ART ROOM."
But who did she hear that from?
A final mystery.
Sakiguchi and the child genius had more or less pinned down her whereabouts,
but they hadn't yet contacted her.
CLATTER
So who tattled on us?

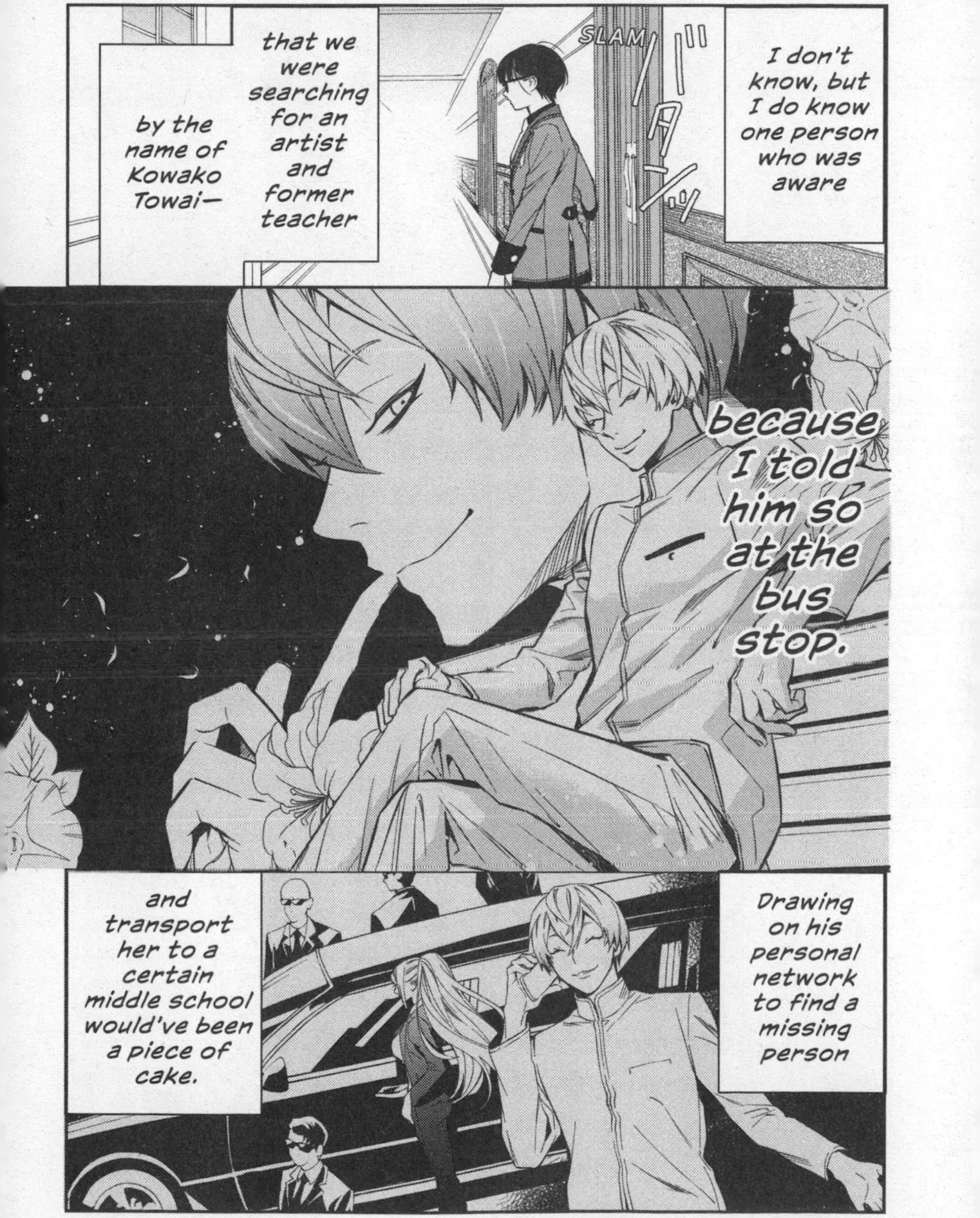
I don't know, but I do know one person who was aware
SLAM
that we were searching for an artist and former teacher
by the name of Kowako Towai—
because I told him so at the bus stop.
Drawing on his personal network to find a missing person
and transport her to a certain middle school would've been a piece of cake.

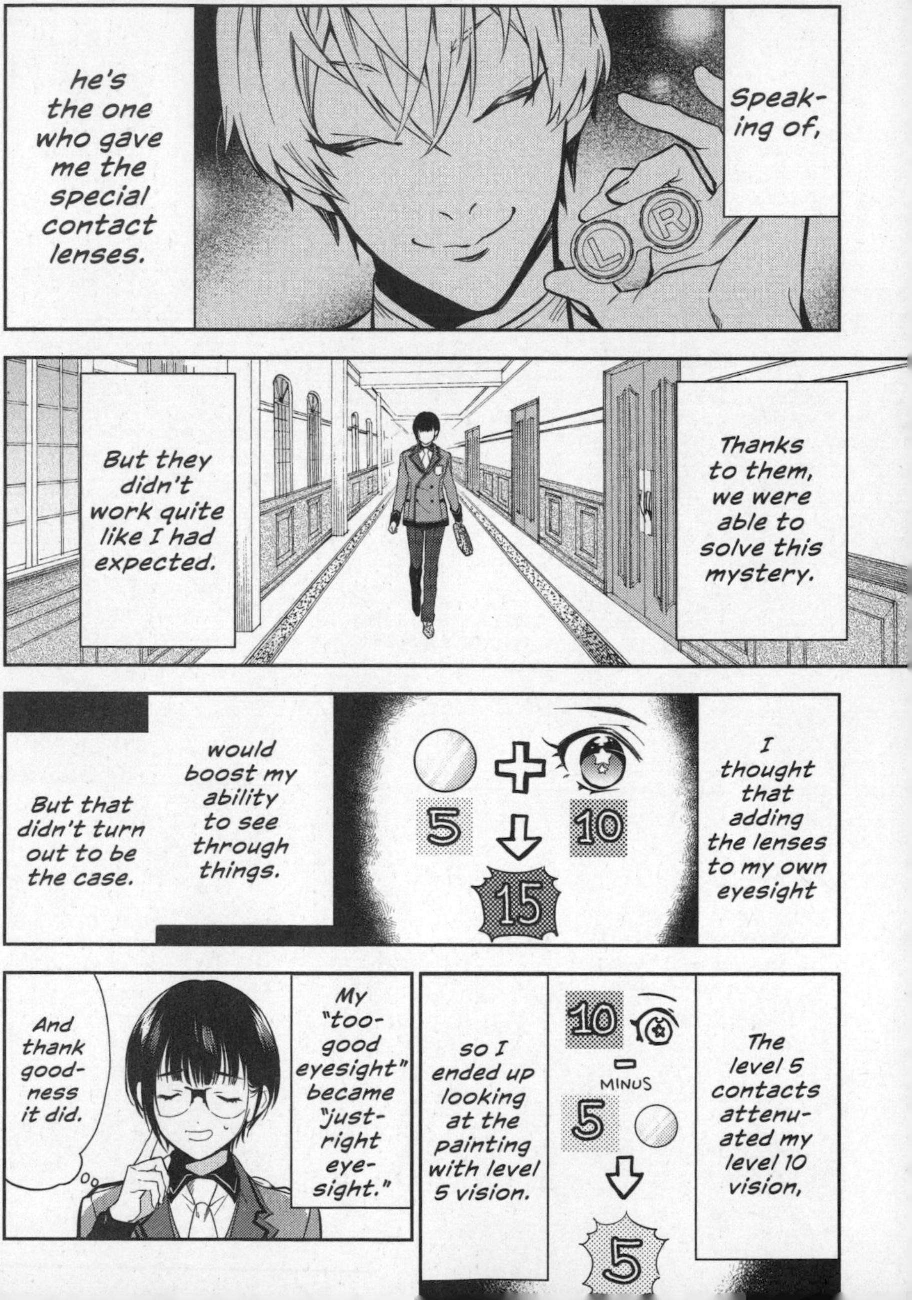
Speaking of,
he's the one who gave me the special contact lenses.
Thanks to them, we were able to solve this mystery.
But they didn't work quite like I had expected.
I thought that adding the lenses to my own eyesight
5
10
15
would boost my ability to see through things.
But that didn't turn out to be the case.
The level 5 contacts attenuated my level 10 vision,
10
MINUS
5
5
so I ended up looking at the painting with level 5 vision.
My "too-good eyesight" became "just-right eyesight."
And thank goodness it did.

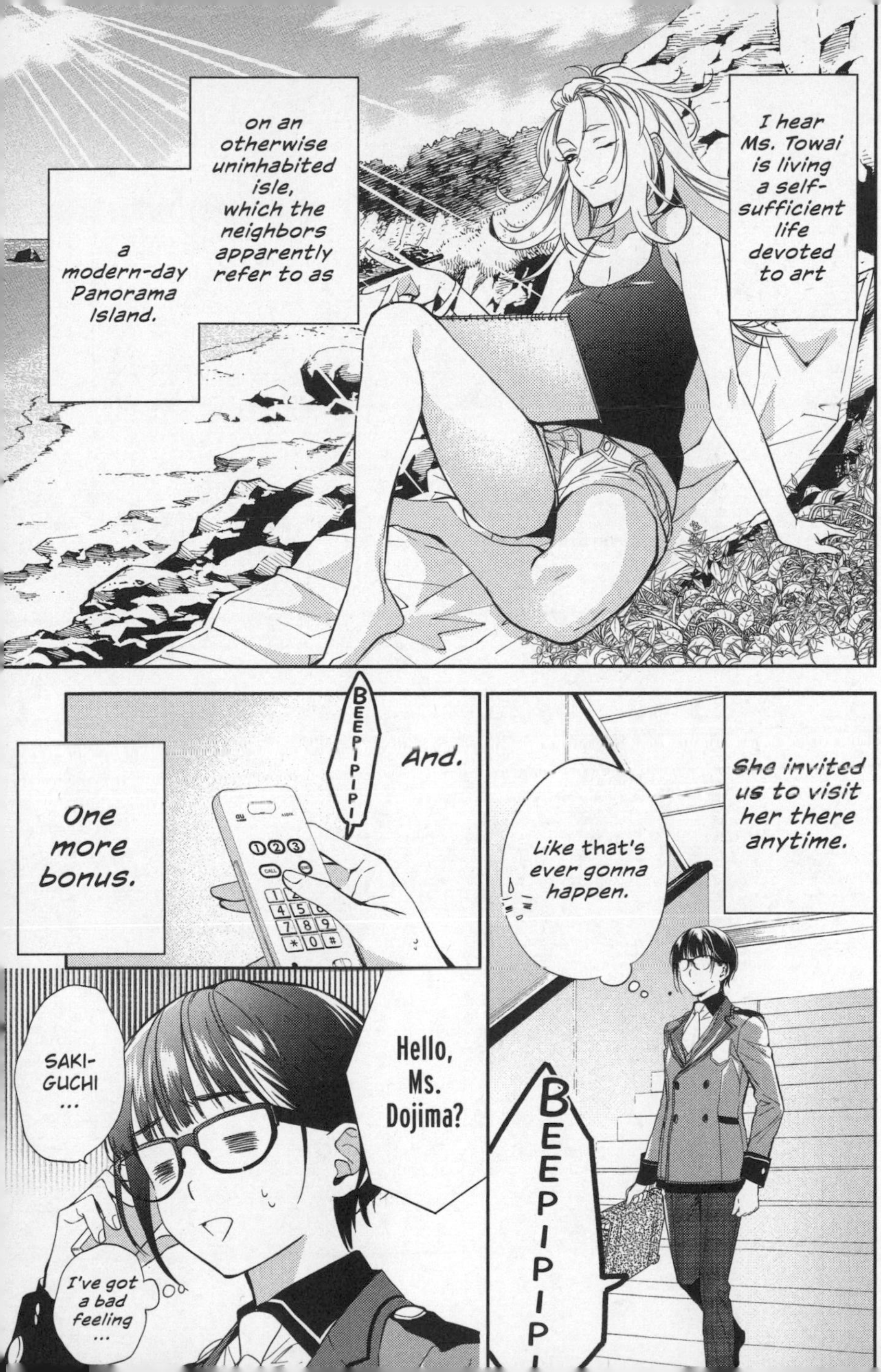
I hear Ms. Towai is living a self-sufficient life devoted to art
on an otherwise uninhabited isle, which the neighbors apparently refer to as
a modern-day Panorama Island.
She invited us to visit her there anytime.
Like that's ever gonna happen.
And.
BEEPIPIPI
One more bonus.
BEEPIPIPI
Hello, Ms. Dojima?
SAKI-GUCHI ...
I've got a bad feeling ...

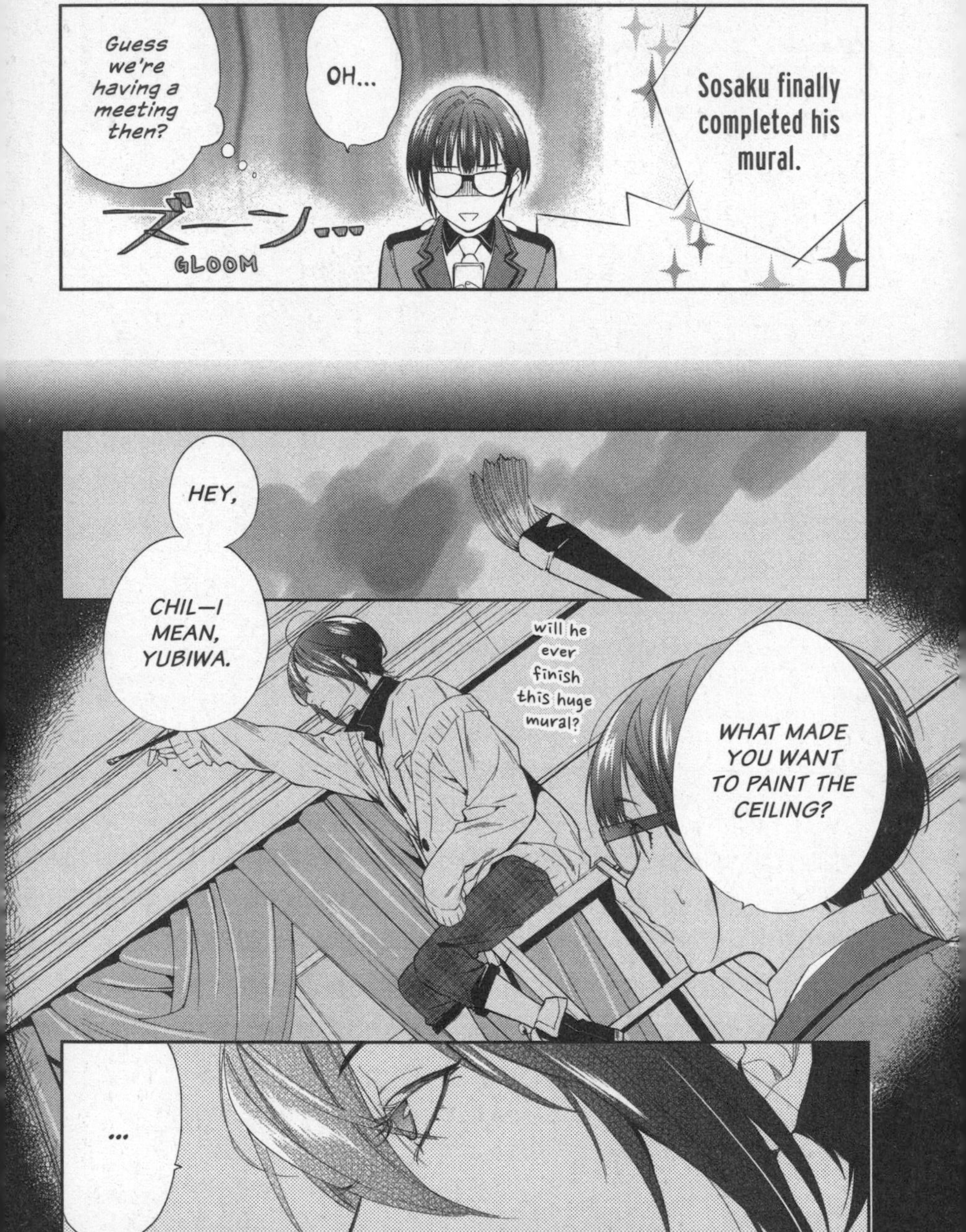
Sosaku finally completed his mural.
OH...
Guess we're having a meeting then?
ズーン...
GLOOM
HEY,
CHIL—I MEAN, YUBIWA.
WHAT MADE YOU WANT TO PAINT THE CEILING?
will he ever finish this huge mural?
...

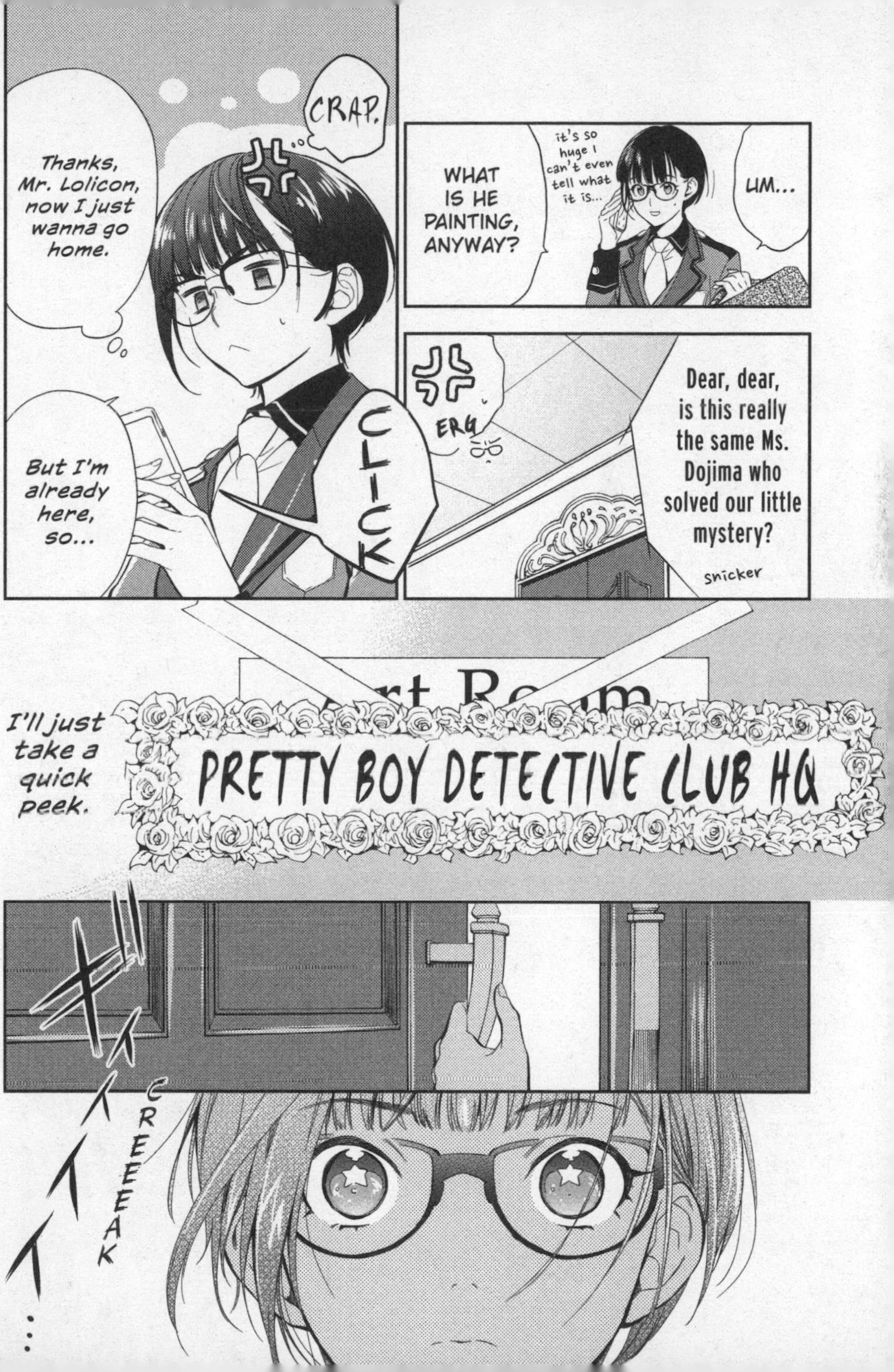
UM...
it's so huge I can't even tell what it is...
WHAT IS HE PAINTING, ANYWAY?
Dear, dear, is this really the same Ms. Dojima who solved our little mystery?
snicker
ERG
CRAP.
Thanks, Mr. Lolicon, now I just wanna go home.
CLICK
But I'm already here, so...
PRETTY BOY DETECTIVE CLUB HQ
I'll just take a quick peek.
CREEEEAK
...

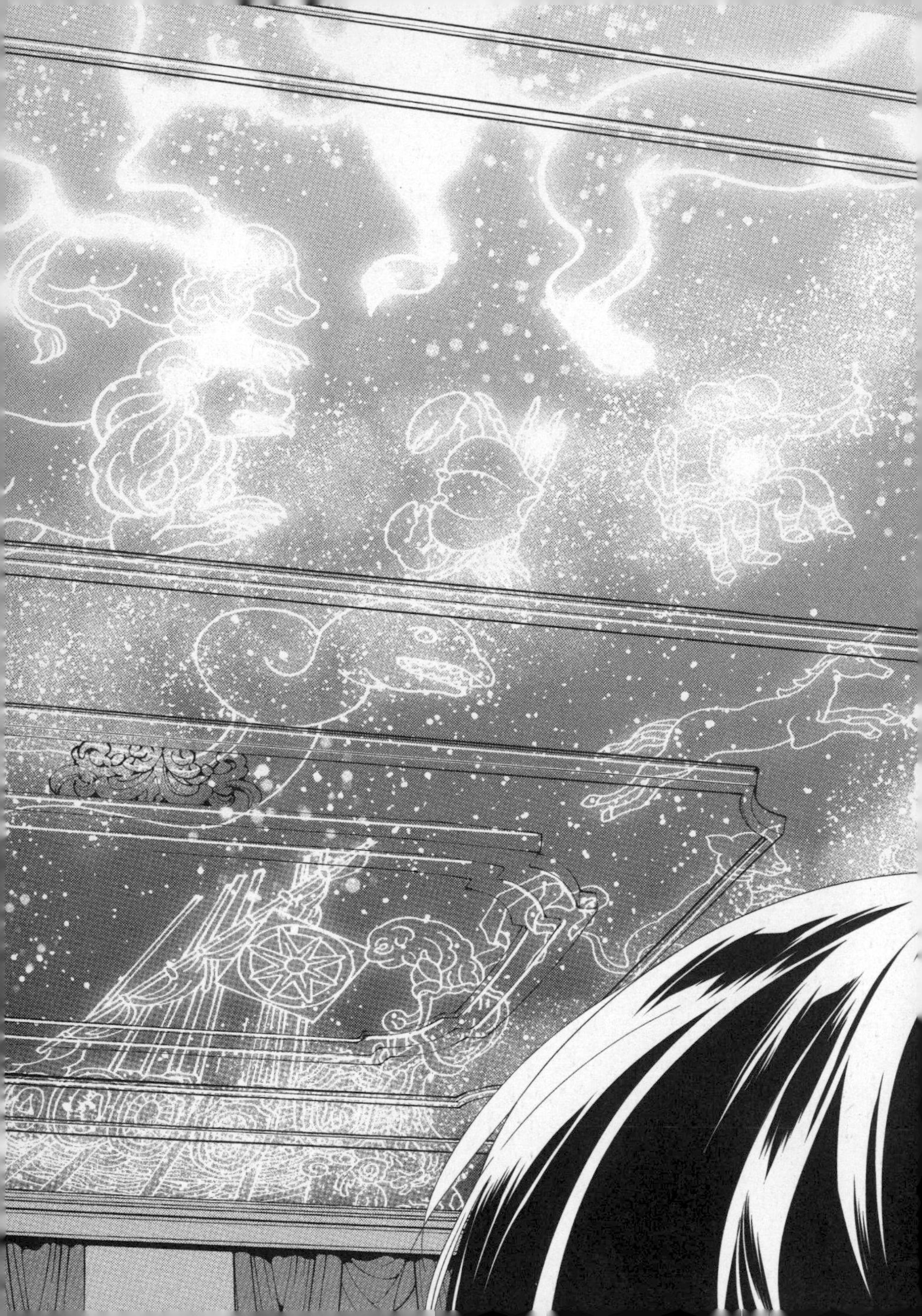

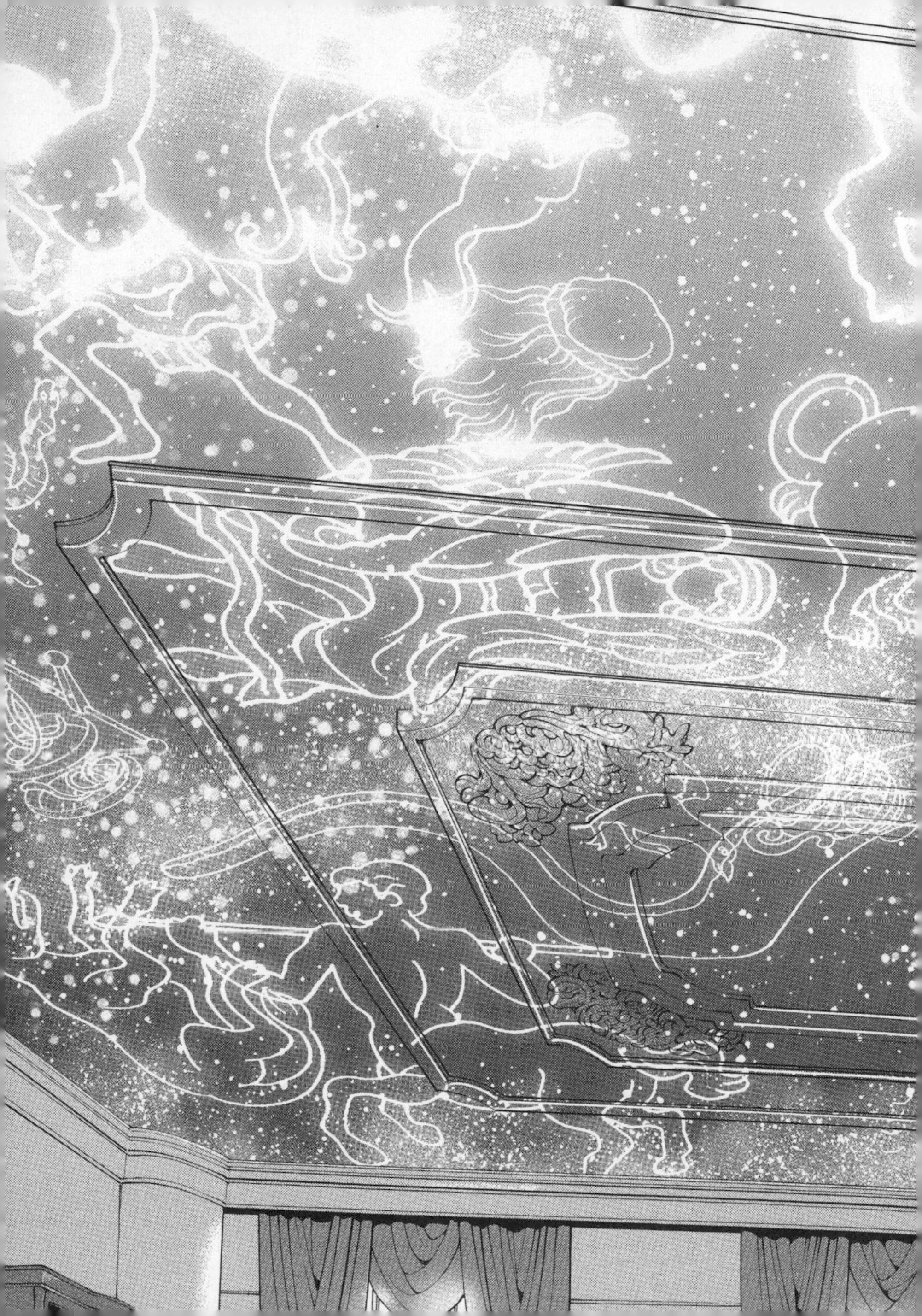

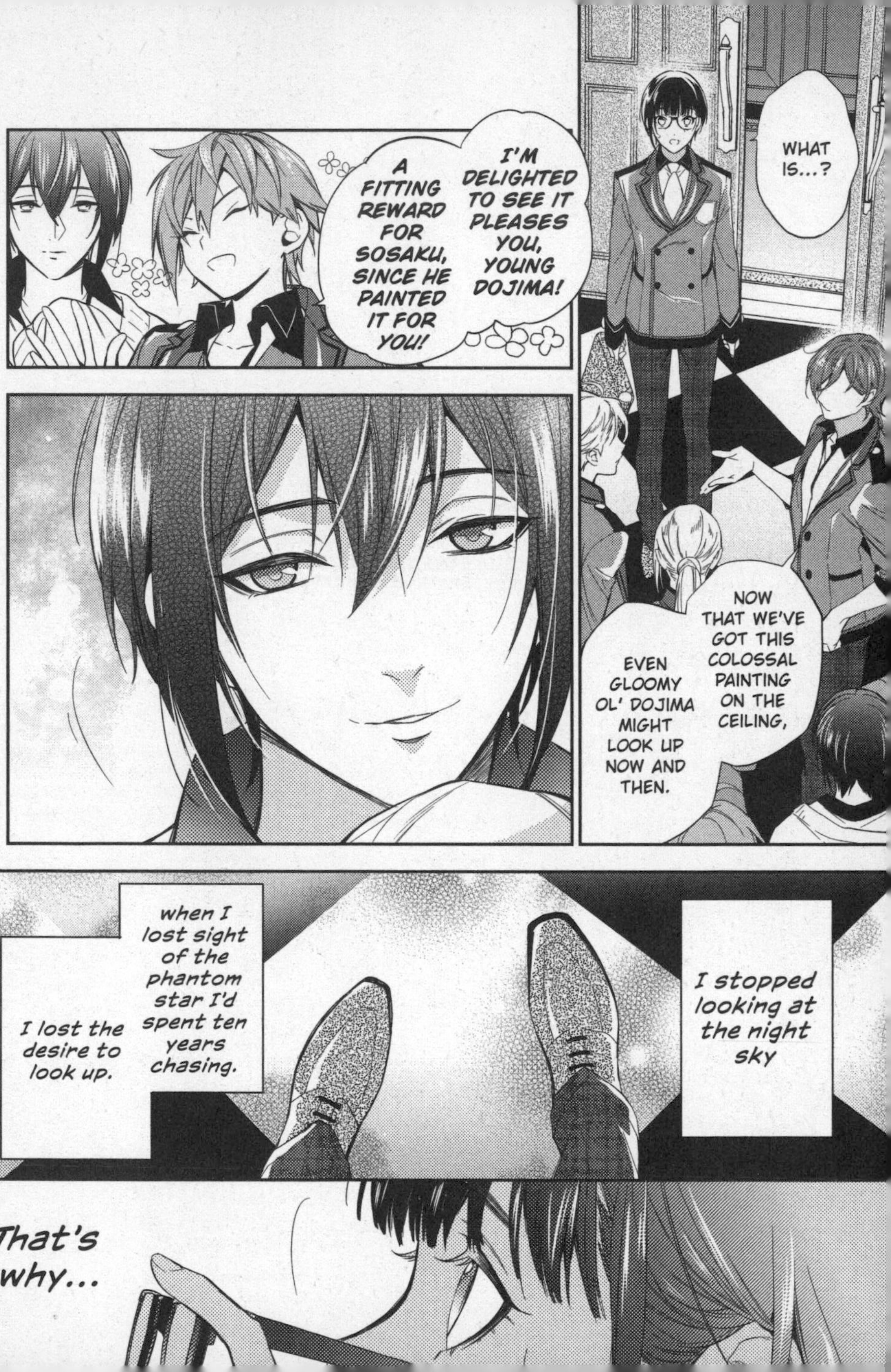
WHAT IS...?
NOW THAT WE'VE GOT THIS COLOSSAL PAINTING ON THE CEILING,
EVEN GLOOMY OL' DOJIMA MIGHT LOOK UP NOW AND THEN.
I'M DELIGHTED TO SEE IT PLEASES YOU, YOUNG DOJIMA!
A FITTING REWARD FOR SOSAKU, SINCE HE PAINTED IT FOR YOU!
I stopped looking at the night sky
when I lost sight of the phantom star I'd spent ten years chasing.
I lost the desire to look up.
That's why...

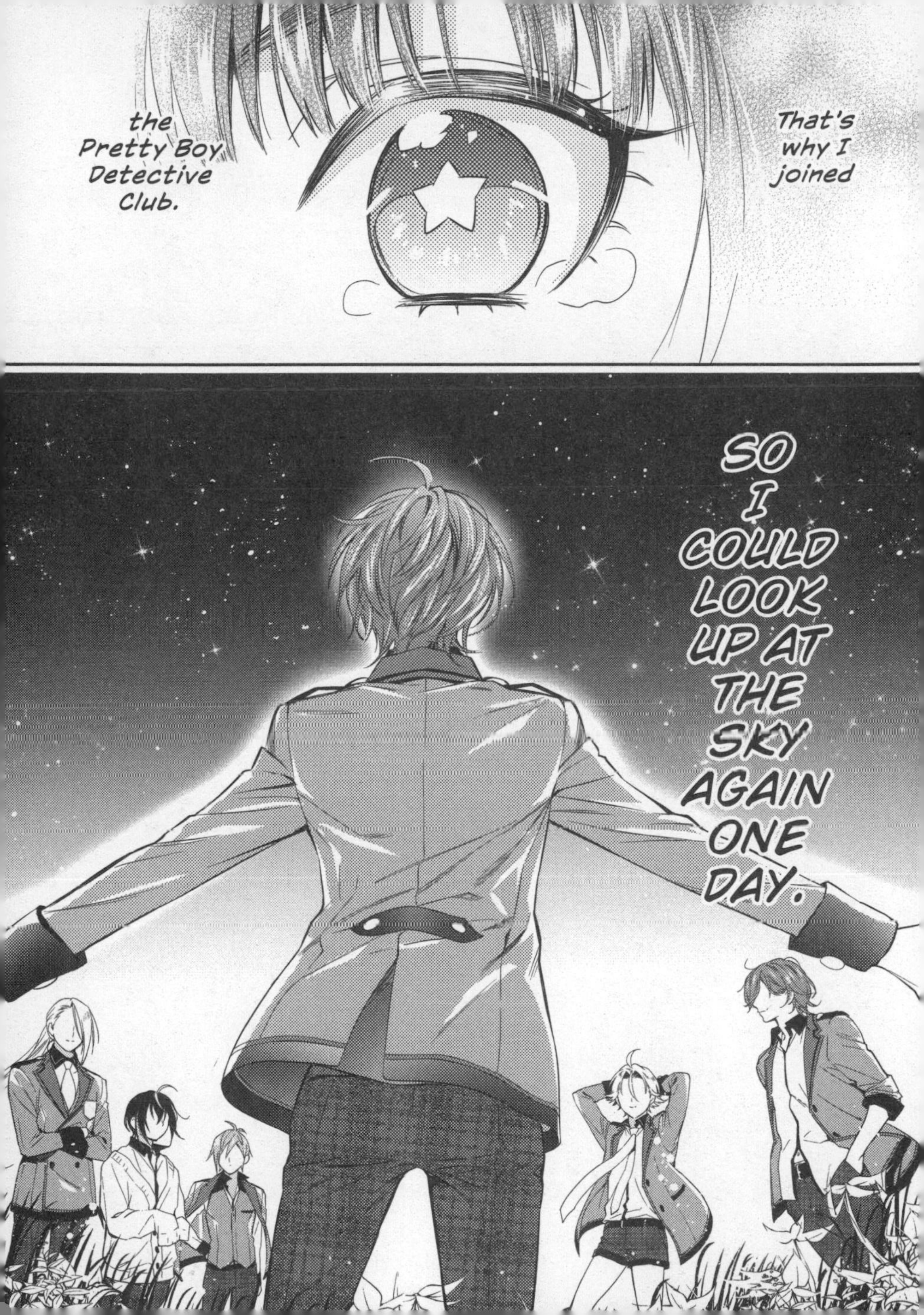
That's why I joined
the Pretty Boy Detective Club.
SO I COULD LOOK UP AT THE SKY AGAIN ONE DAY.

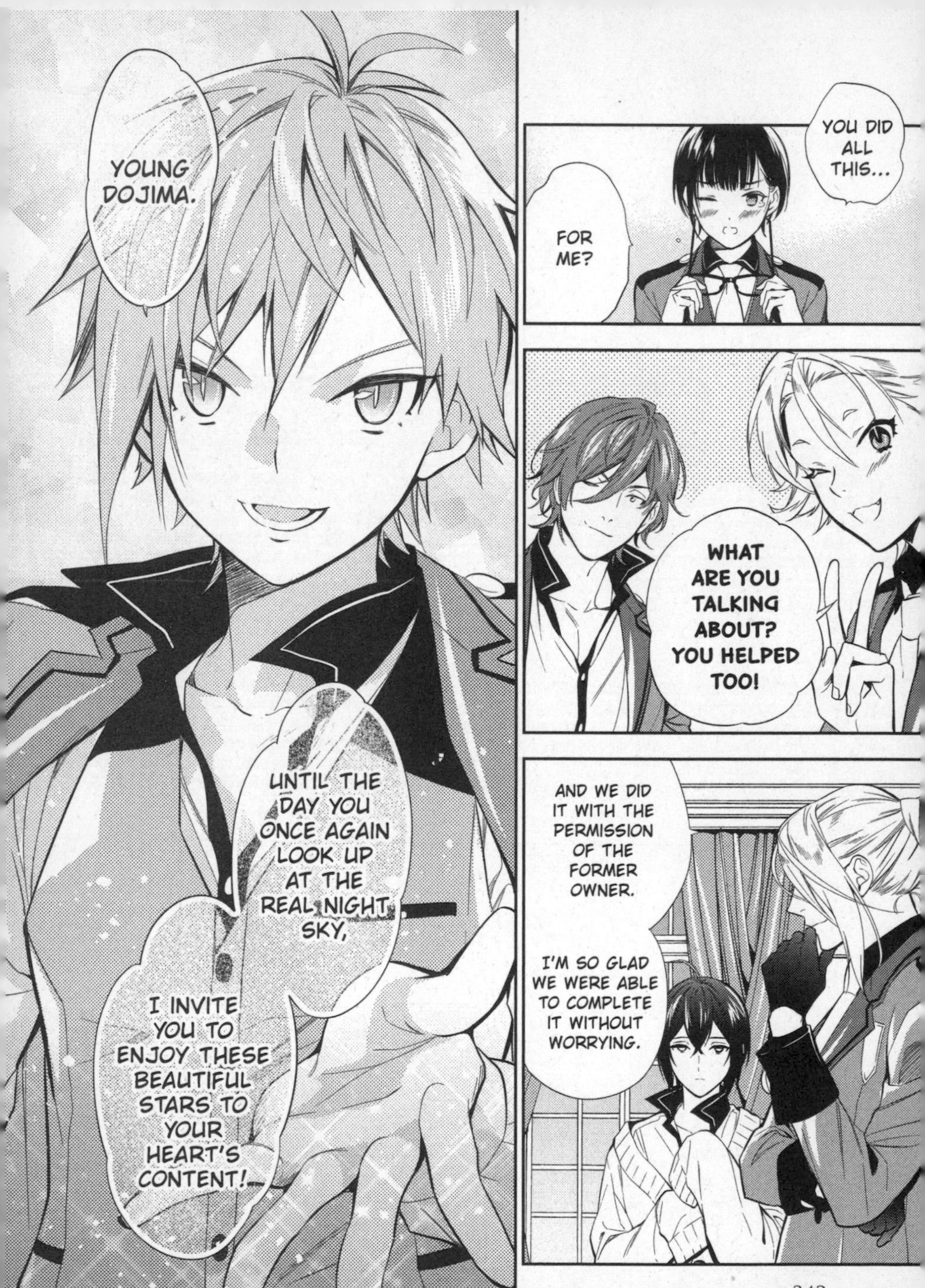
YOU DID ALL THIS...
FOR ME?
WHAT ARE YOU TALKING ABOUT? YOU HELPED TOO!
AND WE DID IT WITH THE PERMISSION OF THE FORMER OWNER.
I'M SO GLAD WE WERE ABLE TO COMPLETE IT WITHOUT WORRYING.
YOUNG DOJIMA.
UNTIL THE DAY YOU ONCE AGAIN LOOK UP AT THE REAL NIGHT SKY,
I INVITE YOU TO ENJOY THESE BEAUTIFUL STARS TO YOUR HEART'S CONTENT!

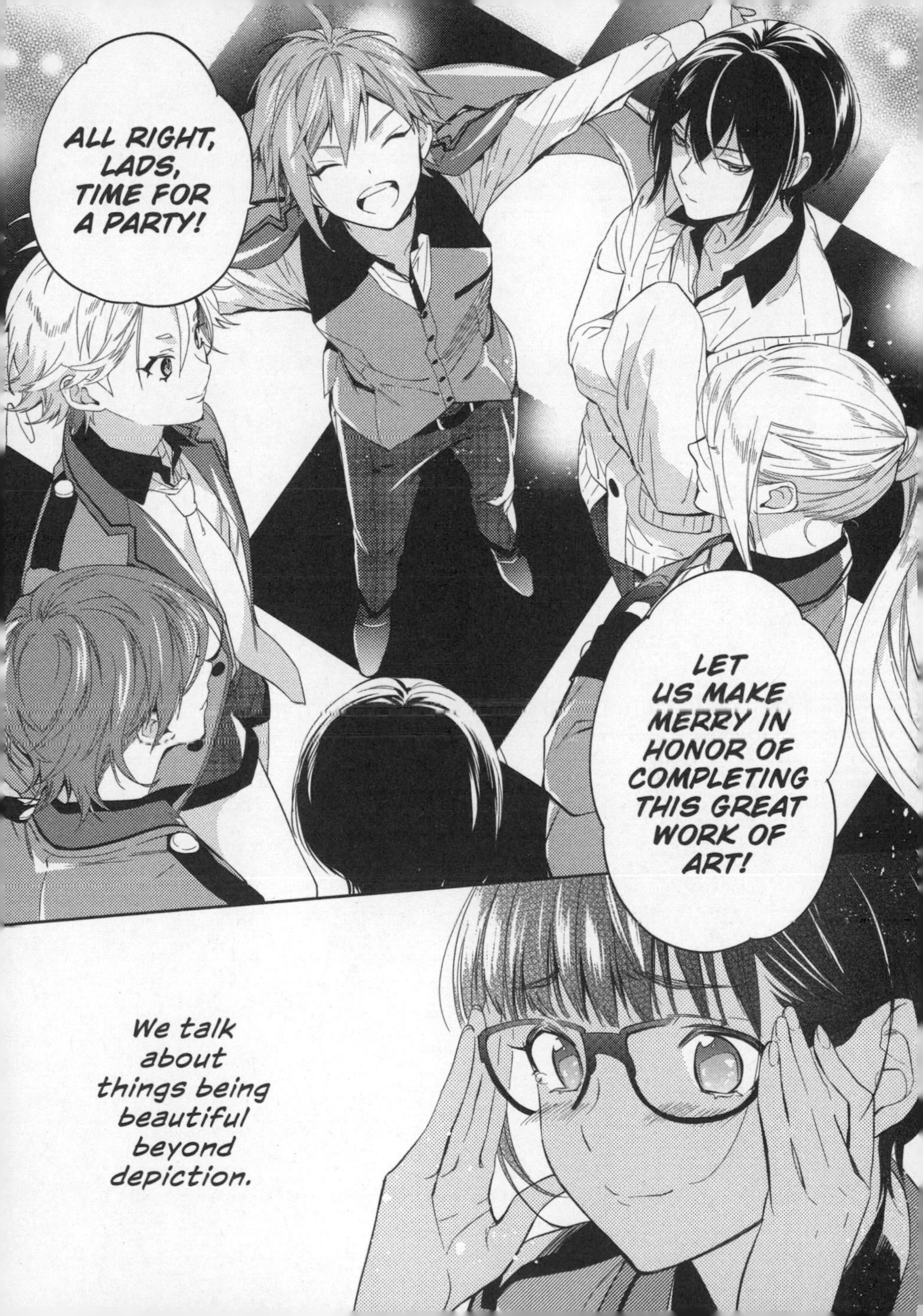
ALL RIGHT, LADS, TIME FOR A PARTY!
LET US MAKE MERRY IN HONOR OF COMPLETING THIS GREAT WORK OF ART!
We talk about things being beautiful beyond depiction.

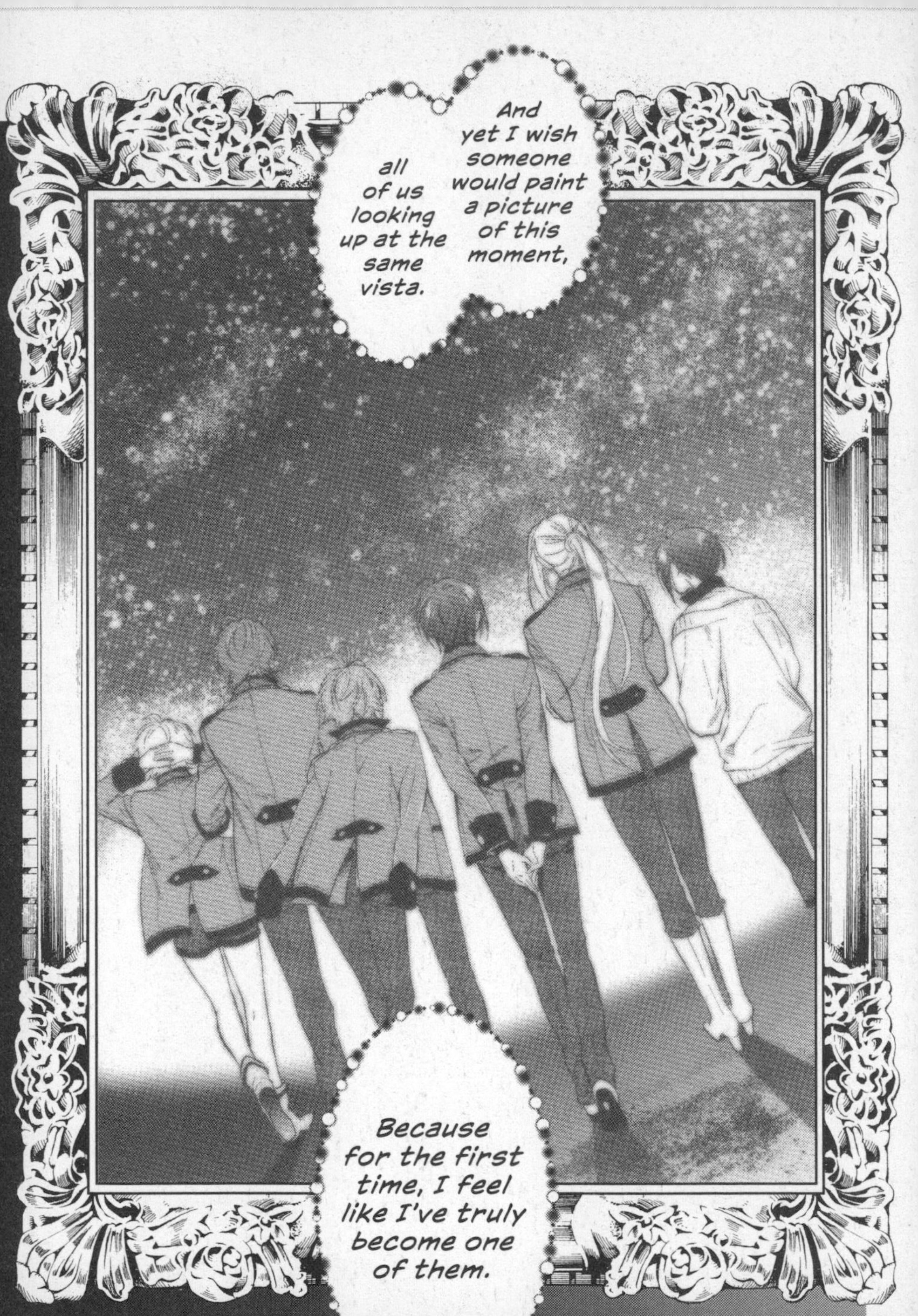
And yet I wish someone would paint a picture of this moment,
all of us looking up at the same vista.
Because for the first time, I feel like I've truly become one of them.

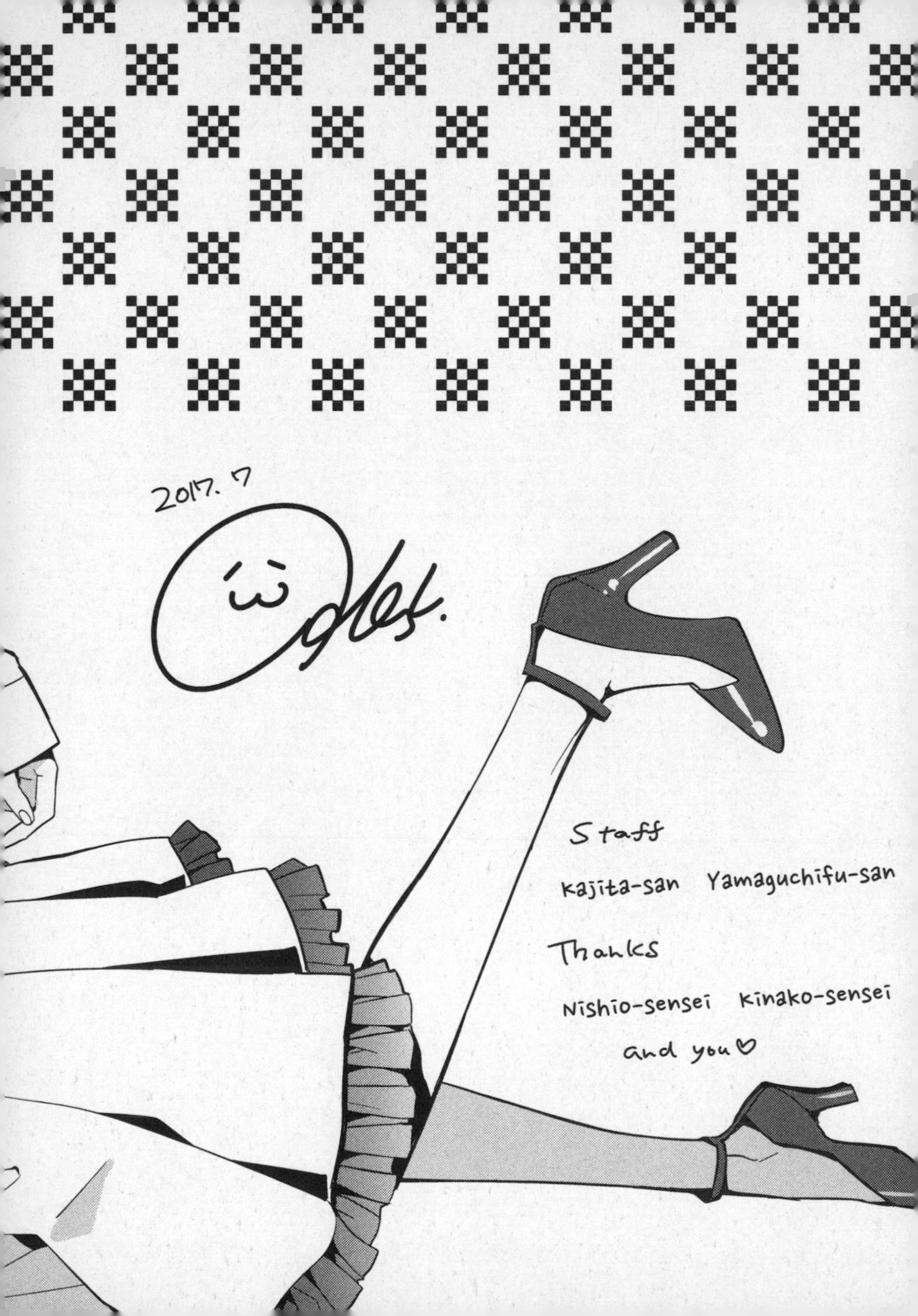
2017. 7
Staff
Kajita-san Yamaguchifu-san
Thanks
Nishio-sensei Kinako-sensei
and you♡

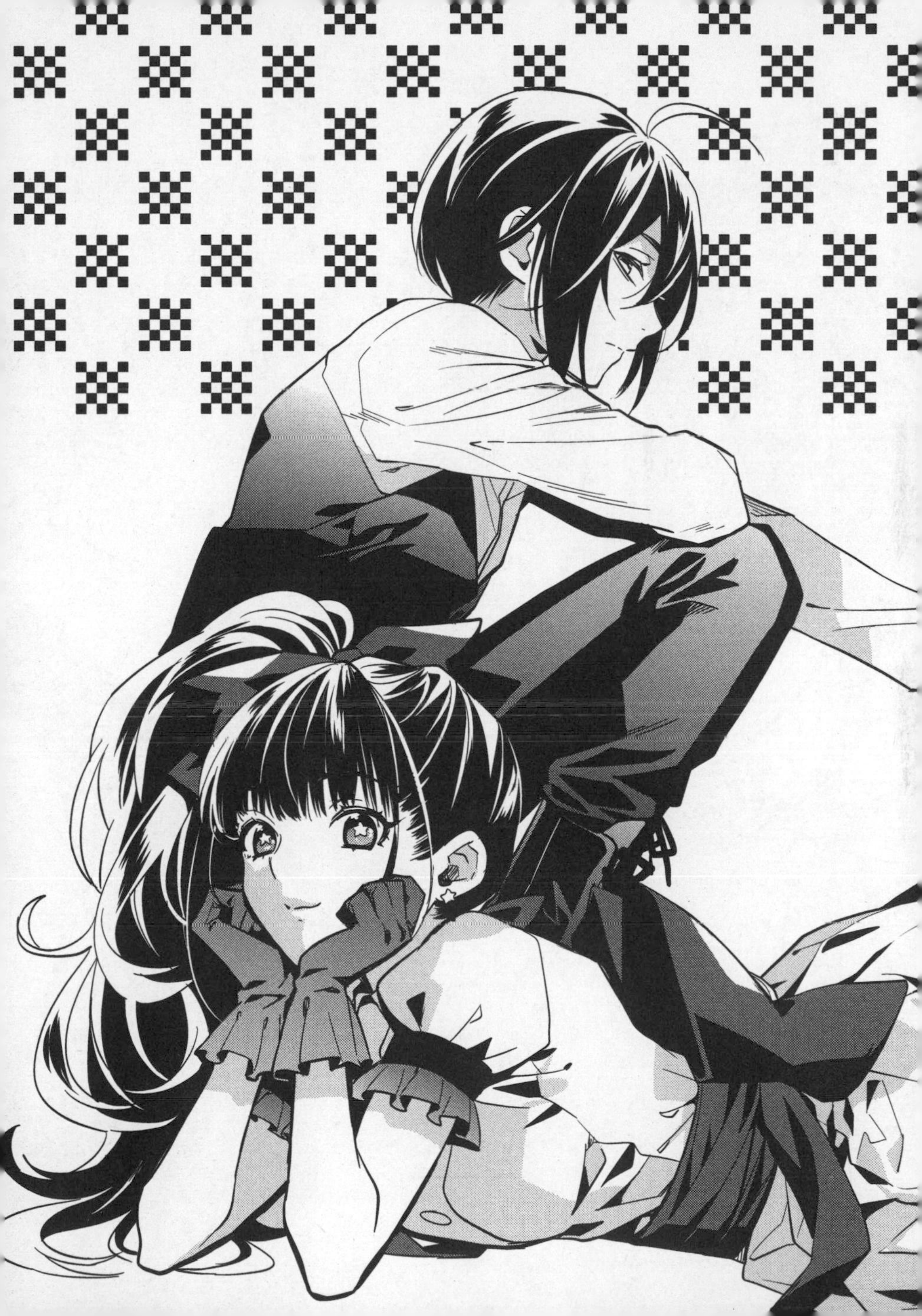

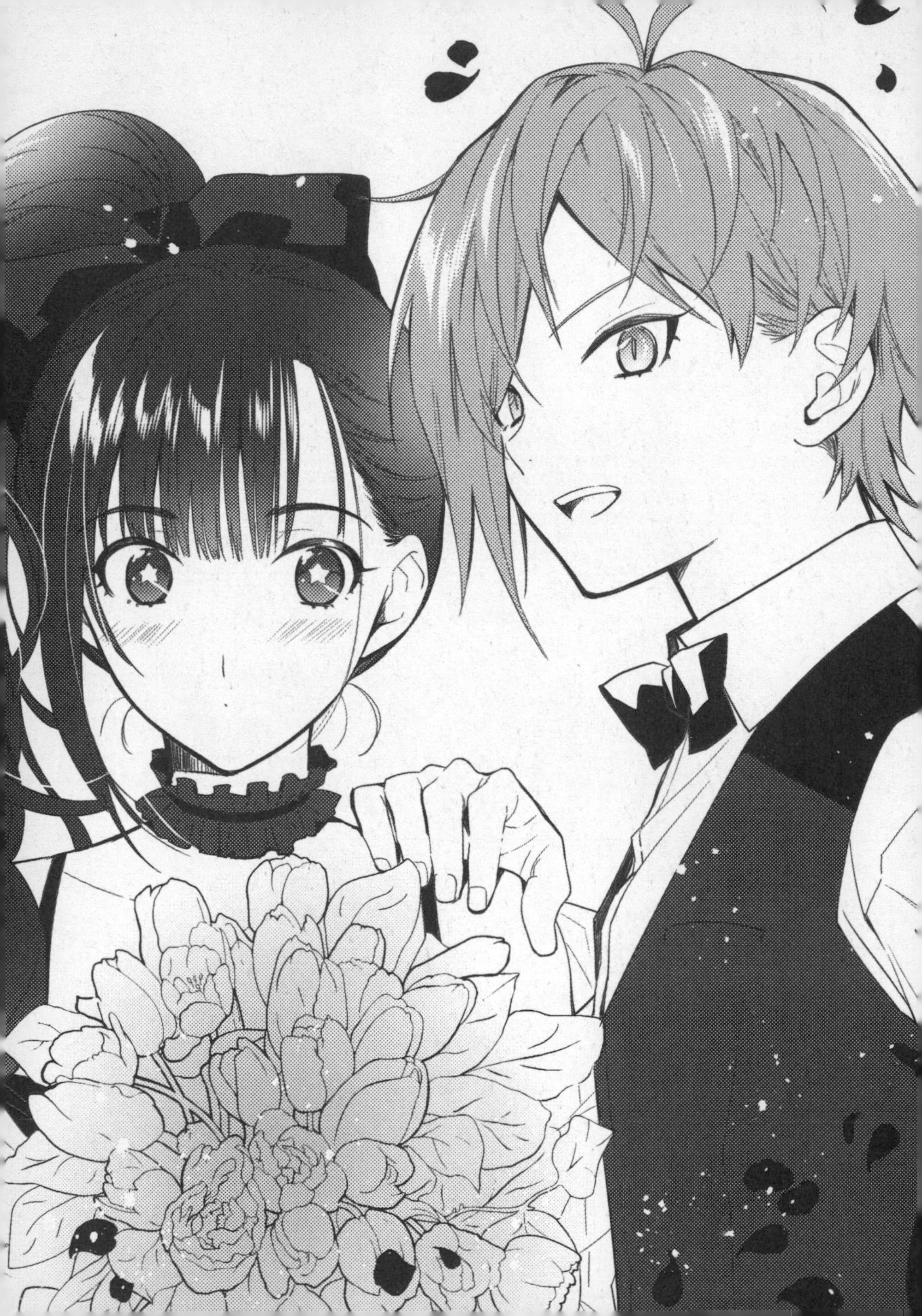

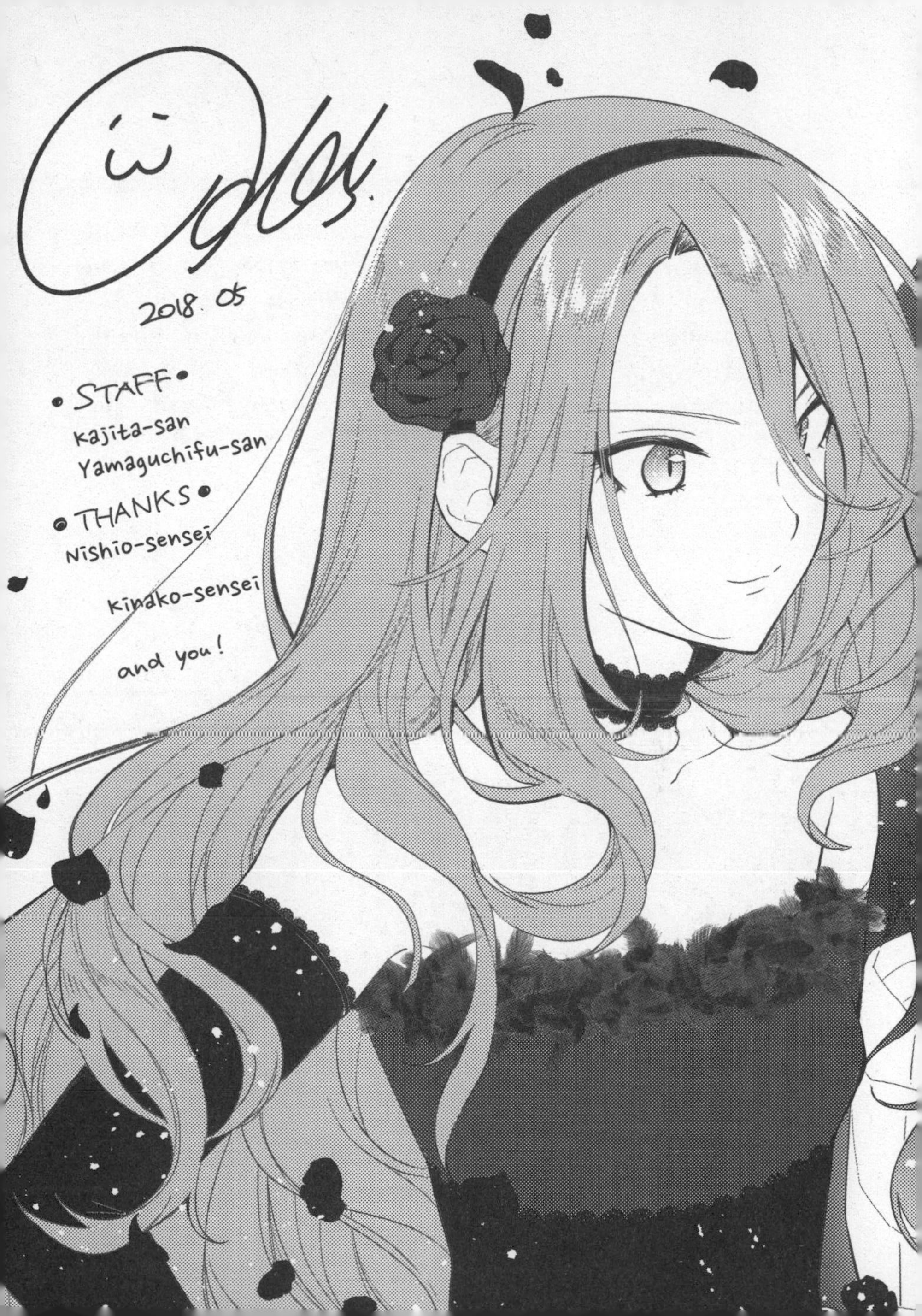
2018.05
• STAFF •
kajita-san
Yamaguchifu-san
• THANKS •
Nishio-sensei
kinako-sensei
and you!

JOIN THE CLUB

Ten years ago, Mayumi Dojima saw a star...and she's been searching for it ever since. The mysterious organization that solves (and causes?) all the problems at Yubiwa Academy—the *Pretty Boy Detective Club* is on the case! Five beautiful youths, each more eccentric than the last, united only by their devotion to the aesthetics of mystery-solving. Together they find much, much more than they bargained for.

★

Read the original novels!

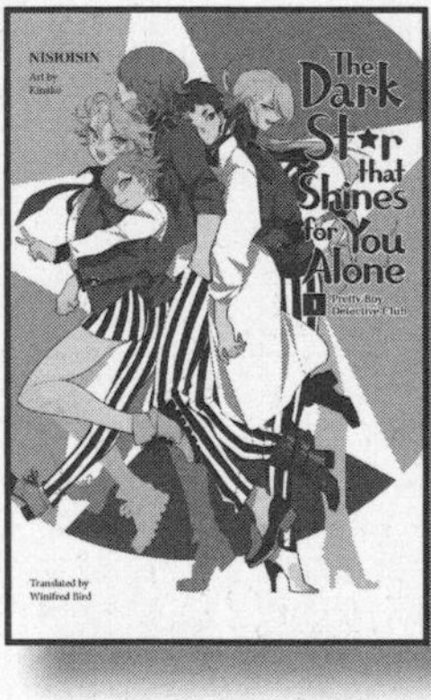
NISIOISIN
The Dark Star that Shines for You Alone
1

The Dark Star that Shines for You Alone

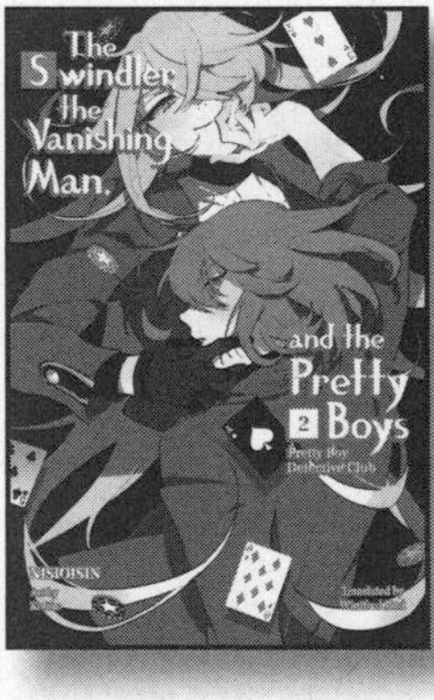
The Swindler, the Vanishing Man, and the Pretty Boys
2

The Swindler, the Vanishing Man, and the Pretty Boys

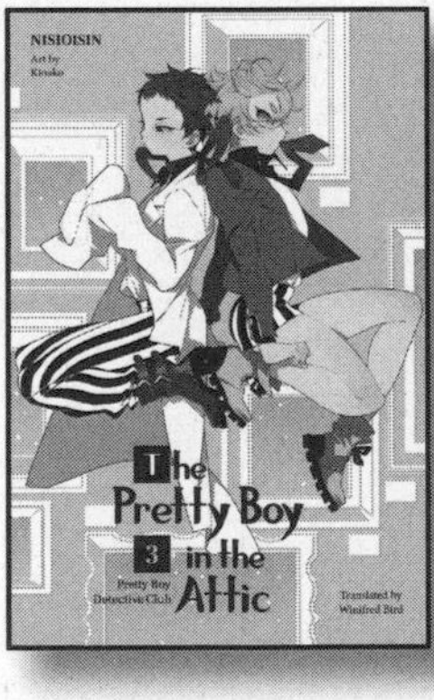
NISIOISIN
The Pretty Boy in the Attic
3

The Pretty Boy in the Attic

AVAILABLE NOW!

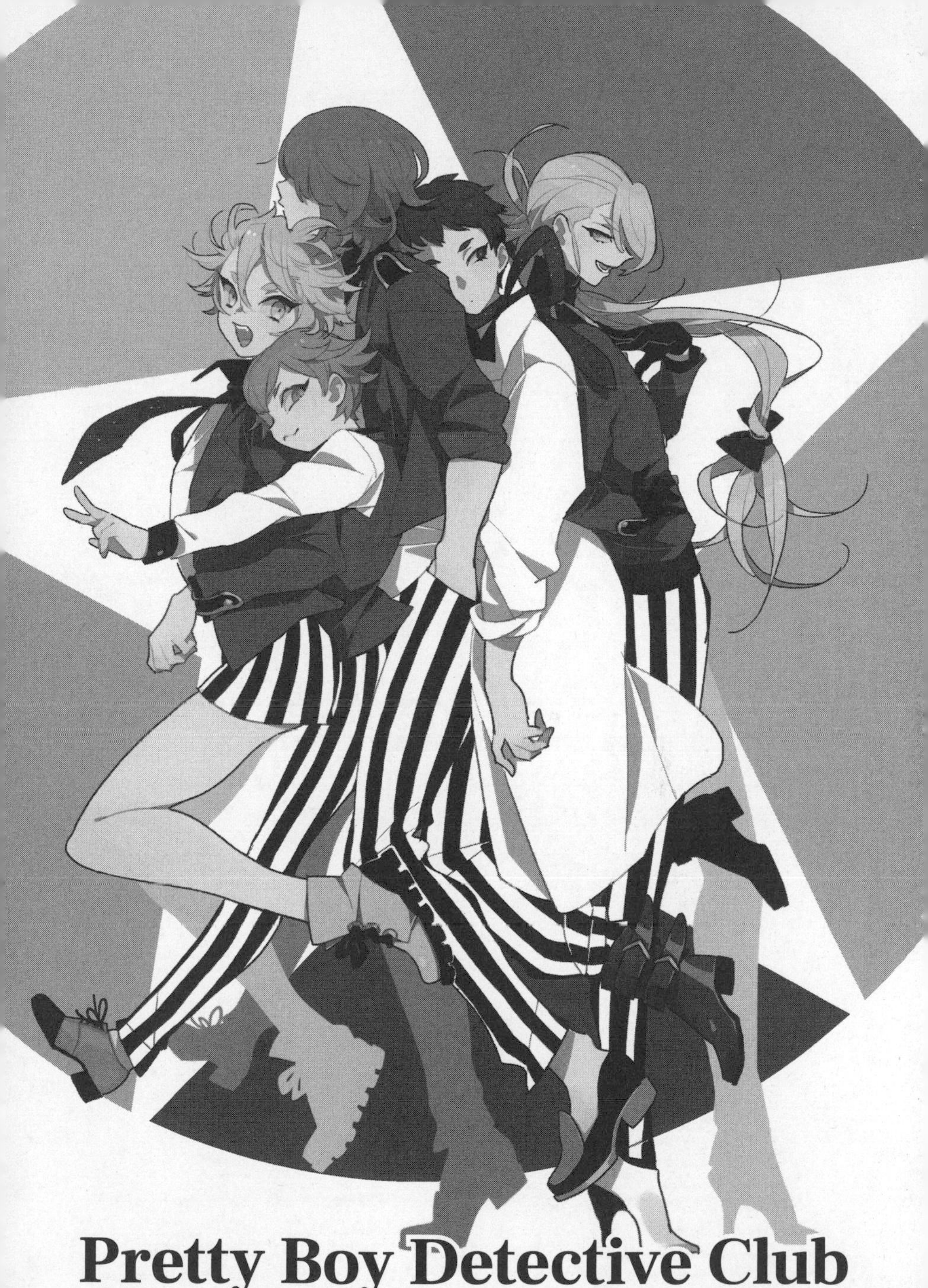

Pretty Boy Detective Club

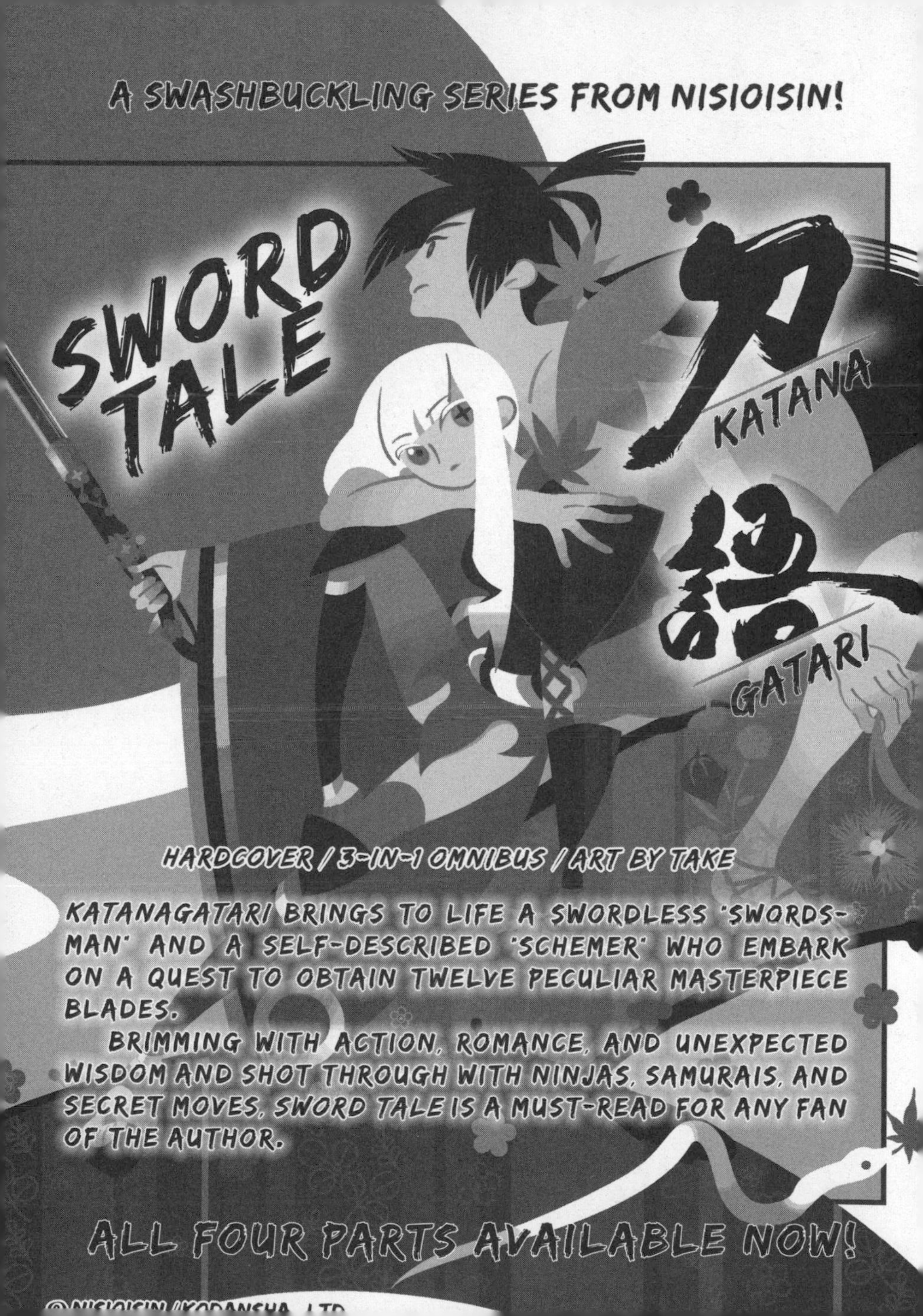
A SWASHBUCKLING SERIES FROM NISIOISIN!
SWORD TALE
刀語
KATANA
GATARI
HARDCOVER / 3-IN-1 OMNIBUS / ART BY TAKE
KATANAGATARI BRINGS TO LIFE A SWORDLESS "SWORDSMAN" AND A SELF-DESCRIBED "SCHEMER" WHO EMBARK ON A QUEST TO OBTAIN TWELVE PECULIAR MASTERPIECE BLADES.
BRIMMING WITH ACTION, ROMANCE, AND UNEXPECTED WISDOM AND SHOT THROUGH WITH NINJAS, SAMURAIS, AND SECRET MOVES, SWORD TALE IS A MUST-READ FOR ANY FAN OF THE AUTHOR.
ALL FOUR PARTS AVAILABLE NOW!
© NISIOISIN/KODANSHA, LTD.

SEASON ONE BOX SET
ISBN 978-1-947194-39-7
$105.65 US | 137.65 CAN

SEASON ONE NOW AVAILABLE

KIZUMONOGATARI
WOUND TALE

BAKEMONOGATARI PARTS 1-3
MONSTER TALE

AS A BOX SET!

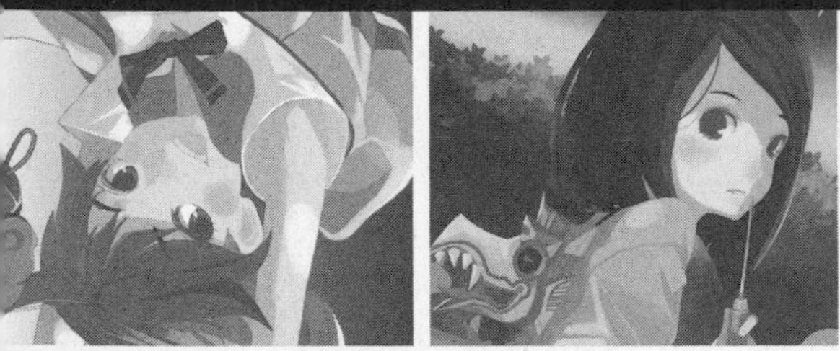

NISEMONOGATARI PARTS 1&2
FAKE TALE

NEKOMONOGATARI
(BLACK) CAT TALE

SEASON TWO BOX SET
ISBN 978-1-949980-06-6
$95.70 US | 125.70 CAN

AND DON'T MISS OUT ON

**NEKOMONOGATARI
(WHITE) CAT TALE**

**KABUKIMONOGATARI
DANDY TALE**

**HANAMONOGATARI
FLOWER TALE**

THE SECOND SEASON!

**OTORIMONOGATARI
DECOY TALE**

**ONIMONOGATARI
DEMON TALE**

**KOIMONOGATARI
LOVE TALE**

1/27

PRETTY BOY DETECTIVE CLUB 2
A Vertical Comics Edition

Editor: Daniel Joseph
Translation: Winifred Bird
Production: Risa Cho
                 Lorina Mapa
Proofreading: Micah Q. Allen

First published in Japan in 2017-2018 by Kodansha, Ltd., Tokyo
Publication rights for this English edition arranged through Kodansha, Ltd., Tokyo
English language version produced by Vertical Comics, an imprint of
Kodansha USA Publishing, LLC

Translation provided by Vertical Comics, 2021
Published by Kodansha USA Publishing, LLC, New York

Originally published in Japanese as *Bishounen Tanteidan* 2, 3 & 4 by Kodansha, Ltd.,
2017, 2018
Bishounen Tanteidan serialized in *ARIA*, Kodansha, Ltd., 2016-

This is a work of fiction.

ISBN: 978-1-64729-076-4

Manufactured in the United States of America

First Edition

Kodansha USA Publishing, LLC
451 Park Avenue South
7th Floor
New York, NY 10016
www.kodansha.us

Vertical books are distributed through Penguin-Random House Publisher Services.